THE COLLECTED WORKS OF
SAMUEL TAYLOR COLERIDGE · 8

LECTURES 1818 – 1819
ON THE HISTORY OF
PHILOSOPHY

General Editor: KATHLEEN COBURN

THE COLLECTED WORKS

4. Pencil and chalk portrait of John Hookham Frere, by Henry Edridge
Reproduced by courtesy of the National Portrait Gallery, London

THE COLLECTED WORKS OF

Samuel Taylor Coleridge

Lectures 1818–1819
On the History of
Philosophy

II

EDITED BY

J. R. de J. Jackson

BOLLINGEN SERIES LXXV

PRINCETON UNIVERSITY PRESS

The Collected Works, sponsored by Bollingen Foundation,
is published by Princeton University Press, 41 William Street,
Princeton, New Jersey
ISBN 0-691-09875-1

Library of Congress Cataloging-in-Publication Data
Coleridge, Samuel Taylor, 1772–1834.
Lectures 1818–1819 on the History of Philosophy / Samuel Taylor
Coleridge; edited by J. R. de J. Jackson.
(The Collected Works of Samuel Taylor Coleridge; 8)
(Bollingen series; 75)
ISBN 0-691-09875-1 (alk. paper)
1. Philosophy—History.   I. Jackson, J. R. de J. (James Robert de
Jager)   II. Title. III. Series.   IV. Series: Bollingen series; 75 V.
Series: Coleridge, Samuel Taylor, 1772–1834. Works. 1969 ; 8.
PR4470.F69   B1583.Z7A5
821'.7 s—dc21   [190]   99-30471

The Collected Works constitutes
the seventy-fifth publication in Bollingen Series

The present work, number 8 of the Collected Works,
is in 2 volumes, this being 8:II

1 3 5 7 9 10 8 6 4 2

THIS EDITION
OF THE WORKS OF
SAMUEL TAYLOR COLERIDGE
IS DEDICATED
IN GRATITUDE TO
THE FAMILY EDITORS
IN EACH GENERATION

CONTENTS

━━━━━━━━━━━■ II ■━━━━━━━━━━━

LIST OF ILLUSTRATIONS

II

LECTURE 11

DATE AND PLACE OF DELIVERY. Monday, 8 March 1819, at the Crown and Anchor Tavern, Strand, London.

SUBJECT. Belief, thought, and opinion from the mid-sixteenth to the mid-seventeenth century, with emphasis on Bacon.

ANNOUNCEMENTS AND ADVERTISEMENTS. The following announcement appeared in the *Morning Chronicle* on Mon 8 Mar: "MR. COLERIDGE'S LECTURE for THIS EVENING has for its subject the Progress of Opinion and Revolutions of Philosophy from Edward VI. to the Republic, or the Golden Age of English Intellect; with especial reference to the Character and Writings of Lord Bacon.— Eight o'clock, at the Crown and Anchor, Strand". A similar notice that appeared the same day in the *Times* omitted the words "and Revolutions of Philosophy" and added "Admission 5s.". An announcement the same day in the *New Times* added to "Lord Bacon" "and the influence of the Calvinistic and Arminian Controversy". It opened its notice of the subject with "The AGE of ELIZABETH, comprising . . . ".

TEXT. Frere MS ff 479–530 and C's draft notes in BM Add MS 47,523 ff 70^v–2^v.

REPORT. BM MS Egerton 3057 ff 23–5^v.

LECTURE 11

At once the most complex and the most individual of creatures, man, taken in the ideal of his humanity, has been not inaptly called the microcosm of the world in compendium, as the point to which all the lines converge from the circumference of nature.[1] This applies to his sum of being, to his powers collectively; but we find him gifted, as it were, with a threefold mind: the one belonging to him specifically, arising, I mean, necessarily out of the peculiar mechanism of his nature, and by this he beholds all things perspectively from his relative position as man; the second, in which those views are again modified, too often disturbed and falsified by his particular constitution and position as this or that particular individual; and the third, which exists in all men [potentially[a]], and in its germ, though it requires both effort from within and auspicious circumstances from without to evolve it into effect. By this third and highest power he places himself on the same point as nature and contemplates all objects, himself included, in their permanent and universal beings and relations.[2] Thus the astronomer places himself in the centre of the system and looks at all the planetary orbs as with the eye of the sun. Happy would it be for us if we could at all times imitate him in his perceptions, in the intellectual or the political world, I mean, to subordinate instead of exclude. Nature excludes nothing. She takes up all, still subjecting the higher to the less so, and ultimately subjecting all to the lower thus taken up. But, alas, the contrary method, exclusion instead of subordination, this and its result present the historian with his principal materials in whatever department his researches are directed.[3] Thus, in our own past

---

[a] MS: prudentially

[1] C had used "microcosm" himself in *TL* as a way of describing how man combined the qualities of plants and animals in the rising scale of nature: "Now, for the first time at the apex of the living pyramid, it is Man and Nature, but Man himself is a syllepsis, a compendium of Nature—the Microcosm!": *SW & F* (*CC*) I 550–1. Cf "the Subsumpsion of nature from the Lichen and Zoophyte upwards in the Man as at once the Epitome

(ανθρωπος ὁ μικροκοσμος [anthropos ho mikrokosmos]) and the Solution or Rationale of the whole System": *SW & F* (*CC*) II 1403.

[2] C offers a more elaborate exposition of "mind in the threefold relation" in *Logic* (*CC*) 43–4, a passage that is in turn part of a synopsis of a more abstract discussion at 40–1.

[3] C's favourite objection to the presumption of empirical philosophy, that

route, we find a long period from the first Christian century to the sixth distinguished by a vain attempt to substitute philosophy for religion, and, following, a more injurious endeavour to make religion supersede philosophy. As this is an error which is in truth never out of date, because religion is the interest of all men and among those who are incapable of the higher paths of intellect there are too many too proud to feel their capability[b], I may be allowed to dwell awhile on this.

What had been recorded by some individual[c] celebrated for purity and Christian virtues as useful discipline for himself as a part of ascetic piety, was soon recommended as laws for all men, and by degrees enforced as such; and when it happened to meet with a congenial disposition and with warm sensibility, it produced all the extravagancies which had deterred the sober from, and invited the visionary to, superstitions in various forms in all ages of the world.[4] I was struck, in looking over some memorandum books, with the character of [St Teresa[d]] who may be fairly taken as the representative of that class of beings who would have religion without any mixture of intellect.[5] I was led to Teresa [of Avila[e]][6] by a letter of hers in which she gives serious advice to her friend Lorenzo to keep holy water [by him, to sprinkle about when he felt any inward confusion[f]] or any under-whispers of temptation, all which she assures him proceed

[b] Meaning seems to require "the limits of their capability" or "incapability"?

[c] MS: individuals

[d] Blank space left in ms for about 8 letters; omission supplied by inference from following sentence

[e] Blank space left in ms for about 13 letters; omission supplied conjecturally in *P Lects* (313) although corresponding passage in N 18 (*CN* III 3909) does not style her so

[f] Blank space left in ms for about 58 letters; omission supplied from corresponding passage in N 18 (*CN* III 3909)

while claiming to argue without bias from observation of sense experience it ignored the unavoidable bias that was caused by the mind's observing some things rather than other things. Cf his sense of the consequences: "all *our* Thoughts are in the language of the old Logicians *inadequate*: i.e. no *thought*, which I have, of any *thing* comprizes the whole of that Thing. I have a distinct Thought of a Rose-Tree; but what countless properties and goings-on of that plant are there, not included in my *Thought* of it?" (*CL* II 1195: to Thomas Clarkson 13 Oct 1806). Cf *BL* (*CC*) I 111–12 where the effect of unselective perception from the top of St Paul's is imagined as resulting in "complete light-headedness".

[4] The treatment of the rise of monasticism in Gibbon ch 37 had developed this theme.

[5] C's N 18 contains a number of entries (*CN* III 3907, 3909, 3911, 3917, 3922, and 3925) on St Teresa, made in Jun and Jul 1810 when he was reading and annotating RS's copy of *The Works of the Holy Mother St. Teresa* (2 vols London 1669–75). The book is now in PML; for the annotations see *CM* (*CC*) V.

[6] From this point to the end of the paragraph C is quoting (var and with omissions) from N 18 (*CN* III 3909).

from the pressure of some evil spirit felt by the soul, though not evidenced by the senses. This led me to reflect on the importance of any act in strengthening and enlivening the will, and I could not but think, what if a mind like hers had attached anything like a religious meaning to the Aeolian harp as she did to the crucifix and the holy water. What endless religious applications and accommodations all its irregular tones would produce![7]

Her character will give the character of the whole class of those who from real piety opposed the revolution[g]. She was indeed framed by nature and favoured by a very hot-bed in a hot-house of circumstances to become a mystic saint of the first magnitude, a mighty mother [of spiritual transports, the *materia prestabilita*[8] of divine fusions, infusions, and confusions[h]]. First, she was a woman; secondly, a lady tenderly and affectionately [reared—no toil[i]], no sobering or deadening reality of physical privation or pain to draw off her self-consciousness of her inward goings on[j], [of her thoughts and sensations. Thirdly, under a very fond father and mother, both of them strictly pious, and the mother romantic to boot. Fourthly, she had early sympathy[k]] from her brothers and sisters and made a convert at eight years old of her favourite brother. Next, she was a Spanish lady—reflect on the full import of that word, [the religion, the government, the manners, the climate, the constitution, the books implied in it[l]]. Again, accustomed to read the lives of saints and martyrs who had fought against or suffered under the Moors. At eight years old, she and her brother were engaged to run away and go to Africa and obtain the crown of martyrdom, a subject which has occasioned . . . .[9] She regarded

---

[g] For "Reformation"?

[h] Blank space left in ms for about 42 letters; omission supplied from corresponding passage in N 18 (*CN* III 3911 f 58)

[i] Corrected to accord with N 18 (*CN* III 3911 f 58). MS: real—no dull

[j] MS: goings on and

[k] Blank space left in ms for about 52 letters; omission supplied by adapting corresponding passage in N 18 (*CN* III 3911 f 58)

[l] Blank space left in ms for about 64 letters; omission supplied from N 18 (*CN* III 3911 f 58)

---

[7] Cf C's own applications of the metaphor of the Aeolian harp in *Dejection: an Ode* and *The Eolian Harp* (*PW*—EHC—I 362–8 and 100–2); the theological speculation of the latter seems applicable to what he imagines of St Teresa: "And what if all of animated nature | Be but organic Harps diversely fram'd, | That tremble into thought, as o'er them sweeps | Plastic and vast, one intellectual breeze, | At once the Soul of each, and God of all?" (44–8). From this point to the end of the next paragraph C quotes (var) from N 18 again: *CN* III 3911, an entry dated 25 Jun 1810 and itself transcribed (see *CN* III 3911n) from the marginalia in *The Works of . . . St. Teresa*.

[8] "Pre-established matter".

[9] Blank space left in ms for about 69

the martyrs with more envy than admiration, they were so very unlucky[m] in getting an eternal heaven at so easy a price. In the habit, and that too without the will or knowledge of a superstitious [father[n]], of reading volumes of romance and chivalry to her mother (before the appearance of *Don Quixote*), and this all night long to herself, she had added all fancy could do. By the [corruption of a light-minded but favourite cousin and[o]] her [female[p]] servants, it seems she opened her fearful heart to a Spanish lover, doubtless in the true [Oroondates[q]][10] style and the giving audience [to some dying swain through the barred windows, or having received a lover's messages[r]] of flames and flaming conceits and anguishing despair[s], these seem to have been the mortal sins of which she bitterly accuses herself together with, perhaps, a few warm fancies and earthly loves[t], but above all which she considers her greatest crime her aversion at fifteen years old to shut [herself up for ever in a nunnery, to which her father likewise was obstinately averse. He had, doubtless, sense enough, with all his superstition[u]] to perceive how utterly unfit such a nursery [of inward fancies and outward privations were to a brain, heart, and bodily constitution like those of innocent, loving, and high-[v]]impassioned

[m] For "lucky"
[n] Corrected to accord with corresponding passage in N 18 (*CN* III 3911 f 58[v]). MS: fear
[o] Blank space left in ms for about 27 letters; omission supplied from N 18 (*CN* III 3911 f 58[v])
[p] Corrected to accord with N 18 (*CN* III 3911 f 58[v]). MS: familiar
[q] Blank space left in ms for about 16 letters; omitted name supplied from N 18 (*CN* III 3911 f 58[v])
[r] Blank space left in ms for about 33 letters; omission supplied from N 18 (*CN* III 3911 f 58[v])
[s] N 18: "Anguish, and Despair"
[t] N 18: "fancies of earthy Love"
[u] Blank space left in ms for about 62 letters; omission supplied from corresponding passage in N 18 (*CN* III 3911 f 58[v])
[v] Blank space left in ms for about 42 letters; omission supplied from N 18 (*CN* III 3911 f 58[v])

letters; the corresponding passage in N 18 has no intervening matter. *P Lects* (314) supplied the omission conjecturally with "[a poem by the poet, Crashaw, 'The Flaming Heart']", referring to Richard Crashaw (?1612–49) *The Flaming Heart, upon the Book and Picture of the Seraphical Saint Teresa*. C knew the poem from *B Poets*; he does not mention Crashaw at this point in the N 18 entry, but he is shortly to quote from him (see 466 below).

[10] Oroondates is the hero of the romance *Cassandre* (10 vols 1644–50) by Gauthier de Costes, Seigneur de la Calprenède. *Cassandre* had been popular in the English translation (1667) of Sir Charles Cotterell. C's reference may also include the unconventional but moral letter of "Statira" to "Oroondates" in which a lady of modest fortune proposes marriage to a richer gentleman; it appeared in *Spectator* (II 280–2) No 199 (18 Oct 1711), was likely to be familiar to C's audience, and fits his theme admirably. *P Lects* (448n) notes the reappearance of Oroondates in Charlotte Lennox *The Female Quixote* (1752).

Teresa. What could come of it [but a despairing anguish-stricken sinner or a mad saint^w]? This frame of such exquisite [sensibility by nature and by education shaken and ruined by the violence done to her nature^x]; but her obstinate resolve to become a nun against her own wishes, and against her fears, arose out of a resolve of duty, finishing in a burning fever [which ended in madness for many months or a state very like it, and which left her brain unsettled as is evidenced^y] from the frequent parox-ysms [or fainting fits to which she was ever after subject. Previously to this step^z] she had been reading to her over-religious uncle books of the most gloomy kind, of death, hell, and judgment, which made a fearful [impression on her tender mind, because out of her exceeding desire^a] to give pleasure, she had affected to take a delight in reading them to him, and thus combined an act of the will with the emotions otherwise pro-ceeding. [She at length resolved on nunhood, she says, because she thought it could not be worse than the pains of Purgatory^b] and not so long, and [that a Purgatory for this life was a cheap expiation in exchange for Hell for ever!!^{c}] Combine these causes only and you will see how al-most impossible it was that a [maiden^d] so innocent and so susceptible, of an imagination so lively by nature, and so fever-kindled by disease and its occasions, [and thus so well furnished with the requisite images and preconceptions, should not mistake, and often, the less painful and in such a frame the sometimes^e] pleasurable approaches to bodily [deli-quium, and her imperfect fainting-fits for divine transports, and momen-tary union with God—especially if with a thoughtful yet pure psychol-ogy you join the force of suppressed instincts stirring in the heart and bodily frame, of a mind unconscious of their nature and these in the keenly-sensitive body, in the innocent and loving soul of a Teresa, with

^{w} MS has "by dispelling" followed by blank space for about 71 letters, followed in turn by "than this"; emendations and omission supplied from N 18 (*CN* III 3911 f 58^v)

^{x} Blank space left in ms for about 50 letters, followed by "and by the violence done to nature"; omission and emendation supplied from N 18 (*CN* III 3911 ff 58^v–9)

^{y} Blank space left in ms for about 74 letters; omission supplied from N 18 (*CN* III 3911 f 59)

^{z} Blank space left in ms for about 52 letters; omission supplied, slightly adapted, from N 18 (*CN* III 3911 f 59)

^{a} Blank space left in ms for about 42 letters; omission supplied from N 18 (*CN* III 3911 f 59)

^{b} Blank space left in ms for about 55 letters; omission supplied from N 18 (*CN* III 3911 f 59)

^{c} MS: "the" followed by blank space for about 56 letters; emendation and omission sup-plied from N 18 (*CN* III 3911 f 59)

^{d} Corrected to accord with N 18: "a young Spanish Maiden" (*CN* III 3911 f 59). MS: man

^{e} Blank space left in ms for about 42 letters; omission supplied from N 18 (*CN* III 3911 f 59^v)

"all her thirsts, and lives, and deaths of love"[11]—and what remains unsolved, for which the credulity of the many and the knavery of a few will not furnish*f*] ample explanation.

But what required the concurrence of many causes to produce in one, by infection will spread over many, till at last mankind become almost divided into knaves, dupes, and visionaries; and such must be the necessary effect of an attempt to disunite religion, the highest object of our nature, from the reason which is its highest faculty. But even in this attempt, which was too successful, if only instead of religion we put superstition, it had in truth borrowed from a former attempt, namely that of substituting philosophy for religion. It had borrowed the theurgic [rites*g*] in one of their great purposes, that is, not to subdue nature and ["]call forth spirits [from the vasty deep"*h*],[12] but to control evil demons that were supposed to be forever hovering round the poor Christian or like [Satan at the ear of Eve[13] infusing inordinate thoughts and sinful desires*i*].

Were it only, therefore, for their endeavours to reunite reason and religion by a due subordination of the former to the latter, we owe a tribute of respect to the Schoolmen from the thirteenth and fourteenth century. Then, one general ill consequence of this was a direct application of the studies to the forms*j* of logical thinking, and because they were treated as more than forms of thinking, therefore sophistically. This is most true, and that the [revival of ancient and classical literature became the object of utter distaste and the subject of incessant complaint*k*] to the great pioneers and chieftains of the Reformation. Yet is this to be carefully distinguished from the works themselves of the most eminent Schoolmen, as Thomas Aquinas, Scotus, and Occam,[14] whom those who have never

---

f Blank space left in ms for about 92 letters; omission supplied from N 18 (*CN* III 3911 f 59ᵛ)

g Corrected to accord with corresponding passage in draft ms (498 below). MS: right

h Blank space left in ms for about 15 letters; omission supplied from draft ms (498 below)

i Blank space left in ms for about 27 letters; omission supplied from draft ms (498 below)

j Corresponding phrase in draft ms (498 below): mere forms

k Blank space left in ms for about 74 letters; omission supplied from draft ms (498 below)

---

[11] Crashaw *The Flaming Heart* 95–8 (var); quoted as part of "The Life of Crashaw" in *B Poets* IV 703.

[12] Shakespeare *1 Henry IV* III i 53 (var).

[13] Cf Milton *Paradise Lost* 4.799–802: "him there they found | Squat like a Toad, close at the eare of *Eve*; | Assaying by his Devilish art to reach | The Organs of her Fancie . . .".

[14] This conjunction of Duns Scotus and Occam may be merely the consequence of listing prominent Scholastic philosophers, but cf the reference in *CN* IV 5087 f 45 (Dec 1823) to Occam as Scotus's "great Scholar & *seeming* Antagonist".

read their works are ever the most apt to accuse[l] and speak with contempt of. I indeed am persuaded that to the Scholastic philosophy the Reformation is attributable, far more than to the revival of classical literature, except as far, indeed, as it produced a general impulse and awakening over society, nay, even more to the Scholastic philosophy than to the genial school of Platonism in Italy.

In the life of Baxter written by himself, speaking of the great obligations he had to the Schoolmen, he particularly instances this, that ever afterwards [they[m]] rendered all indistinctness of means[n] intolerable to him. It enforced on him, it introduced into his mind, the necessity of tracing every position as far back as either duty permitted or it was not demonstrably beyond further pursuit.[15] But I think facts would bear me out in my assertion[16] that the Platonism, perhaps I might call it the Plotinism rather, of the great Tuscan scholars under the great [Cosimo[o]] seems to have been unfavourable to the Reformation, strikingly so as compared with Scholastic philosophy which was logical and analytic.[17] [The mysticism of the former[18] was flexible to all superstitions, and if it engendered any dislike[p]] to those of the Church, it was because there was not enough in it. They preferred paganism and were more in danger of becoming polytheists than [Protestants[q]]; and it is well known that the greater part of them confessed to their intimates an utter disbelief of Christianity and disavowed all attachment to it except as a substitute for the more malleable Jupiters and Junos who could mean anything the philosopher chose.[19] Even to this day the far greater number of converts

---

[l] Cf draft ms (498 below): abuse

[m] MS: he

[n] For "meaning" or "meanings"?

[o] Blank space left in ms for about 12 letters; omission conjecturally supplied from parallel passage in Lect 10 (429 above)

[p] Blank space left in ms for about 72 letters; omission supplied, slightly adapted, from corresponding passage in N 29 (*CN* III 4497)

[q] Corrected to accord with N 29 (*CN* III 4497). MS: Plotinists

---

[15] Perhaps Richard Baxter (1615–91) *Reliquiae Baxterianae* bk 1 pt 1 p 6: "because I thought they narrowly searched after Truth, and brought Things out of the darkness of Confusion: For I could never from my first Studies endure *Confusion*! Till *Equivocals* were *explained*, and *Definition* and *Distinction* led the way, I had rather hold my Tongue than speak! . . . I never thought I understood any thing till I could *anatomize* it, and see the *parts distinctly*, and the *Conjunction* of the parts as they make up the whole. *Distinc-* tion and *Method* seemed to me of that necessity, that without them I could not be said to know . . .".

[16] The passage, from this point to "the great supports of the Roman religion", is a re-wording with various phrases exactly quoted, of an entry in *CN* III 4497 (N 29: Mar 1819). The entry is headed "Mem. for the Philos. Notes in flexible-covered ~~poek~~ red-leathered Book.—"

[17] Cf 237–8 and 327 above.

[18] I.e. the "great Tuscan scholars".

[19] Cf *C&S* (*CC*) 64–5. The imputa-

to the Romish Church among the educated class are drawn into it by the attractive [Pietism[r]] in that Church, by that [*vie intérieure*,[20] that San Teresianism[s]] that attracted our [Crashaw[t]].[21] And the revived [Proclo-plotinism . . .[u]] an enthusiastic man. Add too with what favour, with what unmingled [applause[v]], the Cabalistic writings of [Reuchlin[w]],[22] all that was visionary and magical, were received with popes, cardinals, and bishops; and that Luther and the first leaders of the Reformation in Germany opposed the Schoolmen as the great supports of the Roman religion.[23] This seems to have been confined to that particular time and did not extend into England; on the contrary our great divines found in the writings of the Schoolmen the strongest testimonies in their favour.[24]

There are three great instructive events in history, the reflection on which perhaps more than on any other part of human history will repay us by the lessons of wisdom and caution which they imply: I mean the Reformation, the Civil War,[25] and the French Revolution. We are now come to that period of time in which we are to speak of the state in which the Reformation had left the minds of the educated class in Europe. As I have already spoken of two opposite extremes, so we may divide philo-

---

[r] Corrected to accord with N 29 (*CN* III 4497). MS: poetism

[s] Blank space left in ms for about 14 letters; omission supplied from N 29 (*CN* III 4497)

[t] MS, unpunctuated, corrected to accord with N 29 (*CN* III 4497). MS: Cassius

[u] Blank space left in ms for about 9 letters; omission partly supplied from longer corresponding passage in N 29 (*CN* III 4497): "the revived Proclo-plotinism is multiplying nominal Catholics among the young men throughout Germany". Some phrase such as "proved attractive to" seems to be needed

[v] Corrected to accord with N 29 (*CN* III 4497). MS: authorities

[w] Blank space left in ms for about 15 letters; omission supplied from N 29 (*CN* III 4497)

---

tion of polytheism probably carries with it Gibbon's view that by believing in more gods the polytheists came to believe less in each and were relatively indifferent to religion (cf 222–4 above).

[20] The "inner life". In the course of looking through N 18 for the materials concerning St Teresa C may well have noted his characterisation of St John "who had sympathized more deeply [than St Matthew] with the vie interieure of his Master's doctrines" (*CN* III 3879 f 40: Jun 1810). The French phrase is unusual for him.

[21] See 466 above. Crashaw was converted to Roman Catholicism by 1646 and his poetry on St Teresa was written prior to his conversion.

[22] For Reuchlin see 434–7 above. In the N 29 entry C specifies the writings as

De verbo mirifico and *De arte cabbalistica: CN* III 4497.

[23] By "Roman religion" C appears to refer to a tendency that he still identifies with Roman Catholicism to mingle non-Christian or even anti-Christian elements with Christianity.

[24] By "their" C means the Schoolmen. Cf *CM* (*CC*) II 260 where C combines the Schoolmen with the Fathers of the church: "Even in Donne, . . . still more in Bishops Andrews and Hackett, there is a strong *patristic* leaven—. In Jeremy Taylor, this Taste for the Fathers, and all the Saints and Schoolmen before the Reformation amounted to a dislike of the Divines of the Continental protestant Churches, Lutheran or Calvinist . . .".

[25] I.e. the Civil War in England of 1642–6, 1648–51.

sophy before the time I am now speaking of, and the period since then, into two classes.

During the whole of the Middle Ages and almost down to the time of the Restoration of Charles II we discover everywhere metaphysics, always acute and frequently profound, but throughout estranged from, not merely experimental physics generally, but from its most intimate connective, experimental psychology; while from the Restoration we have the opposite extreme, namely experimental physics and a truly enlightened though empirical [and mechanical[x]] psychology, estranged from and in utter contempt of all metaphysics. From the former we are to deduce the explanation of a [phenomenon[y]] which must strike every student of the reigns of Henry VIII, Queen Elizabeth, and Charles I, I mean the astonishing credulity displayed by men of learning and in many respects of profound research.[26] I do not speak too strongly when I say it would be difficult to find any old woman who with a grave face would relate the stories to be found in Luther and the divines of the English Church, but especially among the Puritans, combined with so much political wisdom, so much ecclesiastical research, and so much genuine piety, that a man must be thoughtless indeed who could find a recurrence of such facts and not seek for their explanation. That explanation is undoubtedly to be found mainly in the cause I have now stated, namely, the absence of all psychological knowledge, or that knowledge by which a man learns the reaction of his thoughts upon outward objects equally with the action of outward objects through his senses on his thoughts. A large number of the tales which Luther tells of himself, and which Baxter records both of himself and of others, will be explained at once as occurring in those imperfect states of sleep which are the true matrix, the true birthplaces, of all the ghosts and apparitions that history has recorded.[27]

We find for instance that in the story told of Dion and the spirit, the fury that he beheld at the end of the room,[28] or the appearance of the spirit

---

[x] Blank space left in ms for about 13 letters; omission conjecturally supplied from parallel passage in *CM* (*CC*) I 281

[y] MS: phenomena

[26] C had been reading about witchcraft, especially the 17th-century version, in 1818. See esp *CN* III 4390–6 and nn (Mar 1818) and *CL* IV 844 (to Thomas Boosey, Jr? 25 Feb 1818) as part of his preparation for his 1818 lects on European literature: see *Lects 1808–1819* (*CC*) II 199–211 and nn.

[27] C treats this theme more fully in *Friend* (*CC*) I 144–7 and, in 1821, in *Blackwood's Magazine*: see *SW & F*

(*CC*) II 928–32. For Luther's tales, see *Friend* (*CC*) I 137–43; for C's reading of Andrew Baxter *An Enquiry into the Nature of the Human Soul* (2 vols 3rd ed London 1745), see *CN* I 188 and n.

[28] See Plutarch *Lives* VI 117, "Life of Dion" 55. Dion is described (tr) as "sitting late in the day . . . alone and lost in thought" when he saw "at the other end of the colonnade" "a woman of lofty stature, in garb and countenance exactly

of Caesar to Brutus,[29] or that which . . . [z] has recorded of himself, or which the great [Lord Lyttleton[a]][30] has related, all have happened under one set of circumstances. They were anxious, weary, in cold and bodily discomfort, the consequence of which is that the objects from without, weakened in their influences on the senses, and the sensations, meantime, from within being strongly excited, the thoughts convert themselves into images, the man believing himself to be awake, precisely by the same law as our thoughts convert themselves into images the moment we fall asleep, and which, no less dreams[b], no longer strike us with their wonderful nature from their frequency. From this one circumstance, that all the well-recorded stories took place under the same circumstances, we could scarcely hesitate as to their solution. And when a story has once had any ground of this kind, and falls into a state of society where the love of the miraculous is uppermost, it will be indeed difficult; in a very short time, a month's time and the travel of twenty miles will convert it into a wonder which I will defy all the philosophers in the world to explain. We are lucky, therefore, when we get hold of a well-attested fact, especially when we can discover it in a disguise when it has passed over

---

[z] Blank space left in ms for about 23 letters; *P Lects* (319) conjecturally supplied "[Captain Lyon]", drawing on parallel discussion in *TT* (*CC*) I 51; OB proposed "[Bishop Berkeley]", drawing on parallel discussion in *TT* (*CC*) II 37

[a] Blank space left in ms for about 18 letters; omission conjecturally supplied from parallel passage in *TT* (*CC*) I 17

[b] *P Lects* (319) emended to: "and which [are] no less [real than if they were actual]. Dreams"

---

like a tragic Fury, sweeping the house with a sort of broom".

[29] See Plutarch *Lives* VI 205–7, "Life of Brutus" 36. Tr: Brutus "had in his hands the conduct of a life and death struggle, and was anxiously forecasting the future". He was alone at night, "meditating and reflecting", when he saw the "monstrous and fearful shape" that said "I am thy evil genius, Brutus, and thou shalt see me at Philippi". Shakespeare's representation of the incident, in *Julius Caesar* IV iii, would have been familiar.

[30] Thomas Lyttelton, 2nd Baron Lyttelton (1744–79), is more usually remembered for being "wicked" than for being "great"—a slip of the tongue for "late" perhaps—and is to be distinguished from his father, George Lyttelton (1709–73), the politician and author. C would have known the father's verse

and annotated his *History of the Life of King Henry the Second* (3rd ed London 1769) and he seems unlikely to have confused the two men. However, no ghost story is traditionally associated with the first Lord Lyttelton, and one of the most famous ghost stories is told of the second. According to a correspondent who quoted from a document left in Lord Lyttelton's house "as a heir-loom", Lord Lyttelton "had not been long returned from Ireland, and frequently had been seized with suffocating fits. He was attacked several times by them in the course of the preceding month. While in his house . . . he dreamt, three days before his death, 'he saw a Bird fluttering, and afterwards a Woman appeared in white apparel, and said, "Prepare to die, you will not exist three days"'": *G Mag* LXXXVI (2) (1816) 422.

many shapes and poured itself into the right one out of a multitude of mouths.[31]

Fearful, however, was one of the results. It revived the notions of witchcraft combined with all the horrors which the weaker and more powerful religion[c] could give to it. How it ought to humble us when we reflect that it was not in the Dark Ages, that it was not in countries struggling only out of barbarism, but in the very morning, in the brightness of reviving letters, in the age of a Kepler and a Galileo, when every department of human intellect was felt and supported in its greatest splendour, it was then that the dreadful contagion of witchcraft and persecution of witches raged, not in one country, but passed like a postillion through all Europe, till it died in North America among the Puritans of New England. No country seems free from its ravages.[32] Some of our greatest divines were the warmest advocates of these persecutions, nay, boldly asserted that he who disbelieved in witchcraft could not believe in a God.[33] In one city alone in Germany, in five years three thousand women and children, for there were many children among them, were put to death by public execution.[34] And the noble Jesuit who first raised himself against it,[35] or rather next to [John Wier[d]][36] did so, on being questioned by a prince how he came to have grey hairs, answered it was the witches that had turned him grey. A smile being provoked, he answered with a sigh, "So many hundreds have I attended to the stake after confession, with a certainty that every human being was perfectly innocent".[37] I mention this as a

---

[c] Corresponding passage in ms report (502 below): a purer and reforming Religion
[d] Blank space left in ms for about 8 letters

---

[31] C brings together a set of examples that overlaps substantially with these in a discussion of ghosts he is reported to have had on 9 Jan 1823: *TT* (*CC*) I 16–17. He analysed one of his own nightmares in the same spirit in *CN* III 4046 (25 Jan 1811).

[32] Cf C's Lect 12 in *Lects 1808–1819* (*CC*) II 199–211 and nn, much of which was based on *CN* III 4390–6.

[33] Cf John Webster *The Displaying of Supposed Witchcraft* 37 where Casaubon *Of Credulity and Incredulity* 7 and Glanvil *A Blow at Modern Saducism* preface are cited as making this accusation unwarrantably.

[34] The anonymous ed of Friedrich Spee *Trutz Nachtigal* (Berlin 1817) gives some details (xi–xii), mentioning the inclusion of women, children aged from 8

to 14, members of the clergy, nobility, etc. during the years 1627–9, and a total number of deaths of about 1687. C is perhaps recalling the passage approximately. A detached title-page of *Trutz Nachtigal* with a note by C written on it is in the Coleridge Collection at VCL, but the rest of his copy has not been traced.

[35] Friedrich Spee (1591–1635), author of *Cautio criminalis* (1631). According to the editorial preface to *Trutz Nachtigal* (viii) he was the first significant opponent of the witchcraft trials in Germany.

[36] John Wierus or Johann Wier (1515–88), sceptical of the convictions for witchcraft, although, like Spee, not of witchcraft itself, author of *De praestigiis daemonum* (1563).

[37] Cf *Trutz Nachtigal* xv–xvi: "Jo-

proof that it is not by learning merely, no, nor even by knowledge of experimental physics, that the most disgraceful enthusiasm can at all times be prevented. The sole prevention in reality is the recurrence to our highest philosophy: know thyself, study thy own nature, but above all do no evil under the impression that you are serving God thereby.

More innocent at least, if equally wild, was one of the two divisions of philosophy, namely, the mystical, which at the time I am now speaking of was so far useful that it was the antagonist to the excess of the former. It is very difficult to trace the origin of mysticism in Europe, for this reason, not that it is difficult to explain any visionary tendency of man, a progressive animal while he is in the lower states of the progress, but from an uncommon uniformity in likeness of the opinions which men [widely*e*], apparently even to craziness, [entertained*f*], from the mysteries of [Samothrace*g*] founded shortly after Homer by the Phoenicians in all probability, and which seem to have continued to the very remotest time of Platonism, and to have initiated almost all the remaining pagan world.[38] There were certainly societies formed, which under various names, some known, some unknown, carried down these principles in a degraded form, which in the time when they were doing their destined

---

e MS: wide   *f* MS: entertain
g Blank space left in ms for about 13 letters

---

hann Philipp von Schönborn, nachher Bischof von Wirzburg und zuletzt Churfurst von Mainz kam in seinen jüngern Jahren, als Canonicus zu Wirzburg lebend, zufällig mit Ihm [Spee] in vertraulichen Umgang, und da er ihn als ein Jüngling fragte: warum doch der liebe geistliche Vater ein graueres Haupthaar habe, als es seinem Alter nach seyn sollte, erwiederte ihm dieser: 'Dieses sey ihm von den Hexen gekommen, die er zum Scheiterhaufen begleitet habe'" ("John Philipp von Schönborn, later bishop of Würzburg and eventually elector of Mainz, when he was living in his earlier years as a canon in Würzburg, by chance fell into familiar conversation with him, and when he asked him, he being a young man, why the dear holy father had a grayer head of hair than was appropriate for his age, he made this reply, 'That he had come by it from the witches whom he had accompanied to the funeral pile'").

[38] C is known to have read F. W. J. von Schelling *Ueber die Gottheiten* and at least part of George Stanley Faber *A Dissertation on the Mysteries of the Cabiri* (2 vols Oxford 1803). Of these, Schelling's essay mattered more to him; he seems to have been trying to acquire a copy for the first time in 1817 (*CL* IV 738: to Thomas Boosey [14 Jun]) and he proposed to illustrate "The Superstitions, distinct from Religion" by referring to "the Cabiric Mysteries" in his notes for Lect 2 of the 1818 series on European literature (see *CN* III 4384 f 149^v and n—N 29: Jan 1818—and *Lects 1808–1819—CC—*II 77). William Warburton *Divine Legation of Moses Demonstrated* (2 vols London 1738–41), a book that C seems to have dipped into recently (see *CN* III 4322: 1816–17), also contains an essay on the Greek mysteries in which it is maintained that the mysteries opposed "the Error of Polytheism" (I 152).

work had perhaps preserved Greece from falling into that barbarism which in all other countries has been the effect of . . .[h] polytheism. Look to the names of the gods worshipped at [Samothrace, the Cabiri[i]][39] and you will well understand what they are, if you will conceive a system of pantheism, which, describing [fire[j]] as a living power, gave a history of its manifestations.[40] The three lower gods[41] . . .[k] with their . . .[l] were the first three. The [theurgic] gods, that is, those who were the workings of the Deity in manifesting itself in the formation of the world. They were otherwise called the magic gods,[42] and it is very curious that the name may be traced in almost all the superstitions of the world, wherever the Phoenicians or after them the Greeks had pierced. Thus we have still the ghebers or fire-worshippers in Persia;[43] we have the [good companions[m]]

[h] Blank space left in ms for about 14 letters
[i] Blank space left in ms for about 14 letters; omission supplied conjecturally by OB; *P Lects* (321) proposed "[Alexandria]". Remainder of paragraph very imperfectly recorded; in *P Lects* omissions conjecturally supplied from "On the Prometheus of Aeschylus" and from *LR* I 184–9 (cf *MC* 191–4), derived ultimately perhaps from parallel material in C's annotations of George Stanley Faber *A Dissertation on the Mysteries of the Cabiri* (Oxford 1803) in *CM* (*CC*) II 574–85
[j] MS: air
[k] Blank space left in ms for about 37 letters
[l] Blank space left in ms for about 15 letters
[m] Blank space left in ms for about 12 letters; omission supplied from corresponding passage in ms report (502 below)

[39] Schelling *Ueber die Gottheiten* 10–11 and nn discusses the first three names and their Hebrew roots.
[40] Schelling has a long note on the role of Hephaestus as the living power of fire (*Ueber die Gottheiten* 67–74). The reporter perhaps misheard "fire" as "air".
[41] According to Schelling *Ueber die Gottheiten* 6–7, the first three were Axieros (Demeter), Axiokersa (Persephone), and Axiokersos (Hades); to these some added Kasmilos (Mercury). Cf *Ueber die Gottheiten* 20: "So bilden also die drey ersten samothracischen Götter dieselbe Folge und Verkettung, in der wir auch sonst überall Demeter, Persephone and Dionysos finden. Es folgt die vierte Gestalt, Kasmilos genannt, gewöhnlicher Kadmilos, auch Camillus" ("So therefore the three first Samothracian deities form the same sequence and inter-relationship. The fourth figure follows, called Kasmilos, more usually Kadmilos, also Camillus").

[42] MS: "theologic gods". Cf Schelling *Ueber die Gottheiten* 17: "Zauber aber oder Zauberin (denn diess bedeuten die Wörter), kann sowohl Demeter als Persephone genannt werden" ("However both Demeter and Persephone can be called magic or sorceress—because the words mean this—"). See also 17–18 and nn, with reference to Creuzer's authority, and 63–4, and, on the theurgic function of the gods, 26–7.
[43] Cf Schelling *Ueber die Gottheiten* 112: "Wie man nun in jene *Chaberin*, welche die Perser selbst und ihre Priester seyn sollen, nicht umhin kann, die jetzt noch so genannten Ghebern zu erkennen, so muss auch wohl dieser Name zuletzt mit dem Kabiren-Namen einer und derselbe seyn" ("Now, just as in those 'chaberin' which should be the Persians themselves and their priests we cannot help recognising the now so-called Ghebers, so must this name also have once been one and the same with the name of

or fairies of [Scotland and England[n]]; the [miners[o]] in the north of [Europe[p]]; and, what is remarkable, [Georg[q]] Agricola, in his account of the mines, states there . . .[r] as appearing in the same form in which the . . .[s] are found on [medals and coins[t]] namely as . . .[u] signifying the deities that were bringing out disorder into order.[44] To trace it somewhat further, another of their nature was the [peri[v]],[45] a name still found in the valleys of Persia, and from that the fairies of Europe. The third name of [the Cabiri[w]] was [boni socii, the good neighbours[x]], which is still a name for the fairies in Scotland and in the north of England.[46]

[n] Insertion supplied conjecturally from ms report (502 below)
[o] Blank space left in ms for about 10 letters; omission supplied from ms report (502 below)
[p] Blank space left in ms for about 11 letters; omission supplied from ms report (502 below)
[q] Blank space left in ms for about 10 letters
[r] Blank space left in ms for about 12 letters
[s] Blank space left in ms for about 28 letters
[t] Blank space left in ms for about 12 letters, preceded by "metals in"
[u] Blank space left in ms for about 84 letters
[v] Blank space left in ms for about 13 letters
[w] Blank space left in ms for about 10 letters
[x] MS: bonae societae, the good members

---

the Cabiri"). He adds (112): "Nach der Parsischen Feuer-Religion waren die Schmiede unrein, weil sie das Feuer entweihten. Daher der verächtliche Begriff, der mit dem Wort Ghebr verbunden war und bis auf den heutigen Tag im ganzen Morgenlande fortdauert. Also Ghebern sind eigentlich Schmiede, die das Feuer verunreinigen, und mit diesem Namen werden eben die belegt, welche der alten Parsenlehre treu das Feuer heilig halten . . ." ("According to the Parsee fire-religion the smiths were unclean because they polluted fire. Hence the scornful idea that was linked to the word 'gheber' and which continues to this day throughout the entire east. So 'ghebers' are really smiths who pollute fire and those were also burdened with this name, who, true to the old Parsee-teaching, regarded fire as holy . . .").
[44] Cf Schelling *Ueber die Gottheiten* 35: "Auch an unsre Bergmännlein dürfen wir erinnern, von denen noch unser treuherziger Landsmann Georg Agricola zu erzählen weiss; denn auch sie sind ja so zu reden Söhne des Hephästos, die mit Metallen Verkehr haben und sogar Waf-

fen aus ihnen verfertigen" ("We may remember too our dwarf miners, about whom our ingenuous compatriot Georg Agricola also used to tell, because they were, so to speak, sons of Hephaestus who had business with metals and even manufactured weapons out of them"). Cf 94 where, in a note, Schelling quotes from Georg Agricola (or Georg Bauer) *De re metallica* (1556); no evidence has been found that C was directly acquainted with Agricola's book.
[45] Cf Schelling *Ueber die Gottheiten* 65: "Wegen der Freja, *frie, fri* bedarf es nicht einmal der Erinnerung an die persischen Peris . . . oder Feen" ("Concerning Freja (the goddess), 'frie', 'fri', a reminder of the Persian Peris . . . or fairies is scarcely needed").
[46] Schelling discusses the Cabiri in the context of the relations of gods to human beings; see *Ueber die Gottheiten* 107, 110–11 and, for Roman household gods, 115. In "The Historie and Gests of Maxilian" (*SW & F—CC*—II 979*) C compares the *boni socii* to the "Robin Good Fellows" of England and the "'Practical Jokers' of *all* places".

But their doctrines were still more resembling; it is impossible to read Paracelsus[47] and compare it with what remains in [Varro^y][48] and elsewhere in the doctrines taught in the mysteries, without perceiving their identity. A system of pantheism it was, but not irreligious. These powers had a certain dim personality attributed to them and if we could conceive them as [Varro^z] did, capable of being combined with true religious faith, for [Varro^a] tells us that the three first of their divinities answered to the . . .^{b} or the [hunger^c] represented the . . .^{d} or that which the yearning after being called forth,[49] and the Pluto. He then tells us that the next trinity answers to the Jupiter, to the Apollo, but according to others, the Bacchus and to the Venus or universal love; but the most mysterious consequence of which cannot be explained but by supposing some connection [between] the Phoenicians and the Jews. They introduce a wonderful character, the [Cadmilus^e], who, we are told, is the first that calls out the lower

^{y} MS: Paley. Material attributed to him here and in what follows belongs to Varro; see e.g. *CM* (*CC*) ɪɪ 575–6 and n

^{z} MS: Paley

^{a} MS: Paley

^{b} Blank space left in ms for about 10 letters

^{c} MS: danger

^{d} Blank space left in ms for about 13 letters; cf parallel passage in *CM* (*CC*) ɪɪ 575–6, quoted in n 51 below.

^{e} Blank space left for about 12 letters; omission conjecturally supplied from parallel passage, written no earlier than 1825, in *CM* (*CC*) ɪɪ 583

[47] Cf Schelling *Ueber die Gottheiten* 94: "Auch aus Theophr. Paracelsus wäre viel von den *Pygmaeis* anzuführen, das er doch wohl nicht blos aus seinem Gehirn, sondern aus gemeiner Volkssage genommen" ("There is also much concerning the 'pygmies' in Theophr. Paracelsus that might be quoted, which certainly is not entirely derived from his brain but also from folklore"). For C's interest in the contribution of Paracelsus, cf *CM* (*CC*) ɪɪɪ 682: "The time will come when Paracelsus will be unanimously acknowleged . . . either as a Repository of the Arcana dispersed thro' Christendom by the abolition of the Samothracian—~~or~~ Cabiric Mysteries, or as the greatest Physiologist since the Christian Æra".

[48] Throughout this paragraph ms records C's ref as having been to Paley. Since the ref to Paley is not only wrong but incongruous, given C's knowledge of Paley's writings and his repeatedly ex-

pressed distaste for them, a reporter's error seems likely. The name needed, however it failed to be communicated, was Varro. Both Schelling and Faber cite Marcus Terentius Varro (116–27 B.C.) as an authority, referring to his *De lingua latina* of which bks 5–10 survive and *Antiquitates rerum divinarum et humanarum*, which is known only through quotations from fragmentary extracts (C was to regret its loss in *CN* ɪᴠ 5232), so the phrase "what remains in" is appropriate.

[49] Cf the Appendix to "On the Prometheus of Aeschylus" where C refers to "Esurience, ποθος, Yearning CERES": *SW & F* (*CC*) ɪɪ 1289. Schelling (*Ueber die Gottheiten* 15–17 and 59–61) states that the names of all three gods in the Samothracian mysteries meant hunger or yearning and cites Varro (60).

trinity, which is the first, says [Varro*f*],[50] [because*g*] the lower, and raises it into light. But this is the same with the second or with the higher or heavenly trinity. And as lights were still celebrated, not as having appeared, but as again appearing as the infant Bacchus, who was to perform for man what as the Mercury he had performed for nature before he came into light and consciousness, namely, to bring back the human soul again, the rites of this infant Bacchus were celebrated as the redeemer to come.[51] So that they divided their religion into seven deities. We have already an eighth that was yet to appear.[52] The three first were the [theurgic*h*] deities representing, in short, the different processes of nature from [an unreal*i*] real or merely potential state,[53] from the chaos in which in all countries had originated nothing, to the appearance of the deity in his full manifestation as conscious will, intellect, and action, and lastly as a redemptive process by which the spirit of man was to be called up again into its higher and heavenly state.

Such were the doctrines taught by . . .*j*, but blended with a multitude of the wildest chemical fancies which, however, as mysticism was not connected with . . .*k* was obliged to apply itself to external objects of na-

---

f MS: Paley

g MS: becomes

h MS: Theologic

i MS: an known real

j Blank space left in ms for about 12 letters; *P Lects* (323) conjecturally supplied "[Giordano Bruno]"; OB proposed "[the mystics and visionaries]"

k Blank space left in ms for about 23 letters; needed meaning is perhaps something like "abstract ideas"

---

[50] Cf Schelling *Ueber die Gottheiten* 104–5 where Augustine's objections to Varro's analogical divinities are quoted from *City of God* 7.28.

[51] C discusses the two trinities or triads he mistakenly attributes to Varro in similar terms in a marginal comment on Faber (*CM—CC—*II 575–6): "The 3 first Cabiri are physiological Deities, Gods of Chaos—then comes the caller forth, the *Word*, Hermes, Mercury—then appear the supreme Triad, in which the Hermes appears again as Apollo, or Minerva—& lastly, the mysterious 8th, in which he is again to appear, as the infant Bacchus, the Son of a most high of a mortal Mother". Cf *CM* (*CC*) II 583: "the eight Cabiri were as follows:—Axieros, Axiokersos, and Axiokersa . . . the infernal Trinity—or dim Personëities of the Chaos in the throes of self-organization—

corresponding according to Varro to Pluto, Vulcan and Proserpine—4th the Camillus . . . the Mercury of the Greeks . . . who under other names fills the second place of the Superior and consequently later Trinity—namely, Jove, Minerva (sometimes named Apollo, Helios, or the Sun) and Venus, or *the Spirit*, the Source of Life and Love—lastly, and as the eighth . . . the same Cadmilus or Mercury . . .". C appears to be drawing on Schelling *Ueber die Gottheiten* 20–1, 29–30, 74–5, and 104–5.

[52] Cf Schelling *Ueber die Gottheiten* 21: "Denn ihre Zahl wird sehr bestimmt auf sieben angegeben, denen ein achter beygestellt ist" ("For their number is given very definitely as seven, to which an eighth is added").

[53] Cf 79 above.

ture, but it was applied in the same way, and, where a modern chemist would talk of attractions and affinity and so forth, [the alchemists*ᶦ*] talked of . . .*ᵐ*; but it was in a belief that every being, however apparently inanimate, had a life if it could be called forth, and that all along that was called but the law of likeness. In short, the groundwork of their philosophy was that the law of likeness, arising from what is called the polar principle, that is, that in order to manifest itself every power must appear in two opposites, but these two opposites having a ground of identity were constantly striving to reunite, but not being permitted to pass back to their original state which would amount to annihilation they pressed forward and the two formed a third something, and in this manner they traced in their . . .*ⁿ* philosophy all the facts in nature, and oftentimes with most wonderful and happy effects.[54] Such was the character of [Giordano Bruno*ᵒ*], a man who possessed a genius perhaps fully equal to that of any philosopher of more known name.[55] He was a tutor to our famous Sir Philip Sidney and his friend Lord [Brooke*ᵖ*];[56] he came over into Eng-

---

ᶦ Blank space left in ms for about 12 letters

ᵐ Blank space left in ms for about 12 letters

ⁿ Blank space left in ms for about 11 letters

ᵒ Blank space left in ms for about 11 letters; omission here, and those later in paragraph, supplied from parallel materials in N 21 f 27 (*CN* I 928), in *Friend* (*CC*) I 117*–18*, and in *SW & F* (*CC*) II 896*

ᵖ MS: Bruce

[54] Cf the account of polarity in *Friend* (*CC*) I 94 and 94*.

[55] C had announced his intention of giving "an account of the life of Giordano Bruno" (?1548–1601) in *Friend* (*CC*) I 117*–18*, II 81*–2*, but found it difficult to gain access to his works—see e.g. *CL* IV 656 (to J. H. Frere 16 Jul 1816) where he mentions a failed attempt to borrow some of them. He read Tennemann's account (IX 372–420), in which Tennemann not only complains of the inaccessibility of the books but also admits his inability to read Italian. C's comment expresses his disappointment: "the article of Giordano Bruno especially heartless & superficial—a mere *skim* from one or two only *ʄ* of Bruno's writings—while his interesting attempts in Logic and Mnemonic are passed over altogether—tho' they would have thrown a light on his whole philosophy.—O for a real Life of Bruno, and analysis of his Writings!" Tennemann pays tribute (IX 390) to Jacobi's discussion of Bruno (in *Ueber die*

Lehre des Spinoza 261–77—including a long quotation from *De la causa, principio, ed uno*—and VII–XII) with which C was also familiar. For Bruno's role in C's thinking see esp *BL* (*CC*) I 144–6 and n. In *SW & F* (*CC*) II 894*–7*, C carries his description of Bruno a little farther. In what follows he relies very largely on entries made in N 21 in Apr 1801 (*CN* I 928 and 929).

[56] C as usual is anxious to interest his audience in the English involvement in the history of philosophy. In *CN* III 4034 (1810) he had said of Sidney (1554–86): "he dwells in our thoughts as in an ~~empyrean~~ element of his own effluviation, a divine Empyræum of Love and Wonder, ever like some rare Balsam insulated by an atmosphere of its own delightful Odors". Sir Fulke Greville, 1st Baron Brooke (1554–1628), was the author of tragedies, poems, and a life of Sidney; C had annotated his *Certaine Learned and Elegant Workes* (1633).

land, and one of his exceedingly rare works, which is called the [*Ember Week^q*],[57] describes London as it then was in the time of our Elizabeth, and with all the feelings [with^r] which an Italian accustomed to the splendid feelings and lovely climate of Italy might be supposed to be impressed. This man though a pantheist was religious. He provoked the priests; he was seized at Rome; and in the year 1601 was burnt for an atheist.[58] Before his death he wrote a Latin poem which I think in grandeur of moral has been rarely surpassed. He says,

"To . . .^s, or let them desire to be carried beyond the flaming walls of the world, but we have been gifted with that genius that not blind to the light the sun not deaf . . .^t and to the influences of the Gods. We care not what the opinion of fools is concerning . . .^u diviners. Neither genius nor reason will condemn me nor the cultivated mind of true learning but the superciliousness . . .^v that salute the [reader] of a book from the threshold . . .^w let the sun proceed . . .^x moreover, the species or the form of truth sought for, found, and manifested, will bear me up, and though no one understand me yet if with nature I am wise and under the Deity, that verily is more than enough."[59]

---

^q Blank space left in ms for about 14 letters
^r Sense seems to require the insertion. Note also the rather limp repetition of "feelings" in the following line where a word such as "scenery" might be expected.
^s Blank space left in ms for about 78 letters
^t Blank space left in ms for about 68 letters
^u Blank space left in ms for about 42 letters
^v Blank space left in ms for about 48 letters
^w Blank space left in ms for about 75 letters. MS has "writer", but Bruno's text warrants "reader"; cf n 59 below
^x Blank space left in ms for about 66 letters

---

[57] *La cena de la ceneri* (1584).

[58] It is not certain whether Bruno was burnt alive or after death.

[59] Seven of the eight stanzas of the ode, "Daedalias vacuis plumas", had been included by C in *Omniana* in 1812 where he drew on Bruno *De monade* . . . . *De innumerabilibus immenso* (1591): see *SW & F (CC)* I 318–19 and n. The reporter caught only fragments of C's translation; a complete prose tr (from *SW & F—CC*—I 319) is provided here in its place, but it is impossible to be sure of C's own exact wording.

"Let others desire to fasten Daedalus' feathers to their bare shoulders or seek to be uplifted by the powerful wings of the clouds, let them seek the oarage of the winds or to be carried along in the groove of a fiery orbit, or crave the winged steed of Bellerophon.

"But we have been gifted with such a genius (as unafraid we look upon our fate and the shadows before us) that, not blind to the light of the sun, not deaf to the clear voices of nature, we meet God's gifts with no unthankful heart.

"We care not what the opinion of fools is concerning us, nor what place they think we merit. We soar above them on surer wings. Of what is beyond the clouds, beyond the paths of the winds, we have seen as much as suffices.

"Many will climb thither, with us as leaders, by the ladder set up firmly in their own breasts, which God and his gift of a vigorous mind will provide, not ghosts [adopting C's emendation of

In this mode the brave man passed to his death an atheist, and it would be well if all the priests of Rome could have acquired his genuine piety according to his own apprehensions. His philosophy he has himself stated in these terms: there is throughout all nature an aptitude implanted that all things may be to each and to all, for everything that exists in some time strives to be always, everything that perceives anywhere strives to perceive everywhere and to become that universally whatever it has as an individual; in short, each part of nature contains in itself a germ of the omnipresence, inasmuch as it still strives to be the whole, and what it cannot possess at any one moment it attempts to possess by a perpetual succession of development.[60] His notions are oftentimes highly grand. He considers himself as the reviver of the Pythagorean system of the universe, and consequently opposed himself to Aristotle. But he was the first, I think, of the moderns who asserted the immensity or infinity of the universe, a praise that has been given falsely to Descartes. He warmly defended and supported the Copernican system,[61] and many parts of his chemistry seemed wonderful in his age as anticipations of modern discoveries. He refers everything to invisible fluids or light. Whatever is not light, he says, is a fluid, but this fluid is capable of existing in fixation; or as a fluid or a higher form it is capable of combining with light and then constitutes fire. He affirms the existence of an absolute vacuum, which is

---

manes for *mens*], feathers, fire, wind, clouds, spirits, the phantasms of soothsayers.

"Not quickening sense nor reason will condemn me, nor the clear wisdom of a cultivated mind, but the raised eyebrow of the treacherous sycophant, equipped not with scales, balance, steelyard, observation, but with a crop of miracles.

"Here is no place for the eulogy of a versifying grammarian, the Greeklings' clumsy tongues, the epistles of [scribblers] who salute the reader from the book's threshold, the testimonies of [critics] howling at Zoilus, Momus, Mastix, and their tribe.

"Naked let the sun come forth, unadorned by mists! The trappings of horses are not for human backs! Let the vision of truth, sought for, found, and manifested, bear me onward! Though no one understand me, yet if with nature I am wise, and under the Deity, that surely is more than enough."

[60] Cf *CN* I 928 where C translates freely and with interpolations from *De immenso*, the second item in *De monade* (tr *CN* I 928n): "[This] appetite was implanted so that *everything* may fit itself to *separate things* and to each individual thing. It seeks to be *always* what it is *at some moment*. It tends to see *everywhere* something *somewhere*, to hold *universally* something grasped *particularly*, to enjoy *as a whole* what it enjoys in *part*."

[61] Cf *CN* I 928 f 28ᵛ, referring to *De immenso*: "The second Book is wholly in answer to the Aristotelian Arguments against the Pythagorean system of the Universe. | The Third Book | Utters a sublime panegyric on Nicolaus Copernicus .... The only real fault, he finds, is Copernicus's limitation of the Universe by his Octava Sphæra—Des Cartes not the first therefore ...." For Descartes's priority, cf *SW & F (CC)* I 314 where C objects to the claim made for him in the "Supplement to the Scotch Encyclopædia Britannica".

necessary to motion but of which God is the sole plenitude, and he especially explains gravity as being the necessary consequence of attraction
and repulsion in a system which could exist only as far as there was a central body.[62] The doctrine of astronomy which he teaches has been [re-
vived[y]] even I believe of late years, namely that the sun owes its light and
so forth entirely to its mass, which again is reciprocally the cause and effect of its being the central body[63] and (which is strange, for situate in
Italy he was not likely to observe the Aurora Borealis) he states that every
planet produces from itself necessarily an accumulation of inflammable
matter which floating in the higher regions will give at times a light of its
own, and that the sun, from the immense mass which it possesses beyond
that of all the other planets collectively, has its light by no novelty or difference of formation, but solely by the production which is common to
all matters of the air which he distinguishes—particularly the oxygen
(and describes it with the greatest accuracy) and the substance which he
more properly calls the air, the nitrogen.[64] This he supposes thinning,
[or[z]] still disposing of more and more light, till at last in the higher regions it becomes light altogether; and to this light in its different passages
from a state of fixation upwards to its appearance as light properly, he
gives many of the most striking attributes of our modern electricity.[65] His
poetry will place him high, for there are few . . .[a].[66]

---

[y] MS: reviled   [z] MS: on
[a] Blank space left in ms for about 19 letters

---

[62] The anticipations C had in mind seem to have been theories of gravity, po-larity, and fluidity; in *CN* I 928 ff 28[v]–29 he gives examples of the opinions in question, e.g. "the Sun's motion", "Whatever is not Light, is aqueous", "Gravity &c he explains by Affinity & Repulsion—". Tennemann, whose rele-vant volume had not been published at the time C made his notes on Bruno, sin-gles out the same points about Bruno's scientific views (see Tennemann IX 375, 411–13).

[63] For a discussion of C's interest in the theory put forward by Lorenz Oken in his *Erste Ideen zur Theorie des Lichts* (Jena 1808) that light is "propagated by the interaction between the sun and the planet", see Raimonda Modiano *Cole-ridge and the Concept of Nature* (London 1985) 142–3.

[64] C's awareness of contemporary theories of the aurora borealis or North-ern Lights would have included Erasmus Darwin's suggestion that the phenomena were caused by hydrogen (*Botanic Gar-den* I 18n) and HD's hypothesis that elec-tricity was the cause (mentioned in *CN* II 1974 and n: Mar 1804). For the scientific implications of such theorising see Le-vere 181–4.

[65] Thinking again, presumably, of the notes made in *CN* I 928, and particularly of a passage from *De immenso* 6.14 which is tr in the note: "Hence the aethe-rial heat, the pure air, and the living fire is fused, as it were, in a complete body of creatures. Secretly commingled and in-grafted, the marvellous union of this great spirit, and the fire of Life stands forth above the orders of simple air."

[66] C had quoted from *De immenso* at length in *Friend* (*CC*) I 115–16, II 79*–80*, drawing upon his transcription of it in *CN* I 928, and urging that "the sub-lime piety of the passage" excused "some intermixture of error".

Of a very different character from Bruno was a man whose very name would excite a smile in many, but I confess [is] far from doing it in me, for I have felt my own mind much indebted to him.[67] And why, indeed, should I be ashamed of my [old[b]] friend Jacob Behmen?[68] Many, indeed, and gross, were his delusions, and such as furnished frequent occasion for the triumph of the learned over the poor ignorant shoemaker who had dared think for himself; but while we remember that those delusions were such as might be anticipated from his utter want of all intellectual discipline and from his ignorance of rational psychology, let it not be forgotten, as I have noticed more than once, that the latter defect he had in common with the most learned theologians of his age. Neither with books nor with book-learned men was he conversant. A meek and shy quietist, his intellectual powers were never stimulated into feverous energy by crowds of proselytes or by the ambition of proselyting. He was an enthusiast in the strictest sense, as not merely distinguished, but as contradistinguished, from a fanatic.[69]

[70]Whoever is acquainted with the history of philosophy during the last two or three centuries, cannot but admit that there appears to have existed a sort of secret and tacit compact among the learned not to pass beyond a certain limit in speculative science. The privilege of free thought so highly extolled, has at no time been held valid in actual practice except within this limit, and not a single stride beyond it has ever been ventured without bringing obloquy on the transgressor. The few men of genius

[b] MS: own

[67] The remainder of this paragraph and the following four paragraphs are taken with some variations from *BL* (*CC*) I 146–51.

[68] Jakob Böhme (1575–1624), the shoemaker mystic of Görlitz. C normally uses the English version of his name, Jacob Behmen, as it had appeared on the English translation of his works. In calling Böhme "my old friend" C perhaps acknowledges that his enthusiasm for the "Teutonic theosophist" was a matter of recent public record and responds to the generally disparaging comments the reviews had made on it (for which, see e.g. *CCH* 298, 305, and 357.)

[69] In *BL* (*CC*) I 30–1 C had already distinguished between "enthusiasm" and "fanaticism", concluding his remarks by saying "The sanity of the mind is between superstition with fanaticism on the one hand; and enthusiasm with indiffer-ence and a diseased slowness to action on the other". He had also praised enthusiasm and distinguished it from fanaticism in *LS* (*CC*) 23. The distinction is recurrent; cf e.g. *CM* (*CC*) I 818: ". . . Bunyan was a man of too much Genius to be a Fanatic. No two qualities more contrary than Genius and Fanaticism/Enthusiasm indeed—θεος εν ἡμιν [*God in* us]—is almost a Synonime of Genius—the moral *Life* in the intellectual *Light*, the Will in the Reason . . .". Cf *Friend* (*CC*) I 432–3 and 432*.

[70] Most of the paragraph in *BL* (*CC*) I 147–9 and n to which this paragraph corresponds is a tr, var, from Schelling *Darlegung* 154–5. In *BL* (*CC*) I 147, C had drawn attention to his source: ". . . I in part translate the following observations from a contemporary writer of the Continent . . .".

among the learned class who actually did overstep this boundary, as Bacon and others, anxiously avoided the appearance of having so done.[71] Therefore the true depth of science, and the penetration to the inmost centre from which all the lines of knowledge diverge to their ever distant circumference, was abandoned to the illiterate and the simple, whom unstilled yearning and an original ebulliency of spirit had urged to the investigation of the indwelling and living ground of all things. These then, because their names had never been enrolled in the guilds of the learned, were persecuted by the registered liverymen as interlopers on their rights and privileges. All without distinction were branded as fanatics and phantasts; not only those whose wild and exorbitant imaginations had actually engendered only extravagant and grotesque phantasms, whose productions were for the most part poor copies and gross caricatures of genuine inspiration, but the truly inspired likewise, the originals themselves, and this for no other reason but because they were the unlearned men of humble and obscure occupations. When and from whom among the literati by profession have we ever heard the divine doxology repeated, "I thank thee, O Father, Lord of Heaven and Earth, because thou hast hid these things from the wise and prudent and hast revealed them unto babes"?[72] No, the haughty priests of learning not only banished from the schools and marts of science all who had dared draw living waters from the fountain,[73] but drove them out of the very temple which meantime the buyers and sellers and money-changers were suffered to make a den of thieves.[74]

And yet it would not be easy to discover any substantial distinction, ground for this contemptuous pride, in those literati who have most distinguished themselves by their scorn of Behmen, De Thoyras, George Fox[75] and others, unless it be that they could write orthographically,

---

[71] The introduction of Bacon as a specific example is a departure from the text of *BL* (and of Schelling) and helps to prepare the way for the discussion of Bacon that follows (486–92 below).

[72] Luke 10.21 (var).

[73] Cf Jer 2.13: "they have forsaken me the fountain of living waters".

[74] Matt 21.12–13 (var).

[75] In *BL* the name De Thoyras appears at this point where Taulerus seems to be meant. Johannes Tauler (c 1300–61), the Dominican monk of Strasburg, noted for his emphasis on virtuous life rather than on metaphysics and known through his surviving sermons. C does not often

mention him and in 1817 seems to have known him only at second hand. (On 20 Jun 1817 C asked HCR about his writings, saying, "Mr Tieck mentioned an old German Divine—Was it Tauler?" and adds an inquiry about followers of Böhme and anecdotes about Bruno: *CL* IV 742. In 1821 he evidently obtained "short specimens from the very rare Works of J. Tauler" (*CL* v 205: to John Murray [26 Jan 1822]). Cf a marginal comment on Jacob Rhenferd *Opera philologica* (Utrecht 1722) 204–8 (*CM—CC—*IV): "the Mystics of the middle Ages from Hugo de Sancto Victore to Tauler, or the Protestant Masters

make smooth periods, and had the fashions of authorship almost literally at their fingers' ends, while the latter, in simplicity of soul, made their words immediate echoes of their feelings. Hence the frequency of those phrases among which [some] have been mistaken for pretences to immediate inspiration, as, for instance, "It was delivered unto me", "I strove not to speak", "I said, I will be silent, but the word was in my heart as a burning fire", and so forth.[76] Hence, too, the unwillingness to give offence; hence the foresight and the dread of the clamours which would be raised against them, so frequently avowed in the writings of these men, and expressed, as was natural, in the words of the only book with which they were familiar. "Woe is me that I am become a man of strife and a man of contention, I love peace, the souls of men are dear unto me, yet because I seek for light everyone of them doth curse me".[77] Oh, it requires deeper feeling and a strong[er] imagination than belong to most of those to whom reasoning and fluent expression have been as a trade learned in boyhood, to conceive with what might, with what inward strivings and commotion, the perception of a new and vital truth takes possession of an uneducated man of genius.

His meditations are almost inevitably employed on the eternal or the everlasting, for "the world is not his friend, nor the world's law".[78] Need we then be surprised that under an excitement at once so strong and so unusual the man's body should sympathise with the struggles of his mind, or that he should at times be so far deluded as to mistake the tumultuous sensations of his nerves and the co-existing spectres of his fancy as parts or symbols of the truths which were opening on him? But one assertion I will venture to make as suggested by my own experience, that there exist folios on the human understanding and the nature of man which would have a far juster claim to their high rank and celebrity if in the whole huge

---

of the interior way, as Behmen, Zinzendorf &c . . ." and a note in the endpapers on Tennemann VIII 956 (*CM—CC—v*) where Tauler is mentioned in the course of an objection to Tennemann's treatment of mysticism. George Fox (1624–91), the founder of the Society of Friends. In 1802 C had confided in his friend John Prior Estlin, a Unitarian minister: "My creed is very simple—my confession of Faith very brief. I approve altogether & embrace entirely the *Religion* of the Quakers, but exceedingly dislike the *sect*, & their own notions of their own Religion.—By Quakerism I understand the opinions of George Fox . . ." (*CL* II 893: 7 Dec 1802).

[76] *BL* (*CC*) I 150n remarks that these seem to be "formulaic phrases".

[77] A variant on Jer 15.10: "Woe is me, my mother, that thou hast borne me a man of strife and a man of contention to the whole earth! I have neither lent on usury, nor men have lent to me on usury; yet every one of them doth curse me."

[78] Shakespeare *Romeo and Juliet* V i 72 (var), the words applied by Romeo to the poor apothecary he persuades to sell him poison.

volume there could be found as much fullness of heart and intellect as burst forth in many a simple page of George Fox, Jacob Behmen, and even of Behmen's commentator, the warm and fervent William Law.[79]

He was indeed a stupendous human being.[80] Had he received the discipline of education, above all, had he possessed the knowledge which would have guarded him against his own delusions, I scarcely know whether we should have had reason to attribute greater genius even to Plato himself. When I consider that this ignorant man by the result of his own meditations presented the Newtonian system in a clearness which it certainly had never before appeared in, not even to Copernicus himself or to the learned Bruno;[81] when I trace in him the love of action and that constant sense of the truth that all nature is in a perpetual evolution, that two great powers are for ever working, manifesting themselves alike in the apparently inadequate and inanimated, and in intellectual nature, namely, the powers by which each particular endeavours to detach itself from nature and the counteracting powers by which nature is still bringing back each of her creatures into itself. This led him assuredly into anticipations and views of truth which will detract from many modern discoveries some part at least of their originality, but, above all, that spirit of love which runs through him, that dread of contempt, that belief that the potential works in us even as the actual is working on us, and that not only man but every creature contains in itself a higher being, which is, indeed, bedimmed under the lustre of the immediate and sensual being which is, as it were, its husk and outward covering, but which in moments of tranquillity most frequently appears in the voice of conscience, but often in high aspirations and in feelings of faith that remain afterwards as sentiments and thoughts of consolation. When I find this animating his whole language, presenting everywhere a being who had forgotten himself in the love by which he possessed all things, I again and again wish that some more enlightened friend had been present and had rescued this

---

[79] William Law (1686–1761), best known for his *Serious Call to a Devout and Holy Life* (1728), was also author of the life of Böhme in *The Works of Jacob Behmen* ed G. Ward and T. Langcake (4 vols 1764–81).

[80] I.e. Böhme.

[81] What C means by the Newtonian system here is suggested by a passage in *AR* (*CC*) 236: "The dependence of the Understanding on the representations of the Senses, and its consequent posteriority thereto, as contrasted with the inde-

pendence and antecedency of Reason, are strikingly exemplified in the Ptolemaic System (that truly wonderful product and highest boast of the Faculty, judging according to the Senses!) compared with the Newtonian, as the Offspring of a yet higher Power, arranging, correcting, and annulling the representations of the Senses according to its own inherent Laws and constitutive Ideas." For C's annotations of Böhme see *CM* (*CC*) I 553–696.

man from evils. I mean the error and the delusion which fortunately, however, his own sense of right held from him, for with all this, though he himself prized his system mainly as explaining and inferring all the mysteries of religion, there is, as there was throughout in the philosophy of that time, a tendency to pantheism, or rather it was itself a disguised pantheism.[82] In short, with the exception of those who have strictly followed the Scriptures and who will not cheat themselves by explaining this away into a metaphor and that into an accommodation, I know none who have avoided one or the other of two evils: the one making the world have the same relation to God as a watch has to a watchmaker, in truth giving all up to secondary causes, and rendering the omnipresence of the great Being the ground of all things as well as their Creator, a mere word of honour and of pomp in the state-room of the intellect; or the opposite error of carrying the omnipresence into a condition of nature-with-God[c], and involving all those fearful consequences from which, as I before said, the best refuge is not to see them. From this I cannot excuse Behmen's writings any more than I can praise or attempt or pretend to understand many of the strange fancies by which he has represented his truths. Sometimes, indeed, one can guess at the meaning; sometimes it is utter darkness. And altogether he represents a great mirror, but placed in the shade; all the objects of nature seem to pass by, but they are reflected in shadow and dimly, but now and then a light passes along and the mirror in the shade flashes and seems to lighten from out of its retirement.[83]

At this time, when the downfall of the Scholastic philosophy and the emancipation from the superstitions in at least the northern parts of Europe had left the mind open and almost impelled it to real silence, there arose our great Lord Bacon, and, at the same time nearly with him, the famous Kepler;[84] two men, one of whom we all know as the beginning of truly scientific astronomy,[85] of that science which possesses power and

---

[c] MS: nature with God

[82] Cf *CM* (*CC*) I 602, a note dated 27 Aug 1818: "What resemblance it [Böhme's error] may have to the system of Giordano Bruno, I have read too few of Bruno's writings to say, and read them at a time, when I was not competent to ask the question, but was myself intoxicated with the vernal fragrance & effluvia from the flowers and first-fruits of Pantheism, unaware of its bitter root . . .".

[83] Cf *CM* (*CC*) I 619: "Behmen often

starts a difficulty, which he cannot solve, or solves but very imperfectly. . . . The κατάβασις τῶν πνευμάτων ὥστε ὕλη γένεσθαι [descent of spirits to become matter] . . . is an Idea, the Flash of which he has often reflected in his Mirror, but never mastered or kept fast hold of."

[84] Johannes Kepler (1571–1630), whom C had recently eulogised in *Friend* (*CC*) I 485–6.

[85] By "truly scientific astronomy" C seems to mean Kepler's laws of planetary

prophecy and which will for ever remain the greatest monument of human greatness, because by laws demonstrably drawn out of his own mind he has, in that mind, not only [lit^d], but as far as his own purposes require it, controlled the mighty orbs of nature; and Lord Bacon, who appeared not for any one purpose but to purify the whole of the mind from all its errors by having given first that complete analysis of the human soul without which we might have gone on forever weighing one thing after another in scales which we had never examined, and thus constantly perhaps mistaking as existing in the thing weighed that which was really owing to the scales themselves.[86]

I have, in the beginning of this lecture, referred in part to it when I spoke of the threefold powers with which man was gifted and of the evils which had arisen from their confusion. Lord Bacon has been commonly understood as if in his system itself he had deduced the propriety of a mode of philosophising of which, indeed, there are found in his own writings not any specimens but some recommendations which it is difficult to suppose that he himself could have been in earnest with. His own philosophy is this: he demands, indeed, experiment as the true groundwork of all real knowledge, but what does he mean by experiment? He himself strongly contrasts it with the gossiping with nature, as he calls it, of the alchemists, the putting one thing to another in order to see if anything would come out of it. No, he requires some well-grounded purpose in the mind, some self-consistent anticipation of the result, in short, the *prudens* [*quaestio^e*], the prudent forethought and enquiry which he declares to be [*dimidium scientiae^f*], the one half of one science. He expressly says, "We do not aim at science either by the senses or by instruments so much as by experiments, for the subtlety of experiments is far greater than that of the sense though aided with the most exquisite instruments. For we

---

^{d} OB conjecturally emended to "[lighted]". MS: light
^{e} Blank space left in ms for about 15 letters; omission supplied from parallel passage in *Friend (CC)* I 489
^{f} Blank space left in ms for about 14 letters; omission supplied from *Friend (CC)* I 489

---

motion, which he, like the *Naturphilosophen*, believed had anticipated Newton on gravitation. See Levere 74–5 and 143–4. Astronomy is a "monument of human greatness" because it is derived from mathematical reasoning rather than from observation of phenomena. In *TL* (*SW & F—CC*—I 519*) C had called it "the sublime science of astronomy, having for its objects the vast masses which 'God placed in the firmament of the heaven to be for *signs* and for seasons, for days and years'". His sustained reverence for astronomy was a point of difference between him and the mechanistic astronomers of the Enlightenment.

[86] In *Friend (CC)* I 472–95 C had used Bacon as the central exemplar of his "Essays on the Principles of Method". The "compleat analysis of the human soul" was to be found in his *Novum organum* and *Advancement of Learning*.

speak of those experiments which have been preconceived and[g] knowingly placed and arranged to the intention and that for the purpose of that which is sought for according to art. Therefore", says he, "we do not attribute much to the immediate and proper perception of the sense, but we deduce the matter to this point, that the sense can judge only of the experiment, but it is the experiment which must inform us of the law which is the thing itself."[87] In this instance, Lord Bacon's fondness for [pungent antitheses[h]] has perhaps rather obscured his meaning; but the sense is this, that our perception can apprehend through the organs of sense only the phenomena evoked by the experiment, but that same power of mind, which out of its own laws has proposed the experiment, can judge whether in nature there is a law correspondent to the same. In order, therefore, to explain the different errors of men, he says that there is a power which can give birth to this question; he calls this the [*lux intellectus*, the *lumen siccum*[i]],[88] the pure and impersonal reason freed from all the personal idols which this great legislator of science then enumerates, namely the idols of the den, of the theatre, and of the market-place[89] he means, freed from the passions, the prejudices, the peculiar habits, of the human understanding natural or acquired, but, above all, pure from the delusions which lead men to take the forms [and[j]] mechanism [of their own mere reflective faculty[k]], as a measure of nature and the Deity. In short, to use the bold but happy phrase of a late ingenious French writer, he guards you against the man particular as contrasted with the general man,[90] and most truly and in strict consonance in this with Plato does the immortal

[g] MS: and that
[h] Blank space left in ms for about 15 letters; omission supplied from parallel passage in *Friend* (*CC*) I 489
[i] Corrected to accord with *Friend* (*CC*) I 490
[j] Corrected to accord with *Friend* (*CC*) I 490
[k] Blank space left in ms for about 72 letters; omission supplied from *Friend* (*CC*) I 490, slightly adapted

[87] Translated from the Latin of Bacon *Distributio operis*: *Works* (1740) I 15 (var) that was given in *Friend* (*CC*) I 489. C continues to quote loosely or paraphrase *Friend* (*CC*) I 489–91 to the end of the paragraph.
[88] Literally "light of the mind", the "dry light", phrases from Bacon *Novum organum* bk 1 aph 49: *Works* (1740) I 279 (Spedding IV 57).
[89] Bacon *Novum organum* bk 1 aphs 39–44: *Works* (1740) I 277–8: "*idola specûs*", "*idola theatri*", "*idola fori*"

(Spedding IV 53–4).
[90] C often uses this example, sometimes, as in *Friend* (*CC*) I 490, quoting the phrase in French. Various promising candidates, Helvétius and Rousseau among them, have been looked through but the author remains unidentified. The distinction may be derived from Rousseau's distinction between the "volonté générale" and the "volonté particulière" (the general will and the particular or individual will: see e.g. *Émile* bk 5).

Verulam[91] [teach that the human understanding, even independent of the causes that always, previously to its purification by philosophy[l]], render that more or less turbid or uneven [, that our understanding[m]] not only reflects the object[s] subjectively, [but that it is itself only a phenomenon of the inner sense and requires the same corrections as the appearances transmitted by the[n]] outward senses. But that there is potentially, if not actually, in every rational being, a somewhat, call it what you will, the purest reason, the spirit of true light and intellectual [intuition, and that in this are to be found the indispensable conditions of all science, whether meditative, contemplative, or experimental, is often[o]] expressed and everywhere supposed by Lord Bacon. And that this is not only the right but the [possible[p]] nature of the human mind, to which it is capable of being restored, is implied in the various remedies prescribed by him for its diseases, [and in the various means of neutralising or converting into useful instrumentality the imperfections which cannot be removed. There is a sublime truth contained in his favourite phrase—*Idola intellectus*.[92] . . . Nay, he has shown and established[q]] the true criterion between the ideas of the mind and the idols, namely that the former are manifested by their adequacy to those ideas in nature which in and through them are contemplated.

This therefore is the true Baconic philosophy. It consists in this, in a profound meditation on those laws which the pure reason in man reveals to him, with the confident anticipation and faith that to this will be found to correspond certain laws in nature. If there be aught that can be said to be purely in the human mind, it is surely those acts of its own imagination which the mathematician avails himself of; for I need not, I am sure, tell you that a line upon a slate is but a picture of that act of the imagination which the mathematician alone consults.[93] That it is the picture only,

---

[l]   Blank space left in ms for about 63 letters; omission supplied from *Friend* (*CC*) I 491
[m]   Necessary missing phrase inserted from *Friend* (*CC*) I 491
[n]   Blank space left in ms for about 46 letters; omission supplied by a shortened version of corresponding passage in *Friend* (*CC*) I 491
[o]   Blank space left in ms for about 77 letters; omission supplied by a shortened version of corresponding passage in *Friend* (*CC*) I 491
[p]   Corrected to accord with *Friend* (*CC*) I 491. MS: visible
[q]   Blank space left in ms for about 146 letters; omission supplied by a shortened version of corresponding passage in *Friend* (*CC*) I 491

[91]   In *Friend* (*CC*) I 490, on which C is drawing, Heraclitus is paired with Plato "among the ancients" and the Scottish philosopher Dugald Stewart (1753–1828) with Bacon "among the moderns".
[92]   "Intellectual idols"; e.g. *De aug-* *mentis scientiarum* bk 5 ch 4: *Works* (1740) I 154 (Spedding I 643).
[93]   For C's views at about this time on the nature of the mathematical line, see *CN* IV 4513 and n (Apr 1819).

is evident, for never could we learn the act of the imagination or form an idea of a line in the mathematical sense from that picture of it which we draw beforehand, otherwise how could we draw it without depth or breadth? It becomes evidently, too, an act of the imagination. Out of these simple acts, the mind, still proceeding, raises that wonderful superstructure of geometry, and then looking abroad into nature finds that in its own nature it has been fathoming nature, and that nature itself is but the greater mirror in which he beholds his own present and his own past being in the law, and learns to reverence, while he feels, the necessity of that one great Being whose eternal reason is the ground and absolute condition of the ideas in the mind, and no less the ground and the absolute cause of all the correspondent realities in nature, the reality of nature for ever consisting in the law by which each thing is that which it is.[94]

Hence, and so has Lord Bacon told us, all science approaches to its perfection in proportion as it immaterialises objects.[95] For instance, in the motion of the heavenly bodies we in reality consider only a few abstractions of mass, distance, and so forth. The whole [phenomenon[r]] of light, the materiality of which itself has been more than once doubted of, [is[s]] nothing but a sublime geometry drawn by its rays; while in magnetism, the [phenomenon[r]] is altogether lost, and the whole process by which we trace it is the power of intellect. We know it not as visible but by its powers; if instead of this we are to substitute the common notion of Lord Bacon[96] that you are to watch everything without having any reason for so doing, and that after you have collected the facts that belong to any subject, if any person could divide them and tell what could be contradicted, then you may proceed to the theory, which must necessarily be

---

[r] MS: phenomena   [s] MS: as   [t] MS: phenomena

[94] Anticipations of the phraseology of this sentence had appeared in *BL* (*CC*) ii 62 and *Friend* (*CC*) i 112 and ii 79.

[95] Cf *BL* (*CC*) i 256: "The highest perfection of natural philosophy would consist in the perfect spiritualization of all the laws of nature into laws of intuition and intellect. The phænomena (*the material*) must wholly disappear, and the laws alone (*the formal*) must remain." In *BL*, C was translating a passage from Schelling (*Philosophische Schriften*— Landshut 1809—i 332); here he seems to attribute an anticipation of Schelling's argument to Bacon, thinking, perhaps, of the implication of the remark in *Novum*

organum: "Optime autem cedit inquisitio naturalis, quando physicum terminatur in mathematico" ("inquiries into nature have the best result, when they begin with physics and end in mathematics") *Works* (1740) i 317; Spedding iv 126.

[96] I.e. the notion that people commonly have of his views. Cf *TM* (*SW & F—CC—*i 661–2): "Those who talk superficially about Bacon's philosophy, that is to say, nineteen-twentieths of those who talk about it at all, know little more than his induction, and the application which he makes of his own method, to particular classes of physical facts . . .".

false if you omit any one term; and consequently (as in all physical things the difference between them and the mathematical is that in the mathematical you can control them because they are the things of your will), it follows necessarily, then, there can be no such thing as a physical theory.[97] Nothing remains, therefore, but either an hypothesis which, if it is a thing, is part of the problem, or the discovery of some law, by which our knowledge proceeds from the centre and diverges towards, by a constant approximation, an ever distant circumference, but feeling its progress as it moves and still increasing in power as it travels onward.

For this a very ingenious man, and a man who had a particular talent for discovery and the whole history of whose very active life is the best answer to his own recommendation, has proposed the following, and I must again repeat that this is most frequently the opinion now of Lord Bacon's philosophy: he says that before a foundation can be laid "upon which anything like a sound and [stable[u]] theory can be [constituted"[v]], you are to make yourself acquainted with a certain number of facts, which I think contain[w] three and twenty pages, of which I will give you one small specimen —you are to be acquainted with [x]["]the history of pot-

---

[u] Corrected to accord with corresponding passage in *Friend* (*CC*) I 484*. MS: staple
[v] Corrected to accord with *Friend* (*CC*) I 484*. MS: constructed
[w] *P Lects* (334–5) emended to "[the lists of] which I think contain"
[x] The whole quotation, of which reporter caught only fragments, had appeared in *Friend* (*CC*) I 484* and runs as follows: " 'The history of potters, tobacco-pipe-makers, glaziers, glass-grinders, looking-glass makers or foilers, spectacle-makers and optic-glass-makers, makers of counterfeit pearl and precious stones, bugle-makers, lamp-blowers, colour-makers, colour-grinders, glass-painters, enamellers, varnishers, colour-sellers, *painters, limners, picture-drawers, makers of baby-heads, of little bowling-stones or marbles*, fustian-makers (query whether *poets* are included in this trade?), music-masters, tinsey-makers, and taggers.—The history of schoolmasters, writing-masters, printers, book-binders, stage-players, dancing-masters, and vaulters, *apothecaries, chirurgeons, seamsters, butchers, barbers, laundresses,* and *cosmetics!* &c. &c. &c. &c. (the true nature of which being actually determined) WILL HUGELY FACILITATE OUR INQUIRIES IN PHILOSOPHY!!!'

"As a summary of Dr. R. Hooke's multifarious recipe for the growth of Science may be fairly placed that of the celebrated Dr. WATTS for the improvement of the mind, which was thought, by Dr. KNOX, to be worthy of insertion in the *Elegant* Extracts, vol. ii. p. 456, under the head of

DIRECTIONS CONCERNING OUR IDEAS

'Furnish yourselves with *a rich variety of Ideas*. Acquaint yourself with *things* ancient and modern; *things* natural, civil, and religious; *things* of your native land, and of foreign countries; *things* domestic and national; *things* present, past, and future; and above all, be well acquainted with God and yourselves; with animal nature, and the workings of your own spirit. *Such a general acquaintance with things will be of very great advantage.*' "

[97] Because the phenomena to be observed before a generalisation can be attempted are inexhaustible.

ters, tobacco-pipe makers, . . .*y* or furriers, spectacle makers . . .*z* picture drawers, makers of baby heads, of little bowling stones . . .*a*. I do not know whether poets deal in this trade music masters . . .*b* butchers, builders, . . .*c* and cosmetics &c &c &c, the truth of which", he concludes, "being all . . .*d*98 in philosophy as a summary of Doctor . . .*e* [multifarious*f*] recipe . . .*g* which was thought by Doctor . . .*h* to be worthy of insertion . . .*i* directions concerning our ideas furnish yourselves", for it is worth listening to, "furnish yourselves with a rich variety of ideas: acquaint yourselves with things ancient and modern, things natural, civil, and religious; things of your own native land, and of foreign countries; things domestic and national; things past, present, and future; and above all be well acquainted with God and yourselves; learn animal nature and the working of your own spirits . . .*j*. Such a general acquaintance with things will be of very great advantage."99 Certainly a most incomparable lesson.100   ✦

No, the truth is that let any unprejudiced naturalist turn even to Lord Bacon's own questions and proposals for the investigation of greater problems*k* or to [his Discourse*l*] [on the Winds*m*] or enquire of his own experience or historical recollection whether any important discovery was ever made in this way. For though Lord Bacon never so far deviates from his own principles as not to admonish his readers that the particu-

---

y Blank space left in ms for about 141 letters
z Blank space left in ms for about 176 letters
a Blank space left in ms for about 62 letters
b Blank space left in ms for about 112 letters
c Blank space left in ms for about 13 letters
d Blank space left in ms for about 117 letters
e Blank space left in ms for about 8 letters   *f* MS: Metaphors
g Blank space left in ms for about 109 letters
h Blank space left in ms for about 8 letters
i Blank space left in ms for about 106 letters
j Blank space left in ms for about 20 letters
k Corresponding passage in *Friend* (*CC*) I 483 has "single problems"
l Corrected to accord with *Friend* (*CC*) I 483. MS: discoverer
m Blank space left in ms for about 70 letters; omission supplied from *Friend* (*CC*) I 483

98 The passage is quoted from *Friend* (*CC*) I 484* which in turn is quoted from Robert Hooke *A General Scheme, or Idea of the Present State of Natural Philosophy* in *Posthumous Works* (London 1705) 24–6 (var).

99 The two quotations are from Isaac Watts *The Improvement of the Mind* (London 1741), quoted from *Elegant Extracts; or, Useful and Entertaining Passages in Prose* ed Vicesimus Knox (1752–1821) (London 1784) bk 2 sec 397 p 456 (var) which is quoted in turn from *Friend* (*CC*) I 484*.

100 The paragraph as a whole is a quotation from *Friend* (*CC*) I 484* (var).

lars are [thus[n]] to be collected, only[o] that by [careful selection they may be concentrated into universals[p]]; yet so immense is their number, and so various and almost endless the relations in which each is to be separately considered, that the life of an antediluvian [patriarch would be expended, and his strength and spirits have been wasted, in merely polling the votes, and long before he could commence the process of simplification[q]], or have arrived in sight [of[r]] the law which was [to reward the toils of the over-tasked Psyche[s]].[101]

[102]I trust I yield to none in my veneration for Lord Bacon's writings. Proud of his name we all must be as men of science; as Englishmen we might be almost vain of him. But I will not suffer nationality so far to bribe me as not to confess that there are points [in the character of our Verulam, from which we turn to the life and labours[t]] of John Kepler as from gloom to sunshine. The beginning and the close of his life were clouded with poverty and domestic troubles while [the intermediate years were comprised within the most tumultuous period of the history of his country, when the furies of religious and political discord[u]] had left neither his head nor heart for the Muses. But Kepler seemed born to prove that true genius could overcome all obstacles.[103] [If he gives an account of his modes of proceeding, and of the views under which they first occurred to his mind, how unostentatiously and[v]] *in transitu*, as it were, does he introduce himself to our notice: [and yet never fails to present the liv-

---

[n] Corrected to accord with *Friend* (*CC*) I 484. MS: those

[o] MS: only—

[p] Blank space left in ms for about 84 letters; omission supplied from corresponding passage in *Friend* (*CC*) I 484

[q] Blank space left in ms for about 114 letters; omission supplied from *Friend* (*CC*) I 485

[r] MS: in

[s] Blank space left in ms for about 84 letters; omission supplied from corresponding passage in *Friend* (*CC*) I 485

[t] Blank space left in ms for about 99 letters; omission supplied from *Friend* (*CC*) I 485

[u] Blank space left in ms for about 84 letters; omission supplied from *Friend* (*CC*) I 485

[v] Blank space left in ms for about 84 letters; omission supplied from *Friend* (*CC*) I 485

---

[101] The paragraph is quoted from *Friend* (*CC*) I 483–5 (var). At 485* and n, C refers to Apuleius's tale of Cupid and Psyche in *Metamorphoses* bks 5 and 6.

[102] The paragraph down to "of the originals themselves" (494 line 3) is a quotation from *Friend* (*CC*) I 485–7 (var).

[103] Cf Goethe *Zur Farbenlehre* II 247: "Der Anfang und das Ende seines Lebens werden durch Familienverhältnisse verkümmert, seine mittlere Zeit fällt in die unruhigste Epoche, und doch dringt sein glückliches Naturell durch" ("The beginning and the end of his life were complicated by family obligations, his middle time coincided with the most unquiet epoch, and nevertheless his cheerful temperament won through").

ing germ out of which the genuine method, as the inner form of the tree of science^w], springs up! With what affectionate reverence does he express himself of his master and immediate predecessor, Tycho Brahe![104] How often and how gladly [does he speak of Copernicus! and with what fervent tones of faith and consolation does he proclaim the historic fact that the great men of all ages have prepared the way for each other^x], as pioneers and heralds! Equally just to the ancients and to his [contemporaries, how circumstantially, and with what exactness of detail, does Kepler demonstrate that Euclid copernicises![105] And how elegant the compliments which he addresses to Porta! With what cordiality he thanks him for the invention of the camera obscura, as enlarging his views into the laws of vision![106] But while^y] we cannot avoid contrasting this generous enthusiasm [with Lord Bacon's cold invidious treatment of Gilbert,[107] and his assertion that the works^z] of Plato and Aristotle had been carried down by the stream of time, like straws, by their levity alone, when things of weight and worth sunk to the bottom; and truly so calumniously does he everywhere speak of Plato that we are obliged to believe that the manifold occupations and anxieties to which his public and professional duties engaged him and his courtly, [alas!^a], his [servile, prostitute, and mendicant ambition, entangled him in his after years, though

---

^w Blank space left in ms for about 108 letters; omission supplied from *Friend* (*CC*) I 485

^x Blank space left in ms for about 106 letters; omission supplied from *Friend* (*CC*) I 486

^y Blank space left in ms for about 200 letters; omission supplied from corresponding passage, slightly shortened, in *Friend* (*CC*) I 486

^z Blank space left in ms for about 205 letters; omission supplied from *Friend* (*CC*) I 486

^a Corrected to accord with *Friend* (*CC*) I 486. MS: at least

---

[104] Tycho Brahe (1546–1601), Danish astronomer, whose *Astronomiae instauratae progymnasmata* (2 vols 1602–3) was edited by Kepler. Cf Goethe *Zur Farbenlehre* II 248: "Wie verehrt er seinen Meister und Vorgesetzten Tycho!" ("How he reveres Tycho, his master and predecessor!")

[105] Cf Goethe *Zur Farbenlehre* II 249: "Wie umständlich und genau zeigt Keppler, dass Euklides Copernikisire" ("How comprehensively and precisely does Kepler demonstrate that Euclid Copernicises"). *OED* cites C for its first instance of "Copernicize".

[106] The acknowledgment is recorded in Goethe *Zur Farbenlehre* II 249: "Eben so verhält er sich zu seinen Zeitgenossen. Dem Wilhelm Porta ertheilt er die anmuthigsten Lobsprüche, den herzlichsten Dank für die Entdeckung der *Camera obscura*, für die dadurch auf einmal erweiterte Einsicht in die Gesetze des Sehens" ("He behaved in just this way to his contemporaries. He gave the most grateful eulogy to William Porta, the sincerest thanks for the discovery of the *camera obscura*, for the immediately broadened insight into the laws of vision that this achieved"). Giambattista della Porta (?1538–1615) was the Neapolitan author of *Magia naturalis* (1558).

[107] William Gilbert (1540–1603), author of *De magnete* (London 1600).

we should avow our conviction that he[b]] must have derived his opinions of Plato and Aristotle from any source rather than from a dispassionate study of the originals themselves. This, however, would have been a trifle, but was not true of the great men themselves. Plato and Aristotle were abundantly the falsifiers of [earlier[c]] systems, but it is not a trifle that those are the parts in Lord Bacon's character, and those the passages in his writings which have been of late more read, and which are more in the mouths and minds of the common race of modern materialists than his invaluable system, which differs in no other respect from that of [Plato[d]] except as the objects were different, except as far as that the mind was the great object in Plato and what I may call the ideal, while the philosophy and the correspondence of the laws of nature to the ideas of the pure reason the object of Lord Bacon. But unfortunately men had been, as it were, satiated with the admiration of the great men of old; the mind wanted to act upon its own stores, upon its own faculties, and with this there was much of the insolence of youth. Had it remained there we should have indeed only had to travel a long road before we came back again and found we might have spared ourselves the trouble, but it unfortunately extended into the moral and political character of nations. Nothing was to have been known before, nothing was to be valued, all was to be created anew; and from this moment the mind was led to the revival of systems which the better feelings of mankind had exploded for many many centuries, and new systems that had not the least claim to originality but which have a most dreadful claim to history from the effects they have produced.

These will form the subject of my next lecture, when I shall trace the state of mind in the Civil Wars under Charles I, and from thence the progress of materialism and infidelity on to the time immediately before the French Revolution. And I beg to conclude with one remark, namely, that the influences of philosophy must not be sought for either in the lives of philosophers themselves, or in the immediate effect of their writings upon the students of speculative knowledge. No, we must look for it everywhere, only not in their own shape, for it becomes active by being diluted. It combines itself as a colour, as it were, lying on the public mind, as a sort of preparation for receiving thought in a particular way and excluding particular views, and in this way its effect has been great, indeed great in past times for good, but great likewise in recent times for evil,

---

[b] Blank space left in ms for about 86 letters; omission supplied from corresponding passage, slightly shortened, in *Friend* (*CC*) I 486

[c] MS: their

[d] MS: Plato's

and if anyone would doubt the truth of what I say, let him look at the disputes in the time of Charles I and detract from the controversies of the Calvinists and Arminians all that belongs to the Christian gospel and leave nothing behind but the metaphysics, and I suspect that spite of the theological phrases, he has left at least four-fifths of the whole work untouched, and that Christianity might fairly give up her claim to the bitterest controversies and resign them again to the Schools.[108]

[108] Cf *C&S* (*CC*) 134–5: "It is . . . my full conviction that the rites and doctrines . . . of the Catholics . . . if they were fairly, and in the light of a sound philosophy, compared with either of the two main divisions of Protestantism, as it now exists in this country, *i.e.* with the fashionable doctrines and interpretations of the Arminian and Grotian school on the one hand, and with the tenets and language of the modern Calvinists on the other, an enlightened disciple of John and of Paul would be perplexed, which of the three to prefer as the least unlike the profound and sublime system, he had learnt from his great masters." Cf *CN* III 3963 (N 18: Jul 1810) where the Arminian and Calvinist differences are stated.

DRAFT MS

BM Add MS 47,523 (N 25) ff 70ᵛ–2ᵛ

[f 70ᵛ] [a]+8 March. 1819. From Edward VI to the ~~elose~~ close ⟨of the Reign⟩ of James the first: or the age of Elizabeth, the golden Age of English Intellect.[+]

Chapter of Contents

Introduction—The times immediately before and after the Reformation rapidly, compressly, but vividly characterized in contrast with the same of the French Revolution—[1]

~~2.~~ Philosophy proved to have been indirectly yet properly the Cause of the Reformation, and not polite or classic Literature—other than as subordinate tho' necessary ally.—Else why not in Italy?—and why was it so *near* to it in Spain?—and why most successful in its Birth-place, Germany?— See p. 84 Meiners Lebenb[b]: Vol I.[2] Besides, the vigor, *thorny husk* of Scholastic Philosophy *What* a common sense did it not produce? comp.[c] with the *effete* C. s.[d] of our days—a young *Lover* ✳ [3] old Debauchee—

Extremes meet—instanced for the 35967845th time in the actual Hypereleutherism,[4] the licentious παρρησια[5] of the Schools by virtue of their outward Badge of unconditional Slavery.

[a] The "plus" signs (here and following "Intellect") seem to indicate a heading or title
[b] For "Lebensbeschreibungen"
[c] For "compared"
[d] For "Common sense"

[1] In the lect at 468 above C adds the Civil War to the Reformation and the French Revolution to comprise the "three great instructive events in history". Cf the same formulation at 499 below.

[2] The reference to Meiners (I 84–5) is to a discussion of the state of German intellectual life in the fifteenth century in which the unsophisticated level of polite learning is contrasted with its counterparts in Italy and France.

[3] "As contrasted with".

[4] An extreme form of zeal for freedom. The word is not recorded in *OED*, although "eleutherism" is, the first instance being dated 1802.

[5] "Outspokenness", "frankness", "freedom of speech"; claimed as a privilege by the ancient Athenians.

"Physic*as, Platonic*as, Mathematic*as, theologic*as, chaldaic*as, orphic*as, magic*as, cabbalistic*as, paradox*as dogmatic*as, parad:*e* sceptic*as, heretic*as, imo, βλασφημουσα/ς, sine periculo, sine scandalo defendere et sustinere ~~poterant~~, homini scholastico licebat, sint modo prefixa hæc vel hujusmodi verba—

"In his omnibus nihil assertive vel probabiliter pono, nisi quatenus id vel verum vel probabile judicat sacrosancta ecclesia catholica, et caput ejus bene meritum, summus pontifex &c—et ~~si~~ quascunque conclusiones condemnabit ille, istae jam a me condemnatæ fuere et condemnantur et revocantur—[″]⁶

[f 71]   Monday, 8 March, 1819. Crown and Anchor.

Subject—~~Virtually complex in~~ At once the most complex and the most individual of Creatures Man, in the Ideal of his Humanity, has been not inaptly called the Microcosm, or the World in compendium, as the point to which all the lines converge from the circumference of Nature. This of course applies to his sum of Being, to his powers and qualities collectively. But if we confine ourselves to his Intellect exclusively, we find him gifted as it were with a ~~two~~ threefold mind, the one [? ~~perspective~~] belonging to him specifically, arising necessarily out of his peculiar mechanism, and by which he beholds all things from the perspective of his relative position ⟨as a man:⟩ the second, in which these views are again modified & too often disturbed and falsified, by his particular constitution and position, as this or that particular individual—and the third, which exists in all men *potentially* and in its germ tho' it requires effort ~~from within~~ and favoring circumstances to evolve it into act—by this he places himself on the same point with Nature, and contemplates all objects, himself included, in their permanent and universal being and relations. Thus the Astronomer places himself in the centre, and looks at all the planetary orbs as with a solar Eye. Happy would it [f 71ᵛ] be for him,

---

e For "paradoxas"

⁶ Meiners (ɪɪ 17n with considerable variations), from the second section of Pico della Mirandola's theses (for which see 499* below and *CN* ɪ 374 and n). Tr: "[conclusions] physical, Platonic, mathematical, theological, chaldaic, orphic, magical, cabbalistic, [in] dogmatic paradoxes, sceptical paradoxes, heretical, and indeed blasphemous ~~would be~~ were allowed to be defended and maintained by a scholastic man without danger or scandal, if only prefaced with these words or something similar—In all this I place nothing assertively or as probable, except in so far as it may be judged either true or probable by the most holy catholic church, and its meritorious head, the supreme pontiff, etc—and ~~if~~ whatever conclusions he may condemn, those had already been condemned by me and are condemned and revoked." Pico was claiming the freedom previously allowed during the Scholastic period.

if he could at all times imitate the wisdom of Nature and take her law for his legislative maxim, whether he is legislating in the intellectual or in the political world—namely, to subordinate instead of excluding—Alas! the ~~er~~ contrary method, exclusion instead of subordination, and its results, presents the Historian with his principal materials, in whatever domain of human History his researches may have been directed.—Thus in reviewing our own road, we find a long period from the first christian Century, to the sixth, distinguished by the ~~vain~~ attempt to substitute Philosophy for Religion, and a following of more than equal length by a still more injurious endeavour to make Religion supersede Philosophy—*Teresa*: & what ascetic for indiv.*ᶠ* made law for all.

Yet in doing this too successfully if only for Religion we read Superstition, it had had*ᵍ* in truth borrowed from the former attempt its theurgic rites, in one of their purposes—not indeed to subdue Nature and call forth Spirits from the vasty Deep, but yet to controll evil Demons that were supposed to be for ever hovering round [f 72] the poor Christian, and like Satan at the ear of eve infusing inordinate thoughts & sinful desires.—

*ʰ*Were it only therefore for their endeavour to re-unite both, by the due subordination of the latter to the former, we owe the tribute of respect to the memory of the Schoolmen from the 13 to the 15ᵗʰ century.*ⁱ*⁷

That one general ill consequence of this was a most depraved direction of their Studies, to the mere forms of logical, & because treated as more than forms of logic, sophistical thinking, is most true—and at the revival of ancient and classical Literature became the object of utter distaste & the subject of incessant complaint to the great Pioneers and Chieftains of the Reformation—. Yet is this abuse to be carefully distinguished with the works themselves of the most eminent Schoolmen,—Thomas Aquinas, Scotus, and Ockham, whom those who have never read them are most apt to abuse—(—Baxter's—) and secondly, I am persuaded that to the scholastic Philosophy the Reformation is attributable far more than to the revival of Letters, except *as it awakened*, in polite Literature, or even to the more genial school of the Platonists as it flourished in Italy.—*

---

* Philos.' influence to be detected only in degree—*ʲ*

ᶠ For "asceticism for the individual"?

ᵍ For "had"

ʰ⁻ⁱ Passage marked in ms for transposition to follow paragraph that precedes it and it has accordingly been so transposed here

ʲ Note given in text with a horizontal line above and another below to set it off

⁷ In lect (466 above) the wording is "from the thirteenth and fourteenth".

The 3 great instructive Events, the Reformation, the Civil War, and the French Revolution—

The state in which the Reformation had left the public mind—(*)^k Metaphysics estranged from experimental psychology & from the Revolution vice versâ.—[f 72^v] The reaction began with the Mystics who tho' they arose among the Sects of Protestantism were by no means congenial with it—By reviving the theurgy of the Samothracian Mysteries without its temples they turned their attention perforce to experiment—

[*] Innocent VIII, who first approved and then condemned Johannes Picus, Count Mirandula's, 900 propositions, at once brought him in—guilty and not guiltless, was the same Pope who did not indeed *first* set on foot, but who first made universal, spread and authorized the Witch-processes—all before him is so trifling as to be = 0. Yet this very Man who sincerely believed that Christendom was invaded, and above all that Germany was deluged by Wizards and Witches,—and by his instruments, the Witch-inquisitors &c renewed the sacrifices of Moloch, or rather those of the Mexican Tescalipoca, and in number & cruelty reduced both to Flea bites by ~~the~~ comparison—this very man was the Lover of Learning, the Strenuous Patron & munificent Rewarder of all the most celebrated Italian Literati, as Politian &c!![8]

^{k} C has a footnote indicator at this point, the ink smeared, perhaps in an attempt to remove it. Possibly evidence of a change of mind about its position

[8] Tennemann (IX 149–50) records that in 1486 Pope Innocent VIII permitted Pico to defend 900 theses in Rome but that in the end the debate was not allowed to take place. C's source, however, is again Meiners's longer account of Pico's life and writings (II 4–110) which is followed (II 111–221) by an account of the life and writings of Politian. Meiners (II 14–28) discusses Pico's theses in some detail and mentions the Pope's equivocal patronage of them; when he turns to Politian he raises the question of the contemporaneous witch trials (II 124): "geschah es während dieser Reise nach Rom, dass der Pabst Innocenz VIII, eben der, welcher die meisten Hexenrichter nach Deutschland sandte, und fast ganz Deutschland mit Unholden und Zauberwerken erfüllt glaubte, den Politian vor einer erlauchten Versammlung auffoderte, dass er die historischen Werke der Griechen, in welchen die Thaten und Schicksale der Römer erzählt wurden, in das Lateinische übersetzen, und dadurch gemeinnütziger machen möchte" ("it happened during this journey to Rome that Pope Innocent VIII, the very one who sent most of the witch-trial judges to Germany and believed that almost all Germany was filled with demons and sorceries, invited Politian before an illustrious assembly and desired that he translate into Latin the historical works of the Greeks in which the deeds and fates of the Romans were described and thereby make them more widely useful"). C included details of the witch craze in his lect at 471–2 above, drawing there on the account provided by Spee. For the example of Moloch see Lev 18.21 and 2 Kings 23.10. Tescalipoca or Tezcatlipoca, the Aztec god associated with the introduction of human sacrifice into central Mexico whose worship was at its height at about the same period as the witchhunts of Europe. In *Lects 1795 (CC)* 142–3 and n, C had related human sacrifice in Mexico to idolatry, drawing on information in F. S. Clavigero *The History of Mexico* tr Charles Cullen (2 vols London 1787) and in *Friend (CC)* I 223 he had casually associated it with despotism.

Agrippa—and considered as an Antidote to the blind confidence in the understanding deserve notice—BRUNO—

Behmen—& Biographia Lit.

Then Lord Bacon—

Then the controversy between the Arminian & Calvinist—

MS REPORT

BM MS Egerton 3057 ff 23–5ᵛ

[f 23]   Philosophy Lecture 11th March 8th 1819^a

Mʳ Coleridge commenting generally upon the errors of the Roman Catholics—read a considerable portion of the history of Sᵗᵃ Theresa of Spain—in a letter to a friend she begs him always to keep holy water by him, as the sprinkling of it would not fail to drive away those unseen and eviil^b spirits which often attack our souls—a great number of the converts to this ⟨Catholic⟩ Faith may be attributed to its attractive outward shew, but in its errors we feel the necessary and fatal consequences of separating Religion the highest object of our nature from Reason its highest faculty, for^c the reunion of these we owe some praise to the schoolmen of the 13 and 14th Centˢ. I am persuaded said Mʳ C that to the scholastic philosophy the Reformation is more attributable than to the revival of Classic literature, or to the Genial schools of platonism which followed that philosophy in Italy except as far as these gave a general impulse to all Europe—The Mysticism of Plato or rather Protinus^d tended more to create Polytheism than Protestanism, while the schoolmen being more logical, were also more favorable to it—There are Three great events in history, the contemplation of which may afford us more than ordinary instruction The Reformation—The civil war and the French Revolution— and with these eras we may divide Philosophy into two classes—The one possessing Metaphysics acute and profound but estranged [f 23ᵛ] from experimental physics & psychology—(psychology says Chambers is the knowledge of the soul as anatomy is of the body[1]) flourished during the middle ages and until the restoration of Charles—The other without

---

^{a} "1819" scribbled so as to be almost illegible ^{b} For "evil"
^{c} "for" written over another word now illegible ^{d} For "Plotinus"

[1]Chambers *Cyclopaedia*, article "Psychology": "Anthropology, or the science which considers man, consists of two parts: the first treating of the body, and the parts belonging thereto, called *anatomy*; and the second of the soul, called *psychology*". The explanatory reference seems to be the reporter's, not C's.

501

metaphysics but possessing psycology has then its beginning—M^r C— described Psycology as that knowledge by which a man learns the reaction of his thoughts upon outward objects equally with the action of outward objects upon his thoughts—The years previous^e to Charles & even during the Reformation are characterized by an astonishing credulity in men even of ability & research this may be attributed to the absence of all psychological knowledge—one fearful result was the revival of witchcraft—it ought to humble us to think that this was not an age of barbarism, but during the revival of letters, at the time of a Galileo, and under a purer and reforming Religion—This witchcraft was predominant throughout Europe—no country seems to have been free from its ravages—it traversed all until it was lost in the wilds of North America—so general and so disgraceful was this enthusiasm, that it was boldly proclaimed, he who did not believe in witchcraft could not believe in a God—O man does not this teach you humility—if thou canst know thy self—study thy own nature but above all do no evil with the notion you are serving God thereby—More innocent was that division of Philosophy the Mystic as it was hostile to the former infatuation—The origin of Mysticism is [f 24] obscure, soon after the time of Homer the Phoenicians appear to have formed mystic societies—the Deities that arose with them assimalate with The Heathen Mythology but it is better worthy of observation that the names of their Gods may still be traced distinctly in the world—viz. in the Ghebers or Fire Worshippers of Persia—the Miners in the North of Europe—The Fairies of England and the Good companions or fairies of Scotland—Giordana Bruno a preceptor of Sir Ph— Sidney—was put to death at Rome as an Atheist but we need no other refutation of this than a knowledge of the man and of his confessional—he considered himself the revivor of Pythagorean Tenets—his phylosophy is grand and dignified—his system of astronomy has been revived of later years—he attributes to each planet its collection ⟨and frequent dispersion⟩ of light—in its appearance to us similar to the Aurora Borealis— he considers the Sun from its immensity at once cause and effect—and in size sufficient to render perpetual that accumulation and dispersion of light which he gives to all matter—Lord Bacon and Krepler were cotemporaries—to the latter we ow that astronomy which solved prophecy and power—to the former the purify^{gf}—of every thing appertain^{gg} to the human intellect—his philosophy demands experiment as the true

---

^{e} Two preceding words crossed out indecipherably ^{f} For "purifying"
^{g} For "appertaining"

Groundwork of all knowledge—but requiring at the [h]same time some well known pre⟨sumption⟩[i] in the mind, of the result—the sense can judge of the experiment but the experiment must prove the law—he also considers that all Science approaches to its perfection as it immaterializes objects—astronomy—light & magnetism prove this—[f 24[v]] speaking of the system, he says the Science of light is but a real geometry of rays—No man said M[r] C— can surpass me in admiration of Lord Bacon but my nationality does not so blind me as to prevent my confessing that from him on many points I turn to Kreppler as from Gloom to sunshine—for Lord B— speaks very calumniously of Plato and Aristotle—and believes their works to have been only carried down the Stream of Time like straws from their lightness while those of profound and true thinkings have sunk to the bottom—

[j]M[r] C— lecture for this evening is on Dogmatical Materialism—in its relations to Physiology as well as to the religious, moral, and common sense of mankind; of the misnomer in entitling it scepticism; and the contrast between this empirical dogmatism & scepticism of any kind, much more philosophical scepticism—The grounds, occasions and influence of materialism have long occupied the first place in M[r] C.[s] researches & reflections, more especially during the last 2 years, and from its paramount importance [f 25[v]][k] in this country, and at the present time, he must defer the consideration of the Critical Philosophy of Kant & Schelling's philosophy of Nature till Monday Sennight—

Monday March 15th

[h–i] Words seem to have been inserted later in space too small for them

[j] Final paragraph written on both sides of a smaller slip of paper mounted between reports of Lect 11 and Lect 12

[k] Remaining text written with paper turned upside down

LECTURE 12

DATE AND PLACE OF DELIVERY. Monday, 15 March 1819, at the Crown and Anchor Tavern, Strand, London.

SUBJECT. Philosophy from the Restoration to the end of the French Revolution.

ANNOUNCEMENTS AND ADVERTISEMENTS. The *Courier* of Wed 10 Mar completed an announcement of the literary lect for 11 Mar (among news items) as follows: "On Monday, 15th March, the State of Speculative Opinion, from the Restoration to the close of the French Revolution; and Monday, 22d March, the Philosophical Series will be concluded with a Review of the preceding Course, and the Moral and Practical Application of the Whole. Crown and Anchor, Strand. Admission, Five Shillings". The date mentioned for the final lect was a week too early. The *Times* of Mon 15 Mar carried the following announcement: "MR. COLERIDGE'S LECTURE for THIS EVENING is on DOGMATIC MATERIALISM, in its relations to PHYSIOLOGY, as well as to the religious, moral and common sense of mankind; of the misnomer in entitling it scepticism; and the contrast between this empirical dogmatism and scepticism of any kind, much more philosophical scepticism. The grounds, occasions, and influence of materialism have long occupied the first place in Mr. Coleridge's researches and reflections, more especially during the last two years, and from its paramount importance in this country, and at the present time, he must defer the consideration of the Critical Philosophy of Kant and Schelling's Philosophy of Nature to Monday se'ennight. Crown and Anchor, Strand. Admission 5s. The lecture will commence at a quarter after eight precisely." The similar announcement in the *Morning Chronicle* of the same day, with substantive variants that suggest that C had himself provided a slightly different text, was as follows: "MR. COLERIDGE'S LECTURE for THIS EVENING is, On MATERIALISM and EMPIRICAL DOGMATISM in relation to PHYSIOLOGY, as well as to the religious, moral and common sense of Mankind; of the misnomer in entitling it scepticism, and the contrast between it and scepticism of any kind—much more philosophical scepticism. The grounds, occasions and influence of Materialism, from Hobbes to the present hour, have long occupied the first place in Mr. Coleridge's reflections and researches, more especially during the last two years; and persuaded of its deep interest in this country and of its paramount importance to the Students in all the learned professions, Mr. C will defer the account of the critical system of Kant and Schelling's Natur-philosophie, or revived Plotinism, to Monday se'nnight.—Admission, 5s.—N.B. Commences at one-quarter after eight precisely.—Crown and Anchor, Strand." A similar announcement appeared in the *New Times* for 15 Mar, and an abbreviated version (stopping short at "during the last two years", but providing information about price, place and time) in the *Courier*, placed among the news items.

TEXT. Frere MS ff 531–91 and C's draft notes in BM Add MS 47,523 ff 73–6.

REPORT. BM MS Egerton 3057 ff 26–7^v.

BACKGROUND AND CIRCUMSTANCES. For C's sense of the currency of his topic, see his letter to Mudford of [13 Mar]: "Of what transcendent general interest the subject is (Materialism in relation to Logic and Physiology as well as to morals & religion) you know & feel . . ." (*CL* IV 928).

506

LECTURE 12

It is a wonderful property of the human mind, that when once a momentum has been given to it in a fresh direction, it pursues the new path with obstinate perseverance in all conceivable directions[a] to its utmost extremes.[1] And by the striking consequences which arise out of those extremes, it is first awakened to its error, and either recalled to some former track or to some new pursuits which it immediately receives and admits to the same monopoly. Thus in the thirteenth century the first science which roused the intellects of man from the torpor of barbarism [was[b]] as we have seen in all countries ever has been and ever must be the case, the science of metaphysics [and ontology[c]]. We first seek at home and what wonder the [truths that appeared to reveal the secret depths of our own souls[d]] should take possession of the whole mind, and all truths appear trivial which could not be either evolved out of simple principles by the same process or at least brought under the same forms of thought by perceived or imagined analogies? And so in fact it was.

For more than two centuries[e] [mcn[f]] continued to invoke the oracle of their own spirits, not only concerning [its[g]] own forms and mode of being, but likewise concerning the laws of external nature. All attempts at [philosophical explication were commenced by a mere[h]] effort of the understanding, as the power of abstraction; or by the imagination transferring its own experiences to every object presented from without.[2] By the

---

[a]   *SW & F (CC)* I 495: "bearings"
[b]   Corrected to accord with corresponding passage in *SW & F (CC)* I 496. MS: which
[c]   Corrected to accord with *SW & F (CC)* I 496. MS, unpunctuated: the non-intellica
[d]   Blank space left in ms for about 14 letters; omission supplied from *SW & F (CC)* I 496
[e]   *SW & F (CC)* I 496: "For more than a century"
[f]   Corrected to accord with *SW & F (CC)* I 496. MS: man
[g]   Corrected to accord with *SW & F (CC)* I 496. MS: their
[h]   Blank space left in ms for about 94 letters; omission supplied from *SW & F (CC)* I 496

[1] The sentence is translated from Heinrich Steffens *Beyträge zur innern Naturgeschichte der Erde* (Freiburg 1801) 37. From the beginning of the lect to almost the end of the fifth paragraph is quoted from the unpublished *TL: SW & F (CC)* I 495–500 (var). It seems likely that C read from the ms. The same material also appears in a report of C's logic class of 1822: see *SW & F (CC)* II 1013–20.

[2] C treats this topic at greater length in *CN* IV 4910 f 73 (N 29: Jul 1822), in a passage that begins: "Were there no other operative causes, as there are many, for the partial diffusion and sudden decay of

former, the understanding or abstracting powers, a class of phenomena was in the first place abstracted, and fixed in some general term; of course this term could designate only the impressions made by the outward objects, and so far, therefore, the effects of those objects, but having been thus generalised in a term they were then made to occupy the place of their own causes under the name of occult qualities. Thus the properties peculiar to gold were abstracted from those it possessed in common with other bodies, and then generalised in the term ["aureity"[i]]; and the enquirer was instructed that the essence of gold, or the cause which constituted the peculiar substance called gold, was the power of [aureity[j]].[3] By the latter, that is, by the imagination, thought and will were superadded to this occult [quality[k]], and every form of nature had its appropriate spirit, to be controlled or conciliated by an appropriate [ceremonial[l]], and this was entitled the substantial form. Thus physic became a dull [poetry, and the art of medicine, for physiology could scarcely be said to exist[m]] [was a system of magic blended with traditional empiricism[n]]. Thus the forms of thought proceeded to act in their own emptiness, with no attempt to fill or substantiate them by the information of the senses, and all the branches of science formed so many sections of logic and metaphysics.

And so it continued till the time the Reformation sounded the second trumpet and the authority of the Schools sunk with that of the [hierarchy[o]], under the intellectual courage and activity which this great revolution had inspired.[4] Powers[p] once awakened cannot rest in one object. All the sciences partook of the new influence and the world of the [experimental philosophy was soon mapped out for posterity[q]] by the com-

---

[i] Blank space left in ms for about 13 letters; omission supplied from *SW & F (CC)* I 496
[j] Blank space left in ms for about 13 letters; omission supplied from *SW & F (CC)* I 496
[k] Corrected to accord with *SW & F (CC)* I 496. MS: nature
[l] Corrected to accord with *SW & F (CC)* I 496. MS: Psychology
[m] Blank space left in ms for about 13 letters, followed by "and physiology"; omission supplied and text emended to accord with *SW & F (CC)* I 496
[n] Blank space left in ms for about 10 letters; omission supplied from *SW & F (CC)* I 496
[o] Corrected to accord with *SW & F (CC)* I 497. MS: higher arcade
[p] *SW & F (CC)* I 497: "Power"
[q] Blank space left in ms for about 11 letters; omission supplied from *SW & F (CC)* I 497

Platonism in the 16th and 17th Centuries, its obscure and in part erroneous exploration of *Matter*, and the frequency with which the Platonists confounded Matter with Body, would have sufficed".

[3] Cf *CN* III 4352 (N 21½: Apr 1817) where C remarks on the loss incurred by the modern metaphysician "from not dar-

ing to adopt the *ivitates* and ëitates of the Schoolmen—as objectivity, subjectivity, negativity, positivity./—"

[4] Cf Rev 8.8: "And the second angel sounded, and as it were a great mountain burning with fire was cast into the sea: and the third part of the sea became blood . . .".

prehensive and enterprising genius of Bacon. [r]An experiment, [as[s]] an organ of reason, not less distinguished from the blind or dreaming [industry[t]] of the alchemists than opposed to the barren subtleties of the Schoolmen, was called forth, and more than this, the laws explained by which experiment could be dignified into scientific experience.[5] But no sooner [was the impulse given, than the same propensity was made manifest of[u]] looking at all things in the one point of view which chanced to be the predominant attraction. No sooner, I observed, had Lord Bacon convinced his contemporaries of the necessity of consulting their senses as well as their understandings, but at the same time of consulting their reason equally with their senses, than the same propensity of moving in one path and that to the extreme was made manifest.[6] Our Gilbert, a man of genuine philosophical genius, had no sooner [multiplied the facts of magnetism, and extended our knowledge concerning the property of[v]] the magnetic bodies, but all things in heaven and in earth and in the water beneath the earth were resolved into magnetic influences.

Shortly afterwards a new light was struck by [Harriott[7] and[w]] Descartes, [with their contemporaries, or immediate predecessors, and the restoration of ancient geometry[x]], aided by the modern invention of algebra, placed the science of [mechanism[y]] on the philosophic throne. How widely this domination spread, and how long continued, if, indeed, even now it can be said to have abdicated its pretensions, I need not remind you of. The sublime discoveries Newton taught, which are not less wonderful than fruitful, [the application of the higher mathesis to the

---

[r] C incorporates note from *SW & F (CC)* I 497n into main text

[s] MS: is

[t] Corrected to accord with corresponding passage in *SW & F (CC)* I 497n. MS: history

[u] Blank space left in ms for about 90 letters; omission supplied from *SW & F (CC)* I 497

[v] Blank space left in ms for about 153 letters, preceded by "magnified"; correction and omission supplied from *SW & F (CC)* I 497

[w] Blank space left in ms for about 11 letters; omission supplied from *SW & F (CC)* I 497

[x] Blank space left in ms for about 109 letters; omission supplied from *SW & F (CC)* I 497–8

[y] Corrected to accord with *SW & F (CC)* I 498. MS: Mechanics

[5] This sentence is an interpolation into the *TL* text.

[6] This sentence is an interpolation into the *TL* text.

[7] Thomas Harriott (1560–1621), mathematician and astronomer whose posthumously published work on algebra, *Artis analyticae praxis* (1631), is said (by e.g. *DNB*) to have laid the foundation for subsequent work by Descartes; according to Rees's *Cyclopaedia* (article "Harriott") his work was attributed to Descartes until "the piracy was discovered and made known by Dr. Wallis, in his History of Algebra".

movements of the celestial bodies,[8] and to the laws of light[z]], gave almost a religious sanction to the corpuscular [system and mechanical theory. It became synonymous with philosophy itself. It was the sole portal[a]] at which truth was permitted to enter. The human body itself was treated of as a hydraulic machine, the operations of medicine were solved, and too often directed [by reference] partly [to] gravitation[b] and the laws of motion, and partly by chemistry, which itself, as far as its theory was concerned, was but a branch of mechanics working by imaginary wedges, angles, and spheres. Should you chance to put your hand at any time on *The Principles of Philosophy* by [La Forge[c]], you may see the phenomena of sleep explained and the results demonstrated by mathematical calculation.[9] In short, from the time of [Kepler[d]], whose mind was not comprehended in the vortex for he erred in the other extreme, but from the time of [Kepler[e]] to Newton and from that to Hartley,[10] [not only all things in external nature, but the subtlest mysteries of life,[f]] organisation, [and[g]] even of the intellect and moral being, were conjured within the magic circle of mathematical [formulae[h]]. But now a light was struck by the discovery of electricity[11] and, in every sense of the word, it may be affirmed to have [electrified[i]] the whole [frame[j]] of natural philosophy.

---

[z] Blank space left left in ms for about 87 letters; omission supplied from corresponding passage, slightly adapted, in *SW & F (CC)* I 498

[a] Blank space left in ms for about 108 letters; omission supplied from *SW & F (CC)* I 498

[b] Corrected to accord with *SW & F (CC)* I 498. MS: directed partly by gravitation

[c] Blank space left in ms for about 11 letters, preceded by "De"; correction and omission supplied from *SW & F (CC)* I 498

[d] Corrected to accord with *SW & F (CC)* I 498n. MS: Cooper

[e] Corrected to accord with *SW & F (CC)* I 498. MS: Cooper

[f] Blank space left in ms for about 12 letters; omission supplied from *SW & F (CC)* I 498

[g] Insertion follows *SW & F (CC)* I 498

[h] Corrected to accord with *SW & F (CC)* I 498. MS, unpunctuated: formality

[i] Insertion follows *SW & F (CC)* I 499

[j] Corrected to accord with *SW & F (CC)* I 499. MS: form

---

[8] The sentence to this point may be an adaptation of Steffens *Beyträge* 37.

[9] A version of this garbled reference to Louis de La Forge (fl 1650–70) had appeared in *BL (CC)* I 93–4 and n. La Forge edited two of Descartes's works but not *The Principles of Philosophy* (*Principia philosophiae*); C seems to have had in mind three engravings representing the contrast between the brains of sleeping and waking subjects that appear on pp 120–1 of Descartes *Tractatus de homine* (Amsterdam 1677), published with notes by La Forge. See *SW & F (CC)* I 498 and n.

[10] From Kepler (1571–1630) to Newton (1642–1727) to David Hartley (1705–57).

[11] C's location of the discovery of electricity after Hartley but before the development of pneumatic chemistry (for which see the note following) suggests that he was thinking of Benjamin Franklin's experiments in the 1750s rather than of the work of Galvani and Volta at the end of the century.

Close on its heels followed the momentous discovery of the [gases[k]], and composition of water, and the doctrine of latent heat by Black.[12] The scientific world had been prepared for a new [dynasty; accordingly, as soon as Lavoisier had reduced the infinite variety of chemical phenomena to the actions, reactions, and interchanges of a few elementary substances[l]], or [at[m]] least excited the expectation that this would be effected, a hope shot up almost instantly and as rapidly ripened into a full faith that this had been effected.[13] Henceforward a new path became the common road as in the former instances to all the departments of knowledge; and even to this moment it has been pursued with an eagerness and almost epidemic enthusiasm which characterise[n] the spirit of this age. Many and inauspicious have been the inroads of this new conqueror into the territories of [other sciences; and strange alterations have been made in less harmless points than those of[o]] terminology, in homage to a life of whatever importance yet unsettled[p], in the very ferment of imperfect[q] discoveries, either without a theory, or by a theory maintained by compromise. Yet this very circumstance has favoured [its[r]] encroachments, by the gratifications which its novelty affords to our curiosity, and by the genial[s] excitement which an unsettled mind is sure to inspire. And he who supposes science possesses an immunity [from influences[t]] like this knows little of human nature and how impossible it is for man to separate part of its nature wholly and entirely from the remaining parts. All

---

[k] Corrected to accord with *SW & F (CC)* I 499. MS: causes

[l] Blank space left in ms for about 90 letters; omission supplied from *SW & F (CC)* I 499

[m] Insertion follows *SW & F (CC)* I 499

[n] Corrected to accord with *SW & F (CC)* I 499. MS: characterises

[o] Blank space left in ms for about 13 letters, preceded by "our"; correction and omission supplied from *SW & F (CC)* I 499

[p] Corresponding clause in *SW & F (CC)* I 499: "in homage to an art unsettled"

[q] Corrected to accord with *SW & F (CC)* I 499. MS: imperfections

[r] Corrected to accord with *SW & F (CC)* I 499. MS: it,

[s] Corresponding passage in *SW & F (CC)* I 500: "keener interest and higher"

[t] Blank space left in ms for about 13 letters, preceded by "of"; correction and omission supplied, slightly adapted, from *SW & F (CC)* I 500

---

[12] Joseph Black (1728–99), whose 1754 medical dissertation at Edinburgh "opened the door to pneumatic chemistry" (*DNB*). The article "Heat" in Rees's *Cyclopaedia* says of "latent heat": "This phrase was first used by Dr. Black. It was suggested from the discovery, that a large quantity of heat sometimes disappears, or is absorbed by a body, without any increase of temperature . . . . The heat which disappears in these cases is called *latent*."

[13] Antoine Laurent Lavoisier (1743–94), still in C's time the dominant figure in chemistry, against whose influence C's friends, Beddoes and HD, and others, struggled. See Levere 172–4. This sentence and the next are based on Steffens *Beyträge* 37–8.

these causes, however, [like[u]] every political event, from their magnitude, have had one tendency, that of drawing men from attention to their own minds to external objects, and giving them a pre-disposition to receive as the more true that which in any way makes a more vivid impression. Consequently a system that supplies image after image to the senses, however little connected they may be by any necessary copula[v], will be a formidable rival for another which can pretend only to a logical adherence of conceptions, and which demand[s] from men the most difficult effort in nature, that of truly and earnestly thinking.[14]

In the commencement of literature, men remained for a time in that unity with nature which gladly concedes to nature the life, thought, and even purposes, of man, and on the other hand gives to man himself a disposition to regard himself as a part of nature. Soon, however, he must have begun to detach himself; his dreams, the very delusions of his senses which he became acquainted with by experience, must have forced him to make a distinction between the object perceived and the percipient. Nothing, however, enabled him to determine to one of these a priority over the other; they were both strictly co-existent.[15] And it seems remarkable, both in ancient and in modern times, the first philosophy was that of idealism, that which [began[w]] with a courageous scepticism, which I think Descartes has beautifully stated when he himself gave a beautiful example of it in what he called voluntary doubt, a self-determined indetermination, expressing at the same time its utter difference from the scepticism of vanity or irreligion: "Nec [tamen in eo scepticos imitabar, qui dubitant tantum ut dubitent, et preter incertitudinem ipsam nihil quaerunt. Nam contra totus in eo eram ut aliquid certi reperirem[x]]."[16] "Nor yet", says he, "did I in this imitate the sceptics who

---

[u] MS: of
[v] MS: copular
[w] MS: beginning
[x] Blank space left in ms for about 196 letters; omission supplied from corresponding passage in *BL* (*CC*) I 258

[14] A recurrent theme. Cf e.g. his recent generalisation about the French Enlightenment, in *LS* (*CC*) 74: "Flattered and dazzled by the real or supposed discoveries, which it had made, the more the understanding was enriched, the more did it become debased; till science itself put on a selfish and sensual character .... *Worth* was degraded into a lazy synonyme of *value*; and value was exclusively attached to the interest of the senses." Cf his account of the scientific consequences of "habitual slavery to the eye" in *TL: SW & F* (*CC*) I 525.

[15] The topic had been treated at length in *BL* (*CC*) I 255–9.

[16] The same passage, from Descartes *De methodo* in *Opera philosophica* (Amsterdam 1685), was quoted without tr in *BL* (*CC*) I 258. It had been entered in a notebook in 1801; see *CN* I 914 and n (N 21).

doubt only for doubting's sake and seek nothing but a distinction [by^y] uncertainty, for, on the contrary, my whole soul was engaged in this, the hope of discovering something certain." In the pursuit of this, therefore, it was evident that success depended on an austere and faithful adherence to the principle of the mind, with a careful separation and exclusion of all which appertains to the external world (as far as this was considered, not as a philosophy, but as a mere introduction or discipline of the mind previous to the discovery of truth). As a natural philosopher who directs his views wholly to external objects avoids, above all things, the intermixture of mind and [its^z] properties in his knowledge, as, for instance, all arbitrary occult qualities, and the substitution of final for efficient causes, so on the other hand the philosopher who begins with the mind is equally anxious to exclude all [interpolation of the objective into the subjective principles of his science^a]; he will be equally careful to [exercise] [an absolute and scientific scepticism to which the mind voluntarily determines itself for the specific purpose of future certainty^b], and by the purification of his mind of all that does not belong to the mind itself, he acquires a true sense both of its strength and of its weakness.[17]

We have seen in an earlier lecture, that about five hundred years before Christ, Leucippus founded the [atomic^c] system or pure materialism in direct opposition to the [Eleatic^d] philosophy or pure idealism,[18] and that within the next hundred years, at a period rendered uncertain by the extraordinary longevity of the individual, this was enlarged by Democritus. And during the interval from 312 to 270 years before Christ, it was brought to that state of completion by Epicurus[19] to which it was restored by Gassendi, who was born in a village of Provence in 1592,[20] and was

---

^{y} Corrected to accord with *BL* (*CC*) I 258. MS: of

^{z} MS: the

^{a} Blank space left in ms for about 90 letters, preceded by "mental"; correction and omission supplied from corresponding passage in *BL* (*CC*) I 258

^{b} Blank space left in ms for about 89 letters; omission supplied from what appears to be corresponding passage in *BL* (*CC*) I 258

^{c} MS: Academic

^{d} MS: Eclectic

---

[17] The distinction being made here between the method of the (idealist) philosopher and the natural philosopher or scientist adds a practical application to the subjective and objective starting points discussed in *BL* (*CC*) I 255–9.

[18] See Lect 3, 134–7 above.

[19] See Lect 6, 271–7 above.

[20] Cf Tennemann (x 142): "Pierre Gassendi war im Jahre 1592 in einem Dorfe der Provence Chantersier, nicht weit von Digne geboren" ("Pierre Gassendi was born in the year 1592 in a Provençal village called Chantersier [i.e. Champtercier] not far from Digne"). C had made use of Gassendi for his unpublished "Outlines of the History of Logic" in about 1803 (see *SW & F—CC—*I 123–40) and had made notes on his work as early as 1801 in connection with his reading of Hobbes at the time (see *CN* I 937 G and n), but his reference to him

after Gassendi especially applied to the explanation of humanity by Hobbes, who was born at Malmesbury four years before Gassendi, and who almost rivalled [Democritus*e*] in the length of his life.[21] The three ancient philosophers[22] declared the inherence of [motion*f*], and the essence at least of life and of sensation in the atoms which they assumed, though they made a difference with regard to those atoms which will not be well understood unless we give the history of those atoms themselves.

The [Eleatics*g*] had begun[23] by demonstrating the inconsistencies that arise out of the position of motion, arising from the arguments against the real external existence of space. Having shown that space involved a contradiction of a something that had the properties of nothing,[24] of course that it was a nonentity, they then deduced that as motion was inconceivable without the belief of space, so neither motion nor space possessed any reality. The materialists who followed, and who were perhaps first materialists by this outrage on their common sense, were not able to combat the [Eleatic*h*] philosophers in subtlety of reasoning, and they cut the knot which they could not solve, and took for granted at once the exis-

---

e Blank space left in ms for about 12 letters; omission supplied from corresponding passage in draft ms (542 below)
f Corrected to accord with draft ms (542 below). MS: the notion
g MS: Eclectics
h MS: Eclectic

---

here was probably a symptom of his responding to the analysis of Gassendi's restoration of Epicurus's atomism or materialism in Tennemann x 149, 150–2, and 157–62. Cf C's later tribute to Gassendi in *CN* iv 5123 and 5125 (Feb 1824). C had mentioned Gassendi and Hobbes as a representative pair of materialists in *BL* (*CC*) i 90.

[21] Hobbes lived to be 91; Bayle (article "Democritus") collects and comments on the conflicting accounts of Democritus's age at death, including the authority of Diodorus Siculus (90 years) and Lucian (104 years). Tennemann (i 271 and n) also discusses the problem without offering specific ages.

[22] I.e. Leucippus, Epicurus, and Democritus.

[23] In returning to the ancient precedents for materialism, C recapitulates a topic that he had previously discussed in Lect 3 (134–8 above) and once more depends for his information on Tennemann

i 258–84. C's analysis of the metaphysical weakness of the materialism of Leucippus and Democritus had been offered briefly in *BL* (*CC*) i 133 and in *Friend* (*CC*) i 462–3 (where Plato's attention to it is mentioned). Tennemann's account is a clear and detailed compilation from the records of Aristotle, Plutarch, and others (whom he cites, paraphrases, and often quotes in their original text); C picks out what he needs, emphasising the arbitrary nature of materialist assumptions more than he had in Lect 3 (and more than Tennemann does—although he too mentions it at i 260) because he wishes now to connect them to modern materialism. In what follows a few specific parallel passages from Tennemann are provided in the notes, but there is also a general dependence on Tennemann at 515–17 below.

[24] The paragraph to this point follows the argument of the third paragraph of Tennemann i 258.

tence of matter and motion without further explanation.[25] But still there were two properties of matter which demanded some solution, and those were the partibility which it presented even to the senses, and its resistance.[26] Now no hypothesis suggested itself, more probable, more plausible at least than that of atoms, to answer both; for while their extreme multitude and minuteness seemed everywhere to account to the professors of matter for its divisibility, on the other hand their hardness, which they were obliged, like motion, to declare to be inherent and essential, they gave as the true cause of the resistance of matter.[27] So that these atoms, in truth, were in the first place a pure fiction, for no man ever pretended to have seen an ultimate particle. It was merely a supposition derived from another supposition, namely, that of external matter. But, in the next place, it was to account for partibility by the very circumstance of being impartible.[28] If they were asked how it was that matter was divisible, they answered, "In consequence of the infinite multitude of ultimate particles of which it was composed"; if they were asked how those particles came to be ultimate, and why they stopped, there the answer then was, if they were atheists, as in our sense of the word the old materialists were, "It was an inherent eternal property". If they were theists, "It was a miracle, God has made them", and who shall pretend, as a late writer has said, to quarrel with any decree of God's?[29] Certainly not, but we may quarrel with a man who chooses to affirm a miracle on his own authority. This, however, was the ground of atoms. It was nothing more than an hypothesis to [suppose[i]] in one thing the partibility of matter by the amazing smallness of it, and the resistance or impenetrability of matter by its hardness.

But these atoms still, when they had them, would only account for a certain number of things either shapeless or of the same shape; but among the phenomena of matter the most impressive was the manifoldness of forms. This again the system of materialism found the means of explaining by a variety of figures. Some of them were angular, and some were round, and these last forms, namely the round atoms and bodies com-

---

[i] MS: expose

[25] See 134–6 above.

[26] The sentence draws on the first paragraph of Tennemann I 261.

[27] This sentence and the preceding one are closely related to materials in Tennemann I 262–3.

[28] This presentation of objections to atomic theory resembles the account given of it in *BL* (*CC*) I 133 where C was drawing on various passages in

Schelling. Cf the more delicate exploration of *CM* (*CC*) III 915–16, an annotation to Henry More *The Second Lash of Alazanomastix* (Cambridge 1651) 93.

[29] The "late writer" has not been identified. Cf the unnamed "Divine" who said of the murder committed by Jael "that he wanted no better morality than that . . . the *Bible* had declared it worthy to be praised": *SW & F* (*CC*) II 1140.

posed of them, the ancient materialists regarded as motive atoms or self-motive powers; in short, the souls and principles of all thought and motion were, according to them, round atoms. And inasmuch as the element of fire was supposed to be composed of those round atoms, likewise the soul, therefore, was according to them of a fiery nature.[30] In the form of warmth, these round atoms appeared as life, that is, where a sufficient quantity was accumulated; for in inanimate substances, says Democritus, there is still a certain quantum of warmth, because there are no bodies without [a] certain roundness, but they are not vital. In this sense, Democritus says, there is a soul in all things, all things have a sensation in kind, but the inanimate things have only a momentary sensation, which, being interrupted by other elementary atoms not round, prevent[s] all consciousness and all memory and even all marks of life. Yet interior sensations or impressions they derived from atoms or their components that were of like nature[j] with the sentient, and all life was but sensation which modified, how has not been preserved[k]. Thus then, the round atoms, according to Democritus, constituted souls, or the power of sensation and voluntary motion. But all mind is sensation which, modified in the brain we are not told how, becomes thinking, but if modified in the region of the breast becomes feeling, and in the abdomen it shows itself only as growth or the obscure sensation of life. The mode, the process of perception he explained by the effluvia, the images from every body,[31] every body, according to him, sending forth images of each of its component

---

[j] Draft ms (543 below): compounds of like nature

[k] C seems to have said "life" instead of "mind", echoing the word in his previous sentence, and then to have broken off and made a fresh start. Corresponding passage in draft ms (543 below): and all mind is but sensation, which modified (how we are not told) in the Brain becomes Thinking

[30] Cf Tennemann (i 265–6): "Wahrscheinlich aber legte er [Leucipp] allen Atomen nicht in gleichem Grade Bewegkraft bey, sondern die runden, die Bestandtheile des Feuers, können wegen ihrer Gestalt am leichtesten Bewegung empfangen und mittheilen. Daher bestehet die Seele aus solchen runden Atomen" ("But he [Leucippus] probably did not attribute the power of motion to all atoms in the same degree, rather the round ones, the components of fire, because of their shape could most easily receive and impart motion. Therefore the soul is constituted from such round atoms"). Cf also Tennemann (i 269): "runde Atomen wären ihre Bestand-theile, weil diese am leichtesten sich bewegen lassen, und in andere Körper eindringen können. Von der Art war aber auch das Feuer. Die Seele ist also ein feuriges Wesen . . ." ("round atoms were their components, because these allowed themselves to be moved most easily and were able to penetrate other bodies. But fire was also of that kind. The soul is therefore a fiery being . . .").

[31] Cf Tennemann (i 283): "Von allen Körpern gehen gewisse Ausflüsse, welche mit ihnen Aehnlichkeit haben, oder Bilder . . . aus . . ." ("Certain emanations or images flow from all bodies which have a likeness to them . . .").

elements and these falling on an organ of the same element, as, for instance, water falling on the eye (which he says is essentially water) constitutes sight; the air falling on the ear constitutes sound, and so forth;[32] but this we may safely omit. It is sufficient for our purposes to know that the fundamental positions of ancient materialism were, first, that motion and sensation are properties of a specific kind of atoms and that mind is but a species of sensation, and all the processes of perception and of reflection purely passive, and all the acts, or more accurately, all the phenomena or appearances of life (just as the seeming acts of a dream), are wholly mechanical or produced by necessitating antecedents. Lastly, that the distinction between these ancient materialists and the moderns from Hobbes lies mainly in this one position, that the ancients accounted for the soul, as the common principle of life, thought, and voluntary motion, from a peculiar sort of atoms, namely, the round atoms or fire-composing corpuscles, while the moderns make the same things result from the [organisation[l]] of atoms, without any assumption of a particular species, or, if of any, yet not *ab origine*,[33] and consequently not immutably peculiar, but the peculiarity itself produced by this self all working[m] organisation. In this assertion, however, I beg to be understood as speaking of the opinion common to all, and the organisation as being the predominant thought; though in connection with organisation, the successors of Hobbes have not at all confined themselves to his scheme of successive corpuscles propagating motion like billiard balls, but [animal[n]] spirits, that is, irrational[o] and inanimate solids, thawed down and distilled, or filtrated into living and intelligent fluids that etch and re-etch engravings on the brain, for themselves to look at, according to the pure materialists, though they were intended [for the[p]] soul to contemplate by their first inventor. We have, too, what comes nearest to the ancient notion of hollow tubes which had been regarded formerly as tools, and we have had, too, electric light, at once the immediate object and the ultimate

[l] Corrected to accord with draft ms (543 below). MS: organism
[m] *P Lects* (348) emended to "self-all-working"; draft ms (543 below) differs considerably: assumption ⟨of a particular species or if of any⟩ of aboriginal and consequently immutable peculiarity of figures in this Species—⟨& consequently, the non-assertion of inherent Life.⟩
[n] Corrected to accord with draft ms (543 below). MS: they had had their
[o] Corrected to accord with draft ms (543 below). MS: their irrational
[p] Corrected to accord with draft ms (543 below). MS: by their

[32] Cf Tennemann (I 284): "jene Bilder ... drücken sich in dem Wasser des Auges ab, und bilden dadurch Kopien von den Dingen. Das Hören geschiehet vermittelst der Luft" ("these images impress themselves on the water of the eye and depict copies of the things thereby. Hearing seems to be mediated by the air").

[33] "From the beginning".

organ of inward vision, which rises to the [brain*q*] like an Aurora Borealis, and there disporting in various shapes, as the balance of plus and
minus or negative and positive is destroyed or re-established, images out
both past and present.[34]

But all these had been proffered as auxiliaries, themselves [the products of organisation; and my former assertion remains true*r*], that the
modern scheme of materialism differs from that of Democritus by representing life, mind, and will as the result of organisation, not as pre-
existing in the specific [atoms so organised*s*].

To the best of my knowledge, Descartes was the first philosopher who
introduced the absolute and essential [heterogeneity*t*] of the soul as intelligence, and of body as matter.[35] The [Eleatics*u*] deduced matter, and
with it the mind as the mere process of thought. Democritus and his followers deduced the mind as resulting from the body. While the Platonists
had founded a system which at all events had the merits of being extremely poetical, and which has been far more accurately as well as beautifully given by Milton than you will find it in [Brucker*v*][36] or all the writers of philosophical history:

---

q Corrected to accord with draft ms (544 below). MS: line
r Reporter seems to have missed a line, perhaps in transcription; omission supplied from
draft ms (544 below)
s Corrected to accord with draft ms (544 below). MS: atom as the organization
t MS: heterogenei
u MS: Eclectics
v MS: Brooker

---

[34] C is re-using the statement in *BL*
(*CC*) I 100–1: "it is to be observed, that
Aristotle's positions on this subject are
unmixed with fiction. The wise Stagyrite
speaks of no successive particles propagating motion like billiard balls (as
Hobbs;) nor of nervous or animal spirits,
where inanimate and irrational solids are
thawed down, and distilled, or filtrated by
ascension, into living and intelligent fluids, that etch and re-etch engravings on
the brain, (as the followers of Des Cartes,
and the humoral pathologists in general;)
nor of an oscillating ether which was to
effect the same service for the nerves of
the brain considered as solid fibres, as the
animal spirits perform for them under the
notion of hollow tubes (as *Hartley*
teaches)—nor finally, (with yet more recent dreamers) of chemical compositions
by elective affinity, or of an electric light
at once the immediate object and the ultimate organ of inward vision, which

rises to the brain like an Aurora Borealis,
and there disporting in various shapes (as
the balance of plus and minus, or negative and positive, is destroyed or re-
established) images out both past and
present." C now repeats his mistaken attribution of the billiard-ball image to
Hobbes; he omits the mistaken attribution of the hollow tubes notion to Hartley. See *BL* (*CC*) I 101n.

[35] The sentence is repeated (var) from
BL (*CC*) I 129, the beginning of a chapter on the dualism of Descartes, for which
see esp *Principia philosophiae* (1644) pt
1 secs 8, 53, 63–4, and pt 2 secs 1–2, and
Meditations (1641) pts 2 and 6. C returns
to the subject at 565 below and later treats
it in much greater detail in *CN* IV 4910
(Jul 1822).

[36] I.e. Brucker *Historia critica philosophiae*, the best known comprehensive
authority, for which see Introduction
xlvi–xlvii above.

Oh Adam, one Almighty is, from whom
All things proceed, and up to him return,
If not depraved from good, created all
Such to perfection, one first matter all,
Indued with various forms, various degrees
Of substance, and, in things that live, of life;
But more refined, more spiritous, and pure,
As nearer to him placed, or nearer tending,
Each in their several active spheres assigned,
Till body up to spirit work, in bounds,
Proportioned to each kind. So from the root
Springs lighter the green stalk, from thence the leaves
More aery, last the bright consummate flower
Spirits odorous breathes; flowers and their fruit,
Man's nourishment, by gradual scale sublimed
To vital spirits aspire, to animal,
To intellectual, give both life and sense,
Fancy and understanding, whence the soul
Reason receives, and reason is her being
Discursive, or intuitive. . . .[37]

Now Descartes had taught an absolute and essential diversity of the soul as [intelligence[w]] and of the body as matter. The assumption and the form of speaking had remained, [though[x]] the denial of all other properties to matter[y] but that of extension, on which denial the whole system of this diversity is grounded, has been long exploded.[38] For since impenetrability is intelligible only as a mode of resistance, its admission places the essence of matter in an act or power, which it possesses in common with spirit;[39] and body and spirit are therefore no longer absolutely het-

[w] MS: intelligent   [x] MS: to   [y] MS: to that of matter

[37] Milton *Paradise Lost* 5.469–88 (var). The quotation had been used as an epigraph to ch 13 in *BL (CC)* I 295. From this point to "a defunct matter" C resumes his quotation from *BL (CC)* I 129–36 (var including some interpolations of new matter). The notes here are heavily dependent on those of the *BL* editors, but provide less detail about the texts of C's sources than they do.

[38] By Leibniz especially, in *Lettre sur la question si l'essence du corps consiste dans l'étendue* (Paris 1691).

[39] Drawing, as is noted in G. N. G. Orsini *Coleridge and German Idealism* (Carbondale and Edwardsville 1969) 199–200, on Kant *Metaphysische Anfangsgründe der Naturwissenschaft* (2nd ed Riga 1787) 81–2: "das so genannte Solide oder die absolute Undurchdringlichkeit, als ein leerer Begriff, aus der Naturwissenschaft verwiesen und an ihrer Statt zurücktreibende Kraft gesetzt, dagegen aber die wahre und unmittelbare Anziehung gegen alle Vernünfteleyen einer sich selbst missverstehenden Metaphysik vertheidigt, und, als Grundkraft, selbst zur Möglichkeit des Begriffs von Materie für nothwendig erklärt wird" ("the so-called solid, or absolute impen-

erogeneous, but may without any absurdity be supposed to be different modes, or degrees in perfection, of a common substratum,[40] as I have just read described in the lines of Milton. To this possibility, however, it was not the fashion to advert. The soul was a thinking substance, and body a space-filling substance; yet the apparent action of each on the other pressed heavily on the philosopher on the one hand, and no less heavily on the other hand pressed the evident truth that the law of causality and effect holds only between homogeneous things, that is to say, things having some common property, and cannot extend from one world into another its opposite.[41] A close analysis evinced it to be no less absurd than the question whether a man's affection for his wife lay north-east or south-west of the love he bore towards his child, for if matter be defined as a space-filling substance, it is evident that what cannot apply to what he predicates of space, can in no degree apply to what is material. Leibnitz's doctrine of a pre-established harmony, which he certainly borrowed from Spinoza,[42] who had taken the hint from Descartes' animal machine,[43] was, in its common interpretation, too strange to survive the inventor. The next hypothesis, therefore, was that of recurrence to, and

---

etrability, is banished from natural science as an empty concept, and in its stead repulsive force is posited. On the other hand, the true and immediate attraction is defended against all the sophistries of a metaphysics that misunderstands itself, and this attraction is explained as a fundamental force necessary even to the possibility of the concept of matter"): tr James Ellington in Immanuel Kant *Metaphysical Foundations of Natural Science* (Indianapolis and New York 1970) 77.

[40] The word may be derived from C's German reading; see *BL* (*CC*) I 143n. *OED* cites C as its earliest instance of "substrate" from "substratum".

[41] The sentence is a paraphrase of Schelling *System des transcendentalen Idealismus* (Tübingen 1800) 112–13.

[42] As is pointed out in *BL* (*CC*) I 130n–1n, C seems to have been influenced in his otherwise puzzling view of Leibniz's indebtedness to Spinoza by Jacobi *Ueber die Lehre des Spinoza* 361–97 and perhaps by Schelling *Ideen zu einer Philosophie der Natur* (Landshut 1803) 14. Ten-

nemann, responding to the claim that Leibniz was dependent on Spinoza, acknowledges a resemblance but insists also on a significant difference (XI 155–7; cf X 374 and 396); Bayle had given prominence to the question in the long note H to his article "Rorarius".

[43] The animal "machines" (*BL* has the plural form) are in *De methodo* pt 5; for Spinoza's indebtedness to Descartes, acknowledged most obviously in his *Renati des Cartes principiorum philosophiae pars I et II more geometrico demonstratae* (1663), see also *SW & F* (*CC*) I 623 and n. As is pointed out in *BL* (*CC*) I 130n–1n, C had earlier objected in a marginal note on Descartes *Opera philosophica* (3 pts in 1 vol Amsterdam 1685, 1677, 1685) to the view that Leibniz was dependent here on Spinoza, asking whether Descartes's Article 16 was "not a clear & distinct statement of the Theory": *CM* (*CC*) II 172. C repeats this comment later in a note to his treatise "On the Passions": *SW & F* (*CC*) II 1421*.

afterwards the hypothesis of, hylozoism, or that every particle of matter is essentially, though not apparently, alive. But this was found to be the death of all essential[z] physiology,[44] and indeed of all physical science; for science requires a limitation of terms, and cannot consist with the arbitrary power of multiplying attributes by occult qualities. Besides, the system of life in matter answers no purpose, unless a difficulty can be solved by multiplying it, or that we can acquire a clearer notion of our soul by being told that we have a million souls and that every atom of our bodies has a soul of its own. But it is here, as it is in many other cases; man, while he was persuaded that he had a soul and that he had a body, and that his soul was gifted with a faculty of perceiving external objects through the medium of that body or by its organs, was satisfied. All was clear. But when he came to ask, what form has this copula?[a] Is the soul diverse from the body, and if so how can diverse powers act and react on each other? And if it be the same, in what point or degree shall we place the soul, and where the body? Then it is as if the sediment were at the bottom of a vessel, all the water above being clear and transparent, but we are not satisfied on account of the sediment; out we cannot take it, and the best we can do is to shake it up, not diminishing it by the least degree, but for our pains rendering the whole water turbid.[45]

Still, I deny yet that it is the duty of man to despair to solve a problem till its impossibility is demonstrated. How matter can ever unite with perception, how being ever transform itself into knowing, is conceivable only on one [condition[b]], that is, if it can be shown that the *vis representativa*, or the sentient, is itself a species of matter, either as a property, or attribute, or a self subsistence.[46] Now, that it is a property is an assumption of materialism, of which, permit me to say thus much in praise, that it is a system which could not but be patronised if it performed what it promises. But how any affection from without could metamorphose itself into perception or will, the materialist has not only left incomprehensible as he found it, but has made it a comprehensible absurdity. For, grant that an object from without could act upon the conscious self as on a consubstantial object, yet such an affection would only engender something homogeneous with itself. Motion could only propagate motion,

---

[z] Mishearing of "rational"?   [a] MS unpunctuated
[b] MS: position

[44] *BL* (*CC*) I 132 reads "rational physiology". The sentence, as McFarland pointed out (356) is a translation of Kant *Metaphysische Anfangsgründe* 121.

[45] A notebook entry of 1801 (*CN* I 920) lies behind this passage from *BL*.

[46] Most of this sentence and all of the next are loosely translated from Schelling *System* 113.

matter has no inward. We remove one surface but to meet with another, we can but divide a particle into particles, and each particle has the power of being again divided. Let any reflecting mind make the experiment of explaining to itself the evidence of our sensuous intuitions from the hypothesis that in any given perception there is a something which has been communicated to it by an impact or an impression *ab extra*.[47] In the first place, by the impact on the percipient or *ens representans*, not the object itself, but only its action or effect, will pass into the same.[48] Not the iron tongue but its vibrations pass into the metal of the bell. Now in our immediate perception, it is not the mere power or act of the object, but it is the object itself, which is immediately present.[49] We might attempt to explain this result by a chain of deductions and conclusions, but that, first, the faculties of deducing and concluding would demand an explanation, and, secondly, there is no such intermediation by logic as cause and effect. It is the object itself, not the product of a syllogism, which is present to our consciousness. Or would we explain this supervention of the object by the sensation, by a productive faculty set in motion by an impulse, still the transition into the percipient of the object itself from which the impulse proceeded assumes a power that can permeate and wholly possess the soul,

> And like a God by spiritual art,
> Be all in all and all in every part.[50]

And how came the percipient here? And what is become of the wonder-promising matter that was to perform all these marvels by force of mere figure, weight, and motion? The most consistent proceeding of the dogmatic materialist would be to fall back into the common rank of soul-and-bodyists, to affect the mysterious, and declare the whole process a revelation given and not to be understood,[51] which it would be profane to examine too closely. But a revelation unconfirmed by miracles and a faith not commanded by the conscience a philosopher may venture to pass by without suspecting himself of any irreligious tendency. Thus, as materialism has been generally taught, it is utterly unintelligible and owes

[47] "From without".

[48] The sentence is translated from Schelling *System* 149, the "*ens representans*" or "representing being" replacing Schelling's "vorstellende Wesen".

[49] The sentence is translated from Schelling *System* 149, the image of the bell being added by C. From the beginning of the next sentence to the quotation from Cowley is a slightly abbreviated paraphrase of Schelling *System* 149–50.

[50] Adaptation of Abraham Cowley *All-over Love* 9–10: *Works* (7th ed London 1681) M2ʳ.

[51] C omits the Latin of *BL*—"Datur non intelligitur"—making allowance for his lect audience.

all its proselytes to the propensity so common among men to mistake distinct images for clear conceptions, and, vice versa, to reject as inconceivable whatever from its own nature is unimaginable.[52] But as soon as it becomes intelligible it ceases to be materialism. In order to explain thinking as a material phenomenon it is necessary to refine matter into a mere modification of intelligence with the two-fold function of appearing and perceiving. Even so did Spinoza. Even so did Priestley; in his controversy with Price, he stripped matter of all its material properties, substituted spiritual powers, and, when we expected to find a body, behold, we had nothing but its ghost, the apparition of a defunct matter.[53]

Let us then re-trace our history. Throughout the whole we have discovered nothing like thought. The earliest materialists began with declaring all who differed from them truly out of their senses. They themselves, however, began with hypothesis and they moved forwards, as a materialist ever must do, by a succession of [leaps[c]], as, for instance, from an atom, fiction the first, to atoms of various figures, fiction the second; amongst these, round atoms constituting the element of fire, fiction the third; then, that the element of fire is the principle of the soul, or thinking, which is the fourth fiction. That sensation and thought are precisely the same, which at all events is but an assertion, then that this same sensation, whatever it be, if it be below my heart is to be one thing, and if it be in the region of my heart another, but at once becomes philosophical and intellectual as soon as it passes into the marrow of my skull. These may be placed each as a separate law and fiction and the whole comes at last to what? Not to anything that was meant by "matter" in the first sense

---

[c] Insertion based on ms report (548 below). MS: laws

[52] The same distinction appears in a letter of 30 May 1815 to WW: "the philosophy of mechanism which in every thing that is most worthy of the human Intellect strikes *Death*, and cheats itself by mistaking clear Images for distinct conceptions . . .": *CL* IV 575. About a year later C also distinguished between "definite Conceptions" and ideas: "As Space to Places, so an Idea to definite Conceptions (= Begriffen—[)] As Places to the Forms and Bodies contained therein, so is a Conception to the ~~Objects in Concreto~~ Intuitions & Images": *SW & F (CC)* I 426. This sentence and the next are loosely translated from Schelling *System* 113.

[53] Joseph Priestley and Richard Price in *A Free Discussion of the Doctrines of Materialism and Philosophical Necessity, in a Correspondence between Dr. Price and Dr. Priestley* (1778). C had declared himself "a compleat Necessitarian" in 1794 (*CL* I 137: to RS 11 Dec); his subsequent change of heart was combined with contempt for its proponents. See e.g. *CN* IV 5059 f 57ᵛ (1823–4) where he inveighs against the danger of disendowing the clergy: "a mortal Dry-rot in the beams and timbers of the Edifice!—And here I might expose at large the pernicious sophistry of Priestley, Price, and others . . .". For evidence of his earlier loss of sympathy with Price see *CN* II 2892 (Oct 1806).

of the word. But without the slightest instruction given even in the meaning of terms, without one practical consequence in science or in philosophy being deducible, and with an outrage to common sense and to morality, it formed a complete circle of dogmatic, mere unsupported, assertions.

The moderns were ashamed of these angular and these round atoms,
and they had substituted therefore for it, organisation some, and others
life or a vital principle.[d] We will examine both. First, then, what is this
organisation? For we have been assured, not in old times but even in our
own, that mind is a function of the brain, that all our moral and intellectual being are the effects of organisation;[54] which I confess has always
had much the same effect upon my mind as if a man should say that building with all the included handicraft of plastering, sawing, planing, etc.,
were the offspring of the house, and that the mason and carpenter were
the [result of a suite of chambers, with the passages and staircases that
led to them[e]]; for to make A the offspring of B, where the very existence
of B as B presupposes the existence of A, [is preposterous in the literal
sense of the word, and a consummate instance of the *hysteron proteron*[f]]
in logic. For what, again I say, is organisation? Not the mere arrangement
of parts as means to an end, for in that sense I should call my watch organisation or a steam-engine organisation; but we agree these are machines not organisations. It appears, then, that if I am to attach any meaning at all to the word "organisation" it must be distinct from mechanism
in this, that in all machines I suppose the power to be from without, that
if I take my watch there is nothing in the component parts of this watch
that constitutes it peculiarly fit for a watch, or produce[s] it.[55] There is
nothing in the steam-engine which of itself, independent of its position,
would account for that position at all. Organisation, therefore, must not
only be an arrangement of parts together as means to an end, but it must
be such an interdependence of parts, each of which in its turn being means
to an end, as arises from within. The moment a man dies we can scarcely
say he remains organised in the proper sense. The powers of chemistry

---

[d] Comma in ms
[e] Blank space left in ms for about 116 letters; omission supplied from corresponding passage in *SW & F* (*CC*) I 502
[f] Blank space left in ms for about 100 letters; omission supplied from *SW & F* (*CC*) I
502

[54] For the "supposition" that "life"
was the "result of organisation" see
below 525. For the remainder of the sentence and the two sentences that follow
he quotes (var) from the unpublished *TL*:
SW & F (*CC*) I 502.
[55] In the related discussion in *TL*

(*SW & F—CC*—I 511*) C defines these
terms as follows: "we may say that whatever is organized from without, is a product of mechanism; whatever is mecha-
nised from within, is a production of
organization".

are beginning to show us that no force, not even mechanical . . .^{g}; to say, therefore, that life is the result of organisation, and yet at the same time to admit that organisation is distinguished from mechanism only by life, is assuredly what I before said: to affirm a thing to be its own parent, or to determine the parent to be the child of his own child. In every instance we may indeed account for the difference of qualities, difference of powers, from organisation, but even there we do it only [metaphorically^h], not in the strict sense of the word, for it is in all times incomparably more probable . . .^{i} and considered with regard to the universe produces the power itself. At all events, in order to justify materialism and in materialism the assertion that life, and, much more, that thought or will, are the results of organisation, it would be necessary to call for a fact of organisation subsisting prior to life, prior to some one of the properties of life. If indeed you could do that, and then present a life resulting from it, we will cheerfully agree with you. But if you can show an arrangement of means to an end without life and declare it not to be mechanism, and if, by the superadding the idea of life, that is, a power from within, you constitute an organisation, it follows self-evidently that not life is the result of organisation but that organisation is in some way or other dependent on life as its cause.

We come then to what is life. Almost all the attempts that I have seen to explain its nature presuppose the arbitrary disposition of all that surrounds us into things with life and things without life, a division which is certainly quite sufficient for the common usage but far too indeterminate for a philosopher. [The positions of science must be tried on the jeweller's scales, not like the mixed commodities^j] of the market, on the [weighbridge^k] of common opinion,^{56} yet such [h]as been the procedure in the present instance, by crazy^l logic which begins [with begging the ques-

---

^{g} Blank space left in ms for about 25 letters; *P Lects* (354) conjecturally supplied "[power, can *make* life.]"

^{h} Blank space left in ms for about 13 letters; omission supplied conjecturally from *P Lects* (354). OB proposed "[loosely]"

^{i} Blank space left in ms for about 100 letters; *P Lects* (354) supplied following passage, slightly adapted, from "Monologues of S.T. Coleridge" of 1822–3 (*SW & F—CC—*II 1032): "[that the qualities and powers, e.g. of reproduction and irritability, are only manifestations of sensibility, which, therefore, alone is properly life,]"

^{j} Blank space left in ms for about 62 letters; omission supplied from corresponding passage in *SW & F (CC)* I 488

^{k} Corrected to accord with *SW & F (CC)* I 488. MS: waverings

^{l} Corresponding passage in *SW & F (CC)* I 488: "an easy"

---

^{56} The metaphor, used again in *Logic* (*CC*) 113 and *CN* IV 4786 may be derived from a similar though not identical distinction in Kant *Träume eines Geistersehers* pt 1 ch 4 *VS* II 304.

tion, and then moving in a circle, comes round to the point where it began; each of the two divisions[m]] has been made to define the others by a mere re-assertion of their assumed contrariety. [The physiologist has luminously explained Y plus X by informing us that it is a somewhat that is the antithesis of Y minus X; and if we ask, what then is Y − X? the answer is, the antithesis of Y + X—a reciprocation of great service, that may remind us of the twin sisters in the fable of the Lamiae[n]], with but one eye between them both, which each borrowed from the other as the other happened to want it, but with this [additional disadvantage, that in the present case it is after all but an eye of glass[o],][57] for instance. Now that I may not be supposed to have stated . . .[p] for my knowledge and acquaintance with the subject does not permit me to read it with . . .[q] I find this definition: "Life is the sum of all the functions by which death is resisted".[58] I could not after a long pause but ask myself, what is the meaning? This life is the sum of all the functions by which death is resisted, that is, that life consists in being able to live; and more was I surprised when I observed the whimsical gravity with which the author has informed us that hitherto life had been sought for in abstract considerations, as if four more inveterate abstractions could be brought together than the words life, death, function, and resistance.[59]

[m] Blank space left in ms for about 67 letters; omission supplied from *SW & F (CC)* I 489

[n] Blank space left in ms for about 107 letters, punctuated by words "we are plainly", followed by another space for about 105 letters; omissions supplied from *SW & F (CC)* I 489 in which intervening phrase, perhaps a result of C's variant wording, does not appear

[o] Blank space left in ms for about 110 letters; omission supplied, probably only partly, from *SW & F (CC)* I 489

[p] Blank space left in ms for about 137 letters; *P Lects* (355) conjecturally inserted "[the position unfairly]"

[q] Blank space left in ms for about 142 letters; *P Lects* (355) adapted *SW & F (CC)* I 489: "The definitions themselves will best demonstrate our meaning. I will begin with that given by Bichat" as "[complete assurance, I turn to a work by the eminent French physiologist, Bichat, where]" and emends preceding verb "read" to "[treat]"

[57] The fable is more familiar as the fable of the Graiae, but cf a standard schoolbook well known to C, Andrew Tooke *The Pantheon* (London 1809) 242: "There were other *Gorgons* beside, born of the same parents, who were called *Lamiae*, or *Empusae*. They had only one eye, and one tooth, common to them all . . . and, whichsoever of them went abroad, she used them."

[58] Marie François Xavier Bichat (1771–1802), an anonymous tr (by F. Gold) of whose *Recherches physio-*

logiques sur la vie et la mort (1800) had appeared in 1815. C's reference is to the opening sentence: "The definition of life is usually sought for in abstract considerations; it will be found, if I mistake not, in the following general expression:— Life consists in the sum of the functions, by which death is resisted": *Physiological Researches on Life and Death* (London and Bristol 1815) 21.

[59] The paragraph up to this point is a loose quotation from *TL: SW & F (CC)* I 488–9.

This is the vilest form, however, of modern materialism, that is, asserting a fact in other words and then putting the synonyms in place of the cause and the definition. Others have taken and observed some particular function of life as [nutrition[r]], or assimilation, for the production of life or growth, as their act of life. Now in the first place, this would be a definition of the lowest species only of living things. It might describe a fungus, but assuredly it could not describe a living man.[60] Consequently it could be no definition of life as a principle of all the other vital functions. In addition to this, the assimilation, but in truth it merely tells us one thing that life enables animals to [do[s]], not in reality what life itself is. For if that be the case assimilation or [nutrition[r]][61] would convey to us some notion of life, whereas we are obliged to preassume a notion of life as known to understand the difference between . . .[t]. A better definition certainly, as might be expected from the truly great man who produced it, is the power of resisting putrescence,[62] for this is not like the former, wholly unfruitful. But even this definition need only be resolved into a higher formula to be found to contain little; for if we say that everything strives to preserve the state in which it is, or nothing changes its state but with some resistance, that will be found equally applicable to every process in chemistry as attacked by mechanical powers and weakened, and again by those of mechanism.[v] Everything in nature, and not a living body only, tends to preserve its state, and all we can learn is that life is a particular state. That is, the knowledge is assumed in the very definition which was supposed to give it, but in truth it was not by the great founder supposed to give it. He knew too well what he was about; he merely pointed out as a description, as that most marked property which involved in itself the most fearful consequences and above all others that which

[r] MS: attrition

[s] MS: die

[t] MS: attrition

[u] Blank space left in ms for about 97 letters; *P Lects* (356) adapted material from Lect 13 and proposed "[the *natura naturata* and the *natura naturans*]". OB conjecturally offered "[the animate and the inanimate]", adopting terms used later in Lect 12 (at 528 below); C himself also refers in *SW & F* (*CC*) I 491 to "the arbitrary division of all things into living and lifeless"

[v] MS unpunctuated. Sentence remains rather incoherent

[60] The example of the fungus is used in *TL: SW & F* (*CC*) I 490.

[61] "Assimilation" and "nutrition", synonyms in the scientific literature of the time, are treated at greater length in *TL: SW & F* (*CC*) I 490.

[62] The definition ("that which prevents decomposition, putredini contrarium") is attributed to the German physician G. E. Stahl "and his followers" in William Lawrence *An Introduction* (London 1816) 129. C cites it as "the definition of Life, as consisting in antiputrescence, or the power of resisting putrefaction" in *SW & F* (*CC*) I 494.

will for ever immortalise his name, an assertion justified by all facts and by all logic from within and without, that to explain organisation itself we must assume a principle of life independent of organisation.[63]

Now where shall we seek for this principle of life? We will suppose, for instance, that it is probable that without any reason we had made these arbitrary assertions of not merely a distinction in degree but of a distinction in kind between inanimate and animate body. We may suppose, for instance, with Newton, that in nature there is a continual antagonism going on between an universal life and each individual composing it.[64] We will suppose that there is a tendency throughout nature perpetually to individuate, that is, in each component part of nature to acquire individuality, but which is as harmoniously counteracted by an attempt of nature to recall it again to the common organisation.[65] Would there be aught very extraordinary in this? Certainly not in the first instance, because mechanism itself implies organisation in the higher sense of the word, namely a power from within; for after the watch-maker has placed the watch in its due positions, he looks to that power from within belonging to all, the gravity which itself of course can never be the result of any mechanism; for if you explained it by a subtle fluid, for instance, you would be asked the cause of that subtle fluid gravitating, and you must have another and another, and at last you would be asked by what logic you connect power within, or why a thick body should be dull and spirits of wine light and even intellectual.[66] These were answers to no pur-

[63] C is objecting to what he regards as Lawrence's misrepresentation of Stahl. The *TL* text is more explicit: "while I disclaim the error of Stahl in deriving the phenomena of life from the unconscious actions of the rational soul, I repel with still greater earnestness the assertion and even the supposition that the functions are the offspring of the structure, and 'Life the result of organization,' connected with it as effect with cause" (*SW & F—CC—*i 501–2).

[64] A parallel passage in *TL* makes C's meaning clearer: "The tendency to individuation, more or less obscure, more or less obvious, constitutes the common character of all classes, as far as they maintain for themselves a distinction from the universal life of the planet; while the degrees, both of intensity and extension, to which this tendency is realized, form the species, and their ranks in the great scale of ascent and expansion"

(*SW & F—CC—*i 516). Newton's supposition remains unidentified, but see n 67 below.

[65] C discusses "tendency to individuation" more fully in *TL* (see esp *SW & F—CC—*i 516–18); in doing so he was heavily dependent on Steffens *Beyträge*.

[66] Cf *TT* (*CC*) i 393 and n: "It seems to me a great delusion to call or suppose the imagination of a subtle fluid, or molecules penetrable with the same, a legitimate hypothesis". C had expressed dissatisfaction long before with Newton's hypothesis of "subtile and elastic fluid" in a note that he contributed to RS *Joan of Arc* (Bristol and London 1796) 41n–2n and he discusses it in connection with John Abernethy in *TL*: *SW & F* (*CC*) i 532 and n. For an extensive contemporary comment on "subtle fluid", perhaps prompted by his recent mention of it in this lect, see *CN* iv 4518 and n and

pose. Mechanism leads to organisation[w], and there seems no contradiction in the supposition that mechanism, in the strict sense of the word, is nothing but the negative of organisation; for the absence of mechanism will not presuppose organisation, but organisation ceasing, mechanism commences. In short, there is through all nature, and we must assume it as a ground of all reasoning, a perpetual tendency at once to individualise and yet to universalise, or to keep[x], even as we find in the solar system a perpetual tendency in each planet to preserve its own individual path, with a counter-tendency which of itself would lead it into the common solar centre.[67] Suppose this, as I believe we must in all reasoning, to take place in the world, where would be at all the extravagance of lugging in the more subtle parts of inanimate nature and in tracing their analogies and comparing them with those of life in ourselves? Certainly if a man were to say *bona fide* that that which is . . .[y] machine accumulated is the same thing as that life which is within me, he might as well have called his life by any thicker fluid or any other unappropriate thing. But if, in proportion as life becomes less the object of the senses, in proportion as it is less capable of appearing fixed, and as the body retains more and more of those properties which I notice in life and that therefore it is not impossible but that in a still higher evolution of the universal nature it may appear as life, I know no logic on earth that would point out any defect in this reasoning. It may be indeed said, but where would you get this? If it be said that here is an organisation like the steam engine, and I procure a state which in a higher state is life, and as soon as I put it in the machine plays, that would not be tenable, because it would leave organisation unaccounted for; for organisation has no other meaning than a power which, instead of moving in a straight line as the mechanism does,

---

[w] *P Lects* (357) conjecturally emended to "[no] organization"

[x] Direction of sentence changed in mid-stream? *P Lects* (357) emended to "keep [a balance]"

[y] Blank space left in ms for about 19 letters; *P Lects* (357) supplied omission with term adapted from C's "Monologues" of 1822–3 (*SW & F—CC*—II 1029): "[in corallighine slime]"

4521 and n (N 27: Apr 1819).

[67] Cf Newton *Principia mathematica* def 5 (*Mathematical Principles* tr Andrew Motte ed Florian Cajori—Berkeley and Los Angeles 1934—2): "*A centripetal force is that by which bodies are drawn or impelled, or any way tend, towards a point as to a centre*". In a fragment on "animal magnetism" dated 8 Jul 1817, C had rendered it as "all Bodies tend to their centers in the direct proportion of their relative masses": *SW & F* (*CC*) I 590. The rather idiosyncratic linking of this law with individuation here suggests that it may have been what C had in mind at 528 above, where he attributed to Newton the supposition "that in nature there is a continual antagonism going on between a universal life and each individual composing it".

moves round upon itself in a circle, and though it is an act of subsisting, being the act of self-reproduction, is at each moment of our life the identical same act as that by which it was first established, if ever there was a first in reality. No, that we should not do, nor do I believe that has been asserted; but it is easy, when a man is anxious to express his thoughts, to take one illustration and pin it down to the literal words, and to draw from it all the consequences that may be drawn from every simile, a sort of procedure which excites my indignation where it does not excite my ridicule. And as I said to a man, "I have presented a simile as a simile just as I present a candle for a light[; you may use it to see with or snuff it out and have the benefit of darkness^z] or of the stench for your pains".[68] In truth there are two errors. The one places the centre in the circumference, as the man who affirms life to be in the organisation, whereas the organisation is nothing but the consequence of life, nothing but the means by which and through which it displays itself. It is in truth its effects formed by the infinity of radii which proceed from that as a centre and which take[n] collectively [form^a] the circumference. The man, therefore, who states life to proceed from organisation acts as a mathematician would who should be mad enough to assert the centre was placed in the circumference. On the other hand, one who would bring life from without, either in the shape of a soul or any other, would commit an equal fault in logic, namely, he would make the centre out of the circumference and besides that, very unnecessarily I think, confound animal life with the soul and the intellectual faculties.[69] For I think too highly of my responsible nature to confound it with a something by which I am not distinguished from the merest animal. Whatever life is in its present state, it cannot be brought to account for that which more especially constitutes us man.

Now I am to state the effects of materialism in its different relations, and first with respect to science. There are three forms under one or the other of which all science must proceed: those are, theory, hypothesis, or law.[70] And it is in my intention to prove that by neither the first nor the

---

^{z} Blank space left in ms for about 120 letters ^{a} MS: from

[68] The reading offered here adapts the suggestion of John Beer "Ice and Spring: Coleridge's Imaginative Education" in *Coleridge's Variety* ed John Beer (London 1974) 63–5, in which the "man" is considered possibly to have been Mr Boyer at Christ's Hospital and the source of the metaphor to have been Böhme *Aurora* ch 8 secs 14–17.

[69] This reasoning resembles the longer discussion of the relative priorities of subjective and objective in *BL* (*CC*) I 255–8; for a parallel discussion of the nature of mathematics see *BL* (*CC*) I 248–50 and nn.

[70] In *CN* IV 4649 (1820) C offers two formulaic developments of this series of distinctions: "Anticipation : Idea :: Theory : Law" and "Genius : Anticipation :: Cleverness : Theory".

last of these can a materialist reason, and only by the second which is hypothesis, and that arbitrarily and most groundlessly. First, then, theory, the origin of the word. [θεωρειν, *contemplari*[b]], is to see, as from an [eminence a[c]] number of objects together in such a manner as to perceive their relations to each other. A perfect theory, therefore, is possible in mathematics only, the mathematician creating his terms, that is, determining that his imagination has had such and such acts, for instance, such and such lines.[71] He himself forms the terms with which he composes his proposition, and consequently he knows well that there can be no more than those and no less, for there being that exact number constitutes the proposition. But he, of course, can never know by any possibility that he has exhausted all the terms.[72] If, for instance, in the composition and decomposition of water (which is generally believed, and which I think a late very eminent physician declared to have an evidence fully equal to the mathematical science), we are told: by the combustion of hydrogen and oxygen water is produced. Again, that if water is decomposed in a particular manner, a certain proportion is oxygen and another hydrogen, and that the quantities lost and gained will be perfectly equal [to the sum[d]].[73] But here it is clear, in the first instance, that the electrical spark is not taken in, or is taken in as a mechanical agent; it may be so, but we

---

[b] MS: "theorem contemplarii"   [c] MS: immense
[d] MS, unpunctuated: at the sun

---

[71] C had discussed the relations of theory and law at length in *Friend* (*CC*) I 459–65; although he mentions hypothesis in the course of that discussion he does not distinguish clearly between it and theory. He defines it carefully in *CN* III 3587 (Jul–Sept 1809) to mean a supposition arising from a fact; his example is gravitation: "That certain Bodies fall toward the Center [of] the largest body near them, as a stone to the Earth, is a *fact* . . . that this is universal and the ground of all the celestial motions is imagined . . . . Gravitation therefore is a just philosophical Hypothesis . . .".
[72] Cf *TT* (*CC*) I 394–5: "The use of a Theory in the real sciences is to help the investigator to a complete view of all the hitherto discovered parts relating to it; it is a collected View, θεωρια, of all he yet knows in *one*. Of course, whilst any facts remain unknown, no theory can be exactly true, because every new part must necessarily displace the relation of all the

others. A theory therefore only helps investigation: it cannot invent or discover. The only true theories are geometrical; because in geometry premises are true and unalterable." Cf *Friend* (*CC*) I 476–7.
[73] Cf *Logic* (*CC*) 192: "like the late ingenious but somewhat overhasty Dr Beddoes, gravely derive the evidence of the elements of geometry by Euclid from the very same source and place it on the same scale with the elements of chemistry by Lavoisier and [assert] that we have exactly the same certainty and the same kind of certainty in affirming that water is a compound body constituted by the combination of oxygen gas with hydrogen gas in the proportion of twenty-seven to seventy-three, as in the mathematical position that a circle is formed by the circumvolution of a straight line fixed at one end . . .". The reference is to C's old friend and mentor Thomas Beddoes *Observations* esp 108–11 and 15.

know that the contrary theory, namely, that oxygen itself is only water combined with positive electricity, has been supported by very ingenious men, and we have never heard of any mathematical demonstration or position whatever.[74] Consequently a perfect theory is impossible in physics,[75] but as far as we may essentially conclude for our purposes we have seen [that, of] the objects which belonged to them, though it can never produce more than probability, we shall discover some one, which being taken for granted will serve as a support to all the rest, will enable us to classify and to understand them. And therefore, out of every theory as far as it is a just or plausible theory, there arises a just or a plausible hypothesis; an hypothesis being only that fact which, in a multitude of facts, is observed as common to them all, and which, being ascertained, the order and relation of all will be secured. But a law will arise from an hypothesis only when, having been once given, it at once supersedes both hypothesis and theory. From a perfect theory arises an hypothesis, that which we "place under" all;[76] from a steadfast hypothesis arises a law; and from a primary independent or absolute law a system.

Thus Sir Isaac Newton. Contemplating the abstracts of material bodies, as weight, mass, and motion, and the conditions of a perfect theory as far as bodies are considered exclusively under the conceptions of weight, mass, and motion, he made the bodies mathematical; for he contemplated them under those conditions only which he could state abstractly and as parts of a definition. From this arose his hypothesis of gravity, and from this again finally the law of gravitation; and thenceforward neither theory nor hypothesis were further regarded.[77] Nothing but

---

[74] A symptom of C's continuing interest in opposition to the chemistry of Lavoisier and in the experiments on oxygen conducted by HD: see Levere 188–91 and nn. Cf *TL*: "Already our more truly philosophical naturalists (Ritter, for instance), have begun to generalize the four great elements of the chemical nomenclature, carbon, azote, oxygen, and hydrogen: the two former as the positive and negative poles of the magnetic axis, or as the power of fixity and mobility; and the two latter as the opposite poles, or plus and minus states of cosmical electricity ..." (*SW & F—CC—*I 524). C's knowledge of the work of Johann Wilhelm Ritter (1776–1810), a German experimenter with electricity, seems to have been at second-hand by way of Steffens.

[75] C makes the same point in *Friend* (*CC*) I 476–7 and in a long note (477*) quotes from a recently published "exposition of the impossibility of a perfect *Theory* in Physics".

[76] Cf *BL* (*CC*) I 101: "*supposition*, i.e. a fact *placed under* a number of facts".

[77] C seems here to be thinking of "Rule III" in "Rules of Reasoning in Philosophy" in Newton *Principia* bk 3 (*Mathematical Principles* 398–400), where the steps from empirical observation to a received law that includes phenomena that cannot be observed is discussed in careful detail. The rule itself is: "The qualities of bodies, which admit neither intensification nor remission of degrees, and which are found to belong to all bodies within the reach of our experiments, are to be esteemed the universal

the law was at all paid attention to; with the law dwelt power and prophecy, and by exclusive attention to the law it has been that late disciples of Sir Isaac Newton, [Laplace*e*] and others, have removed all the apparent difficulties in the theory of gravitation and turned them into the strongest confirmations of the same, as they must. But the progress of all great science is to labour at a law.[78] The question then is, will ever physics define . . .*f* not as the heavenly bodies in abstract but competent to the same bodies? I answer . . .*g* and the other instruments, impossible that we should ever acquire through mere observation perfect theory, or, in other words, we can never be sure we have exhausted all the terms, that is, that we have present to our knowledge all the agents and their relations. But whether physics may or may not be ultimately elevated into science and prophetic power, proceeding in the opposite direction, that is, from law to hypothesis, and from hypothesis to theory, the last of which will be . . .*h*, will depend of course upon the discovery or non-discovery of such a centre, and this again on the . . .*i*, and this again on whether the forms of the human conscience . . .*j mutatis mutandis*, and whether an absolute is contemplable in every dependent and finite; but this is to conceal that scarcely had the present state of physics been removed from a law than the heavenly bodies appeared in the time of Kepler.

Now it is clear that the materialist excludes all facts that are not immediately the objects of his senses. By his very hypothesis he cannot have a theory, for he determines first of all rather to place effect for cause than to concede any one thing which his reason dictates if only his senses do not at the same time give him a picture of it. The law which is to come,

---

e MS, reflecting C's anglicised pronunciation of French name, perhaps: replace
f Blank space left in ms for about 113 letters
g Blank space left in ms for about 80 letters
h Blank space left in ms for about 77 letters
i Blank space left in ms for about 15 letters
j Blank space left in ms for about 103 letters

---

qualities of all bodies whatsoever". C valued Newton's reservations; see e.g. his mention of "Gravitation in the first and purest sense of the word as solicitously determined by Sir I. Newton": *SW & F (CC)* I 590.

[78] Cf *SW & F (CC)* I 574*, a note of c Mar 1817: "Long after Sir I. Newton, Astronomers were perplexed by certain anomalies in the Moon's Motion. We will suppose it to have been questioned, whether these were not delusions arising from the senses, the position, perspective &c of the Observers?—La Place succeeded in reducing them to, and deducing them out of, the common Law of Gravitation—& the Phænomena were at once understood & *substantiated*." Cf *SW & F (CC)* I 678. For Pierre Simon, Marquis de Laplace (1749–1827), see *Traité de mécanique céleste* (5 vols Paris [1799]–1825), bk 5. Levere (251n) observes that C is likely to have known Laplace's argument only by report.

which is to fulfil, how this can ever arise from mechanism, which must be dependent constantly upon the accidents of the external world and therefore of all others the least fit to control it, it would be useless to speak, but [hypotheses[k]] or sub-fictions may be had in abundance. There may be atoms counteracted by atoms, and these again counteracted by yet finer, and so on to infinity; and if only you will grant three or four moderate requests such as those [Leucippus[l]] demanded: first of all, atoms, some one of which is a great deal larger than the others and having common powers of attraction and repulsion, and these so and so modified, then he will make a picture out of it, having taken care that all the contents of the picture shall be put in the definitions and the assumptions before given.[79]

But if even in science it be pernicious, what must its effects be in morals and in religion? In religion it necessarily will lead either to atheism or to superstition: to atheism if it be driven into all its consequences. For a man who affirms boldly that what the senses have not given to his mind (which mind itself is but, like the senses, an organisation of his body) that he will regard for nothing but words, that is, he will look for those impressions of the senses which he is aware of, and those are only the motions of articulated air; such a man cannot pretend to believe in a God.[80] Consequently (God forbid I should say a man may not be very virtuous and pious in consequence and that the human heart will not often rescue the human head), but, I say, as a consequence reasonable, a man cannot profess to believe in a God unless at the same time he professes to have seen him and been acquainted with him. If he does that it is what we should call superstitious; and, if without thinking, if he is a dogmatic materialist . . .[m] by a corrupt and ignorant hierarchy, he will worship statues and imagine the same power into those statues which the more philosophic materialist imagines in his composition of particles, which are called [atoms[n]]. But this would be nothing if it only left something in us to force a belief of God which cannot be destroyed without destroying the basis of all truth. That is, it destroys the possibility of free agency, it destroys the great distinction between the mere human and the mere animals of nature, namely, the powers of originating an act.[81] All things are brought, even the powers of life are brought, into a common link of causes

---

[k] MS: hypothesis   [l] MS: Lycurgus
[m] Blank space left in ms for about 80 letters   [n] MS: organs

[79] See 513–17 above, where the discussion of Leucippus and Democritus merges their teaching in a single account.
[80] Cf *LS* (*CC*) 112: "the godless materialist, as the only consistent because the only consequent reasoner".
[81] The determinist position against which C had argued in *BL* (*CC*) I 89–139.

and effect that we observe in a machine, and all the powers of thought into those of life, being all reasoned away into modes of sensation, and the will itself nothing but a current, a fancy, determined by the accidental copulations of certain internal stimuli. With such a being, to talk of a difference between good and evil would be to blame a stone for being round or angular; the thought itself is repulsive. No, the man forfeits that high principle of nature, his free agency, which, though it reveals itself principally in his moral conduct, yet is still at work in all departments of his being. It is by his bold denial of this, by an inward assertion "I am not the creature of nature merely, nor a subject of nature, but I detach myself from her; I oppose myself as man to nature, and my destination is to conquer and subdue her, and my destination is to be lord of light and fire and the elements; and what my mind can comprehend, that I will make my eye to see, and what my eye can see, my mind shall instruct me to reach through the means of my hand, so that everywhere the lower part of my nature shall be taken up into the higher. And why? Because I am a free being I can esteem, I can revere myself, and as such a being I dare look forward to permanence. As I have never yet called this body 'I', but only mine, even as I call my clothes so, I dare look forward to a continued consciousness, to a continued progression of my powers; for I am capable of the highest distinction, that of being the object of the approbation of the God of the universe, which no mechanism can be. Nay, further, I am the cause of the creation of the world. For what cause? To a being whose ideas are infinitely more substantial than the things which are the results or are created from them, what motive to create things that are not capable of right or wrong? What was there in them? Not reality. They existed with an infinitely greater reality in the mind. The Deity knew in that which was God himself, which could come from God only, the will and power of becoming worthy of a return to that Maker." This, I say, is so sacred a privilege that whatever dares to tell us that we are like the trees or like the streams, links in an inevitable chain, and that the assassin is no more worthy of abhorrence than the dagger with which he murders his benefactor, that man I say teaches treason against human nature and against the God of human nature.[82]

---

[82] Cf the emblem of "philanthropic justice" presented by the monster Blasphemy in C's "allegoric vision" "Superstition, Religion, Atheism" in 1811: "in which was figured a murdered body, and beside it the assassin before the judgment seat, on which philosophy was imaged sitting, with a label from her mouth, sentencing the dagger to be hung, because neither less nor more guilty than the assassin whom fate had necessitated to necessitate his dagger to stab his friend, the idea of whose wife or wealth had formed the irresistible motive ..." (*EOT— CC*—II 268). Cf *Friend* (*CC*) I 107–8, II 72.

Shall I be told this is scepticism only? Oh, we have met with nothing like scepticism here, we have met with "truth", with nothing but the most dogmatic assertions from the time of Leucippus to Hobbes, who was so far from anything like scepticism that he told Doctor [Wallis[o]] that he could demonstrate all Euclid was nonsense because he himself admitted that the eternal truth of [mathematics[p]] would be subversive of materialism.[83] And from Hobbes to [Condillac[q]], who, having this objection made to him, that if all things were dispositions of material particles, or the result of them, you might ask what colour such a virtue was, answered with coolness, "Yes, and very properly too, for as such a virtuous action is nothing but a generic term for so many particular acts, which particular acts are but so many combinations of motions of a particular man, which particular man must at that time have had such a coat on with such and such impressions joining with that motion; such was the colour of his coat, such was the colour of the action". One would be surprised at this, but looking into Condillac's *Logic* you will find it asserted.[84]

What! We have been told that a truly great man, Professor Kant, has

---

[o] MS: Willis
[p] Corrected to accord with sense and with corresponding passage in ms report (549 below). MS: metaphysics
[q] Blank space left in ms for about 10 letters; omission supplied by inference from quotation that follows

[83] Cf *Friend (CC)* I 32: "But when the philosopher of Malmesbury waged war with Wallis and the fundamental truths of pure geometry, every instance of his gross ignorance and utter misconception of the very elements of the science he proposed to confute, furnished an unanswerable fact in proof of his high presumption; and the confident and insulting language of the attack leaves the judicious reader in as little doubt of his gross arrogance". C made a number of entries in N 21 and N 22 in 1801 (*CN* I 912, 937 E–G) on the controversy between Hobbes and John Wallis (1616–1703). In *Elenchus geometriae Hobbianae* (1655), Wallis, the Savilian Professor of geometry, had exposed the weaknesses of the geometrical solutions in Hobbes *De corpore politico* (1655).

[84] Étienne Bonnot de Condillac *La logique* pt 1 ch 6 in *Oeuvres complètes* (23 vols Paris 1798) XXII 56, where Condillac responds to the question "de

quelle couleur est la vertu, de quelle couleur est le vice" ("what is the character of virtue, what is the character of vice") by saying "la vertu consiste dans l'habitude des bonnes actions, comme le vice consiste dans l'habitude des mauvaises. Or ces habitudes et ces actions sont visibles" ("Virtue consists in the habit of doing good deeds, as vice consists in the habit of doing bad ones. Now these habits and deeds are visible"). C's translation of "couleur" as "colour" and "habitude" as "clothing" may be a jest or perhaps merely uncertain French; it is certainly presented with humorous exaggeration in a parallel quotation in *LS* (*CC*) 102. In Tennemann (XI 289 and 293n–4n) Condillac is introduced as the most important proponent in France of Lockean empiricism and as having gone farther than Locke in insisting that sensation was the only source of our ideas. Tennemann's view is probably similar to C's here.

justified this scepticism.[85] Now that requires an answer.[86] Kant has told us that there are certain great truths which, though they are born in the reason as ideas even as the mathematical theorems are in the pure understanding, do not yet, and cannot, derive their reality from the reason; that in and of themselves, as far as the reason was concerned merely, we should say we cannot help, from the nature of our reason, having such ideas, and an existence therefore in the reason they undoubtedly have. But whether there be any reality correspondent to them, whether the being of God has likewise an existence, that not our reason can assure us. We believe it because it is not a mere idea but a fact that our [conscience[r]] bids us do unto others as we would be done by, and in all things to make that a maxim of our conduct which we can conceive without a contradiction as being the law of all rational being. This, says he, is a fact. But this being the case, there is a difference between regret and remorse which is another fact,[87] and these would be nonsense, they would not be facts, if there were not a free will, but [for] there being a free will we should fall into an endless contradiction of nature,[88] for one part of our nature forces us to demand a value in things, that is, their consequences with regard to our happiness. Another part of our nature demands that there should be a worth in things.[89] I will explain myself in a moment. A man in a moment

[r] MS: consciousness

[85] Kant himself mentions this claim in a footnote to "Was heisst: sich im Denken orientieren?" *VS* iii 81n–2n— the work from which C begins to quote adjacent passages at 539–40 below.

[86] The summary of Kant's position that follows is a reasonable generalisation and is consistent with the views expounded popularly in "Was heisst . . ." and more systematically in *C d r V*.

[87] The distinction is recurrent in C, most elaborately in *Lects 1808–1819* (*CC*) i 63–4: "Where ever we are distinctly conscious, that our Will has had no share direct or indirect in the production of a given event or circumstance, that is painful and calamitous to ourselves or others, we feel *Regret . . .*" (63). Cf *AR* (*CC*) 128, on a criminal whose conscience is awakened: "you hear no *regrets* from him. Remorse extinguishes all Regret; and Remorse is the *implicit* Creed of the Guilty".

[88] Cf C's marginal comment on Christoph Friedrich Nicolai *Ueber meine*

gelehrte Bildung (Berlin and Stettin 1799) 20–1: "The whole of Kant's System of Theology proceeds on this plain Principle: *That*, the non-existence of which would involve the non-existence of ~~that~~ some other, which we *know* to exist, must itself have existence. Thus we *know* the existence of the Law of Conscience, 'Love thy neighbour as thyself', & the *generic* distinction between Regret & Remorse. Now this would involve a contradiction, if Free Will did not exist— & by the same Process, from Free Will, a super-sensuous Nature is deduced; & again from this Immortality & a God": *CM* (*CC*) iii 956. C is drawing on the arguments of Kant in "Der einzig mögliche Beweisgrund zu einer Demonstration des Daseyns Gottes" *VS* ii 55–246 and *C d r V* 294–315.

[89] C had treated the distinction between worth and value in *LS* (*CC*) 74 and n. Kant considers it ("Würde", "Preiss") in *Grundlegung zur Metaphysik der Sitten* esp 77. For discussion of the distinc-

of hatred and revenge stabs me with a dagger. He happens to have opened an impostume and brings about my health. That act is of value. Do I therefore love the man, or feel grateful to him? No. I feel grateful to Providence for using such an agent, but for him nothing but detestation. Why? Because one part of my nature demanded worth and could not be satisfied with the value only.[90] Again, no man can pretend without insincerity to say he could . . .*s* productive of no consequence, but arising from the mind like a bubble of water bursting into nothing; no, however pure they were, however great the worth in the agent, we should still complain of the want of value.

Now our will is to a certain degree in our power, and where it is not it is owing to some prior fault of ours; but the consequences of that will are not in our power, and hence there arises a moral interest that a Being should be assumed in whom is the only will, and the power that involves all consequences as one and the same; which being supposed, it then follows immediately that he who . . .*t* and the consequences because his will marches under the banners of omnipotence. This is Kant's scepticism. It is a modest humility with regard to the powers of the intellect. It was a means of curbing the pride of dogmaticism, because he had seen that Descartes and others had their doctrines turned round and used by Spinoza and used . . .*u*, that is, an unconscious something that being everywhere is nowhere, that being everything it is nothing.

---

s Blank space left in ms for about 120 letters
t Blank space left in ms for about 21 letters
u Blank space left in ms for about 104 letters

---

tion in a religious context see *Friend* (*CC*) I 440; cf *Friend* (*CC*) II 350–1, *EOT* (*CC*) II 320, *LS* (*CC*) 189, 211, *AR* (*CC*) 6–7 and n, and *C&S* (*CC*) 168.

[90] C had discussed aspects of this problem at several points in *BL* (*CC*), esp I 89–90, 130–1, and 202–4. On the issue that "the existence of a being, the ground of all existence, was not yet the existence of a moral creator, and governor", he had quoted in translation from Kant "Der einzig mögliche Beweisgrund" *VS* II 102–3 (although in this instance he quoted at second hand from Jacobi's quotation of it in *Ueber die Lehre* 354n–5n, verifying his quotation against his copy of Kant). The pertinent part of the quotation is as follows: "In the position, that all reality is either contained *in* the neces-

sary being as an *attribute*, or exists *through* him, as its *ground*, it remains undecided whether the properties of intelligence and will are to be referred to the Supreme Being in the former or only in the latter sense; as inherent attributes, or only as *consequences* that have existence in other things *through* him. Thus organization, and motion, are regarded as *from* God not *in* God. Were the latter the truth, then notwithstanding all the preeminence which must be assigned to the ETERNAL FIRST from the sufficiency, unity, and independence of his being, as the dread ground of the universe, his nature would yet fall far short of that, which we are bound to comprehend in the idea of GOD": *BL* (*CC*) I 201.

But what does he say of another kind of assertion? I will as literally as I can translate his words. "When", he says, "the reason in things which concern super-sensual objects, such as the existence of God and a future state, is denied, the right which belongs to her to speak first, then there is the door open to all fanaticism, to all superstition, and to atheism itself.[91] I know not", says he, "but in some of the late writings of Jacobi and [Mendelssohn[v]] I have heard of a philosophy which demonstrates the non-existence of a Deity or at least asserts certain things which, being granted, such an idea becomes impossible. I have seen them say that it is directly against reason to believe in a soul or in a free will, that all consequent reasonings must necessarily lead to Spinozism"[92] (that is to say to matter and thought being one and the same thing and matter having the priority so as to produce thought, by organisation). He goes on thus, "But that reason can easily give her full assent to that which it is not in her power to produce, that having herself produced the idea of a supreme Being, of a free will, and of a future state, as a consequence she can then without pretending herself to prove the reality, gratefully receive such proof from revelation or from a moral and its dictates"[93]—this I can un-

[v] Blank space left in ms for about 21 letters; omission supplied from passage in Kant being quoted

[91] Kant "Was heisst . . ." *VS* III 80: "Wenn also der Vernunft in Sachen, welche übersinnliche Gegenstände betreffen, als das Daseyn Gottes und die künftige Welt, das ihr zustehende Recht *zuerst* zu sprechen bestritten wird; so ist aller Schwärmerei, Aberglauben, ja selbst der Atheisterei eine weite Pforte geöfnet" ("If therefore the reason attempts to address itself first of all to matters that concern immaterial topics such as the existence of God and the world to come, a wide door is opened to all fanaticism, superstition, and, indeed, atheism").

[92] C paraphrases Kant "Was heisst . . ." *VS* III 80–2: "Und doch scheint in der *Jacobischen* und *Mendelssohnischen* Streitigkeit alles auf diesen Umsturz, ich weiss nicht recht, ob blos der *Vernunfteinsicht* und des Wissens (durch vermeinte Stärke in der Speculation), oder auch sogar des *Vernunftglaubens*, und dagegen auf die Errichtung eines andern Glaubens, den sich ein jeder nach seinem Belieben machen kann, angelegt. Man sollte beinahe auf das Letztere schliessen, wenn man den *spinozistischen* Begriff von Gott, als den einzigen, mit allen Grundsätzen der Vernunft übereinstimmigen, und dennoch verwerflichen Begriff aufgestellt sieht" ("And yet in the controversy between Jacobi and Mendelssohn it seems that everything depends upon this overthrow, I do not rightly know, whether simply of rational insight and of knowledge—through supposed strength in speculation—or also indeed of rational belief, and on the contrary on the establishment of another belief which anyone can make according to his preference. One might almost settle for the latter if one saw the Spinozistic concept of God as the only one that was consistent with all the principles of reason and nevertheless established the objectionable concept").

[93] C paraphrases freely from Kant "Was heisst . . ." *VS* III 82: "Denn ob es sich gleich mit dem Vernunftglauben ganz wohl verträgt, einzuräumen: dass speculative Vernunft selbst nicht einmal die *Möglichkeit* eines Wesens, wie wir uns Gott denken müssen, einzusehen im

derstand. But when a man tells me that it is against his reason to believe such things, that all argument proves the contrary, and yet pretends to believe it from a principle of faith, I am very glad that one thought remains to me: that he may be a fanatic and not a hypocrite, but one or the other must he be as none but a hypocrite or a fanatic would pretend to believe by faith not only what is above his reason but directly against it.

Indeed I know no better definition of it, and if you will allow me I will conclude with one little allegory, if I may so express myself, by which some time ago I endeavoured to express my opinion between the materialist who would have nothing but what proceeded from his senses, and the philosopher who thought it not beneath him to look at the other part of his nature, namely, his mind, and to see whether there he might not lead to some law which would render the objection from the other part of his nature intelligible. I have said, "Imagine the unlettered African[, or rude yet musing Indian, poring over an illumined manuscript of the inspired volume, with the vague[w]] yet deep impression that his fates and fortunes are in some unknown manner connected with its contents. Every [tint[x]], every [group[y]] [of characters has its several dream. Say that after long and dissatisfying toils, he begins to sort, first the paragraphs that appear to resemble each other, then the lines, the words—nay, that he has at length discovered that the whole is formed by the recurrence and interchanges of a limited number of ciphers, letters, marks, and points[z]], which however in the very height and utmost [perfection of his attainment, he makes twentifold more numerous than they are, by classing every different form of the same character, intentional or accidental, as a separate element. And the whole is without soul or substance, a talisman of superstition, a mockery of science: or employed perhaps at last to

---

[w] Blank space left in ms for about 112 letters; omission supplied from passage being quoted, *Friend* (*CC*) I 512

[x] MS: tent

[y] MS: grove

[z] Blank space left in ms for about 108 letters; omission supplied from passage being quoted, *Friend* (*CC*) I 512–13

Stande sey; so kann es doch mit gar keinem Glauben und überall mit keinem Fürwahrhalten eines Daseyns zusammen bestehen, dass Vernunft gar die *Unmöglichkeit* eines Gegenstandes einsehen und dennoch, aus anderen Quellen, die Wirklichkeit desselben erkennen könnte" ("But if it is entirely consistent with rational belief to concede that spec- ulative reason itself is never in a position to see into the *possibility* of a being such as we must think God is for us, so can it concede, even with no faith, and above all with no proof of a design, that reason may be able to recognise even the *impossibility* of the topic and nevertheless from other sources to recognise its reality").

feather the arrows of death, or to shine and flutter amid the plumes of savage vanity*a*]. The poor Indian too truly represents the state of learned [and systematic ignorance*b*], arrangement guided by the light of [no leading idea, mere orderliness without method!

But see! the friendly missionary arrives*c*]. He explains to him the nature of written words, translates them for him into his native sounds, and thence into the thoughts of his heart—how many of these thoughts [then first*d*] evolved into consciousness; henceforward the book is unsealed for him; the depth is opened out; he communes [with*e*] the spirit of the volume as a living oracle. The words become transparent, and he sees them as though he saw them not."[94] And then too shall we be in that state to which science in all its form[s] is gradually leading us; then will the other great Bible of God, the book of nature[95] become transparent to us when we regard the forms of matter as words, as symbols valuable only for the meaning which they convey to us, only for the life which they speak of, and venerable only as being the expression, an unrolled but yet a glorious fragment, of the wisdom of the supreme Being.

---

a Blank space left in ms for about 113 letters; omission supplied from *Friend* (*CC*) I 513

b Blank space left in ms for about 11 letters followed by "ignorant"; omission and correction supplied from *Friend* (*CC*) I 513

c Blank space left in ms for about 120 letters; omission supplied from *Friend* (*CC*) I 513

d Corrected to accord with *Friend* (*CC*) I 513. MS: have

e MS: on

[94] The quotation is from *Friend* (*CC*) I 512–13 (var).

[95] Cf *LS* (*CC*) 70: "Let it not weary you if I digress for a few moments to another book, likewise a revelation of God—the great book of his servant Nature. That in its obvious sense and literal interpretation it declares the being and attributes of the Almighty Father, none but the *fool in heart* has ever dared gainsay. But it has been the music of gentle and pious minds in all ages, it is the *poetry* of all human nature, to read it likewise in a figurative sense, and to find therein correspondencies and symbols of the spiritual world."

DRAFT MS

BM Add MS 47,523 (N 25), ff 73–6

[f 73]   Materialism
Monday, 15th March, 1819

We have seen in an early lecture that about 500 years before Christ Leucippus founded the atomic scheme, or pure Materialism, in direct opposition to the Eleatic Philosophy, or pure Idealism—and that within the
next 100 years, at a period rendered uncertain by the general inaccuracy
of ancient chronology and the extraordinary longevity of the Individual
this System was enlarged and modified by Democritus—and that during
the interval from 322 to 270 before the birth of Christ it was [? for]
brought to that state of completion by Epicurus, in which at the period to
which we have now advanced it was restored by Gassendi, who was born
in a village of Provence in the year 1592, and especially applied to the
Anthropology, or the explanation of Human Nature by Hobbes who was
born at Malmesbury 4 years before the birth of Gassendi ⟨1588⟩ & who
almost rivalled his great predecessor, Democritus, in the date to which
his life extended—But tho' the senior of Gassendi, as a man, he was his
Junior as a Philosopher—Oft The 3 ancient Philosophers all alike either
declared or implied an inherence of motion and the essence at least of life
and sentiency in the atoms—tho' in the round atoms & bodies composed
of them they regarded as motive or self motive Powers and Souls, or Principles, of Thought & Motion—[f 73ᵛ] Of these same round atoms the element of Fire was composed—the Soul therefore was a fiery nature. A In
the form of Warmth it appears as Life, i.e. when a sufficient quantity is
accumulated—for in inanimate Substances a certain quantum of Warmth
is inherent & specific, but not enough to reveal themselves as vitals. In
this sense Democritus affirmed, that there is a Soul in all things/—(Here
his different figures of Atoms entangles his Materialism in difficulties not
necessary)—All things therefore have sensation in kind—but the inanimate only momentary & interrupted by the intervenience of the other elementary atoms—All mind is sensation is impression from Atoms or their

542

compounds of like nature with the sentient—and all mind is but sensation, which modified (how we are not told) in the Brain becomes Thinking, but in the region of the Breast is Feeling, and in the abdomen shews itself as growth or obscure sensation of Life—the mode and process of Perception by Effluvia of Images from every body, every body sending forth ειδωλα[1] of each of its component Elements, and falling on an organ of the same elements—these the watery Eidola on the eye which is essentially water, the airy on the Ear which is essentially aeriform &c &c, we may safely omit—It is sufficient for our purposes to know that the fundamental Positions of Ancient Materialism are—first, that motion and sensation are properties of atoms—and that mind is but a species of sensation—and all the processes of Perception & of Reflection purely passive, and all the Acts (or more [f 74] accurately, all the Phænomena or Appearances of Life, just as the seeming acts in a Dream) are wholly mechanical or produced by necessitating antecedents ~~as Billiard Balls~~.—Lastly, that the distinction between these ancient Materialists, & the moderns from Hobbes[2] lies mainly in this one position that the ancients accounted for ~~Life~~ the Soul as the common Principle of Life, Thought and voluntary Motion from a peculiar sort of Atoms, namely the round or fire-composing corpuscles, while the Moderns make the same things result from the organization of ~~the~~ Atoms without any assumption ⟨of a particular species or ~~if~~ of any⟩ ~~of~~ aboriginal and consequently immutable peculiarity of figures in this Species—⟨& consequently, the non-assertion of inherent Life.⟩ In this assertion, however, I beg to be understood as speaking of the ~~principle⟨al⟩ & most celebrated Materialistic~~ opinion common to all; tho' in connection with organization the successors of Hobbes have not all confined themselves to ⟨his scheme of⟩ successive corpuscles propagating motion like Billiard Balls; but animal Spirits—that is, inanimate and irrational fluids thawed down, and then either distilled or else filtrated by ascension into living and intelligent fluids that etch and re-etching engravings on the Brain, ~~which~~ for themselves to look at—according to the pure[a] Materialists, tho' they were intended for the Soul by the first Inventor—We have had too, which comes nearest to the ancient, an oscillating Ether vibrating along these strings which in the system spirits had been regarded as [tubes], and finally, electric matter, the immediate object and the ultimate Organ of inward vision which rises

---

[a] Word is C's inserted correction of another now illegible word—"pre"?

[1] *Eidola*, "images".   wards.
[2] I.e. the moderns, from Hobbes on-

to the Brain like an Aurora[b] Borealis and there disporting in various Shapes, as the balance of + and minus is destroyed or re-established, images [f 74ᵛ] out both past and present.

But all these have been proffered as auxiliaries only, themselves the products of Organization: and my former assertion remains true, that the modern scheme of Materialism ~~is distinct~~ differs from that of Democritus by representing Life, ~~as well as~~ Mind, and Will as the result of Organization, not as pre-existing in the specific atoms so organized.—(Here turn to Lit. Life p. 128.)[3]

First then what is organization? Is it the same as Mechanism? Or not? If not, where lies the difference?

and secondly Life—

All attempts to explain its nature pre-suppose the arbitrary division of all that surrounds us into Things with Life and Things without Life— — far too indeterminate and diffluent for a Philosopher. The positions of Science must be weighed on Jewellers' scales not like the mixt commodities of the market on the way-bridge of common opinion & vulgar usage—.—Yet such has been the procedure in the present instance. By an easy Logic which begins with begging the question and then moving in a circle ends where and *as* it began, each of the two divisions has been made to define the other by a mere re-assertion of their assumed contrariety. The Theorist has explained $Y + X$ by informing us that it is the opposite of $Y - X$: and if we ask, what then is $Y - X$, we are told that it is the opposite of $Y + X$! a reciprocation of good services, that may remind us of the twin Sisters in the [f 75] fable of the Lamiæ, with but one eye between them both which each borrowed from the other as either happened to want it, but with this additional disadvantage in the present ⟨case,⟩ that this one eye is after all but an eye of Glass!— —Bichat's— ["]Life is the sum of all the Functions by which Death is resisted"—i.e. Life consists in being able to live!—/ the whimsical preface[c] that Life had life had hitherto been sought for in *abstract* considerations: as if 4 more inveterate abstractions could be brought together than Life, Death, Function and Resistance—

This is the purest form of modern Materialism—others take ⱥ some particular Function, as Nutrition, or assimilation for the purposes of Reproduction & growth—in the first place, a definition of the lowest species only of living things, as a Fungus—& consequently no definition of LIFE

---

[b] Word miswritten or blotted so as to resemble "Aurola"   [c] For "pretence"?

[3] In the lect at 518 above, C incorporates first a sentence from *BL* and then at 519–21 above a more substantial passage. C's page number refers to the 1817 ed.

as the principle of all the ~~Fun~~ vital functions of the noblest—But in truth, it merely tells us one thing that life enables animals to do—not what life itself is—*

A definition must be ~~the~~ such an Idea of the thing defined as being admitted all its properties and functions are admitted by implication/

[f 75ᵛ] Theory—Hypothesis—Law—One or the other of these you must reason by, unless you give up all pretence to Reason—And by the second only can a Materialist reason—

Effects in Politics—I have before spoken of—viz. Now as a Body is the aggregate of atoms, ~~each are~~ all equal in dignity &c—

In Religion, either Superstition or Atheism, at all events, preclusive of all morals as precluding the possibility of Free Will—Here the ~~objection~~ answer of Lawrence—and the Reply from Kant—

To End with an account of Scepticism, as the first effort of psychological Science—& then of philosophical Scepticism, as the ~~truest~~ friend both of Science & Religion & necessary in initio—[4]

The only argument that ever really disturbs men of sincere & sober minds is that drawn from the seeming growth and decay of the mind with the body—This however a mere sophisma ειδωλατρειας—seu phantasiæ.[5] For first it asserts universally what in any sense is true only partially, of certain faculties—& again of all what holds good only of some. Secondly, it presumes the truth of materialism which yet was the point to be proved—it is more than a petitio principii,[6] it is a petitio finis in principio or rather ab initio.[7] [f 76] For suppose the fact that A and B. thrive or decay together, it does not follow that B is the cause of A—the Organization of the Mind—the same phænomena would take place if A were the cause of B—the mind or power ab intra,[8] the efficient cause of the Organization[9]—Nay, all the analogy of Nature is in favor of the latter—and organization itself only so distinguishable from mechanism—and so too it would be, tho' A and B. acted ~~without~~ each per se by a pre-estab-

---

* A better definition—the power of resisting putrescence—for it is not like the former wholly unfruitful—but yet it need only be resolved into a higher formula to found[d] = 0—for in this it would be found = disposition to preserve its present state—

[d] For "be found"?

[4] "From the outset".

[5] "A mere image-serving sophism—or fantasy". C's version in Lect 13 (581 below) is "a mere sophism of the fancy".

[6] A "begging of the question".

[7] A "begging of the end in the principle or rather from the beginning". Cf Lect 13 at 582 below: "It assumes the conclusion as the very ground upon which it is to begin".

[8] "From within".

[9] The paragraph to this point is absorbed and greatly enlarged in Lect 13 at 581–2 below.

lished Harmony, as suggested by Spinoza & taught at large by Leibnitz—
a doctrine which those are most likely to find absurd who least understand the difficulties of the ~~two~~ three other systems—namely, ~~Bod~~ Mind
result of Org. = Materialism; Body result of Mind = Idealism: and physical influx, or action and reaction of Mind, and Body, immediately or by
some κοινον τι ψυχοειδες.[10] Now a phænomenon that admits of an
equal solution from four different Hypotheses cannot prove the exclusive
truth of any one of them.

---

[10] "Common spiritual entity".

MS REPORT

BM MS Egerton 3057 ff 26–7ᵛ

[f 26]   Mʳ Coleridge—Philosophy Lecture 12ᵗʰ

March 15—1819

In the 13ᵗʰ Centʸ the first science that roused the torpor of mankind was metaphysics & ontology and for more than two Centurys men continued to consult the organization of their own beings—this internal research then gave place to physics—and traditional Magic blended with empiricism (or quackery)—and this again continued until the reformation sounded the second trumpet and the Authority of the schools sunk with that of the hierarchy—we next find the discovery of Magnetism leading philosophy—Descartes ⟨(Who has beautifully described the discipline of the mind prior to its receiving Philosophy.)⟩ seized^a mechanism and then with its influence extending to the present hour, electricity assumed the philosophic throne—thus did Mʳ C— in an interesting manner trace the history of the various Causes, which have drawn men from their own mind to the contemplation of ~~outward~~ external objects—It is remarkable that the first philosophy both Ancient and Modern was idealism and as the Newtonian Philosophy excludes every thing external—so did the Platonic set aside all the objective—in 1592, Gasander of Provence restored the Materialism of Epicurus—which was continued by Hobbs—⟨~~three~~⟩ the ⟨three⟩ ancient ~~materialists~~ philosophers maintained an inherency of motion and the essence of life in the atoms they assumed [f 26ᵛ] and their disputations having determined that space was a nonentity—it followed that as motion was dependant upon space it must be equally nothing^b— the materialists thus finding their senses offended cut the knot altogether ⟨and took for granted the existence of both—thus⟩—~~and~~ their ground of atoms was an hypothesis to explain the partibility of matter and its impenetrability from its hardness—they agreed that round atoms constituted warmth—the fire—the life—the soul—they gave to ⟨all⟩ external nature something of a Soul but not sufficient to produce life—Democri-

---

^{a} "adopted" written under the word, in pencil in another hand
^{b} "non existent" written in pencil above "nothing" in another hand

tus said the soul was the power of sensation or voluntary motion—and if modified in the brain—caused thinking—if in the breast—feeling—if in the abdomen—growth—and thus motion and sensation were properties of different kinds of Atoms & Mind but a species of sensation and not the fundamental power—the distinction between these and Hobbs—consists chiefly on this point—~~they~~ Hobbs yields the absurdity of round atoms and accounts for the Soul as the common power of life ~~and~~ which is the general organization of atoms not peculiar forms—still they make every part of matter essentially tho— not apparently alive and thus revive the hypothesis of the ancients—Materialism sprung from hypothesis and went forwards as it always must by leaps and fictions—ending in dogmatical and unsupported assertion without one practicable deducible result and to [f 27] the sacrifice of common sense and morality—some assume organization and others life or vital principle—What is organization?—it is not mechanism—all machines—a watch has the power from without—it is not ~~made~~ merely an arangement of parts as means to an end but such a mixture of parts each in itself means and end—to say that organization is life and that life only differs in it from mechanizm is to make a child its own parent—you must first prove organization existing prior to life and life consequent upon it—if organization is ⟨not⟩ dependant upon life as its cause—what is life?—life is the sum of all the functions by which death is resisted,—is one of the absurd answers of these materialists—~~thus they say~~ in other words only life is being able to live—this is the purest form of modern materialists—⟨[c]the⟩ assertion of a fact, and then the giving of synonomy for[d] the proof—others say it is the power of resisting putrescence—but this will be found equally applicable in chemistry and mechanism—for every thing in nature endeavours to preserve the state in which it is—where then shall we seek for the principle of life as a principle?[e]—there is in all nature a perpetual tendancy to individualize [f 27ᵛ] and to universallize—as in the planetary system, while each in retaining its own orbit has always an inclination and a leaning to the centre—organization implies ⟨the⟩ revolving in a circle and within itself—and not an impulse forwards as in mechanics—it certainly is the effect and not the cause of life—it is like placing the centre in the circumference—The effects of Materialism in its various relations were—1ˢᵗ on Science—in Science there are three forms—Theory hypotheses—and law—the materialists cannot reason but upon hypotheses and then only arbitrarily—a perfect theory must embrace all the

---

[c] "viz" inserted in pencil, possibly in a different hand   [d] "as" written above line
[e] Question-mark seems to have been inserted later

terms that can belong to the object of the theory ⟨and have present to our knowledge all the relations & properties⟩—and thus only can a perfect theory exist in mathematics—an hypothesis is a fact deducible from theory among a number of facts embracing all—from a stedfast hypothesis arises a law and from a perfect law—a system—Newtons correctness was well proved & traced thro—the four points—the Materialists cannot have a theoretic hypothesis—it is only on the weak foundation of subfictions of fluids actuated by finer fluids—but law wh is to possess prophecy and power they cannot lay claim to—we often find the human heart saving the human head. M^r C commented beautifully upon the free agency of Man and contended any destruction of this free will was a treason against—Nature—human Nature & the God of human Nature—is this scepticism—no—it is dogmatical assertion—one of these Materialists owning mathematics were against his doctrines offered to demonstrate as nonsense the whole of Euclid—Mr C. concluded with an Allegory shewing the distinction between the naturalist who judges wholly from the senses & the true philosopher who argues from his reason

LECTURE 13

DATE AND PLACE OF DELIVERY. Monday, 22 March 1819, at the Crown and Anchor Tavern, Strand, London.

SUBJECT. German philosophy as a response to Locke.

ANNOUNCEMENTS AND ADVERTISEMENTS. The *Courier* for Sat 20 Mar carried the following announcement among its news items: "Mr. COLERIDGE'S Lecture, on Monday Evening next, is, the German Philosophers in relation to LOCKE, or LEIBNITZ, KANT, AND SCHELLING. On Thursday, *Don Quixote*, and on Monday, the 29th March, Mr. COLERIDGE *will deliver his last Address as a Public Lecturer*, with a Review and Application of the whole preceding Course of Philosophical History. Eight o'clock; Crown and Anchor, Strand.—N.B. The Lecture on Dogmatic Materialism (the doctrine, namely, that life and mind exist only as results of organization) with the History and Influences of Empirical Dogmatism, from DEMOCRITUS to the present day, is preparing for the press, with notes and additions." On Mon 22 Mar, the *Morning Chronicle* carried a briefer announcement in which "in relation to LOCKE" appeared as "and its bearings on Locke", "of Philosophical History" was omitted and the announcement of the forthcoming publication of the previous lect was shortened to "The Lecture on Dogmatical Materialism with Notes, is preparing for the Press". The *Times* announcement on the same day was very similar, but read "with its bearings on the System of Locke, comprising the systems of Leibnitz, Kant and Schelling" and referring to the "Lecture on the History and Influences of dogmatical Materialism". The *New Times* carried a slightly abridged version on 22 Mar.

TEXT. Frere MS ff 594–643 and C's draft notes in BM Add MS 47,523 ff 76^v–81.

REPORT. BM MS Egerton 3057 ff 28–31^v.

LECTURE 13

I trust that the very nature of the subjects on which I am to address you will of themselves inform you that, without compromising the very ends for which I stand here, you must derive your best amusement from that degree of information which it will be in my power to impart. The subject itself cannot be ornamented or impassioned without placing you in the very state of mind subversive of the objects which I have in view. There are few pursuits more instructive and not many more entertaining, I own, than that of retracing the progress of a living language for a few centuries, and its improvement as an organ and a vehicle of thought by desynonymising[a] words.[1] Thus as late as the Restoration, for instance, "ingenuous" and "ingenious", "ingenuity" and "ingenuousness" were used indifferently the one for the other.[2] "Propriety" was the common term for propriety of behaviour, for instance, and for property in the sense of estate or ownership. Thus from the Latin *magister*, softened by the Italians into [*maestr*[b]], we have made "mister" as well as "master", and thence "miss" and "mistress", and use them as contradistinctions of age;[3] and it would have been quite in the course of the progress of language if another pronunciation which actually exists, ["meester"[c]],[4] had been

---

[a] MS: desynomizing
[b] Corrected to accord with corresponding passage in draft ms (592 below). MS: master
[c] Corrected to accord with draft ms (592 below). MS: Massiter

[1] A reiteration of the recommendation of a historical dictionary at 212–13 above.
[2] In annotations to his reading, C often remarks on the earlier indiscriminate use of these words. See, e.g., *CM* (*CC*) I 258 and n on an instance in Baxter *Reliquiae*: "One of the very few improvements in our language since the time of the Restoration is the separation of 'ingenious' and 'ingenuous'. The prior writers confound them." Cf *CM* (*CC*) II 822. Johnson *Dictionary* had recorded the different meanings without commenting on either desynonymisation or improvement.
[3] In *CM* (*CC*) III 889, C remarks: "It is the tendency of all Languages to avail

them of the opportunities given by accidental differences of pronunciation and Spelling to make a word multiply on itself/ ex. gr. Propriety, Property; Mister and Master". In his discussion of desynonymisation in *BL* (*CC*) I 82*–3*, C had included a footnote that offers most of the instances used here; they reappear in *CN* III 4397 f 49ᵛ in notes for his literary lect of 10 Mar 1818. C was later to exploit the etymology of "propriety" himself when he adopted it as a term to place beside "nationalty" in *C&S* (*CC*) 35–6.
[4] In his notes (at 592 below), C's wording concerning "meester" is "as it actually exists in our provincial rustic dialect"; *The English Dialect Dictionary*

553

adopted by some great writer, Chaucer for instance, to express mastership instead of servant.

This is the progress of language. As society introduces new relations it introduces new distinctions, and either new words are introduced or different pronunciations. Now the duty of a philosopher is to aid and complete this process as his subject demands; and a distinction has perhaps almost already begun to carry an adjective to a substantive. We should say, and be perfectly intelligible, that Cowley was [a] fanciful, Milton [an imaginative] poet[d]. The philosopher proceeds and establishes the same meaning, in fancy and imagination;[5] for active philosophical language differs from common language in this only, or mainly at least, that philosophical language does that more accurately and by an express compact which [is[e]] unconsciously and as it were by a tacit compact aimed at and in part accomplished by the common language, though with less precision and consistency. Thus, in the philosophic world, each contributing consistently to the finishing of that work, the rudiments of which each man at large is unconsciously aiding to furnish, the mighty machinery goes on, at once the [consequence and the mark[f]] of the mind, the mind of the nation which speaks it.

I have from the commencement of this course been honoured and supported by the respectful attention of my auditors, so much that it might well seem at once unseemly and unthankful to request it on a particular occasion, but I may request you to think with me to produce not a mere passive listening but an active concurrence for a few minutes while I define a few terms which, once thoroughly understood and then borne in mind, you will find little difficulty in following me or accompanying me through the present lecture. And here let me observe that the definitions of those terms are offered to you as verbal not as real definitions, as explaining the sense in which certain terms are to be constantly employed, not as positively affirming the truth and reality of the sense so expressed.[6]

---

[d] Corrected to accord with draft ms (592 below). MS: was fanciful Milton imaginary Poets

[e] MS: it

[f] Blank space left in ms for about 16 letters followed by "of the symptoms"; omission and correction supplied from corresponding passage in draft ms (593 below)

---

ed Joseph Wright (6 vols London and New York 1898–1905) in its article "MASTER" records the variants "mēster", "meeaster" and "measter" for northern counties (Lancashire, N. Yorkshire and Derbyshire).

[5] An adaptation of another part of his

discussion of desynonymisation in *BL* (*CC*) ɪ 84.

[6] By a verbal definition C means what in *CM* (*CC*) ɪɪɪ 261 he calls "a mere Verbal, or Dictionary, Definition", i.e. a definition that indicates the meaning that an author is giving to a word. A real defini-

I have named the pursuit of language entertaining as well as instructive, and in a great number of instances it really is so; but in all those subjects which require the mind to turn its attention inward upon its own operations it cannot be done without thought; and thinking is an effort which habit only can render other than vain. I proceed then to the definitions.[7]

First, that which appears by weight, or what in chemistry is called ponderable substance, is in philosophic language body. Second, that which appears, but not by weight, or the imponderable substance, is matter. (Thus sunshine we should not in common language call a body, though we might not hesitate to call it a material phenomenon, but the painter alludes to a body of sunshine because he alludes to the body laid on to produce the resemblance.)[8] Thirdly, that [which[g]] does not appear, which has no outwardness, but must be either known or inferred but cannot be directly perceived, we call spirit, or power.[9] Fourthly, in speaking of the

[g] Corrected to accord with draft ms (593 below). MS: what

tion by contrast defines the nature of the thing to which the word refers. Cf *TT* (*CC*) II 71: "To know any thing for certain is to have a clear insight into the inseparability of the predicate from the subject (the matter from the form), and *vice versâ*. This is a verbal definition,—a *real* definition of a thing absolutely known is impossible. I *know* a circle, when I perceive that the equality of all possible radii from the centre to the circumference is inseparable from the idea of a circle." Leibniz *Nouveaux essais sur l'entendement humain* (1765) bk 3 ch 3 sec 18 had introduced the distinction as one between real and nominal definitions.

[7] For a ms note to copy G of *SM* outlining a set of definitions parallel to the ones that follow here, see *LS* (*CC*) 81n. For C's most precise, if terse, attempt at them, which arises from his own struggle with Kant *Metaphysische Anfangsgründe der Naturwissenschaft*, see *CM* (*CC*) III 277–8.

[8] The relationship of body to matter is treated in slightly different but usefully consistent terms in *CN* IV 4923 (N 29, dated by the eds as belonging to 1822): "When we *think* Body in the abstract, we call the result Matter: when we *imagine* Matter in the concrete, we call it Body: i.e. Matter is the abstract Notion, or το πανκοινον, *of* Body.—This is the best

scholastic definition of Matter—But a more serviceable explanation and more consistent with the subjects and occasions, on which we might use the word, *material*, where we could not say either spiritual, or bodily, is this—that Matter is an abstraction (of the attention) from the substance (= *esse*) of Body to the appearance (= *videri*), or a Thinking of the appearance abstractedly from the substance. In this sense Matter is not a Universal or πανκοινον: for the appearance may be determinate or indeterminate, seen or thought of (= Anschauung oder Begriff), so that it be *appearance* only.—Thus: I might hold Light incorporeal, Lux = vis incorporea—but no one will deny, that the phænomenon of Light = Lumen, is a material phænomenon.—So the Rain-bow, the Reflection from the Glass, &c are not bodily but yet *material*. I have only to add that by *appearing* as the translation of *videri* I mean a sensuous appearance, or an appearing to the outward Sense."

[9] Examples would be magnetic power and the force of gravity. Whether C means to exclude the human soul and the power of life from what he is about to call "the aggregate of phenomena ponderable and imponderable" is not made entirely clear but it seems consistent with his discussion of "Mind" in the next paragraph but one.

world without us as distinguished from ourselves, the aggregate of [phe-nomena[h]] ponderable and imponderable, is called nature in the passive sense, in the language of the old schools *natura* [*naturata*, while the sum or aggregate of the powers inferred as the sufficient[i]] causes of the for-mer, which by Aristotle and his followers were called the [substantial forms[j]],[10] was nature in the active sense or *natura natur*[*ans*[k]].[11] Fifthly, on the other hand, when reflecting on ourselves as intelligences, and therefore individualising spiritual powers[l],[12] that which affirms its own existence and, whether mediately or immediately, that of [other[m]] beings, we call mind. I believe if you ask yourselves you will find that is the strict sense which you have been accustomed consciously or unconsciously to attach to the word. Lastly, we contradistinguish the mind or the percipi-ent power from that which it perceives; the former has been, very conve-niently I think, entitled the subject and the latter the object.[13] Hence the mind may be defined [as[n]] a subject which has its own object.[14] And

[h] MS: phenomenon
[i] Blank space left in ms for about 60 letters, followed by "efficient"; omission and cor-rection supplied from corresponding passage in draft ms (594 below)
[j] Corrected to accord with draft ms (594 below). MS: actual fluid
[k] MS: naturems
[l] Draft ms (594 below): Spirit or Power
[m] Corrected to accord with corresponding passage in draft ms (594 below). MS: our
[n] MS: to

[10] Cf *SW & F* (*CC*) I 496 where, in a discussion of alchemy, C explains the term: "the inquirer was instructed that the Essence of Gold, or the cause which con-stituted the peculiar modification of mat-ter called gold, was the power of aureity. By the latter, i.e. by the imagination, thought and will were superadded to the occult quality, and every form of nature had its appropriate Spirit, to be controlled or conciliated by an appropriate ceremo-nial. This was entitled its SUBSTANTIAL FORM." C comments at some length on "the Substantial Forms of the Peripatetic [i.e. Aristotelian] School" in similar terms in an annotation to the BM copy of Johann Nicolaus Tetens *Philosophische Versuche* (2 vols Leipzig 1777) I xxxi, xxxiii.
[11] This is one of C's most explicit def-initions of the distinction between *natura naturata* and *natura naturans*, separating the former, ponderable and imponder-able but in either case apparent as phe-nomena, from the latter, not apparent but

known or inferred. His almost contempo-rary glossary of the terms in *SW & F* (*CC*) I 688 situates them more precisely in the Spinozan context from which they are derived (Spinoza *Ethica* pt 1 props 29 and 31). Cf *CN* III 4397 f 50[v] (Mar 1818) for their aesthetic implications.
[12] C concedes that mind is included in *natura naturans* as an instance of spirit or power, just as our bodies may be consid-ered individually by us as instances of *natura naturata*.
[13] C had himself "re-introduced" these Scholastic terms in *BL* (*CC*) I 172, but as the eds point out (I 172n–3n) the mediaeval meaning had been reversed by modern thinkers and C followed the modern practice.
[14] Cf the Schellingian passage in *BL* (*CC*) I 252: "All knowledge rests on the coincidence of an object with a subject", derived from Schelling's "Alles Wissen beruht auf der Uebereinstimmung eines Objectiven mit einem Subjectiven".

hence those who attribute a reality to bodies and to material phenomena, independent of the mind that perceives them, and yet assert equally an independent reality of the mind itself, namely, those who believe in both immaterial and corporeal substances, or, in the language of the day, in soul and body both, would define the body as merely [and purely objective; while[o]] an idealist would declare the material and corporeal world to be wholly [subjective[p]], that is, to exist only as far as it is perceived. In other words he, the idealist, [concedes[q]] a real existence to two terms only—to the *natura naturans*, in Berkeley's language, to God,[15] and to the finite minds on which it acts, and [the *natura naturata*[r]], or the bodily world, being the result, even as the [tune[s]] between the wind and the Eolian harp. I remember when I was yet young this fancy struck me wonderfully, and here are some verses I wrote on the subject:

> And what if all of animated nature
> Be but organic harps diversely framed
> That tremble into thought as o'er them sweeps
> Plastic and vast one intellectual breeze
> At once the soul of each and God of all.[16]

Now in and from this last view, that of the idealists I mean, arises the difficulty and perplexity of our metaphysical vocabulary. As long as the subject, that is the percipient, was opposed to the object, namely the thing perceived, all was clear.[17] Again, in considering the finite [mind or soul as self-percipient[t]] or as the subject [capable[u]] of becoming an immediate object to itself[v], but incapable of being an immediate object to any one

[o] Blank space left in ms for about 90 letters; omission supplied from corresponding passage, slightly adapted, in draft ms (594 below)
[p] Corrected to accord with draft ms (594 below). MS: subject
[q] Corrected to accord with draft ms (594 below). MS: conceives
[r] Blank space left in ms for about 15 letters; omission supplied from draft ms (594 below)
[s] Corrected to accord with draft ms (594 below). MS: tone
[t] Blank space left in ms for about 100 letters; omission supplied from draft ms (594 below)
[u] Word supplied from draft ms (594 below)
[v] MS redundantly repeats: but incapable of being an immediate object to itself

[15] Cf C's definition of Berkeleianism, in a note on Blanco White probably written in 1825: "in which the Accidents have their subsistence in the Percipient, and their specific cause in the supersensual Motors, of all whose formative motions God is the Sustainer, the Sustenance, and perpetual originating Pulse and Impulse" (*CM—CC*—I 525). C's awareness of this question is revealed as early as 1796 in a letter to Thelwall (*CL* I 278: 17 Dec).

[16] *The Eolian Harp* 44–8 (*PW*—EHC—I 102 var), first published in 1796.

[17] C had offered such an opposition in *BL* (*CC*) I 252–60 where, relying heavily on Schelling's analysis, he discusses the subjective and objective alternatives in our understanding of the way we know.

other finite subject, there would be no great difficulty. A man's thoughts are known only to God and himself, as reduced [to] a rule [for the convenience of reasoning, as we use the marks and letters in algebra[w]]. But when not only the mind's self-consciousness, but all other things perceived by it are regarded as modifications of itself, as disguised but actual modes of self-perception, then the whole ground of the difference between subject and object appears [gone[x]]; all is subject[y], and the sole distinction is, first, between that which not only is but is thought of by us as being such, and that which indeed truly is so no less than the former, but which we think of as being the contrary.[18] By way of illustration: man contemplates the image of his friend. Not only his recollection of the friend is in his mind, but he contemplates it as such; but when his friend is present, though according to the idealist that impression is as much in his mind as the former, he yet considers it to be external and independent of himself. Secondly, the distinction between that[z] which all men are by the common necessity constrained so to imagine, and that which is accidental and individual, as, for instance, all men in a sane state are compelled to see the objects which all others at least see around them, as compared with the man who, in a fever or delirium, blends objects which no man else perceives, so that one of the elder idealists will state the subject according to his view of it, that when we are awake we have a dream in common, when asleep every man has a dream of his own; that is, when we are awake we have a world in common, and when we are asleep every man has a world of his own.[19]

We have only to reverse this order of thought and we shall have the op-

---

[w] Blank space left in ms for about 81 letters, following "as a rule"; omission and correction supplied from corresponding passage in draft ms (595 below)
[x] Corrected to accord with draft ms (595 below). MS: good
[y] Draft ms (595 below): subjective
[z] MS, redundantly: that between that

[18] A few months later C returned to this issue in a more thorough-going spirit: "A position, which occurred to me 20 years ago as an objection to Idealism (as Berkley's &c) recurs with additional weight to me as often as I think on the subject.—Idealism & Materialism are both grounded in the impossibility of inter-mutual action between things altogether heterogeneous—and here again it is assumed by both parties that *Perception* is but a sort of, or at least an immediate derivative from, *Sensation*—so that the changes or modifications of the Percipient's own Being are exclusively the objects of his perception. But is not this gratuitous? Is not sensibility just as mysterious, equally *datum*, haud intellectum [*given*, scarcely understood], as Percipiency?" (*CN* IV 4540 and n: Jun 1819). For evidence of C's early awareness of the problem, see e.g. *CL* I 278 (to John Thelwall: 17 Dec 1796).

[19] *Spectator* (IV 229) No 487 for 18 Sept 1712 reported the saying of Heraclitus as it is recorded by Plutarch (*Moralia* 166c): "*That all Men whilst they are awake are in one common World; but that each of them, when he is asleep, is in a World of his own*". Cf *LS* (*CC*) 18n and *BL* (*CC*) I 262 and II 63–4.

posite result, that of the materialist. All [here*a*] is merged in the objective, as the former in the subjective, and these reduced, as before, into the general and permanent, and the particular [and*b*] transitory. The thoughts of a ta[b]le, according to the materialist, differ from the ta[b]le itself, not by essential invisibility or by being essentially imponderable, but only because this portion of the brain is too thin and subtle to be perceptible of weight, and it is truly owing to the defect of our organs that we cannot weigh our thoughts or measure our perceptions.[20]

Henceforward [, therefore, "objective" acquired two meanings, the first being the reality of any thing, outwardly correspondent to our perception, or notion*c*], thereof, independent of the perception itself; and the second meaning, the universality of the perception as arising out of inherent laws of human nature in opposition to the accidental state of any one individual percipient. That grass is green is an instance of the former; that it appears yellow to a man in the jaundice, if such be the fact, would be an instance of the latter.[21]

Still, most serious difficulties [were*d*] started and have been stated with incomparable clearness by Lord Bacon in his *Novum organum*. It is [this*e*]: that the human understanding itself is but an individuality in nature, having its own peculiar organisation and modifying all objects, even its own form of self-consciousness no less than the forms seen as external by its own peculiar appropriate perspective. In the language of our British Plato, there are not only idols of the den, the theatre, and the market-place, the idols or delusions of our passions, of our imagination, and of custom and habit, but idols of the [race, *idola tribus^f*],[22] and consequently the utmost that rational conviction can arrive to is not that this

---

a Corrected to accord with corresponding passage in draft ms (595 below). MS: that

b Missing word supplied from draft ms (595 below)

c Blank space left in ms for about 17 letters, followed by "or motions"; omission and correction supplied from draft ms (595 below)

d Draft ms (595 below): a most serious difficulty started

e Corrected to accord with corresponding passage in draft ms (595 below). MS: thus

f Corrected to accord with draft ms (595 below) and parallel passage in *SW & F (CC)* II 929. MS: res idola toribus

[20] Cf *BL (CC)* I 261–2: "It is the table itself, which the man of common sense believes himself to see, not the phantom of a table, from which he may argumentatively deduce the reality of a table, which he does not see". MS: differs.

[21] The two senses of "objective" are alluded to e.g. in *Logic (CC)* 43*. On the effects of jaundice, see *CN* III 4309 and n (N 22: Feb 1816) and II 2439 (N 17: 9 Feb 1805); it is the example of illusion used by Descartes in *Discourse on Method*: *D Phil Writings* I 130–1.

[22] For C's recent expositions of the "idols" of Bacon ("our British Plato"), see *Friend (CC)* I 491–3, drawing on *Novum organum* bk 1 aphs 23 and 39 (*Works*—1740—I 276–7; Spedding I 163–4), and "General Introduction to the *Encyclopaedia Metropolitana*" in *SW & F (CC)* II 929.

or that is true by any inherent necessity, but only that it is for man; that he is compelled so to perceive and so to conceive and the deductions thus drawn can be questioned only by those who admit themselves to be deranged, that is, not in the same order with their fellow men. To what an extent this position has been carried by ancient and by modern sceptics, it will be sufficient that I remind you by one observation of Mr. Hume in the *Essays* in the form in which they first appeared, namely, that if spiders had been theologians, they would have been under the necessity of concluding that the world had been spun, and that—though a [philosophical lecture will be no sufficient excuse for repeating blasphemy, and I stop.*g*][23]

One question would*h* occur to every reflecting hearer, "Pray, would this spider have the power of [doubting*i*] its own perception and conclusion?["] If so, and if the spider be but a nickname for a rational being, proposed for misleading the fancy by a verbal association, and the spider means no more than a serious sober man arguing in defence of his Maker, must there not be some other faculty above this mechanism, by which man is adapted to his present circumstances? Must there not be some power, [call it*j*] with Lord Bacon the [*lumen siccum*k], the pure light,[24]

---

g Blank space left in ms for about 13 letters, preceded by "philosopher". MS unpunctuated and unparagraphed; omission and correction supplied from draft ms (596 below)

h MS: ⟨would⟩ would

i Corrected to accord with corresponding passage in draft ms (596 below). MS: fitting

j Corrected to accord with draft ms (596 below). MS: calling

k Blank space left in ms for about 13 letters, following "Roman"; omission and correction supplied from draft ms (596 below)

---

[23] David Hume *Dialogues concerning Natural Religion* (1779 pt 7; ed Norman Kemp Smith—2nd ed London 1947—180): "The BRAHMINS assert, that the world arose from an infinite spider, who spun this whole complicated mass from his bowels, and annihilates afterwards the whole or any part of it, by absorbing it again, and resolving it into his own essence. Here is a species of cosmogony, which appears to us ridiculous; because a spider is a little contemptible animal, whose operations we are never likely to take for a model of the whole universe. But still here is a new species of analogy, even in our globe. And were there a planet wholly inhabited by spiders (which is very possible), this inference would there appear as natural and irrefragable as that which in our planet ascribes the origin of all things to design and intelligence . . .". C mentions the vulnerability of "the Admirers of Proofs *a posteriori* ~~of~~ for the existence of God" to Hume's observation, and identifies Paley *Natural Theology* as an instance, in a note to Tennemann II endpapers. The omitted "blasphemy" is presumably Hume's immediately following remark (180–1): "Why an orderly system may not be spun from the belly as well as from the brain, it will be difficult for him to give a satisfactory reason". For C's sense of the dangerous consequences of this position, see *CM* (*CC*) III 848.

[24] Literally "dry light", for which see Bacon e.g. *Novum organum* bk 1 aph 49 in *Works* (1740) I 279: "Intellectus humanus luminis sicci non est; sed recipit infusionem a voluntate & affectibus; id

with [Lord Herbert call it reason,[25] with Kant[l]] call it a faith [of] reason?[26] Must there not be some power that stands in [some union with[m]], in some participation of the external and the universal, by which man is enabled to question, nay, to contradict the irresistible impressions of his own senses, the necessary deductions of his own understanding, to [challenge[n]] and disqualify them as partial and [incompetent[o]]? Think you that the man who even first dared suggest to his own mind the thought that the sun did not really rise, did not really move through the heavens but that this was the first prospect of his eye and his position only? Think you that

[l] Blank space left in ms for about 17 letters, followed by "call it a faith a reason"; omission is supplied by adapting slightly the following corresponding passage from draft ms (596 below): call it reason with Lord Herbert, or call it the Faith of Reason with Kant

[m] Corrected to accord with draft ms (596 below). MS: human nature

[n] Corrected to accord with draft ms (596 below). MS: change

[o] Blank space left in ms for about 10 letters; omission supplied from draft ms (596 below)

quod generat *ad quod vult scientias*" ("The human understanding is no dry light, but receives an infusion from the will and affections; whence proceed sciences which may be called 'sciences as one would'"): tr Spedding IV 57. Cf *SW & F (CC)* I 635 and n.

[25] C rarely mentions Edward Herbert, 1st Baron Herbert of Cherbury (1583–1648). In *CL* II 681–2 (to J. Wedgwood 18 Feb 1801) he had objected to Sir James Mackintosh's attribution of the doctrine of innate ideas to Descartes, arguing that Herbert had "assigned" them in his *De veritate* (1624) and noting Locke's reference to them and adding classical precedents. Locke discusses Herbert's treatment of "aliquod supremum numen", "a highest command" that is placed in human minds by God, but treats it dismissively. In an annotation, dated 6 Mar 1824, to a flyleaf of the Houghton Library copy of John Smith *Select Discourses* (London 1660) C is more particular: "Lord Herbert was at the entrance ⟨of,⟩ nay, already some paces within, the Shaft and Adit of the Minde, but he turned abruptly back—and the Honor of establish⟨ing⟩ a compleat Propædia of Philosophy was reserved for Immanuel Kant a century or more afterwards". The increasing specificity of C's remarks on Herbert may owe something

to Tennemann's detailed account of him (x 112–40) where the term "eine höchste Vernunft" ("a supreme reason") is cited from *De veritate* (London 1656) 135 and 136 (x 131).

[26] Cf e.g. Kant "Was heisst: sich im Denken orientiren?" in *VS* III 79: "Ein reiner Vernunftglaube ist . . . der Wegweiser oder Compass, wodurch der speculative Denker sich auf seinen Vernunftstreifereien im Felde übersinnlicher Gegenstände orientiren, der Mensch von gemeiner, doch (moralisch) gesunder Vernunft aber seinen Weg, sowohl in theoretischer als praktischer Absicht, dem ganzen Zwecke seiner Bestimmung völlig angemessen vorzeichnen kann; und dieser Vernunftglaube ist es auch, der jedem anderen Glauben, ja jeder Offenbarung, zum Grunde gelegt werden muss" ("A pure faith of reason is the guide or compass by means of which the speculative thinker orientates himself on his intellectual excursions in the field of suprasensual circumstances; the man of ordinary yet—morally—healthy reason, however, can mark out his way in a theoretical as well as in a practical project fully conformable to the whole purpose of his destiny; and it is also this faith of reason, that must be laid as the foundation for every other belief, even for every revelation").

a man who, diseased and beholding plainly before him such and such objects, dared say that these things are not so, was not at the same time conscious of something nobler than his perceptions themselves?[27] Could a machine or any part of a machine pass out of itself? If it can, what becomes of the famous doctrine that our ideas have no other pretence to truth except as [they are[p]] generalisations or classifications and impressions passively perceived through the mechanisms of sense and sensation?[28] But I need not inform you that a numerous class of modern philosophers assert no such faculty exists;[29] the notion is a mere abortion of pride engendered in the imagination.[30] But still, though I call, not improperly, this class numerous, they yet appear numerous in consequence of their fewness, of their contrariety of opinions to the feelings of mankind in general; which makes me wonder so many would be found entertaining such doctrines. Still, I say, it must make us pause that positions asserted to differ from noise only by the sounds being articulated, that positions which are affirmed to have no origin in kind but delusion, and which, traced to their source, will be found to arise from sophisms of the mere imagination, that these absurd doctrines should have been held not only by the mass of mankind in all ages, but by the best and the wisest, even by those whom these very philosophers are obliged to place

---

[p] Corrected to accord with draft ms (596 below). MS: their

[27] Cf the parallel use of the example in *SW & F* (*CC*) I 589: "the discovery of Copernicus, . . . its broad blank contradiction to the apparent evidence of the Senses . . .". The observation is related to the imagining of Adam watching the first sunset (*TT*—*CC*—I 245 and n) which in turn takes up Hume's comments on expectations of sunrise and on Adam's lack of knowledge of the properties of water and fire (in *An Enquiry concerning Human Understanding* sec 4 pt 1), but also to the problem of the astronomer's point of view which is mentioned above (461) and in *TT* (*CC*) I 249.

[28] Or as C had formulated it in terms derived from Aristotle *De anima* in *BL* (*CC*) I 141: "*nihil in intellectu quod non prius in sensu*" ("there is nothing in the mind that was not previously in the sense"). There he links the theory to David Hartley and to Etienne Bonnot de Condillac (1715–80) as modern exponents of the philosophy of Locke. In *Logic* (*CC*) 134 he calls it "the rule of

common sense". For his views on its practical inadequacy see *CN* III 4047 ff 138ᵛ–40ᵛ (N 18: Jan 1811).

[29] The faculty to which C refers is one that allows us access to knowledge that is not derived from sense perception. He had attacked the mechanical assumptions of association theory in greater detail in *BL* (*CC*) I 106–28, using the writing of David Hartley as his example. As he admits in *BL* (*CC*) I 187, C had himself once been an enthusiastic Hartleian; Joseph Priestley (1733–1804), the Unitarian scientist and philosopher, had been an influential exponent of Hartley's views; and C was inclined to regard the "Common Sense" school of philosophy in Scotland—particularly as represented by Thomas Reid (1710–96), James Beattie (1735–1803), and Dugald Stewart (1753–1828)—as being mere followers of Hartley.

[30] Here using "imagination" ironically as the "modern philosophers" do, to mean something contrary to fact.

[foremost*q*] in their list whenever they have occasion to enumerate the chief luminaries and benefactors of the race. That these absurd positions should be the groundwork of all law, so inwoven in all language that we may fairly*r* find a materialist or an atheist to talk consistently with his own opinions any five minutes; and that they should be taken for granted in every thing that distinguishes man from the brute, even in the degree in which he is so distinguished, for these philosophers are compelled by their own principles to deny any distinction between us and the brute in kind. However, be this as it may, the facts remain as I have stated; and if I have succeeded in rendering them intelligible and comparatively short, they will explain the subjects of this lecture which is the object with which I have stated them.

I am so deeply impressed with the benefit which we all receive by the associations of love and honour with the names of great men in past times, how much they make up the historical feeling of a country and give to every individual who has cultivated his intellect a pride of heraldry far beyond that which a descendant of Julius Caesar would enjoy if he contemplated his own family merely from himself, that I shrink from violating any genuine persuasion in favour of a man's greatness and never indeed approach to it unless where I can at the same moment offer him a substitute and feel at least in my own mind the belief that the pain he suffers at the moment will be more than compensated by the pleasure that follows.[31] This I certainly feel, more especially, when I speak of Mr. Locke. My conscience bears me witness that it is not from any neglect of studying his writings or of seeking for assistance from those who have professed to do so, but sincerity compels me to say that after all the study and all the assistance I could never discover any one thing to account for that prodigious impression that seems to have been made, either in the novelty of the sentiments or in the system of those which are peculiar, to him.

I verily believe myself that the case stood thus: we were becoming a commercial people; we were becoming a free people in enjoyment, as we had always been in right. Mr. Locke's name, and his services, which of themselves would be sufficient to immortalise him, had connected his

---

q Corrected to accord with draft ms (596 below). MS: forward
r For "scarcely" or "hardly"?

[31] On "the true historical feeling" of a nation, cf *Friend* (*CC*) I 447 and *C&S* (*CC*) 67 where C associates it with heraldry. Descent from Julius Caesar is presumably offered as a family connection more splendid than could be claimed by any English nobleman, and one that could in fact be claimed by no one, Caesar's only child, Caesarion, having died without issue.

name with that of freedom and that of the Revolution from the natural attachment of old and established learned bodies to old and established political bodies which had been their protectors. It was not to be wondered that those who were supposed to teach the philosophy of past times were found mainly amongst those who supported the old forms of government; it was . . .*s* and that the same great revolution was to go on in mind that had been going on in state affairs, and that as King William had completely done away with all the despotism of the Stuarts, so Mr. Locke had done away altogether with the nonsense of the Schoolmen and the universalists. In consequence of which, people read who had never once examined the subject or thought about it, and found some monstrous absurdities that they themselves had never heard of before, and they found them most ably confuted. To those absurdities they attributed all they had connected in their own minds with the abuses and miseries of former ages, utterly neglecting the good at the time. They had considered this as a new light stepping into the world; and it is not once or two or three times that I have heard it stated, when I referred to the writers before William III: "Oh, you forget there was no light till Locke".[32] Milton, Shakespeare, and so on were forgotten. They were poets, but it is clear the reign of good sense came in with Locke.

Now one of the followers of Locke, Hume, who has carried the premises to the natural consequences, has allowed that he did not com-

---

s Blank space left in ms for about 13 letters; *P Lects* (376) altered conjecturally to "[also to be expected] and [stated]"

[32] C's most extensive discussion of Locke's reputation and its causes is to be found in the series of letters he wrote to Josiah Wedgwood in 1801 (*CL* II 677–703). In them he drew upon materials in Maass *Versuch über die Einbildungskraft* as is recorded in *BL* (*CC*) I 89n and ff. His summation here is more closely related to his recent account of the growth of Locke's reputation, in *LS* (*CC*) 108–10, where the contemporaneous political and commercial development of England is stressed. Years earlier C had anticipated the unfavourable impression his criticisms of Locke might make. In his draft letter to Josiah Wedgwood of Feb 1801 (*CL* II 700) e.g. he says: "I feel deeply, my dear Sir! what ungracious words I am writing; in how unamiable a Light I am placing myself. I hazard the danger of being considered one of those trifling men who whenever a System has gained the applause of mankind hunt out in obscure corners of obscure Books for paragraphs in which that System may seem to have been anticipated; or perhaps some sentence of half [a] dozen words, in the intellectual Loins of which the System had lain snug in *homuncular* perfection. This is indeed vile in any case, but when that System is the work of our Countryman; when the Name, from which we attempt to detract, has been venerable for a century in the Land of our Fathers & Forefathers, it is most vile. But I trust, that this can never be fairly applied to the present Instance—on the contrary I seem to myself as far as these facts have not been noticed, to have done a good work, in restoring a name [Descartes], to which Englishmen have been especially unjust, to the honors which belong to it."

pletely understand the first book of Locke, what was understood and what overthrown.[33] But I believe it may be traced historically nearer, that Descartes was the first man who made a direct division between man and nature, the first man who made nature utterly lifeless and Godless, considered it as the subject of merely mechanical laws. And having emptied it of all [its[r]] life and all that makes it nature in reality, he referred all the rest to what he called "spirit", consequently the faculty of spirit, in relation to this "matter".[34] What must be then the perception? What was it then to perceive? Why, it was not, for mechanical laws prevented his admission of that, not as the old Platonists would have said, perceiving the things outward; physiology had advanced too far to render that attainable. He therefore conceived what he called "material ideas", that is, as he supposed there [were[u]] in the soul causative powers which produced images for it, so that there [were[v]] in the brain certain [moulds[w]] that pre-existed in itself and which determined it to receive such and such impressions rather than others, and these he had called "material ideas".[35] And in consequence of their origin being in the organisation itself, he had named

---

[r] MS: his   [u] MS: was   [v] MS: was
[w] Corrected to accord with parallel passage in *BL* (*CC*) I 98*. MS: modes

---

[33] C is probably referring to the conclusion of a footnote in Hume *An Enquiry concerning Human Understanding* sec 2 in Hume *Enquiries* 22n: "To be ingenuous, I must own it to be my opinion, that LOCKE was betrayed into this question [concerning 'innate ideas'] by the schoolmen, who, making use of undefined terms, draw out their disputes to a tedious length, without ever touching the point in question. A like ambiguity and circumlocution run through that philosopher's reasonings on this as well as most other subjects."

[34] Cf *BL* (*CC*) I 129: "To the best of my knowledge Des Cartes was the first philosopher, who introduced the absolute and essential heterogeneity of the soul as intelligence, and the body as matter". For comment on the consequences to "spirit" and "matter" see 519–20 above where C quotes from *BL* (*CC*) I 129–31.

[35] Cf *BL* (*CC*) I 98* and n where Descartes is credited with "having introduced into his philosophy the fanciful hypothesis of *material ideas*, or certain configurations of the brain, which were as so many moulds to the influxes of the external world . . .". Descartes does not himself use either the French or Latin equivalents of the term "material ideas", but he does at several points discuss the actions of the brain in physiological terms. *BL* (*CC*) I 98*n suggests Descartes *Treatise of Man* tr Thomas Steele Hall (Cambridge MA 1972) 84–8 (equivalent to *D Phil Writings* I 102–6) as an e.g.; cf *D Phil Writings* II 59–62 and 187–8 for others. C adds (*BL*—*CC*—I 98*): ". . . Mr Locke adopted the term, but extended its signification to whatever is the immediate object of the mind's attention or consciousness". The eds refer to *Essay concerning Human Understanding* bk 2 passim and Intro to sec 8 where "idea" is defined as "whatsoever is the *object* of the understanding when a man thinks . . . whatever is meant by *phantasm, notion, species,* or *whatever it is which the mind can be employed about in thinking . . .*" (Locke *Essay* I 32). For C's confusion over La Forge's presentation of Descartes, see 510 n 9 above.

them "innate ideas", in both senses: first of all, the true ideas, or spiritual ones, he conceived as having their birthplace in the mind; and those "material ideas" he considered innate, as having their birthplace in the organisation. But the Jesuit [Voetius[x]],[36] before Locke wrote, had attacked this on the ground that Locke proceeds on. But the answer Descartes makes, who was a truly great man, is this: "I said innate not [connate[y]], I spoke of the birthplace not the time. Do you suppose that either I or any man in his senses, nay, I will add, that any man out of his senses, could imagine such an absurdity as that men heard before they heard, that they had images before they saw? These things are too absurd to be attributed to any man in his senses, much more to a philosopher."[37] But still, admitting that, and taking Descartes without his material hypothesis at all, nothing can be more simple than what he says, or more agreeable to common sense. And what indeed was not first said by Descartes, it would be difficult to find anywhere among the Schoolmen in which you will not find the same things said, or among the ancient metaphysicians, which is simply this: that there must be a difference in the perceptions of a mouse and a man, but this difference cannot be in the object perceived, but in the percipient; that, therefore, says Descartes, we have reason to suppose that there are two sorts of ideas or thoughts. If, says he, two really be, these are Descartes' own words (I am now speaking logically and as a grammarian, not as a mathematician), if there are two differences, one is of those thoughts or images in which we are conscious of being passive, those which are impressed upon us whether we will or no, and those, as appearing to have their causes externally, we call "external ideas"; but, says he, there are others in which the mind is conscious of its own activity, and, tracing its own operations, forms notions which, from the place of their origin, we call "innate ideas".[38] He then goes on with a definition

---

[x] MS: Grotius   [y] MS: quallate

[36] Cf *Logic* (*CC*) 184* where the same material appears and the name, Voetius, is given. Gysbertus Voetius (1588–1676) was not a Jesuit but a Dutch Calvinist; Descartes does reply to objections raised by him in his *Epistola . . . ad . . . Gisbertum Voetium*, but the objections to which C is about to turn were to another controversialist whose identity is uncertain.

[37] A paraphrase or rough summing up of Descartes's reply in articles 12 and 13 of *Notae in programma quoddam* (*Comments on a Certain Broadsheet*) (1648).

In *Logic* 184* C had provided his own Latin rendering of the first sentence: "Innatas non connatas dixi, locum non tempus oriundi".

[38] C's reference here is difficult to pin down. He seems to be summing up material in his letter to Wedgwood of 24 Feb 1801 (see esp *CL* II 688) and again paraphrasing Descartes rather than quoting him. Articles 12 and 13 in *Explicatio mentis humanae* to which Descartes was responding are as follows: "Mens non indiget ideis, vel notionibus, vel axiomatis innatis: sed sola ejus facultas cogitandi,

which is noticeable (you may see it in his answer to [Voetius^z]) by being word for word the same as Locke's definition of the [ideas of] reflection, so that in truth the man of straw that was to be thrown down never existed,[39] but the real assertion to be opposed was not merely in substance but *totidem verbis et [ratione^a]*[40] the idea in Locke's ["ideas of] reflection".[41]

---

^{z} MS: Boetius ^{a} Blank space left in ms for about 15 letters

---

ipsi, ad actiones suas peragendas, sufficit" (art 12); and "Atque ideo omnes communes notiones, menti insculptae, ex rerum observatione vel traditione originem ducunt" (art 13) ("The mind has no need of ideas, or notions, or axioms which are innate: its faculty of thinking is all it needs for performing its own acts"; and "Thus all common notions which are engraved in the mind have their origin in observation of things or in verbal instruction"): tr John Cottingham *D Phil Writings* I 295. The comment by Descartes which C sums up is part of the response to art 13; C had quoted it (var) in his letter to Wedgwood of Feb 1801 (*CL* II 692): "quod nempe *judicemus*, has vel illas Ideas, quas nunc habemus cogitationi nostrae praesentes, ad res quasdam extra nos positas referri—non quia istae res extra nos menti nostrae per organa illas ipsas Ideas sensuum immiserunt; sed quia *aliquid* tamen immittitur, quod menti occasionem dedit ad ipsas per innatam sibi facultatem, hoc tempore potius quam alio efformandas" ("We make such a judgement not because these things transmit the ideas to our mind through the sense organs, but because they transmit something which, at exactly that moment, gives the mind occasion to form these ideas by means of the faculty innate to it"): tr *D Phil Writings* I 304. To this may be added Descartes' response to art 12 which C seems to have had in mind in his letter to Wedgwood: tr "In article *twelve* the author's disagreement with me seems to be merely verbal. When he says that the mind has no need of ideas, or notions, or axioms which are innate, while admitting that the mind has the power of thinking (presumably natural or innate), he is plainly saying the

same thing as I, though verbally denying it. I have never written or taken the view that the mind requires innate ideas which are something distinct from its own faculty of thinking. I did, however, observe that there were certain thoughts within me which neither came to me from external objects nor were determined by my will, but which came solely from the power of thinking within me; so I applied the term 'innate' to the ideas or notions which are forms of these thoughts in order to distinguish them from others, which I called 'adventitious' or 'made up'. This is the same sense as that in which we say that generosity is 'innate' in certain families, or that certain diseases such as gout or stones are innate in others: it is not so much that the babies of such families suffer from these diseases in their mother's womb, but simply that they are born with a certain 'faculty' or tendency to contract them" (*D Phil Writings* I 303–4).

[39] Cf *CL* II 686 (to J. Wedgwood 24 Feb 1801): "these Innate Ideas were Men of Straw".

[40] "In so many words and with the same argument".

[41] For the definition, see Locke *Essay* I 123 bk 2 ch 1 sec 4: "the other fountain from which experience furnisheth the understanding with ideas is,—the perception of the operations of our own mind within us, as it is employed about the ideas it has got;—which operations, when the soul comes to reflect on and consider, do furnish the understanding with another set of ideas, which could not be had from things without. And such are *perception, thinking, doubting, believing, reasoning, knowing, willing,* and all the different actings of our own minds;—

The abuse of the word "idea" by Descartes and Locke I shall not further speak of, and therefore I simply say, and most happy should I be to stand corrected by any man who could give me better information, that if you only substitute for the phrase, the ideas being derived from the senses or impressed upon the mind or in any way supposed to be brought in, for nothing can be more mechanical or pagan-like than the phrases used in the *Essay on the Human Understanding*, if for this you only substitute the word "elicit", namely, that there are no conceptions of our mind relatively to external objects but what are elicited by their circumstances and by what are supposed to be correspondent to them, there would be nothing found in Locke but what is perfectly just, but at the same time I must say nothing but what is perfectly what had been taught from the beginning of time to the end.[42] And with regard to the rest, the grammatical part,[43] I think I took the fairest way of convincing myself that a man could. I took the abridgement of his work published at Cambridge for the use of the young men at the university, and, having it interleaved from Descartes and with no other guide, I wrote opposite to each paragraph the precise same thing written before, not by accident, not a sort of hint that had been given, but directly and connectedly the same.[44] The question, therefore, amounts precisely to this: Mr. Locke's phrases seem to say that the sun, the rain, the manure, and so on, had made the wheat, had made the bar-

which we being conscious of, and observing in ourselves, do from these receive into our understandings as distinct ideas as we do from bodies affecting our senses. This source of ideas every man has wholly in himself; and though it be not sense, as having nothing to do with external objects, yet it is very like it, and might properly enough be called *internal sense*. But as I call the other Sensation, so I call this REFLECTION, the ideas it affords being such only as the mind gets by reflecting on its own operations within itself." Or is C thinking rather of Locke's definition (*CL* II 683) in his second letter to Stillingfleet?

[42] For evidence of C's continued struggle with this issue, see *CN* III 3268: "Important Hint suggested itself to me, 10th Feb. 1808. The powers of conscious intellect increase by the accession of an organon or new word—try this in that abominable word, Idea/ how have I been struggling to get rid of it, & to find some exact word for each exact meaning—but no!—look into Bacon, Hooker, Milton,

and the best Writers before Locke—& then *report.*—"

[43] Books I and II of *An Essay concerning Human Understanding* are entitled "Neither Principles nor Ideas are Innate" and "Of Ideas" respectively; Books III and IV are entitled "Of Words" and "Of Knowledge and Probability". It is not clear whether by "the grammatical part" C means Books III and IV or just Book III.

[44] In *CL* II 679 (to J. Wedgwood 18 Feb 1801) C says of his first serious study of Locke, ". . . I took Locke from my Landlord's Shelf, & read it attentively.—" The most likely abridgement for him to have had interleaved was *A Syllabus of Locke's Essay on the Human Understanding* (1796), a book still being republished at the end of the 1820s. C's copy is not known. Alternatives that went through many editions were [J. Wynne] *An Abridgment of Locke's Essay concerning Humane Understanding* (1696) and [Sir Geoffrey Gilbert] *An Abstract of the Essay of Human Understanding* (1709).

ley, and so forth; but we cannot believe that a man who was certainly a very wise man in his generation could have meant this and that he was only misled in the expressions from his not being made apprehensive of the consequences to be deduced from them. If for this you substitute the assertion that a grain of wheat might remain for ever and be perfectly useless and to all purposes non-apparent, had it not been that the congenial sunshine and proper soil called it forth, everything in Locke would be perfectly rational.[45] I am only standing in amazement to know what is added to it, for never have I been able to learn, from repeated questioning these, what was done[b]. The only answer has been, "Did not he overthrow innate ideas?"

Locke is no materialist. He teaches no doctrine[s] of infidelity, whatever may be deduced from them. In his controversy with the Bishop of Worcester, speaking of substance, where the Bishop says substance can never be brought to an image, ["*sine re substante*"[c]] that which stands under every possible image, precluded this. What is Locke's answer? "I never denied the mind could form a just image of itself by reflection and deduction",[46] so that in truth those who have drawn the doctrines of mere

[b] *P Lects* (379) silently emended to "from repeatedly questioning these Lockians what was done"; OB suggested "[from repeated questioning, please, what was done]"

[c] Blank space left in ms for about 48 letters; omitted passage is perhaps to be found in passage Locke quoted from Stillingfleet, or a variant of it, for which see n 46 below

[45] Cf C's ms note on the first fly-leaf of John Petvin *Letters concerning Mind* (London 1750), the copy now in the Huntington Library: "the whole scheme of Locke is an Hĕtĕrozētēsis—by which the Sun, Rain, Air, Soil &c are made to *constitute* the germs (as of Wheat, Oat, or Rye) ⟨of⟩ the *growth* & *manifestation* of which they are the efficient *Conditions*.—Instead of the words, 'give, convey' and the like, write wherever they occur, 'excite, awaken, bring into consciousness' or words equivalent—& little will remain in Locke's Essay to be complained of, but its dullness & superficiality . . ." (*CM—CC*—IV). By "Hĕtĕrozētēsis" (not in *OED* but a recognisable combination of Greek words) C seems to mean an investigation in which the terms used are heterogeneous.

[46] In his answer to Edward Stillingfleet, bp of Worcester (1635–99) *A Discourse in Vindication of the Doctrine of the Trinity* (1696), *A Letter to the Right Reverend Edward Ld Bishop of Worcester* (London 1697), Locke quotes Stillingfleet as follows: "The Idea of Substance . . . is nothing but the supposed, but unknown Support of those Qualities we find existing, which we imagine cannot subsist, *sine re substante*; which, according to the true import of the Word, is in plain English, standing under or upholding" (42–3). Locke sums up Stillingfleet's objection: "Your Lordships Argument . . . stands thus, *If the general Idea of Substance be grounded upon plain and evident Reason, then we must allow an Idea of Substance, which comes not in by* Sensation *or* Reflection" (38). Locke's reply, ending with phrases reminiscent of the ones that C employs, is: "All the Ideas of all the sensible Qualities of a Cher[r]y, come into my Mind by Sensation; the Ideas of *Perceiving, Thinking, Reasoning, Knowing*, &c. come into my Mind by *Reflection* . . . as your Lordship well expresses it, *We find that we can have no true Conception of any Modes or Accidents, but we must conceive a* Substratum *or* Subject, *wherein they are*; i.e. That they cannot exist or

materialism from Locke certainly drew what he never intended to draw. And with regard to the rest, I remain as before; I have not yet been able to discover the ground, or any ground, why I should calumniate all the great men that went before him in compliment to any one idol, however deserving of praise in other respects, as to say that, because Locke told us in defining words we ought to have distinct images or conceptions, . . .[d] which Cicero never heard of and which was a strange thing to Plato. But I can very easily understand that men with far less merit than Locke, and even men who wrote more entertainingly, for that is a great thing, when a book has once got a character, if it should be so dull that nobody should read it afterwards it saves the reputation for centuries; this we have had instances of in others.[47] Many circumstances combined at the time. The first was that Descartes had had his physical prophecies and other parts of his mechanical system overthrown by Sir Isaac Newton, but the . . .[e] as Locke's ideas of reflection; therefore one great man had overthrown the physical parts and another the [metaphysical[f]] parts, and to that circumstance we owe entirely the custom of talking of Locke and Newton, to that accident entirely.[48] The next thing was that Voltaire and others before him both in France and in Germany had held up [Leibniz[g]], a truly

---

[d] Blank space left in ms for about 60 letters; *P Lects* (379) conjecturally inserted "[and therefore we ought to have an image or a conception of an idea]"; OB proposed "[we should despise Cicero or Plato for a fallacious doctrine]"

[e] Blank space left in ms for about 72 letters; *P Lects* (380) supplied "[metaphysical parts, it was said, by Locke; though rather it was the case that his (Descartes') epistemological theory of innate ideas turned up in another form]", adapting very freely material in *CL* II 701 and ms report (600 below)

[f] Corrected to accord with corresponding passage in ms report (600 below). MS: mathematical

[g] Blank space left in ms for about 13 letters; omission supplied from parallel passages in *CL* II 702 and ms report (601 below)

---

subsist of themselves. Hence the Mind perceives their necessary Connection with Inherence or being Supported, which being a relative Idea . . . the Mind frames the *correlative* Idea of a *Support*. For I never denied, That the Mind could frame to it self Ideas of Relation, but have shewed the quite contrary in my Chapters about *Relation*" (40). Locke returns to the dispute about substance in *Reply to the Right Reverend the Lord Bishop of Worcester's Answer to His Second Letter* (London 1699) 372–92.

[47] This paragraph and the following three paragraphs are derived from the much more detailed discussion of the topic in C's letter to J. Wedgwood of Feb 1801 (*CL* II 697–703). Examples of parallel phrasing are recorded in the notes that follow.

[48] Cf *CL* II 702: "Sir Isaac Newton had recently overthrown the whole system of Cartesian Physics, & Mr Locke was believed to have driven the plough of Ruin over the Cartesian Metaphysics.— This was a complete Triumph of the English over the French / the true origin of the union, now proverbial, of the two names—Newton & Locke."

great man, but as a sort of rival to our Newton, and anyone who has read the literary and scientific history of that time well knows that nothing in politics could excite more fury than the controversy concerning the [infinitesimal[h]], as to who was the inventor, this again interested the natural feelings. But Leibniz . . .[i]; and here again there was another connection made between Locke and Newton. He was opposed to Leibniz and the . . .[j] which had been invented by our Newton.[49]

At that time, too, we know well the very great heats that there were between the high church and the low church, and at the same time the existence of a middle party who, while they kept to the church, yet still favoured all the tolerant opinions and [what was in general] terms[k] the most rational way of interpreting the religion. But Locke was . . .[l], while the clergy at large and the religious people found that, in an age when the philosophers were beginning to be notorious as infidels, there was a man of true piety who wrote very edifying comments (as they really are) on the Scriptures,[50] and those won that party; while the infidels, such as

---

[h] Corrected to accord with corresponding passage in *CL* II 702. MS: arithmetic

[i] Blank space left in ms for about 63 letters preceded by "supposed"; corresponding passage in *CL* II 702 seems too long to be what was omitted but probably conveys general sense of the sentence: "not only opposed the Philosophy of Locke, but was believed & spoken of as a mere reviewer of the exploded Cartesian Metaphysics"

[j] Blank space left in ms for about 11 letters; *P Lects* (380) conjecturally supplied "[calculus of fluxions]". C seems not to use this term elsewhere although he refers e.g. to "the Differential Analysis" (*CM—CC*—I 739). In each case he means calculus

[k] *P Lects* (380) silently emended to "in general what was termed". MS: in general in what was in terms

[l] Blank space left in ms for about 14 letters; OB conjecturally supplied "[both pious and rational]", in keeping with gist of *CL* II 702: "Mr Locke, that greatest of Philosophers & yet pious Believer"

---

[49] Cf *CL* II 702: "After this came Leibnitz, & the Dispute concerning the Invention of the Infinitesimal &c and the bitterness & contempt with which this great man was treated not only by Newton's Understrappers, but by the whole English Literary Public, have not even yet wholly subsided.—Now Leibnitz not only opposed the Philosophy of Locke, but was believed & spoken of as a mere reviewer of the exploded Cartesian Metaphysics . . . . Leibnitz's notions of Plenum, pre-established Harmony &c were misrepresented with the most ludicrous blunders by Maclaurin & other Lockists—& Voltaire in that jumble of Ignorance, Wickedness, & Folly, which with his usual Impudence he entitled a *Philosophical* Dictionary, made it epidemic with all the No-thinking Freethinkers throughout Europe, to consider Locke's Essay as a modest common sense System . . .". Colin MacLaurin (1698–1746), was a Scottish philosopher and scientist who contributed to the fluxional calculus; Voltaire's *Dictionnaire philosophique portatif* first appeared in 1764, in London.

[50] By Locke's comments on the Scriptures C presumably means *The Reasonableness of Christianity, as Delivered in the Scriptures* (1695) and *A Vindication of the Reasonableness of Christianity* (1695), both works that were regarded

Voltaire and others, cried him up beyond all bounds.[51] He was the true modest man; he had referred all things to the effects, to mind ... [Hume*m*,] who, smiling at Mr. Locke's deductions, said they were merely amulets against priestcraft,[52] take them in the lowest sense which Locke did not intend.

If you doubt, just refer to the beginning of Hume's essay on cause and effect;[53] you will find immediately the channels made on Locke's opinions. Everywhere it is, you have no real truth but what is derived from your senses, it is in vain to talk of your ideas of reflection for what are they? They must have been originally in our senses or there is no ground for them.

So many circumstances combined together as to make it a kind of national pride in the first place, and secondly, the interest of almost each of the parties to cry [up*n*] Mr. Locke. And the effect is shown more especially, that the most ingenious, I think some of the finest, works of philosophy for that period, those produced by the great Stillingfleet and others, were not merely put at once as trash out of fashion, but it was said

---

m Blank space left in ms for about 36 letters   *n* MS: out

---

as having Socinian or Unitarian implications, and perhaps his posthumously published paraphrasis of St Paul's Epistles which appeared from 1705 to 1707. C does not seem to have mentioned this aspect of Locke's career elsewhere.

[51] Cf *LS* (*CC*) 109–10: "the *sensible* Christians ... with the numerous and mighty Sect of their admirers, delighted with the discovery that they could purchase the decencies and the *creditableness* of religion at so small an expenditure of faith, extolled the work for its pious *conclusions*: while the Infidels, wiser in their generation than the children (at least than these *nominal* children) of light, eulogized it with no less zeal for the sake of its principles and assumptions, and with the foresight of those obvious and only *legitimate* conclusions, that might and would be deduced from them". Cf *TT* (*CC*) I 563, a parallel account of remarks made in a conversation in 1810. Voltaire praised Locke on a number of occasions. The 13th Letter of his *Lettres philosophiques* (*Lettres ecrites de Londres sur les Anglois*—Basle 1734—) is devoted to Locke who is referred to in the following terms (91): "Jamais il ne fut

peut-être un esprit plus sage, plus méthodique, un Logicien plus exact que Mr. Locke" ("There has perhaps never been a wiser, a more methodical spirit, a more exact logician, than Mr. Locke"); and (96–7) "Locke, après avoir ruiné les idées innées ... ayant bien établi que toutes nos idées nous viennent par les sens ..." ("Locke, after having overthrown innate ideas ... having established convincingly that all our ideas come to us by way of the senses").

[52] Hume's closest approach to such a statement seems to be his comment on Locke's discussion of innate ideas, in *An Enquiry concerning Human Understanding*, for which see 565 n 33 above.

[53] Meaning, probably, *A Treatise of Human Nature* bk 1 pt 3 sec 15, "Rules by which to Judge of Causes and Effects", a discussion that is conducted entirely in terms of "objects", "observation", and "phenomena". But C might also have had in mind pt 3 sec 14, "Of the Idea of Necessary Connection", or even the whole of pt 3, "Of Knowledge and Probability", where the same tendency to depend only on the evidence of the senses is steadily displayed.

that Stillingfleet had died of a broken heart in consequence of his defeat by Locke; though wherein the man was to become defeated till we can find how Locke differed from others is for other considerations.[54] I can therefore say this finally with regard to Locke, that it was at the beginning of a time when they felt one thing: that the great advantage was to convince mankind that the whole process of reacting[o] upon their own thoughts or endeavouring to deduce any truth from them was mere presumption, and henceforward men were to be entirely under the guidance of their senses. This was most favourable to a country already busy with politics, busy with commerce, and [in] which yet there was a pride in nature [so] that a man would not like to remain ignorant of that which had been called the queen of sciences,[55] which was supposed above all things to [elevate[p]] the mind, which had produced a word which a man had overthrown,[56] had . . .[q] that of "philosopher". What a delight to find it all nonsense, that there was nothing but what a man in three hours might know as well as the Archbishop of Canterbury!

[57] This exactly suited the state of the nation, and I believe it was a

---

o For "reflecting"?   *p* MS: alleviate
q Blank space left in ms for about 12 letters

---

[54] C is reported as having praised Stillingfleet's role in the controversy with Locke, in a conversation with HCR on 23 Dec 1810 (see *TT—CC—*ı 563) and he refers to it pointedly as "the asserted and generally believed defeat of the Bishop of Worcester (the excellent Stillingfleet)" in *LS* (*CC*) 105. The death of Stillingfleet's second wife in 1697 is now more usually taken to be the cause of the "broken heart" of which he is said to have died in 1699, and even *A New and General Biographical Dictionary* (new ed 15 vols London 1798) xiv 182 expresses scepticism: "some have imagined, that being pressed with clearer and closer reasoning by Locke, than he had been accustomed to from his other adversaries, it created in him a chagrin which shortened his life. There is, however, no occasion to suppose this: for he had been subject to the gout near twenty years . . .". But the story persisted; see e.g. Isaac D'Israeli *The Literary Character* (3rd ed 2 vols London 1822) ı 151: ". . . Bishop STILLINGFLEET's end was hastened by LOCKE's confutation of his metaphysics".

[55] I.e. theology. Cf *CL* ıv 863 (to H. J.

Rose 23 May 1818): "Is there . . . *any one Science* which has for its specific object to be supplemental of all the other Sciences? In its highest sense, *Theology* (or the cognitio *logica* τοῦ A = Ω [the *logical* recognition of the fact that Alpha = Omega]) is that science. If then the somewhat you now seek for under the name of Philosophy is not to be found in the science of Theology, it is to be found—nowhere." Cf *C&S* (*CC*) 46 for a reiteration of this opinion.

[56] By "a word", does C mean the term "innate ideas"?

[57] In this paragraph C takes up a theme that he had recently introduced in his discussion of the difference between genius, talent, sense, and cleverness, as they are variously exhibited in Germany, England, and France (see *Friend—CC—*ı 419–23). Here his emphasis shifts from comparison for the sake of illustration to the part played by national circumstances, national histories, and the intervention of Providence. For a contrary but related view that had stressed the complexities of national character, see *CN* ıı 2598 (May–Aug 1805).

symptom of that state of providential government of the world which observed the nearer union of the kingdoms of Europe to each other. What in a former time had been distinctions co-existing in each country were now to be a distinction of whole countries. Formerly we were to have the men who employed their senses chiefly, and those again who employed their brains and their spirits, all in one country. The time had come when, by a subdivision of labour, one country was to employ its brains, another its hands, and another its senses. There was a subdivision among the countries which before had been made between the inhabitants of several countries, and this was evident in Germany. Germany never had the advantages that this country has, never had that fulness of occupation by commerce, never that deep interest in the affairs of the whole which constitutes the pride, and is perpetually improving the faculties, of Englishmen, who still carry their country home to their fireside. But on the other hand, it had many and great advantages of its own: it was the number of its universities, and the circumstance that the learned or studied men formed a sort of middle class of society correspondent to our middle class, and the very absence of nationality gave to the Germans as they became cosmopolites as they are the only [writers who feel as men*r*], the only writers truly impartial in their accounts of other nations. If they err it has been from want of information or wrong premises, but never from any national feeling whatsoever. And the same cause, rendering the outward world of less importance to them, rendered each man of more advantage to them, made them a thinking metaphysical people. In other words, their defect (for in every nation and every individual, put your hand upon the defect of a nation, and you will find there its excellence, and upon its excellence you will find there its defect), so it is the defect of Germany to be forever reasoning and thinking, and in other countries, perhaps happier, to have a great aversion to thinking at all.[58]

Now Leibniz first opposed Lockean philosophy as then understood in the simplest manner in which it could be. Mr. Locke's followers had repeated, there is nothing in the mind which was not before in the senses. Leibniz added [*praeter ipsum intellectum*s], except the mind itself;[59] and

---

r Blank space left in ms for about 24 letters; omission supplied from corresponding passage in ms report (600 below)

s Blank space left in ms for about 12 letters; omission supplied from parallel passage in *BL* (*CC*) I 141

---

[58] A joke at the expense of himself and his listeners?

[59] In *Logic* (*CC*) 226, C was to attribute the statement of Locke's followers, "Nihil in intellectu quod non *prius* in sensu" to the schools of Aristotle and Epicurus, emphasising the traditional nature of Locke's view. Leibniz's modifi-

he then proceeds, in his new language,[60] to demonstrate in the most beautiful manner that all those puzzling laws which appeared, which Locke had in vain endeavoured to draw from external objects[61] (while in truth the very first process presupposed the knowledge of the contrary, as, for instance, the very first process to limit a space presupposes the want of limit: if I draw in my imagination a circle or a sphere, I must have a preconception of the unlimited before I can examine the limit[t] itself), he showed that all the subjects at all in controversy were the operations of the intellect itself, that they were not indeed things but they were acts of mind, or forms.[62] And in a manner that was as elegant as really it was forcible in demonstration, he showed that there were two points in which Mr. Locke's philosophy was altogether disorder; in that, first of all, which I have just now mentioned, that every one of those experiences to which he refers presupposed a certain something in the mind as the condition of that experience. And he admits, as Kant has afterwards done,[63]

---

[t] MS: limits

---

cation, "Nihil est in intellectu, quod non fuerit in sensu, excipe: nisi ipse intellectus", appears in his detailed commentary on Locke, his *Nouveaux essais sur l'entendement humain* bk 2 ch 1 sec 8. Cf *BL* (*CC*) I 141–2 and n.

[60] Is "new language" a slip on the part of the reporter? "New essays", for "*Nouveaux essais*", would seem less odd. It is possible, however, that C is referring to Leibniz's rewriting of Locke's argument, for which see the following note.

[61] Leibniz *Nouveaux essais*, which follow the structure of Locke *Essay* section by section, are presented as a dialogue between two friends, Philalethes and Theophilus (the "friend of truth" and the "friend of God") who represent respectively the views of Locke and the views of Leibniz. C's appreciation of the "beautiful manner" of Leibniz's demonstration is in accord with his recommendation elsewhere of dialogue, a form which he said, e.g. in about 1803, "gives an excellent grace to the writings of Plato": *SW & F* (*CC*) I 131.

[62] C appears to be summing up the nature of Leibniz's argument rather than referring to a particular part of it; the chapter "Of Infinity" (bk 1 ch 17), however, is an example of what he seems to have in

mind.

[63] Probably a reference to Kant's remarks near the end of *C d r V* (882–3): "*In Ansehung des Ursprungs* reiner Vernunfterkenntnisse, ob sie aus der Erfahrung abgeleitet, oder, unabhängig von ihr, in der Vernunft ihre Quelle haben. Aristoteles kann als das Haupt der Empiristen, Plato aber der Noologisten angesehen werden. Locke, der in neueren Zeiten dem ersteren, und Leibnitz, der dem letzteren (obzwar in einer genugsamen Entfernung von dessen mystischem Systeme) folgete, haben es gleichwohl in diesem Streite noch zu keiner Entscheidung bringen können. Wenigstens vorfuhr Epicur seinerseits viel consequenter nach seinem Sensualsystem (denn er ging mit seinen Schlüssen niemals über die Grenze der Erfahrung hinaus), als Aristoteles und Locke, (vornehmlich aber der letztere) der, nachdem er alle Begriffe und Grundsätze von der Erfahrung abgeleitet hatte, so weit im Gebrauche derselben geht, dass er behauptet, man könne das Daseyn Gottes und die Unsterblichkeit der Seele (obzwar beide Gegenstände ganz ausser den Grenzen möglicher Erfahrung liegen) eben so evident beweisen als irgend einen mathematischen Lehrsatz"

that Locke was not unaware of this; that though it did not enter into his plan, and though it was afterwards received by many of his followers, yet he speaks of predisposing causes in the mind which would really amount to no more than this, the acts of the mind itself.[64]

The next point which he pressed on the Lockeans is this: all we know of matter and the external world is transient, and to everything which refers to reality we attribute a something particular, the dependence upon particular time, particular space, whereas there are a whole class of truths which are distinguished by their universality, by their necessity.[65] As, for instance, I will take two truths, but of which every man that now hears me is as much convinced practically of one as the other, namely, the first, the sun will rise tomorrow, and second, that the two sides of a triangle continue greater than the third side. We are convinced of it, but we feel the diversity of the two propositions. There is no absurdity, however wild, if a man were to say, "It is my opinion that the sun will not rise tomorrow, that in the night the system will be destroyed", there is no absurdity in the thing. But should a man tell you that in a month or two the two sides of a triangle will be less than the third, then you know he is teaching a language he does not understand, for madness could not conceive or attach a meaning to the words. Where is this to be derived from? The nature of the mind itself. What is this mind? Reduce it to a result of the or-

---

("*In respect of the origin* of the modes of 'knowledge through pure reason', the question is as to whether they are derived from experience, or whether in independence of experience they have their origin in reason. *Aristotle* may be regarded as the chief of the *empiricists*, and *Plato* as the chief of the *noologists*. *Locke*, who in modern times followed Aristotle, and *Leibniz*, who followed Plato (although in considerable disagreement with his mystical system), have not been able to bring this conflict to any definitive conclusion. However we may regard Epicurus, he was at least much more consistent in this sensual system than Aristotle or Locke, inasmuch as he never sought to pass by inference beyond the limits of experience. This is especially true as regards Locke, who, after having derived all concepts and principles from experience, goes so far in the use of them as to assert that we can prove the existence of God and the immortality of the soul with the same conclusiveness as any mathematical proposition—though both lie entirely outside the limits of possible experience": tr Kemp Smith 667–8).

[64] C is presumably referring to a passage in *Nouveaux essais* bk 2 ch 1 sec 2 that immediately precedes the quotation from Leibniz at the beginning of the paragraph: "Il y a tousjours une disposition particuliere à l'action et à une action plustost qu'à l'autre" ("There is always a specific disposition to action, and to one action rather than another"). C used the term "predisposing cause" elsewhere, e.g. in "On the Passions" in 1828: ". . . I take each Impetite and ~~seek for~~ endeavor to shew, of what Passion or Passions it is the predisposing Cause, or an ingredient, materia subjecta, in the constitution of such passions . . ." (*SW & F—CC—*II 1447).

[65] For the remainder of this paragraph C appears to be thinking of the argument in Leibniz *Nouveaux essais* bk 1 ch 1 on the possibility of innate principles in the mind, or even of bk 1 as a whole. The examples of the sunrise and triangle that follow, however, are not in Leibniz.

ganisation of matter, and it must inevitably partake of all that is transitory in this matter of which it is a property. Suppose it to be the mind itself and not matter, then we ask, what in the name of wonder can be the organs of a mind? What is the mechanism of the mind? What are these but vague words that can after all come to nothing more than what we express by the word "ideas"? What we know of our own mind we know by its thoughts. What are the thoughts? Are they, for instance, particles or corpuscles? We are [so*u*] apt to use words derived from external objects, that I verily believe that many a man before he asked himself the question would imagine his mind made of thoughts, as a wall is of bricks, till he asks whether he ever separated a thought from a thought, whether there was a meaning in the word "thought", except as the mind thinking in such a situation; whether a notion of any plurality, or anything we can call construction, takes place in our experience. We are aware of no such thing; the mind passes on, and in vain would it be to distinguish thought from thought till we had reduced it to words, and by distinction of pen or of printer we had made them visible. Then our eyes recognise the character[s], find out divisions, but the senses discover none. Such might be called the philosophy of Leibniz in relation to Mr. Locke; a far higher ground is taken as he stands on his own system.

I have not felt myself allowed, from the limits which my lectures have placed round me, to enter particularly on Spinoza, because the substance of his life, I could have said, I have been obliged to anticipate first in the [account*v*] of the Eleatic school, the idealists of old, and secondly in the [account*w*] of the new Platonists;[66] but great impressions has Spinoza made on the minds of the learned and an impression on the theologians. And the theologic hatred of his name is one of the most incomprehensible parts of philosophic researches;[67] for Spinoza was originally a Jew,

---

u MS: too   *v* MS: perhaps as abbreviation: act   *w* MS: act

[66] See above perhaps 122–5, 133–4, and 192–4. Tennemann (vi 175n) mentions "einen versteckten Spinozismus" ("a concealed Spinozism") in Plotinus. C had recently written a much longer account of Spinoza's life and thought (for which see *SW & F—CC*—I 607–24 and nn). The information about him in this paragraph is all to be found there, generally with more circumstantial detail.

[67] The religious opposition to Spinoza is also deplored by Tennemann (x 381): "Kein Philosoph hat das Schicksal gehabt, auf eine so entgegengesetzte Weise behandelt zu werden, als Spinoza" ("No philosopher has had the fate to be treated in so contentious a manner as Spinoza"). Cf Tennemann (x 482): "Aber sehr spät ist durch Spinozas metaphysisches System der Vernunft ein reeller Nutzen geleistet worden, weil er lange Zeit hindurch als ein Atheist verschrieen [war] . . ." ("But only very recently has a genuine usefulness been recognised in Spinoza's metaphysical system of the reason, because for a long time he was decried as an atheist . . .").

and he held the opinions of the most learned Jews, particularly the Cabalistic philosophers. Next, he was of the most pure and exemplary life,
and it has been said of him, if he did not think as a Christian, he felt and
acted like one.[68] Thirdly, so far from proselyting, this man published not[x]
a system (it was a posthumous work published against his will),[69] but
what is still more strong, he was offered by a German prince a high salary
with perfect permission to preach his doctrines without the least danger;
instead of accepting this, he wrote to the prince to reprimand him for his
neglect of his duty, and ask him what right he had to abuse the confidence
the fathers of Germans had placed in him, opposite to their wish.[70] And
if we come at last to the man's own professions and service, I have no
doubt they were [sincere[y]]; I have seen many questions . . .[z] to believe
that not only the immediate publishers of Spinoza's writings, but that
Spinoza did think that his system was identical with but that of Christianity, on so subtle a point that at least it was pantheism, but in the most
religious form in which it could appear.[71] For making the Deity that

---

[x] MS: published—not a system
[y] *P Lects* (385) conjecturally inserted "[severely orthodox]"; OB suggested "no doubt
[what] they were"
[z] Blank space left in ms for about 62 letters; *P Lects* (385) supplied omission by adapting parallel material in *BL* (*CC*) I 152: "[raised as to the compatibility of Spinozism with
religion, natural and revealed, and now am persuaded]"

---

[68] C derived the details of Spinoza's
life from the biographical account by Johannes Colerus (1647–1707); Tennemann (x 377n, 380n) cites it and recom-
mends it but C had read it for himself in
French tr in Spinoza *Opera* and H. E. G.
Paulus (2 vols Jena 1802–3) II 591–665;
cf his "Note on Spinoza" in *SW & F* (*CC*)
I in the course of which (619) C attributes
to "the pious BOERHAAVE" the remark
"Eheu! quantus est in infidelitate suâ
Christianus!" ("Alas, how Christian he is
in his infidelity!") A few years later C
was to express an even less qualified
enthusiasm: "Man perhaps never approached nearer to a moral harmony,
than in the instance of Benedict Spinoza"
(*CN* IV 5123 f107[v]—N 29: Jan–Feb
1824—).
[69] Spinoza's avoidance of public
recognition is recorded in a note to
Colerus's life (Spinoza *Opera* II 640n).
Cf C's marginal comment on Spinoza in
Argens *Kabbalistische Briefe* (*CM*—

CC—I 104): "If ever man of Genius was
free from the lust of a wide reputation,
Spinoza was he. . . . He queried, whether
those who thought enough to understand
his work would not—without the work
arrive of themselves at the same truths—
& wished it to be suppressed."
[70] The exchange of letters concerning
the invitation to Spinoza to occupy the
Chair of Philosophy at Heidelberg in
1673 is given in Spinoza *Opera* I 638–
40; Colerus also mentions the incident
(Spinoza *Opera* II 628). The German
prince was the Elector Palatine, Karl
Ludwig (1617–80).
[71] The sentence seems to have been
garbled; C's meaning appears to have
been that Spinoza and his publishers
thought that his system was all but identical with that of Christianity and that in
so far as it differed it did so on so subtle
a point that at least it was pantheism. In
his "Note on Spinoza" (*SW & F*—*CC*—
I 615–16) C argues that Spinoza's views,

which is independent, which is certain in and of itself and needs no argument, but which is implied in all other truth, and by making all other truths dependent upon that, beyond any other system of pantheism it divided the Deity from the creature. On the other hand, I am far from hiding the inevitable consequences of pantheism in all cases, whether the pantheism of India, or the solitary [case[a]] of Spinoza.[72] He erred, however, where thousands had erred before him, in Christian charity communicating his opinions to those only from whom he expected information.[73] And to end all, the quiet family in which he lived when he was too ill to attend publicly, he still kept regularly to their duty, and when they came[b] home as regularly examined them and made them repeat the sermon and comment upon it according to their impressions. A character like that, so unlike a[n] infidel, scarcely exists, and I cannot understand the cause [why, as Lessing observes, is no man to speak of Spinoza but[c]] as a dead dog.[74]

At this time [Jacobi] had the courage to say that Spinoza's arguments were inevitable were it not that the system of [Spinozism[d]] could not be

---

[a] MS: classes

[b] MS: come

[c] Blank space left in ms for about 21 letters; omission supplied from corresponding passage in ms report (601 below)

[d] Blank space left in ms for about 13 letters; P Lects (386) supplied omission by inference

---

while unacceptable now because of their pantheistic tendency, did not differ materially from the views of contemporary Arminian clergymen such as Hugo Grotius and those of modern Unitarians.

[72] P Lects (385) emended the text to read "solitary cases [like that] of Spinoza". Some alteration does seem to be required and this one provides for a plausible contrast between the pantheism of a whole culture (India) and the pantheism of an individual (solitary) reasoner. The possibility of the reporter's mishearing or misunderstanding, however, should probably be considered as well; "solitary classes" as a slip for "substances" or even "substantiality", referring to Spinoza's definition of God, "substantiam constatem infinitis attributis" ("a substance consisting in infinite attributes") would perhaps be more characteristic of C.

[73] For a detailed explanation of Spinoza's "error" see CL iv 849 (to Pryce [Apr 1818]): "The πρῶτον ψεῦδος [fundamental mistake] of Spinoza is not his first definition; but one in which all his Antagonists were as deeply immerged as himself. He alone had the philosophic courage to be consequent. We need only correct the convenient clinamina [evasions] of the Theistic Philosophers to reduce all their systems into Spinosism. The πρῶτον ψεῦδος consists in the assumed Idea of a pure independent Object—in assuming a Substance beyond the I; of which therefore the I could only be a modification."

[74] Lessing is so quoted—"Reden die Leute doch immer von Spinoza, wie von einem todten Hunde" ("But the people always talk about Spinoza as if about a dead dog")—in [F. H. Jacobi] Ueber die Lehre des Spinoza 38. C's copy is in the BM.

defended.[75] He had (that is, Spinoza) affirmed there were . . .*e* transitory as the waves of the sea, having no other qualities naturally but what arise externally from their relation to each other.[76] Leibniz [taught*f*] the system of Spinoza, namely that the Deity, as the great Mind, not merely modified into thoughts as our minds do, but gave each thought a reality, and that the Deity was really different from all creatures by that thing, [the preconception of things conceived*g*]; His thoughts were more real than the effects of them, that therefore he gave a reality to those thoughts, and that whatever was possible became real, not merely as thoughts, nor yet by a participation of the reality, but by a communication of this reality to that which was so thought by the Deity.[77] And when he was

e Blank space left in ms for about 17 letters
f MS: thought
g Blank space left in ms for about 16 letters; omission conjecturally supplied from roughly corresponding passage in ms report (601 below)

[75] For [Jacobi], ms reads "Leibnitz", but no such statement has been found in him. His attitude to Spinoza is expressed in a letter to Placcius of 14 Feb 1678, where he says that Spinoza "has occasionally beautiful thoughts . . . yet, nevertheless, his main doctrines are not capable of the least proof, and, in fact, are not proved by him despite his claim to have given the demonstration" (tr Held Herbert Wildon Carr in his *Leibniz*—London 1929—25). It seems likely that here C intended to refer to Jacobi, from whom he had just quoted Lessing's remark in the previous sentence, rather than Leibniz who comes in quite naturally a few lines later; again possibly a reporter's slip in the transcription of the shorthand. C had recently summed up Jacobi's views on Spinoza elsewhere in a parallel way, drawing on Jacobi *Ueber die Lehre des Spinoza* 223ff as follows: "first, that the System of Spinoza is atheistic; secondly, that it is a strictly consequent and the only strictly consequent Production of *demonstrative* or *ratiocinative* Theology; that all other works, that profess to demonstrate the existence and attributes of God, whether a priori or a posteriori, and which rest ~~our~~ the truths of natural Religion on grounds of Reason or ~~Understan~~ Reflection, may be driven by fair argument to the same conclusions; and that their Authors from Aristotle to

Locke &, Leibnitz, and ~~from~~ Wolff, and from Wolff to Reimarus and Paley have saved their religion at the expence of their Logic" (*SW & F—CC*—1 620). For other acknowledgments of the force of Spinoza's argument, see e.g. *CL* IV 548 (to R. H. Brabant [10 Mar 1815]) and *Logic (CC)* 208.

[76] C is presumably thinking of Spinoza's discussion of "bodies" in *Ethica* pt 2 prop 13 and of the explanatory material that follows it. Cf e.g. lemma 1: "*Bodies are distinguished from one another by reason of motion and rest, speed and slowness, and not by reason of substance*". And lemma 3: "*A body which moves or is at rest must be determined to motion or rest by another body, which has also been determined to motion or rest by another, and that again by another, and so on to infinity*": tr Edwin Curley *Collected Works of Spinoza* (2 vols Princeton 1985–) 1 458–9.

[77] Cf *BL (CC)* 1 130–1: "Leibnitz's doctrine of a pre-established harmony, which he certainly borrowed from Spinoza . . . was in its *common* interpretation too strange to survive the inventor—too repugnant to our *common sense* . . .". On the other hand, as the editors of *BL (CC)* point out (1 130n–1n), C takes issue with this view in a marginal note on Descartes in *CM (CC)* II 172 where he finds the precedent for Leibniz rather in Descartes

called on to explain the nature of the body and its relation to the mind, he first of all joined with Spinoza in overthrowing the doctrine of Descartes. And here, if you will permit me, I will pause for a few moments on this, the most interesting part of the subject as referring to the doctrine of materialism.

The only argument that I believe ever really disturbs men of sincere and sober minds is that which is derived from the seeming truth of a decay of the mind with the body.[78] We see it, they say, grow with the body, with the organisation. As the organisation is affected, we see it affected, and when that decays, this decays. This is, however, a mere sophism of the fancy. For first, it asserts universally what in any sense is true only partially; and certain faculties of memory may awaken into judgment and seem to increase. Again, it asserts of all, what holds good only of some. A man from the time he has the use of his will devotes it entirely to his bodily pleasure, or to his ambition, or power, or a desire of making money constantly, and thus he occupies his mind from youth till he is feeble; and do you wonder at last, when the whole joke is discovered, when the pleasure is no longer pleasure, when the ambition has sickened, and when money is representative of the world with the folly of men, do you wonder that a mind so naked of all that could remain and be permanent, felt at the same time a necessity of withdrawing all attention from the organs of outward perception, which presented no symbols of aught that any longer interested it?[79] But compare such a mind with Newton, with Leibniz who died fainting away in the act of a great discovery.[80] Or trace the

---

De passionibus animae pt 1 art 16: *Opera philosophica* II 8ᵃ. McFarland (271–4) lays out the reasons why readers of C's time tended to regard Leibniz's philosophy as being akin to Spinoza's and provides arguments against sharing their view.

[78] The concern to which C alludes here is the fear that the mind like the body is mortal. Cf *CN* III 4356 (N 25: Aug 1817): "To me therefore, & I believe to all men, the best proof of immortality is the fact, that the presumption of it is the at the bottom of every hope, fear, and action. Suppose for a moment an intuitive certainty that we should cease to be at a given time—the *Whole* feeling of futurity would be extinguished at the first feeling of such a certainty—and the mind would have no motive for not dying at the same moment."

[79] C reflects on the relationship of the mind to the body in a more speculative spirit in *CM* (*CC*) II 1185–7.

[80] Newton, who died at the age of 84, was active to the end, presiding over a meeting of the Royal Society about three weeks before his death. Leibniz died at 70 having been engaged for the two preceding years in his famous theological correspondence with Samuel Clarke (1675–1729); his first biographer recorded that on the day of his death he made two attempts to write but desisted on finding that the results were illegible. C's information will have been derived from Brucker's account which is quoted in Leibniz *Opera omnia* ed Ludovicus Dutens (6 vols Geneva 1768) I xcix. C was to take issue with Kant on the conjunction of bodily and mental decline: see *CM* (*CC*) III 323–4.

history of the great Greek philosophers and poets; refer to Titian and Michael Angelo;[81] and there see whether or no the picture of an old age of manhood and that which had been used to what was noble, praiseworthy, and permanent, does not present a different picture. Or go into humble life; take the true modest Christian who has passed a life of struggle with self-will, who has watched to love his neighbour as himself, and who entertains a constant faith that not merely the outward body and clothings but the greater part of our intellectual vanity will be as useless in the state into which he is passing as the thoughts of a grub which has passed three years in the mud would be to the butterfly when risen out of the stream, but who had [passed] the time, in what? In rendering[h] the will productive, in giving the will a causative power and fitting it for a higher state. Take the . . .[i] of which man is born; observe the glory with which it is conquered; and then tell us that because the memory of some insignificant circumstance is weakened, or that the man can no longer talk so as to excite applauses, therefore the whole mind is gone. No, when we are most and best ourselves, all that remains and all that could decay is but the cracks on the caterpillar's skin; it is the loss of the caterpillar faculty which the new life of society is beginning to do without.

But again it is the truth it presumes, a truth of materialism which yet, after the point allowed it, is more than a . . .[j]; it is a begging of the question. It assumes the conclusion as the very ground upon which it is to begin; for suppose a fact, that A and B live and decay together, surely it does not follow therefore that B is the cause of A! . . .[k]. If the mind or the power from within . . .[l], nay, all the analogy of nature is in favour . . .[m], and in the other from without, and so to[o] it would be though A and B taken as the mind and the organisation . . .[n] the mind and body immediately by a miracle, according to Descartes,[82] or by some common thing

---

[h] MS: past the time, in what? In redering
[i] Blank space left in ms for about 12 letters; *P Lects* (387) conjecturally supplied "[flesh]" and OB "[dust]"
[j] Blank space left in ms for about 14 letters
[k] Blank space left in ms for about 54 letters
[l] Blank space left in ms for about 36 letters
[m] Blank space left in ms for about 36 letters
[n] Blank space left in ms for about 162 letters

---

[81] Titian died of the plague when he is believed to have been 99; he had continued to win commissions for painting. Michelangelo lived to be almost 90 and was still engaged in architectural projects, most notably the construction of St Peter's in Rome.

[82] Descartes does not refer to a miracle explicitly, but C may have had in mind his acknowledgment of the need for the continuing involvement of God in the world: "to be kept in existence we need the continual action of the original cause" (tr *D Phil Writings* II 254: 5th set of Replies to Objections to Third Meditation 9).

between partaking of the nature both of body and soul according to one Doctor Henry More.[83] Now a phenomenon that admits of equal solution from four different hypotheses cannot in any common sense be thought to prove the truth of any one of them. Why then does it strike [us]? The answer is simply this, because the impressions upon our senses are always more vivid and connected with sensation than those connected with thought, and this all must be struck with[o] who mistake vivid pictures for clear perceptions.[84] The very circumstances of this bribery in favour of the doctrine, contrasted with the fact that the doctrine is held in abhorrence by mankind in general, is decisive of it, for we act against a bribe in our nature. This forms the last part of the Leibnizian philosophy which rejecting . . .[p] this was however too opposite to common sense[85] and for Leibniz to Kant and Voltaire . . .[q] was all that remained,[86] the rest was falling apace into the Eclectic system . . .[r] and from that which instead of being any philosophy at all was a direct unmanning of the mind and rendering it incapable of any systematic thinking.[87]

---

[o] MS: with it   [p] Blank space left in ms for about 98 letters
[q] Blank space left in ms for about 40 letters
[r] Blank space left in ms for about 84 letters

[83] Tennemann (x 517–18 and n) discusses this concept of More's, citing More's "immortalitas animi" ("immortality of the soul") from his *Philosophische Werke* II 300, but he treats him rather dismissively (518): "es sind grösstentheils Träume mit wenigen Wahrheiten vermischt" ("they are for the most part dreams with a few truths intermingled"). However, the relationship of body to soul is discussed in relevant detail by C in *CN* IV 4910 (N 29: dated by the eds Jul 1822), and C had read More for himself; see *CM* (*CC*) III 906–29. In the course of this passage WW's treatment of the development of the soul in his *Ode: Intimations of Immortality* is compared with stanzas 5–7 of More's *The Pre-existence of the Soul* which are said to be "prefigured in coarser Clay, ~~and~~ by a less mastering hand & with a less lofty Spirit, yet excellent in its own kind . . .". Later in the same entry (f 73) he says "In Henry More who blended the Doctrine of Des Cartes (viz. that Matter is mere extension, and that Body and Soul or Spirit are ~~b~~ essentially heterogeneous, with ~~his~~ the Notions of Plotinus . . .". C's marginalia on More's poem (*CM*—*CC*—III 911–14) are more critical. In *CN* IV 5079 (Dec 1823), C categorises More as a "Cartesian Platonist".

[84] C often complains of the philosophical and theological consequences of our reliance on vivid sense impressions, particularly on those of sight, what he calls at one point "the tyranny of the Eye": *SW & F* (*CC*) II 900.

[85] Part of the missing passage may perhaps be provided by C's comment on Leibniz in *BL* (*CC*) I 130–1 which concludes with a similar phrase; see 580 n 77 above. The nature of the pre-established harmony is outlined in the lect at 580 above.

[86] The missing passages make confident reconstruction of the sentence impossible. C seems to mean that Leibniz's philosophy was regarded as "opposite to common sense" from Leibniz's time to Kant's and that in the meantime the scepticism of Voltaire "was all that remained".

[87] For the Eclectic system, see above 314–25. But cf also *BL* (*CC*) I 292: "But the worst and widest impediment still re-

In this wretched state was not only Germany when Kant arose.[88] His merits consisted in three things: namely, the first was that he examined the faculties critically before he hazarded any opinions concerning the positions which such faculties had led men to establish. He entered into a real examination of the balance before he would suffer any weights to be put in the scale, and [this[s]] he did, as alone could be done [at[t]] that time, upon the ground of reflection taking the human mind only as far as it became an object of reflection.[89] In this way he saw that there were two classes of truth received by men: the one, he observed, were truths of experience and were uncertain in the conviction, and which increased by accumulation, so that what was but faintly believed for the first month became more the second, and more the third, and perhaps many centuries passed[u] before it came to full perception, and even here in England was susceptible of alteration and change. Other truths he perceived to be immediately insusceptible to the conviction they produced; the moment they were understood they were as certain as they would be after 100 years of attention.[90] He perceived that the one were necessarily particu-

<hr>

[s] MS: thus   [t] MS: of   [u] MS: past

<hr>

mains. It is the predominance of a popular philosophy, at once the counterfeit and the mortal enemy of all true and manly metaphysical research. It is that corruption, introduced by certain immethodical aphorisming Eclectics, who, dismissing not only all system, but all logical connection, pick and choose whatever is most plausible and showy; who select, whatever words can have some semblance of sense attached to them without the least expenditure of thought . . . . This alas! is an irremediable disease, for it brings with it, not so much an indisposition to any particular system, but an utter loss of taste and faculty for all system and for all philosophy." C was drawing on Schelling for this passage: see *BL* (*CC*) I 292n.

[88] C's description of the impact of Kant's contribution may be compared with his partly parallel account of his own first experience of Kant (in *BL—CC*—I 153–5). His exploration of the "wretched" condition of German philosophy had begun as early as his interview with Klopstock in 1798, in his report of which he insists, contrary to Klopstock's opinion, on Kant's new ascendancy:

"there is not a single professor who is not, either a Kantean, or a disciple of Fichte, whose system is built on the Kantean, and presupposes its truth; or lastly who, though an antagonist of Kant as to his theoretical work, has not embraced wholly or in part his moral system, and adopted part of his nomenclature": *BL* (*CC*) II 199–200.

[89] Kant's examination led to his distinction between the two faculties of the mind, the reason and the understanding, which is developed at length in *C d r V* and became a fundamental theme for C's own thought from about 1801 onwards (see e.g. *CL* II 706–7: to Thomas Poole [16 Mar 1801]). Its importance and implications occupied much of his *Logic* and had been introduced without specific reference to Kant as being "encouraged and confirmed by the authority of our genuine divines, and philosophers, before the revolution [of 1688]": *BL* (*CC*) I 173.

[90] The two classes of truth are knowledge *a posteriori* and knowledge *a priori*. C frequently discusses them and attempted various comprehensible definitions. Knowledge *a posteriori* he calls

lar the other universal, the one necessarily contingent, the others bearing in themselves the absurdity of their contrary; and he affirmed therefore that here we had found a criterion of the acts of the mind or the forms which arise out of the mechanism of the mind itself and of this, if I may so call it, "substance" of reality which the sensations gave to us.

But still he carried this to a great extent, for while he admitted that there was a power in the reason of producing ideas, to which there were no actual correspondents in outward nature, and therefore they were only to be regarded as regulative, he was then asked, or rather he asked himself, what would become of the ideas of God, of the free will, of immortality,[91] for these too were the offspring of the reason and these too it would be said were merely regulative forms to which no outward or real correspondent could be expected. Here, then, he disclosed what I may call the [proof*] of his Christianity which rendered him truly deserving the name

---

ᵛ MS: roof

"the image in the mind correspondent to the outward object consequent on the presence of that object": *Logic* (*CC*) 220–1. C had offered a definition of the more difficult concept of knowledge *a priori* in *Omniana* in 1812 (*SW & F—CC*—I 334*) and repeated it (var) in *BL* (*CC*) I 293*: "by knowledge, *a priori*, we do not mean that we can know any thing previously to experience, which would be a contradiction in terms; but that having once known it by occasion of experience, (i.e. something acting upon us from without) we then know, that it must have pre-existed, or the experience itself would have been impossible. By experience only I know, that I have eyes; but then my reason convinces me, that I must have had eyes in order to the experience." Later, more succinctly, he offers "KNOWLEGE *a priori*—whatever we may determine from the mere *possibility* of the thought" (*SW & F—CC*—I 690) and provides the German text of Kant *Metaphysische Anfangsgründe der Naturwissenschaft* (Riga 1787) ix. Cf *C d r V* 3–5 and *Logic* (*CC*) 139 and 178. Kant's brief definition in *C d r V* 2 treats both terms together: "ein [Erkenntniss] von der Erfahrung und selbst von allen Eindrücken der Sinne unabhängiges Erkenntniss gebe. Man nennt solche

ERKENNTNISSE *a priori*, und unterscheidet sie von den *empirischen*, die ihre Quellen *a posteriori*, nämlich in der Erfahrung, haben" ("knowledge that is . . . independent of experience and even of all impressions of the senses. Such knowledge is entitled *a priori*, and distinguished from the *empirical*, which has its sources *a posteriori*, that is, in experience": tr Kemp Smith 42–3). As examples of knowledge *a priori* Kant offers e.g. *C d r V* 15 and 17: "der Satz 7 + 5 = 12", "dass in allen Veränderungen der körperlichen Welt die Quantität der Materie unverändert bleibe", and "in aller Mittheilung der Bewegung, Wirkung und Gegenwirkung jederzeit einander gleich seyn müssen" ("the proposition that 7 + 5 = 12", "that in all changes in the material world the quantity of matter remains the same", and "that in all communication of motion, action and reaction must always be equal": tr Kemp Smith 52 and 54).

[91] Cf Kant *C d r V* 7: "Diese unvermeidlichen Aufgaben der reinen Vernunft selbst, sind *Gott, Freyheit* und *Unsterblichkeit*" ("These unavoidable problems set by pure reason itself are *God, freedom*, and *immortality*": tr Kemp Smith 46).

philosopher and not the analysis of the mind. He says, in my . . .*w* into the whole human being. There is yet another, and not only another but a far higher and nobler, constituent of his being, his will, the "practical reason", and this does not announce itself by arguing but by direct command and precept: thou shalt do to others as thou wouldst be done by, thou shalt act so that there shall be no contradiction in thy being.[92] And from this he deduced a direct moral necessity for the belief or the faith of reason;[93] and having first shown that though the reason could bring nothing positively coercive in proof of religious truth, which if it could it would cease to be religion and become mathematical, yet [he*x*] demonstrated nothing could be said with reason against them, and that on the other hand there was all the analogy, all the harmony of nature, all moral interests, and last of all there was a positive command which if he disobeys he is at once a traitor to his nature, nay, even to his common nature.[94]

Such [were*y*], I think, the great merits of Kant. I have not mentioned a particular merit he had, namely, that by the first clearly showing the nature of space and time as habits, not of thinking as Leibniz supposed,[95]

---

w Blank space left in ms for about 15 letters; *P Lects* (389) conjecturally supplied "[Critique of the Pure Reason we have not entered]"; corresponding passage in ms report (601 below): now have I been giving you a new analysis of man as far as his intellect is concerned

x MS: they

y MS: was

[92] C seems here to be paraphrasing Kant rather than quoting him, although *P Lects* (389) silently supplies quotation marks. In presenting Kant's moral views in such a Christian guise, using the terms of Christ's "golden rule" from Matt 7.12 and 5.43, C had the warrant at least of *Grundlegung zur Metaphysik der Sitten* 13: "So sind ohne Zweifel auch die Schriftstellen zu verstehen, darin geboten wird, seinen Nächsten, selbst unsern Feind, zu lieben" ("It is in this manner [i.e. desiring his happiness], undoubtedly, that we are to understand those passages of Scripture also in which we are commanded to love our neighbour, even our enemy": tr Abbott in Kant's *Critique of Practical Reason* 15). But he was inclined to emphasise the religious implications of Kant's writing because he believed that he had been obliged to avoid expressing his actual religious convictions because he had written "in imminent danger of persecution during the reign of the late king of Prussia [Freder-

ick the Great], that strange compound of lawless debauchery, and priest-ridden superstition . . .": *BL* (*CC*) I 154.

[93] For the "faith of reason" see 561 n 26 above.

[94] I.e. the "practical reason". C had considered the sense in which reason and religion should be considered as differing "only as a two-fold application of the same power" in *LS* (*CC*) 59–65, a passage in which he makes extensive use of Kant's distinction between reason and understanding without referring to Kant by name. Kant's views are set out systematically in his *Die Religion innerhalb der Grenzen der blossen Vernunft* (2nd ed Königsberg 1794); for C's annotations, see *CM* (*CC*) III 304–13. This work helped to reassure C about Kant's intentions; for his continued struggle with what seemed its shortcomings, see *AR* (*CC*) li–lii.

[95] Kant himself had taken issue with Leibniz on this question; see particularly *C d r V* 320–36. Cf *Logic* (*CC*) 159–60:

[but of^z] the perception he secured it . . .^{a} the Platonist of a pre-existent light on the one hand,[96] and the degrading notions of the materialists which considered it as chemistry or an empirical proof.[97] This was a great merit, but still greater was it that he determined the nature of religious truth and its connection with the understanding, and made it felt to the full that the reason itself, considered as merely intellectual, was but a subordinate part of our nature; that there was a higher part, the will and the conscience, and that if the intellect of man was the cherub that flew with man^b, it flew after the flaming seraph and but followed its track; that to be good is and ever will be not a mere consequence of being wise but a necessary condition of the process. In short, he determined the true meaning of philosophy, for all our knowledge may be well comprised in two terms: the one, philology, that is to say, all the pursuits in which the intellect of man is concerned, in which he has a desire of arriving at that which the logos or intellectual power can communicate;[98] the other is

^{z} MS: by
^{a} Blank space left in ms for about 86 letters
^{b} *P Lects* (390), following ms report (601 below), emended to "wings"

"Leibniz was so far in the right that he denied the subsistence of space independent of the mind; but he grievously erred in representing it as nothing more than a confused perception arising out of the indistinctness of all particular figures whether from the distance or the minuteness of the objects".

[96] An apparently parallel passage in *Logic* (*CC*) 146 suggests what C had in mind here. Speaking of Polemo, but seeming in fact to mean Speusippus, C says: "All knowledge is excited or occasioned by experience, but all knowledge is not derived from experience, such, for instance, is the knowledge of the conditions that render experience itself possible, and which must therefore be supposed to exist previous to experience, in the same manner as the eyes must pre-exist to the act of seeing, though without that act of seeing we never should have learnt that we possessed eyes". A similar point is made without any explicit Platonist association in *BL* (*CC*) I 123.

[97] C's readiness to use the term "materialists" to designate a thinker whether ancient or modern who "would have nothing but what proceeded from his

senses" makes his reference vague. The mention of chemistry, however, suggests the *Naturphilosophen* to whose speculations he introduced C. A. Tulk in a letter of Sept and Nov 1817 (*CL* IV 767–76). For a relevant general summation of C's views on perception see *Logic* (*CC*) 135–6.

[98] C does not often define philology so capaciously. He praises Porson as a philologist (*SW & F*—*CC*—II 859) and he certainly was an admirer of Porson's intellect, but the correction he makes in the ms of "Confessions of an Inquiring Spirit" ("I ~~must begin by describing it~~ [the Bible] ~~as a mere Scholar or~~ [? ~~Litterateur~~] speak now in the assumed character of an uninterested Critic or Philologist": *SW & F*—*CC*—II 1120) seems more typical of his attitude. The more comprehensive sense of the word is apparent, however, in a marginal note on Tennemann III 26–7: "That Aristotle did not, and as a mere tho' most eminent Philologist, ⟨could not,⟩ *behold* the *Ideas* of the divine Philosopher [Plato], is most true . . ." (*CM*—*CC*—V). The distinction between philology and philosophy is made in parallel terms in a marginal note

philosophy, or that which comprises the logos, and, including it, at the same time subordinates it to the will, and thus combining the other, is philosophy the love of wisdom with the wisdom of love.[99]

My time will not permit me to enter into any account of [Schelling[c]] as I intended, but in truth I should be puzzled to give you a true account. For I might at one time refer you to Kant, and there I should say what [Schelling[d]] appears at one time; another time to Spinoza as applied to philosophy;[100] and then again I should find him in the writings of Plotinus and still more of Proclus,[101] but most in the writings of a Jesuit who

---

[c] Blank space left in ms for about 10 letters; omission supplied from corresponding material in ms report (602 below)

[d] Blank space left in ms for about 10 letters; omission supplied from ms report (602 below)

---

on John Petvin's remark in his *Letters concerning Mind* (London 1750) 73, "PHILO-SOPHY is nothing but the LOVE OF TRUTH . . .", to which C responds: "O no! no! This were Philo*logy*—Philoso*phy* is the Love of Truth in the speculative, + Goodness in the practical, = Wisdom" (*CM—CC*—IV).

[99] For C's views on the role of the Logos in philosophy, see e.g. *Logic (CC)* 32–4.

[100] The phrase "as applied to philosophy" seems meant to avoid the implication that Schelling's religious beliefs resembled Spinoza's. Cf, however, the private comment: "This is the Basis of the Schellingian Atheism, Σπινοσισμος πολυσαρκος or the *cloathed* Skeleton of Spinoza!" (*CM—CC*—III 123). The unpredictable changes of course in Schelling's philosophical career were generally recognised. Hegel was to say of him that he conducted his education in public. His Kantian phase (in which he was also deeply influenced by Fichte) is exemplified in *Ueber die Möglichkeit einer Form der Philosophie überhaupt* (1795); with *Vom Ich als Princip der Philosophie* (1795) the influence of Spinoza appears and it is even more markedly evident in "Aphorismen zur Einleitung in die Naturphilosophie" *Jahrbücher der Medicin als Wissenschaft* ed A. F. Marcus and Schelling (3 vols Tübingen 1805–8) I 3–12, a work of which C had recently complained at some length in

CN III 4445 (N 27: Oct 1818), and in *Briefe über Dogmatismus und Kriticismus* (1796).

[101] According to HCR, C in a conversation of 3 May 1812 stated that "when many years ago he began to think on philosophy he set out from a passage in Proclus at the point where Schelling appears to be" (*On Books and Their Writers* ed Edith J. Morley—3 vols London 1938— I 70). At that time C's acquaintance with Schelling may have been limited to *System des transcendentalen Idealismus* (Tübingen 1800); it seems to have been only slightly enlarged by the time he began to write *Biographia Literaria* (see *BL—CC*—I 164 and n). But what lies behind C's attention to the affinity of Schelling's thought to Plotinus and Proclus is made much clearer by his comment in *CN* III 4424 and n (N L: 1818) on Francesco Patrizi or Franciscus Patrizius (1413–92) whose "The Oracles of Zoroaster" appears in Thomas Stanley *The History of the Chaldaick Philosophy* (1701) 48–51, appended to Stanley. In a letter to JHG of 30 Sept 1818 (*CL* IV 874), in which he explains his disillusionment with Schelling, C says: "You will find, as I have before mentioned to you, the entire principia philosophiae Schellingianae [Schellingian principles of philosophy] in the fragments collected by Fr. Patricius from the Pagan and Christian Neo-platonists, Proclus, Hermias, Simplicius, Damascius, Synesius,

opposed the Protestants I think about the time of James I but got silenced for it,[102] for his great object, like that of [Schelling[e],] was to justify the worship of saints by endeavouring to convince the world that God consisted in the saints, an opinion which I believe so completely won [Schelling's[f]] heart, that the last act of his life was a most extraordinary one, namely, that this Roman Catholic pantheist[103] who with a rosary in one hand and a Bible in the other had received a call from [Munich[g]] to [Jena[h]] which is a Protestant town under Protestant government, and he accepted it under these conditions, that he was to have two professions, that of philosophy and that of theology, that a church should be given him to preach in [on] the weekdays, and all for the purpose of convincing the

[e] Blank space left in ms for about 10 letters
[f] Blank space left in ms for about 10 letters
[g] Blank space left in ms for about 8 letters   [h] MS: Yenna

& others ejusdem farinae [of the same stuff], as Oracles of Zoroaster—the inconsistencies of which betray the variety of the Forgers, yet strangely co-exist in the works of Schelling, Baader & Oken. This however the Zoroastrian & Schellingian Oracles have in common— that Polarity is asserted of the Absolute, of the Monad: (= Oken's +0). The inconsistency Schelling has contrived to hide from himself by the artifice of making all knowledge bi-polar, Transcendental Idealism as one Pole and Nature as the other . . .". Cf *CN* III 4445 and n and 4449 and n.

[102] A parallel passage in *CL* IV 883 (to C. A. Tulk [24 Nov 1818]) identifies C's "Jesuit": "Thomas De Albo, or White, an English Jesuit (I believe) made the same attempt [as Schelling's defence of polytheism]". White (1593–1676), a theological controversialist, was the author of about forty books, including *De mundo dialogi tres* (1642), a work to which Hobbes replied in his "Anti-White" in 1642–3 (which remained unpublished until 1973). White was not a Jesuit but received part of his education from Jesuit teachers. C does not mention him anywhere else and his resemblance to Schelling seems in C's view to be merely that he was a Roman Catholic (see n 103 below) whose philosophical speculations led him to be suspected of atheism.

[103] Cf *CL* IV 883 (to C. A. Tulk [24 Nov 1818]): "Schelling is a zealous Roman-Catholic, and not the first Philosopher who has adapted this sort of Plotinised Spinozism for the defence of the Polytheism and Charms of the Church of Rome". On another occasion C had referred to "the celebrated Schelling, the ἀρχ[?as]ασπιστης [chief shield-bearer] of Catholicism on the Continent, a profest Believer in the miracles and mysteries of Christianity . . .": *SW & F* (*CC*) I 622. Cf *CM* (*CC*) II 187–8. He was mistaken about Schelling, however. HCR recorded a meeting that he himself had with Schelling in 1829 of which he says: "The most agreeable part of his conversation was that which showed me I was wrong in supposing him to have become a Roman Catholic. On the contrary, he spoke in a tone of seeming disappointment both of Schlegel and of Tieck for their change" (*Diary, Reminiscences, and Correspondence* ed T. Sadler—3 vols London 1869—II 446). The religious allegiance of the Jena circle was always difficult to be sure of, and it has been maintained that Schelling himself was mistaken about Tieck's. (See Edgar Anthony Lang *Ludwig Tieck's Early Concept of Catholic Clergy and Church*—New York 1936— xii–xiii.)

young men that their salvation was concerned in their becoming papists;[104] and . . .[i] has described well the old system. He says, "When I was
young and used to see the ceremonies of the Catholics, we used to go
home, put on some shirts, and act through the whole ceremonies with
wonderful delight, and I find . . .[j] and the new converts were doing the
same thing, for they well knew if they held but a tenth part of what they
thought it must be a bad heretic indeed that would not believe without
. . .[k] any inquisition that it was mere mockery[105] or as one of the [disci-
ples of Schelling[l]] told me [in Rome after long argument[m]], "You think
only of one sort of religion, but you know in our country we distinguish
sciences into two kinds; every man has his bread science and at the same

---

  [i] Blank space left in ms for about 10 letters
  [j] Blank space left in ms for about 13 letters
  [k] Blank space left in ms for about 17 letters
  [l] Blank space left in ms for about 13 letters; omission conjecturally adapted from corresponding material in ms report (602 below): one of his disciples
  [m] Blank space left in ms for about 22 letters; omission conjecturally supplied from ms
report (602 below)

---

[104] By "the last act of his life" C
seems to mean the most recent one.
Schelling did not in fact accept the invitation to Jena, but he was offered the
chair of logic and metaphysics there in
1816 and evidently considered it in
somewhat the spirit in which C describes
it. In a letter to his brother Karl, undated
but apparently written in late Jan or early
Feb 1816 he writes: "Wieder blos Lehrer
der Philosophie zu sein, würde mich
nicht in so hohem Grade reizen, aber der
allmähliche und schickliche Uebergang,
den ich dort zur Theologie machen könnte und zu dem ich auf jeden Fall die Mit-
tel mir ausbedingen würde, der Gedanke,
dadurch unter göttlichem Segen für ganz
Deutschland etwas Entscheidendes zu
thun und ein wohltätiges Licht anzu-
stecken, wogegen die erste noch in der
Jugend hervorgebrachte Bewegung nur
ein unlauteres Feuer war . . ." ("To be a
teacher of philosophy again would not
delight me to so great a degree, but the
gradual and easy transition to theology
which I would be able to effect there and
for which in any case I would make the
means a condition, the thought that in
that way, with the blessing of God, I
should be able to do something decisive

for all Germany and light a beneficent
light by contrast with which the first
movement produced in youth is only an
impure fire . . .": tr [G. L. Plitt] *Aus
Schellings Leben. In Briefen*—3 vols
Leipzig 1869–70—II 366). These negotiations were known about outside of
Schelling's immediate circle. See e.g.
Briefe von und an Hegel ed Johannes
Hoffmeister (3rd ed 4 vols Hamburg
1969) II 73 (to Karl Friedrich Ernst
Frommann 14 Apr 1816): "Mit Jena,
scheint es, hat die Regierung in Weimar
wieder weitaussehendere Plane. Goethe
hat, wie ich höre, viel mit Einrichtung,
Vereinigung und Erweiterung der dorti-
gen Sammlungen zu tun. Von anderer
Seite vernehme ich, dass Schelling dahin
berufen worden, der es aber ablehnte"
("For Jena, it seems, the Weimar regime
again has most far-sighted plans. I hear
that Goethe has much to do with the in-
stalling, systematizing and enlarging
of the collections there. From another
source I learn that Schelling has been invited there but that he has declined").

[105] Schelling is not the author of this
reminiscence, but the true one has resisted identification.

time his . . .*ⁿ* science, his dwelling*ᵒ* or hobby horse. Now it is so with me",
says he, "I am teaching religion, I . . .*ᵖ*, but my bread is a Roman Catholic
Church, and I prefer that to the other doctrines because it is more like the
ancient pagans."[106]

On Monday I deliver my last lecture and my last address to you and
the public as a lecturer, with a review of all the preceding course and the
application of it.

ⁿ Blank space left in ms for about 12 letters; *P Lects* (391) conjecturally supplied
"['Liebling']", relying probably on word "darling" in ms report (602 below)

ᵒ OB emended to "[darling]", also relying, presumably, on ms report (602 below)

ᵖ Blank space left in ms for about 11 letters

[106] No further evidence of this disciple of Schelling's has come to light. The reported conversation with him bears some resemblance to the conversation C had in Rome about the worship of saints: "—I doubt not, that Poetry is guilty of bringing in the Invocation of Saints/ i.e. that it began in Hymns, with no other than poetic Truth. Were I a Romanist, I should rest much of my Defence on the agreement of the Greek Church with the most obnoxious Tenets of the Roman/ I once told a Prelate at Rome—Prove to me that the Invocation of Saints is not Idolatry, & I will become a Catholic—" (marginal note in Jean de Thévenot *The Travels . . . into the Levant*—London 1687—I 82–3: BM copy; see *CM— CC—*v). The only prelate in whose company C is reported to have been is Joseph, Cardinal Fesch (1763–1839), in whose suite he is said to have left Rome in 1806 (*BL—CC—*I 217 and n and *TT—CC—*II 477–8). Cf another such conversation reported in *TT (CC)* I 8.

DRAFT MS

BM Add MS 47,523 (N 25), ff 76ᵛ–81

[f 76ᵛ] Monday, 22 March, 1819
Locke, Leibnitz, Kant, Schelling.[1]

ᵃ⟨* or rather *begin here*⟩ Few pursuits are more instructive and not many more ~~amusing~~ entertaining than that of retracing the progress of any living Language for a few centuries, and its improvement as an organ & vehicle of thought by desnyonimizing [f 77] words—Thus as late as the Restoration ingenious and ingenuous, ingenuity and ingenuousness were used indifferently—Propriety was the common term for Propriety, of behaviour for instance, and Property in the sense of an estate or ownership.—thus from Magister softened by the Italian into Maestr we have Made Mister, as well as Master—and thence Miss and Mistress, and use them as contra-distinctions of age—and it would have been quite in the course of language, if another pronunciation, Meester for instance, as it actually exists in our provincial rustic dialect, had been appropriated to ~~the sense of~~ the expression of Mastership in opposition to Servant.—Now the business and duty of the Philosopher ~~and Philologist~~ is to aid and ~~perfect~~ compleat this process—as his Subject demands—and ~~where~~ a distinction that is perhaps already begun in the adjective to carry on into ~~the~~ its substantive likewise—thus, ~~in~~ common language gives ~~ano~~ a very different sense to the adjectives, fanciful and imaginative—Cowley a fanciful but Milton an imaginative Poet—The Philosoph⫲er proceeds & carries on the distinction with the substantives, Fancy and Imagination. [f 76ᵛ] ᵇ⟨For philos. differs etc.⟩ ⟨Begin⟩ ~~For~~ philosophical differs from common language in this only, that it does that more ~~precisely~~ accurately and by an express pre-agreement which is unconsciously and as it were

---

ᵃ Beginning of new paragraph indicated in margin at this point. C marked ms for re-arrangement, changing his mind once in the process, dropping on f 76ᵛ first to "~~For philosophical differs~~" and then to "Few pursuits". Arrangement provided here follows his last decision. Foliation indicators are provided whenever text begins to be found on a different folio and allow reader to reconstruct original order of the ms

ᵇ In marking transposition C repeats "For philos. differs &c"

[1] The philosophers named in the advance publicity as the subjects of the lect.

by a tacit compact aimed at and in part accomplished, tho' with less precision and consistency in the common language of every civilized nation at least. [f 77] Thus in the philosophic world each contributing consciously to ~~what in society at large each is~~ to^c the finishing of the work, ⟨the rudiments of⟩ which in society at large each is unconsciously ~~beginning~~ aiding to furnish, the mighty Machine goes on—at once the consequence & the mark of the Mind of the Nation which speaks it.—

I have named the pursuit ~~amusing~~ entertaining as well as instructive; and ~~so~~ in the great number of instances it really is so—but in all these subjects, which ~~so~~ require the mind to turn its attention inward, in upon its own operations, it cannot be done without *Thought*—and Thinking is an *effort* which habit only can make pleasurable—

[f 76ᵛ] ⟨continued from the bottom of the page opposite⟩

* ^dI have from the commencement of this course been both honored and supported by the respectful attention of my Auditors, that it might well seem at once unthankful and superfluous to request it on any particular occasion—. Yet ~~for me~~ I will venture to entreat you, not indeed to attend to me, but to *think* with me, to produce in your ~~minds~~ selves not a mere passive ~~submission~~ Listning but an active concurrence, for a few minutes: while I define a few Terms, which once thoroughly understood and then borne in mind, you will, I dare promise myself, find little difficulty in following or accompanying me thro' the ~~remaini~~ whole of the present Lecture. And here to prevent all misunderstanding let me observe that the following definitions are offered to you as verbal not real, as explaining the sense in which certain terms are employed by me not as affirming the truth and reality of the sense so expressed.

[f 77ᵛ]   ~~1. That which must be known or inferred, but cannot~~

1. That which appears by weight, or what in Chemistry is called ponderable substance, is Body.

2. That which appears but not by weight, or the imponderable substances, is Matter. (Thus, Sunshine we should not in common language call a body, tho' we ~~might~~ should not hesitate to call it a material phænomenon; but the Painter speaks familiarly of *a body* of sunshine, alluding to the paint laid on to produce that resemblance.)

3. That which does not appear, which has no outwardness, but must be either known or inferred, is Spirit or Power.

4. In speaking of the World without us ~~us~~ as distinguished from ourselves, the aggregate of ~~two~~ *former* phænomena ponderable and imponderable is Nature in the passive sense, in the language of the Schools,

---

^c Redundant "to" in C's correction
^d In marking transposition, C repeats "I have from the commencement etc.*"

Natura Naturata—while the sum or aggregate of the Powers inferred as the sufficient causes of the former (by Aristotle and his followers entitled, the substantial forms) is Nature in the active sense, or Natura Naturans.

5. ⟨ On the other hand, when we are reflecting on ourselves, ⟨as intelligen⟨ces, & therfore⟩ and individualizing Spirit or Power, that which affirms its own existence and mediately or immediately that of other beings, is Mind

[f 78]   6. Lastly, when we contra-distinguish the Mind or Percipient Power from that which it perceives, it the former has been (and very conveniently) entitled the Subject—while and the latter the Object. Hence both matter and body may be defined conjointly as merely objective, the Mind may be defined, a Subject which is its own Object. And hence those who attribute a reality to bodies and to material phænomena, independent of the mind that perceives them, and yet assert equally an the independent reality of the Mind, i.e. those who believe in both Mind and Body immaterial and material corporeal substances, would define the latter as merel purely and merely Objective; while an Idealist, or what is called a Berkleian ᵉtho', as we have seen, the doctrine was taught & fully developed more than 2000 years before Bishop Berkley was born)—an Idealist, I say, would declare the material & corporeal world to be wholly subjective, that is, to exist only as far as it is perceived—. In other words, he concedes a real existence to two Terms only—to the Natura Naturans, in the language of Berkley to God, and to the finite minds on which it acts, the Natura Naturata being the result—as the Tune between the Wind & the Eolian Harp.

> And what if all of animated Nature
> Be but organic Harps diversly frameᶠ
> That tremble into thought as o'er them sweeps
> Plastic and vast one intellectual Breeze
> At once the Soul of each & God of All—

[f 78ᵛ]   7. Now from in and from this last view arises the whole difficulty and perplexity of the metaphysical Vocabulary. While As long as the *Subject*, i.e. the individual Mind Percipient was opposed to the *Object*, i.e. the Perceptum² all was clear. Again, in considering the ⟨finite⟩ Mind or Soul as self-percipient or a Subject capable of becoming an ⟨immediate⟩ Object to itself, but incapable of being an immediate Object to

---

ᵉ MS omits needed opening parenthesis   ᶠ For "framed"

² The "thing perceived".

any other finite Subject, there is no great difficulty. It is b̶u̶t̶ ⟨only⟩ but the position—A man's thoughts are known only to God and himself, reduced to a ⟨general⟩ formula—for the convenience of reasoning—as we use marks and letters in Algebra. But when not only the mind's self-consciousness, but all other things perceived by it are regarded as modifications of itself, as disguised but actual modes of the Self-perception, then the whole d̶i̶s̶t̶i̶n̶c̶t̶i̶o̶n̶ ground of the d̶i̶s̶t̶i̶n̶c̶t̶i̶o̶n̶fference between Subject and Object is gone—all *is* subjective ∫ and the sole distinction is 1. between that which not only is but is thought of us[g] as being such—and that which indeed truly *is* so no less than the former, but which we a̶r̶e̶ think of as being the contrary—and 2. of the latter, that which all men are by a common necessity constrained so to imagine, and that which is accidental & individual—as forms in fever—[? T̶h̶i̶s̶] We have only to reverse this order of Thought, and [f 79] we have the opposite results of Materialism. All here is merged in the Objective, and this again distinguished, as before into the general & permanent, and the particular & transitory. ⟨The⟩ Thought̶s̶ ̶a̶n̶d̶ ̶I̶m̶a̶g̶e̶ of a Table differs from the Table itself, not by essential invisibility or even by being essentially imponderable; but by being too minute to be seen by us, too thin and subtle to be perceptibly weighed—

Henceforward therefore Objective acquired two meanings, the first being the reality of any thing, outwardly correspondent to our perception, or notion thereof, a̶n̶d̶ independent of the perception itself—and the second, the universality of the perception as arising out of the inherent Laws of Human Nature in opposition to the accidental state of the individual percipient.—That Grass is green, is an instance of the one; that it appears yellow to a man in the jaundice (if such be the fact) is an instance of the other.

Still, however, a most serious difficulty started, & has been stated with incomparable fullness and clearness by Lord Bacon in his Novum [f 79ᵛ] Organum.—It is this—that the Human Understanding itself is but an individuality in Nature, having its own idiosyncracy or peculiar organism, and modifying all objects, its e̶l̶f̶ own forms of Self-consciousness no less than forms seen as external, by its own appropriate perspective. In the language of our British Plato there are not only Idols of the Den, the Theatre, and the Market-place but Idols of the *race*—and consequently the utmost that rational conviction can amount to, is not that this or that is true, by any inherent necessity but only that is[h] true for Man—that he is by the very mechanism of his nature compelled so to perceive and con-

---

[g] For "by us"?   [h] For "it is"?

ceive. To what an extent this has been carried both by ancient and by modern sceptics, it will be sufficient that I remind you by the one observation of M[r] Hume's in his Essays as they first appeared—that if Spiders had been Theologians, they would have been under the necessity of concluded[i], that the World was spun and that—but a philosophical [f 80] Lecture will be no sufficient excuse for repeating Blasphemy, & I stop—

One *question*, however, would occur to every reflecting Hearer of such a ~~remar~~ position/ "pray, would this theological Spider have the power likewise of doubting its own necessary perception and conclusion["]/ if so, and if this Spider therefore be but a nick-name for a ~~man~~ rational Being, imposed for the purpose of misleading the fancy by a mere *verbal* association, must there not be some other faculty above this mechanism by which man is adapted to his present circumstances? some power, call it ~~reason~~ with Lord Bacon the lumen siccum, or pure Light, call it reason ⟨with Lord Herbert,⟩ or call it the Faith of Reason with Kant, that stands in some union with, some participation of the Eternal & Universal, by which Man is enabled to question, nay, to contradict, the ~~necessary~~ irresistible impressions of his own senses, ~~the~~ nay, the necessary deductions of his own Understanding—to challenge & disqualify them, as partial and incompetent. Can a machine or any part of a machine pass out of itself—[f 80[v]] and if so, what becomes of the famous Doctrine, that our Ideas have no other pretence to Truth except as they are generalizations or classifications of impressions passively received thro' the mechanism of the organs of sense & sensation?—I need not inform ⟨you⟩ that a numerous class of modern Philosophers answer—No such faculty exists— the notion is a mere abortion of Pride engendered on the Imagination— ~~bu~~ but still tho' numerous I called this class, they ~~are~~ yet ⟨appear⟩ numerous (paradoxical as it may sound) in consequence of their paucity—and of the contrariancy of their doctrine to the feelings of Mankind in general which makes us wonder that *so many* could be found entertaining such a doctrine—but still it must make us pause, that positions asserted to differ from noise only by the sounds being articulated should have been held ~~by~~ not only by the Mass of Mankind in all ages, but by the best & wisest, even by those whom these very philosophers are obliged to place foremost in their list, whenever they have occasion to enumerate the Luminaries and [f 81] benefactors of the race—that these absurd positions should be the ground work of all Law, inwoven in all language, & taken for granted in every thing which distinguishes man from

---

[i] For "concluding"?

the brute—even in the degree in which he is so distinguished/ for they are compelled by their principles to deny any distinction in kind?— —

However, be this as it may, the facts remain as stated by me—& if I have succeeded in rendering them intelligible, a comparatively short account will suffice to explain to you the character of the different systems announced as the Subject of my Lectures—& I shall be found to have economized my Time even by the length of my introductory matter—

First, of Locke,

MS REPORT

BM MS Egerton 3057 ff 28–31^v

[f 28] Mr Coleridge—Philosophy Lecture 13th March 22 1819

There is scarcely a more instructive or entertaining subject than the tracing the progress of any living language by the *de-synonimization* of words and it is the business and duty of the philosopher to aid this progress as far as his subject will allow—. The ~~attention~~ kindness said M^r C with wh^a you always honor me may seem to render it useless for me now to entreat your attention—but it is not your ears only I would engage, for a few minutes let me ask you to think with me, while I explain some terms in philosophy on which will rest greatly the sense of this lecture—1st That ⟨~~substance~~⟩ which is actually a substance & in chemistry would be called ponderable is in Philosophy—body—2nd That ⟨~~substance~~⟩ which is without perceptible weight and termed the imponderable—is Matter— such as the Sunshine—3rd That which does not appear & has no outwardness & which must be known or inferred—is Spirit or Power—4thly The aggregate of the sums ponderable and imponderable is—Nature passive—& the aggregate of the sums inferred is Nature in the active sense—5^{thly} when inwardly then is Spirit and Power, that wh affirms its own existence is Mind immediate—6^{ly}—when we contradistinguish the percipient from the thing perceived—the former is termed subjective— the latter objective—the Idealist ~~on the former ground~~ would declare the whole corporeal & mental world to be subjective—now in and from this last error arises the whole difficulty of our Metaphysical vocabulary—as long as the subject was opposed to the object [f 28^v] all was clear but when not only the minds self consciousness—and consciousness of others is regarded as the result of sense—^{b}—every thing becomes subjective—these idealists make a distinction between that which all men are constrained to believe or imagine & that which is accidental thus they say when awake all men have a dream in common but that when asleep each has a world or dream of his own—if you reverse these tenets, you have the Materialists—who consider the thought of a table only to so far dif-

---

^{a} For "which" ^{b} Two lines deleted indecipherably

598

fer from the table itself, as our organs are defective & which we cannot weigh—Hume in one of his essays tells us that if a Spider were a theologian he would maintain the world was spun—if this spider be only to conceal his own doubts but a philosophical lecture will not excuse me for introducing blasphemy & I shall stop—We do not find here the "true sight" of Bacon—the "reason" of Lord Herbert or the "Faith of Reason" of Kant must there not be some power call it what you will which communicates with our Nature [?ɏ] which enables us to dread & feel the errors & falacies of such reasoning—it is lamentable to find such delusions so often existing in those persons whose names we are compelled to bring forward as luminaries in the philosophy & literature of the world—⟨Lord Bacon says the human mind itself is but an outward form⟩—It [is]^c always painful to me sd^d M^r C— to mention a name, which is highly valued by the world, when my opinions upon it do not coincide with the general feel^{ge}—& this is the case when ⟨I⟩^{f} bring Mr Lock before you—My conscience bears me witness it is not from any want of studying his works or those who have studied him—but sincerity compels me to say that I never could account [f 29] for the impression they made or discover the novelty of his sentiments or the justice of his opinions—As William the 3$^{rd.}$ had done away with the tyranny of the Stewarts so was Mr Locke to do away with all the absurdities of the schoolmen & the universities—Hume one of the followers of Locke has carried his premises to their natural consequence ⟨he confesses he cant see the object of the first book of Locke—historically it may be thus accounted for⟩—Descartes was the first who made a direct distinction between Man & Nature—he therefore supposes in the Soul a causative power—adapting mechanical laws and material ideas—he first used the term "innate" and gave an innate spiritual which had its origin in the mind and he had also the innate material idea—Descartes is indeed a great Man—he thus replied to Mr Lockes fancied refutation of his system—and proves Locke not only to be the refuter but the absolute instigator & only possessor of any such ideas as he attempted to destroy I said innate—not connate—I said the birth place not the time—it is absurd to say men had sight before they saw or hearing before they could hear—but still there must be a difference between a mouse and a man—it is the percipient not the object of perception that varies—there are two ideas—those thoughts which we are conscious to be passive—and those in which the mind feels its own activity forming notions—which come

---

^{c} MS has a letter at this point that may be either "G" or "Y" ^{d} For "said"
^{e} For "feeling" ^{f} Insertion in pencil above line, possibly in a different hand

immediately from the place of their origin & these Descartes calls innate ideas—

[f 29ᵛ]   But Locke has not even originality for Boetius a Jesuit attacked Des Cartes on the self same subjects before him—and his answer is the same as Lockes since adopted definition of the powers of refection—Mʳ Coleridge observes nothing in Locke but what is perfectly just if you substitute for his definition of ideas being derived from the senses or brought in by them—the word elicited—for indeed all thoughts are elicited from the objects of the senses—or what is a thought can you in your mind divide one thought from another—no but commit your thought to paper or in words make it tangible to the senses and the difficulty is vanished— Mʳ C— had a Copy of Lockes Essay on the Understanding interleaved and against each particular paragraph he wrote what Descartes & others had ~~said~~ before promulgated—Locke says—it is the manure the tillage &c that produces the oat or wheat—but if you say that it was the sunshine & the dews that called the seedᵍ into life which would otherwise have rotted in the manure—it is much more intelligible—indeed his terms throughout are mechanical & waggon like—it may be shortly said he did not destroy the Innate Ideas he combatted—for such never had any existence—he is not a materialist—although too material in his words— Newton had overthrown the mechanical, the physical part of Descartes & Locke thus attacking this [f 30] Metaphysical philosophy—we have these two names linked as the destroyers of another great man and Mʳ Locke may be here ⟨a⟩ long time preserved—but we have yet to trace the causes of the deep impressions he made upon the mind—and first we find him cried up by all parties, each could see sufficient in him to have the desire of claiming him and thus it became the interest of all to follow him—finally it was the beginning of a time when all seem to have agreed upon one theory—Voltaire taught that things were known only by the senses & we ⟨as a nation⟩ were gratified as a bustling political & commercial people with the thought that a few hours could make us fit for ⟨the⟩ See of Canterbury or place us upon an equalityʰ with a life of Study.

In Germany they have or had nothing of this intensity of nationallity— the learned men formed a middle class—and their numerous universities and want of commercial bustle have tended to make them a thinking metaphysical & cosmographical people—the Germans are the only writers who feel as men & who write impartially upon & of other nations— but when you lay your hand upon an excellence you may be almost certain of embracing ⟨also⟩ its defect—

ᵍ "grain" written above line in pencil in a different hand
ʰ "equality" scribbled over another word—"equivalent"?

[f 30ᵛ] Leibnitz—to the opinion that there was nothing in the mind which was not before in the Senses—added "but the mind itself"—he opposed the Lockeyan Philosophy and shewed some points deficient in it—

Spinoza was a Jew—he was of a most exemplary life—& had no wish to make proselytes—he refused the offer of protection from a German Prince if he would preach his doctrines—indeed they were never published till after his death—his System was pantheism, but in its best form—& he erred only where thousands have erred before him ⟨and erred with a Christian feeling⟩—he communicated only his opinions where he could obtain information—why then as Lessing observes is no man to speak of Spinoza but as a dead dog—

Leibnitz taught—that the Deity had a preconception of the things conceived and thus gave [? His] thoughts a reallity without partaking of the reallity—or any communication with it—thus stamping a reallity upon His thoughts & rendering all things possible with the possibility of thought—

Why does Materialism strike us? because we are apt to mistake outward appearance for quick perceptions—the senses are at all times sooner acted upon through Sensation than the thoughts can be

[f 31]   Among the Merits of Kant may be reckoned 1ˢᵗ that he examined critically the faculties before he hazarded any opinion upon what those faculties had established among men—thus he saw two classes of truths received—1ˢᵗ Truths of experience—but still uncertain—acquiring stability & belief with time—but often ultimately controverted—& 2ⁿᵈ other truths immediate and ⟨as⟩ fully believed as so soon as understood as they wd be in a thousand years—the one universal the other contingent—he allowed the possibility in the mind of producg[i] ideas wh had no relation to outward nature—but he said now have I been giving you a new analysis of man as far as his intellect is concerned—but there is yet a higher constituent of his Nature—his will which, as he is commanded to do this & that, is belief on the faith reason religious truths would become mathematical if they could be proved by reason—but equally is yet it beyond Reason to controvert them—however his great merit is the having determined the nature of Religious truths & its connection with the understandg[j] if the intellect be were the cherub that flew with wings—it still flew after the flaming Seraph and in its course—in short he describes the one philosophy in which the intellectual powers are concerned as a logos—the other as subjugating this logos to the will & thus combined as the union of love—

---

[i] For "producing"   [j] For "understanding"

Schelling Ӏ must ⟨be⟩ briefly mentioned—his doctrines may be found in the lower platonism in Spinoza &c he is a Roman Catholic Pantheist with the Rosary in one hand and the bible of Spinoza in the other [f 31ᵛ] [? but*k*] still he worshipped Saints as the only means of addressing God [? at/out] on earth—

When Mʳ C was in Rome—he met with one of his disciples who after a long argument—confessed—that although he openly followed the Roman Church as his bread—yet that Atheism was the darling of his heart but the Roman Ch was the most like Paganism—Mʳ C— beautifully demonstrated that in the decay of nature or of substance the Mind does not die away—but that when it appears to slacken tis only as the cracks in the catapillars skin when changing & which he no more needs as the buterfly thus is immortallity—the inward Psych*l* of our frames—

Advertisement—Mʳ C. lectures this even*gm* on the German Philosophy with its bearings on the stem*n* of Locke—comprising the system of Leibnitz—Kant & Schelling—on Monday next Mʳ C— will deliver his last address a public lecturer with a review & application of the whole preceeding course—The Lecture on the history & influence of Dogmatical Materialism with notes is preparing for the press—

LECTURE 14

DATE AND PLACE OF DELIVERY. Monday, 29 March 1819, at the Crown and Anchor Tavern, Strand, London.

SUBJECT. Review of the entire course.

ANNOUNCEMENTS AND ADVERTISEMENTS. On Sat 27 Mar the *Courier* carried the following announcement among its news items: "On Monday evening, MR. COLERIDGE'S last Lecture, with a Review and Application of his Preceding Labours, as a Public Lecturer. Eight o'clock, Crown and Anchor, Strand." On Mon 29 Mar the *Morning Chronicle* carried a similar announcement: "THIS EVENING, Mr. COLERIDGE'S LAST LECTURE, with a Review and Application of his preceding Labours as a Public Lecturer.—Eight o'clock; Crown and Anchor, Strand." This announcement also appeared in the *Times* and in the *New Times*.

TEXT. C's draft notes in BM Add MS 47,523 ff 81^v–4^v.

REPORT. BM MS Egerton 3057 ff 32–5.

BACKGROUND AND CIRCUMSTANCES. Despite the announcement that this lect was to be C's last as a public lecturer and despite his own evident wish that it might be, he was already negotiating for another series to be given at the Russell Institution (see *CL* IV 925: to J. Britton 28 Feb 1819), although these negotiations seem to have been unsuccessful. His lect in 1825 to the Royal Society of Literature should perhaps be regarded as a private one, open only to members of the Society.

LECTURE 14

DRAFT MS

BM Add MS 47,523 (N 25), ff 81ᵛ–4ᵛ

[f 81ᵛ] Monday, 29 March, 1819

Fourteenth of the Phil. Course and the Last (O pray Heaven, that it may indeed be the Last) of All. Absit omen de morte secundâ: de primâ sufficiet, sit modo post obitum ἀταραξια.[1]

~~As images of Place are the best helps of Recollection, next to a healthy state of the digestive functions, mental and bodily, I shall begin my brief recapitulation of the ⟨great⟩ outstanding points of the History of Philosophy~~

~~I have~~ My address of this evening must consist of two parts/ as the concluding Lecture ~~of the~~ on the History of Phil. ~~Course I must place before you the~~ its great outstanding Points, ~~of~~ to and thro' which I have led you, league by league, I must place at once before you as in ⱥ the simple Map of a *Sampler*[2]—and as the last Lecture, I would fain impress those truths deducible from both my Courses, & ~~which are~~ the objects common to both.—And first then of the first—as next to a healthy state of the digestive powers mental and bodily, the best aids of the Memory are supplied, it is said, by IMAGES OF PLACE,[3] I will end as ⱦ my first Lecture

---

[1] "May this not be an omen of another death to follow: as for the first, it will be enough if only after death there is peace." In *CN* III 4504n, where this tr is provided, C's enigmatic observation is associated with Rev 2.11—". . . He that overcometh shall not be hurt of the second death"—and Rev 20.14: "And death and hell were cast into the lake of fire. This is the second death", and with the announcements in the newspapers of this lect as being C's last and as his "farewell address to his auditors". His series of literary lects had ended 25 Mar.

[2] A sampler as in the sense of a child's display piece of skill at embroidery?

[3] In *BL* (*CC*) I 128, C had commented on memory in more detail: "Sound logic, as the habitual subordination of the individual to the species, and of the species to the genus; philosophical knowledge of facts under the relation of cause and effect; a chearful and communicative temper that disposes us to notice the similarities and contrasts of things, that we may be able to illustrate the one by the other; a quiet conscience; a condition free from anxieties, sound health, and above all (as

began—~~by~~ and again put before your eyes the Country of the Patriarchs, [f 82] from the Euphrates to the Hellespont/ ~~but more specially the Coasts of~~ ⟨Land of⟩ ~~Palestine and Syria~~ emphatically entitled in the eldest national Document, the Tents of Shem— —[4]

For here dwelt the ~~Semitic~~ Nations whose ~~Languages~~ ⟨Tongues,⟩ ~~have~~ Languages as manifest Dialects of the same original Tongue, have been well & aptly entitled the *Semitic* Languages, as the Hebrew, Arabic, and Syro-chaldaic, in order to distinguish them from the Tartar, Chinese, Hindostanic &c better than the far too vague and general term of Oriental Languages—⟨The⟩ Language of a race is its character—[a]⟨The Literature of⟩ The Semitic Nations[b] were and to this day ~~are~~ is characterized by being—1. *imperative*[c], and ~~oracular~~ assertory (Thou shalt—thou shalt not—*I am*[5]) or *narrative* in the simple form of Chronicles, as in the Hist. Books of the O.T.[6]—or *cumulative*[d], as in the instance of the Proverbs and the more didactic Psalms—. No where do we perceive any *connection* between sentence & sentence but that afforded by Imagination & Excitement—namely, the *poetic* connection—.[7] And such is the appropriate Language of Religion—assumed or imitated in all religious rites even by the nations of opposite character—and need I say, the most proper repository wherein to place Truths too awfully important & necessary to the Human Race to be trusted to the stumblings & alternate Pro- and Re-gression of [f 82ᵛ] the growing Intellect of Man/—As early as *these*[e] we hear from the same authority of another Race, the Descendants of Japhet—~~one branch~~ distinguished not only by their migratory tendency but by their common direction *westwards* ~~the~~ one branch, ~~N.W.~~ more northerly—and the other ~~S.W.~~ more to South—& ~~in a~~ this latter branch splits again into the two names of Greeks & Romans—and ~~in~~ the full understanding of the peculiar national traits that occasioned & justify the

---

[a] Indecipherable mark in ms may have been meant to indicate beginning of new paragraph
[b] C meant to change "Nations" to "Nation"?
[c] Underlining to indicate italics very faint
[d] Underlining to indicate italics very faint
[e] Underlining to indicate italics very faint

---

far as relates to passive remembrance) a healthy digestion; *these* are the best, these are the only ARTS OF MEMORY". C's addition of the "IMAGES OF PLACE" here is probably a good-humoured allusion to the current schemes of artificial memory (see *BL*—*CC*—I 127n) that he himself rejected and a graceful excuse for his own resumption of geography.

[4] For C's opening remarks on the "historical and theoretical" role of the Hebrews, see 49 above. C returns here to the materials used in his eighth lect at 347–9 above.

[5] E.g. as in the Ten Commandments (Exod 20.1–17) and in God's answer to Moses, "I AM THAT I AM" (Exod 3.14). Cf *BL* (*CC*) I 275* and n.

[6] Old Testament.

[7] In Lect 10 at 422 above, C had stressed "the power and force of Greek and Roman connection" and its efficacy as a safeguard against "the mere aphorism style of the oriental nations . . .".

contrast of Jew and Greek—is the condition and the foundation-stone of all philosophical Insight into the History of Philosophy, which was ~~even more~~ no less exclusively indigenous in Greece, ⟨in the Isles of the Gentiles,⟩ as Revelation was during the same period appropriate to the Tents of Shem— —[8]

~~The~~ We saw the ~~dawning~~ commencement in the Ionic School.[9] The first ⟨and most important⟩ step was taken by Thales, in proposing the problem of the origin & constituent laws of the material World to be solved by the efforts & researches of the Understanding, without recourse to Tradition or Mythology.[10]—A further advance was made by ~~this~~ the[f] second Master[11] of the same School—he discovered that the solution of phænomena could not be found in phænomena, as the sol.[g] would be part of the problem to be solved[12]—and the third,[13] in whom the Ionic Sect reached its summit, discovered that neither [f 83] could any finite power by itself account for the appearances—for to account for a thing &c— —He therefore ~~attributed the~~ sought for it *in* certain abstractions, making ~~the~~ all things proceed from the oppositions & reconciliations of the Finite & the Infinite—~~to~~ which he considered as real Powers, having an objective existence.—[14]

In the Italian School, & the Person of Pythagoras, Philosophy as it first obtained an appropriate name, so it here first ascended with a full face— He saw, that either the problem was insolvible, not merely as of infinite solution from its complexity (for if only we were progressive, this would be well) but because it was impossible to determine the first step, if the solution was to be sought for from the senses or what are called facts of outward Experience. In the mind or no where—[15]

But yet not in the mind ~~generally~~ as individual—It was therefore to be assumed, that a somewhat under that name was that was not individual— and in this, or the pure Reason, to be found if at all—But he saw that this could not be any fraction of our Nature—but moral [f 83ᵛ] as well as

---

[f] Word written over cancellation that precedes it   [g] For "solution"

[8] C follows closely the materials presented in Lect 8 at 347ff above.

[9] In Lect 8 at 347 above, C associates the Ionic School or Ionians with the descendants of Japhet.

[10] C had described this aspect of Thales's contribution at greater length in his second lect at 61–2 above.

[11] Anaximander. Cf 30 n 40 above.

[12] The observation of "the immediate followers of Thales" on the solution of phenomena had been discussed at the beginning of C's fourth lect, at 169 above.

[13] By "third" master one would expect C to mean Anaximenes, but elsewhere (e.g. *CN* III 4445—N 27: Oct 1819—) he attributes the doctrine in question, conventionally, to Anaximander.

[14] Appearances, or "visibility", and the finite and the infinite, or the "distinguishable" and the "indistinguishable", had been discussed at greater length in the second lect at 63–4 above.

[15] C's account of Pythagoras's reasoning on this point had been given in the second lect; see 74–5 above.

intellectual—that it must be not *philosophylogy* merely but philosophy including philology—& thaten that a moral previous discipline was indispensable—[16]

On these premises he sought in the Ideas manifested in the Reason for the Laws of the World—and taught the adoration of the Deity as the common ground of both[17]—and in the belief of Kepler who adopted the same principles,[18] the success was answerable—

But soon the party-spirit of human nature appeared—[19]

The Eleatic began by taking the Intellect exclusively—[20]

The Corpuscular Philosophers the very Contrary—[21]

The Sceptics arose out of, and triumphed over, the contradictions & uncertainties of Both—[22]

While the Sophists taking up the Philosophy of the latter made it the pandar to the worst passions, and by mob-flattery hastened the ruin of the State—[23]

[f 84]   Socrates attempted a compromise by excluding all earnest investigation except into human nature—

The proper study of mankind is Man[24]—but by his own oscillating between the good and the useful, whether erime guilt was or was not more and other than an error in calculation, he but gave rise to new schisms— the Stoic Bully and the Cyrenaic Sensualist—[25]

Lastly, Philosophy seemed to rest fall into two great domains, & there to rest—those who grounded all hope of knowlege on observation, and the power of generalizing and classifying, arranged themselves under

---

[16] The moral aspect of reason had also been stressed in the second lect at 79 above.

[17] Pythagoras's separation of both the reason and the world from the idea of God had been explored in the second lect at 79–80 above.

[18] The connection between Kepler's study of the planets and "Pythagorean harmonies and numbers" had been pointed out in the fifth lect at 236 above.

[19] In Lect 4 C did not allege "party-spirit" in his presentation of the Eleatics, the "Corpuscular Philosophers" and the Sceptics, but he had stressed the moral character of Pythagoras's philosophy and "the transition from thence to speculative philosophy, disjoined from the moral" in Lect 3 at 118–19 above.

[20] For C's previous presentation of the Eleatics, see 122ff above.

[21] For C's previous account of the Corpuscular Philosophers, i.e. the atom-

ists led by Democritus and Leucippus, see 134–7 above.

[22] For C's previous account of the Sceptics, see 253ff above.

[23] For C's previous account of the Sophists, see 138ff above; it includes the claim that Sophism was "a working agent in precipitating" the fall of "a debauched state" (140).

[24] Socrates's concentration on human nature is stressed in similar terms in Lect 3, at 142–4 above.

[25] The connection between Socrates's "oscillating", first mentioned in Lect 3 as his "vacillating" (148 above), and the Cyrenaics had been pursued in Lect 4 at 179–81 above, where the Cynics, the precursors of the Stoics, are mentioned (181). The detailed discussion of the Stoics, including mention of their Cyrenaic affinities, was provided in Lect 6 at 276–80.

[? the] Aristotle—while those who remained faithful to the principles of Pythagoras, who sought for the only true science, & in it for Power and Prophecy in Laws, and Laws in the Ideas revealed thro' the pure Reason, marshalled under Plato—[26]

This was the ne plus ultra[27]—the Romans realized but did not invent— and Christianity brought Religion—defined as this morning[28]—and Vice—Superstition—and the Decline of Philosophy—[29]

[f 84ᵛ] The N.W. Branch of the Iapetidæ—[30]

~~Religion deprived of Philosophy—~~

The Schoolmen modified the Peripatetic Phil—& excited a necessity for rational conviction, & organized the barbarous Languages with the connections of the Greeks—and thus by distinction without division ac- comodated it to the characteristics of Gothic [? Freedom]/[31]

The Platonists brooded over the birth of Genius & the Fine Arts[32]— And the very discoveries, owing to this, brought back the materialism of Democr. & Epicur[33]—the Sceptics, ~~and~~ the Sophists—in short all that tribe which had their Triumph in the French Revolution—[34]

Then Lay Sermon[35]

Then apply—
the prevailence of idolizing [? shewyness] of the Day—
&c &c—

---

[26] This characterisation of Plato's and Aristotle's philosophies is in accord with the much more elaborate descriptions of them in Lects 4 and 5 (182–94 and 221–36).

[27] "That beyond which one can go no farther".

[28] The preceding day, 28 Mar 1819, C had given an inscribed copy of Richard Field *Of the Church* to DC (see *CL* IV 929) and it is possible that the definition of religion came up as part of a conver- sation the following morning. In a frag- ment probably of 1821 (with wm of 1821) C attempts a combined definition of religion, the church, and Christianity, that may include the essence of the defi- nition he alludes to here: "RELIGION de- fined, or the Idea of Religion, and that it comprehends or implies Revelation. (The ~~phrase~~ epithet, *revealed*, ⟨prefixed to⟩ religion, ⟨may be allowed as⟩ declara- tory of one of its essential characters; ⟨but⟩ otherwise ⟨it is⟩ a pleonasm in speech.)" (*SW & F—CC*—II 906.)

[29] This view of the Roman role in the history of philosophy is conventional and compatible with C's earlier discussions, but he had not made this particular point previously.

[30] C had discussed the "north-western race" of the Japetidae in Lect 8 at 347–9 above.

[31] C's account of the Schoolmen's adoption of Aristotelianism (the Peri- patetic Philosophy) had appeared in Lect 9 at 373–89 above; their concentration on distinctions was taken up at 386–9 above, their improvement of the connec- tive force of language and the role of Gothic genius in Lect 10 at 422–4 above.

[32] C had connected the revival of the fine arts in the Renaissance with Platon- ism in his fourth lect at 194–6 above.

[33] Democritus and Epicurus.

[34] The course of the revival of materi- alism up to his own time was traced by C in Lect 12 at 513ff above. He had previ- ously mentioned the French Revolution as a consequence of "mechanical philos- ophy" in Lect 5 at 240–1 above.

[35] See Introduction cxliv–cxlv above.

MS REPORT

BM MS Egerton 3057 ff 32–5

[f 32] Mr Coleridge—Philosophy Lecture 14—29 March 1819—

We have said M^r C— passed through a long and wandering road, which has often ~~seemed~~ appeared to turn back upon itself, and not without its chasms—I must now present you a simple Map and as Place is said most to assist the memory I shall begin as I did before by laying before you the tents of Shem, the Countries from Tigris to Euphrates called the Semite Nations. the language of a Nation is its character and their language is either mandatory or narrative—as I am the Lord the^a God or in the historical books and psalms of the sacred writings and therefore these sacred writings were more properly placed in their hands than where the growing intellect of man was in its progress perpetually stumbling—The descendants of Iaphet distinguished by their migratory lives are the forefathers of European Nations—from one division of which the Greeks & Romans immediately proceeded—to the former our present considerations are chiefly drawn—and as we find Religion in Judea, so do we find Philosophy in Greece, equally indigenous—in Thales, we have the commencement—he began the great search after cause by casting off all history [f 32^v] and tradition—and is at the head of the Ionic School—In Pythagoras—who is at the head of the Italian School philosophy obtained its appropriate name and rose with its full face—for he combined morality and taught ⟨that⟩ the adoration of the Deity contained the law of the mind and the success of the intellect and led to that love of wisdom which is the union of our intellect and our will—and this Keppler afterwards supported—here philosophy appeared to have taken a certain & confident path, but the restless spirit of human nature arose in the Eleatic sect and Sophistry lent her aid ⟨in pander^gb the worst passions & thus effected the overthrow not only of philosophy but Greece herself⟩—Socrates was followed by the Stoic bully and Sirenaic sensualist—The divine Plato and Aristotle now lead and divide philosophy—and next we see Christianity bringing ~~philosophy~~ Religion to her assistance and with this phi-

---

^a For "thy"   ^b For "pandering"

610

5. Manuscript report, in an unknown hand, of Lecture 14
BM MS Egerton 3057 f 32
The British Library; reproduced by kind permission

losophy received at once its object & completion—but soon after came superstition, allied with magic and imposture—a pause an interregnum now took place—Religion was next to exist without any philosophy at all and persecution supported the seperation—the schoolmen at length arose, moderated the Parapetetic philosophy and prepared the [f 33] way for the overthrow of scepticism—they were the great agents also of modifying the languages of the North to the South—We next find Platonism brooding over the birth of genius and reviving with the restoration of literature and the fine arts—and this is the point when her pre-eminence over the cramped philosophy of Aristotle is most conspicuous—she shone forth in a Giotto and Michael Angelo—producing some of the highest possible efforts—but again the Materialists and Idealists arose with all that train of error which we have traced down to the French Revolution—But the main object of this brief attempt is to induce you to ask yourselves whether God has not made you more than objects of sense and whether there is not a something within you like the expression that pervades the intelligent countenance—Mr C. here gave a beautiful description of the mind as distinct from the senses illustrating the reason which is the minds eye also as the attribute of the Deity[1]—how greatly different is this from the late systems of French and perhaps more general phylosophy—with the loss of the life and the Spirit [f 33^v] of Nature, this philosophy has maybe produced a few new mechanical inventions—cer-

---

[1] Cf the passage in *LS* (*CC*) 69–70 (Appendix C of *The Statesman's Manual*): "the REASON without being either the SENSE, the UNDERSTANDING or the IMAGINATION contains all three within itself, even as the mind contains its thoughts, and is present in and through them all; or as the expression pervades the different features of an intelligent countenance. Each individual must bear witness of it to his own mind, even as he describes life and light: and with the silence of light it describes itself, and dwells in *us* only as far as we dwell in *it*. It cannot in strict language be called a faculty, much less a personal property, of any human mind! He, with whom it is present, can as little appropriate it, whether totally or by partition, as he can claim ownership in the breathing air or make an inclosure in the cope of heaven. | The object of the preceding discourse was to recommend the Bible, as the end and center of our reading and meditation.

I can truly affirm of myself, that my studies have been profitable and availing to me only so far, as I have endeavoured to use all my other knowledge as a glass enabling me to receive more light in a wider field of vision from the word of God. If you have accompanied me thus far, thoughtful reader! Let it not weary you if I digress for a few moments to another book, likewise a revelation of God—the great book of his servant Nature. That in its obvious sense and literal interpretation it declares the being and attributes of the Almighty Father, none but the *fool in heart* has ever dared gainsay. But it has been the music of gentle and pious minds in all ages, it is the *poetry* of all human nature, to read it likewise in a figurative sense, and to find therein correspondencies and symbols of the spiritual world." Was this the passage that C intended to refer to (at 609 above)? Cf also *Lects 1795* (*CC*) I 94.

tainly even those are not discoveries—and instead of human Nature we have a French Nature which we may sum up as the Caput Mortuum of a French ferocity, audacity, frivolity, immorality, and corruption[2]—but we must learn to search & know our internal selves and why when we have this power of judging should we take the assertion or belief of another— the poet Daniel says, "unless man can ⟨rise above⟩[c] himself how mean a thing is man⟨!⟩"[3]—Lorenzo the Magnificent & Cosmo the benefactor of his country delighted in the Study of human Nature—Luther & Erasmus underwent the hardest campaign—such Men loved Metaphysics, and in the Court of our own Elizabeth—Sir P. Sydney & others resorted to a philosopher[4]— —we are peculiarly called upon to this study—are we in the unceasing change of all sublunary things to im⟨a⟩gine ⟨that⟩ the soul

---

[c] "rise above" inserted in another hand

[2] Cf *LS* (*CC*) 76–7: "Prurient, bustling, and revolutionary, this French wisdom has never more than grazed the surfaces of knowledge. As political economy, in its zeal for the increase of food it habitually overlooked the qualities and even the sensations of those that were to feed on it. As ethical philosophy, it recognized no duties which it could not reduce into debtor and creditor accounts on the ledgers of self-love, where no coin was sterling which could not be rendered into *agreeable sensations*. And even in its height of self-complacency as chemical art, greatly am I deceived if it has not from the very beginning mistaken the products of destruction, cadavera rerum [dead bodies of things], for the elements of composition: and most assuredly it has dearly purchased a few brilliant inventions at the loss of all communion with life and the spirit of nature. As the process, such the result! a heartless frivolity alternating with a sentimentality as heartless—an ignorant contempt of antiquity—a neglect of moral self-discipline—a deadening of the religious sense, even in the less reflecting forms of natural piety—a scornful reprobation of all consolations and secret refreshings from above—and as the caput mortuum of human nature evaporated, a French nature of rapacity, levity, ferocity, and presumption."

[3] C had used this quotation in a longer passage from Samuel Daniel *Epistle to the Lady Margaret, Countess of Cumberland* stanza 12 (*Poetical Works*—2 vols London 1718—II 354) as an epigraph to *Friend* (*CC*) I 100: "Knowing the Heart of Man is set to be | The Centre of this World, about the which | These Revolutions of Disturbances | Still roul; where all th' Aspects of Misery | Predominate: Whose strong Effects are such, | As he must bear, b'ing pow'rless to redress: | And that unless above himself he can | Erect himself, how poor a Thing is Man!" The reporter may have caught only the end of the quotation. The concluding exclamation mark seems to have been inserted by another hand.

[4] C had used a similar group of exemplars in *LS* (*CC*) 101–2: "The magnificent son of Cosmo was wont to discourse with Ficino, Politian, and the princely Mirandula on the *Ideas* of Will, God, and Immortality. The accomplished author of the Arcadia, the star of serenest brilliance in the glorious constellation of Elizabeth's court, our England's Sir Philip Sydney! He the paramount gentleman of Europe, the poet, warrior, and statesman, held high converse with Spencer on the *Idea* of Supersensual beauty; on all 'earthly fair and amiable,' as the *Symbol* of that Idea; and on Music and Poesy as its living *Educts!*" The passage was repeated with slight variations in *C&S* (*CC*) 64–5. Cf *LS* (*CC*) 172–3.

whose nature will not so far flatter us as to allow the hope of her one day being Nothing—is alone in this world—[f 34] and without a sympathizing feeling throughout Nature—if self knowledge prevent this unmeaning blank is not it a delightful desirable object— —M^r C considers Modern Metaphysical philosophy as perfectly erroneous, the formation of ideas from outward objects will not be allowed by him to the extent some require—for if you rob me of my senses I have still my mind says M^r C— but this argument is very defective—he should take away the senses at the birth to make good his ground—and then describe that mind so divided—its extent and capacity may be fairly doubted or denied—[5]

Again if men do not acquire the habit of reflection or of tracing to each faculty of the mind all they see and hear how useless must be our reading and our daily intercourse with the world & human Nature[6]—I have often admired for instance the beauty of Popes description of a moonlight night one part of wh describes the north Pole as ~~guilt~~ gilt with stars innumerable—this to one who had never [f 34^v] left the Southern Hemisphere would be almost nonsense—but the elegance of the langu⟨a⟩ge & the thoughts have pleased me[7]—Mr C. strongly reprobated those works of modern times which under the false garb of morality and virtue appeal only to the lowest senses often tis true disguised in language fair, deceiving and the more dangerous, while a Fielding ⟨is neglected⟩ whose genuine bursts of humour sweep away occasional grossness & which by the pure mind is passed by not because it is bad but offensive—and where

---

[5] The reporter's objection may have been warranted by what C actually said in the lect. C does take the problem into account elsewhere, however, most notably in ch 9 of *BL*.

[6] In the notes for the thirteenth lect in his series on European literature in 1818, C had developed the implications of this view for the poet: "Poetry . . . is purely *human*—all its materials are *from* the mind, and all the products are *for* the mind. It is the Apotheosis of the former state—viz. Order and Passion—*N.b.* how by excitement of the Associative Power Passion itself imitates Order, and the *order* resulting produces a pleasurable *Passion* (whence Metre) and thus elevates the Mind by making its feelings the Objects of its reflection/and how recalling the Sights and Sounds that had accompanied the occasions of the original passion it impregnates them with an interest not their own by means of the Pas-

sions, and yet tempers the passion by the calming power which all *distinct* images exert on the human soul" (*CN* III 4397— N 22: Mar 1818—); cf *Lects 1808–1819* (*CC*) II 218 and *BL* (*CC*) II 54.

[7] In *BL* (*CC*) I 40* C had said of the lines from Alexander Pope tr *Iliad* VIII 691–2, "Around her throne the vivid planets roll, | And stars unnumber'd gild the glowing pole", "it is difficult to determine whether . . . the sense, or the diction be the more absurd". HCR recorded an earlier instance of C's analysing the passage in a lect in 1812, and introducing "this censure with a very insincere eulogium" (*Lects 1808–1819—CC—*I 406). On these occasions C had been complaining of Pope's meaningless diction, choosing a generally admired passage on purpose; here his comment is on the relationship of actual human experience to imagination and he is content to exploit the popularity of the lines.

the intellect is preeminently conspicuous instead of that sensual feeling so often pervading other & much more admired works[8]—but should you meet with a work where your understanding is appealed to through your senses and your conscience through your feelings then you will be grateful when you can bring reflection to your reading and you will feel as I do now after my twofold lectures, that delightful harmony which ever will be found where philosophy [35] is united with such poetry as Milton and Shakespear[9]—or those who have endeavoured to reconcile all the powers of our nature into one harmony and to gather that harmony round the cradle of Moral will—

---

[8] Cf C's marginal comment in a copy of *The History of Tom Jones*: ". . . I do loathe the cant which can recommend Pamela and Clarissa Harlowe as strictly moral, though they poison the imagination of the young with continued doses of *tinct. lyttae* [an aphrodisiac], while Tom Jones is prohibited as loose. I do not speak of young women;—but a young man whose heart or feelings can be injured, or even his passions excited, by aught in this novel, is already thoroughly corrupt. There is a cheerful, sun-shiny, breezy spirit that prevails everywhere, strongly contrasted with the close, hot, day-dreamy continuity of Richardson. Every indiscretion, every immoral act, of Tom Jones . . . is so instantly punished by embarrassment and unanticipated evil consequences of his folly, that the reader's mind is not left for a moment to dwell or run riot on the criminal indulgence itself" (*CM—CC*—II 693). Cf *TT* (*CC*) II 295. C is reported by HCR as having expressed the essence of this view as early as 1808: see *Lects 1808–1819* (*CC*) I 118–19.

[9] In the notes for his 1808 lects on the principles of poetry C had said of Shakespeare: "he—previously to his Drama—gave proof of a ~~thinking~~ most profound, energetic & philosophical mind, without which he might have been a very delightful Poet, but not the great dramatic Poet/but this he possessed in so eminent a degree that it is to be feared &c &c—if—" (*CN* III 3290 f 16—N 25: Mar 1808—). The unconventional association of Milton and Shakespeare as philosopher-poets had been offered previously as an example of the assertion (in *BL—CC*—II 25–8): "No man was ever yet a great poet, without being at the same time a profound philosopher": ". . . Shakspeare, no mere child of nature; no automaton of genius; no passive vehicle of inspiration possessed by the spirit, not possessing it; first studied patiently, meditated deeply, understood minutely, till knowledge become habitual and intuitive wedded itself to his habitual feelings, and at length gave birth to that stupendous power, by which he stands alone, with no equal or second in his own class; to that power, which seated him on one of the two glory-smitten summits of the poetic mountain, with Milton as his compeer not rival. While the former darts himself forth, and passes into all the forms of human character and passion, the one Proteus of the fire and the flood; the other attracts all forms and things to himself, into the unity of his own IDEAL." For relevant precedents for valuing the relationship of philosophy and poetry see *CN* I 383 (N 21: Jan–May 1799) and *CN* II 2194 (N 21: Sept–Oct 1808).

APPENDIX A
THE FRERE MANUSCRIPT

THE FRERE MANUSCRIPT

VCL MS BT 23

The Frere ms consists of 12 unnumbered booklets of loose leaves that have been gathered together in paper covers and sewn with pink ribbon. Each booklet contains a transcription from the shorthand report of one lect, Lects 1 and 14 being omitted, not having been reported. The texts seem to have been written out as fair copy and contain a number of corrections by the transcribers. The recto and the verso of each folio of the booklets has had a frame or lozenge drawn upon it in brown pencil to provide a margin for the text, and the text was evidently written within the frame, only the rectos of the folios being used. The folios are foliated in pencil in a single sequence from 1 to 643 in the upper right-hand corners of the rectos, and they are "paginated" in ink, booklet by booklet, the numbers being centred below the text of the rectos. There were three transcribers, whose identity remains unknown. Their handwriting is relatively clear and regular, but it is sometimes ambiguous (especially in its capitalisation and punctuation) and it often seems to struggle with their uncertainty about the shorthand text they are expanding, an uncertainty that in turn may be derived from uncertainty about what the shorthand reporter or reporters heard. Hyphens are sometimes omitted from the ends of lines and catchwords are used at the end of each page. Spaces left by the transcribers for passages that had been missed by the reporters are indicated uniformly by three points of ellipsis (. . .); the textual notes to the main text record the varying sizes of these spaces. The text is written throughout in ink, but it has been annotated in pencil. With the exception of a few apparently random pencil marks, the pencilled annotations are recorded in the textual notes; those that are proposed as insertions are so described but are not inserted into the text itself in angle brackets (⟨ ⟩), that device being reserved for insertions by the transcribers. Some of the annotations have been ascribed with a measure of uncertainty to JHG and EHC. For further discussion of the Frere ms see lxviii–lxxii above.

Lect 2. Booklet [2]: in a marbled paper cover, coral in colour, with dark blue veining. The cover is labelled "Lecture | by | S. T. Coleridge Esqr |

28.th Decr 1818". Page size: 21 x 33.3 cm. The booklet contains 56 folios, foliated 1 to 56 and paginated 1 to 56. Transcribers A and B both contribute.

Lect 3. Booklet [3]: in a marbled paper cover, greenish blue in colour, with dark blue veining. The cover is labelled "Mr Coleridge's Lecture | 4.th January 1819". Page size: 20 x 33 cm. The booklet contains 64 folios, foliated 57 to 118 and paginated 1 to 63 (no page having been numbered 53). Transcribers B and C both contribute.

Lect 4. Booklet [4]: in a marbled paper cover, green and yellow in colour. The cover is labelled "Mr Coleridges Lecture | Monday 11th January 1819". Page size: 21 x 33 cm. The booklet contains 53 folios, foliated 119 to 171 and paginated 1 to 53. The hand is Transcriber B's.

Lect 5. Booklet [5]: in a marbled paper cover, pink and dark blue in colour. The cover is labelled "Mr Coleridge's Lecture | 18.th January 1819". Page size: 21 x 33.5 cm. The booklet contains 60 folios, foliated 172 to 231 and paginated 1 to 60 at the bottom centre. The fourth folio is bound out of order after the fifth and sixth (which lacks pagination); the foliation does not record the discrepancy. Transcribers B and C both contribute.

Lect 6. Booklet [6]: in a marbled paper cover, brown and blue in colour. The cover is labelled "Mr Coleridge's | Lecture | Monday 25th January 1819". Page size: 20.5 x 33 cm. The booklet contains 66 folios, foliated 232 to 297 and paginated 1 to 63 (the numbers 37 and 38 having been repeated in the sequence); the foliation is not affected by the discrepancy. The hand is Transcriber B's.

Lect 7. Booklet [7]: in a marbled paper cover, gray and blue in colour. The cover is labelled "Mr Coleridges Lecture | Monday 8th February 1819". Page size: 21 x 33.5 cm. The booklet contains 44 folios, foliated 298 to 341 and paginated 1 to 44. Pages 17 and 18 are misbound and appear between pages 20 and 21; the foliation ignores the discrepancy. The hand is Transcriber B's.

Lect 8. Booklet [8]: in a marbled paper cover, brown in colour with dark blue veining. The cover is labelled "Mr Coleridge's Lecture | Monday February 15th 1819". Page size: 20.5 x 33.5 cm. The booklet contains 38 folios, foliated 342 to 378 and paginated 1 to 37. The final folio being left blank apart from its frame is unfoliated and unpaginated. The hand is Transcriber B's.

Lect 9. Booklet [9]: in a marbled paper cover, gray and red in colour. The cover is labelled "M.ʳ Coleridges Lecture | Monday 22ⁿᵈ February | 1819". Page size: 20.5 x 33.5 cm. The booklet contains 46 folios, foliated 379 to 424 and paginated 1 to 46 (page 21 having been numbered 20, reduplicating the number on the preceding page). The hand is Transcriber B's.

Lect 10. Booklet [10]: in a marbled paper cover, pink and brown in colour with dark blue veining. The cover is labelled "Mʳ Coleridges Lecture | Monday 1ˢᵗ March 1819". Page size 21 x 33 cm. The booklet contains 54 folios, foliated 425 to 478 and paginated 1 to 54. The hand is Transcriber B's.

Lect 11. Booklet [11]: in a marbled paper cover, mauve and brown in colour with dark blue veining. The cover is labelled "M.ʳ Coleridges Lecture | Monday 8 March 1819". Page size: 20.5 x 33.5 cm. The booklet contains 53 folios, foliated 479 to 530 and paginated 1 to 52. The final folio being left blank apart from its frame has been left unfoliated and unpaginated. The hand is Transcriber B's.

Lect 12. Booklet [12]: in a marbled paper cover, coral in colour with dark blue veining. The cover is labelled "M.ʳ Coleridge's Lecture | 15ᵗʰ March | 1819". Page size: 21 x 33 cm. The booklet contains 61 folios, foliated 531 to 591 and paginated 1 to 61. The hand is Transcriber A's.

Lect 13. Booklet [13]: in a marbled paper cover, brown and mauve in colour with dark blue veining. The cover is labelled "M.ʳ Coleridges Lecture | Monday 22.ᵈ March 1819". Page size: 21 x 33 cm. The booklet contains 52 folios, foliated 592 to 643 and paginated 1 to 52. The hand is Transcriber B's.

LECTURE 2

[f 1]   Lecture
                                  by
                          S. T. Coleridge Esqr
                      Monday 28th December 1818

In the ancient world there were two nations that seem particularly to deserve the attention of the historical Critic from their opposition in character, the Hebrew race and the Greek—in the one we find a nation purely
historical and theocratical their history is traced consistently and regularly from the earliest period—all their institutions according to their own
history were derived not from themselves or from any genius arising in
themselves but from a supernatural agency—their very beginning supernatural—their passing into a nation supernatural—their whole Legisla-
ture one with their religion—and this character continues throughout
their whole history to a certain period—intensely bearing the marks of
one family and all their writers attribute their different excellencies not
to any natural faculties but to some especial inspiration so that there does
not even remain a vague tradition in the ancient [f 2] Jewish Writers of
any man whom in our modern phrase we should call a man of genius referring thereby to his natural or acquired advantages—

   On the other hand we find a nation whose ⟨first⟩ historians not to say
their Poets appear with a perfection that has been a model for all succeeding times—and yet strange to say those very men appear about as
much perplexed concerning their origin as we at this present time do and
in the various criticisms concerning the planting of Greece each position
has its own and almost equal authorities or what is still more common the
authority of the same writer brought against himself—but in this nation
we find after a certain period every perfection appearing to rise out of the
people and out of their circumstances—I do not mean to say as the Athenians said of themselves when they called themselves Grass-hoppers that
they were born out of the earth—Undoubtedly they derived their instruction or rather the stimulants to it and the excitements of it from various causes but still as soon as it came into Greece it became so modified
so extremely altered by the character of the people [f 3] that it required

622

all the researches of the learned to discover the affinity between the Greek opinions and their immediate sources whatever they were.—

One cannot help thinking provided the mind is before hand impressed with a belief of a providence guiding this great drama of the world to its conclusion that as opposites are in constant tendency to union and as it is the opposite poles of a magnet and not the similar ones which attract each other that a certain unity is to be expected from the very circumstance of opposition and that these are as it were imperfect halves which after a series of ages each maturing and perfecting are at length to meet in some one point comprising the excellencies of both.

We know in truth—when I say know I use the word in the sense of sound history, we cannot be said to know anything of Greece before the writings of Homer but these themselves are our history it is true that Thucydides and Herodotus the earliest historians of the Greeks speak of those poems as written by one man called Homer but it is equally true that Thucydides [f 4] attributes the Iliad[a] so called to the same person which I believe there is not now a scholar in Europe that supposes to have been possible to belong to the same period. This however would not interest us much upon the present occasion were it not for a passage in Herodotus which declares speaking of the earliest Colony of the Greeks that Greece seems to have been gradually peopled by a conflux of tribes but as far as we can discover tribes of the same race which is concluded from this circumstance only that the Conquerors or those that came latest introduced no order of Nobility made no distinction between themselves and those they had conquered a clear proof that they had the same language and some marks at least of the same origination for in all Countries in Europe a Nobility may be traced to the circumstance originally of a conquered Nation the conquerors assuming to themselves[b] certain superiority of course but contriving certain distinctions from the natural love of the Country they had left to be known by it to all ages afterwards—such is the case with Poland, such manifestly the case in Hungary and so it appears [f 5] to have been in our own Country—From no such circumstance having taken place in Greece though it is evident that there were wave after wave of new Colonists into Greece it seems equally clear that they were of the same origin—

Herodotus has observed that the[c] the first race to whom he refers knew no Gods by name but secretly acknowledged the Gods whom in their lan-

---

[a] "Iliad" crossed out in pencil and "Hymns" inserted in a different hand. "Iliad" occupies space too large for it and the writing seems to have been inserted later

[b] "a" written in pencil above space between "themselves" and "certain"

[c] "Pelasgians" inserted in pencil, in space left for word of that size

guage they so called because they were the arrangers those that brought every thing into the world and the separaters of things but that in after time persons came among them who spoke of other Gods whom they rejected and lastly of the God Dionysius or Bacchus upon which they were advised to consult the Oracle of Dodona which appears from plain proof to have been brought at least from Egypt and being asked whether or no they should worship their Gods by any particular names They were answered in the affirmative and he says from that time the Greeks began to call their Gods by name but adds immediately afterwards that their theogony and Mythology as it existed in his time was first brought in by Hesiod and by Homer I think I may venture to appeal [f 6] to the natural sense of every man whether or no in such an age and with such difficult means of communication it was possible for any two poets (poets generally not being the most active sort of people in the world) to alter at once the whole religion of a people not residing in any one place but scattered over the Islands of Greece and over the Provinces of Minor Asia—though I profess myself perfectly sceptical neither decided to the one side nor the other of the great controversy concerning whether the Iliad of Homer was a Poem written by one man or whether it is a choice of an immense number of poems written upon the same subject strung together by Pisistratus or some other in the same manner though with a worthier motive than Macpherson strung together a number of Scotch poems and called it the Epic poem of Temora but I can see no probability of the Homer being a particular person rather what is already hazarded respecting Orpheus and Musæus and so forth I should say it implied a fraternity of men who had wandered through the Countries and by the charms of music and whatever else could work upon the minds of a rude [f 7] people gradually introduced those traditions or this properly speaking poetic and sensuous mode of propagating truths which Herodotus attributes to Homer—Be it so—we know well that the antiquity of Homer's Poems was such as completely to perplex the first historical investigators of Greece

The question then is at what time the Mysteries ~~histories~~ *d* were formed—I will not deny that many and great authorities of the moderns are inclined to suppose that the earliest of the mysteries those of Samo-

---

d Blank space left for a word between "the" and "~~histories~~", perhaps for missed adjective modifying "histories". "Mysteries" seems to have been inserted and perhaps "histories" then cancelled. Facing page, in pencil (probably in the hand of JHG): The Mysteries of Samothrace appear to be a relic of the Orphic Institutions in Thrace—Samothrace was the Mona of the Orphic Druids and seemed by its similar situation from the Revolution which accompanied the introduction of the Bacchic Rites a Revolution which extended over the whole Northern Continent from Thrace to Thebes— | tecting Penthia | Disjecta nos lini mina | Thracis et imperium Lycurgi | at Athens there are the evident traces of a compromise— (see Ouvaroff) by which the Bacchic rites were *engrafted upon* ⟨superadded to⟩ those of Ceres

thrace[e] were anterior to Homer or at least contemporary with him but I confess I have never discovered any sufficient proof on the contrary it appears to me clear that the very purpose of those mysteries, the very interest which they excited in the minds of thinking men was that of counteracting this popular theology which afterwards the Philosophers without exception opposed and as considering it entirely destructive of all morality.

Here permit me to notice the tendency of a number of writings of men deserving of all veneration especially on the Continent to justify this Idolatry—They consider it as they say as the natural and [f 8] the best possible means of representing important truths to the minds of an ignorant people—how it is said could these ignorant people understand abstract truths—how is it possible that it could be done but by cloathing them in forms of sight and sound and in short variously symbolizing them to their senses and apprehensions in short it is the old papistical argument of pictures and images poor mens books—certainly if the matter were really so—if this was a right and proper mode of instructing mankind and if its effects were those of progression that by these means they would gradually become capable of less gross images and then of more ⟨and more⟩ generalization till at last they rose to correct ideas of what they were and whence they were and what was to become of them—we must think it strange that in our own religion from the very beginning to the thunders of Sinai and to the more efficient promises rather than maledictions of the Christian religion this one object should be constantly in view to overthrow this as the source of every thing that is wicked and every thing that is degrading and strange it is that such men as . . .[f] and other men of whose learning [f 9] I speak with the highest honor and reverence should not have asked themselves what came of this—did any progression take place—take Egypt[g] did it follow that the Egyptian people from observing and worshipping a Deity according to their account in Ibis's—in crocodiles and in the Nile and so forth rose lastly to consider the whole world as a kind of language—as the painted vale[h] of Isis in which the Almighty was speaking to them—History shews to us the contrary—Juvenal tells us of the wars between the . . . Gods and the . . . Gods[i] and shews us as the Bible indeed has done with higher authority all the sensuality that followed—need we wonder that sensuality should follow

---

[e] "Simo", at end of line, altered in pencil to "Samo-"

[f] Blank space left at end of line and beginning of next. "Creuzer" pencilled into one, perhaps in the hand of EHC, the other left blank

[g] Comma inserted in different ink, rather carelessly written

[h] Corrected in pencil to "veil"

[i] Spaces left for missing adjectives. On opposite page in pencil, annotation, probably by EHC: ? per XIII 41

from directly appealing to the senses and instead of weaning man from that which was his fall^j gradually strengthening it^k and upon the same pretext—^{l}I am afraid lest the illustration that now occurs to me should be too light for the subject^m but it is really such^n as^o the old story of the man who being extremely weary on the road got up at the back of a Coach and being told it was going the direct contrary way over the same ground he had already gone said "however I shall be rested [f 10] during the time"— most assuredly all this is utterly vain the true origin ^{p}and I mention this because it is quite necessary for the understanding both of the rise and of the necessity of Philosophy in the Pagan world—^{q} the true cause seems to have been this that very early in ⟨the history of⟩ mankind there seems to have been a division among them—the one attending more to their moral feelings^r and to the manifest good consequences of it in the world yielded to the traditions of their ancestors and found themselves happy— the^s opinions were perfectly congruous with their moral feelings and the great character of that people was that they made their hearts the interpreters of their hands^t—To know that a thing was right and congruous to their moral nature they held as the evidence of its truth and this by a most excellent logic for unless they supposed themselves to be either infinite in one extreme or beasts in the other they must believe themselves to be progressive but whatever is progressive must have a dim horizon as well as a clear vicinity and what truth has more right to be obscure to us than that which [f 11] when we arrive at will be the very perfection of our being and in the bold phrase of antiquity our union with the Author of that being—

The other race determined that their imagination^u as the Scriptures properly call it^v but which they deemed their understanding or their reason should be the judge of all things^w and rejecting the traditions of their ancestors and history, they followed the natural leadings of the imagina-

---

^{j} Comma inserted in pencil

^{k} Comma inserted in pencil

^{l} Opening parenthesis inserted in pencil

^{m} Pencilled closing parenthesis inserted and then crossed out

^{n} Closing parenthesis inserted in pencil and then crossed out

^{o} Overwritten boldly in pencil "as", inserted pencilled closing parenthesis having partly obscured word

$^{p-q}$ Pencilled parentheses inserted

^{r} Altered in pencil to "feeling"

^{s} Altered in pencil to "their"

^{t} Altered in pencil to "heads", probably in the hand of JHG, and in the margin a pencil "q" (for "query"?), possibly in the hand of EHC

^{u} Comma inserted in pencil

^{v} Comma inserted in pencil

^{w} Comma inserted in pencil

tion or fancy governed by the law of association.—they^x were themselves alive and that they knew though they did not understand the mode—they moved in consequence of that life and acted—wherever therefore they saw motion they supposed that in some way or other there was a vital or motive [f 12] power and denying all else but the very law of mind by which we must necessarily generalize ^{y}that is when we look at an immense number of things be impressed by that which is common to them all rather than by that which is particular to any one^z—they conceived that the whole world—every thing, must have a motive power—when they contemplated this motive power with regard to particular individuals they called it soul—if with ⟨reference to⟩ anything which occupied a large importance and comprehended many souls they would call it a God but when they raised their senseous^a imagination to the utmost and conceived the indefinite idea of an All they carried on the same analogy and the All was God: and this I am sorry to say has imposed upon many thinkers in modern times as if it were the all things and God of the Christian, whereas in truth it was nothing more than a common feeling,^{b} as I move in consequence of having life^c so in another way the tree shoot^d out, the rivers flow and so forth^e and what is true of each part must be true of the whole—^{f} but with regard to any conscience any of those attributes which properly form a religion^g so far from that being felt the very contrary was felt^h it was in truth made by a tremendous blasphemy the cause of all evil—The thing would be well^i it was said^j but there was such a necessary intractability of matter that many things could not be [f 13] reconciled^k and at length came that curious notion which seems to have originated all^l without exception^m of the Theogenes^n or Theologies of the Pagan Nations^o that good came out of evil^p the better out of the worse—

^{x} Altered in pencil to "They"
$^{y-z}$ Pencilled parentheses inserted
^{a} Corrected in pencil to "sensuous"
^{b} Comma crossed out in pencil
^{c} Comma inserted in pencil
^{d} Corrected in pencil to "shoots"
^{e} Comma inserted in pencil
^{f} Full stop or dash inserted in pencil
^{g} Comma inserted in pencil
^{h} Full stop inserted in pencil and "it" altered to "It" in pencil
^{i} Comma inserted in pencil
^{j} Comma inserted in pencil
^{k} Comma inserted in pencil
^{l} Comma inserted in pencil
^{m} Comma inserted in pencil
^{n} Altered in pencil to "Theogenies"
^{o} Comma inserted in pencil
^{p} Comma inserted in pencil

at first it was all night and chaos—then in the course of things by a strange unintelligible fatality, *q*but something must be unintelligible when men put down that*r* the mere nature of the intellect which arises from a far grander source—the depth, the unfathomable depth of the will*s*, this was to bring forth an egg which brought forth love or the organising power*t* and then love produced hatred a very strange thing certainly*u* and then these two points by constantly intermingling and balancing each other produced a long series of times*v* out of which the world existed—this*w* is not the Greek Theology merely*x* it is a fair account of the Egyptian of the Indian [f 14] and of every other, but I speak of Greece because it was the only Country that dared ask itself why—all the other Countries as the Jews for instance had received that which they held by admission of a revelation and all the Nations besides Greece that we know of had received their constitutions and their opinions either by conquest or by imposture*y* that is by pretence to revelation—the Greeks alone stood by themselves and having first out of limited monarchies or rather monarchies by tradition formed themselves *z*there is here a gap in history out of what monarchies*a* but*b* so the fact is*c* having formed themselves at once simultaneously as it were into Republics—*d*and this not in one part of Greece merely but nearly at the same time in all parts of the Peloponnesus and Major and Minor Greece*e* so that the same men who derived their power not from the people who were the representatives of the reason*f* were designated [f 15] as Tyrants and however beneficent in their conduct did not still escape a certain mark of infamy

In Greece, legislation was the first step towards philosophy or rather it was the first dawning or appearance of it—after Lycurgus came Solon and others and then arose Thales—I have stated before that I did not con-

---

q–s Parentheses inserted in pencil. In right-hand margin, in pencil, probably in the hand of JHG: a very long note is wanted here—

r "as" inserted above line in pencil, between "that" and "the". In right-hand margin appears pencilled "?"

t Comma inserted in pencil
u Comma inserted in pencil
v Altered to "q atoms" in pencil (for "query atoms")
w Altered to "This" in pencil
x Comma inserted in pencil
y Dash inserted in pencil
z–a Parentheses inserted in pencil
b Comma inserted in pencil
c Comma inserted in pencil
d Comma inserted in pencil and dash obliterated in pencil
e Comma inserted in pencil
f "of the reason" underlined in pencil; faint pencilled question-mark appears in right-hand margin

sider Thales as the Ancients did not properly a Philosopher—they called him sophos a wise man and placed him at the head of the seven wise men of Greece who however according to another tradition reduced themselves to three[g] two Tyrants it appears having frightened them into acknowledging them among their order—In these we find I think three characteristics—there is an extreme wicked[h] hilarity—I do not know what to call it[i] more they seem to be like a cheerful man placed among those whom he could not bring up to himself [f 16] and who was content to live quietly and happily among them and to give what knowledge he could—but if you take the coarsest comparisons as given by Stanley and others in their account of their sayings and anecdotes there is one characteristic of uncommon cheerfulness with occasionally a disguised sneer at the superstitions of the people—In another sense they appear to have been men religious according to the best notions of their Countrymen, their[j] morals are pure but all bordering on the prudential never referring to the principle in the heart but always referring to the consequences in short I think that almost every rule of prudence in life may be collected from the sayings attributed to the seven sages I think if I mistake not that I have made a note of a few of them—

[f 17]   Psittacus[k]—"Power shews the man"—[l]what is best[m]—to do the present well.[n]

Thales—"what is the strangest thing?—a Tyrant of a tolerably good old age—"what is the happiest Ruler? him for and not whom the Subjects are afraid. So Bias answered to a man who had proposed to him to drink up the sea—"with all my heart if you on your part will promise to stop up the rivers while I am doing it"[o]—To rascals who were praying during a storm "for mercy sake be quiet—why should you put the Gods in mind of you we are bad enough already"—I mention these instances of that sort of witty character which belongs to them—To a rogue asking concerning wisdom and piety he was silent and being asked why he did not speak he said "hold your tongue—it is no matter to you"[p]—So "bet-

---

[g] Altered in pencil to "q 5," (for "query 5")

[h] "wicked" crossed out in pencil and "q" (for "query") pencilled into left-hand margin

[i] Comma inserted in pencil

[j] Altered in pencil to "Their" and preceded by pencilled inserted comma

[k] Altered in pencil to "Pittacus"

[l] Opening quotation-mark inserted in pencil

[m] Question-mark inserted in pencil

[n] Closing quotation-mark inserted in pencil

[o] Pencilled vertical line in right-hand margin beside this answer and query sign, with below it, in pencil, probably in the hand of JHG, "dele" (for "delete"?)

[p] Last six words of answer crossed out in pencil; inserted in pencil above them, probably in the hand of JHG: they are things that you have no concern in

ter to decide a quarrel between enemies than friends for in the latter case you [f 18] are sure to make one friend an enemy whereas in the other case you may possibly make one enemy a friend"—this[q] is strongly the character of the homeric Ulysses—where the shrewdness of cunning is placed for what should have been morality—but throughout in the character of the Homeric Ulysses you find a shrewdness and reference to consequences—so[r] "a good Republic it is better to fear the Laws and not the Rulers[s] or according to another tradition to love your Country or[t] the Magistrates but fear the Law alone[u] and in that law your own conscience

Cleobulus "Oh beware of the calumny of friends never mind what your enemy says—never be tempted to join in the laugh of derision"—Periander when he was asked what was the best ⟨Government⟩ said "that Democracy which comes nearest to an Aristocracy"—

[f 19]   [v]Anacharsis says artists contend that—which is very strange that those who are no artists at all and know nothing about art are best able to determine—I give these specimens of the character to show that it was so far from Philosophic that is getting to the origin and principle of things that it was what we should naturally expect from men of a sound and healthful mind and quick observation of what was before them in life and a facility in generalising it and deducing the wisest remarks

Thales by the admission of all Antiquity was the first who even in Physics even in natural Philosophy instead of resting with traditions asked himself what could have been the origin of things but I do not give him the name of a Philosopher because his enquiries such as they were were confined wholly to material causes and this is to be observed that Aristotle himself in speaking of Thales and those of his time has said ⟨that⟩ they confined themselves wholly to material elements while Plutarch condemns them[w] for having mistaken principles as to the true origin [f 20] of things for elements or those first materials which appear in consequence still[x] however the step was great for that Thales learnt this from Egypt and so forth I regard as mere fancy[y] the mere jargon of the later Platonists[z] and for this plain reason that the causes assigned for in-

---

[q] Altered in pencil to "This"
[r] Altered in pencil to "So in" with pencilled caret of insertion and query mark in right-hand margin
[s] Semi-colon inserted in pencil
[t] "or" altered in pencil to "to honor", the "to" being very faint
[u] Comma inserted in pencil
[v] Hand changes to that of Transcriber B; a vertical line is pencilled in left-hand margin beside first four lines
[w] Pencilled in margin, probably in the hand of JHG: note & quotation wanted
[x] Altered in pencil to "Still"
[y] Comma inserted in pencil
[z] Comma inserted in pencil

stance why he made water the origin of things has nothing in it historical—nothing historical—nothing that reminds one of the books of the Indians or the fragments of the Babylonians which we have—no he gives
you the first reasons as we should say or experiments or observations
which any man would be struck with—he says[a] while we see that all
things begin in a sort of fluid state we perceive that water nourishes all
things and that such and such plants though fed only with water will yet
grow[b] and[c] no wonder[d] that in that state of Science not knowing the composition of water and little knowing how many things [f 21] might be contained in it that when he saw things growing in water he supposed that it
passed into earth and produced all things and so forth—[e]no wonder that
when he had dared separate himself from tradition he should yet be able
to go no further Those are the very reasons which are assigned by Thales
without the least traditional or historical Character whatsoever for the last
and all the other things which are found in him amount to nothing more
than this that he was a very worthy good man who believed the religion
of his Country in the best form in which it appeared and thought no more
about it but most assuredly combined it with his philosophy as Linnæus
and John Hunter may be supposed to have done the one with physiology
and the other with natural history—The [f 22] disciples of Thales made
one advance still further going[f] onwards they perceived that no one element no phenomenon nothing visible could be the cause the[g] visibility
there must be certainly something unseen to be the cause of something
seen[h] for this reason that you were no wiser than if you attributed the thing
to water—then the question would arise what is water and so ad infinitum and though you went on as some moderns would do

> Fleas bite little Dogs and less fleas bite them
> And so you go on *ad infinitum*[i]

it is merely pushing off the thing under the sophism of something less till
you have wearied out the man[j] and then say [k]well Sir we must stop here

---

[a] Comma inserted in pencil
[b] Comma inserted in pencil
[c] Comma inserted in pencil
[d] Comma inserted in pencil
[e] Dash partly overwritten by "no"
[f] Altered in pencil to "further. Going"
[g] "of" inserted in pencil above line between "cause" and "the" and pencilled query mark in right-hand margin
[h] Semi-colon inserted in pencil
[i] Vertical pencil line drawn to the right of these lines, and in margin, also in pencil, prob-ably in the hand of JHG, query mark and very faintly ["delete"]
[j] Comma inserted in pencil
[k] Opening quotation-marks inserted in pencil

for we cannot go further not that we are one whit nearer the point than we were before"—this*l* appears to have been the case with the man who endeavoured to resolve this into the distinguishable and indistinguishable [f 23] the*m* only thing that he could discover was that fluid was somewhat the parts*n* of which could not be distinguished by figures, ⟨it was something that had no figure⟩ of its own but constantly took that which the vessel in which it was contained or the banks impressed upon it—from this he divided things into two the distinguishable and the indistinguishable or as he called it the finite and the infinite but apparently a man staggering with a new idea and relapsing*o* of which we have had some later instances even in the works of John Hunter of a man having an idea *p*greater than the sum total of his intellectual knowledge or that of his age was equal to*q* presenting it with a flash and again falling down to the common feeling of his Country or like a bird that having been limed as it were upon a hedge or twigs by more than usual force of genius gets himself loose [f 24] and yet still feels the lime hanging on its wings and with a sort of imperfect flutter and fright drops and again tries to rise*r* and produces that which for the world is a glorious light but for dull men a matter of endless difference of opinion and of controversy

These ideas as far as they were speculative I have introduced as the dawning of philosophy—as far as they did not refer to the mind at all but were sought only in observation I consider the authors of them as not yet Philosophers—the man to whom the name seems due first of all was Pythagoras something like one of the most extraordinary human beings that has ever astonished and perplexed the world—As to the Oracles which announced his birth I mention them only as shewing the great sensation he produced upon posterity more so more*s* striking because it is not certain that he ever himself wrote any thing and that even [f 25] what his opinions were was already matter of almost as much obscurity in the time of Plato and Aristotle as it is in the time in which we live—Now there must have been something extraordinary in that man who has filled the world with his fame in such a way that no man who has read is not familiar with the name of Pythagoras—he*t* was born according to the best

---

l "before—this" altered in pencil to "before'—This"

m "able" of "indistinguishable" on f 22 used as catchword, but entire word repeated at beginning of f 23; "indistinguishable the" altered in pencil to "indistinguishable. The"

n Pencilled question-mark in left-hand margin directed probably at "parts" which could be mistaken for "pacts"

o Comma inserted in pencil

p-q Parentheses inserted in pencil

r Comma inserted in pencil

s Altered in pencil to "⟨the⟩ more so ⟨the⟩ more"

t Altered in pencil to "He"

accounts at Samos under particular advantages as for instance that he was a man of wealth that it was in a Town then extremely thriving as a commercial Town—that he had early opportunities of conversing with Mariners and of course early took in the desire of seeing more than a [? narrow] Island could produce to him What his travels were is a subject of controversy on which I know no better canon of criticism than this that where there is a general tradition and there is neither impossibility nor improbability in the circumstance that we ought to believe it [f 26] upon the plan of the law Courts it is the best evidence we have I therefore do not doubt that Pythagoras went to Egypt and I can see no reason why from Egypt under the troubles of that time he might not have gone to Babylon and when I have told my authority that Prince of English solid good sense Selden I can venture to say that I see neither in the chronology nor any other circumstance any one reason to object to his having been at Babylon in the time of the Prophet Ezekiel except that I must honestly add that I have not any one reason for it—but according to the tradition which it has been latterly fashionable to deny for what reason I know not. to those who admit that he was in Egypt that he went through Persia to India I concede for I conceive it may be somewhat to concede that I have discovered what I may call a presumptive argument for in[u] the Pythagorean doctrine with respect to[v] all of which except the first principles of it [f 27] I profess not to understand what has been recorded by the latest Platonists—Pythagoras held that there were ten bodies or kinds of bodies in the Universe according to the common interpretation the planets then known—the moon—the Sun the Comets and so forth but these unfortunately made up but nine in consequence of which he made up a tenth to complete the ten which he called an Antitheton or counter earth and its invisibility to us he ascribed to its being always on the directly opposite side of the World from the Sun as he held the doctrine of the Centrality of the Sun and the motion of the Planets round it—it is said this Antitheton or Counter earth was in direct opposition always to our earth and consequently always invisible to it

The common doctrine of Pythagoras that is of the metempsychosis or wandering of Souls from one body to another we all know—but it is very striking that Colonel Sims who went into Burman and who [f 28] in his travels never appears to have had any thought of Pythagoras or Pythagorean Philosophy in his mind when the circumstance that the Burmans together with the transmigration of souls and the abhorrence of particular kinds of food particularly beans hold ten bodies and in order to

---

[u] Altered in pencil to "⟨in⟩ in the"
[v] Indecipherable pencilled insertion appears above "to all"—short word such as "its"?

make out the number they hold a sort of shadow earth that was almost opposite so that it could never be seen but it is likewise mentioned by Laertius of Pythagoras that he brought in an explanation of the eclipses this is certainly a most singular circumstance With regard to the transmigration of souls we may suppose it was a common feeling spread through many nations but the peculiar circumstance of this counter earth joined with such a number of Pythagorean Doctrines not found in Hindostan tends I think to prove two things first of all that what the Burmans say is true that the Religion of Buddha which they profess and which has no Castes at least no compulsory ones which tend to stop the [f 29] progression of mankind and to make man degraded and unprogressive (I refer to the system of castes and so forth) was the original and that the others are derived from them—As it would be absurd to suppose that Pythagoras really passed down into Siam and Ava and so forth I apprehend that their account is true that such as they are the original inhabitants of Hindostan were and that the castes of India and the other institutions prevailing there are the natural effect of a comparatively civilised people being conquered as the Indians in the Peninsula appear to have been repeatedly by men more warlike but less civilised and contriving every scheme possible to preserve the civilisation ⟨existing⟩ among themselves from being overwhelmed by conquests for[w] instance Herodotus tells us there were castes in Egypt but that they[x] were after the race of the woolly haired men—it appears as if they were over run by some conqueror and history records such events and the account of Herodotus that the ancient Egyptians were woolly haired men is a convincing proof that they were over run by another nation and that the attempts of [f 30] Priests and Leaders to preserve their arts and sciences founded the institution of Castes in which a man was compelled to teach his child his own art and that Son was compelled to follow it certainly a mode of arresting Barbarism to a certain extent but when carried beyond that tending to evil

The very different character of the Laws in Birman with regard to the Priesthood where there are none of those ferocious institutions raising up one body of men above another and punishing the least insult in the most inhuman manner present the Idea of a Nation not conquered when a nation is conquered it is no longer a matter of Government or established power whether you shall respect your Priest or your Teacher but it is left

[w] Altered in pencil to "conquests. For". On facing page pencilled, probably in the hand of JHG: It will appear I think a very bold assumption to infer from such slender premises that the establishment of Castes in India was posterior to the time of Pythagoras

[x] Small pencilled "x" at this point, and in right-hand margin pencilled "q the passage" (for query or quote the passage?)

entirely to your sensibility or sense of honor in all such Countries the Priests have become powerful.[y] I hope I may say this for a Philosophical purpose—it is seen throughout Europe in Catholic Countries on the Continent the more powerful people take part rather with the Government than with the Priesthood—they enter warmly into the feelings of Government to Check the presumption of the Priesthood on [f 31] the same ground that all our Ancestors before the Reformation were as anti-papistic as the best Protestant is in these days and they were as eager to join with the Government to prevent any encroachment by the Priesthood but where it becomes a matter of choice it becomes a matter of honor and the Catholics are most bigotted and adhere to the greatest extravagances of their system in that Country in which the Government happens to be Protestant—In all countries a conquest checks the power of the Priesthood[z] and upon that ground I consider it extremely probable that Pythagoras among his travels really had been in India—however this is but of comparatively little importance compared with his philosophical efforts and which he displayed assuredly after his return first he left [a]it is said[b] his native Country on account of the tyranny of Polycrates not that he so much disliked being under Polycrates who was a mild and wise Governor though not by the choice of the people but because he saw that there would be factions [f 32] and Revolutions inconsistent with his purpose and he transplanted himself to the South of Italy then called Magna Græca afterwards called Groto[c] and there he began to develope the great plans he had conceived during his travels

The mode in which he did it is certainly most exemplary—he first addressed himself to the people of all classes to the highest first with regard to their Morals and used every possible persuasion with great eloquence and (what all tradition agrees in) a remarkably beautiful and majestic person which joined to that greatest of all possible influences the evident palpable disinterestedness of the man enabled him to bring about a reform in their conduct and to convince them of the miseries they suffered not from badness or wickedness but from the real state of ignorance that precluded the opening of any better.[d] After having made himself popular as all disinterested men that speak to the heart of man are sure to do he then

---

[y] Last four words underlined in pencil. Pencilled, probably in the hand of JHG, on facing page: on such points it is difficult to generalize the priesthood in England were sufficiently powerful before the conquest—the proposition as it stands seems exclusive

[z] Pencilled, probably in the hand of JHG, in right-hand margin: something seems wanting in the chain of argument Here

[a-b] Parentheses inserted in pencil

[c] Corrected in pencil to "Croton", perhaps in EHC's hand

[d] Pencilled query mark inserted

opened a plan of education It appears that he was requested [f 33] by the people to give them constitutions but instead of that he told them that those things were perfectly indifferent in their state—he should make no alteration in Constitutions for that if they were ignorant and incapable of self government they must have Government in some way and if the men who governed them were no better than themselves they must be miserable—that for fools to chuse wise men and vicious men to choose virtuous ones or the majority of men to chuse the man to govern them was so opposite to nature and to the experience of all who know the manner in which fathers govern their children men govern beasts and to the fact that the herd does not choose its Shepherd and so forth that he utterly rejected this idea as factious and one that would ultimately reduce their Country to ruin and Slavery

The great object was to begin with the highest and to educate them and on this he opened an institution the purpose of which was to educate all that were well disposed who felt a craving *e*for that is the best beginning of every thing to feel ourselves dissatisfied with [f 34] what we are*f* all that felt a wish to be something more and that conjoined with a sense of duty were invited to come to him—it appears that it became the fashion but of the multitude of Candidates he chose those only whom his observation in life which gives to many men a physiognomic power had selected and those he arranged into different classes still beginning with the moral character—The first thing was to instruct them in the Government of their appetites next in the Government of their understandings by silence thirdly in the government of their wills and after they had passed through this severe probation then he communicated to them those truths concerning nature and their future destination which he himself possessed still directing all to the purposes of beneficence and of acting immediately upon their fellow Citizens who had not been perhaps capable of this species of education but it was amongst the great Pythagorean symbols so to convey truth in part as that it might make the mind [f 35] susceptible hereafter of another portion—to tell truth but so at the same time to convey it as to prepare the mind for greater truths was the grand maxim of what may be called moral politics

Happy perhaps it may appear that it would have been for mankind had this prospered that ⟨in⟩ one point of view it deserved to prosper is evident from this that by the tradition of all antiquity those who remained after its violent subversion were attached to each other beyond the love of brothers but like all secret bands all secret associations it carried its own

---

e–f Parentheses inserted in pencil

poison with ⟨it⟩ it embraced too many things or rather two things incongruous—the one was that of preparing a man to be governed the other that of governing but the ultimate object which indeed spread to a great extent at that time as it appears through Magna Græca (so that from the Pythagorean band all the Cities took all their Majistrates and so forth) naturally placed that object first—still there was the practical view at a time when the speculative view or the practical view each singly might have been effectual but both [f 36] combined they were incompatible with each other and doubtless one of the causes of the sudden destruction of the Pythagorean band under such amiable auspices as it began was that politics were at the head—The question was what is to be done in this City and what in that City and beneficent and benevolent as this was it took the men out of their proper place namely that of working on*g* not for the present time but*h* as a humble component part of a system that was to extend to all times*i* of course its prosperity brought about its fall*j* the more honorable it was to be a Pythagorean the more competitors there were for it among those men who were rejected some probably wise men*k* others perhaps unwise men*l* some were made Enemies*m* that was the manifest influence though no constituted power ⟨no positive power⟩ was pretended to*n* yet it was more odious for that very reason it was a something behind the Throne (to use one of our own English phrases) and it was in the power of any demagogue to rouse [f 37] the people at any particular time of discontent and the greater part of them were murdered *o*and according to the best reports Pythagoras himself*p* in the Insurrection against them—

There is one point more in Pythagoras's character before I proceed to those doctrines worthy noticing—We hear of Thales Theocritus Anaxander*q* and Simonides*r* Contemporaries of Pythagoras but we hear of nothing miraculous about them whereas of Pythagoras the accounts are full of miracles that he worked—he was a Prophet he was one born of the Gods and himself a God—this is certainly a remarkable feature I have subtracted from all those accounts every thing that is found in the lower

---

g Comma inserted in pencil
h Comma inserted in pencil
i Semi-colon inserted in pencil
j Comma inserted in pencil
k Comma inserted in pencil
l Comma inserted in pencil
m Comma inserted in pencil
n Comma inserted in pencil
o-p Parentheses inserted in pencil
q Corrected in pencil to "Anaximander", probably in the hand of EHC
r "Simonides" cancelled in pencil and "q Anaximenes" written above it (for "query Anaximenes"?), probably in the hand of EHC

Platonists—they wanted to set up a man against our Saviour no matter where they found him—they brought together all sorts of tales to shew that one of their Philosophers had had inspiration had had communication with the Deity and was capable of attesting it by miracles—all this I [f 38] put for nothing but there does appear from Aristotle from Plato and what we should call grave Writers sufficient evidence that the tradition^s in their time was of numerous miracles worked by Pythagoras and by him communicated to Epaminondas^t and others.

With respect to the miracles which have been stated it requires perhaps almost an apology to enter into the question except to determine whether Pythagoras had a spice of the impostor and the Mountebank which would be no great wonder recollecting what we have heard as to the founders of Alchemy but in the accounts there is something so very congruous with late facts which have come forwards and the admission of the thing would explain so many things in ancient history without recourse to that which is very undesirable saying "Oh it is a lie—it is an untruth and so on that I cannot help mentioning it—If it were possible for a man of sense to believe . . ."^{u} the supposed discoverer of Animal Magnetism one tittle^v beyond what his assertions have been attested and accredited by such men as Cuvier Blümenburg Hoffer Ryve^w and many others [f 39] of those great men most of whom gave the best test certainly of their sincerity by having opposed it publicly and privately for so many years with the greatest zeal in their publications lectures and so on but who as you may find in the last edition of the text book of all the authors in Europe have made three distinct recantations of their former writings that though it is to the stupor of all physiology though contradicted by all our theoretical opinions before yet the facts are as undeniable as they are surprising—

Those facts as you all well know consist in this that one human being has the power of acting upon another under certain conditions by the power of the will assisted by certain gesticulations—Now it is certainly—I speak not as a man who has been a witness in any way but as an historical critic that is most assuredly a fact—men who would be believed in every other matter such men as Cuvier Blümenberg Ryve and others have asserted things and given details which so precisely resemble the accounts stated by the [f 40] ancient priesthood of the manner in which the persons that went to the Oracles were acted upon such as being

---

^{s} "tradition" appears to replace an erased word
^{t} Altered in pencil to "Epimenides"
^{u} Space left in ms; "Mesmer" pencilled in, perhaps in EHC's hand
^{v} Uncrossed first "t" of "tittle" completed in pencil
^{w} "Hufeland" written below line in bottom margin and question-mark above it, both in pencil, perhaps in EHC's hand

wrapped in medicated skins exposed to certain gases from the earth and in various ways particularly in one part of Plato thrown by the power of others by motions into a state of sleep in which sleep they returned answers and those answers were afterwards collected and reported to them when they awoke as prophecies joined with the circumstance that the first magnetisers who appear to have been discontented unless they had carried it to the highest extreme brought about in too many (which has indeed occasioned laws in Germany) instances of melancholy and madness during life this may be compared with the Greek proverb that when a man was seen moody and melancholy it was said "surely you have been in the cave of Trophonius and have been in the charmed sleep there" I mention it not in any degree as of perfect [f 41] conviction but as deserving of our attention more than it has hitherto received particularly as in the miracles ascribed to Pythagoras supposing these things to be true there is scarcely one of them that would not admit an easy explanation—Now as according to Philodemus such things were taught in the mysteries—as Philodemus's account of the mysteries in Egypt corresponds exactly *though they were never understood before* to the statement of the facts that have been made recently it does appear to me not improbable that Pythagoras who went as it appears to all these oracles every where had for his object the acquirement of those powers—whether trick whether powers of acting upon the imagination I will not decide but only this that if facts we all admit be true and if they be referable to the imagination the imagination is an extraordinary power and very well worth looking into

[f 42]   *But now for Pythagoras as a Philosopher—we have seen him as a moralist and as an Educator—what then entitled him to be distinguished from the great men of Egypt and India and those before him, this plainly, that he went back into the reason of man* and that his first principle was that that which was in part the effect certainly of other circumstances could never contain pure truth or be the cause of them—he saw clearly that objects at a distance were different from objects that were near he perceived very well that what he called the outward object was in part the product of his own mind and the natural and common phenomenon of dreams joined with the morbid phenomenon of fever and delirium still brought further conviction that there must be a principle in the mind productive of these things or a third principle balancing them and producing a common third by meeting together he appears to have been the first who had proposed this problem distinctly to himself who sought in his own mind for the Laws of the universe and [f 43] without entertaining or rather

---

x–y Parentheses inserted in pencil   *z* Transcriber A resumes
a "man" underlined in pencil

~~or rather~~ distressing you with an account of Pythagorean numbers and
harmonies it will be sufficient to state this one thing as the introduction
to all the Philosophers that he began that position the carrying on of which
by Plato and the division or schism from which by Aristotle constituted
the two classes of Philosophers or rather of Philosophy which remain to
this day and if we were to live a thousand or ten thousand years ever
would remain, for in this it consists—I do not look on Materialism on the
doctrine of atoms as Philosophy at all[b] inasmuch as it is pure assumption—for instance a man says "if you will suppose matter dispersed all
over space"—without asking himself what he means by matter or what
he means by space and if you will only grant me that this matter has two
powers"—without asking what he means by that "attraction and repulsion and then only grant me that by some happy accident some of those
atoms"—but why they should have those properties [f 44] "may happen
to be a great deal bigger than others for which no more reason can be assigned than for the laws of gravitation and repulsion—"the bodies would
be projected straight forward by one contrivance and then by the larger
bodies be counteracted by the other and then you would have the
world"—in short you have precisely this if only the world had been from
the beginning then it would be[c] for it is plain that all which is now in the
world is presupposed to account for the world[d] so that in truth this is one
of those numerous instances in all books of materialists without exception in which the solution is itself a part of the problem[e] therefore I say I
do not consider this as deserving the name of philosophy—it is an anti-
philosophy arising out of a thorough coldness of the moral feeling and
the habit of looking so intensely at the external world with all the powers of the heart fixed upon it that at last the man does not deserve to be
considered merely as having self love[f] that supposes a reflex[g] he becomes
a mere lover of self but of philosophy that which admits an appeal to the
[f 45] inner being, there have been and always will be two kinds—the
one that which considers the principles of pure reason as purely contemplative and the objects of them in the external world as entirely devoid of
life and moving by certain mechanical Laws though those laws themselves originated in a higher ~~place~~ principle that is the one—the other is
that which considering that the world[h] can act upon another but by some
law of likeness, that no man would think of saying that a thought for instance was a shield or that his love for his sister was[i] north east for in-

---

[b] Comma inserted in pencil   [c] Comma inserted in pencil
[d] Comma inserted in pencil   [e] Comma inserted in pencil
[f] Comma inserted in pencil   [g] Comma inserted in pencil
[h] Query mark pencilled in right-hand margin   [i] Comma inserted in pencil

stance[j] of his affection for his child or his wife[k] who[l] even seeing that between things manifestly incongruous there can be no action whatsoever[m]
concluded that which acted upon the other must be homogeneous—must
be of the same kind they therefore thought[n] at least Pythagoras who was
the originator[o] conceived that that in the soul of man, which was not of
the individual[p] which no man could call his own but in consequence of
which [f 46] he was a man and without it would not have been, must necessarily be of the same nature and kind with those laws of the universe
which acted upon him and which he alone was capable of beholding—
he saw that the animals perceived the effects and acted upon the effects
but it was clear that they knew nothing of the laws for even men who were
capable of reflecting for the greater part thought little of them and that
those Laws [q]take gravitation for instance or any other law[r] were utterly
beyond the reach of the senses—utterly beyond the reach of the understanding even though all the objects of the understanding as far as they
consisted in the outward world were to be deduced from them—he therefore supposed that what in men the ideas were as we should say those in
the world were the laws that the ideas partook according to the power of
the man of a constitutive character in the same manner as the laws did in
external nature but how should he convey the nature of this best to the
mind and it appeared to him that he should best do it by numbers and figures for obser[f 47]ving that in numbers considered philosophically there
was a perpetual reference to an unity that was yet infinite and yet that in
each number there was an integral or individual that still contained in its
nature something progressive that went beyond it, he conceived this was
the best symbol if I may so say of the representation of the laws of nature
considered as homogeneous with the pure reason in man Leading from
this ground therefore he appears to have found that all truth, all certainty
must be in this and on trying it both with numbers and with figures and
perceiving that there arose from it a sense utterly unlike that which any
experience however perfect could give that instead of high probability
there came at once a sense of certainty that denied the opposite which was
out of all time, out of all space, out of all accident, he is reported and it is
the sublimest era of human nature when Pythagoras exclaimed "Eu-

---

[j] Comma inserted in pencil
[k] Dash inserted in pencil
[l] Comma inserted in pencil
[m] Comma inserted in pencil
[n] Comma inserted in pencil
[o] Comma inserted in pencil
[p] Comma inserted in pencil
[q-r] Parentheses inserted in pencil

reka"[s]—I have found, for it assuredly was no less for the heathen world than to have found the principle of humanity itself—all that distinguishes us from the [f 48] animal essentially, all that carries us beyond the blind present into the ever opening future—he found a something that was above time, above accident, it was drawn from the fountain of truth that was inexhaustible and this was in man but it was not in his . . . for he saw it—it was not in his understanding for he had not deduced it from any thing but it was in the mind—it must be I only can perceive it in this point and it is an impossibility that aught else can give me conviction

If the Sophist would say but why do you believe the mind—the first answer doubtless would be why should I not and for this reason that it is free from all causes of doubt—but the next is this that you are asking an absurdity you are asking for a first to be a second—a faith I must have in something for that is implied in the very term of first—that which is the ground cannot have a ground under it and thus Pythagoras commenced philosophy in the faith of the human reason revealed to himself by purity of the moral character—the faith of that reason in its own dictates—On this [f 49] plan he founded the grand system of the Deity as the Monas not as the one but as that which without any numbers and perfectly distinct from numbers was yet the ground and by its will the cause of all numbers and in the manifestation of the Godhead[t] he represented it by the famous triad three while the world as a dim reflex of that was his God in the tetrameter or the four—

Doubtless since that time philosophy has been divided from science and I should have done wrongly if I had represented Pythagoras as having achieved that distinction—in the nature of things both must have been combined but it is most worthy of notice that the mathematical sciences and the arithmetical upon which we pride ourselves and which are the bulwarks against modern infidels, who denying all other certainty are yet obliged to yield to this did not commence as they would have them commence in abstraction by the senses[u] though that circle has not all its radia equal[v] it is as good as if it had thus[w] man must be taught [f 50] that these sciences commenced far deeper that it is ludicrous to suppose that Pythagoras on finding out what his eye sight must have informed every man that lines drawn from the middle of a circle were pretty nearly equal

---

[s] "Eureka" underlined in pencil and alongside in right-hand margin pencilled, probably in the hand of JHG: this story I believe belongs to Archimedes and the problem of Hieros Crown.

[t] Pencilled, probably in the hand of JHG, in right-hand margin: this requires a note

[u] Comma inserted in pencil

[v] Comma inserted in pencil

[w] Comma inserted in pencil

should have felt any rapture but he felt that it could not be otherwise that he had discovered not merely that which was to be learnt from external objects but that it was the law and the rule of those objects—well might he exclaim Eureka when he found in after discoveries that applying those numbers drawn abstractedly from his own reason to the laws of external nature and her motions he perceived the direct contrary to what the wisest of men had done before him that instead of supposing the earth fixed and the heavenly bodies (as our senses shew us) moving around us he saw by laws derived from his own reason that the sum was fixed and further that all matter has its number and that the external phenomena themselves were as nothing [f 51] of which no man could say they are but only that they have been but that they were the perpetual language of those numbers and finally he resolved all this into a power which to the honor of Pythagoras did not in the least partake of Pantheism but still kept the Deity at a distance from his works—this entitles this man to our gratitude

As to the idea that Pythagoras had learnt this in Egypt India and so forth and that it was part of the knowledge of those times that may be dismissed in a very few words Thales had been in Egypt it appears and instructed by the Priests and yet though he possessed as it appears certain experimental mathematical knowledge such as a Carpenter might have with us yet still he had learned nothing of science properly so called—what the state of information must have been when Pythagoras after having travelled through Egypt Persia and India came back and was transported and offered a hecatomb on having discovered the thirty seventh proposition of Euclid[x] is a pretty good answer to those [f 52] men who would suppose a high state of knowledge in scientific men who were nobody knows who but such an idea has been carried to a most extravagant height by some of our modern contenders for Indian Wisdom—Was it to be supposed that Pythagoras who had passed his life in seeking knowledge wherever he went should when he came back express a delight amounting to rapture at the very elements of geometry if geometry had been already carried to a system—no doubtless the state of India and Egypt was precisely what may be expressed and which the Bible fully expresses elsewhere a state of high civilization ⟨and of all that can arise out of civilization⟩ but without any cultivation whatsoever—man was in all things drawn towards his senses—brought into the bonds of society by conquest or imposture or whatever other cause the many were working for the pride or the superstition of the few as is shewn in the pyramids and they pro-

---

[x] Pencilled in right-hand and bottom margin, probably in the hand of JHG: This supposes that Pythagoras had nothing of the Mountebank about him—a point which is stated above to be somewhat doubtful.

ceeded as far as the outward man could do by imitation as for instance the formation of the body just as many men in the present day [f 53] the Russians for instance will do and frequently those who are most incapable of anything original and just as the new Hollanders do they were able to do all that was done well but the countenance that impressive somewhat which gives the mind—In vain have we looked for any specimens of that in Egyptian Architecture—even if you go back to the remotest times and seek it between Egypt and Ethiopia no where does there appear science but all tradition and history—It is remarkable the earliest writers say that the Egyptians were a very historical ⟨people⟩ for wherever they went they saw upon their pillars the history of their times—what those histories must be that were written on pillars we may by consulting common sense easily learn—I confess that in my opinion those hieroglyphics have excited a great deal more attention than anything but their antiquity could call for—what little we know after all the learned disquisitions into the properties of bodies and so forth seems to end in a much greater probability that it was a rude invention of the first times in Egypt to represent their thoughts by images by visual images and that [f 54] this was doubtless first of all what they called Chiaro-logical—a man was put for man—afterwards by some observable property in which they perceived an analogy as for instance that a scull represented death that emblem was employed afterwards as they began to be somewhat more refined by some knowledge of natural history their further ideas were combined in a tedious game called the . . .*y* or a meditation of death where there is a man standing thinking—there is a man for a man—a book for a book—on the table before him is a skull which by a natural image in all nations represents death but on the skull a butterfly here you see at once there is a man meditating on death and immortality—but for the language in general I think even Scaliger though of a very contrary opinion himself has brought sufficient things to prove that great part of it was much what we have seen at Carrington Bowles's and so forth those curious letters written half with images—an eye to signify an I a U and a tree to signify a yew tree—a [f 55] hawk or a species of Sparrow-hawk was the Representative as we know for the soul but it appears that . . . was the name of both for the Hawk and the soul so exactly as in Greek the Butterfly was called Psyche and at the same time the soul was called Psyche and it appears that the hieroglyphics were made up from these three sources which of itself proves a very low state of science and how very little Greece could have properly gained from these three sources.

---

y "μελέτη θανάτου" inserted into space in pencil, probably in the hand of EHC

One other argument I think is perfectly satisfying that all the pretended obligations of Greece to these three Countries are during the period while Greece itself was compleatly ignorant but in all that makes Greece Greece to us we find it the great light of the world the beating pulse that power which was predetermined by Almighty Providence to gradually evolve all that could be evolved out of corrupt nature by its own reason while on the opposite ground there was a nation bred up by inspiration in a Child like form in obedience and in the exercise of the Will till at length the two great component parts of our nature in [f 56] the unity of which all its excellency and all its hopes depend namely that of the will in the one as the higher and more especially Godlike and the reason in the other as the compeer but yet second to that will were to unite and to prepare the world for the reception of its Redeemer which took place just at the time when the traditions of history and the Oracles of the Jews had combined with the philosophy of the Grecians and prepared the Jews themselves for understanding their own scriptures in a more spiritual light and the Greeks to give to their speculations that were but the shadows of thought before—a reality in that which alone is properly real—ᶻ

ᶻ In remaining space, pencilled, probably in the hand of JHG: ?—the motive of Pythagoras travels? | ? What was the wisdom of the Egyptians which Moses had learnt?

LECTURE 3

^aM.^r Coleridges Lecture.
Monday 4.th January 1819.

In my last address I understand that that part of the Lecture which referred to the peculiar arithmetical metaphysics of Pythagoras was not fully understood and as it will lead me immediately to the purpose of the present I will take the opportunity of attempting to explain myself—There is no one among us who feels the least inclination to call a Cudgel a Bruise or a Sword a wound or the pain the reason is evidenty this because a Cudgel and a Sword are separate and distinct images to the senses but we all of us and in all languages call the sensation heat or cold and the outward cause of it by the same names and inevitable as this is it has produced a great confusion of thought not indeed in the palpable instance which I have now mentioned but in many others and yet as common to all Nations and arising out of the nature of the human mind may well be believed to refer to some important truth [f 58] We know that Chemistry found itself soon compelled to frame a different word for the cause to distinguish it from the sensation it was produced to effect and hence we have the word calorif or calorific We know too that in the first edition of Newtons optics he had spoken of radii colorati colored rays which he altered afterwards to radii colorati formati^b color making rays—Now it appears that Pythagoras had proceeded upon this opinion that those unknown somethings powers or whatever you may call them that manifest themselves in the intellect of man or what in the language of the old philosophy would be called the intelligible world as numbers and the [? essential] powers of numbers these same manifest themselves to us and are the objects of our senses I mean as creative and organizing powers in short that the very powers which in men reflect and contemplate are in their essence the same as those powers which in nature produce the objects contemplated—This position did indeed appear to be deducible from that

---

^a Transcriber B's hand
^b Pencilled correction "? colorere formants" (for "colores formantes"?) inserted above line, probably by EHC

of the Ionic school I mean that of Thales that there is no action but from like on like [f 59] that no substances or beings essentially dissimilar could possibly be made sensible of each others existence or in any way act thereon

This involves an essential I know not how I can avoid using a pedantic word . . .*c* a sameness of the conceiver of the idea and the law corresponding to the idea—in the language of the old philosophy they would say that the eye could not possibly perceive light but by having in its own essence something luciferous—that the ear could not have been the organ of hearing but by having in its essence and not by mechanism something conformed to the air—The obstacle to the acceptance of this position is to be found in the fancy and imagination as far as they take their materials from the senses which constantly present the Soul the percipient as a sort of inner more subtle body a kind of under waistcoat as it were to the bodily garment and the mind itself as a Vessel or at best a mode sometimes even as a blank tablet in short to take the meaning of all inclusively as a passive receiver which in fact however as we may convince ourselves [f 60] by a little self examination is nothing more than the craving for our image—we have been accustomed by all our affections by all our wants to seek after outward images and by the love of association therefore*d* to whole truth we attach that particular condition of truth which belongs to sensible bodies or to ~~the~~ bodies which can be touched The first education which we receive—that from our mothers is given to us by touch—the whole of its process is nothing more than*e* to express myself boldly*f* an extended touch by promise—the sense itself—the sense of vision itself is only acquired by a continued recollection of touch*g* no wonder therefore that beginning in the animal state we should carry this onward through the whole of our being however remote it may be from the true purposes of it therefore an image supporting something*h* (which in itself is a contradiction for an image always supposes a superfices and a something supported*i* and is asked for under the name of a substance*j* is construed into an Agent when we can no longer boldly bring forwards a thing for it*k* and this agent is contradistinguished from [f 61] an act as if these

c "homogeneity" inserted in pencil, probably by EHC
d Comma inserted in pencil
e Comma inserted in pencil
f Comma inserted in pencil
g Comma or full stop inserted in pencil
h Comma inserted in pencil
i Comma inserted in pencil
j Comma inserted in pencil
k Semi-colon inserted in pencil

oppositions of our human language and thoughts were really the true conditions and the very essence of our being but[l] to comprehend the Philosophy of Pythagoras ~~as~~ the mind itself must be conceived of and the numbers of Pythagoras and the Cabalist with the equivalent ideas of the Platonists as not so properly acts of the reason in their sense I mean as they are of reason itself in Act

Now this the writers of the history of the Philosophers have clearly not mastered and I believe it is from this want of distinction between the two opposite poles—of all human thought namely the objective and the subjective that is to say the supposed external cause and that modification of the mind itself of which alone we are conscious which is the result of it that has occasioned all their confusion and contradictions in the accounts of the ancient Philosophers—thus the very best Writer on Philosophic history we have hitherto had[m] Teneman[n] charges Pythagoras and the great men following him with having turned into objective different things that were purely subjective but the very contrary appears to have been the object of Pythagoras [f 62] himself and of those who immediately followed him namely to shew that in the essence both object and subject were united in one that there was one principle which produced the object of perception and that the same principle at the other pole produced the contemplation of that object—whether this be true or false such was evidently their opinion and it is necessary to be understood in order to the comprehension of the progress of Philosophy for in this in truth did philosophy begin in the distinction between the subject and the object— how many centuries we might say millenia might the race of men go on without ever asking themselves the question whether the sensation which was all to them was one and the same with that external something which was the occasion of it—to both they gave the same names and he who first (to use a former illustration) distinguished heat from the supposed power externally which he called calorif might have been truly said to have begun philosophy and the whole progress from that time to this present moment is nothing more than an attempt to reconcile the same—there are therefore essentially but three kinds of [f 63] philosophers and more are not possible—the one is those who give the whole to the subject and make the object a mere result involved in it—Secondly those who give the whole to the object and make the subject that is the reflecting and contemplating feeling part the mere result of that and lastly those who in very different ways have attempted to reconcile these two opposites and bring them into one

---

[l] Emended in pencil to "being. But"   [m] Comma inserted in pencil
                                    [n] Comma inserted in pencil

It may appear to us [o]owing to the advantages of our education and of living in the present state of advanced knowledge that we do—in certain things at least[p] extraordinary that any man should confuse the distinction between the external Cause and the effect upon ourselves and yet in the writing of Ocullus[q] Lucanus the authenticity of which as the immediate follower of Pythagoras I reject not from the arguments brought against it by Teneman or the circumstance that it is in the Attic instead of Doric dialect but because the whole tone is opposite and inconsistent with the Pythagorean Philosophy of which he is a professed follower yet he after having given some instances which were fair and which were probably parts of the traditional doctrines of Pythagoras proceeds to carry it on [r]as dull men never know when to leave off at the [f 64] proper time[s] by saying after what he says of the different senses and the conformity to the objects "Now honey is a particular substance, it produces an extreme sense of sweetness on the palate and everybody knows it is extremely sweet in itself." Now this confusion or rather this strange division of the same things expressed in different words will at once shew at least this how natural such a blunder is to the human mind when it first begins to think and at once establishes to me a proof that this work of Ocullus Lucanus was that of an early but very rude Grammarian who had taken into his head to imitate or to take upon himself the name of some great man that had been recorded by tradition

But we will return to the progress of philosophy. Of Pythagoras I have said that we[t] are abandoned necessarily I will not say absolutely to conjecture but to that state that not unfrequently occurs in human life in which it is necessary for a man to have discovered by other means the truth of a particular position in order to learn with certainty whether a prior writer has or has not taught it—I wish I could as successfully [f 65] and as confidently clear the character of Pythagoras from the charge of a pretended Magician and impostor as I think I could from all charges of mere vulgar pantheism or what may be called fanatical philosophy he seems to me to have attempted at least the union of the two opposites which he distinctly understood namely the objects of contemplation and the contemplative power itself

After him—immediately after him and according to Chronology while he was yet alive arose the founders of the Eleatic School—the moral Philosophy of Pythagoras which Teneman brings forward as exhibiting the intense state of thinking seems to me rather to prove the highest of all that

[o–p] Parentheses inserted in pencil   [q] Corrected in pencil to "Ocellus"
[r–s] Parentheses inserted in pencil
[t] "we" underlined in pencil and "we" written in pencil in margin

has been ever attributed to Pythagoras nay to explain the ground of the high admiration in which his name was held by posterity through so many ages speculatively considered he admitted that moral acts form an object of philosophic contemplation equally with all other acts and he determined their Law which in an Arithmetical metaphor according to the language and symbol of his own choice he declared to be [f 66] a proportion a harmony a something which containing no principle of contradiction in itself was susceptible of becoming the law of any rational being in whatever circumstances—but this he thought of so little practical importance that he rested the whole chance of bringing men into a moral state upon education and on this ground that virtue so far from being learned by any theory could only be known by the practice of virtue—that there was no power of educing virtue out of any thing else but itself nay more that there was that which is supposed in all virtue namely an act of the Will but if you prefix or presuppose any act influencing the Will necessarily we see at once that it is no longer the Will but an impulse—a billiard ball moving against another billiard ball and we lose the very notion of will in consequence of which he very wisely rested the whole upon a process of education which in its first elements should be delivered from the Gods in other words that it should be found [f 67] in our nature and from the constant tradition of our ancestors guarding us against any doubt lest it should be a delusion in our minds that there was such a thing as virtue and that once fixed what were the means of educing it—As I shall have to speak of this hereafter I will only say that in the case of Pythagoras—with whatever human infirmity his institutions might have been mixed yet the record of all ages that even the fragments and relicts of the scattered societies were distinguished by sanctity of manner intense friendship to each other and the principle that they would love all men either for what they were or for what they might be is a strong proof that they had proceeded upon the right ground namely that of deducing the true character of man as he ought to be not in the first instance from the intellect but from a higher principle and then to employ the intellect as constantly educing this and bringing it into more and into more perfection

Pythagoras remains to us therefore highly estimable and chiefly as a moral character and it is interesting to us to see [f 68] the transition from thence to speculative philosophy disjoined from the moral in the first instance and we return to the old difficulty of the subjective and the objective nor will it appear to you unnoticeable that the first school which formed itself instead of acceding to what we might have expected perhaps at the first thought namely that the objects of the sense should at first

have overpowered the minds of men and have presented themselves—
no—the Eleatic school writings of which are reduced but to a few fragments but of no sect of Philosophy have we so clear and distinct notions
doubtless from the simplicity of their system at once by what may be
called a Courage and perhaps an effrontery of the human mind dared decide the question by rejecting all that was objective as real and affirmed
that the whole existed only in the mind and for the mind that all the multitude of objects that appear to us are founded in delusion and that in mind
itself was to be found the sole reality of things Xenophones[u] the founder
was born at Colophon a City of some note in Asia [f 69] Minor coeval
with Pythagoras from thence he migrated to . . .[v] a newly founded Town
by . . . in South Italy[w] where he lived to a long old age without any direct
Master he had acquainted himself with the opinion of Thales . . .[x] as well
as those of Pythagoras which he refers to indeed in one of the elegies
which he wrote against Hesiod and Homer and the fragments of which
though not containing the name yet evidently referring to Pythagoras is
⟨preserved in Diogenes Laertius in his life of Pythagoras—and⟩ here permit me to refer to the former lecture in which I ventured in opposition to
several Writers particularly to a man of great learning Kreitzer to place
the institution of the . . . mysteries and the Eleusinian at a lower date than
that of Homer and Hesiod for I cannot but observe that the very first effect of Philosophy was a determined warfare against the gross and crude
theology which Theocritus[y] tells us was first introduced into Greece by
Homer and Hesiod whether it was possible that two single individuals
could produce such an effect over the people so scattered some being in
. . . in Asia Minor others [f 70] in the . . . or in the Islands and others again
in South Italy is a question well deserving of thought and whether it
would not be more rational to some extent at least to do what all scholars
have lately found themselves compelled to do with regard to the Hymns
of Homer so to refer the effects to Bands of men lately call Homeridæ,
and who may have been assembled like other persons who sung together
on the same subjects this however seems confirmed by Heredotus when
he tells us that those who had been placed before Homer generally he believed to have lived after him now it would be difficult to conjecture
whom he could mean if it was not the names of Orpheus . . . and the other

[u] Corrected in pencil to "Xenophanes"
[v] "Elia or Velia" inserted in pencil, probably by EHC
[w] "of the Phocians" written above line in pencil, probably by EHC
[x] ", Pherycides and Anaximander" inserted in pencil, probably by EHC
[y] Name underlined, query mark written in margin, and over it "Herodotus", all in pencil, probably in the hand of JHG

Mystical poets who endeavored to give to the Homeric theology a more spiritual and lofty meaning[z]

To turn to Xenophanes the sanctity of his life is extolled by Plato and Aristotle and the same (I mention it for a particular reason) is expressed of all the rest of the disciples of these and the following sects they were eminently good men Zeno the disciple of . . .[a] and Zeno's friend . . .[b] who went together [f 71] with him to Athens in the 80th Olympiad 460 years before Christ were probably from 25 to 30 years younger than Zenocrates[c]—Nearly at the same time or a little later . . .[d] under whose command the great Naval Victory was obtained over the Athenians according to Appollodorus he was in the height of his celebrity about 476 years before Christ these four illustrious contemporaries were all writers or Authors Xenophanes and . . .[e] her[f] metrical compositions which however are more valued for their philosophy than their Poetry while Zeno and Melesius wrote in prose—of these works we have but a few fragments remaining and as I observed before it is to their extreme simplicity we owe our account of them The Eleatic system consisted in the blank denial of any true reality in the supposed objects of the Senses or of any proper correspondence in external nature to its perceptions[g] that is[h] they not only supposed[i] which it was easy to prove[j] that the external object could not be exactly that which it was seen to be[k] because the question would immediately arise [f 72] at what distance is it seen by an eye[l] how organized[m] that which is at a distance will appear round which nearer will appear square[n] that which appears with one shape to a perfect eye will to an eye distempered appear with another—No—that would have been

---

[z] On verso page in pencil (now very faint) probably in the hand of JHG: I cannot persuade myself that the Orphic establishments in Thrace were posterior to the Homeric writing—that the poems which in Herodotus's time passed under the names of Orpheus Musæus etc were posterior to the Homeric poetry is I think obvious—and it is equally clear that after the last of the Homeric compositions there existed a mystical & philosophical school of poetry a sort of [? Euripidean] school—

[a] "Xenophanes" inserted in pencil, probably by EHC

[b] "Parmenides" inserted in pencil, probably by EHC

[c] Corrected in pencil to "Xenophanes", probably by EHC

[d] "Milissus of Samos" inserted in pencil, probably by EHC

[e] "Parmenides" inserted in pencil, probably by EHC

[f] Corrected in pencil to "in"

[g] Comma inserted in pencil

[h] Comma inserted in pencil

[i] Comma inserted in pencil

[j] Comma inserted in pencil

[k] Comma inserted in pencil

[l] Comma inserted in pencil

[m] Comma inserted in pencil

[n] Comma inserted in pencil

merely that in external nature there does exist a positive correspondence but they denied this altogether all preceding reasoners whether Naturalists as I call the Ionic school or . . .*o* had proposed to themselves however to trace the birth and the growth of things—the problem was whence and how things became or as perhaps I might say more intelligibly how things came to be—all of them grounded their opinions on this axiom that from nothing nothing can come but the Eleatic school deduced or believed itself to deduce from the same axiom the impossibility of any change any true transition from any one thing or estate to another in other words they reduced the argument to two positions—nothing can arise out of nothing the first—secondly neither out of any thing can any thing arise or begin to be for this [f 73] itself would be a creation—the first position they did not attempt to prove they took it as conceded by all the second they endeavored to demonstrate by various turns of Logic as for example What arises out of another must be either like or unlike it—if like it must have like properties and then there is merely a numerical difference between the producing cause and the product and no reason why priority should be assigned to one rather than the other but chiefly they endeavored to recommend their opinion by calling into question all the conceptions of the mind that accompany our knowledge of change and above all the conception of motion

These Sophisms concerning motion have been preserved to to us it would be wasting time to detail them to you and wearisome—it is sufficient to state the result that they all proceed upon a manifest Sophism which takes for granted the thing in question and requires for the objects which are no longer phenomena or appearances *p*that which can appear to the senses*q* all the qualities of phenomena as for instance a Tortoise shall set off after a Hare—or a Hare shall set off after a Tortoise but the Tortoise shall have [f 74] a yard given him in the advantage then the demonstration is that there must be a given portion of time in which the Hare takes half the length of the Tortoise in the mean time the Tortoise would have gone on a certain portion that the Hare must take another half and the Tortoise must have gone on a certain period the Hare must go on halving and the demonstration is that he can never arrive at the Tortoise the consequence is this that the very impossibility of finding an image that could present a Sophism to the mind without an absurdity is a compleat detection of it for we see at once that there was no necessity of taking the Hare and the Tortoise for it was evident upon the same grounds that nothing could move at all by any possibility—Why already the Hare was made an absurdity and the Tortoise was made an absurdity for they both occupied a certain quantum of space without any regard to the minimum and consequently the Hare did not move a half inch at a time in the end—but here as the Hare occupied a certain quantity of space which set at defiance the whole calculation of the philosopher he required all the properties of phenomena when he had himself reduced [f 75] Space to a mere idea of the mind which never can be apprehended or even imagined by the senses consequently he brought two different things into the argument namely space,ʳ or rather he punned upon the word space he took space in the first place to mean an image presented by the imagination and then he took it for a Metaphysical possibility of motion and no wonder that from two things so perfectly heterogeneous he could produce nothing but absurdity

This is sufficient not to add another which has false logic in it—namely that while he required a minimum of the one he took an indefinite quantity of the other or allowed no minimum in the other case as for instance a wheel may move—Supposing a Wheel to have on the top of it the letter A and at the bottom B you may suppose it to move so rapidly that at the same moment perceptibly by man it shall cease to move at all and appear motionless what does that prove why that it has gone beyond the bounds of perception or imagination and after that we are forbidden by sound sense to apply the Law of phenomena [f 76] to it otherwise than by analogy but that analogy which we draw from the objects of the senses it would be absurd to bring against the objects of the senses

This I mention as having been brought forwards by a Philosopher who really thought well who having spoken the arguments of some philosophers against motion related the story that Diogenes rising up and walking along the room said—thus I confute the arguments of a Zeno recited that the Disciples of Zeno might have kicked him down stairs to which it might have been replied we understand that as well as you and we will give you the advantage of the phenomenon of motion but our difficulty is how to reconcile it with our reason and this is the point in which alone you are to consider these things you are to consider them as you do the strange cases put in our old books of arithmetic or other imaginary things in the books of old Schoolmen as exercises of the reason itself not to be looked at for that particular case or to be supposed Zeno was that Madman . . . [f 77] but as a process of science in which it is perfectly different essentially different from that and a mere record of experiment it is an attempt of man out of long experience in which he is perpetually float-

ʳ Comma may be only an accidental speck of ink

ing to arrive at some fixture from whence he can command experience and when we consider what an elevation that is of human nature how it rises so essentially above the animal creation how it entitles us to be called the delegated Lords of nature and of light fire and the elements and enables us to send our fleets over the elements which as individuals would destroy us in a few moments to act on that fire which is to tremendous animals fly before it with a terror neither Sword nor Spear could inflict we may be well grateful for every preparatory exercise of the mind that can lead to this for experience can only tell us to expect the future from the past with a perfect ignorance of all by which the future will be modified and made different from the past it is only in Science that depends power of prophecy that which enables the sage in his closet to foretel with a confidence grounded on the most awful of pledges "as sure as God liveth so it will be if the laws of nature proceed [f 78] as they now are"

I have a particular object in attempting to impress this on your minds because in the early histories of the Philosophers we meet with so many things which might excite contempt such as to draw away our minds from the important steps which they made towards the state in which we now are—too apt we are to confound the truth perceived with those rude illustrations of the truth which their experimental knowledge afforded to them and where therefore it requires that moderating recollection what the object was for which these men were laboring and above all that they of all the earth only labored in vain[s]

However there was one point assumed in the whole of this Philosophy and which appears to have been common to all the elder Philosophers for though I am myself inclined to except Heraclitus and Pythagoras I am bound in historical fidelity to admit they were otherwise interpreted and that it is evident that their disciples understood them according to the common opinion which is this—they all took[t] for granted the identity of God and the World [f 79] This is the point which forms the true interest of this lecture for upon it depends the whole intelligibity of philosophy hereafter—there is an evident truism when examined in all the Dogmatas of the elder Philosophers as far as they reason namely—they call the World . . . the Universe of all—the whole—and then they deduce with an inevitable force of conviction that it must have had neither beginning nor can have ending that is involved in it that is evident—that nothing can come from nothing and therefore the Universe being the whole it

---

[s] Vertical line and query mark in pencil in right-hand margin beside last three lines of the paragraph

[t] "they all took" underlined in pencil and "that they had taken" written in pencil in right-hand margin, probably in the hand of JHG

must have been eternal and must forever continue but the main question which did not occur to them was whether or no the Deity *u*which yet they admitted*v* was essentially distinct from the World or not—Now to us bred up as we have been nothing can appear more easy than this—it must even appear strange that man should have confounded the maker the Creator and the Work and yet when Plato teaches another doctrine he expressly says it was a Wisdom derived from the Gods which had been received from the Barbarous Nations [f 80] whom in another place he calls the Holy Nations it was an idea so bold that it does not appear that it ever did suggest itself to any human mind unassisted by Revelation—We who have been accustomed from our Childhood almost from our infancy to speak of God our Creator and to reverence him as being infinitely above the World and altogether and essentially diverse from it—We may wonder that others should think differently and much could I wish I had the power to impress upon your imaginations the feelings of difference in the minds of those who were without those advantages and had not been born in Christian Countries as we are—Nay if I could point out to you the state of Countries nominally Christian in which the Clergy of the Country have been more attentive for their Saints their Altars and their particular Worship than to impress the great grounds of Religion on the mind and you would see not only how difficult an idea this was to form but likewise how speedily the mind [f 81] as if wearied falls away from it to sink into the ease of sensuality and . . . conceive at once that that immense universe those thousands of worlds with all their infinite varieties of action forms of life destinations births deaths that these all should be subject to the power as they originated in the Will of one Being and that that Being who possesses in itself what was a reason and by the contemplation of which we alone know what reason can be—*w*the contemplation I say for I speak not too boldly that the ground the cause the Governor of all this Universe was wise and good in the sense which men understand the word though they can never arrive at so stupenduous a truth that as when it did seize hold of the mind of man it possessed it with a species of inspiration so without other aid than that which human reason could give it appears never to have arrived at the heart of man and yet it might seem wonderfully easy

I wish to give a striking instance of [f 82] what the human reason of itself I will not say could arrive at but I speak more safely of what it ever did arrive at for there is not a more frequent delusion or one that it was more fashionable about a hundred years ago in the time of the Chubbs

---

u–v Parentheses inserted in pencil
w In right-hand margin, in pencil, probably in the hand of JHG: a note wanted.

and Morgans more frequently to bring forward what they called natural proofs of Religion the object of which was to shew the inutility of Christianity that it was of no value and it is astonishing with what coolness they proceed to give demonstrative proofs which no man could reject of the being and attributes of God and a future state it might have been a matter of surprise that the Philosophers of old did not arrive at this that they were extremely puzzled that when Simonides was asked the question he required day after day to solve it and that the arguments which they bring forwards independent of Revelation the Philosophers of old would have treated either with abundant contempt or as mere proofs of what they admitted namely that for every motion in nature there was a motive power that when a man said he could prove . . . over the person but not the intention they would say [f 83] all the . . . just as bees in a bee hive all pursue one object and from thence would produce a system of . . . which alone could have been derived from such an argument while the arguments of a higher kind go into pantheism which again instantly brought round the effect of . . . and when we find that History attests the statement that there was but one nation upon earth that did for any time resist the seduction of . . . and that nation only by a miraculous interposition of providence we must be blind with Conceit or ignorant of history not to feel that the very first foundation of what we call natural religion is in truth Revelation that natural religion is a word without name . . . is the result of nature and such it has been shewn in all ages and the effect of . . . in all ages has been in the under states of life cruelty and brutality in the higher states selfishness and Sensuality here there is no doubt that good men for thank heaven there is a glorious inconsistency [f 84] in human nature through the mercy of our Creator a mans head will frame this and that cobweb but his heart will whisper better things his moral feelings will wish them and he will contradict himself and with the common sophistry try to reconcile the one with the other and thus it is with the natural influence of Pantheism or the belief of God as identical with the world there will be motives when^x the reverence of that something which instinctively we must conceive of as greater than ourselves and then all the aggregate of things that we behold will excite feelings of devotion and awe and these will produce fragments of true religious feeling but for a few philosophers while mankind at large are better logicians made so by their animal nature and will in the very same moment be sinking into the worst excesses and the blindest superstition accompanied with the most accursed moral practices^y

^{x} Word may be "where"
^{y} Vertical line drawn in pencil in right-hand margin beside last three lines of the paragraph

We have in this Work which I have now before me an extract from a great poem of India where Pantheism has displayed [f 85] its banners and waved in victory over three hundred millions of men and this has been published in England as a proof of sublimity beyond the excellence of Milton in the true adoration of the supreme being it is an address to the Pantheistic God compare it with the feelings you have all been taught in your Catechism

"Oh Mighty Spirit behold the wonders of an awful countenance what troubled minds of the Celestial bands I see . . .[z] [f 87] thyself." Now this is said and it is published by the authority of the East India Company I find for which certainly we are much obliged to them for it is a very interesting poem but with a declaration "I should not fear to place in opposition to the 1st and 6th . . .[a] that however is a piece of taste but the result is more serious and to us I think more comfortable namely that in the utmost attempts of a Pantheistic philosophy to reduce Religion to any objects of the senses ⟨or⟩ any object to be apprehended by men and that is more than the indistinct conception of the whole the infinite of a something that works like gravitation works without any consciousness this it gives in the most striking manner and when we find how anxious the Ancient Sages of India with this opinion were to impress a belief of an unity for that the reason of man of itself necessarily tends to do and yet to bring it down to the practical and moral point so as to make it the subject of influence on the Will or moral being they were distracted [f 88] into the most ridiculous forms and we begin to pay some compliment to those Theologicians who by dropping the one part in thing and hiding it altogether from the multitude[b] presented only to them fairies and . . . and for every object presented to them a sort of life and passions and motions attending it which affected themselves for that be assured is the utmost height human nature has arrived at by its own powers that first of all the highest and best of men felt by an impulse from their reason and necessity to seek an unity and those who felt wisely like Plato and Socrates feeling the difficulties of this looked forward to that being of whom this necessity and their reason was a presentiment to instruct them and expected with reverence and hope that an instructor would come but with regard to the others it fell into a multitude of forms so that at length the theologists themselves were weary of counting them and it has become a matter of dispute whether there were twenty thirty forty or fifty [f 89] thousand of the Roman and Greek Deities

---

[z] Page and a half of ms, including all of f 86, left blank to allow for later insertion of quoted passage

[a] Space left for two and a half lines to allow for later insertion of quoted passage

[b] Vertical line drawn in pencil in right-hand margin beside last three lines

This however must not be said without in some measure retrieving the character of Zeno Xenophanes and others from whose history I have been led to this digression there are found in their Fragments opinions which proceeded from the heart rather than the system and every where you perceive that their object was noble it was an excess—it was an extreme indeed but it was from an honorable impulse and with a praise worthy object men were entirely under the tyranny of their Senses they attacked the very first elements of the senses they endeavored to convince them of their fallacy and how little in themselves they could be relied upon and so far they shook the great superstition of human nature and prepared for better things and all that we can expect ⟨of⟩ our fellow creatures collectively is not that they should do the whole*c* which must be ever left to providence who educes good out of evil and wisdom out of folly but that they should [f 90] in one division of the army or in the other be working towards it and thus it is these noble opinions this inward piety even contradictory to their opinions this shock ⟨which⟩ they all expressed at the degradation of the objects of human admiration by the poets*d* which has preserved them from the name of Sophists this I say and this alone for I have only to mention the opposite to the scheme of the Eleatic School or Zeno namely Democritus and his subjects and his system of atoms to exhibit the true occasion of the Sophists as far as it was occasioned by intellectual causes Democritus took the direct opposite system to that of Zeno instead of rejecting the objective instead of placing all reality in the mind itself and in what he called the whole he placed the whole in the outward object and in the parts and considering that he had two things to solve the first was the impenetrability of things if they were to be parts for if there was to be no penetrability*e* where was to be the end we should go on from little to less and from less to less and so forth and at the same time the power of composition both these he discovered as he imagined in the notion of an Atom an Atom was to explain two things [f 91] which experience had shewn him in nature the first was that things were divisible that they were capable *f*which as a thought is not*g* of being dissolved into parts and separated one part from the other and the next is of their resistance of all power of cohesion in order to do this he combined the two notions of hardness and separability in supposing matter to be a composition of atoms—if he was asked why there was a resistance made to matter by matter why one subject opposed another he referred it to the

---

c Comma inserted in pencil
d Caret and query mark in pencil in right-hand margin over erasure that seems to have read "poets"
e Altered in pencil to "impenetrability"
f–g Parentheses inserted in pencil

impenetrability of atoms if he was asked why matter was capable of being divided as for instance any thing being crushed the answer was the same—the atoms are divided from each other though they themselves are irresistible[h]—something however was required why these atoms came together at all how they came to connect and form essence into order[i] to this he was obliged to imagine that is to invent a power the very thing which he had been anxious to avoid which he called gravity a something which was no longer either an [f 92] atom or any thing capable of being conceived of by the mind but a notion altogether borrowed from what he found within himself namely the sense of power and out of this came the whole notable system of material or mechanic philosophy I mean permit me to say the mechanic philosophy take as the base and ground work of human knowledge ⟨in⟩ itself as ~~an~~ instrumental[j] it cannot be too highly valued but it began with a perfect fiction as complete a dream as ever formed any imagined image for if you made it of any size . . . and if this is to be answered it must be by a Miracle—that is by a power but of a different kind having preternaturally given it a degree of hardness which though essentially it would not have had yet by that act of power it was[k] chosen to possess thereby directly introducing what it was wished to avoid and even when they had had this fiction upon which the whole was grounded what was to be done with it—the atoms would remain harmless atoms as harmless—I wish all nonsense was equally [f 93] so—no there must be another datum given namely that they were to have two powers attraction and repulsion to attract and to repel and that the result of this should be another power gravitation there was a second violent assumption but the third is most wonderful of all for all this would do nothing but by accident one atom was larger than the rest consequently having a larger force and that being the case it is as easy as can be—it is only to see how things are and then put that as the cause by which they became to be—it is sufficient if you call the sun the largest atom and the stars smaller atoms and apportion the degrees of attraction and repulsion and it is as easy as can be—It is only to make three perfectly arbitrary and contradictory positions and the whole is done—all that can be lamented is that so much time should have been wasted for it is simply saying why the truth was that the causes of things were that they were and something or other must have been and that something or other must have been the

***

[h] Corrected to "indivisible" in pencil, probably in the hand of JHG

[i] "in order" written in pencil above line, probably in the hand of JHG, and caret below line, also in pencil. Substitution for "into order" presumably being suggested

[j] "means" inserted in pencil, probably in the hand of JHG

[k] Query mark written in pencil in right-hand margin

cause—no more is gained for no man can understand [f 94] more by an atom than by something ⟨no man can understand more by attraction & repulsion placed in an atom than by something or nothing⟩ and so on for this reason that the moment he comes to explain the words he refers only to certain appearances which are generalized under those words and if he means more than that he travels out of the system the case comes to a power altogether unmechanical which is necessary for the first step of every mechanical reason—exactly as every man making a machine goes on the presumption of gravitation and would laugh if you asked him what machine that was—he would say if it was so there must have been another gravitation and so on ad infinitum for a machine never could originate its motion in any mechanical principle

Still it is observable that Democritus himself was none of the modern Atheists none of the materialists his reason indeed out of two difficulties or of two absurdities I may say[^l] have chosen the one he chose materialism instead of Spinosism and therein he has made the better choice because by leading men more to exercise their senses and to acquire experience concerning the bodies in nature and their [f 95] operations he then led us to science and in all ages therefore his name has been and deserves to be venerated but his feelings show him entitled to it—the very absurdities which he labors through in order to produce an object for the hopes and fears of men his contrivance of a particular kind of spherical atom out[^m] of which the time was made which was to be different from the atom of matter his notion that those atoms could not be divided or dissolved[^n] his notion that certain effluxes which came from and produced Gods and Demons which [^o]whatever their origin[^p] were beings of high perfection in short all the Religion that could be produced on this principle that the effect was more noble than the cause all this Democritus did with hearty good will but still the consequence of these struggles of Human Reason with itself the calling in question on the part of his School and that of . . . and attempting to originate them in the objects of the senses on the one hand . . . the denial of motion and in short all of those things which it is not [f 96] in our power to disbelieve however we try on the part of Zeno had produced a sceptical turn in the minds of men in that upon which the state of society must always depend namely the tone of mind the better educated man has to prepare . . .[^q] for the extraordinary victories which

[^l]: "may" inserted in pencil, probably in the hand of JHG
[^m]: "ot" overwritten to make "out"
[^n]: Comma inserted in pencil
[^o-p]: Parentheses inserted in pencil
[^q]: Indecipherable comment inserted in pencil in right-hand margin, probably in the hand of JHG. Perhaps "Hiatus considerabilis"?

the Athenians joined with the other Greeks but in which the Athenians preserved their . . . splendid victories the romantic character of those Victories the constant appeal to them in the orations before the people joined with the Democratic Government and the lessening ascendancy of the gentry or higher classes over the populace luxury increased rapidly by a new communication with Persia and the East through the rich Commercial towns of Minor Asia with luxury selfishness and a disposition to enjoy life rather than think about it made an admirable ground for a system which not[r] in point of intellect was[s] much different or much worse than had gone before but was utterly different by its object which was that of loosening the [f 97] human mind from all control except from that of a calculation which was left to every mans own choice what degree of enjoyment he was likely to have from this or that mode—Various have been the pictures given us ⟨by⟩ Plato Aristotle and other Sophists but I know none equal in fidelity and liveliness to that given by a Jewish writer whose work is in the Apocrypha under the name of the wisdom of Solomon where speaking of these sophists he said "For they said reasoning with themselves but not aright our life is short and tedious and in the death of man there is no remedy neither was there any man known to have returned from the grave"—The first thing is reducing all things to the mere experience of the senses "For we are born at all adventure and we shall be hereafter as though they had never been—for the breath in our nostrils is as smoke and a little spark in the morning of our heart—Which being extinguished our body shall be turned into ashes and our spirit shall vanish as the soft air—And our name shall be forgotten in time" sufficient to shew [f 98] that from all the objects of the senses we have nothing but corruptibility and why should we suppose we are formed not merely because we have life and spirit so has a tree in its way so the beast and yet they die they pass into ashes and their Spirit whatever it is blends into the common Air into that great Abyss which the religious men call Deity and there is an end of it but still the mind of man aims for preeminence and even in that state too noble to be utterly debased by such opinions he wishes to live in his children he wishes to live in the recollection and blessings of his posterity No the Sophists say "Our name shall be forgotten in time and no man shall have our works in remembrance and our life shall pass away as the trace of a cloud and shall be dispersed as a mist that is driven away with the beams of the Sun and overcome with the heat thereof For our time is a very shadow that passeth away—and after our end there is no returning—for it is fast sealed so that no man cometh again Come on therefore" This is the natural result [f 99] and excellent good

---

[r] "not" crossed out in pencil
[s] "not" inserted in pencil, probably in the hand of JHG

logic too according to this notion "Come on therefore let us enjoy the good things that are present and let us speedily use the creatures like as in youth. Let us fill ourselves with costly wine and ointments and let no flower of the spring pass by us—Let us crown ourselves with rose buds before they be withered—Let none of us go without his part of our voluptuousness let us leave tokens of our joyfulness in every place for this is our portion and our lot is this" Then the Writer with a beautiful insight into human nature shows how close the cruelty follows on sensuality and that hardening of the mind with*t* sensuality in all its forms is most sure to produce "Let us oppress the poor righteous man let us not spare the Widow nor reverence the ancient grey hairs of the aged—let our strength be the law of Justice for that which is feeble is found to be nothing worth—Therefore let us lie in wait for the righteous because he is not for our turn"—if this should appear to be a picture drawn from an enemy permit [f 100] me to give you the evidence of a Sophist in his own words and I will trust to your recollection to compare them with the part of the Scripture which I have just read*u* [f 101] among you"—This I believe is the earliest so it is the best exposition of right as it is disjoined from duty I wish we heard less of it in the present day—that this was not a mere accompaniment of a debauched state but that it was truly and effectually a working agent in precipitating its fall we have every testimony that History can give us and as if the Almighty either by direct interference as in the case of the Hebrews or by particular providence never left man wholly without an aid in the worst times and if he*v* refused it left him wholly without excuse*w* at that time and in this age was Socrates born whose whole life was one contest against the Sophists but who yet marked the necessity of Revelation by an intermixture of weakness nay even of sophistry in his own mode of contending against them he did the best it was*x* for unassisted man to do he lived holily and died magnanimously and he who judges us by the love in our hearts when we have in the hour . . . we may safely look for our reward he was [f 102] a man *y*if I may speak of him as a man and as far as we can learn of his biographer Xenophon or the more suspicious representations of Plato who however is very faithful in his portraits*z* generally appears to have possessed a fine and active but yet not very powerful imagination—an imagination instrumental and illus-

---

t "with" corrected in pencil to "which", probably in the hand of JHG
u Remainder of page left blank to accommodate missing quotation
v "(viz) man" written in pencil in right-hand margin and marked for insertion at this point, probably in the hand of JHG
w Semi-colon inserted in pencil
x "possible" inserted in pencil, probably in the hand of JHG
y-z Parentheses inserted in pencil and "one who" added in pencil, probably in the hand of JHG

trative rather than predominant and creative but beyond all doubt what characterized him was—pardon the play[a] on words the human excellence of common sense naturally and by observation he excelled in this and cultivated it—there was in his character an exquisite balance and equilibrium and harmony of all the various faculties so that every where his mind acted by a sort of tact as it were rather than arithmetically or by examining the process this without genius would have been the character of a wise natural unaffected man but Socrates doubtless possessed genius in a high degree a peculiar turn for contemplation not for the purposes of physical truth but in aid of prior truths or antici[f 103]pations[b] found in his own nature by meditation—He meditated observed the goings on of his mind started questions to himself as far as by himself he could decide them he did but then modestly went forth among mankind and still questioned every where how far general experience authorized him to generalize those truths. His genius ⟨too⟩ and this turn for observation arising from meditation was thereby distinguished from that of Xenophonic observation[c] This turn for meditative observation was connected in him as we find it in others of our times with a species of humour and keen perception of the extravagant the irrational the absurd and with the freedom of a republican city it led him frequently into good humoured conversations with his fellow citizens you all allow[d] with the Sophists and with their disciples that so hard is it for virtue to wrestle with Vice or Goodsense with Folly without receiving some stain on its outward garments it cannot be denied I fear that from this practice he fell at times into the very errors he was opposing—at all events by his example [f 104] he gave currency to a mode of argument which may be as easily perhaps more easily adapted to delusion than sound conviction it has the misfortune at least by entangling a man in a number of questions the answers to which he does not anticipate of leaving a final conviction as if the man were cheated in the conclusion though he could see no mode afterwards to escape from it but with minds truly ingenuous nothing is more desirable than this method of leading the mind to a consciousness of its own ignorance by degrees and of securing every step behind before there was any undue progress forwards these are the faults and excellence of the Socratic mode as they appear to me

But this was not all—⟨all⟩ these qualities would not of themselves have

---

[a] Word underlined in pencil and query mark in pencil in right-hand margin

[b] Although catchword on f 102 is "pations", f 103 gives whole word "anticipations"

[c] "Xenophonic observation" underlined and query mark in right-hand margin, both in pencil

[d] "you all allow" underlined and altered to "you will allow", in pencil, probably in the hand of JHG, and cancelled pencilled query mark in right-hand margin

formed a Socrates he had and in that all of his contemporaries and all who followed joined a deep nay what our enlightened men of the present day would perhaps call a superstitious and earnest piety which disposed [f 105] him to the reverence of the unknown whatever it were nay even to a reverence of the best*e* signs of it however he might disapprove of them which secured his fellow creatures from being merely as the beasts that perish—he was in every sense of the word a religious man and as the natural result of Religion combined a firm love of his fellow creatures

I should be thought to have omitted a very important or at least interesting part of the disquisition if I did not say a few words on the Demon of Socrates—he thought himself and he asserted himself to be accompanied by a Demon as he called it it gave him no light no insight it was as evidently not conscious for it never decided on the right or wrong of any action but it was a precentiae*f* preventiae presentiment which whenever he was about to do that which would be injurious either temporally or morally withheld him—nor was this all but in a passage where he endeavors to explain it *g*[f 106] if that indeed may be called explanation which commences with a full acknowledgement that it was utterly inexplicable to him that he was as much surprized and unable to account for it as those who related it—that it—that it had an influence upon those around him and he introduces an instance of a young man who had been a sensualist who ⟨had declared he⟩ had heard from others the doctrines which Socrates had taught and was disposed to ridicule and laugh at them that ⟨where*h*⟩ he heard them himself he was impressed not intellectually by an insight into the truth but in a manner he could not account for but when introduced to Socrates he felt a change in his mind a predisposition to receive the truth so utterly different from any thing which a pleasing appearance could produce or impress upon him as to induce him with the belief that there was something divine nay says Socrates as if he was preparing for credulity which his love [f 107] of truth would not permit him to avoid exciting nay I have known my friends by being in the house where I was to feel suddenly on my entering it an influence on their minds which they had not in the moments before been conscious of and an influence of its own kind—As I am utterly incapable of explaining this fact I mention it only to express one conviction of mine that it is always easy to say I do not understand it and till I have the means of so doing here I will rest unless there be some manifest conviction brought to me of ei-

---

e "best" underlined in pencil with query mark in pencil in right-hand margin
f "precentiae" underlined in pencil with a query mark in pencil in right-hand margin
g Hand changes to that of Transcriber C
h "where" altered in pencil to "when"

ther intentional or unintentional imposture it is easy to say with Gibbon there is a middle state . . . and bring Socrates as an example this is easily said but where are the proofs of it what is there in Socrates's whole character which should lead him to assert it if false without deriving any consequences [f 108] from it without any wish to excite a sect instead of referring it to any inspiration to declare it inexplicable to have mentioned it as wishing to have it explained

I say general truths are good—things in themselves but must be applied casually[i] or else they would come from being generals to mere nothings[j] I say I cannot pretend to limit the powers of Providence I can on the contrary see very substantial motives for the supposition that while God acted directly upon the chosen nation as preparing a Receptacle for that Religion which was to spread over all mankind He did not in the meantime wholly abandon those who were hereafter to be taken into his Church but in other ways so distinguishable from the truths of Revelation and the miracles that accompanied it as not to hazard the least confusion and yet a sufficient [f 109] pledge that his Providence was universal and that wherever there was a heart that truly loved Him there His assistance was given either by the means of nature or by Inspirations of which we are not capable of judging

The clamour of the Sophists against Socrates and his death or what it might be truly called his martyrdom I will not detail to you you must be all acquainted with them from childhood—it is sufficient to state that in his philosophy he had the design and he certainly produced the effect of making the moral being of man the especial and single object of thought and of human institution disheartened by the gross-incongruity of the opinions of the elder philosophers seeing no good arising at that time perhaps despairing far too early of any good which might arise from their physical astrono[f 110]mical[k] and astrological speculations he said whether these things be true or not and whether anything or nothing is to come out of them still man must be man before generally they can receive any advantage our great object at present is to render ourselves susceptible of any truths for good purposes which God may hereafter grant us the proper knowledge of mankind is man—Consequently all his reasoning and I may add all his sophistry tend to this one point to withdraw the

---

[i] "casually" altered in pencil to "cautiously" in an unidentified hand

[j] "from being . . . mere nothings" underlined in pencil; "note wanted" written in pencil in right-hand margin, probably in the hand of JHG

[k] Ink page number for this page jumps to 55 from 53, 54 having been written by mistake on blank verso of p 53. Catchword on f 109, "mical" followed on f 110 by full word "astronomical"

human mind from all other subjects as of main or important[l] interest till it had entered into that the last the most important both his death and his condition—the state of his own moral being from[m] the influence of Socrates from the celebrity if I may say so of his death, from the hasty repentance of the Athenians afterwards this undoubtedly produced on the Pagan World a greater [f 111] effect than any other single event can be supposed to do it undoubtedly did draw the mind of Plato and others to more and more speculations concerning the heart of man and when at last the whole came to be this that with the better and profounder kind it excited an anticipation of some clearer knowledge which doubless[n] prepared greatly for the reception of Christianity in the Lower orders who were incapable of understanding these abstract speculations still produced a sense of their necessity which made them receive Christianity with gratitude and with fervor

This must be stated as a defect likewise as indeed is the case in the writings before the time of Socrates and even in a number of the Theologues[o] of Plato himself there is a confusion arising from the word Happiness—Happiness is every where stated as the aim of man the last aim but with Socrates as with the writers much [f 112] later than he indeed hitherto no proper distinction has been made what is properly meant by happiness and if it were required of me to attempt to impress upon the minds of others the importance of words and the truth of old Hobbes's maxim that how easily from mistakes in words men fall into mistakes in the most important things, I know not a more impressive instance than this of the word Happiness—There are four perfectly distinct states we need only appeal to our own consciences to know their distinctions namely that of a bodily ... in other words a perfect correspondence of the external stimulants to the frame to be stimulated producing an aggregate of bodily pleasurable sensations has on the second a certain joyousness ... as where Pythagoras descovered the proposition that made him cry out Eureka and this every man who has intellectual [f 113] intellectual[p] light will refuse to consider—I do consider analogous to the pleasure of eating venison or enjoying anything else bodily—he calls it intellectual pleasure forgetting he must find something in common ... the third is a speculative point which arises from the consideration of our extreme de-

---

[l] Suggested corrections "mean" and "un" (for "mean or unimportant") written in pencil above line probably in the hand of JHG

[m] Altered to "From" in pencil

[n] Altered in pencil to "doubtless"

[o] Altered in pencil to "Dialogues", probably in the hand of JHG

[p] No catchword at end of f 112 and f 113 repeats "intellectual" as if the first instance had been catchword

pendance upon external things that a man has reason to congratulate himself on having been born in such an hour and climate under such and such circumstances and under such auspicious circumstances this the ancients called . . .*q* that is when the Gods were favorable to them and we call it Happiness when things happen well—the fourth I cannot otherwise express than in the words of the Liturgy—as "the peace of God" which every man who has ⟨had⟩ an approving conscience must [f 114] must know*r* how infinitely it is degraded from being combined in one . . . with eating and drinking or whatever follows.

Now Socrates was constantly vacillating at one time things were to be revered and honoured for their utility which at times meant the quantum of agreeable sensations sometimes other things were evil and then it signified an intellectual harmony at other times he has a still higher flight and he speaks with true piety of blessedness but*s* again relapses and considers this but another mode of pleasure the consequence of this was shown his disciples immediately I am not speaking of those who became so eminent to themselves as Plato and Aristotle for they are subjects each of a separate consideration but of Aristippus and Antisthenes*t*—a poor man of a morose [f 115] constitution originally who understood from Socrates that happiness consisted in independance—in the being free from all ⟨the⟩ anxieties after pleasure and equally with the others made pleasure or the absence of pain their happiness and from thence founded the Sect of the Cynics which threw off . . . denied all the civilities of life and the courtesies because they led to Falsehood and in short became a mendicant friar under pretence of morality covering an intense selfishness and evidencing it by two things the gratifying it of*u* human malignity by perpetually sneering at the vices of others and maintaining himself by the booty gained from this gratification—on the other extreme arose Aristippus who was a man of rank and fashion and of chearful temper and he considering as was very fairly deduced from it that with regard to pleasure the [f 116] question is not what sort but how much for if it is pleasure why ask what sort it is that is dependant upon accidents one man may say I delight in Milton and Shakspeare more than Turtle or Venison another man that is not my case for myself I think a good dish of turtle and a good bottle of port afterwards give me much more delight

---

q "q Ευδαιμονια or Ευτυχια" inserted in space in pencil, probably in the hand of JHG, the "q" standing, presumably, for "query"

r Repetition again results from mistake with catchword

s Letter obliterated between "blessedness" and "but"

t Apart from first letter, "Antisthenes" written in ink in another hand over an erasure, probably by JHG

u "of" inserted in ink over an erasure, probably by JHG

question is not what sort but how much for if it is pleasure why ask what sort it is that is dependant upon accidents one man may say I delight in Milton and Shakspeare more than Turtle or Venison another man that is not my case for myself I think a good dish of turtle and a good bottle of port afterwards give me much more delight than I receive from Milton and Shakspeare you must not dispute about tastes and if a taste for Milton is the same as a taste for Venison there is no objection to be found in the argument at least it is perfectly clear that if they are all diffe- rent species of pleasure the question of what kind it is must be referred to the accident of the organs which are to be the means of conveying it and the only

61

6. Frere manuscript, transcriber C's hand. VCL MS BT 23 f 116
Victoria University Library, Toronto; reproduced by kind permission

than I receive from Milton and Shakspeare you must not dispute about tastes and if a taste for Milton is the same as a taste for Venison there is no objection to be found in the argument at least it is perfectly clear that if they are all different species of pleasure the question of what kind it is must be referred to the accident of the organs which are to be the means of conveying it and the [f 117] only result which is universal to all men is how much of it there is therefore from the laxity of the Socratic moral with regard to the subject of utility and out of that to the word Happiness Eudamonismas and the system which has been since called ... all the Sophists whom Socrates had done so much to destroy reappeared in a short time and the name of the Epicureans no longer sceptical ... degraded idea and with it corruption and sensuality which first produced the utter downfall of Grecian greatness and Greek Liberty then did they pass over to avenge the Greeks on their Conquerers the Romans and to produce the same effects in a more disgusting form till the time came when human nature presented one of the most hateful objects human nature could do namely a power upon earth [f 118] a nature above animals with superior powers to do yet exerting all those powers to cultivate the very worst ⟨passions with the very worst⟩^{v} objects of the beasts that perish such was the point that history gives it of the system of pleasure as the great object of morals and which has been now speciously called the calculations of utility upon the sound ~~of~~ basis of Self-Love—

---

^{v} Insertion in ink may be in the hand of JHG

LECTURE 4

ᵂMʳ Coleridges Lecture
Monday 11ᵗʰ January 1819.

An indolent man lying on his Sofa and yawning is said to have exclaimed
. . . I wish this was being at Work—something like a similar feeling I may
express I wish that the subject of philosophy were as amusing to us as it
is important but we must take it as it is consoling ourselves with this that
every pleasure that is procured by attempting at something beyond . . . In
the important stage in the history of philosophy on which we are now
standing it will be convenient to take a rapid review of what I have hitherto laid before you—I began with Thales or the Ionic Sect and shewed
that these differed from their predecessors and were therefore entitled to
be mentioned as forming the path—the transit to philosophy rather
[f 120] than philosophers themselves by seeking for the origin of things
in their own observations and in the force of their own understandings instead of deriving them from history and religious tradition—The good
which this exertion of the human intellect brought with it appeared in the
immediate followers of Thales himself—they had already detected two
great truths neither of which have yet been used to their full extent and
which like many truths of the elder mathematicians are to produce their
effects thousands of years after them first that the final solution of phenomena cannot itself be a phenomenon and next the law that Action and
re-action can only take place between things similar in essence—Such
were their merits—Pythagoras the proper founder of Philosophy proposed the whole problem the attempt to solve which constitutes the
philosopher namely the connexion of the visible thing the phenomenon
with the invisible thing under a cause common to both and above both—
unfortunately our knowledge of the particulars of [f 121] this great man
and his opinions are and must remain matter of conjecture—in other
words with him as with others in history we must have discovered the
truth ourselves by other means before out of the mass of traditions assertions and fables we can discriminate what really was Pythagorean ⟨and

ᵂ Hand of Transcriber B

671

this great man and his opinions are and must remain matter of conjecture - in other words with him as with others in history we must have discovered the truth ourselves by other means before out of the mass of traditions assertions and fables we can discriminate so what really was Pythagorean. and that it was Pythagorean After him philosophy split immediately into two sects, the Eleatic under Zeno who allowed the World to possess no reality and the Corpuscular under Democritus who allowed of the existence of body the ultimate ground of which body he placed in atoms. Then arose Anaxagoras who in many respects resembled our own *Locke* he attempted and in part did reconcile both parties. he introduced the Nous and supreme mind but he still retained matter and he still retained   as acting upon matter and from the mind he deduced all in matter that was formed - proportion aptitude and so forth

          In this manner he reconciled the best feelings of men inwardly and of a moral nature their feelings having outward morality but he did not solve any of the difficulties

3

that it was Pythagorean⟩—After him philosophy split immediately into two sects the Eleatic under Zeno who allowed the World to possess no reality and the Corpuscular under Democritus who allowed of the existence of body the ultimate ground of which body he placed in atoms— Then arose Anaxagoras who in many respects resembled our own lot[x] he attempted and in part did reconcile both parties—he introduced the nouse[y] and supreme mind but he still retained matter and he still retained . . . as acting upon matter and from the mind he deduced all in matter that was formed—proportion aptitude and so forth.

In this manner he reconciled the best feelings of men inwardly and of a moral nature their feelings having outward morality but he did not solve any of the dif[f 122]ficulties for if he was asked what becomes of this matter after you have taken away the properties he would be at a loss to decide the question for a thing without any property at all is tantamount to nothing—were he asked what property is it essential to matter—what is the meaning of the word you use and as you take two powers first matter and then intellect and the one independent of the other how do you explain the possibility of the action of the one upon the other—to all this Anaxagoras would certainly have no answer to return and the fact is that while it did honor to his heart to have secured in his philosophy an object for the best moral feelings of mankind and in itself most advantageous inasmuch as philosophy cultivated in parts is much better than philosophy not cultivated at all by securing an object for the contemplation of the human mind when dwelling on its own highest faculties still I say so lame was the system of the world which he brought forward that not only Aristotle but Plato himself complains of him that [f 123] his nouse or supreme reason was a mere hypothesis to solve a few impossibilities but never introduced when he could do without it—as long as ever Mechanical causes could explain the thing so long the nouse was not heard of when a miracle was to be worked then only when he had no further reason to give this nouse was introduced. This matter has certainly led the way to those who beginning with an acknowledgment of the supreme reason attribute it so much to second causes that it becomes a matter of wonder what was remaining to the first cause or wherein the necessity could consist—for if matter in itself without reason and without benevolence could by any positions into which it might be placed act wisely and act benevolently common sense would say if now it is possible why not always possible—the very answer to that would imply immediately the very contrary namely that it was not possible for it is evident that it

[x] "Locke" written beside "lot" in right-hand margin, perhaps by EHC
[y] "nouse" altered in pencil to "Nous"

cannot be incompatible with matter universally with every particle the matter may be sup[f 124]posed to have for any given time—it is very true that taking any one particle of matter it could not be supposed to originate in itself but that this must be derived not from any thing out of matter but from matter itself is implied in the very supposition that matter has it and that therefore it is a property not at all contradictory to matter but that which may be connected with it therefore I say that Anaxagoras provided a scheme which had some disadvantages and some advantages— it had sundry advantages in as much as for those who did not think very deeply it offered no outrage to their moral or religious feelings and on the other hand it was better than the Eleatic School the Idealists because it left a world of observation open to the mind and was at least neutral if not favorable to experimental philosophy—From these disputes however for I cannot say that his doctrines had real influence upon Society but that while the good man prided himself upon his consciousness that there was a supreme reason the bad man took advantage of the logic of what he ought from his own principles to have concluded—though I [f 125] say I cannot find that he produced any great effect on Society—that whatever it was seems to have given way to the corruption of manners introduced by the sudden prosperity and ambition and democratic fury of the Greek States had the whole progress of philosophy been confined to the history of Greece I should not hesitate in affirming that it had been an evil for mankind if only for this reason—that it was joined with that corruption the principal cause of the origin of the Sophists—men who no sooner had discovered that the reason and the reasoning faculties had power in themselves but they abused it to the worst purposes of the worst passions namely as I have shewn in a former lecture to unsettle all the moral feelings—all that bound man to man upon the score of a crude speculation which was then beginning only to found itself—from the corruption of morals and manners doubtless the Sophists began though like worms they not only increased the putridity that produced them but made it additionally contagious yet it was from the reputation of preceding philosophers [f 126] had gained—it was from the confusion of mind produced from the opposition of the Sects—the Eleatic who denied all credit to the senses and the sect of Democritus who placed all in the senses that these men borrowed their Armour—the state of things as presented to us by history ⟨is shocking—perhaps nothing in history⟩ to a reflecting mind so shocking for you find states enjoying every blessing of heaven in a lovely climate with competency of life high guides of nature—those highly cultivated with objects of patriotism that still tended to expand each mind nearer falling into a sympathy with the whole—a dignity derived even from an unhappy source but then common to the whole World that of slavery and yet instead of aught moral that should have followed this the historians represent them as utterly false incapable of all trust—cruel in their private life and debauchees and in their public life open to every man who could bribe them either on the one side by money or on the other by that worst of all bribes to a corrupt people the flattery and gratification of their pride and their rapacity—

[f 127]   In this emergency Providence vouchsafed to raise up Socrates who attributing the unsettled state of his Countrymen in great part to the application of the mind^z by^a those who ought to have been their instructors and who were best fitted both morally and intellectually to have become such—attributing it I say to their application to objects which he deemed placed beyond all but conjecture namely the organization of things and the laws of the World and in part to the neglect which thence arose in the media of the intercourse between man and man namely language and the connexion of thoughts^b lived and died in the unwearied effort to convince his Countrymen that the proper object of mankind was the knowledge of man and again in his modes of impressing this truth he endeavored to teach all with whom he conversed that it was idle to argue without previous definitions of the terms used by the disputants and that the only way to arrive at a just definition was by a fair induction of all the particulars which could not be gained but by looking at them without prejudice and with a mind weaned from its selfish passions—but I endeavored [f 128] to shew and I believe proved in my former lecture that Socrates himself was not free from the errors which it was his object to oppose and I must not say that without adding his imperishable glory to have opposed in so many and in such important points—for little and with a poor spirit does he estimate the merits of a great man by the mere quantum of direct truth which he happens to teach first or detract from that merit by the quantum of error with which that truth was mingled through human imperfections and the state of the times in which he lived—No these are but small and comparatively trifling portions of a great mans merits—it is to have awakened an idea—to have excited a Spirit to have opened a road and to have given the first impulse to it—he is working in hundreds in after ages who are working in his Spirit and to him they will all in proportion as they possess his genius give praise and honor—not that this and that was done well or this or that erroneously but that it was done at all—that it was attempted that the path was

---

^{z} Indistinct pencilling seems to intend alteration of "mind" to "minds"
^{a} "by" altered in pencil to "of"
^{b} "Socrates" written above line, perhaps by EHC

opened—that the light was given—that the impulse was provided [f 129] the power of doing this constitutes the power of a great man—I could not mention the name of Socrates with any thing that resembles detraction without saving myself from the infamy by this explanation

The Socratic method safe in his hands and in those of men as pure as himself was certainly too near to a sort of special pleading by not presenting the whole at first to the person who was to be converted but entrapping him into concessions as to the result of which he was to be kept in the dark—This I have mentioned chiefly for its historic importance for in his hands as we shall see hereafter it was admirably adapted—there is a greater defect that which admits of no compliment though all that I have said before fully applies to it he began to think deeply of that which men ought really to exist in and to pursue—he seriously proposed to himself and to his fellow Citizens the question what is the summum bonum—what is that highest good that ultimate aim to which all the detail of our efforts and of our withholdings are to be considered as instrumental—as secondary [f 130] as mere means—Now here there does certainly appear in the Socratic doctrines a considerable vascilation[c] Socrates appears to have felt it not without considerable irritation natural to a good mind which had not yet perfectly cleared the doubt—he says I devote to the furies the man who first made the distinction between the useful and the honorable but it was not a man that made the distinction—it was human nature that had made it it was the corruptions of human nature it was all the circumstances in contradiction to the higher destinies of men and which were constantly making conquests wide and near moving all nations I may say which had made the distinction before him and which with an imperative voice still continued amidst the shouts and triumphs of wickedness and the groans of oppressed virtue—amidst all that was good in the good and all that was evil in the evil called aloud—yea with the most piercing of ⟨all⟩ invocations that of inward prayer to the unknown being—unknown yet wished for did it call till He who alone could give the answer to it appeared in his Son and introduced the decision by the voice of ~~the~~ revealed religion.

[f 131]   The great point which Socrates laid down was this that ignorance was the ground of all vice and therein of all misery and that knowledge on the contrary was the source of all virtue and therein of all happiness—to this object he constantly tended but it was evident to a thinking man that either it was an argument in circle or it led to the destruction of the very essence of virtue for if he meant which he could not

---

[c] Altered in pencil to "vacilation"

that no man does a crime knowing it to be a crime and knowing that its effects will be a[d] disproportionate one[e] to the misery to his future being[f] compared to the gratification he immediately receives from it—it is notoriously false every drunkard that lifts with trembling hands his glass to his lips and even sheds tears over it knowing the anguish it will occasion is a proof against it—⟨No—⟩ it is impossible as the whole experience of the World shews—it is not an ignorance of the effects that will arise from it but to get rid of the pain arising from the want of it and that just in proportion as the pleasure declines so the temptation as it is called or the motive becomes equal—then does the impulse then does the goad become most tremendous—not a single ray of pleasure before hand but the daily round of habit from behind that presses on the human mind—[f 132] it could not be taken therefore in this sense for we all know—we are so well persuaded in our own mind that what we call criminals are aware at the time they commit the crime both of its criminality and of its consequences to themselves that wherever we can make out a fair case of compleat ignorance we acquit the being of guilt and place him either as an idiot or a madman or as by law we do as a child So little is it possible that in this sense vice can originate properly speaking in ignorance but if on the other hand Socrates meant that vice was not possible was not compatible with the clear perfect insight into the very nature of the action of the Soul and such a commanding idea ⟨to⟩ the mind as comprizes a perfect science— how is this to be given for his great doctrine was that it could be taught— the only answer to be made was it must be given with a mind predisposed to it and hence he uses the word apathia not ignoria for ignorance—this is merely a concession of the point in dispute for then there is something attached to knowledge and the condition of it—not knowledge itself which is necessary to make this knowledge efficacious or influential so that in truth [f 133] we see that knowledge without this is without avail so on the other hand we see this without knowledge is of great avail and therefore the foundation of virtue must be laid in something to which knowledge indeed as highly natural which in its general effects must lead to knowledge but which in itself is a higher principle than knowledge namely placed in the Will if I may venture to use such a phrase and in that religion which is inate[g] in man only because it is felt by the very necessity of it

In his own logic therefore he failed for the whole as we shall see presently consisted and first led to a just system of reasoning—Now in all just generalization the genus or kind ought to contain the essential of

---

[d] "a" cancelled in pencil   [e] "one" cancelled in pencil
[f] "being" altered in pencil to "Being"   [g] Altered to "innate" in pencil

each Species and not a mere quality common to the species either accidentally or because that quality is universal as for instance if I were to
generalize trees from their uprightness or from their possibilities or any
number of different trees by the accident of their having the same color—
thus again if I were to generalize sugar and sugar of lead because they
have the same color both are sweet to the taste both look exactly alike
both are chrystallized both frangible by [f 134] the touch but the one being
nutritious and the other a deadly poison every man would admit with me
that I should have made a false generalization Now some error like this
Socrates seems to have fallen into in the ground work of his argument
namely that pleasure is the ultimate object of all our pursuits—or as we
should now say, "happiness Oh happiness our end and aim" and so
forth—It will be instructive to ask whether pleasure is properly capable
of being designated[h] of all the pursuits of men whether it is a fit generalization—whether I have a right for instance strictly speaking for I am
now not talking for common life but with an attempt at least toward philosophy—have we a right I say to talk in one word of the pleasure of a
good conscience and the pleasure of a good dinner as a similar good—
because both are what a man would rather wish than avoid—is that a sufficient generalization or more so in truth than the circumstance of the
shape and taste of the Sugar and the sugar of lead—I seem to myself to
feel the contrary and just before I came here I lit on an old pocket book
which for years had been thrown by and in it there is a conversation
[f 135] which I had at Keswick with a man of great notoriety in the present day as a Critic—Having expressed my convictions to this purport he
answered that he saw no greater impropriety in calling that particular state
of being which we experience from an approving conscience *this* pleasure and a different state of being which we possess during the gratification of any appetite that[i] pleasure than in pointing to brandy and saying
this fluid and then to water and saying that fluid—In other words I replied
you contend that pleasure is a general term in short the genus generalis-
simum of whatever is desirable for our nature even as you make pain the
general term of the contrary? Even so he said and why not—I answered
for three reasons—first because according to your own concession we already possess such a term in the word good—Pleasure therefore in this
sense becomes a mere lazy Synonime whereas it is the business of the
philosopher to desynonymize words originally equivalent therein following and impelling the natural progress of language in civilized Societies I wish we say that such a thing were as pleasant to me as I know it

---

[h] "as the object" inserted in pencil, perhaps by EHC
[i] "that" underlined in pencil

[f 136] to be good—This medicine is exceedingly unpleasant but it is very good for me—Thus you make the same confusion as if you were to use Wine which is the general term of all fermented liquors procured from grapes as a synonime with fluid—You may call Burgundy and Claret this and that fluid—but what if you were to call the Seltzer and the Bath waters this and that Wine—That is the true Sophism—you use that which is not properly general but universal and you apply it as if it were general—you use pleasure in the same sense as a man would do who having called Burgundy and Claret this and that fluid because the genus was known to be the same should proceed to call the Bath and Seltzer Waters this and that Wine in spite of the known essential differences between them—But thirdly and of most importance there is an equivocation in the main word of the definition—Viz. *desirable* by means of which you assume all that ought to be proved and prejudice the very point in dispute between us—For desirable means either that which actually I do desire or that which I know I ought to desire though perhaps [f 137] I am not virtuous enough actually to will it—Oh if this were but virtue might the voluptuary say while embracing an enamoured wanton You pre assume I say that *Good* is nothing more than a reflex idea of the mind after a survey and calculation of agreeable or delightful sensations included within any given time—the whole of our life for instance—Now this I utterly deny—*I know—intuitively know*—that there is a power essential to my nature and which constitutes it human nature the voice of which is I ought I should I ought not I should not and that this voice is original and self-existent not an echo of a prior voice—I mean the voice of prudential self-love but the very source out of which selflove itself must flow and I am a wicked man I feel myself say if I call that good which I feel I desire instead of endeavoring to desire that only which I know to be *good*. If you answer I do not understand what this good is which determines what is desirable instead of desiring it meaning from it we are both in the same predicament—for it is *the Peace of God* which passeth all *understanding*—But if you persist [f 138] in telling me that you are conscious of nothing in your nature which gives any meaning or correspondency to what I have said and that my words are no more than articulated sounds that knock loudly at the portal of your ears and when you open it there is *nothing*—if this be indeed the case as God forbid it should—but if it really be so I can only say I pity you from my inmost Soul—There is a point which is above all intellect and there are truths derived from that point which must be presumed and which if a man denies we say it is not the question whether you can or cannot conceive a straight line or a curved line or that two straight lines cannot include a Space for that Society en-

titles me to tell you You do not understand my words or you wilfully tell a falsehood there is a will a consciousness of something which independent of desire dictates what is desirable and when such principles are denied you may at least candidly say we differ on principles and charitably think that man must be made a better before he can be made a wiser man

This vascilation[j] sometimes inclining and more frequently inclining to the moral [f 139] side at other times seeming at once to incline to the prudential and by prudence to win over and bribe advocates for virtue Socrates seems to have proceeded even with the same temper which we are told was attributed to him with some tenderness of reproach by an Indian Philosopher Calamus who speaking of . . . and other great men said that they were men of great parts and wise men but they paid too much obedience to the laws which could only mean in teaching truth—they were too favorable to the prejudices and customs of those around them alluding doubtless to their toleration of idolatry—The results were seen immediately—could there be a doubt of the truth of my statement it would be answered as I stated before by the circumstance that immediately after the death of Socrates and while his memory was preserved in equal love and veneration by all his disciples they split into three parts one who took the side of virtue and who understood Socrates in the highest sense namely Antisthenes who founded the Cynic School but with a [f 140] perverse Spirit refused all compliance with the very means of virtue and compelled virtue as it were to turn out of doors her best householder prudence . . . if by any means it might scare any and Aristippus who took the principle of selflove and as a man who felt in himself in the enjoyment of good health good fortune and high connexions that he was doing no great harm in the World and thought as many men of the kind have that to live well and comfortably was the great end of life he founded a system since repeated by a French Philosopher that the ground of all morality was selflove but that well calculated—in short he left to every man to determine whether virtue or vice would be likely to be most agreeable in the long run with only two small defects in the argument—the first was how far this system was likely to prepare in the mind any great harbour for that which was to render selflove well calculated—whether the motives you could address to a man in good health and so forth in life and in the enjoyment of the pleasures of life to urge him to the difficult task of thinking [f 141] reading meditating—denying himself those pleasures—sacrificing that and so forth when all that you had to tell him was at last go on just as you are now only as you go on look round you a lit-

---

[j] Altered in pencil to "vacilation"

tle—naturally I try to do that but I may die tomorrow and my mode^k is a short life and a merry one—This is one tremendous defect in that system and the other is that it precludes that very thing in which man is made—for in the name of wonder what is it? Is reason given us to be nothing more than instinct? Instinct guides the animal safely to chuse the food which is healthful to reject that which is injurious to it—it guides it in building its nest appropriate to its wants—everywhere it governs it with regard first to its own safety and secondly the preservation of its species if reason is to be the mere substitute of this—for this is all self love can it tend to an equality with instinct—how comes it that man should be such an unfortunate being as to be stripped of that which leads according to this system to his highest [f 142] good and gives him no compensation whatever by any further objects—instead therefore of his looking on his reason as an advantage he must necessarily look on it as a curse of nature subjecting him to endless wanderings to superstitions to every species of bewilderment from which animals are secure—if he would be at peace with his own mind and with the providence that placed him there^l he must say my nature has been placed above instinct—there is a faculty given to me under conditions and those conditions observed under which it was given will enable me to reconquer for myself as a part of my own nature all that which nature has given in the form of instinct but even there I should have had my labor for my pains were it not that all that this instinct could give me is but the step the ladder to something infinitely higher—Yet I say these two the Cynic and the Cyrenaic sect the sect of those who menaced and frowned upon all the social comforts and all progress of civilization and that which flattered all and every individual [f 143] in it did the disciples of Socrates divide into with the exception of . . . who appeared the true portraits of their Master in this especial thing first they avoided all speculative things all natural philosophy except in subjects of experience and that their morality was derived according to experience ⟨and applied according to experience⟩ which as it fell into such hands as Xenophon was applied most admirably but principles of morals and religion you will seek for in vain and for our present time their writings are of most importance to us as they furnish us with a test of what in the writings of Plato is Socratic and this the more so in Xenophon from a fact which was generally believed by Ancients and according to my own feeling is not slightly confirmed by certain parts of Xenophons own writing that he was at enmity with Plato himself consequently wherever we find the same sentiments attributed to Socrates as are in Plato the same

---

^{k} Altered in pencil to "motto" ^{l} Altered in pencil to "here"

substance of reasoning we may fairly conclude it to [f 144] be Socratic—
then the ordinance being Plato's I do not find any reason myself to suppose there was any serious or intentional deviation from the doctrines of
Socrates to be found in Plato no difference but though*ᵐ* the manner in
which it was given and in this sense I understand the story related concerning Socrates who had of the two dialogues of Plato published before
his death said how many fine things this young man has attributed to me
which do not belong to me but had this regarded any essentials of
Socrates's doctrines had there been any thing in the doctrines of Plato
contrary to them Xenophon would have noticed and resented it and this
not having been done—I think we may fairly rely on the works of Plato
as containing the true opinions of Socrates. I say this because I shall have
afterwards to shew my opinion *ⁿ*paradoxical as it may be*ᵒ* that the works
of Plato contain the opinions of Socrates but they by no means convey
the opinions of Plato I do not mean that they convey different opinions
but they do not convey the [f 145] peculiar opinions of Plato

Plato! I really feel unaffectedly an awe when I mention his name—
when I consider what associations are connected with it—that it is the
characteristic of ages and men that they love and honor the name of Plato
this great man for he truly was such was born at the commencement of
that wide wasting Peloponessan*ᵖ* war which was the true source of ⟨the⟩
destruction of Greece as far as Greece was to be destroyed—that is as far
as Greece was a phenomenon in the world and affecting it is that even
when it was in its very height—in its utmost excellence and producing
those ideas of moral excellence in all the objects of thought—in all the
great principles of Government in all that is to [? convince] and elevate
the mind—the fine arts and the preparations at least for religion at this
very time this destruction was already beginning and preannounced as if
to say for this alone was it created a phenomenon which if it had been of
long endurement would have been utterly [f 146] mischievous appointed
for a particular purpose the hot bed to present impulses for all after generations but not to be imitated but to be mimicked only to the degradation of itself. Such appears to me to have been the Republic of Greece
they were the producers of all that men were afterwards to follow to perfect to diffuse but arose out of a state of society which nothing but that
fulness of genius that paucity of life which is as it were insensible to de-
formity and to pain could have rendered tolerable and which we looking
at coolly cannot but fall into the same feelings as . . . and at the same time
the utmost caprice of immorality and cruelty but at the time too was the

---

ᵐ Altered in pencil to "through"   *ⁿ⁻ᵒ* Parentheses inserted in pencil
ᵖ Altered in pencil to "Peloponesian"

man born who above all others deserved to be called the Prophet and the preparer for the new world to which his writings and still more his spirit had led and it is for something better and yet for something better against which the local polytheism of Greece and Rome struggled for a while but at last was forced to give way to the higher evidence of Christianity for which I have historical evidence [f 147] to prove that Platonism at least predisposed the most effective means

Plato was born a man of rank descended on the side of his Father from the famous Codrus the ideal of a Patriotic King while his mother descended from a Brother of the great Solon he was wealthy as an Athenian at least and who can blame him in taking a pride in his Ancestry which is apparent in his writings but still as if genius dwelt in that descent eminent as a Poet Orator Statesman may we not rather wonder that this man with such advantages took no part in the politics of his Country—he— so eloquent—so gifted by nature personally and by fortune in circumstances—surely here at least we may admit the presence of a higher genius and not improbably the Poetic in the first instance for Plato was a Poet of such excellence as would have stood all other competition but that of his being a Philosopher—his poetic genius imported in him those deep impressions and the love of them which mocking all comparison with after objects leaves behind it*q* [f 148] thirst for something not attained to which nothing in life is found commensurate and which still impels the Soul to pursue—His Tutor Cratylus under whom he studied the philosophy of Heraclitus and Hermodorus gave him all the knowledge that was then to be obtained but in his twentieth year he attached himself to Socrates who soon mastered his whole esteem and affections though it is plain the opinions of Socrates were not commensurate with the whole of his genius After the . . . Plato fled to Megara where Euclid taught a disciple of Socrates—thence he travelled to Italy Cyrenica a famous Colony of the Greeks in Africa to Egypt and to Sicily—One of the chief objects of his travels was and of this we have ample authority to acquaint himself more particularly with ⟨the Pythagorean philosophy and its sources⟩—the same spirit he formed his intimate friendships with . . . both were and continued to be Pythagorean and both men of high rank and estimation in their Country the fame of . . . as a Magician we learn from Horace and Plato speaks of . . . not only as distinguished for [f 149] rank property and the . . . it is worthy notice too that Plato brought back certain writings of the . . . with which Aristotle enriched his library—I mention these facts because I may as well say if I were to give my con-

---

q Catchword, "it", not repeated on f 148

ception of Platos character as far as any great mans character can be conceived of comparatively I should say that it was a combination of Pythagoras with Socrates—the good sense of Socrates and the moral objects he had especially in view but not as Socrates did limiting it to the human being but with a full impression that to understand any one thing well we must at the same moment be struggling to understand the spirit of the whole

On Plato's return from Egypt he visited Sicily and . . . he arrived again at Athens where either in his own garden or in a gymnasium or place of exercise in the suburbs he formed the great philosophic school ~~from~~ which from that place has been called the Academy—his Lectures were of two kinds popular and scientific or . . . and desultory. [f 150] The object of this display—first all we are to remember the fate of Anaxagoras who would have lost his life had he not fled and of Socrates who had fled—in a republic where the Mob were to be the judge a mans innocence was of little avail—it was simply as we should say the daily papers have expressed such and such a feeling for or against a man—prejudice was their Judge Jury and Executioner—no wonder if the Philosophers felt themselves bound in the strict sense to be prudent and reserved if it was only to spare their Countrymen the guilt of repeating the murder of a Socrates but there was another motive likewise and this is in more especial connexion with my present purpose he wished to diffuse as much knowledge among all who were desirous of any as they were capable of receiving and then out of those to select such minds as had manifested a peculiar susceptibility and therefore were worthy of being selected to undergo as the criterion a certain moral discipline rendering them capable of being those of whom Plato could say the truth [f 151] without conveying falsehood I do not believe that there was in Plato at least—whatever there might have been in the mysteries the least desire of witholding any truth from those who were capable of receiving it but that there did dwell on his mind a sense of high responsibility not to do mischief and arm fools with fire under the pretence of conveying truth—he would not set the temples of his native Country on fire simply to bring about what? the destruction of something imperfect for that which was fiendish but as it is with nature in the Beech tree as I have somewhere observed she retains the old leaves upon the tree through the Winter till the new ones arise and as the slow buds prevail and push off the old ones at the time that their successors are already there to take their places for be assured that dry leaves for human nature are better than mere nakedness

Here interrupted by the voyages to Italy with his love for Dion and his zeal for ... he lived in an even course to a good old age and died in his eighty first year—what remains of him [f 152] are his works and his spirit—I have already dared to say that his works convey to us a full and adequate idea of Plato's eloquence—of his exquisite dramatic talent—of his powers of producing a perfect model of conversation among men of rank worthy of that rank by the objects concerning which they conversed that they present the perfection of all that can be wished for in style—in presentation of images in the form in which truth can be presented and I believe too that they convey with little—perhaps with no exceptions what Plato thought only not all that he thought Floyer Sydenham has given so perfectly just an account of the style of Plato's dialogues that it would be idle in me to attempt to give you a better and it is so clear it is well worthy of your attention—The most general division of his writings is into those of a Sceptical and those of a dogmatical kind. In the former nothing is expressly proved or asserted—as some *'philosophical question is considered and examined & the reader is left*' to himself to draw such conclusions and to discover such truths as [f 153] the philosopher means to insinuate—This is done either in the way of enquiry or in that of controversy and dispute—In the way of controversy are carried on all such dialogues as tend to eradicate false opinions and that is done either indirectly by involving them in difficulties and embarrassing the maintainers of them or directly by confuting them—In the way of enquiry proceed those dialogues whose tendency is to raise in the mind right opinions which is effected either by exciting to the pursuit of some part of wisdom and by shewing in what manner to investigate it or by leading the way and helping the mind forward in the search—The dialogues of the other kind namely the dogmatical or didactic teach explicitly some kind of doctrine and this they do either by laying it down in the authoritative way or by proving it in the way of reason and of argument In the authoritative way the doctrine is delivered sometimes by the speaker himself Magisterially and at other times as derived to him by tradition from wise men—The argumentative or demonstrative method of [f 154] teaching used by Plato proceeds either through analytical reasoning resolving things into their principles and from known or allowed truths tracing out the unknown or through induction from a multitude of particulars inferring some general thing in which they all agree according to this division is formed the following scheme or table—

r–s Passage seems to have been inserted later into space too small for it

Dialogue[r]	Sceptical	Disputative	Embarrassing / Confuting
		Inquisitive	Exciting / Assisting
	Dogmatical	Demonstrative	Analytical / Inductional
		Authoritative	Magisterial / Traditional

The Philosopher in thus varying his manner and diversifying his writings into these several kinds ⟨means⟩ not merely to entertain the reader with their variety nor to teach him on different occasions with more or less plainness and perspicuity nor yet to insinuate different degrees of certainty in the doctrines themselves but he takes this method as a consummate Master [f 155] of the art of composition in the dialogue way of writing and from the different characters of the Speakers as from different elements in the frame of these dramatic dialogues or from different ingredients in their mixture he produces some peculiar genius and turn of temper as it were in each Socrates indeed is in almost all of them the principal Speaker but when he falls into the company of some arrogant Sophist when the modest wisdom and clear science of the one are contrasted with the confident ignorance and the blind opiniativeness of the other—dispute and controversy must of course arise where the false pretender cannot fail of being either puzzled or confuted—to puzzle him only is sufficient if there be no other persons present because such a man can never be confuted in his own opinion but when there is an audience round them in danger of being misled by Sophistry into error then is the true Philosopher to exert his utmost and the vain Sophist must be convinced and exposed In some dialogues Plato represents his [f 156] great Master mixing in conversation with young men of the best families in the commonwealth When these persons happen to have docile dispositions and fair minds there is occasion given to the philosopher to call forth the latent seeds of Wisdom and to cultivate the noble plants with true doctrine in the affable and familiar way of joint enquiry—To this is owing the inquisitive genius of such dialogues—in which by a seeming equality in the conversation the curiosity or zeal of the mere stranger is excited and that of the disciple is encouraged and by proper questions the mind

---

[r] "Dialogue" written at right angles to rest of text

also is aided and forwarded in the search of truth—At other times the Philosophic hero of these dialogues is introduced in a higher character engaged in discourse with men of more improved understandings and ⟨of⟩ more enlightened minds At such seasons he has an opportunity of teaching in a more explicit manner and of discovering the reasons of things—for to such an audience with all the demonstration possible in the teaching it is due—Hence in the dialogues [f 157] composed of these persons naturally arises the justly argumentative or demonstrative genius— it is of the analytical kind when the principles of mind or of science the leading truths are to be unfolded; and of the inductional kind when any subsequent truth of the same rank with others or any part of science is meant to be displayed—But when the doctrine to be taught admits not of demonstration of which kind is the doctrine of outward nature being only hypothetical and a matter of opinion the doctrine of antiquities being only traditional and a matter of belief and the doctrine of laws being injunctional and the matter of obedience; the air of authority is then assumed: in the former cases the doctrine is traditionally handed down to others from the authority of ancient Sages; but in the latter it is magisterially pronounced with the authority of a Legislator—That this turn may be given to such dialogues with propriety and with justice to the character of the speakers the reasoning Socrates is laid aside or he only sustains some lower and obscure part while that which is the principal or the shining part is allotted to some other philosopher to whom may properly be attributed a more authoritative manner or to such [f 158] an antiquary as may be credited or may be deemed to have received the best information—or finally to such a statesman or politician as may fairly be presumed best qualified for making laws"

Such is a very fair account of the platonic dialogues and this appears to me to have been the object of Plato to have published for the advantage of all his Countrymen that which being studied by docile minds would lead them to seek further all that could be safely entrusted to men at large—he under the name of Socrates and as I have before proved truly representing his opinions has given us in the most enchanting form but all as i̶s̶ the introduction to something—his objects which were first of all to destroy the Sophistic mode of reasoning all those false modes of conception all that want of true induction and of the faculties and habits of true induction which indispose a mans mind for receiving the truth—this might be called the . . . part of his dialogue—he then proceeds to give in various dialogues the best examples of truth pursued either scientifically by assuming some truth which has been admitted [f 159] and from thence deducing the consequences or analytically by taking the fact and dividing it into parts shewing that itself confuted what had been deduced from it—This might be called the logical part of his writings the disciplinary[u] of the intellect and I believe till the time of Lord Bacon there existed nothing to be compared with it for every where is the principle that in the mind itself must you find the ground of the question but that it is from induction and from nature alone that you can receive the answer and lastly his great object was to take without deciding the question the morality of Socrates as it was truly applicable to the best purposes—hence the whole of the substance if I may so say of Plato's purpose may be said to be contained in four of his dialogues—the Theodotus . . . and the De Republica[v]—In the Theodotus he has exposed the Sophists principally but at the same time interwoven as in others of his works with a fair statement of the opinions of preceding philosophers which indeed he has not neglected on any fair opportunity in any of his dialogues [f 160] as if equally willing to do justice to them and preserve proper praise for himself that he might state as it were so far have my predecessors gone . . . by a continued exposition of the arts of the Sophists with a rejection of the same and introducing the plain dictates of common sense in their stead—In the Politicus he considers the application of morality to the highest point in which morality can be shewn in merely practical life and with reference only to the present state namely in that of an enlightened statesman— This he carries on in detail in the De Republica a dialogue admired by all the great men of former ages[w] and I fully believe by all the truly great men of the ages since—here we have all that good sense and wide induction can give—not with regard to the practical for he would greatly mistake the dialogue who supposed Plato believed that Plato thought it all practical but as ideas known to be unapproachable as to realization but they were to be a polar star guiding a mans mind by approximation and there he stopped—The tradition was that he had written a dialogue entitled the Philosopher [f 161] but it was admitted that it was never published the truth is that I believe Plato would have baffled his own purposes had he done so—there he stopped In one of his dialogues—indeed in more than one he has taken care to shew that he intended—namely by pointing out the defects which the highest experience of practical life as merely practical could give by even a tone of detraction but for which he makes Socrates apologize by placing . . . so much below the ideal which he calls the Philosopher that the question must then needs suggest itself

[u] Perhaps "disciplining"
[v] Names of dialogues seem to have been inserted later; "Republica" seems partly erased, then re-written
[w] Word erased and "ages" substituted

what then is the Philosopher—you have raised us to a great height you
have presented it in all its . . . yet you shew us that this is imperfect and
is below the final aim of a man—what is the philosopher—So again with
the great proposition of Socrates—namely with regard to ignorance—it
is ever said ignorant indocility is the cause of all evil and knowledge ⟨of
all⟩ good and philosophy is the only way of attaining that knowledge—
but what this philosophy is you look for in vain in the writings of Plato—
[f 162] I mean—what that is and if a man should take up the writings of
Plato expecting to find the proper system of Platonism he will feel himself much in the same state that our amiable Countryman—our Sweet
Poet and Scholar Gray seems to have found himself after a most laborious and elegant abstract[x] of the writings of Plato—he found excellent
good sense—prudential wisdom for it is wisdom and the true practical
morality and the few passages that could not be brought under this . . . he
honestly declares himself that not being one of the initiated it was utterly
incomprehensible to him and very few they undoubtedly were with the
exception I think of a few pages of the . . . and his juvenile work the Phaedrus—If then as my sons said to me very properly—if then it be true—
that the doctrines of Plato that constitute the proper platonism are not to
be found in his own writings I pray you where are we to find them and
that requires more courage than I can exert without [f 163] some little distress to answer the question—when I say first of all we may find something of them something in the few fragments that are preserved in his
immediate Successors such as . . . and likewise more in the writings of
the new Platonists in the Roman Empire provided we go to the perusal of
their writings aware of their object and in proportion as this was their object and with a tact capable of discovering the passages were such an object would have such an object I mean opposing and setting up a rival to
christianity I should trust more to . . . than to any writers who were determined enemies to Christianity . . . in the writings of . . . who seems almost to have given up the cause of paganism as lost I should trust him according to the authorities he quotes but yet from all together I think that
such a knowledge of Plato's great principles might be gathered as would
be capable of being presented to one who had pursued philosophy in a
form that would leave him no doubt that he had [f 164] apprehended their
true meaning but for us as I cannot pretend to enter into this process nor
would it be a part of my business which is the history of philosophy I must
speak of that which was really influential in Plato and which none will
deny to have originated in Platonism who does not deny the coinciding

---

[x] Word erased and "abstract" substituted

testimony of all antiquity—It is this in common with others but more expressly and purely than any he taught us to seek the principles—that charm and spell by which nature is to be invoked in reason itself but with filial awe . . . the confirmation of those principles of nature by induction but above all this is what I mean—he taught the idea namely the possibility and the duty of all who would arrive at the greatest perfection of the human mind of striving to contemplate things not in the phenomenon—not in their accidents or in their superfices but in their essential powers—first as they exist [f 165] in relation to other powers coexisting with them but lastly and chiefly as they exist in the supreme mind independent of all material division distinct and yet indivisible—This is expressly asserted by . . . and it is the very essential of Platonism when he says that that which exists in the perfection of distinctness and yet without separation either from another or from the supreme cause is an idea what can such an abstract notion as this produce it may be said—what can such a shadow give of formless truth—if it be a truth bring it forward for that very reason were there no others as there are many and better did it produce a great effect—the human passions and human energies do not close on my natural vacuity with any distinct palpable visible forms—the mind always feels itself greater than aught it has done—it begins in the act of perceiving that it must go beyond it in order to comprehend it therefore it is only to that which contains distinct conception in itself and thereby satisfying the intellect [f 166] does at the same time ~~contain distinct conception in itself and thereby satisfying the intellect does at the same time~~ contain in it a plenitude which refuses limitation or division that the soul feels its full faculties called forth

Such is the origin of all great ideas on which . . . works—how the grand idea of the Universe worked in him before it found utterance—in how many obscure and as it were oracular sentences—in what strange symbols did it place itself—all great and bold ideas in their first conception partake in their nature they are utterly . . . it is a glow without light in which light gradually forms itself—our present mode is from light to bring out smoke—to begin with the separate and finite—the distinct and out of that come to what? confusion and if we are rescued from it only by resting contented with shallowness—if I be required to mention facts I think that this will be the most convincing I speak of the connection of speculative opinion especially of Platonic [f 167] idea with the fine Arts at the first awakening of mankind out of the barbarism which followed the subversion of the Roman Empire the . . . was predominant—it was . . . for the divisions and subdivisions—whatever Aristotle might have thought is not for the present subject—but as the doctrines existed in the

Schoolmen they were outlines traced indeed by stiff lifeless divisions and subdivisions ad infinitum—compare the paintings . . . superfices and still outlines wonderfully vivid at times but no life—every figure was imprisoned within its own outline as soon as Platonism began to dawn with . . . then arose the . . . and the others who with all the awkwardness of composition and stiffness of outline of their predecessors gave such a bewitching grace that one remains in looking at the pictures in perfect astonishment how such a feeling of grace could [f 168] be conveyed through such a media—we wonder we do not laugh at the stiff lines and the awkward form and instead of it we find a presence we cannot explain—an expression of something that is equally pleasant to you as in the works of Raphael without ⟨that⟩ which can equally explain—I remember when I was at . . . a picture of one of those old Painters who rose just at the time Platonism began to produce ⟨its effects⟩ in Italy and to actuate the minds of men which was the effect of the appearance of death on all men—different groups of men—men of business—men of pleasure—huntsmen all flying in different directions while the dreadful Goddess descending with a kind of air chilling white with^y her wings expanded and the extremities of the Wings compressed into talons and the only group in which there appeared anything like welcoming her was a group of beggars—the impression was greater I may say than that which any poem had ever made upon me—there from all [f 169] the laws of drawing all the absence of color for you saw no color—if there were any you could not see it—it was gone—it was one mighty idea that spoke to you everywhere the same—In the other pictures the presence of an idea acting of that which was not formed was evident because the forms there outraged all notions of that which was to be impressed had there not been something more—but it was the adoption of a symbol which though not in as polished a language as could be wished for which though in a hoarser voice and less tempered modulation uttered the same words to that mind which is the source of all that we really enjoy or that is worth enjoying— we may find that too in the gratification which of all others is the best symbol perhaps for it is as far as sight is concerned formless and yet contains the principles of form so that in all civilized language we borrow the proportions from it—I mean music—[f 170] it is an innocent recreation and produces infinite joy—while the over busy worldlings are buzzed round by night flies in a sultry climate if we sink into music our childhood comes back . . . moved so deeply as no object in mortal life can move us except by anguish and here it is present with joy—it is joy in all

---

^y Word erased and "with" substituted

its forms—we feel therefore that our being is nobler than its senses and the man of genius devotes himself to produce by all other means whether a Statesman a poet a painter a Statuary or a man of Science this same sort of a something which the mind can know but which it cannot understand of which understanding can be no more than the symbol and is only excellent as being the symbol—it is this same spirit which still craving for something higher than what could be imagined in form this value of the images of form as far as they make us forget ourselves and become mere words unnoticed in that which they convey which works in all men [f 171] more or less and which assuredly in the higher classes of Society in Greece and Rome did that which their own humble feelings and their own solace and affections did for the lower class of mankind—prepare them to be more and more dissatisfied with religion which presented nothing but forms the symbols of which were to be found either in crude phylological[z] speculations—our moral vices still led them to look first to a purer ideal with a desire of connecting with it which is equally taught by Plato—reality and which Plato himself or at least Socrates told us could only be done by the Realizer by him who was the fountain of all and who in the substance superceded the Shadow—I mean the Christian religion—

[z] Attempt made in pencil to change word to "physiological"

LECTURE 5

Mr Coleridges Lecture
                              18.th January 1819.

I have often noticed in conversations I have had with men thinking and
unthinking an universal assent to the proposition that there is a moral government in the World—that things neither happen by chance nor yet by
any blind agency of necessity—those persons to whom I allude will readily and cheerfully admit that not a feather falls from a Sparrows wing but
forms a part in a grand system—and yet if you apply this principle
namely that of a design and final cause in every thing beyond the exact
limits which they have been accustomed to draw it is a possibility—the
man is a fanatic and so forth—nay it is well for him if his orthodoxy be
not suspected—if for instance you speak of an event such as Christianity in which every human being is interested and [f 173] I might add more
by the authority of the Apostle in which the whole creation is interested—
if you confine your observations to the history of the Jews and the Ecclesiastical history as far as they know it it is well but if you presume that
the same providence is at the same time working over the whole of the
World as far as we know it and that Christianity was not welcomed in one
direction only but that from North to South and from South to North from
east to West and from West to East the whole march of human affairs
tended to that one centre in which all men were equally concerned and
interested and apply this principle in any particular—there is immediately a sort of sudden connexion in their minds that you have introduced
between Christianity and the world that they have not been accustomed
to—they raise a sort of paganism—a kind of heathenism is felt Far otherwise were the feelings of the first Christians—they gladly—and I appeal to the writings of all the Fathers of the Church—[f 174] they gladly
appealed to all the workings of Providence out of Polytheism to this one
end when they addressed themselves to the Gentile or Polytheistic nations
with the same warmth and with the same force as they did to the Jews derived from their particular institutions and their particular prophecies—I
mention this to justify the importance I have attached to the appearance
of Platonism in the Greek world

Of Plato himsclf I havc spokcn in my last Lecture—The Scholars of Plato—I mean the immediate scholars of whom we have records Speusippus Xenocrates, . . .[a] and . . .[b] the history of his scholars has been variously divided—by some into four or five Academies by others into three but I think by the most rational into simply the first and second Academy which in truth historically almost (the latter I mean) belonged to Plato— the true division is this that to the time of Arcesilaus the Platonists assumed and asserted a dogmatic tone such as their keen perception of the truths which they taught amply justified—[f 177][c] as manners were debauched and those who called themselves philosophers and by their talents were certainly sure to attract attention and to appear at least to deserve it—as soon as these began to fall in with the age and modified by it began themselves to modify it then the fashion began apparently justified by certain parts of Platos writings to be sceptical upon all occasions and say this is indeed my opinion there are such and such probabilities for it but all these things are opinion and as to certainty it would be impolite—for that in reality is[d] the basis of it—to assert this for depend upon it no man ever in reality speaks of anything with warmth that concerns his permanent being—with a feeling of scepticism at the moment he gives the full force of his conviction at that moment—admitting however that he may be fallible that he does not wish to impose this on the minds of others and that his very dogmata must be divided into two kinds namely the one respecting circumstances in which however [f 175] warm his present convictions are he still has had experience of having had convictions equally positive altered—the other of opinions which say were I to be convinced they were false after I had once entertained them I cannot myself deny that my inmost nature has suffered a dissent and deterioration which makes it utterly inexplicable how I could have ever had a thought concerning which I now doubt—for no man will believe it possible that a simple wheel in a machine existing only in that machine could have a conception of that whole—never we may therefore truly say that the division between the two Schools of Plato which alone deserve to be mentioned is this that the first great men proceeded in the firmness of their conviction of their ends—they had higher notices deeper intuitions than that which mere logic could supply—abundantly willing to acknowledge that in their modes of proving them they might have been defective—the

---

[a] ", Polemo" inserted in space in pencil

[b] "Crantor" inserted in space in pencil

[c] Page 4 misbound between 6 and 7, page 6 left unnumbered; pencilled numbering sequence [f 177] recorded out of usual order

[d] "is" replaces erased word

second Sect which began with Arcesilaus flattered the pride of those about them by [f 176] acknowledging a mere opinion that it would be impolite in good company to suppose that every man ought to do it or that you should be so ungenteel as to say to a man you are a Rogue Sir you are a villain confessed if you do not do this—for if there be nothing infallible in nature if honor—if honesty—if to do to others as you would be done by are not infallible what becomes of your own modesty of your own*e* tolerance nothing remains for you to tolerate—there remains no distinction no criterion upon earth man must be mad not to acknowledge the fallibility of his nature—the fallibility of his judgment—but he must be still more mad I may venture to say if he pretends even to the compliment of being deceived when he himself admits that there is no ground of judging at all and that therefore neither deceit nor conviction can possibly exist—every man who admits that he may be deceived admits at the same time that there is a something upon which he cannot be deceived—doubtless that he will not find in his own individual [f 178] reasoning but he will find it in that principle which is above reasoning—in his moral nature and as long as he remains in any degree what he ought to be—in the contradiction which he finds in certain errors with his own moral nature

Now I say passingly that this distinction the only profitable one of the two academies should be kept in mind by all readers of Cicero for otherwise it will be impossible to understand his various applications of the word Academicus—that the distinction likewise receives a kind of interest from the history of Brutus who we are told was a follower of the academy and certainly in his death and the last speech attributed to him—no honorable one did we not remember he was a Platonist of the School of Arcesilaus namely a Sceptic and in the pusilanimity in which he gave up all hope because a battle ended amiss and in the Suicide by which he ended his life in contradiction to the doctrines of his Master—this would be [f 179] inexplicable if we did not refer to the corruption which had taken place coincident with the general corruption of morals and of moral feeling—The teachers on the contrary of the first Academy appear faithfully to have taught their great Masters philosophy and to have been eminently conducive to the diffusion of it not by*f* any addition or alteration but by that by which a great idea can be taught gradually that is by considering it as a germe which cannot appear at any one moment in all its force but will gradually separate the plenitude of its contents into*g* dis-

---

e "your own" written over erasure
f "by" written over erasure   *g* "into" written over erasure

tinct parts and in proportion to the distinctions that arise will require new
and appropriate terms—it is and let those who exclaim against jargon and
barbarous terms and every new and original mind that appears before
them—let them recollect that the whole process of human intellect is
gradually to desynonymize terms—that words the instruments of communication are the only signs that a finite being can have of its own
thoughts that in proportion as what was conceived as one and identical
becomes several there [f 180] will necessarily arise a term striving to represent that distinction—the whole of the progress of society might be expressed in a dictionary in which I do not say that we should have the practical means of doing so but it is in possibility that a dictionary might be
expressed from the first and simplest terms which would satisfy all the
distinction that occurred to the first men while as they perceived that other
things and yet other things which they had grouped in one mass had each
their distinctive properties when they had experienced the evils arising
from confusing them there would arise a motive for giving a term for each
as warning and safeguard and the whole progress of Society as far as it is
human Society depends upon—it may sound as a paradox[h] but it is still
a very serious truth the process of desynonimizing—that is the feeling
that there is a necessity for two distinct subjects which have hitherto been
comprehended in one—perhaps I may not ⟨make⟩ myself understood I
will endeavor to illustrate ⟨illustrate it by one instance⟩ even so late as the
time of Charles the first and the Republic of England the words compelled
and obliged were perfectly synonimous—Hobbs and other [f 181] men
of his mind took advantage of this one term and contended therefore that
as every body acknowledged that men were obliged to do such and such
things and that if a man were obliged it was synonimous to say he was
compelled there could never arise anything like guilt for who could blame
a man for doing what he was obliged to do since he was compelled to do
it—this fortunately puzzled only a few minds but it convinced only those
who wished to be convinced whose crimes and bad conscience found a
consolation in this while the innocent puzzled began to say there is a defect in our language in this instance they are two perfectly different things
and every man feels them to be different and the best way is to use the
word obliged when we mean what a man ought to do and the word compelled when we mean what a man must do whether he likes it or not and
with this single clearing up of the terms the whole basis fell at once as far
at least as that argument was convincing—This was the merit as it appears from the records of the [f 182] immediate followers of Plato—they

---

[h] "paradox" written partly over erased word—"parody"?

improved the terminology and we have the according testimony of all antiquity that they did not add any thing to Plato's doctrines—I mention this because I propose to build something upon it

Speusippus the nephew[i] and immediate Successor of Plato deserves especial honor from us on other accounts as the first man who attempted an Encyclopedia in the genuine sense of the word—that is a co-organization of the Sciences as so many entire independent systems each having a specific life of its own but all communicating with philosophy as the common centre as the brain if I may say so by means of a philosophic logic as the great sympathetic nerves leading to it A scheme similar to this is attempted at the present time and I wish it all success on account of its scheme—This of itself was a grand conception and a strong proof of the influence of the Platonic philosophy on the minds of those who attended to it—for to impress the importance of Knowledge of various Knowledge for different men was itself a great benefaction but to present the idea that all possible Knowledges were [f 183] but vital parts of some one Knowledge which comprehended them all as in the germ and to which they were all referrable and from which they all derived unity and in that unity light and true insight—this was truly a magnificent conception and this we owe to the reflected light of Plato as reflected from his immediate Successor Speusippus

But more than this—I have spoken of the unwritten dogmata of Plato of those which he would not publish and which were peculiarly and which alone were his own—a strong light I say is let in upon the sacred recesses of this interior doctrine at least a component part we may say which in addition to a few others from a few other sources will almost suffice for some future Cuvier Abernethy or . . . in metaphysics to make up the whole system and reproduce the Platonic philosophy for us as it then existed This fragment has been preserved by Trebellius I refer to the passage in which we are told that the intelligential powers by the Pythagoreans and Anaxagoras ⟨called⟩ the Nous the Logos or the Word of Philo and S! John is [f 184] indeed indivisibly united with but yet not the same as the absolute principle of causation that eternal one the super essential will nor yet though indivisibly one with is it the same as the energy of love—the sanctifying spirit so sublimely described in the Apocrypha under the name of the Wisdom of Solomon remembering that wisdom is the term which the Fathers of the Church made peculiar to the Holy Ghost—if we connect this with the testimony of the Ancients that Speusippus added nothing to his Masters philosophy or the testimony that

---

[i] Letters "ph" seem inserted later into "nephew", perhaps merely supplying temporary deficiency of ink

his true philosophy was not written or found in his public works every scholar acquainted with his works will find here a proof I flatter myself—assuredly a strong presumption of the truth of the seeming paradox maintained by me in my last lecture that Platonism would be sought for in vain in the dialogues of Plato himself which I believe to have been all preparatory—predisciplinary tending to kindle the desire for the philosophy itself in the few minds thereto called tending to remove the obstacles and most fitting to foster the growth of the wings of such minds fluttering [f 185] as it were on the edge of the eagles nest and yet for other minds—invaluable as themselves—as treasures of practical knowledge for men destined by nature and their own purpose exclusively for active life and for the duties of society

On the same ground we may derive from Xenocrates—Speusippus's Successor the proof of another assertion which I hazarded namely that the true idea of Plato's genius and system is to be found in the Union of Pythagoras with Socrates that is the Union of the Speculative physiology of the eldest philosophers with the moral it has been lately called now Anthropologia the anarchy of the Socratic reformation the elder philosophers took the whole world as the object of their philosophy with the inadequate means joined with other worse causes the Sophists availed themselves of that insufficiency to introduce a principle subvertive of all our best moral feelings Socrates rose as a reformer and in the heat of reform he confined all philosophy[j] to the Knowledge of our own nature the proper Knowledge of mankind is [f 186] man"—Plato his great disciple perceived that this were true if it were possible but that the Knowledge of man by himself was not practicable without the Knowledge of other things or rather that man was that being in whom it pleased God that the consciousness of others existence should abide and that therefore without natural philosophy and without the sciences which led to the Knowledge of the objects without us man himself would not be the man—therefore I say that Plato united the elder philosophers with the philosophy of Socrates and this is proved[k] to us not only by the little which the Ancients record of Xenocrates namely that with the Socratic words he united the Pythagorean but by both Xenocrates and Speusippus and likewise by two other followers who have been recorded . . . and . . . and following that maintained fully the immortality of the Soul as the best and worthiest ground of hope and purity of the conscience in combination with a faith in that immortality as the securest source of consolation [f 187] of finite

---

[j] Beginning of "philosophy" covers erasure
[k] "proved" seems written over erasure of longer word

nature—Of the material world as the proximate Cause but by no means as the absolute origin of pain and imperfection in the world and lastly the reconciliation of man and in the human being of the whole creation with the Deity as the only remedy of those evils These doctrines I say were taught by them zealously dogmatically positively and in such a way as to form such a contrast with the doubtful tone expressed on all these points in the dialogues of Plato himself as to render it utterly irreconcileable with the assertion of antiquity that they in no way deviated from their great Master but by the hypothesis which I had the honor of submitting to you in my last lecture namely that in the now published and extant writings of Plato we have not the Platonic system but only the preparation for it and such a preparation as for those who are not disposed to go further would be in itself of great and invaluable gain

The nature of the subject I am sure [f 188] will ⟨convince all my intelligent auditors that it does⟩ not rest with me altogether whether it is more or less interesting I must as an Historian give you the steps ⟨that is to say the important steps⟩ of the progress not of the life of Philosophers but of the life and growth of Philosophy itself and here is a proper place for discussing the question which has been often agitated and I am sorry to say generally very little to the honor of Plato's character—why no doubt having been entertained as to the marks of superiority of Aristotles genius to that of the men whom I have now mentioned Speusippus Xenocrates and their schoolfellows—Plato should yet have preferred Speusippus as his successor passing by the mighty Stagyrite—some have said it is explained Speusippus was his nephew and Plato did this from natural affection for his family which is certainly a very plain and sensible way of explaining the matter only we must forget in the meantime that we are talking of Plato—Others have told us that Plato saw Aristotles great powers and talents and that he envied him I will not condescend to answer that objection—others again have attributed it to some private pique between them or quarrel, which is no otherwise worthy of notice than as it furnishes an opportunity of noticing and guarding against [f 189] that abominable vice of vulgar minds which if they are really in the rank to which they belong—if they appear what they are do no harm at all anymore than the common blackguardisms which are heard in the streets but which unfortunately take place at times in minds who for a little while are lifted up to an apparent possession of the second or third seats in existing reputation—these men have a mighty fancy and produce a great popularity for the time by convincing their hearers or their readers that their betters are not a whit better than themselves that they have just the same bad passions and nothing can be more delightful to a man of that disposition than to read that Shakespear was as foolish as himself or the pleasure of finding that Shakespear was a fool here or Milton made a great blunder there—in short he had a few accidents that lifted him above other men in reputation but in truth put him out of that situation and he was just such a fellow as I am not what I ought to be just what I am when I am what I ought not to be—this is most striking in the comment which I have seen [f 190] made on the writings of great men and I have traced that no work was ⟨ever⟩ immediately popular which did not appeal in some degree to this kind of worthless detraction—having the courage to schoolmaster great men to admit their amazing genius but at the same time to point out the compatibility of it that they were great fools that they were eminent men cannot be denied in some respects but at the same time that their most important actions were guided by the dirtiest means which every man is ashamed of—The same thing may be observed in the history of Painters the great Michael Angelo speaking as a man of great genius would ever speak looking firmly at the ideal and what was excellent in itself the permanent said of Titian—that Man alone deserves to be called a painter because like nature he has operated most powerfully ⟨by⟩ the most powerful agent namely that of color in all its combination with passion but it is a pity that he had not learnt to draw to design that he had not paid more attention to the power of lines—At once Michael Angelo envied him [f 191] it was a business of detraction—because the man was discriminative he was instantly detracted and often have I observed that in real life a man shall give a fair character of one whom he admires and looks up to and in order to reserve himself from the charge of flattery he points out that part which he has not attained—that alone shall be brought forward as a proof the man envied the other such is the spirit which has a bad effect because it prevents men from communicating with men— how well therefore should we attend to and love those anecdotes which are recorded for instance of Raphael who when Michael Angelo came into the Farnesian Palace at Rome which he was at that time painting and finding fault with something Raphael had done or was about to do— Raphael asked how would you do it—he said I cannot tell but give me a bit of pencil or a bit of chalk something like this and he drew a head and they parted—day after day went on and still Raphael did not finish this at length when the whole was done he was asked why this part remained in the state in which it was—[f 192] forbid it Heaven said he that I should dare alter a line of the divine Michael Angelo and there it remains to this day—So is it men of genius feel towards each other and the moment you perceive the slightest spirit of envy in a man be assured he either has no genius or that his genius is dormant at that moment for all genius exists in a participation of a common spirit—in joy individuality is lost and it therefore in youth not from any principle in organization but simply from this that the hardships of life—that the circumstances that have forced a man in upon his little unthinking contemptible self have lessened his power of existing universally it is that only which brings about those passions to have a genius is to live in the universal to know no self but that which is reflected not only from the faces of all around us our fellow creatures but reflected from ~~from~~ the flowers the trees the beasts yea from the very surface of the . . . sands of the desart a man of genius finds a reflex to himself were it only in the mystery of being—

[f 193]   If I were asked to conjecture the reasons which determined Plato in the choice of his successor and which seems so much to have interested antiquity I should not disguise my belief that Plato saw early in Aristotles mind all indeed that was mighty powerful expansive and yet an unfitness for certain more spiritual parts of his system and therefore in coincidence with his own principles he withheld them for what should we suppose that a good and great man would do—Aristotle had been incapable of following Plato to a certain height he did not attribute this to any defect in his own mind but he believed the fault to have been in an extravagance of his Masters genius if Plato were convinced of this doubtless he would have become an Aristotelian but he was not—he remained firm in his intuitions and he believed the point of difference between him and Aristotle to be of an essential importance in short to be fundamental could Plato remaining convinced of the superior truth of his own system have named as his successor a man who had proclaimed his dissent from it and was labouring to put [f 194] another system in its place or if from personal admiration of Aristotle's superior talents he had done so what effect I pray could this have had but that the old Scholars who adhered to their Master Plato would have naturally followed Speusippus who likewise with them adhered and a new sect would have taken possession of the old place and the old Sect of a new place Speusippus would have taught in the Lyceum Aristotle in the groves of Academus so little is it in the power of the individual will to alter the necessity of things

The essential difference of Aristotle to Plato is to form the remainder of this address—conformably with my plan I am briefly to give you the life of Aristotle he was born in Stagyra a border town between Macedon and Thrace in the first year of the 99th Olympiad . . . He went to Athens where during the course of twenty years he attended the school of Plato such a man with such advantages how could it be but he must have proved an Aristotle—After the death of Plato he returned in Company with Xenocrates his fellow Scholar [f 195] or as the Greeks call it . . . after whose tragic fate Aristotle was called by Philip of Macedon to be the tutor of Alexander on the accession . . . once more to Athens and founded the school in the Lyceum—there from the shady walks and alleys of which his philosophy and its . . . Peripateticks or walkers about—before his death he was compelled to flee from Athens in order to avoid an accusation of offending the Religion of the Country in short to avoid the fate of Socrates before him—It would be unpardonable in me considering the different lessons that have been taught in one of our most eloquent historians indeed I may say two I allude to Gibbon principally and likewise to Hume in spirit—I say with my opinions I could not answer it to myself if I avoided taking notice of the boasted tolerance of the ancients with regard to Religion—the tolerant spirit of Polytheism we hear for the purpose of contrasting it at all times with the dreadful intolerance of Christianity [f 196] and truly tolerance they did exert[l] when they were exceedingly amused and delighted with what they tolerated they tolerated with wonderful equanimity . . . frogs in which he brings Bacchus and Hercules and so forth into the shades and makes himself merry with all the vices and with all the caprices of their gods wonderfully tolerant they were with the Birds of Aristophanes which consists in this that two old men flying from the abominable persecutions of . . . having heard of a kingdom of birds repaired thither and on being admitted began to spread the poison of it in the new state to which they were come and proposed that the birds should set up against the Gods and at the same time establish themselves as the supreme monarchs by keeping the Gods from being fed intercepting all the sacrifices and the odours from the burnt offerings and on the other hand keeping men under their [f 197] subjection by preventing the rain and the sun and the other influences—this in every age and with the grossest to a degree that it is perfectly surprizing to imagine that an audience could have borne the established Religion of their Country to be exposed to with every the keenest insult contempt and reprobation applied to all the holiest names before the images of whom their sacrifices were daily offered this was indeed tolerated received with delight and crowned with applauses—but when Anaxagoras taught that there was a supreme mind who would call them to account for all this waste of their devotional feelings he was obliged to fly and when Socrates though in the most tolerant and almost timid form conceivable led even to the great truths which being told this diabolical system of Polytheism must necessarily have fallen he was poisoned and when Aristotle with a much less pure philosophy yet still held that there was a one power to which all

---

[l] "exert" written over erasure

others were answerable [f 198] he called for his illustrations of it and they were so little compatible with the interests of the priests of heathenism at that time that he did not rely even on the favor that he stood in with the greatest monarch of the world but was obliged to fly away to save his head from these tolerant enlightened Grecian Republicans—The truth is let us never degrade ourselves by any pretence of that kind we are none of us tolerant but by a great effort except when we are interested when we are deeply interested in any concern then let us ⟨try to be tolerant & pray hard for it but do not let us⟩ degrade the name and pretend to be tolerant about things in which we do not care a pinch of snuff whether it is one way or the other and then boast ourselves to be the enlightened age I have been oftentimes amused with the triumph that has been made over our Ancestors those men persecuting each other upon some point of Baptism or some controverted opinion with regard to some religious point that we know nothing about and happy it is we live in such an enlightened age but I find those men when [f 199] a law suit comes forward when a tax or aught that interests themselves appears whether an Election business or whatever it is if it interests them what becomes of toleration—let us despise such let us not pretend to be superior to our Ancestors

I must trouble you with one further observation because it arises and is in itself indeed an instructive point for when I mention that Antisthenes was obliged to fly to save his head from the fury of the popular prejudice about his religion upon the same principle that poor Roger Bacon was thrown into a dungeon as they say and we are certain it was so with Galileo because he knew a little more than other people and that of itself if it was not impiety against the better being is always taken as impiety against the mob and just as much in the present time as it ever was for I do not find we are so much wiser in that respect but those very people who drove away Aristotle had repented concerning Socrates, they were ashamed thoroughly [f 200] ashamed of those who had put to death that great and good man—In order to shew it to record it to make it imperative upon posterity they had built a temple to Socrates and the repentance of the Athenians but as soon as another Socrates came there was another murder to be committed the prejudiced of one age are condemned even by the prejudiced of the succeeding age for endless are the motives of folly and the fools join with the Wise in passing sentence on all motives but their own—who cried with greater horror against the murder of the prophets than those who likewise cried out on the most awful occasion Crucify him! Crucify him!—those who pretend to preach up such doctrines as there is no need of impressing this truth or that truth on the present enlightened age—it is pedantry to suppose that the present enlightened nineteenth century should do so and so are the basest flatterers of mankind the wise and the virtuous are always few and it is by few only that the world is progressive depend upon it the majority of mankind till Christianity is more widely diffused in its essence will ever be enjoying [f 201] the conveniences of the advantages of the Wisdom of the few but the wisdom itself it is absolutely mob-adulation to attribute to them

This which I have mentioned is all that is known or credibly recorded of this great mans life if indeed we except Alexander the Greats suspicions of him which he did not live to put into action as of all our worthy men he ended in the final breaking up of an over stimulated and inebriate spirit but as so*[m]* great a mind deserves if it were only conjectural the tracing of its growth we may say and say with probability that from his father an eminent physician young as he was he had acquired a taste for natural history which distinguished him so much throughout for this we are warranted to say by the common experience of mankind and the deep impressions made on the earliest periods of our*[n]* life by what we look up to and admire—A severe student—he seems to have been to Atanea from one circumstance that he was first induced to go to Athens and make himself a Scholar of Plato from the [f 202] report that Plato possessed the best philosophic library at that time—probably a perfect unique for though the works of the poets were in all hands I will not say compared with the modern times since printing was invented but as far as they can be supposed to be in an age when manuscripts only were used—yet philosophic writings were rare and to this circumstance we are to attribute the frequency of the forgeries of them—In this manner he acquired what we may call another characteristic of him as distinct from the ancient philosophers his wide and extensive learning Alexanders favor too which had enabled him to form the greatest library of his own that a private man at that time possessed relating to objects of natural history with a splendour which has been since unexampled and this was the second point of Aristotles character namely experimental knowledge of which he was assuredly the father and I believe there is no intelligent professor of any of the natural sciences that fairly reading the works of [f 203] Aristotle has not expressed a wonder that the man who first broke up the ground should have proceeded so far or not made his acknowledgements for that which though it appears little in the further progress of the science is immense in itself namely the drawing the general scheme the mode of thinking the plan of generalizing by which alone a multitude of facts can be brought under one point of view—thus I have said that Aristotles Character con-

---

[m] "so" written over erasure; "so" also written in pencil in right-hand margin
[n] Word or part of word crossed out indecipherably following "our"

sisted first in his wide knowledge of all that had been brought before him—secondly of his experimental knowledge or his attempts to add from the great source of knowledge—Nature—that which could be added thereto—I have only to add in order to complete his character and the sources of it the dialectic habits and the inductive logic to which during twenty years he had been familiarized in the Platonic school and which had prepared in a mind so capacious and so predisposed the spirit first of observation secondly of discrimination and thirdly of abstraction and of generalization—It will not perhaps be deemed tedious by you if I endeavor to desynonimize [f 204] those two words abstraction and generalization—by abstraction I mean the general faculty or power of the human mind to attend to any one impression of the senses a part only of a multitude as being alone to the particular purpose of the mind this faculty of for instance overlooking in a multitude of horses what each horse has particularly and drawing from it a general notion of what all ⟨the⟩ horses have distinct from all the other animals—I should call the abstracting power when this same power is exerted for the purpose of forming classes so as to fix upon some one thing which a certain number of animals we will say or plants have peculiar to themselves which no other has however many other points there may be in common then we call the same faculty generalization—it is to say generalization cannot ᵒpossibly exist with abstraction but abstraction may exist without generalizationᵖ

These seem to me to have been the ground of Aristotles genius how much he learned and continued to learn under Plato the fact itself that he remained twenty years [f 205] a regular auditor is assuredly sufficient to prove yet doubtless he had already determined and his Master had known that he had determined on a different point of view from that of the Platonic and why should not this consist one man stands on one point and another on another the objects seen are the same they vary only according to the point of perspective so that the one man had the power of increasing the field of vision and though the other would not venture to mount to the height in which he stood because he thought it giddy and insecure he would surely have the advantage of that increase of objects and would be grateful for it and in this point I think Aristotle stood to Plato grateful for the number of facts conceptions possibilities which his everflowing invention presented but like an original genius still bringing them within his own plan of interpretation grateful for his Masters facts and yet still working upon them to bring them into his own construction—The point therefore for us to [f 206] consider is wherein consisted the differ-

---

ᵒ⁻ᵖ Material erased and this passage inserted in its place

ence between the point of view of Plato and of Aristotle[q] for I am sure that you can neither expect nor wish that in the course of an hour and a half I should give you the whole particulars of the Aristotelian Philosophy I am only concerned to do it by my plan as far as it is a living movement in the progress of human philosophy

Plato sought in that which is above our senses he sought in the thinking power itself and still further in the power of will revealed to us by our Moral being the solution both of the Super Sensual that is our Moral and intellectual being and the Sensual or the objects of our senses Aristotle on the contrary began with the Sensual and never received that which was above the Senses but by necessity but as the only remaining hypothesis by which it could be brought within the conceivability of the human mind—in other words Plato began in meditation thought deeply within himself of the goings on of his own mind and of the powers that there were [f 207] in that mind conceived to himself how this could be and if it where what must be the necessary results and agencies of it and then looked abroad to ask if this were a dream or whether it were indeed a revelation from within and a waking reality he employed his observation as the interpreter of his meditation equally free from the fanatic who abandons himself to the wild workings of the Magic Cauldron of his own Brain mistaking every form of delirium for reality and from the cold sensualist who looks at death as the alone real ⟨or⟩[r] life of the World by not considering that the very object was seen to him only by the seeing powers and that a little further consideration would have led him to deduce that that which could make him see it must be an Agent and a power like his own whilst that which [f 208] was ⟨merely seen which was⟩ purely passive could have no other existence than what arose out of an Active power that had produced it

It would be unfair to charge Aristotle with wilful perversion of Plato's meaning at least wilful in that sense of which the mind can be conscious though we all too naturally perhaps where we do not understand a thing think and speak of it with less respect than it deserves it is undoubtedly a fact that all who believe in the doctrines of Plato must believe at the same time that Aristotle has misrepresented Plato's conception or thought but that he grossly misunderstood Plato's words or that he made Plato mean something monstrous in order to substitute Plato's own meaning as his own this I can [f 209] never believe—The difference between Aristotle and Plato is that which will remain as long as we are men and there is any difference between man and man in point of opinion—Plato with

---

[q] "and of Aris" written over erasure   [r] "or" also pencilled in right-hand margin

Pythagoras before him had conceived that the phenomenon or outward appearance all that we call thing or matter are but as it were a language of which the invisible that which is not the object of our senses communicates its existence to our finite beings we need for instance no sort of language to communicate our thoughts to ourselves one thought communicates itself to another in the same mind without any sensible intermedium but as there is individuality in the World arising out of free Agency and that [f 210] each individual has will there arises a necessity that there should be an intermedium by which one mind should be distinguished from another mind different from it and in addition to that by which one thought communicates its existence to another thought in the same mind—Now Plato argued that as was that power in the mind which thinks and images its thoughts—analogous to this was the power in nature which thought and imaged or embodied its thoughts in consequence of which he resolved the ground of all things into the Dynamics but the power regarding the external phenomenon is intelligible only in proportion as the power which [f 211] produced and manifested itself thereby was understood Aristotle on the contrary affirmed that all our knowledge had begun in experience had begun through the senses and that from the senses only we could take our notions of reality—the objects of the senses therefore he declared to be the true realities of nature and with regard to those things which are invisible he resolved them into certain harmonies into certain results and so forth—As however this would necessarily have led to Atheism and an utter destitution[s] of all religion and all morality which it was least in the mind of Aristotle to produce he was obliged to admit that in this reality but not as distinct from it there existed [t][f 212] as he called it an Intileka that is a power which contained in itself as it were a capability of producing all that should be derived from it independent of time I do not know how I can better explain the notion which a great Cardinal is said to have raised a Demon up in order to explain that is the Aristotelian Intileka than by saying I am now standing but no one doubts I have the power in me of sitting that I have the power in me of lying now this something which is equally the—principle of my power of standing or sitting or of all my various actions and which in all those various actions is one and the same Aristotle called the Intelika if he were asked whether it was the same or not with the phenomenon that was produced he would say yes but the consequence was this that the supreme Intelika must necessarily be the same with matter and [f 213] no way properly called its judge or in any other manner its Master or Lord than as the principle of gravitation of this earth which arises out of the complex Intelika of all its atoms can be said to be the Lord of its motions round the Sun no wonder therefore that in different ages there should be so many disputes whether Aristotle was a pious Theist or an Atheist and I firmly believe the truth would be found this that Aristotle wished that he was attached to ⟨a⟩ system and that he was a good and a religious man out of his system—he wished to educe all that was religious and all that gratified the moral feelings and if he did not perceive the inconsistencies of the sophists by which he connected that system with those conclusions it is only a proof that the greatest of men have too great a love for systems of their own creation nor need we wonder when the same error has been carried on through a series of philosophers whom it would have been the last degree of [f 214]*ᵘ* uncharitable calumny to suppose are irreligious for there is thank Heaven a glorious inconsistency in this nature*ᵛ* in which what is good when driven*ʷ* from the head takes place in the heart and still finds its operative place in the whole man this is metaphysics however whatever they were ⟨they⟩ are noticeable ~~only~~ to us only as far as it was the first way in which plainly and distinctly two opposite systems were placed before the mind of the world—one whether or not in order to arrive at the truth we are in the first place for there is no doubt among thinking men that both must be consulted—the question of priority is the point whether or not in the first place and in order to gain the principles of truth we are to go into ourselves and in our own spirits to discover the law by which the whole Universe is acting and then modestly to go forth and question this that and the other how far it will give a favorable response to our own individual conception of that truth [f 215] or whether on the contrary we are to regard with Aristotle the mind as being a blank or empty receiver distinguished from it indeed by a strange and mysterious propensity of being filled—a sort of intellectual vaso vacuo which is to receive here and there from this individual and the other individual a multitude of notices which this same blank tablet this same empty vessel is yet to generalize to assert and finally to present to itself as a reality precisely in the same way in which children might be made to mistake a projected image from a mirror in the air for the real cause of that mirror—

This I say is the first noticeable thing of Aristotle but I can*ˣ* no otherwise call it his merit than that as he gave it the highest perfection which it has ever received and I will venture to challenge any scholar acquainted with the subject to show me from the time of Lord Bacon to the present

---

ᵘ F 213 lacks catchword; f 214 begins by repeating "of"
ᵛ Word written over erasure   *ʷ* Word written over erasure
ˣ Word written over erasure; pencilled "can" in right-hand margin partly erased

day any one opi[f 216]^ynion not in itself too absurd for an Aristotle to
have conceive⟨d⟩ any one opinion upon which they themselves pride
themselves which is not to be found in Aristotle with all the Arguments
which they have brought forward for it more ably and more systematically than it has even been since that time—There are but two possible
philosophies that is seekings after Wisdom for as to the trash which
comes out from a bad heart acting upon a vain and coxcombical head it
is not deserving of attention—that—which a man must call a person a
bad man to listen to with patience ought not to be considered as a matter
of grave discussion the point is when you hear any such thing to say—
Sir we differ in our premises I am an honest man if you tell me Sir for instance that a Nero and a . . . are just as good or that an Assassin is no more
worthy of punishment than the Dagger with which he commits the crime
I should say at once you miss the grounds of all reason go learn your catechism be a better man and it is possible you may be a wiser one at present [f 217] it is impossible to reason with men who deny . . . and without
which they would be scourged out of nature as monsters but in all that
have in any way conceived the human mind sensibly and honestly as far
as the pursuit of truth is honorably entertained there I say I have found
nothing either in the doctrine of association and the various modes in
which they have been applied to the different pursuits and actions of men
or in the schemes of generalization which had not been anticipated by
Aristotle and in most instances without the errors and the absurdities that
in many cases have accompanied them putting that aside great was his
merit in his metaphysics of having framed what may be called a Dictionary for the World in a grand scheme that he drew the generic terms upon
the laws upon which the generic terms were to be formed—Grand too
was this that having been logically exercised upon a variety of the most
important subjects of human thought in the schools [f 218] of Plato and
joining with Plato as an honourable man in indignation at the increasing
influence of the Sophists he began then to abstract the science of Logic
itself he first of all assuredly brought forward to men not merely in practical examples and instances the mode of reasoning rightly but he abstracted from all this the forms of all coherent thinking he discovered the
law of it he shewed as clearly as any man who has acquired for instance
the science of fortification how he must necessarily build what angles he
must necessarily make for such and such reasons and because such and
such objects it will have that it will infringe upon it and have such and
such properties—So Aristotle first of all determined what were the laws

^y Catchword on f 215 is "-nion"; f 216 begins with "opinion"

common to all coherent—thinking and therein he founded not only the science of Logic but with it he made general throughout all the civilized world the terms of connexion we me our as our ands and our^z thes and our [f 219] therefores and so forth—so familiarly we hear them from ~~our~~ infancy that we have no idea of the advanced state in which we stand by those connexions—but take an oriental writing and see how thought is put on thought with little other connective than ad for and compare it with the organized spirit of our writings till the ⟨new⟩ French writings which aimed at destroying all the connexions of thought as the same philosophy strove to destroy all the connexions of society and domestic life I say if we think of this and could be witness of the effect which it produces every hour of our life in our conversation with children in our influence upon servants we should feel ⟨a⟩ proportionate gratitude to that great man who first presented^a to us the science of our own thinking and therein first reduced to law and to foresight for all Law contains in itself the power of foresight all the visionary sophisms by which men might through the medium of words impose false momentary convictions on each other

[f 220]   This was accordingly quite in the character of Aristotle and could scarcely have proceeded from Plato for Aristotle as I have said before was an abstracting and generalizing power in the world he still proceeded from ~~Plato~~ the particular to the universal from the concrete to the abstract so it is no wonder that in his ethics which followed they are still the abstractions from the actions of men and of their consequences and end at last not in morality but in a discreet prudence and enlightened self love from this ⟨he⟩ proceeded increasing his generalizations to Parethics in which he found a proper safeguard for there all that might have been amiss in his philosophics or ethics found its place for parethics consist in reconciling the whole by a generalization of the relations which take place between each and each in their individual relations and between the relation of the whole to them all I need say no further on this than that one of the greatest Statesmen of modern times Mr Burke has spoken the [f 221] highest praise of Aristotle on this point and that all great Statesmen have acknowledged that from the politics of Aristotle we derive not only a better knowledge of all the States of Greece than their historians could have given us but likewise the grounds of all the possibilities under which States can exist and in this a dim prophecy but yet a panegyrical one of our own happy constitution—

I have but one thing more to say—namely that we should look with a

---

^{z} Letter at end of "our" seems erased

^{a} End of "presented" written over erasure; pencilling also erased from right-hand margin

charitable mode of judgment upon the immediate works of Aristotle in our present state of Knowledge—if we did not apportion the proper merit to the Grand Scheme rather than to the extension in all its parts every truly great mind is to be considered in two points of view the first is that in which he may be said to exist universally to act upon all men in all ages and that is the grand idea which he first originates the grand form and scheme of generalization and the next is when quitting the part of the Architect he himself becomes one of the labourers and one of the [f 222] masons there you will find in him the imperfections of course of every human individual and while you give him every praise where he succeeds you will never permit it to detract from his merits where he fails when the great Capella from the meditation on the Pythagorean harmonies and numbers drew forth the scheme of the motion of the Planets and their distances what a petty mind must it be to say still he did not calculate such and such a distance accurately or he left such and such a thing to be done by those who followed him—aye that was his merit—he gave the principle of life ⟨as⟩ a ruling power and then sinking into an individual formed himself a part of the mighty impulse which was to move on for ages without end.

I should be happy if your patience is not exhausted to say a little on the subject of philosophy in general with regard to its influence on Society— it has been commonly supposed—I will not say the same as but certainly under a terribly suspicious rela[f 223]*b*tion to Alchymy or Conjuration or something or other—only this it may be very innocent but as to any utility or influence on society it is a matter out of the question you may go through all the streets of London and enquire at every shop in vain for any philosopher or any thing that philosophers have done that was useful to the happiness of mankind I again do think somewhat differently from this and I will not give you a philosophical reason but an historical one for it I cannot but feel when I look through modern history a powerful coincidence of sundry things with great events of society in which we are interested—as for instance I find to begin with a point I touched on in my last lecture that during the prevalence of the corrupt Aristotelian philosophy—which had passed into endless distinctions and classifications the fine arts partook of the same influence wiry outlines surfaces imprisoned in the outlines without depth—without force it was in painting [f 224] what mere verbiage would be in literature and that with the dawning of the true genius of Giotto and the six other Masters whose works are preserved at the Cemetery of Pisa where . . . with philosophy there the out-

b Catchword on f 222 is "-tion"; f 223 begins with "relation"

ward form was more than indifferent it seemed like the Platonic matter to be untractable and yet there was the power felt and with the power the grace and the life and the influence of Platonic Philosophy this was under the auspices of Lorenzetti the Magnificent and of Leo the 10th with . . . and others carried to its height for the time and the great men the Raphaels and the Michael Angelo's appeared there the mighty spirit still coming from within had succeeded in taming*c* the untractable matter and in reducing external form to a symbol of the inward and imaginable beauty we feel it to this day we feel it for this reason because we look at the forms after we have long satisfied all curiosity concerning mere outlines yet [f 225] still we look and look and feel that these are but symbols full worthy have they expressed themselves why having seen their outlines why having determined what they appeared to the eye do we still continue to muse on them but that there is a divine a something corresponding to within which no image can exhaust but which we are reminded of when in the south of Europe we look at the deep blue sky the same unwearied form presents itself yet still we look on sinking deeper and deeper and therein offering homage to the infinity of our souls which no mere form can satisfy—With the progress and the decline of philosophy came exactly as in the history of philosophy itself the Eclectic school—the men who without any forming principle within were to select the best from every thing they were to make the Helens from all the different beautiful women they were acquainted with the nose from one the eyes from another and the forehead from another and in this [f 226] manner they were to put together the lifeless fragments—the egg-shells to make the living germ of the Phœnix and they succeeded to a certain extend we had fine academic forms and they stood in a kind of middle state which will always please*d* certain minds congenial with them and this I should call the age of the . . . The Eclectic philosophy was followed by the merely mechanical in which in truth the atoms to which they were obliged to admit certain special qualities brought together produced a result and that result led to nothing excellent on the contrary the very principle was that the effect of outward form or symbol was more noble than the cause which produced it and accordingly for nearly half a century or more we had your fine inveterate portraits and in statuary your great marble wigs which led a man to say that they could not have looked more inveterately stupid in real life than they did [f 227]*e* upon the Canvas or in the Mar-

---

c Word written over erasure; "taming" also seems written in right-hand margin, then erased

d Word written over erasure; pencilled word in right-hand margin also erased

e F 226 lacks catchword; f 227 begins by repeating "did"

ble—this was the real state of the arts during the predominance of that kind of Philosophy but at length what was the mark of a better taste flatteringly for us arose with Sir Joshua Reynolds and it is no slight confirmation of my opinion that it is recorded that in evil days and with every obstacle around him he had drank deep of Platonism at least of what is best of all the vital feelings of Platonism in his early youth since that time and now I am happy to see and feel that men are craving for a better diet than the wretched trash they have been fed with for the last century that they will be taught that what is sound must come out of themselves and that they cannot find good with their eyes or with their ears or with their hands that they will not discover them in the crucible or bring them out of a machine but must look into the living soul which God has made His Image in order to learn even in fragments what that power is by which we are to [f 228] execute the delegated power entrusted to us by Him and I feel more when I think that in the Country where this mechanic philosophy was predominant and most idolized it presented a most fearful but a most instructive lesson of its consequences—we have only to put one word for the other and in the mechanical philosophy to give the whole system of the French Revolution—here are certain atoms miraculously invested with certain individual rights from the collection of which all right and wrong is to depend these atoms by a chance and will of their own were to rush together and thus rushing together they were to form a convention and this convention was to make a constitution and this constitution then was to make a contract a very sound^f contract between the major atoms and the minor ones that the minor should govern them but that the major should have a right to knock them on the head whenever they chose and if there was any quarrel the major atoms were to assume the power of repulsion [f 229] suspending ⟨then⟩ the power of attraction and dance the old Hay over again till they formed a new convention which was to form a new constitution which was to make a contract which was to give them the same inherent rights of doing wrong whenever they chose—what can be the consequence of this when look at us—what are we in ourselves if we look at our hands our limbs they are marvellously composed but did we compose them is not the whole power of the Universe concerned in every atom that falls and takes its place as a living particle there—but yet after all what are we can man if he does not raise himself above man above his individual self contemplate himself as aught but an animal different from other animals by having a bewildering self conceit instead of instinct—If he is not man if he is not a living part of the

---

^{f} Word written over erasure; pencilled word in right-hand margin also erased

Universe capable of partaking of the universe and finding himself then only when he does partake in it let us throw aside all our pride all our boastfulness of the image of God—how [f 230] can that be so which considers only the paltry particle and who knows nothing of a whole but as it is produced out of a collision of these nothings which is to make the marvellous integer out of so many thousand noughts—no depend upon it whatever is grand—whatever is truly organic and living—the whole is prior to the parts—that man is unworthy of being a citizen of a State who does not know the citizens are for the sake of the State not the State for the sake of the immediate flux of persons who form at that time the people—who does not know what a poor worthless creature man would be if it were not for the Unity of human nature being preserved from age to age through the Godlike form of the State—who does not carry it further on and judge of all things in proportion as they partake of Unity—who judges of the democratic element as far . . . by the individual . . . who does not reverence Monarchy as far as it again [f 231] tends to draw the mind to the feeling of the one and the magnificent power in the one and reverence in the universe—who does not again feel the same ~~elsewhere~~ elevation of mind in contemplating rank, high birth, aristocracy as principles of preeminence as the thread of cohesion . . . as our very own and on future ages as our reversionary property—it is this—the principle of Unity and that derived from within not from the objects of our senses which deprived of the interpreting power from within are but an Alphabet run mad—are in reality only a tendency like matter itself to be divided and divided ad infinitum in which we have to thank[g] our better nature that though we may perish without end we cannot utterly cease to be—

---

[g] Word written over erasure

LECTURE 6

Mͬ Coleridges Lecture
                    Monday 25ᵗʰ January 1819

It will I conceive be the best arrangement of the subjects of this evenings
discourse if somewhat changing the order in which they had appeared in
the advertisement I begin with the Sceptics for the purpose of taking up
what otherwise I should find no place for and in truth is not of great philosophic consequence the history of the Megaric school of these we have
little more remaining than the names of the Teachers and Founders Euclidas or Euclid—his Scholars . . . Pyrrho^h Stilpo and Clitomachus but
above all Theodorus surnamed the atheist and Pyrrho the founders of the
Sceptics and therein linking onto our immediate subject—All those men
flourished between the 95ᵗʰ and the 120th Olympiad that is to say from
about three hundred and ninety nine years to two hundred and seventy
years before our Lord—from all the accounts [f 233] we have received—
the school appears more probably disputatious than philosophic—Timon
himself a Sceptic talks of the . . . in no very honorable phrases for he says
in three of the Greek Hexameters which among others have been preserved of his what would have been to us invaluable poems—"but I care
nothing for these triflers nor for any that belong to them not . . . whoever
he may be nor yet for the litigious Euclidas who struck the inhabitants or
the school of Megara with radias^i of disputation—in short it was at once
an art and a passion with them—Still however something is to be said . . .
who wrote against Aristotle was a man who is deemed to have done good
service to the science of Logic and we are informed by Plutarch that his
book of sophisms or as we should call them conundrums were merely
logical exercitations which indeed before I met with this passage in
Plutarch I believed to be the Case with the Conundrums of the greatest
poets—the object was to guard the [f 234] minds of the young pupils
against the force of equivocation of double meanings lying hid under the
same word so that an argument or a deduction drawn from one meaning

---

  ^h "Phyrro" correction of partly erased word
  ^i First letter of "radias" blotted and uncertain

715

shall be perfectly correct but from the other shall be perfectly fallacious yet this may by the artifices of words be so disguised that you may trace from a Sophism which is only not what we call a bull on to the finest paralogism which has set nations at War with each other and has disturbed the last Century with factions yet the same sophism shall be at the bottom of both and the difference only is that the one is more happily disguised than the other by words arising out of associations and out of the nature of the subject—Now they thought and permit me to say I fully agree with them that no more happy mode could be perceived of putting the mind on its guard against this delusion which all history shews us has been of such vital importance to men than by presenting an absurdity palpable at first [f 235] sight where the Scholar has no temptation of being misled or actually believing the thing to be so but yet all his ingenuity is exerted to discover where the fault in the argument lies—as for instance when a man says I lie he either lies or he does not lie—if he lies he tells the truth and if he tells the truth he lies a sort of Conundrum every man knows at once the thing must end in nothing that it is an absurdity and yet it will not suggest itself at once to every mind where the logical defect is which in this case for instance would be that here a poetic or passionate use of a phrase is substituted for a logical one that when a man says I lie he uses the present tense figuratively in order to determine the extreme recency of what he has said and the Sophism consists in the man having used bad Grammar and saying I lie which is referrable to the past as a positive act of immediate consciousness for if he said I lied the argument would drop and yet be assured there have been Sophisms [f 236] as gross as that in reality which yet a little better disguised have been productive of all the bad passions that can agitate the human mind and of all the consequences that follow from such passions when men have swords to argue with instead of merely a pen or their tongues

Theodorus deserved mention too for his labors in desynonimizing words—he began with the assertion that properly speaking there are no synonimous and this[j] perhaps applied to a homogeneous language like the Greek may be very nearly true—applied to a language derived from many sources such as is the English it certainly is not strictly true and a very ingenious work on the subject by M[r] William Taylor I believe labors under this mistake that substituting what ought to be and what is desirable for what actually is he has assumed that no two words really are synonimous—I should say that certainly there are several—many in our language and I believe that the more ⟨we move⟩ forward in [f 237]

---

[j] Nearly vertical pencilled line drawn through last letter of "this"

knowledge the more of such[k] we shall discover we shall with every new permanent and just distinction be obliged to use the word in one sense only which unwittingly we have before used in many—The instance that now suggests itself to me is that of obliged and compelled before the time of Charles the first—the words were used as perfectly synonimous till Hobbs having drawn an argument from this that as a man who was obliged was compelled when a man that is compelled cannot be responsible and consequently there can be no real essential distinction between vice and virtue men were obliged to look about them and they found they used one word to express a compulsion from without that which a man cannot prevent and another to express that which he ought not to do and that which he is obliged not to do but by no means compelled to do or to omit—then we began to use the words with a very important difference attached to them and this having come into our language and being that which we are[l] all bred up from infancy to [f 238] discourse it becomes common sense—for often as I have questioned myself what the exact meaning of the words common sense is I can find no other explanation than the following—when that which had been in the schools and was communicable only by a technical language in consequence of its compleat correspondence with the inward and outward experience of all men becomes a part of the general language so that men by the mere mechanism of language[m] can think as a man can do sums by a Carpenters rule then it becomes what we call common sense which is an ever varying thing—what is philosophy in one age is common sense in another and vice versa so that when that which belongs to a few becomes the inheritance of all who are not[n] diseased or pitiably below their fellow creatures in the state of Society which they enjoy in common then philosophy perpetually acts as the pioneer and purveyor of common [f 239] sense—the more industrious philosophy is the larger the sphere of common sense for whenever Philosophy is so intelligible that all men admit it—it becomes then a part of their common thoughts and common language and every man now can say common sense dictates to us that the small speck we call this earth is not the centre of the whole universe round which the other stupendous bodies move but it itself goes round the larger orb and this to an extent of which we are unaware this we are all almost taught—you will scarcely find a person in this Country ignorant of the truth of what was thought such uncommon sense even absurd in a time so recent as that of Charles the second as that Sir Thomas Brown one of the ablest men of the age declared it to be such uncommon nonsense that it was a proof

[k] "such" written over erasure   [l] Vertical line pencilled between "are" and "all"
[m] Second "a" written over erasure   [n] "are not" seems written over erasure

there was no idea so absurd but it was a proof that some philosopher had taught it—this has become the common sense of the Village and of the Cottage such is the [f 240] protruded state of progression in Society and it applies not only to thoughts but to words which on all occasions a man may observe words are things they are the great mighty instruments by which thoughts are excited and by which alone they can be in[o] a rememberable form and delightful it is to listen to the common people—hear them in the streets—overhear them when they are conversing with each other and particularly at any moment when they are interested or animated and you may count on your fingers word after word the history which you can trace and find—how familiar words are with them and how appropriately used which but a century ago were placed as pedantic and fit only for the schools—in some instances even to abuse I grant but what is there in human nature without abuse

We ought not to quit that subject without remembering how much we owe to the institutions of Christianity how clear it is that the history has been ⟨this⟩ from the schools to the pulpit and from the pulpit not by any long circuit but directly to the common people And their degrees of intellect do not so much in this Country at least depend upon the quantum [f 241] of their opportunities with regard to books or to conversation as it does to the zeal and the interest that they feel in their own permanent concerns and I will appeal to common experience whether it be common or whether an instance can be found of a man who having begun to think better of his duties and what he has got to look forward to in life becomes as they say Serious—a regular attendant on his church or on his meeting but that you find that man in the course of a few months wonderfully altered both in his language in his power of connecting words and with that in his power of generalizing and the increase of his intellectual faculties generally—This I say because if we may use the word proud I was about to say but yet pride that has no selfishness is honorable it is a proud distinction because it is a grateful one and our religion from all others that have been revealed has been the faithful guide and the pioneer and companion of civilization—look at the Countries under the influence of Mahometanism look at the Countries under the influence of [f 242] Brahminism[p] and observe how from good it has become less so to the bad and from the bad to the worse with all the natural effects of degraded nature in sensuality[q] cruelty and finally under a familiarity to despotism that last that worst state of man—utter insensibility—in which nothing remains that is human but the forms of superstition—let these men therefore as

----

o "in" written over erasure of longer word   *p* Catchword on f 241: "Brah-"

q Last six letters of "sensuality" written over erasure

friends of logic though little[r] interested with philosophy properly so speaking have our thanks and our honorable remembrance—In their school it appears ⟨that⟩ Pyrrho the founder ⟨of⟩ the Sceptics or the Pyrrhonists was educated—his biography however is stuffed with contradictions and different tales—different individuals of the same name are confounded with him—there appear still all the practical consequences that would follow if this Sceptic was supposed as a man really to believe all that the demonstrators thought and that ⟨on⟩ grounds of logic supposing he alone had as a philosopher imagined [f 243] such a monstrous impossibility as this and that these were past at once into actual matters of fact concerning Pyrrho that because he would call on a man as a philosopher to prove to him the existence of that post out of his own mind that therefore Pyrrho must necessarily run his nose against that post or he was a very inconsistent man—Pyrrho would say I am reasoning on a point of science I believe the post to be there and act on its being there as well as you the dispute is whether you as a philosopher as a scientific man have or have not assumed a light by which you can demonstrate this independent of your natural feelings this is the true doctrine of Pyrrhonism and were it otherwise it would be an affront to the name of philosophy to bring the history of such men or their names into any discussion at all but in that sense M[r] Hume—no one will suspect me of being an advocate of M[r] Humes opinions but I most assuredly do think that he was attacked in a very illogical not to say unhandsome manner both by Priestley and Oswald and [f 244] I grieve to say for the beauty of the book in other respects—by Beattie—it was a book that honoured Beattie from the display of genius and eloquence which shot through and through as it were with a good heart and sincere piety but notwithstanding that M[r] Hume had some right to say it was a great big lie in Octavo as far as it referred to him for it went on the ground that Hume did not believe there was any connection of cause and effect that man could act by whereas it was a proud challenge to your proud dogmatists who conceived all things to be the influence of their reason and particularly those as was the case with ninety nine out of a hundred for whom he wrote compleat . . . who held that all knowledge ⟨was⟩ derived from the senses and that there was no reality in the senses and he cut the matter short by calling on them to prove that the ideas of cause and effect of any reality at all—they may be produced by the mere force of association as the law of association [f 245] in the human mind when two things come together habitually with the one appearing we naturally expect the other and as long as that experi-

---

[r] "little" written over erasure

ence remains uncontradicted so long we act confidently and there we affirm the reality of those ideas I call on you to give up your . . . and allow some other truth than the senses or admit with me there is no philosophic no sciential ground for the arguments of cause and effect—Instead of answering this book a great clamor arose—here is a man denying all cause and effect what will become of all our religion if it stopped there there would be some sense in it—but they went on what was to become of all society—if such opinions were to prevail men would not use their spoons to put their soup into their mouths in short a wonderful number of . . . by telling them there were a great many things not dreamt of in their philosophy—such I have said because I think it a duty owing to every man who has sought for truth however widely what he believed as truth differs from my conceptions—Now something of this I believe [f 246] to have been the case with Pyrrho for his character was most highly revered and from the fragments of Timon which I have mentioned he is spoken of exactly as Socrates whose great object was to withdraw men from vain speculations beyond their powers to the practical duties of life but to prevent especially that feverish positiveness that so often deludes minds under the best impulses into the worst actions to teach men what a difference there is between positiveness and certainty and if they could not arrive at the latter which he professed himself unable to do then to say with Voltaire and the very passage is found in Timon—I neither know nor believe myself to have the means of knowing why the air of Greece is better than the air elsewhere but this I know that we ought to cultivate our Olive Gardens

The Sect of the Sceptics were however obscure and counted of all the sects the fewest great names this arose from the nature and the circumstances of the Grecian [f 247] and of the Roman Republics—there was not any criminality in the first place attached to any direct belief or unbelief while it remained merely philosophical as long as the question was purely metaphysical relative[s] to the Divine nature and not to the Gods of the laws and the establishment for like us the ancients were liberals—enlightened and tolerant men of the very first water as long as the subject in dispute was one in which they had not the slightest degree of interest where indeed any interest was awakened on the subject they could if not burn yet poison and banish and display the usual modes of conviction or deferring or preventing that spread of heresy with as much alacrity and thorough good will as the Inquisition itself—but Scepticism was not in the nature of the times—their very republican habits[t] led them to carry

---

[s] The word partly written over erasure   [t] The word partly written over erasure

into the schools of philosophy the same temper of minds with which they voted in the assemblies—they must be on the one side or the other directly and the [f 248] doctrine which seemed to put a check to all progress of the human mind which it really did or would have done was opposed to their better feelings as well as it was incongruous with their manners or accidental ones—I have mentioned this therefore merely in proof that all the forms of philosophy that are properly philosophy that is to say grounded in any of the operations of reason or of the understanding right or wrong had been developed previous to the appearance of our Lord and I therefore defer the rest to the second part of this discourse the reappearance of philosophy in Christendom where it will be found that from other circumstances the Sceptics then had and continued to play a much more important part though without a single argument . . . philosophy as a striving of the mind—the world of man. In accordance of this plan I defer the detail of their arguments as well as the consequences of them to the era in which they were truly influencial and effective

I proceed therefore now to the Epi[f 249]cureans[u] and the philosophy of Epicurus but in order to do this it will be necessary for me to recur again not to repeat but simply to recur to the Cyrenaic sect whom I spoke of in an earlier lecture as arising out of the ambiguity of Socrates's own doctrine which split itself in his immediate followers into the Cynic sect under Antisthenes and the Cyrenaic or voluptuary sect under Aristippus—the particulars I deferred until the present time—Aristippus himself was not properly the founder of the School he was a courtier a man of fashion a philosopher of the World but his grandson Aristippus became strictly speaking a Master of philosophy and the founder of a particular school—After him came Theodore surnamed the Atheist and the tenets common to them all seem to be these they all alike divided the movements of the mind into pain and pleasure between which stood the states of indifference these movements[v] pain or pleasure originate all in the body they admitted however certain agreeable and disagreeable [f 250] emotions some of them at least did—that had their ground in the Soul such as the laws[w] of our Country but then what they gave with one hand they took away with the other for they declared those emotions to be so faint and ineffective in themselves that unless they were accidentally associated by some bodily feeling they would have no weight and scarcely arrive at consciousness pleasure and the avoidance of its opposite they declared to be the actual only motive the impulse of each mo-

[u] Catchword on f 248: "-cureans"
[v] All but first two letters of "movements" written over erasure
[w] "laws" crossed out in pencil, and "love" written in pencil above

ment and the aggregate of pleasurable sensations the final sum total—I beg to observe for something rests on the distinction the final sum total of these not the coexistence of them at any one time but the final sum total of pleasurable sensation they proposed as the great object of all human thought and action under the name of . . . so far their doctrines do not appear in direct open hostility against all morality however indirectly or by fair deduction they would be found so personally but there was a third [f 251] which renders all sane or safe interpretation impossible—they declared that each individual is as an individual an entire end—to and for himself and that all our objects have no other reality except as the sensations and phantoms in the individuals mind constitute a part of his whole pleasure—but it was objected ᵗᵉ the bodily emotions too often contravene each other and it is hard to reconcile them—this they admitted and to systematize them therefore they said requires prudence but the task being very difficult for that reason and for that reason only prudence becomes virtue so that virtue they defined to be prudence exerted on a difficult subject but as every noticeable time every time of which we can be conscious or remember however short it be must itself be a system of sensations therefore say they we may without impropriety speak of happy moments and he is on the whole the happiest man who has the greatest number of intense enjoyments or of happy moments—it follows from all this [f 252] that there can be no universal criterion either of duty or of virtue or of wisdom because there can be none in the sensations all these have origin and from them they derive their only reality disputemus non de gustibus—we must not dispute about matters of taste each mans appeal is to his own incommunicable peculiarity of feeling I have Cicero for my authority who says . . . they admit of no criterion of judgment except their own innate or incommunicable feelings and undoubtedly this is not so wild as it may seem to be when fairly stated for even in modern times I have met with books which assert the very same things—I have seen a very elaborate work on taste for instance in which the taste of Venison[x] and a taste for Milton and a taste for Religious sentiment have been all treated of as a species of the same genus all originating in the palate [f 253] and the whole system of criticism both in poetry painting statuary and so forth is derived from this grammatical mistake of a taster of and taste for various others past the same inward judgments till the moral being . . . absurdity as well as the baseness which is contained in their notions—what is the consequence of this—I need not say that to the

---

[x] First and last two letters of "Venison" written over erasures

greater part of mankind it would preclude all wish to be better for unless I could demonstrate to a healthy fellow that is for instance in an Ale house or elsewhere enjoying himself over a pot^y of porter that I at that time enjoyed more pleasurable feelings in endeavoring to develope my intellectual faculties^z than he did with his pot of porter or if I said I believe you are as well employed as I am if only you are developing your being in the best way of all by an earnest desire to perform your duty if he says I have neither tasted the sweetness nor felt the smoothness nor seen the colour nor had any other gratification from this sort of duty you talk of what motive [f 254] could I offer to such a man in the world he is the judge of his own sensations I cannot pretend to tell him I think the developement of his intellectual faculties or the keeping sacred the principles of conscience are worthy his notice if I am to reduce him to what I know nothing about whether it will tickle the man or give him a pleasurable sensation or not—the moment I press that I must reason as we all reason— Well Sir taste differs no man is angry with another for liking Beef when he prefers Mutton if our moral duties originate in the same way the same reasoning must follow and as the object of all philosophy is to raise man from a lower state to a higher what must become of that which is incapable of shewing that any one man could gain by the exchange which has not one single Argument that can be offered why he would be at all happier in one state than in the other for every argument would suppose something under the name [f 255] of happiness which did not belong to the sensations and which did not belong to any thing peculiar but which was convincing to all men when it was once offered to them unless that conviction was precluded by their own fault—there are things on which we are entitled to say perhaps Sir I cannot convince you but this I know that you ought to be convinced and philosophy which strikes the words should and ought out of the dictionary and intellect of philosophy is only anti-philosophy and presented in this crude form no man would admit it but when tricked up with all the advantages of a Religion where the grapes from the Vineyard of Revelation are hung on the thorns it is astonishing what a decorous well bred^a courtly amiable and convincing system this can be made to appear even to a majority of mankind

From the Cyrenaic sect arose I [f 256] should say before for it is a necessary part of the proof of it—the Cyrenaic may be taken for a sect who

---

^{y} "pot" seems written over erasure

^{z} "faculties" written over erasure

^{a} Apparent erasure under last letter of "bred"; in right-hand margin "d/" in pencil imperfectly erased

in a plain manner followed the natural consequences of their doctrine they rejected in the first place two of the three divisions of philosophy namely physics and dialectics and retained only the ethics the dialectics they rejected as utterly useless because a man must know his own sensations and all logic consisted in knowing whether a man did or did not look on a thing—the physics they rejected on a higher ground they said it tended to create a belief in any reality out of a mans feeling and therefore troubled his mind and made him anxious but what sect will give up morality—It was a sort of Gourmands Almanac there were many dishes that agreed very well and appeared digestible to many persons and therefore in the form of a question they were all strongly recommended to try and if another found the direct opposite to [f 257] agree with him better they hoped his communication in time for the next edition—This was the sauce they mustered under different forms *b*all pretences*c* to Ethics which are founded on the principle of self gratification I do not say self love that is a subtler point more interesting a great deal here for this is one thing different from the whole history of philosophy that the biography of the Individuals that formed it is infinitely more interesting than the scheme itself two or three must be mentioned—Theodore surnamed the Atheist and . . . first of Theodore he was surnamed the Atheist and undoubtedly the inevitable consequences of the Cyrenaic system must have ⟨been⟩ Atheism for what man would pretend to say that he had any consciousness that he had any sentious*d* perceptions of the objects of Religion however he appears to have been as far as a man of such principles could be yet practically an honest man and it was not for his real Atheism [f 258] but for his sincerity in rejecting the divinity of his Countrys Gods and Goddesses whom he regarded as mere deified men and women afterwards employed in a secondary use and by an after thought as symbols of the power of Nature and consequently he has found many able Advocates in the best fathers of the Christian Church—but though he ought not on this ground to be called an Atheist or perhaps on any yet doubtless a Sceptic or unbeliever—a negative Atheist . . . whether this in its cruder form the Cyrenaic or in its after more prudential shape as the school of Epidorus I feel the greatest respect for Theodorus whose brief creed of his unbelief has been preserved by Plutarch "To the idea*e* of God . . . yet not in time every where present yet not in space acting on all and yet impassive to all

---

b–c Apparent erasure at beginning and end of passage; pencilling erased in right-hand margin

d "sentious" crossed out in pencil and "sensuous" written in pencil above it

e "c" or "e" written above "d" of "idea"

through action . . . [f 259] immutable now for the possibility of a reality
correspondent to this idea I can find no grounds in the terms and in my
understanding no facts . . . senses and I think that what the philosophic
Apostle has said one sentence this is a just comment on by the mere power
of reasoning no man ever yet arrived at God at that Being given by his
conscience and his moral being—then his intellect his senses and all the
objects of both intellect and senses are one continued book for ever calling it forth for ever reminding him of it—for ever bringing it into distinction and comparison but those who think it easy to demonstrate the
being of a Deity are mistaken a very worthy man once expressed to me
his astonishment that any doubt should be felt about it what have you to
conceive of but Infinite Goodness Infinite Wisdom and Infinite power—
and that is God—fortunately the most powerful [f 260] of the Ancients
found this no easy task and poor Theodore who saw clearly by what I
must think a proof of a good heart what he would wish to believe and who
admitting more than his senses and his understanding as that which brings
it into consciousness was perfectly right in affirming that he could find
there no correspondent reality to such an idea were we regardless of the
Anachronism to imagine to ourselves Theodore and the furious compro-
miser who followed him as present at that sublimest moment in the
records of Orators the Oration of Sͭ Paul at Athens when the . . . were we
to consider both these men auditors of this Apostle we should not hesitate in determining which of the two would most probably have been the
disciple of Sͭ Paul—Theodore the honest and reluctant Atheist or . . .
who holding precisely the same premises found a number of courtly ways
of agreeing with the established opinion of [f 261] Society on all occasions next to Theodore was . . . who drew from the same premises the
~~same premises the~~ same melancholy results with respect to the great idol
of their scheme namely Happiness whether understood as the Cyrenaics
that is*f* enjoyment or as their successors the followers of Epicurus that is
pleasurable tranquility I say from the same premises he drew the same
melancholly results with regard to Happiness which Theodore had done
with regard to truth he held this happiness to be demonstrably unattainable nothing could be more legitimate than his deductions were from this
system which since his time has ⟨been⟩ called Eudemonism or that which
places Happiness as the true source and regulator of duties as the object
and the aim of man for rejecting as they did immortality because that
again could be brought under no sensation under no perception thank

---

f "is" written over erasure

their reasonings I had at one time felt [f 262] within myself and gave utterance to them in a few lines under the title of "Human life contemplated on the denial of Immortality"

> "If dead we cease to be; if total gloom
>   Swallow up life's brief flash for aye, we fare
> As Summer gusts, of sudden birth and doom
>   Whose sound and motion not alone declare,
> But *are* their whole of being! If the breath
>   Be life itself and not its task and tent
> If e'en a Soul like Miltons can know death;
>   O man thou vessel purposeless unmeant
> Yet drone-hive strange of phantom purposes
>   Suplus of natures dread activity
> Which as she gazed on some nigh finished vase
> Retreating slow with meditative pause
>   She formed with restless hands unconsciously
> Blank Accident! nothing's anomaly!ᵍ
>   If rootless thus, thus substanceless they state,
> Go weigh thy dreams, and by thy hopes thy fears
> The Counterweights!—Thy laughter and thy tears
>   Mean but themselves, each fittest to create
> And to repay the other! Why rejoices
>   Thy heart with hollow joy for hollow good
>   Why Cowl thy face beneath the mourners hood
> Why waste thy sighs, and thy lamenting voices,

[f 263]

> Image of image Ghost of Ghostly Elf,
> That such a thing as thou, feel'st warm or cold!
> Yet what and whence thy gain, if thou withhold
>   These costless shadows of thy shadowy self
>   Be sad! be glad! be neither! seek, or shun!
>   Thou hast no reason why! Thou canst have none!
>   Thy beings being is contradiction"

When we can conceive a man of eloquence painting life as it really is under all the vices and turpitudes and under all the miseries arising out of these—out of the passions which originate in these sensations taken as the law of action when he perceives how nature still sympathizing with man suffers with . . . and revenges it with marsh fevers how she breathes forth to him in the air and yet she cannot as a mother . . . with his inflic-

---

ᵍ Line written over erasure

tions on his own species when he came to paint a society unregulated by moral principle and describe those who waked to labor in order merely to sleep that they may again rise to labor in all things showed the impossibility that the full developement [f 264] of the frame of man could be arrived at under the state of society which fatally as he deemed was their destiny—who could wonder that such a man infused such melancholy or despair such tedium of life that he was forbidden by the Government by Ptolemy ever to speak in public and was directly banished from Egypt because he told the melancholy truths that must necessarily force themselves upon every thinking and feeling mans mind—were you once to remove a view and belief of a future state then better said he is death than life but how far better would it be never to have been such is the end which is the true and natural conclusion of every voluptuary system for it is a fatal . . . that cannot be evaded—Man must not be man cannot be on a level with the beast either infinitely more blessed than they or incomparably more wretched either above them beyond all measure or deplorably below them, angel he may be fiend he may [f 265] make himself but beast—that is a privilege which a bad man cannot hope for it is a punishment which a good man can never suspect

The transition from this to Epicurus is short as I have hitherto done I begin with his biography he was born in the third year of the 109th Olympiad or about 342 years before Christ—his father . . . was one of the poor men who were sent to Samos as Colonists—the farm allotted to him there being insufficient for his maintenance he endeavored to make up what was wanting as a travelling Schoolmaster or instructor of children— it is not however without interest what is related of Epicurus's mother that she was remarkably superstitious under constant fear of evil or bad spirits haunting her place of abode—profuse in the use of holy water exorcisms &c and that Epicurus when a boy was obliged to recite to her the usual incantations by which the Spirits were to be laid or sent as we say to the Red Sea—this anecdote is interesting as it explains the [f 266] excessive antipathy he had in his after life to the very name of spirits and to every thing that was connected with it in a sort of spite as it were against them he revenged himself on the miseries he suffered in his childhood— It is said that his education having been narrow and in short almost entirely without any masters he received his first impulse from Hesiod when he was twelve years old in a line beginning "First of all things arose Chaos and out of what said the boy did Chaos arise and finding no sort of explanation—it is the same feeling many of us have heard from our own children when we first speak to them of the origin of things—finding no satisfaction he remained perplexed till he fell in with the works of Democritus and appearing to himself to receive great satisfaction from them thenceforward attached himself to the corpuscular philosophy and that of atoms but it is characteristic both of Epicurus and the whole sect that their acquaintance with the writings of the Philosophers whom they opposed was altogether superficial it was Epicurus's pride that he was a self taught man none of your vulgar students who acquire their knowledge from study it all came by force [f 267] of his natural genius true it is he had read a little but all the rest was a perfect creation of his own and he brought forwards according to his own declarations the opinions of other philosophers and enquired concerning them only for the purpose of confuting them this is so strange[h] it might sound I believe it is not uncommon in life for it has happened to me with a man of considerable eminence in the medical world who just after I had quitted college told me that he had some wish to employ a young man of a metaphysical turn to read the books of all former philosophers to him and to give him a syllabus of their opinions which he was not acquainted with for says he I can reconcile the whole to my system and I think it will be doing a great service to confute them when I establish the great doctrine of physics and the understanding of man—This took place with a man who was deemed a great philosopher sometime ago and I believe in the hospitals and elsewhere you may hear his name now—and there was a time when he was a great Poet [f 268] likewise both the one and the other appear to have been in rapid decay but it is truly the case with men when they oppose the sympathies of mankind when they have to bear up against all the connexions which we have formed in the most sacred manner from our homes from our Law Courts from our churches from all that binds us to the earth as it were—Why what is a man to do who has determined to mount a balloon which in truth compleatly raises him from earth but without getting one inch nearer to heaven and then he is to float above and have no other amusement but to look on those below and consider how high he is

Vanity and an earnest desire of . . . were two other qualities universally attributed to Epicurus with the ancients yet with these he had many amiable qualities he was a friendly man weak in constitution and therefore incapable of any of the Cyrenaic maxims it led him very naturally to prize that most which was most in his power that is comfortable tranquility the absence of pain—what sort of ground that is for morality you may well suppose by recollecting [f 269] the old Proverb

[h] Altered in pencil to "⟨not⟩ so strange ⟨as⟩" with pencilled check mark (√) in right-hand margin

"When the Devil was sick the Devil a monk would be!
When the Devil was well the Devil a monk was he!!!"

So it is when a man is in pain or the moment afterwards nothing appears so delightful as mere tranquility to him—let a little new blood out on his nerves and the man doffs aside all tranquillity no—an active life and a merry one—give me a short life and a merry one because then the tone of the one is just as good as the other they are the natural notions and feelings that arise out of the immediate state of the feelings of the mind and so far Epicurus was consistent that while he preferred comfort to enjoyment—and in preferring the pleasures of the mind to those strictly called bodily he however assured you that both one and the other arose entirely in the other and had no other value than the body—began with it and with it ceased altogether—another difference too there was between Epicurus and the philosophers both before him and his contemporaries he attempted to settle himself it appears and establish some [f 270] particular[i] school in various parts of minor Asia without success and then as his last resource went to Athens here he exerted himself and employed the influence and interest of his acquaintance to procure him scholars he became a busy candidate for scholars and he succeeded in bringing them not only together but in organizing them . . . Pythagorean only that every appearance of Religion and Enthusiasm was excluded and all their discipline calculated on the plan of the greatest possible prevention of pain admitting of as much possible enjoyment as was compatible with the absence of pain for in this I repeat consisted the difference and the whole difference between the Cyrenaic and Epicurean that they attached the greatest value to passive pleasure they were for intense happiness and measured it according to its intensity while the Epicureans prized most the absence of uneasiness and that diffused sense of comfort which the act of living is accompanied by when the organs go on in harmony when no one is noticed but the effect of the [f 271] whole is what we call the sensation of happiness—a most desirable thing beyond all doubt the only fault in it is this that nature itself forces us to seek for this happiness in some way or other that it is very absurd to make that to be the principle of regulation which is to be the thing grounded that whether I will or not I cannot help wishing to be happy—there is no man not even a madman but wishes to be happy in some way but unfortunately every man wishes it according to his passion at the moment a man no doubt is influenced by the gratification of some feeling or other to procure pleasure or to get rid of a greater pain when he dashes his head against the wall but where is

---

[i] Catchword on f 269: "par-"

the rule for this no man doubts every sentient being must seek for a pleasurable sensation and avoid a painful sensation but what has this to do with morality—Morality is to be the regulator of this which is only the aggregate of the passions and senses they are the very things the moral principle is to conduct and regulate and the whole argument of self love goes into a perfect circle for if you drive it from one gross form to another less so still you come to the most refined of all—I do it for the pleasures [f 272] of a good conscience I first of all object to the word pleasures it appears such a strange generalization which brings the consistency of having done your duty to the best of your power to the very same class with eating an orange or any grosser gratification but after all that—you do it for this reason only for no other reason but[j] because your conscience would give you a certain quantum of pleasure if ⟨so⟩ you will be greatly deceived your conscience will not be mocked and will tell you essentially and intellectually you are as great a rascal as if you had done the very opposite—no man can have the sensation of an approving conscience in the nature of things but as far as he has consciousness in himself that he did it because it was his duty because it was the will of his maker because he could not do otherwise without introducing a complete contradiction to the love of that being to whom he is worse than a beast if he does not feel love and gratitude and incapability of deriving his happiness from the senses[k] and to the best of his power acting and living and feeling with the consonance of our author There are in short but two systems possible [f 273] that have an essential difference the one is that Virtue is the means the other that it is an absolute end to take Virtue as a precept in order to render it a nature—this is the true problem of all true Philosophy then comes History and the most important comment on History—self knowledge which acknowledges the truth of this position and the moral necessity[l] but at the same time its impracticability by human nature unaided—this is a philosophy which at once reconciles the highest ideal with the truest and profoundest humility and all that is on the one side or on the other is empty pride or bestial degradation—the physiology of Epicurus so fully detailed in Lycurgus I have no concern with that does not come within my plan except as far as it refers to the actual state of things now that I think I may say enough upon when I refer to the part in Lycurgus in which being asked why the earth produced animals answered first of all the mud was a milky substance with which the living things were nourished and that in the former state it was still better for it

[j] "but" seems written over erasure
[k] Last letter of "senses" covered by pencilling
[l] "moral necessity" written over erasure and too large for available space

produced the living things themselves being asked [f 274] why we can see no instances of this at the present he answered we have a clear analogy for that when hens are old they leave of laying now as this was the best philosophy they could bring I hope you will forgive me for not entering into it further—what was further belonged to Democritus not to Epicurus and observe again as in the Cyrenaic sect it was peculiar to the Epicureans indeed the Cyrenaics did modify the opinions of their predecessors as far as their purposes permitted but with Epicurus it was irreligious to alter any form of thinking not to be found in his very voluminous writings and to revere him as a God was the only religion of his followers—that Epicurus was a God—the great Being who had lifted them up above all superstitions who had freed them from being afraid of their mothers and nurses stories of Ghosts and bloody heads and bones but unfortunately he had not freed them from the fear of death had^m not given them one consolation in sickness or pain but to be something more than a beast for no [f 275] conceivable^n reason but that of dying at last and admitting that life ended in nothingness this was Epicureanism no progress was ever made in philosophy in them their effect upon the morality of the Roman people was incalculable it appears that at least ninety nine out of a hundred of his adherents were Cyrenaics or voluptuaries in the grossest sense and yet poor human nature so essentially does it crave after a Religion that he who denied a God who denied Immortality who denied everything that can sooth sorrow or elevate thought—he for lack of a better he must be their God—Epicurus—and his words must be their Oracle and in his wretched hopeless doctrines was their faith to find its necessary object so true it is that to believe nothing or to disbelieve is impossible to man and Infidelity merely shifts the object of faith not the faith itself and merely turns from Paradise to a Slough of Despond At the same time with Epicurus and as if where the poison grew there the antidote was to grow^o Zeno was born at Citium a town in the Isle of Cyprus—his father a merchant a man [f 276] of opulence who in some of his mercantile journies brought with him for his son a collection of the best philosophical writings from Athens this excited the young mans interest and eager to hear either the great Writers themselves or some of their immediate followers he proceeded to Athens and studied for a while in the school of the Cynics under Crates but born as a Gentleman and with all the feelings and habits of a Gentleman we need not wonder that he was soon disgusted—^{p}at this outrage of all the common habits of life which

---

^{m} "had" written over erasure ^{n} Catchword on f 274: "con-"
^{o} "grow" written partly over erasure
^{p} "disgusted—" written over erasure, dash used apparently to fill unneeded space

was prescribed in the Cynic school he formed a scheme of itself in which he endeavored to avoid the faults of the others—the antients have charged him with pride with neglect of acknowledging his intellectual obligations but in all other respects calumny itself has left him unattacked he is every where spoken of as a model of purity piety and disinterestedness—taught in the famous hall of Paintings called the Stoa at Athens from whence the name of his sect and of his followers—in direct opposition [f 277] to Epicurus in all things—as Epicurus rejected Religion in every form except as far as was necessary to secure him from the Magistrates so Zeno appears to have been an Advocate even for its superstitions—The Stoic system likewise was not like the Epicurean formed at once but gradually so much so that Chrysippus is said to have been its founder by many though in truth he appears only the man who brought it into a system and no doubt illustrated and perhaps added to its consistency—the ground work of Stoicism may be found in the few premises of their Philosophy—Philosophy say the Stoics is the science of Wisdom is the supreme and absolutely necessary perfection of man that is not as the Epicureans Cyrenaics, and even Aristotle himself have stated it as a means to an end but as an end in itself to which all other things are indifferent except as means—the reality and the practicability of this absolutely perfect wisdom they asserted and this assertion properly constitutes Stoicism as distinct from all [f 278] other sects—the three divisions, Logic Physic and Ethics they considered all in reference to the attainment of this Ideal to the perfect wise man logic was useful to discover to him the truths of the intellect—Physics in order to act according to nature in all things and Ethics for the exercise of the will in order that it might be a convenient servant to the speculative wisdom which they supposed capable of being contained in humanity—another distinguishing point immediately is that they adopted Aristotles maxim that there is nothing in the intellect which was not previously in the senses in opposition to Plato and the reason was evidently this that they wished to bring all wisdom in its perfect ideal into the form of man but only once allow that there was any truth which had no connexion with the senses there would immediately arise ⟨a⟩ probability that this wisdom might indeed exist in the Author of the Universe but could scarcely [f 279] exist in a finite being hence they rejected whatever was supersensual and the supreme Being itself and described it as an Ether or a Fire and their Gods they considered as like all bodies perishable though after very long intervals hence do their discussions and endless doubts respecting immortality and all those endless contradictions which Plutarch or whoever is the author against the Stoics has collected arise[q] for men who call themselves Stoics have here the greatest eulogists and in their arguments against them they hold it unworthy of a wise man to have any motives at all except that of being wise but as Wisdom was not dependent on Time therefore a man could not be influenced by any considerations with regard to his own continuance in time again for the same reason the Stoics strange is the contradiction they added ~~the~~ reason the greatest and the most obstinate defender of Polytheism their Gods were indeed but men, but they were men who had arisen to a state of perfect wisdom the Supreme Being they did indeed admit a Will and an intelligent Being [f 280] but their notions of his personality were extremely weak extremely contradictory one with the other and though a Stoic would not hesitate to avow his belief in a God yet if he had been asked concerning the living God I fear the answer would have been a most imperfect one and all that forms the true bond between man and his Maker would have been found composed of very slight and rotten threads—hence throughout they confounded God and Nature for this was the grand error of Socrates himself and common to all his disciples as far as they were his exclusively the Stoics adopted it namely that the definition of Virtue is to live according to Nature without considering the double constitution of man his spirit and his body in one part indeed the creature of Nature but in another constituted above Nature its Lord— the Master of light and fire who commands its elements and not merely avails himself of them what then could the Stoics do who had rejected this duplicity—flatter and idolize Nature make [f 281] a false Nature and thus in the effects exchanged vices and give pride and obduracy for effeminacy and selfishness but ending at last in mere selfishness alike in both but alas too often producing despair and a recklessness of all living from finding that impossible and impracticable which yet was constantly spoken of not only as the true object which man ought to ~~do~~ pursue but as the real prize which man could attain and that in so exclusive a form that short of this they denied there was any difference in actions but that the greatest crime and the smallest deviation from the severe rule of reason was[r] to be considered as equally criminal

Such then has been the career of Philosophy it has been presented to you in all its forms in the utmost efforts[s] that unaided men could make use of in Pythagoras and Plato as originating all their systems in the pure reason or in that part of the human being which is above his senses and

[q] Semi-colon inserted in pencil
[r] "was" crossed out in pencil and "were" written in pencil above
[s] "efforts" written partly over erasure

though evoked called forth by them yet still having [f 282] its root and origin ⟨in itself the utmost that the understanding of man⟩ or that faculty by which we arrange and apply as well as remember the notices given us by our senses we then find in the Aristotelian Philosophy the following of Nature according to the senses and a reliance wholly on the senses we then are presented with the Cyrenaic and the Epicurean while at length there remained only the pride of the human will—which dismissing all support of itself affirmed its own deficiency*ᵗ* and made an arbitrary apotheosis of self a complete deification we have seen in all these how hollow it was and its effects will prove it—for nearly half a century there seems to have been a pause of all philosophic thinking painfully endeavored to be counteracted by Cicero—sensuality at home and ferocity abroad—the days all passed by in which their chief Commanders came from the conquests of Kings and Emperors and reverentially laid down their faces before the Jupiter of the Capitol and returned into the rank of private Citizens or to the plough of Lucullus and every great Commander [f 283] aiming to render his whole Country but a Camp his fellow Citizens but his Soldiers and hesitating at no means however atrocious which were to answer this end in short we had Marius and Sylla and Ceasar and Pompey and . . . Augustus and Anthony and the last Massacre . . . in the Country itself a most dreadful contest between unprincipled poverty and unprincipled opulence in this state there seemed to be a pause of all that was good in human nature a state of suspended animation with all the fiends that are permitted to agitate the World as if conscious that their hour was coming in which they must again retire to their prisons were taking their holiday and exercising their Saturnalia—That bright being appeared when nothing short of Divinity could have saved man from this state for where else*ᵘ* was the assistance to be found—the eye which was the light of the body had become filmed and jaundiced the only two nations which possessed intellect and with that intellect [f 284] the power of communicating order and civilization were corrupted and become the vilest of the vile—they had gone to Egypt and brought to Rome their Egyptian Gods they had gone to Persia and introduced the worship of Mithra in all corners of the World—whatever was strange and magical they were all gone to . . . and the best purpose of their own Polytheism of Gods was to furnish jokes for their Comic poets when they had had enough of the Gladiatorial games there was no help from the north and from the South all things and all the best powers of humanity had been

---

ᵗ "suff" written in pencil above "defi" of "deficiency"; "q" for query written in pencil in right-hand margin

ᵘ "else" written over erasure

marching forward to one point and paused at a limit and stood gazing towards that at which they could not arrive and likewise to the North and to the South it looked in vain for any comfort it was not to be found in the dreadful Wildernesses of Germany it would not come from the low voluptuous slavery of the East and of the South. Athens had lost patriotism nay it had lost genius itself and Rome existed only to exhibit one awful act of justice that of the oppressors [f 285] self oppressed and avenging on themselves the cruelties with which they had plundered and then desolated the World at[v] that time came assistance from whence alone it could come from the author of being who alone could regenerate who alone could give the germ of regeneration

It does not belong to me to enter into the depths of Theology I am reverentially believe me for I almost dread to connect the human nature even the most awful name in its purest sense with that of my Redeemer but as he was to[w] perfect man as part of his character I will therefore endeavor to contemplate him for you in that which is a perfect man as a perfect philosopher as he in whom all the rays of truth from all the different Sects concentred but whom none of their errors could reach and who supplied that which was wanting to all for if I even begin I first find that submitting to all righteousness he formed the basis of moral [f 286] obedience[x] almost all the social and natural affections prior to his commencing a teacher of others in the very first act in which he announced his ministry I find him at once taking the divine medium between the opposite and jarring extremes of men—in the marriage feast at Cana he neither came with the gloom and austere self denial without reason of the Cynics and still less with the relaxed morality and sensual principles of the Epicureans yet his first act was that of consecrating and blessing that ceremony which is the foundation of the whole moral being of the World namely Marriage familiarly from which arises the conditions of all progressiveness and without which Man can be nothing but a miserable self contradictory beast—his first act was to give his blessings upon all the innocent enjoyments of social life on the condition of all that could make man capable of those enjoyments his moral and intellectual being—again in opposition to all the pretenders [f 287] of self love with the severity and more than severity of the Stoics we hear him command us to be perfect even as our Heavenly Father is perfect and yet declaring to men that they must perish—utterly perish—if they rely on themselves or if they sought for a realization of that perfection which yet remained ever the only ground of a safe morality in aught but a reliance on a superior power not a mere tame acquiescence in the truth of it but in a total energy of their being without concentration of the Soul to that our intense wish a sense of its utter dependence which is entitled faith—ask and it shall be given to you your reason has informed you what morality is your feelings have instructed you that[y] to do to others as you would that others should do to you and to love your neighbours as yourself but God above all is the sole Ideal of the moral law it is truly the law and the prophets but that this cannot be attained by a mere act of unaided will that this is not to inflate the mind with any pride but only by a sense of its dependence[z] by [f 288] a sense of its utter incapability can it ever command that faith by which it shall ask and have that given—more than this we lead on to the great object of all religion namely a faith in a Supreme Being—how widely different do we find the precepts of our Lord compared with the noblest passages the purest exhibitions of natural Theology in the pagan world prior to his coming—here we find even in the extant writings of Plato himself the To-theon the power which is indeed complimented with intelligence and which appearing in divers forms acquiring divers consciousnesses constitutes a Theology a system of Gods but no where do we find a living God to whom we may be privileged to say Our Father no where is that consistently pressed that he is our God not only the God of the Universe but the Lord God whose voice our parents heard walking in the Garden—not that which connects the humble but awful duties of existing life with the highest aspirations of Religion and which in the love of our earthly parents prepares us for the [f 289] love of our heavenly—that which gives a reality to idea that which gives the dignity of the ideal to reality that which combines all the common Sense of the experimental philosopher with all the greatest prospects of the Platonists—that we find in Christianity and in Christianity alone it is so—With regard to the other great article of faith our immortality the imperishableness of life was indeed taught by many sects but in what form and Spirit of animation that[a] passed out of one organization into another organization without any definite prospect without any certainty so that with many minds the fear of immortality was predominant above the hope of it—through how many forms of untried being may we not pass—but in others again there was a sort of perfect consciousness reserved chiefly in the popular religion which was at the first draught to be Lethe but after a thousand years were

[y] "that" crossed out in pencil

[z] "dependence" partly written over erasure

[a] "that" crossed out in pencil; "they" written above in pencil and crossed out; "we" written in pencil beside it

circled round the souls as if the bodies were to be by that time empty to receive them were to come back and make up the same [f 290] endless and objectless circle but it is in the Christian Religion only and I mention this particularly because from the manner in which Natural Theology in the last Century was said to be the Theology of human nature . . . we are too apt to mistake a great point of our Religion which is this—that immortality is only immortality for us as far as it carries on our consciousness and with our consciousness our conscience that it is truly the resurrection of our body of our personal identity and with it all by which and for which we are to be responsible that there is no metaphysical divisions on which we can safely affirm it is utterly out of the power of man ever to learn or if it were learnt to comprehend—no metaphysical discussions between the Soul and the body as two distinct or two heterogeneous things no we are taught that there is a bond that a finite being has a body and must have a body there are bodies celestial as well as bodies terrestrial and that [f 291] it is only in the body that is in that personal identity that which constitutes every mans self and which as an intelligent being he has the power of communicating to another which constitutes that body—hence are removed all the fears of Pythagorean transmutation hence comes all the healthful and necessary terrors . . . so must we live— that body which is put into the earth will not indeed in that visible shape or those ponderable articles of matter appear but even as when the corn is put in the earth that which is visible passeth away we know not into what forms in the visible world yet there arises the plant healthful or diseased as the seed may be and in which the seed continues—even so in man and this I say is the true supplement even this would be little more than mockery as in truth philosophy itself is nothing but mockery unless it is considered the transit from paganism to religion unless we were told how we could do this with advantage it is as if I say to a man who is paralytic in both arms [f 292] rub your arms against each other—Alas! that is my misery I cannot do it if I say to a man involved in habits of sin who sees the misery of his Vice and yet still goes on from bad to worse—exert your Will—Alas! he would answer that is the dreadful penalty of my crimes I have lost my Will what do I say of the man or take out one . . . in particular or draw your attention to vice when it stares you in your face and when it happens to affront your social advantages when it breaks in upon your strong box or annoys your outward senses or in any way interferes with your plans or your interest why do I draw this one thorn out of the hedge—I say of the whole human race they have lost their Will there is not one that would dare put his hand on his heart and say in all things I act and feel as I know I ought to do unless that man is the most degraded of the degraded and in order to purchase a mere trance of conscience does away all conscience together by declaring that he has no Will at all—this[b] therefore was [f 293] the[c] great object first to shew man that as a Spirit he ought to be an intellectual Will—but a finite Will whose perfection consisted in its being perfectly concentrated with the Will of the great Being—Author and Lord of the Universe next to shew him into what a state he had fallen—that vain were all the Stoic dreams—they would fail him and his own inward conscience would give him the lie till by a trick of pride he had forgot to attend to it forgot his own inward being in the attention he paid to his external . . . and all the air and demeanor of the Wise men—in vain too there it was not life to himself but scourging nature and the vices of his own fellow men in vain would he hope for any relief from the pleasure of the senses pain comes and at all events old age and what a strange relief is that which every year lessens which every year brings you nearer to an opposite state no . . . the eye gives you a power which enables you [f 294] to see but you have not the hand to grasp—and you have not the Wing to soar towards it and what remains for you—this—and by this essentially are you distinguished from the desperate you can ask you can confess you can feel an earnest desire for that which you want and without which you must perish and this is all that is asked of you—ask and it shall be given you—feel deeply that you can do nothing of yourself ask and in that very energy of asking—Oh how we talk of prayer as if it was an easy matter as if it were but the repetition of a few words the pater noster or so—but the energy of the Soul to act is by the divine grace made to be the very means of strength—made to be the very wing by which you are to fly and from which alone you can—but who can ask who does not believe in the Savior—who can expect when he has no consistent conviction that there is that which can and ought to give—it is impossible—therefore [f 295] I call this the supplement of all philosophy ⟨it is to feel that philosophy⟩ itself can only point out a good which by philosophy is unattainable—to feel that we have a disease—to believe that we have ⟨a⟩ physician and in the conjoint action of these to exert that total energy of Soul from which it is as impossible that evil or aught but good can follow—[d]if it be indeed total[e] as that a fountain should send forth sands or a fire produce freezing around it—no not from any external impulses—not from any Agencies that can be sought for these may make men prudent and may make them outside moralists—they may deceive themselves by it fatally but man comes

---

[b] Pencilled line above "this" seems meant to alter it to "This"

[c] F 292 lacks catchword; f 293 repeats "the"

[d-e] Pencilled parentheses inserted

from within and all that is truly human must proceed from within and for him who does not enjoy it there remains but one thing—ardently to desire that which he does not possess and gratefully to look towards that Being who was not only ranked as the only true philosopher but who was [f 296] warmth and vital action yea that light which is the life of every man as well as it is the light of every man that cometh into the World—it is a combination of light and life and this is the true criterion—will you find any pretence to light in that which has really no warmth—there is nothing in it that can be called tangible—nothing which presents motives or shapes itself to human imperfections—allow the light it is moonlight and moths float about in it—Again those who reject all knowledge—who have wonderful incommunicable we know not what—in the recesses of we know not where and who scorn all knowledge and all the means of attaining it—we will say here again you have warmth—this may be a stove of life and crickets and other insects sing their inarticulate songs in it—but you must be as the lark and rise and enjoy the warmth and therein your own being will be made fit for its apportioned*ᶠ* happiness [f 297] and the extension of power which will come when the Spring has been given then only will true philosophy be existing when from philosophy it is passed into that Wisdom which no man has but by the earnest aspirations to be united with the only wise in that moment when the Father shall be all in all—

ᶠ "apportioned" crossed out in pencil; "appointed" written in pencil above

LECTURE 7

Mʳ Coleridges Lecture*g*
Monday 8ᵗʰ February 1819

It is in its very nature a melancholy theme when we have to record the decline and the follies of mankind only, while the good which is going on in the meantime is hidden or appears only by starts to us like the later months of autumn—when the leaves are dropping from the Trees and all nature seems ruined to us while the vegetative powers that are then retiring as it were to their rest and sinking down to their root to reproduce a new world and perhaps in a more glorious form are hidden from our eyes—It is a remarkable circumstance that the most valuable works respecting philosophy in the strict sense of the word are those of the Sceptics in this period of decline [f 299] one valuable fragment indeed alone remains to us from the works of . . . which has been preserved by Phaedrus but the truly important work of . . . is fortunately extant and gives us the full system of scepticism among the ancients perhaps the completest work of philosophy ever executed—This in its detail would require ample mention were it not that in the succeeding lectures the great object will be to exhibit the modern . . . On long reflection I have determined so to divide the course as that the first half of it should present the growth of philosophy as a striving of the human mind and as presenting the utmost that as far as we know human reason itself can atchieve while in the second I endeavored to present the effects of those discoveries made by the ancients in speculative philosophy to demonstrate that nothing as sensual has really been discovered in pure [f 300] speculation*h* by the moderns— at the same time while I humbled the pride of a false originality and took away from infidelity its outward varnish of apparent genius and invention still to maintain the importance of Philosophy itself by exhibiting . . . the historical facts I can prove it to have exerted upon the structure of language upon the language moral feelings and political opinions of the

---

g At top of leaf above frame, "Lect vii" written in pencil in one hand, probably that of JHG, and "Query, vi" in another
h Catchword on f 299: "Specu-"

European nations—for permit me to say that though there was a struggle for a time not between philosophy and religion but between a corrupt philosophy and the Christian religion—yet still when the Victory had been atchieved religion did not grossly enslave her captive—no—she placed her in her proper rank and as Ahasuerus did to Mordecai she threw her own Royal robe around it and made it the overseer of her household—It lost nothing but that which it had itself been seeking after—the head— and the ground—it is impossible to explain the state of philosophy [f 301] at this time in the ancient world without adverting to the spread of Christianity—they are too intimately interwoven to make it possible to treat of either separately—I have the highest respect for the learning the industry and the genius of Mr Gibbon—but I assert no more than I am prepared to prove when I say his celebrated fifteenth chapter of the causes of the spread of Christianity exhibits offences against all the most serious duties of an historian—for if I take the three main duties of an historian who professes to give the causes of any great event those will be admitted to be that the causes assigned should in the first place be true—secondly that no more and no less than their due proportion should be attributed to them—either directly in themselves or indirectly by the omission of other causes still more applicable—lastly that they should be placed in their proper light—Now in all these instances Mr Gibbon appears to me to have grossly [f 302] offended—as for instance when he states that the belief of the last conflagration taught among the Christians was one great cause of the rapid spread of their religion—I would not be thought deficient in respect to a great man—but I declare this is little else than childish—for in order to the belief of a doctrine, naturally we should expect it would be the greater objection more especially with those who possessed against religion that which the platonists and Pythagoreans had told them was . . . no visible causes of decay—that this should at a particular time— within a few years be utterly destroyed—I should have conceived one might fairly place this among the obstacles to Christianity—and assuredly it was so thought of by the Church—for with a charity to private opinions where they did not interfere with the essentials of religion it appears the church tolerated or were indifferent to the opinions of different doctors while innocent or innocuous but as soon as any superstitions were raised on [f 303] this event—any false articles introduced into the Church by the advocates for a millenium—it became a weighty motive with the Church to suppress it—and as to the prophecies in the scriptures and the Sophisms on them it may be worth answering them once for all—in a prophecy of St Matthew of the Seige of Jerusalem being typical of the final dissolution of the world—the language is that of the ancient prophecies and with the numerous converts of Christianity it is not to be wondered at if many of them understood and expected the events according to their own hopes and fears—but that this does not apply in any way to Christianity or what was notoriously taught—is evident in the first place from St Peter—who tells them—what is this to you—whether or no this happens a thousand years hence or to morrow can make no imaginable difference to you the same fate will await you the same reward and the same punishment—and on the other hand with regard to St Matthew [f 304] himself the argument is brought to a very easy conclusion either that Gospel was written before the seige of Jerusalem or afterwards—if it was written before the seige here is a clear prophecy—and that even in minutia—of an event not at all within the bounds of human foresight fulfilled in all its particulars—but if you suppose it written after and that the Evangelist really understood the words he wrote to mean the coincident destination of the whole world it is supposing him to be as great a madman as if a disciple of Brothers or any other fanatic in the present day were to publish a book recording a prophecy that in 1810 all London was to be destroyed by an earth quake and publish it in 1819 as a proof of Brothers having been gifted by divine inspiration—for it supposes a man to put a story not fulfilled as a proof of the prophetic powers of the man who spoke—nothing that I know of can avoid this dilemma—if written before the seige—here [f 305] is a clear prophecy fulfilled in its minutia—and if written after—you must suppose the man a madman—if the words were to be understood as applied to something supposed to have passed the nonfulfilment of which was notorious—I mention this as one instance of the many others of the same kind in the form of sneers

Another fault is that many things are attributed to Christianity which instead of being the effects of Christianity were counteracted by the same—as for instance—the Civil wars—it is notorious that Rome suffered a more quiet decay in consequence of the quiet manners and morals impressed on the minds of men who were taught to obey for conscience sake—But the best answer would be to state the true human rules of the conquest which Christianity made over Polytheism including the philosophy which then marshalled itself on the side of superstition—The first and perhaps the most important is the growing necessity felt in all ranks of a powerful religion in proportion to the unutterable depravity of manners then [f 306] reigning—It is really shocking to human nature to read the accounts given of the manners in the Roman world by Seneca by Tacitus and by others—the manners of Ancient Greece were indeed highly relaxed crimes that may not be uttered were related of their greatest men and the general fashion was to consider them as mere bagatelle—but these were hid under a splendour of Patriotism—of great exploits—of superior eloquence—and we almost forget the Vices of Republican Greece and Rome under their so far heroic virtues as they implied an heroic energy and self control—But when the same heroic virtues which Tacitus says they vexed in order to exhaust, by all the want of noble objects success brought with it—and by the last curse and the due punishment which always[i] attends subjection to military despotism—producing an utter want of all noble objects for the mind—then Vice appeared in its own shape connected with none but its kindred vices and all who pretended to any morality at all shuddered back from them—

[f 307]   In this way we are to explain the very superior moral philosophy of the few moral writers in those times—nay that of the best ancients—I will not undertake to say that nothing of this was borrowed from Christianity—but I think it may be derived from other Causes—and that the cause of Christianity will receive advantage in another way in a still greater degree for the Seneca's the Antonines the Juvenals—felt those vices and expressed their abhorrence of them in tones very different from what are found even in the writings of Plato himself and yet what was the effect—we cannot discover even a check given to the progress of depravity, and the event proved its utter insufficiency—This may be derived from many causes and among others from the success of the Roman arms which had united in one Empire nations so heterogeneous— local faiths so widely diverse that the mob—the population—had no longer any local associations in favor of local Gods—the Jupiter of the Capitol or the Temple [f 308] of Mars in its place referred to histories with which they had no connexion—which inflamed them with no sense of glory—while in the meantime the dreadful despotism of pinching penury contrasted with ⟨consciousness⟩ wealth about them—depriving them of every hope in this life—must unless they ceased to be human beings inspire a wish and a craving for something beyond desire—Before Christianity had appeared already the yearning after a religion for man as man and not as Roman or as Grecian had appeared—already the religion of the Jews had become a superstition in the Roman Metropolis and after the birth of our Saviour—Egypt poured in all her Gods—Persia all her superstitions—and this not among the lowest people but the philosophical—the excellent Emperor Antonine himself previous to his campaign against ... ordered sacrifices to be made to all the Gods—Grecian Roman and Barbarian over the whole Empire—nay he sent to every part of the Empire for priests of each superstition—brought [f 309] them to

---

[i] "always" crowded into space too small for it, probably over erasure

Rome in order to pray in Rome itself to their own particular Gods for his victory and caused expiations and sin offerings to be made successively through all the streets of the Metropolis—so strongly had the desire to bring something that all men could agree in by an attempt to bring them all together worked in one of the most intelligent minds of the time—and this necessity for a Religion comprehending the interests of all mankind with the utter absence excepting*j* Christianity of any one religion which answered to this end—I regard as the first and main cause (human cause) of the spread of Christianity and equally providential with the miraculous evidences which lie as its ground—For what can we ask more what can we think more elevated as a proof of a Religion than a demonstration of its necessity for mankind—a necessity not first felt when it was preached but already discovered so that as it were the very vices of mankind and their own sense of their utter helplessness went before hand as a prayer for its appearance and when it [f 310] appeared and was found adapted to the heart of man in all its recesses surely it was something more than mere human reasoning and yet included it all to say that a religion which so fitted the human heart must have come from that Being that made the human heart—

What perhaps might be placed as second in importance is this—that Christianity being the divine medium between all the opposite doctrines of the different philosophers and comprehending what was true in each— had them with few exceptions all as its pioneers—all as its combatants— If for instance—the Platonists looked forward to a ground out of the objects of the senses and not dependent on mortal life they were asked on what ground do you pretend this—they could appeal only to the desire itself which prompted it—or to what they would call an idea of this— which could not be explained but on the supposition of its truth—Christianity presented the same thing to the wise and to the simple—to all mankind in the very mode [f 311] which was fitted to them all—it presented it to the common people to whom the Gospel was preached by the evidence of their senses and above all by the presumption common to all mankind—that receiving it all men must be happy—while to the learned it presented the same truths authoritatively and upon that authority upon which their own great philosopher had himself rested it finally—In the meantime the Epicureans were fighting for philosophy as ... for instance—and I should say the Epicureans and the Sceptics were the predominant sects with men of rank and genius—the first exposed the folly of Magic and detected its tricks—they held out to ridicule the absurdities

---

j "absence excepting" written partly over erasure

and the immorality of the ancient Polytheism and in every way they convinced men and that too by arguments which have never been bestowed without success that the human reason ⟨in⟩ and of itself cannot go beyond the objects of the senses—it may hope—it may expect—it may pray—but of itself it cannot secure a point beyond that coincidence of external experience with the forms of the mind which constitutes what we ourselves call fact—all [f 312] beyond that are forms we can demonstrate that they are forms—not derived from accident—not originating in education or in prejudices—but necessarily evolved out of the human soul in a given state of cultivation but still their reality remains improved—I can demonstrate for instance that the mathematical circle—and the different truths of Geometry are all inherent in the human reason and in the forms of the mind itself—but ⟨it⟩ would be in vain to seek for a proof of a perfect circle in nature and as vain to attempt an explanation by an actual experiment on the measurement of a Wooden Circle—And if a man asked ⟨do⟩ you believe that there is such a thing as a circle except as an idea you would be puzzled to give any other answer than the negative—Even so is it with all the great moral truths—they show a fitness in the human mind for Religion but the power of doing it is not in the reason that must be given as all things are given from without and it is that which we call a Revelation—and hence it is that I have ventured to call Christianity the proper supplement of Philosophy—that which uniting all that was true in it at the same time [f 313] gave that higher spirit which united it into one systematic and coherent power

There is a fine passage in . . . who has indeed many admirable passages where he says it is easy to show that all the scattered opinions in the different philosophies of the Greeks and Romans are united in Christianity and united without the imperfections with which they at first appeared but to what purposes says he very sensibly would this be who shall make the selection who shall place them in their proper order—but the man who already knows that truth and who is already possessed of the same faith as a Christian—the Helen of Zeuxis is said to have been composed from different features of the most beautiful women of Greece but yet ⟨it⟩ would be strange to say that the Helen of Zeuxis had existed any where but in the picture—or to use another image man is called the microcosm inasmuch as he comprehends in him all the faculties and abilities of the other animals—but no person would say that man existed elsewhere but in man or that those different ⟨powers of the different⟩ animals could [f 316] have been united into one real being otherwise than by some higher cement some copulative as it were which interpenetrated them all and combined them into one and therefore remained as truly original as any component part the excellence of which he might have taken up unto himself

The consideration of the slaves in Rome is likewise a most important one both with regard to Philosophy and to the spread of Christianity the cessation of Wars except at the extreme borders had rendered slaves much more valuable in proportion as they were less easily bought and gained but likewise the nations with whom Rome towards the decline of her republic and in the flourishing time of her Empire were engaged were men who in all but the acts of civilization were in truth equal or superior to Rome itself as Seneca admits when upon a proposal for distinguishing the Slaves by a particular badge he said "O beware how ⟨you⟩ teach them to number themselves these are our equals in power and mind our superiors in Virtue and bodily strength and hereafter are to be our conquerors—In proportion however to the [f 317] value attached to them was the jealousy and it would shock us to have brought before our minds the treatment they received and the various cautions used to prevent their insurrections—what wonder then that a Religion which taught all men to consider themselves as equal before their common judge should find a ready hearing with the oppressed and with the poor This is mentioned by Mr Gibbon but mentioned as an objection and really an objection to it that the Religion of Christianity gave comfort where it was most wanted— but there was another point he has not taken—the consummate wisdom unexampled in the history of mankind with which the Christian Church from its very foundation managed this most difficult point we in our translation and perhaps for very good purposes have rendered the word servants which in the original we know means properly slaves but consider the numbers of the passages addressed to servants the earnest admonitions to them to obey their masters not from worldly fears or hopes but as standing before a great [f 314] Master and one point more particularly I would notice that though christianity instead of lessening came to increase in every way the awful duty that every rational being has to set apart a portion of his time to his permanent interests yet still no direct holiday was prescribed by authority for that sacred portion—no day was by immediate and direct authority appointed as a substitute for the Sabbath—the sacred duty was impressed the duty upon every man as plain as if a voice from Heaven had spoken it but no particular time was there stated the reason is evident—so large a number of the first Christian converts being Slaves there would have been endless quarrels with the Masters endless martyrdoms with the Slaves who had persisted in dedicating that day and in taking away as it would have been said the Masters property but as soon as ever the Christian Religion became the Religion of the

State—then not the duty was taught anew that was ever the same and must be but a particular day [f 315] was apportioned in order to render the Religious duties of each man compatible with his civil duties and with the conveniences of the whole state—then when Christianity became the marked majority of the nation it was declared with full right that that day in which the Christians devoted themselves to the recollection ⟨of the resurrection⟩ of their Redeemer should be the holiday of the State there was no persecution no man was forced to become a Christian thereby it was simply an annunciation of a state fact the majority of the Empire are Christians and consequently they have a right to have their day appointed as a general holiday even as we do in every state—those who are Christians will know how to make use of it those who are not will regulate their worldly affairs by it—I mention this as a peculiar—*k*instance of the Wisdom of the first founders of Christianity and especially so as an instance of the benevolence and the temperance with which Christianity was taught—supposing for instance that all the doctrines [f 318] which benevolent and warm hearted men would consider to be founded in truth as they are indeed if truth were independent of all circumstances had been announced would not the . . . have had an unanswerable argument to the spread of Christianity would it not have been said no wonder you spread when you teach insurrection when you teach the slaves to disobey their Masters and when you teach disobedience on particular days—one man would have said I am a . . . and this is a . . . a second would have said I am a . . . and this is a Friday and I am to worship the sun—and a third I am a Christian and this is the first day of the week and I cannot do any labor others went further and taught them this was a grievous aggression of the rights [f 319] of man a horrible tyranny the consequence would be that from an inner Religion which was to soften all evils for the time and gradually by the means of persuasion to do them away it would have become a vulgar rights of man and in its consequences would have brought disgrace on the sublime truths which it taught and which are so sublime as to render even the supposition painful to a good man that it could have been so

Christianity had among its Chief enemies what would surprize one—the sect that seems to have been in its moral doctrine the nearest to it but which only seems—I mean the Stoics—for as in a former Lecture I dwelt on the principle Pride—in the Stoical system as the ground work of all its splendid pretensions so it joined with that pride a vast deal of worldly motive and hence it became a favorite doctrine of the great men in Rome

---

k Dash and first three letters of "instance" seem to have been written later, dash merely filling unneeded space

who were men in power for of all the Philosophers of Greece the Stoics were the only ones who where they[l] admitted nothing spiritual nothing that was not the object of the senses yet took under their[m] immediate protection all the superstitions of Polytheism and the doctrines connected with the auguries [f 320] and oracles and in short with whatever beauty the human hopes and fears might make from the objects of the senses— It has struck me upon much examination that the Sadducees mentioned in our Sacred Scriptures were a sort of stoicised Jews in[n] this way we can best explain their origin from Sadoc the just man whose doctrine was that no other motive ought to be sought for than the mere sense of right—a Stoical opinion—next that all crimes were equal the smallest offence against the law equally punishable with the greatest and lastly that it was a dangerous doctrine to teach any thing that was at all disconnected from the senses—Now this perfectly corresponds in all its parts both with the history of the Sadducees and their appearance in our gospels—for Josephus says they were a small number of rich men occupying the chief magistracies of the state descended from Sadoc a high flying Stoic and marked for their contempt for all things supposed to be removed from the object of the senses—above all—the notions of spirits and of apparitions or [f 321] beings in a Spiritual state not strictly corporeal—these men were . . . but the more dangerous sect was arising—the rival of Christianity— namely the sect which is said to have begun in . . . about the beginning of the third Century, but which in truth had begun somewhat earlier—it is very difficult to speak accurately of the opinions of a sect whose great pride was to combine and to reconcile all the truths of the other philosophers that had appeared in the World—in that very instance presenting itself as the mimic of Christianity and pretending to do what had been really done by Christianity and the more difficult is it because as their predominant features according to themselves were in the union of Pythagoreanism with Platonism it becomes doubly perplexed to us who are not really well acquainted with what platonism was—It is very easy for those who take the writings of Plato as now extant as containing his own peculiar opinions and [f 322] who regard Socrates as a man of Straw from which Plato as a Ventriloquist made the voice proceed it is easy to do as Teneman has done contrasting it with those doctrines[o] but not so easy to know precisely in what respects particularly it varied from the doctrines of Plato and in what it coincided—As far as I have been able who perhaps have spent more time than ⟨I⟩ should be willing to ac-

[l] "they" written over erasure   [m] "their" altered, perhaps from "the"
[n] "in" written over erasure   [o] Two vertical lines drawn through line in pencil

knowledge in reading the works of these men it is not so much in the opinions themselves as in the extremes to which they carried them—and in the accessions they made . . . that the philosophers called the Eclectics differed from their great predecessors—their great object was to uphold the heathen superstitions—in the then state of the Empire they in common with all others felt the absolute necessity of some one religion which should be common to all men as men—and they hoped by means of a philosophy to bring all religions interpreted in a particular way under some one point of view so that without any mans changing his religion [f 323] every man should find to his own great surprize that in this religion he possessed all the truth in the World—that he might be miserable and hopeless under it—but it was want of a better interpreter—in short that there was one common object in all and that ⟨all⟩ those[p] Religions were but different modes of representing it—With this however they were not content—the mind of man stript of all sane enjoyments from without—without any noble objects had been forced to yearn after a support from a higher cause—this was so strong that the old augurers[q] the common mouths of Superstition—which had been legalized in Rome as the interpreters of the Sybilline leaves and so forth were grown into utter neglect—but from Persia Egypt and other places a perfect stream of Astrologers and nativity casters and magicians or whatever they might have[r] been—inundated Italy—this was too strong to be resisted and this Eclectic system adopted it and we have to contemplate the strange and unnatural union of the abstrusest philosophy [f 324] with the basest[s] superstitions—Many are the difficulties that press on this subject—more so in consequence of the determination which the literati of the last Century and a half have had to consider all the ancient oracles all the facts related concerning extraordinary circumstances among the ancients as mere delusions—as poor conscious tricks of the priesthood—little considering whether it was possible that century after century and century after century—no acknowledged imposture could have prevailed and could have produced such belief in the sacredness of an oath and such a constant superintendance in conscience in an imperfect morality indeed but yet still in a morality as appeared in the Roman Empire for so many centuries—when their generals after conquering Kings came back and humbly ⟨laid⟩ their Fasces at the foot of the Jupiter Capitolinus no—but sure something more—we need not go to[t] revelation but it is not to be believed but that certain powers of nature which [f 325] they interpreted re-

---

[p] "these" altered to "those" [q] End of word erased and replaced
[r] "have" written over erasure [s] Word may be "barest"
[t] "go to" seems written over erasure

ligiously were made use of and the decay of the oracles and the decay of
those things by their own admission seems strongly to prove that circumstances had taken place which ~~had~~ then no longer existed—I could
say[u] more on this subject with reference to an opinion which has strange
to say become quite common even among Christians people that the
human race arose from a state of savagery and then gradually from a mon-
key came up through various states to be man[v]—and being man to form
a state—and being states to improve upon them and so by a certain train
of regular experience to explain all things as they now exist which[w] reminds one of the French lady who hearing a story that a dead man had
walked a league with his head under his arm somebody exclaimed What!
a league! with surprize aye! said the lady, the first step was the thing if
however man began to exist in the infancy of his race he must like every
other animal have been protected by an instinct—but as [f 326] sure as
he was protected by an instinct so surely must it have been a human and
an intellectual instinct—and that this might have existed in imperfect degrees and will go on even to its last decay appears to me I confess not at
all extravagant—and I say this because in the writings of . . . not to mention some striking passages in Plato himself I find references to secret
arts[x] in their mysteries which correspond so strangely and minutely to the
facts which have been lately brought forward on the Continent—and permit me to say I am not passing any judgment on those facts because what
I state will be true whether we take the report of D[r] Franklin and the
philosophers who made their report before the American war or the reports made by the direction of other governments which bear a different
complexion still it remains fact that means exist by which a mutual action of the imagination upon the nervous system and the nervous system
upon the imagination [f 327] will produce most extraordinary phenomena for these phenomena have never been denied the facts themselves
cannot be disputed—the only question has been whether it is necessary
to assume a new principle of physiology or whether what we know of
the human frame and the power of imagination is sufficient to explain the
fact—the facts being the same—now this which I find to have been the
constant practice in their higher mysteries so that . . . declares he has no
confidence in their writings—but such as were composed when he was
in one of those extasies—I conclude that those arts[y] which may be practised among the meanest of men were among the main secrets of the
Eclectics and constituted those pretences to magic and to a divine com-

---

[u] "say" written over erasure   [v] "man" altered, perhaps from "men"
    [w] "which" written over erasure   [x] Word could be "acts"
                    [y] Word could be "acts"

munion which appears everywhere in their writings Appolonius of Tya-
neus One of the great men who was set up as the whole object of this philosophy was to form a rival sect to Christianity and therefore they chose
[f 328] him their great man he appears to have been an extraordinary enthusiast who had proposed early to himself to imitate Pythagoras in which
he travelled to the Indies and worked wonderful miracles and taught great
morality the great object of which was to support the heathen Gods and
the pagans no wonder therefore that the Christian religion when it began
to . . . Queen . . . commanded Philostratus a century afterwards to collect
the facts in consequence of which he went upon his travels after this
pagan . . . and he found some writings of a companion of his namely . . .
he likewise went into the different cities where he performed his works
and he enquired of the temples in which they had been recorded but unfortunately some of the most striking of those miracles are copied almost
word for word from those of the Gospels which we know to be anterior
speaking [f 329] unthinkingly[z]—and to others the best authorities were
the Priests themselves for whose sakes they were worked—A more striking contrast cannot be conceived than that between the miracles of our
Lord in opposition to a priesthood and those miracles which were attested
by the very Priesthood for whose preservation they were worked and yet
Philostratus is honest enough to acknowledge that his different accounts
of the same Miracles were so different he did not know which to choose[a]
from amongst the number—but what could not be done by trick and imposture—for here the Epicureans have assisted the other sect that was to
be done by the highest principles of philosophy and wherein did this consist—Plato had taught men that after going through all the highest exertions of the faculties which nature had given them—cultivating their
senses their understandings[b] their reason and their moral powers—yet
still there was a ground wanting a something that could not be found
within the sphere of [f 330] their knowledge yet knowledge led men to
ask for that ground—and this he placed in the Supreme Being as the final
result of all human effort and human reasoning—The same doctrine was
taught by Plotinus and . . .[c] but with this remarkable inversion of order—
they began first with the knowledge of the Supreme Being not in our
Christian sense of the word not as a belief that such a being exists whom
we are to obey—and under whom perform our duties—but no—by certain . . . men were to arrive at a Communion—that is to say at[d] an intel-

---

[z] Catchword on f 328: "unthink-"   [a] "choose" seems written partly over erasure
[b] "der" in "understandings" seems re-inked; traces of erased pencilling around word
[c] Erased letters faintly visible at beginning of space   [d] "at" written over erasure

lectual a positive possession of this Supreme Being which would supersede all knowledge by giving them a higher one so that what by the efforts of Reason we were to acquire . . . by possession and by all the power . . . of reasoning this was to appear in a blessed vision at once that is the great object—beautiful passages there are in Plotinus—exquisite morality—fine observations so that you would believe him to be a Christian—as indeed his teacher left it [f 331] doubtful whether he was or was not a Christian for his only works as far as we can ascertain were comments on the Scriptures—but this is the difference between the works of Plotinus (and in speaking of Plotinus I speak of almost all that follow him) and those of the Ancient philosophers in the works of Plato and Aristotle you see a painful and laborious attempt to follow thought after thought—and to assist the evolution of the human mind from its simple state of information to the highest extent its faculties will reach but in the ⟨works of⟩ Plotinus it is all beginning—no middle—no progress—all depends upon one assertion—an assertion which undoubtedly had the advantage of putting a stop entirely to all sceptical objections—there is a power which we may arrive at of seeing certain things as facts which neither our senses nor our understanding nor our reason could give us the least conception of—and I point you ⟨to⟩ the means of doing this—you are to consider the social virtues and so on as things which if you are obliged to exercise them you may—but it would be infinitely [f 332] greater virtue in you entirely to abstract yourself and regarding these as utter delusion*e* to give yourself to those rights of subjugating the body in retirement and submitting to certain mystical ordinances which would open a new faculty in you—it would be said Sir if you disbelieve this we have no reason (as John Penn very warmly said in exposing the vain efforts of human reason to arrive at the truth) well but how am I to know you have it or any man Oh! you must seek for it yourself I cannot talk with the blind upon colours the strongest feature in this was in assumption—it attempted at a supernatural something in the commencement and placed it in this light which the Christian Religion had indeed taught—but taught in order to humble man had taught it not as a beginning—but as the final reward of long exertion—In short the Eclectic philosophy might be contrasted in its distinctions alike from genuine Philosophy and Christianity from the genuine Philosophy it stood distinguished ⟨by⟩ its unnatural union [f 333] with Magic and while it pretended to consider the senses as mere delusion and all the impressions on the senses as mere dreams yet with strange inconsistency it was constantly combining itself with all the tricks by which

e Word may be "delusions"

the senses could be acted on this not only in the mean and low adherents of the sect in after times but in Plotinus[f] himself—as for instance—the story of Porphyry of him—⟨that⟩ he said one day of one of his pupils this man is working magically upon me but I will shew him I am his Master he records that . . . but Plotinus has a God that protects him—similar stories are related by Porphyry the immediate friend disciple and companion of Plotinus of his raising up from two mountains the two demons one the Aroes or Love and the other the opposite to love—not to mention the grave manner in which he quotes a passage of Plotinus to him on the subject that four times Plotinus had been united with the Deity as a foretaste of great and wonderful . . . while he himself [f 334] had been but once "which was in my 68th year on the 9th day of such a month" a sort of minuteness in the date of this wonderful event which I cannot but say reminded me of some late stories I have heard of conversions on days hours and so on suddenly coming which disgrace those who know better and know that Christianity is to convince us in spirit and truth and not by tricks on our feelings and not that which every dreamer may mistake or the weakest be most likely to believe the truth—They were distinguished from Christianity ⟨by⟩ this one great point namely that Christianitys ~~this one great point namely that Christianity's~~ great object is to make us fit for Heaven and to make our future state work upon us as a motive for our exertion in the present but the great object of the Eclectic Philosophy was to persuade men Heaven was already practicable on earth not to raise men up to God but by pernicious practices and contrivances of rites to bring God down to man and with this it joined all the artifices that policy could prompt although in the time of Julian [f 335] and again . . . the Christian modes of preaching upon particular days and the administration of holy rites were adopted—The Empire was to be divided and began to be in different parts in all things there was a laborious imitation of Christianity and the better feelings of mankind were to be bribed by a constant appearance of conscientious abstraction and elevation of mind above the senses—this therefore which was the conclusion of a philosophy was to have answered all its purposes—the natural conclusion it would not acknowledge its due subordination the Eclectic Philosophers were not content that Philosophy should be the pioneer and guide to and afterwards the willing servant and help mate of Religion—no—it must make Religion its property Philosophy must be the great mouth of Religion—that which is meant for all mankind and therefore must be understood by all mankind applicable to all the situations of mankind and working by mo-

---

[f] "Plotinus" written partly over erasure

tives in which men might partake that was to be given to the sacred Priesthood under [f 336] the head of the learned of the Philosophers—and yet as they could not bring up the poor and the ignorant to them they were obliged to sink down to the poor and the ignorant and to answer their purposes by the low tricks of Jugglers and the constant pretence of mystery—yet let me not say this without acknowledging that truths are to be found in those writers and in my mind awful truths—I certainly do believe that in the quiet of the Soul truths will be felt and found hopes and impulses which will not arise either in the bustle of occupation—No—nor in the bustle of mere . . . the activity of the understanding—but I contend this is not the mode of beginning a truth nor the means of arriving at the very state it pretends to—let a man follow what the Christian religion has every where impressed—perfect himself in all his duties—acknowledge no duty in any thing which is to abstract him from the love of his neighbour and the fair performance of all his relative obligations to others—let him do the best in his [f 337] power to develope and exercise all his natural faculties—strengthen his understanding—make all that good which nature has given for this world and then in that best quiet of a good conscience—in that Sabbath which hope and faith bring you if he derives hopes more confirmed and fear more fixed—aspirations more lofty—it is his reward and can mislead no man—The very contrary of this was attempted by the mock religion placed as the Rival to Christianity and which has often reminded me of a fable of the Rabbins who say that after the creation of man Nature jealous with the remnant of the delegated power which had been given to it in the preceeding days of the creation attempted to make a man in the same way as that being was formed from whom she had been excluded—and that she succeeded so far as to make an ape the most resembling indeed but the most in Antipodia[g]—the most imitative but likewise the most mischievous and degraded of all her creatures—So with regard to the Eclectic philosophy in which philosophy [f 338] found its dishonorable grave—we find indeed one the nearest to Christianity for it stole from it but at the same time so perverting in its order and so degrading it by the difference of motive—as to have at length no other than the sad memorial that it has too often been seen to reappear in the Christian World of which as with regard to all the other sects of Philosophy my next seven Lectures will give an account and I will intreat your attention in order to state the particular purpose of those Lectures

I shall begin with a brief statement of what was really done by Philo-

---

[g] Last two letters of "Antipodia" are correction

sophy with a short proof that before the birth of our Saviour all philosophy could do or has done had been really atchieved and as well atchieved as Philosophy is confined to the meaning I give it . . . by the efforts of the reason itself as it has ever since been done it was at that time a substitute for Religion among the higher Classes ⟨that⟩ it was no mean substitute a simple fact may inform us namely the great difference [f 339] and superiority of the Greek and Roman states to those of the other parts of the World Judea excepted—The remainder is to shew the reappearance of Philosophy—no longer as the substitute or as the guide but either as the mask or the direct antagonist of the same—still however keeping separate in my mind the great difference in the opinions (often pernicious opinions) of particular men and the general influence of the tendency to Philosophy itself—for as the human mind I shall demonstrate never can in a civilized state be without some Philosophy or other—and it is an utter mistake to suppose its influence is confined to particular classes[h] I shall endeavor to trace as I go on—first in each age what those particular opinions of the Ancients were which in all their Essence were then brought forward and to state their effects upon the nations of Europe at a time since the Aristotelian System and its effects—I shall go to the temporary but brilliant effects of the institution of [f 340] Platonism[i] . . . on ⟨to⟩ a new scheme of Eclecticism and finally to materialism and every where hold in with the two points—first to demonstrate that in those opinions there was nothing new and secondly that such as they were they were highly influencive and connected with the manners nay with the great Political events of mankind in a degree and in a manner which ought to impress on the minds of all statesmen that without a congenial philosophy there can be no general religion[j] that a philosophy among the higher classes is an essential condition to the true state of Religion among all classes and that Religion is the great centre of gravity in all Countries and in all ages and accordingly as it is good or bad whether Religion or irreligion so all the other powers of the State necessarily accomodate themselves to it—so true is it in this as in most other things that what is really influencive is out of sight and [f 341] that the indirect consequences are in almost every instance ten times more important than the direct and apparent ones—These Lectures therefore will of course lead me a great deal more into History and to mark out the effects of opinions upon the minds of men and of countries than upon mere opinions which I shall only have occasion to repeat as proving that whatever merit they might have they have not that of originality—

[h] Final "es" added later to "classes"   [i] Catchword on f 339: "Pla-"
[j] "religion" written partly over erasure

LECTURE 8

[f 342]   Mͬ Coleridges Lecture

Monday 15ᵗʰ February 1819

In the order of Providence as revealed to us by History it seems to have been the final cause of Philosophy to prepare the way to religion—the necessity of some intelligible object of that religious feeling which is the proper characteristic of humanity was indeed the working impulse to philosophical investigation for according to the definition which I have given in the first Lecture of the first part of this Course I have defined Philosophy to mean an attempt to seek after the origin of things and the fundamental laws of the world by the efforts of ⟨the⟩ reason and understanding alone—a religion commensurate with all the wants and with the honorable yearnings of the human being had been announced and we find that from the first preaching of the Gospel to the Antonines [f 343] philosophy as having already performed its functions existed only as an unvegetating^k trunk—there were indeed teachers of the old schools and men eminent as teachers but without any desire or pretence of addition—the Sceptics the most deserving of philosophic celebrity at that time as Sextus and others blunted their own tools by extending their scheme of doubt too far—while they attacked the Dogmati⟨s⟩ts who had confounded the motions of the machine with the stuff upon which it must work and had given a reality to those motions they were successful but at length they carried on their doubts to the form of the Machine itself that is they would leave us to doubt of those things which we cannot doubt because they form the very means of our doubting as for instance against the human reason which must necessarily meet with the argument if you reason rightly you confute yourself and if you reason falsely you only prove yourself to be a blockhead—that in no case can man reason against reason—still however as far as they acted at all which in that unhappy state of mankind [f 344] under the despotism of the Cæsars and the far worse state the insusceptibility of the people of any better Government—as far

---

^k First part of word written over erasure

as they acted at all they and the scoffers such as Lucian and others aided the cause of the Gospel they rendered its opponents ridiculous but in all this there was no proper revolution the revolution commenced with the attempt of the Eclectics under Ammonius Saccas no longer to consider philosophy as a Pioneer to Religion but to drag Religion down into philosophy—there are hopes which he is guilty of treason against human nature who endeavors to damp—but they are hopes—not absolute proofs derived from the sum total of our human nature not from our mere faculties of reasoning—We see every*[l]* where throughout nature an adaptation of means to end if we discover aught the final cause of which is not evident to us it immediately becomes an object of anxious curiosity and scientific research and this is so implanted in our nature that it is quite independent of any particular opinions of philosophers who have prided themselves [f 345] in opinions that reject all intelligence from the Government of the Universe and would subject it to a blind necessity and have yet shewn*[m]* themselves as anxious concerning the spleen or whatever part of the body has not its known and permitted use as the most pious—as the most rational of their fellows of the same profession—The Butterfly is not led in vain for a purpose unknown to itself or unconscious of any particular desire and want to lay its eggs on any particular leaf fitted to sustain the Caterpillar and if this be true through all nature as far as we know it—is it in man—is it in the sole magnificent temple of the world of existence is it in the Holy of Holy in this Temple—is it in the High Priest in the consciousness of nature that nature tells her first and only lie—is it here that she begins to deceive us when she bids us believe that ours is a mixed nature belonging in part to the earth and like it transient but belonging like our reason and like its magnificent products the sciences to [f 346] a higher and more permanent state of existence this would be impossible but observe that it is a reasonable persuasion whereas the Eclectics for the prospect would substitute an insight*[n]*—for a confidence that could result only from the harmony of all our powers and faculties of man en masse if I may venture so to express myself they would present the intellect as sufficient—the tools with which they worked must of course be the mere forms of human thinking—to this they gave not only a true reality as forms of the mind but as impersonal reality they made things of them and consequently fell very far short of the understanding—for every logical generalization or abstraction they obtained a new idea—this is carried so far that in one of the Eclectic philosophers there is not only a Deity for the . . . as they called it but an especial Deity

---

[l] "We see every" written over erasure   *[m]* "shewn" may be written over erasure
[n] "insight" written partly over erasure

for every point of the Mariners compass having its due attributes and all that was to distinguish the . . . as if the philosopher had been writing history instead of investigating [f 347] into the laws of the world—in short the numbers by these means became so monstrous that in the time of Paroclus there became a necessity of generalizing and classifying these classes themselves which he actually did making four classes of Gods the Noetoi who were intelligible—the objects of intellect but themselves above all intelligence what was to be substituted is not known the . . . and intellectual—those who were not only the objects of intelligence but were themselves intelligent—the . . . or those who were . . . and the Inkosmeoi or the . . . each containing numbers numberless at least equal in number to a Lexicon of all possible abstract words but as all this would have been chill and . . . and partook of its origin merely the sport of Logical fancy they were obliged to call in an unfair alliance—they connected philosophy with magic with the power of names and numbers and the whole secret trade which we know little of but which they professed under the name of the . . . what [f 348] it was it is perhaps of little importance to us to know I am inclined to think that mere fancy mere delusion it was not—but that whatever it was it was worthless and in its nature of no true value or capable of originating any serviceable laws to mankind seems evident from its imperminence—The worst of all is they abused the highest prescript of philosophy and religion that of becoming Godlike—the voice both of philosophy and religion teaches us man can become like his Maker only by imitation of his goodness only morally but these men taught that there were modes by which physically man could be taken into the Godhead and the consequence was the most fearful superstition that can be imagined for it is astonishing how little human beings will regard either labor or pain or privation if they can only arrive at any one object of their desire by any other than the appointed means— the poor East Indian will suffer himself to be hung up by hooks—he will walk upon nails turned upwards [f 349] he will sit under a tree with his eyes fixed in one position year after year in the hopes of obtaining this Godlikeness because that is so much more easy after all than to think and to do his duty as a social man—in the former instance he is gratifying his will while he is tormenting himself—in the latter he is obliged to subjugate his will to his reason—the good sense of those about him and the laws of his Country—hence then is the true secret of superstition—it is not whether it demands this sacrifice or that but it does not enforce the principle which gratifies no pride and which when a man has performed it he has simply the consolation that he has performed it—the test of an approving conscience

These men however taken apart from their prejudices were by no means men of light minds or without all the praise that genius misguided can give to them—the more awful therefore is the example to us when accustomed as we are to see superstition appear only in conjunction with ignorance we find that under [f 350] certain circumstances it is capable of being held forth with all the pomp of eloquence with all the pretence of deep research—nay of being brought into a system and advanced as a demonstrated and regular fabric of human reason—it was not therefore Justinian's Edicts merely that suppressed philosophy but it died itself of a natural death from two Causes—first of all from a weariness of mind aided by the fearful political commotions which were then agitating the world an effect which if I have not been misinformed is at this time observable in Germany—for thirty years or more the Germans were philosophy mad—one sect followed another and if Englishmen asked of the weather or enquired of the last nights debate Germans were enquiring concerning the newest philosophy or whether the efforts of the learned Spinosists had produced any thing—The time came of practical danger—of practical effort leaving behind it ⟨as⟩ all such struggles do— expectation that never can be gratified ~~and yet hopes that~~ [f 351] ~~never can be gratified~~ and yet hopes that never can be given up and yet at this present moment to speak of philosophy—it makes a man shrug up his shoulders it is gone by—nothing can be made of it—there have been the greatest genius's of our nature—one system brings on another which is . . . new political pamphlet and so forth—Such is the natural effect of exhausting philosophy when it happens to combine at the same time with political commotion and this I assign as the first cause—The second is that having dragged religion down into philosophy philosophy itself became nothing compared with that which it had unnaturally taken up as a part of itself instead of being its hand maid and subordinate . . . had succeeded in detecting the folly of assigning to the abstraction of the mind personal realities and it was astonishing having reduced his[o] opinions so closely to those of the Christian church how he could remain pagan—but it appeared he preferred the revelation of Hermes . . . [f 352] and . . . the two former of which he could have no possible document to prove having existed as individuals and the latter nothing more than that he did exist to the credibility of the Gospel history—I need not say that at that time when all the powers of the world was on the side of the Christians and all the argument—when the philosophers admitted their argument was contained in Christianity and the only question was which they should chuse

---

[o] "his" may be written over erasure

between the fables of paganism or the attested facts of Christianity the contest could not be with philosophy—therefore as well as of philosophy this may be called no more than the death of the old World—it died self convicted

The materials for the renovated man are two fold—first the laws and customs by which the individuals are to exist as a state and secondly that dignity in each individual which reacting[p] on the State to which it belongs gives to that State itself the moral being The character of the Gothic conquerors gave [f 353] the second the Roman Laws and Institutions supplied the first and the union of both is most pregnantly expressed in the word Christendom—that is a State composed of States as those of individuals professing to be governed by a law superior to each or all collectively even as every single person is so subject—nothing like this do we find in the antient world—I refer you to that incomparable historian Mitford for the document of my assertion—nay that no attempts were ever made at a representative Government in Greece or in Rome though the idea had been given so early as in Thales—marks the deficiency of the very materials for constituting a State like the present the childhood of states like that of individuals promises more than it fulfils for it gives a promise as the representative of universal humanity as every healthy child is but it performs it both in individuals under all the modifications of circumstances and in States likewise as aggregates of individuals under the same compunction but we have one comfort [f 354] that in the existing state of the world we are to remember that the progress of cultivation no longer rests as of yore on the fates of a single people that therefore we may notwithstanding particular progressions be yet in the youth of the process and are not therefore entitled to draw the same depressive results as weigh on all minds during the perusal of the Greek and Roman history—The origin of this State then well deserves a more than common attention and more than ordinary research It is impossible that we can contemplate the present state of the planet without perceiving that Europe is the predominant and influencing power—in vain do we look with hope for aught higher or better but on the other hand idle would be the fears so rationally felt in the Roman times of a worse of a deteriorating power— Take our own Country—a little Island—small at least in dimensions— which a few Centuries ago could scarcely have boasted of more than four or five Millions of people and we find this Country by the combined effects of those institutions which Christianity engrafted [f 355] on Gothic customs and combined by the Copular of a fitting religion has

---

[p] "reacting" partly written over erasure

produced—This Country we find governing the very Waves of the Ocean with a regularity scarcely less than the moon does the tides—We find her by her own children commanding and for the most benevolent purposes a multitude four fold greater than that of her own immediate Subjects— in the East and in the West we see her offspring and empire which if no convulsion of the planets should arise will in the Course of a few cen- turies present as great a multitude speaking the English language and ut- tering the words of a Bacon a Milton and a Shakespear as are contained in the vapid improgressive Empire of China If this be the Case with one Country what must not necessarily be deduced from the prospects of the whole of Christendom combined—it is if aught can be clear to man of the future—evident that the intention of providence is that from the an- cient Roman Empire to which Christianity was first preached should di- verge the rays that are to enlighten and civilize the rest of the planet

[f 356] I mention this in order that we may feel a greater degree of prob- ability in the sketch that I will venture now to present—various have been*q* the disputes of antiquarians concerning the origin of Nations—I have found no reason whatsoever to differ in the least from the plain and simple account given us in our Scriptures—We are told that after a great revolution in the planet which had destroyed all but a few of the race of man the three Children of Noah spread gradually from one point over the Globe the children of Shem were still distinguished in their posterity by the similar nature of their languages which have been from thence called the Shemetic languages as the Hebrew Seraic*r* and so forth—remained near their original station—we are informed too that the . . . or descen- dants of Japheth diverged into two branches but with this remarkable dis- tinction that their instinct or tendency were both westward the one to the South west the Ionias or Ionians or children of Japheth who formed the Greek Islands [f 357] and in a later period possessed Italy and were the founders of the Italian Empire and with a strict conformity to the sa- cred writings did really abide in the tents of Shem—the other or north western race passed into the more barbarous and less favored realms of the North—into Germany and so on into Sweden and there remained in their original simplicity still however hardened by the hardships around them but in all respects most distinguished and even contrasted with that of the savages whom we have found in America—in truth the South west- ern race became civilized to the loss of true cultivation but the North western race appear to have retained their cultivation in spite of the di-

---

q Pencilled cross appears in right-hand margin
r "Seraic" seems to have been partly altered

minishing civilization[s]—the third set the children of Ham seem by providence to have been impelled to the South and there as the inhabitants of
Africa to bear witness to us of that awful prophecy which Christianity the
universal Redeemer has been lately to the undying glory of this nation at
once fulfilling and healing the unhappy slaves that were to [f 358] be servants to their elder brethren till that time when the servant should be as
the Master and the Master as the Servant before the eye of the common
Lord. The children of Shem we find were strictly forbidden to intermarry
with those of Ham or Japheth—we are informed likewise that excepting
the Jews who were prevented by a miraculous interposition of the Arabs
who were equally prevented by a providential course of circumstances
this command was generally disobeyed a mixed race arose who appear
to have spread east and west neither ascending Northward nor descending but forming as it were a mighty Wall or Isthmus between the North
western descendants of Japheth and the South Western under the name
of the Celtic Nations. Against this Wall ignorant of each other the divided
brethren were fighting till at length by their mutual successes they came
themselves into collision—for a long while the Contest was doubtful for
on the part of the Romans into whom the Greeks had flown as the great
Rivers in America flow into yet greater—on the one side there was discipline—there was all the advantage of art and Science—on the other
there [f 359] was superior valour superior morality and a population
wholly applicable to Military purposes so long the contest remained undecided but when from frequent wars and increasing depravity on the part
of the Romans the Germans had acquired Roman discipline had become
themselves Masters in part of Roman knowledge the contest no longer
remained disputable—it was not as we have too commonly been led to
imagine a direct eruption of barbarous Nations which at once overwhelmed a civilized Empire—far from it—all the eruptions that were the
. . . of the Goths and Vandals were in full activity long before—let any
man who has been at Rome compare the Arch of Constantine with that
of Antonine . . . ⟨with the pure works of Greece⟩ and he will see how rapid
the degeneracy had been In truth the Christians naturally predisposed to
the natural morals of the Germans as soon as the Germans themselves had
adopted Christianity became their warm friends and to them they looked
for the fulfilment if not of the prophecies of their interpretation of the
prophecies—A powerful [f 360] party had been formed in Italy nay in
Rome itself and the German party prevailed doubtless with all the horrors which accompany a long and wide extended warfare but by no means

---

[s] "civilization" written over erasure

by all those horrors with which we have been accustomed to consider the event forgetful that our Narrators were Italian Monks or Italian Priests of the Italian party and that the few writings which remain by others of the other party present to us very different results—It was different in different Countries—in Spain for instance the conquerors took the conquered into full partnership adopted their laws and in a short time their language and no other difference remained but what was supplied by heraldry and the pride of families—in other Countries the Conquerors gave the conquered no better terms than those of . . . but still every where Christianity was received and in that a slow but certain cure of the evils which had been inflicted

I have placed the commencement of the modern times as opposed to the ancient in the time of Theodorick the Goth and truly [f 361] I cannot conceive a better characteristic could be afforded of the difference between the modern and the ancient world with respect to philosophy poetry politics Religion and all that is interesting to mankind—I cannot imagine a more expressive symbol and as it were allegory of this than by placing before my eyes the Palace of that imperial Goth . . . running opposite to the Christian Temple . . .*t* that was permitted to overlook the Monarchs palace the sole remaining object of reference and willing submission for in this I seem to have the commencement of the era as in a living symbol—I imagine that Temple too removed with all its Greek and Roman associations and nothing remaining but Christ and the Cross and instead of it a Cathedral like that of York of Milan or of Strasburgh with all its many Chapels its Pillared stems and leaf work roof as if some sacred . . .*u* by permanence into a symbol of the everlasting [f 362] Gospel I hear the choral thanksgiving rolled in peal through its solemn aisles or the Chaunt of penitent and holy piety from . . . and consecrated virgins sobbing and dying away in its dark recesses . . .*v* and the sacramental pledge of peace and mercy—In these assemblies thus collected before my imagination I see and recognize the comparison of that era . . . [f 363] . . .*w* For a time Philosophy must of course have been out of the question—the business of the Schoolmaster was to take its place and where under ⟨a⟩ similar revolution before the time of our Saviour could such a Schoolmaster have been found—we hear of the terrific revolutions produced by the Asiatic Conquerors and the result has been degradation if not utter extinction—here the arts and sciences have appeared to be tram-

---

t Dot at left-hand margin indicates omitted line
u Dots at left-hand margin indicate omitted lines
v Dots at left-hand margin indicate omitted lines
w Dots at left-hand margin indicate omitted lines

pled under foot—fierce Warriors still fiercer from their recent conquests possessed the customs of the world those customs from contempt of those whom they had conquered were suffered to lose their ornaments—their pasture fields to pass into forests and their flocks to be exchanged into wild beasts to furnish more amusement for the warlike spirit of the Victors with all that could bring on an utter decay of the human race [f 364] what do we find continued a traceable progress a mild Schoolmaster was there amidst all the clang of Arms of the terrific sound of the trumpet still the elevation of the cross had a power that tamed the proudest spirit—if at once it could not do away the angry passions if those who had joined in conquering a common foe and then had begun the trade of War with each other what could not be prevented was still alleviated and a single sound of the Ave Maria bell secured for a few hours at least ⟨the⟩ Labourer and the husbandman from their danger—if the turbulent passions of the Chieftains prevented all discipline in the Arts or in philosophy still their religion secured a sanctuary for all the learning that remained in humble monastery—Every where the Church appeared as the combining power—it was an union unknown before but an union so powerfully effective that if we could but dwell upon it forgetful of all heats and differences which the events of two or three centuries passed have occasioned I persuade myself that we should hear and read too with far different feelings the [f 365] stories of Emperors holding the stirrups for the Popes and of Archbishops menacing their Sovereigns—that is one view of the subject—When the Church had gone beyond the due bounds and when having passed as all earthly things do into excess the reaction had begun—but present to ourselves the humble peasantry the peaceful tradesman of the Town trembling to lead out his wares lest the Feudal Lord should pounce upon them . . . gave the only chance of hope for the poor and the humble man to rise into distinction and to sit down in equality with his proud Peers—conceive that it was—however impure in particular dogmas yet still it was religion—the only religion then upon earth—it was learning however defective yet the only learning upon the earth—that it was science which though the links were composed of ignoble matter was still preserving the chain that stood before the Lordly warrior and lowering his spirit presented to all the world the great truth right is greater than might—as sure as you are man there is a power more powerful than brute force and see the Monarch himself obeying it and holding as he holds the stirrup the visible confession that [f 366] the moral and intellectual part of mankind were destined to be the Governors and arms and brute force to be their implements and organs and then we should see justly the sources of the higher arcade[x] and learn to distinguish the benefits derived from an institution during the time to which it was fitted from the disadvantages which announce its decay and in its decay announce that it has already performed the functions for which it was intended and was making way for a new order of things prepared however in a great measure by its own former merits

This is not merely declamation for it is to the Church assuredly that we owe all the origins all the ground works of our present state of Civilization—the land divided among the great Lords by feudal tenures there was none but Master and Slave and to the Bishops to the . . . was alone given the privilege of forming places of refuge where [f 367] the Bishops castle was there and for a certain extent around it was a sacred land—where a church was built there likewise was ground that dare not be encroached on—what wonder then if the poor vassal when his oppressions became greater than he could sustain fled thither—what if a foreigner instead of being submitted to the caprices of savage ignorance had fled at least within the vicinity of reason—the effect was even so—wherever a Bishops Castle was a Town arose and this[y] Town increased into a City— wherever a Church was with a few exceptions a small set of houses arose about it and thus began the greater part of the Towns and almost all the Cities of this Kingdom and in truth of all the rest of Europe—then began the possibility of freedom before that there was freedom indeed—a well balanced freedom between the Monarch and his Peers except that the balance was too often on the side of the Subject but even to a far later period. I am sorry to say we are not to read the panegryricks of [f 368] freedom without remembering it was only freedom for Gentlemen and as low down as the time of Milton and Algernon Sidney and some of our more modern great lovers of modern freedom we find that Gentlemen only are the persons in contemplation and that with the exception of a few levellers even in the turbulent times of Cromwell there was not a man of Sense who would have believed it possible or if possible probable or adviseable that there should be the degree of freedom now possessed in this Kingdom I will venture to say ⟨that⟩ like the trial by Jury which is often talked of as carelessly as freedom . . . that is one of the most difficult problems to solve from so many fine balances and counterbalances—so many things that are met here but the opposing powers are so much the most capricious that by the goodness of Providence it has ripened into present wisdom but above all and which is more than all [f 369] all the imperi-

---

[x] Altered in pencil to "higher=archy"
[y] "this" seems to have been written over erasure

ous circumstances and events drawn from our history—all the imperious circumstances and events drawn from our insular situation all the imperious circumstances and events drawn from the time when our Towns and Cities began to have a greater weight and influence than elsewhere all these combined to produce two effects in the Gentry of the Country a spirit of compromise and in the Country throughout a volunteer spirit without both which it appears to me that the British Constitution first would not be practicable and secondly that not it but a whole area of it would be one of the greatest curses that could be inflicted on a Country because it would quell all real progressive improvement by fixing the sting of disappointment in the public mind

At this time all the philosophy of the World was of course contained in their books of Theology and those existed for the Priests alone and were presented to the [f 370] people at large in the disguise of external ceremonies and of forms but here even in those very doctrines which were connected with those ceremonies lay the seed—the reviviscence of philosophy the Christian Religion I am not speaking now of the pure Gospel but the Christian Religion as a historical fact differed from all the institutions of the Ancients in this point that great truths were connected with all its ceremonies—nay even the very sacred events in which the historical part of Christianity consisted were themselves only so many really real and historical symbols of the great truths which it was the object of Christianity to propagate or rather to speak more truly Christianity first of all destroyed the pernicious distinction between truth and reality and that which was merely speculative—they considered of no weight a moral opinion or a moral feeling deprived of intellect that it was an impossibility in consequence of which as the God of the Christians [f 371] differed from those of the old Philosophers by being no abstraction no blind power but a living God so at all times truths appear as living truths and even in an excess of ceremonies still there was a more or less visible connexion between each ceremony and an opinion represented thereby when therefore chiefly by service of the Jewish Physicians who keeping up connexion with their brethren in different parts of the world who were employed in commerce and even before the seige of Constantinople they having brought into Europe this treasure which excited the restoration of literature even before that they had brought certain stores of philosophy from the Arabs and that the dark ages as they have been called were not darker is certainly in no small measure owing to the service of the poor despised Jews—The Cities as I mentioned before originating in Sacerdotal production because of course the Chief seats of instruction from the

Clergy from these came the Colleges and the Universities those University's [f 372] naturally gave their first attention to the articles of their religion—the point was to bring forward a system of Religion—this was done from the writings of the Fathers—differences arose in consequence not concerning the opinions themselves but concerning the modes of defending them—the Aristotelian Logic which had been brought into Europe from the Arabs supplied an inexhaustable source of disputation—at that time to suppose any other than . . . would have been out of the question when men were content to devote all the powers of mechanism to their Church accustomed to a hardihood of life it was not to be expected that the merely practicable sciences would have effect—that must appear a paradox but though a paradox it is strictly true for every true . . . earlier than what is termed utility—the savage before he ever thinks of making a Coat or Waistcoat fixes a feather in his head [f 373] or the bone of his enemy or the very skin of the wild beast he throws on his shoulders is not for warmth he would despise himself if he was capable of external sense—no it is a mark of power and revenge . . . or a religion where man has been favored with it has in every instance been the foundation and the beginning of his imagination—no wonder therefore that just in proportion as the useful arts would have been most useful were they the less regarded—at the time when men were deficient[z] in the comforts and conveniences and many of the necessaries of life then was it that they became most zealous most earnest about generalities—convictions everything only their present state as if all that is wanted in the present state seemed only to whisper to a man for this reason it is not worth your attention let my affections be given to something that is permanent—to something that is beyond [f 374] this while the more worthy the more pleasant our present circumstances appear unfortunately (I speak as a general tendency) the greater aversion we seem to shew to all ⟨the points of thought a greater objection to all⟩ that is general permanent or fundamental sufficient if only we have that which is at the moment expedient and this is not only the feeling of individuals but it spreads to the feelings of States and therefore as I before vindicated in some measure the image I have presented at least of the hierarchy in the dark ages so in a certain qualified sense I cannot look on the Theological disputations in those times with the contempt it is customary to do I see something awful in the fact that three or four thousand men could collect together in a single place to hear one great Teacher—men barely able to read begging on the road and

---

[z] "deficient" written over erasure

submitting to every species of privation and yet crowding to hear what—
an amusing tale or to see a splendid Tragedy or even to give their attention to some song or ballad? no—to listen with greedy ears to the forms
of their own minds to be told by what laws thoughts are connected with
thoughts—to be made sensible of a certain pride when they could come
to an apparent conclusion [f 375] a certain sense of Victory when they
could detect an inconsequence—I say to see such men poor and with
every privation of life yet disputing as described by the Writers of those
times eagerly in the Streets and with a degree of warmth which we
scarcely hear even on the most important concerns with respect to things
in which they as individuals have no imaginable interest it certainly does
not degrade the men themselves in my mind but most assuredly it greatly
elevates our nature—The consequences more important that result from
this—the peculiar nature of the Schoolmen and of their philosophy and
the manner in which it not only worked onward towards the restoration
of literature which ended in exploding its introduction—these will be the
subjects of my second Lecture which will carry down the history of philosophy from the race of the Schoolmen to the restoration of literature
throughout Europe—

But I cannot conclude without a few remarks on the different position
in which philosophy must now be treated compared with what it has been
in the former course of Lectures—in the former course I considered it as
a growth [f 376] of the human mind that different individuals Thales and
Pythagoras or Plato and Aristotle I regarded as only the same mind and
in different modes or in different periods of its growth and I am satisfied
that from the rude beginning namely the first bidding farewell to mere
tradition and seeking for light in the mind itself to the age of Epicurus
philosophy had formed its circle and appeared in every possible form—
this was my object—in the present so far from having aught new to inform you concerning the opinions themselves it must be my business to
tame the vanity of the moderns by proving to you in every Case I know
of that those men took up such and such opinions but that those opinions
were nothing more than what had been brought forward by such and such
of the antients as far as they were really philosophical—but I have another thing I have to shew the effects of philosophy which I have not had
an opportunity of doing in the very tumultuous very hastening changes
of the Greek and Roman [f 377] Republics there its effects such as they
were were so intermixed with political events with wars with rapid ris-
ings up and as rapid descents—it was impossible to give a fair and convincing statement of what philosophy can do both of good where it is
what it ought to be and deserves the name ⟨and⟩ of evil when it combines

with wrongful causes—*a*this I shall I hope shew that as Religion never can be philosophy because the only true philosophy proposes Religion as its end and supplement so on the other hand there can be no true religion without philosophy—no true feelings and notions of religion among men at large without just notions of Philosophy in the higher classes*b* and I may venture to add likewise that all the great events of Europe have borne so wonderful a coincidence and similarity with the predominating systems of philosophy at the time that if we consider too that those predominant opinions were always prior and fashionable to the event yet stictly*c* homogeneous with the event and the event such [f 378] as we should have been entitled to deduce it would be extravagant if we were to imagine it was altogether vain or like a Weathercock that without affecting the wind simply shews it—Now I trust I shall shew that a true religion will necessarily lead to a just philosophy and on the other hand that Statesmen who have to manage a Constitution founded in the spirit of one philosophy but who do manage it in that directly contrary—or even a Clergy who with one set of opinions are to preach doctrines brought together by men who believe the direct contrary cannot but produce a state either of dissention or of indifference and as one example among a *thousand* think of Frederick the Great of Prussia and Joseph of Austria . . . to manage the constitutions formed by the noble Goths their Ancestors and look at the records of the early parts of the French Revolution for the precise effects produced by the contrast to which I have alluded—

---

a–b Pencilled vertical line in right-hand margin beside passage and, indicating it, a hand with a pointing finger sketched in pencil to its right
  c "stictly" written partly over erasure

LECTURE 9

Mr Coleridges Lecture
Monday 22nd February 1819^d

A series of Lectures on a subject which comprises a space of some thousands of years must be a chain indeed but it cannot be composed of links of the same lustre or of the same metal and yet those are links and cannot be altogether omitted—the history therefore of the scholastic philosophy an important emovement in the progress of the human intellect I cannot pass over though at the same time I can only promise my best endeavors to make it interesting without promising to myself any favorable result but I must rely on your favor and I am . . . uselessness and so forth being connected with the name almost in the Soul of Scholastic philosophy—In a former Lecture upon the Eclectic philosophers or those who were in opposition to philosophy I have shewn not only the immense powers that by some of the great men [f 380] strongly prejudiced in favor of their Ancestorial Religion had been made but likewise the pernicious or utterly worthless results of an attempt to confound Religion with philosophy in order to mix religi^e itself with philosophy for that is the proper character of the efforts of those philosophers after the birth of our Lord— the national religion^f and national religions in general had lost all their influence and those who rejected Christianity had nothing left^g but to try to make an universal religion out of philosophy—Now we are to prepare ourselves for an attempt equally impracticable but equally natural and far more excusable under the circumstances—that of the schoolmen to make philosophy Religion—I know no better description that I could give you than this—As the Eclectic philosophers had confounded them so did they but the Eclectic philosophers attempted to make Religion philosophy— the schoolmens attempt was to convert philosophy into Religion

Now there is not perhaps a truth more important to us than that these

---

^d "Lect 8" written in pencil above pencilled lozenge, probably in the hand of JHG
^e Last two letters of "Religion" missing and others erased; incomplete correction of a mistranscription?
^f Possibly "religious"
^g "left" written partly over erasure

two dearest names [f 381] to human nature philosophy and religion can neither be confounded nor yet can they be separated—if you would confound them you must immediately conjure up imaginary faculties powers of the intellect of an intellectual vision so estranged from intellect that the most eloquent supporters of it are obliged to borrow their metaphors from a rival sense and call it a rival tact a rival intellect in which intellect becomes one with the object of which it is supposed to be the contemplator—in short we must abandon ourselves wholly to visionary speculations to the ennoblement of mere bodily sensations by the connecting with them mere notions and fancies—This must necessarily be the case when you would turn Religion into philosophy—on the other hand if you would have a religion without a philosophy then history will enable me to tell you what the result would be—it was presented in indelible characters very shortly after . . . ⟨the last philosophic schools and⟩ when the very reading of a book tending to learning was complained of by . . . [f 382] when even a philosopher himself and a man of no mean merits Anchion sent forth a pastoral . . . concerning an abomination he had heard of—the introduction of Seneca and Virgil lest it should injure faith— what was the consequence—man was left to combine his senses with his better feelings—the Church had taught him indeed truths of the utmost importance to his well being but by precluding all exercise of intellect had left it to himself to substantiate them or bring them into any form of reflection what the lower classes were on the worship of dead bones and relics on all the blessed influences of that Religion which was to emancipate us from the control of our senses became the means of disturbing . . . the legends of the dark ages will sufficiently inform you but even in its influence upon the higher classes upon those who possessed whatever education was then existing—nay who were themselves the teachers of it the operation of this cause is manifest

During the Roman Empire while [f 383] Christianity was struggling with philosophy and itself fought the enemy with her own weapons we find the great objects of controversy to have been on the Trinity—on those parts of our Religion most removed from our senses—after the first dawnings of intellect dispute will turn to some object of the senses namely on the sacrament and the sacrament itself was turned into a sort if^h I may so say of exponent of that effect for here was the spiritual degraded into an image and secondly the image was unnaturally made to possess Spiritual powers and in that very description I have given you the true character of superstition—man cannot deprive himself of his moral

---

^{h} "if" written partly over erasure

feelings altogether he cannot deprive himself of that instinct which still teaches him that there is a something which is better than his senses or the mere organs of his body can present to him—but he has it in his power to confound what he cannot destroy and to give to the spirit the attributes of the body and to give to the body the attributes of [f 384] the spirit—to make an image real to make a Wafer possess omnipresence and to take a . . . This is the character of superstition in all ages—it is the confounding of the Spiritual with the bodily

Now it being the business of philosophy ever to distinguish without unnaturally dividing it is for this reason that you may trace the world through its whole history and you will find that wherever philosophy has attempted to place itself above Religion or to take Religion in as its parts the consequence has been a dreary scepticism which has ended in a sensual delivery of our own being up to the wants and appetites of the present state—on the other hand when a Religion misunderstanding the holy word *faith* shall attempt to put the extinguisher upon all the powers of the intellect however pure the dogmas may have been in the beginning so assuredly it will become a mere . . . man will differ from the beast only [f 385] by a falsehood and a blunder only because instead of seeing a snake as a snake or a tree as a tree his higher being makes him combine with it something of hope or general fear which is perfectly estranged from the apparent exciting cause—Oh believe me Sirs gross blunders are those which are represented to us in gross forms but the very same in essence lurk under the handsome appearances and cheat many a man who . . . the scorn of his honored mind in a more beggarly dress—so even is it in this the same errors are going on among us and have done and as long as men remain men in their inequalities[i] will do so still—you will have two classes of . . . and the one will when he has seen an Astronomer looking through a Telescope say—Nonsense—the man is a madman what will that pole do with those bits of glass recommend me to my common Senses—I will not believe a Word he says—Another who has attended more or whose fears have been acted on by the fulfilling of an Eclipse predicted [f 386] goes the contrary way—you shall deserve fire and faggot if you do not believe everything the Astronomer tells you—your eyes are the greatest nuisances in the World—they are deceiving you on all occasions they are leading you into ditches and pools wherever you go—let me pore through a telescope—Now what the telescope is to the eye just that faith—that is the energies of our moral feelings are to the rea-

---

[i] Short wavy line drawn between "their" and "inequalities" as if "inequalities" had been inserted later into space too large for it

son—reason is the eye and faith (all the moral anticipation[j]) the telescope—No wonder that when men had placed themselves voluntarily in the dark they began to rub their eyes as in the den of Polyphemus[k] and made sparks such as proceeded from no one thing there is in nature—and such is the case where man rests solely on self or any of those things which God and nature have made to be conjoint

Still there is a noble something in man that cannot be suspended long—that will lift up great weights and the moment that other causes have removed them will play forth at all the pipes—such was the Case in that glory of our kingdom and of human nature—our Alfred—As soon [f 387] as his Victories had procured a small interval of tranquility he began to think whom he was to govern and what the purposes of Government were and it ought to be written in letters of gold what this great Sovereign conceived Government to be—books of politics have been written and have not contained so much wisdom as this one sentiment that it was a substitute for the defects of self government arising out of the imperfections and perverted will of man there is the ground of all true liberty—and there too is the guard against all sedition all false and idle pretences to give freedom—when freedom they cry but license they mean—license they mean when they call for liberty for who lives that must first be wise and good—hence it follows too necessarily that there can be no universal form of liberty no universal constitution—for just in proportion to the increasing quantum of self Government ought to be nay it ever will be the case that such will be the decreasing power of external Government and were the men of [f 388] Algiers by any miracle to be turned into self thinking self governing beings their present Military despotism would be done away probably but whether it would or not it would not make an atom difference for in every country and I would the higher classes[l] felt that—the minority will be influenced by the feelings of the majority . . . is brought back to him—into[m] his very Soul and even into that of his very confederates—Alfred and Charlemagne in different ways the two greatest men of the Modern World sought in their obtaining of power as much as possible to supercede it a grander eulogy cannot be placed on a human being than an individual in that station saying I will exert my whole powers to prevent the necessity of it—he therefore founded or established our Universities—that of Oxford he first brought . . . so did Alfred strive to bring in the Bible as one of interest common

---

[j] "anticipation" written partly over erasure
[k] Name written in space slightly too large for it, as if inserted later
[l] "classes" seems written partly over erasure
[m] "into" written over erasure

to all—not only the jarring states that composed his own [f 389] Realm
but those of his own neighbours and in the same spirit acted his immediate predecessor in Age I mean Charlemagne

The most extraordinary man perhaps of his age and the first philosopher that arose after the suspended animation of Philosophy was Johannes Scotus[n] Originæ of whom we know nothing but that he was an
Englishman—a wonderful man he must have been—who had travelled
according to his own account into Greece into Egypt from Egypt to Italy
and thence through France and back again to England and he says of himself calling heaven to Witness that no Temples were there which were
supposed to contain any valuable works of the ancients which he did not
visit nor was there any man he heard of superior to others whom he did
not pay his address to—He came back to France first and when the no-
bleness of his opinions drew upon him suspicion Charles the Bald unwilling to deliver up his friend and favorite to the irritated Roman Court
and yet [f 390] not daring to disobey it contented himself with forbidding
him to reside at Paris—our Alfred hearing of this invited him to England
and gave him the destiny of establishing or if it be so of re-establishing
the schools at Oxford—His death is scarcely known—it is said he was
assassinated by the Monks with penknives but the operation of his mind
could not be destroyed—he first of all introduced what alone could be interesting at that time—the laws of thinking—he was as Roger Bacon
himself a high Authority has declared the first sound Commentator on
Aristotle and who had read the original writings and from Aristotle he
gave the first simple laws of necessary thinking but so far from being ascribed to Aristotle that he mingled his opinions with those of Platonism
and he endeavored to subordinate the whole to the higher Wisdom he had
learnt from his Religion—in one word and with one exception which he
appears to have been somewhat dazzled with the Splendour of the Eclectic philosophy and in some points to have come too near Pantheism but
with all his practice and his opinions we may say he was a [f 391] Protestant in the present sense of the Word—at least on all the doctrines on
which we call ourselves Protestants—his opinions were the same as ours
and this was the stand he made against transubstantiation—the glorious
zeal with which he stood forward against double predestination—that is
. . . without any respect at all to actions or the enjoyers or sufferers—
these were great measures—but still greater was the merit of the zeal with
which he urged that a true Religion might be above but never could be
contrary to Philosophy and that therefore any act of the Church by which

[n] "Scotus" seems to have been inserted later in space too large for it

an apparent philosophical truth not conceived in truth was declared to be false would strip Religion of intellectual aid and bring it into parity with blind paganism add to this . . . and he was beyond his age as other men have lagged behind—The utmost consolation is to think he was the Companion the Counsellor the friend of Alfred who placed in more genial circumstances could form institutions more lasting than the philosopher in his closet with [f 392] the perishable materials which before printing was known were in his power but do not let us be insufficient in gratitude . . . what was better than all what gales of refreshment from the mere power of talking with a rational being—one perhaps and the very one who like himself was beyond his age and thereby appointed to bring that age forward into the power of producing a nobler . . .

Johannes Scotus Originæ (and we have no better way of describing the philosophic period than by stating the names of those who most distinguished themselves) was followed by . . . who took precisely the same path with himself and whose hours had ⟨been wasted⟩*ᵒ* he again by Abelard and Abelard by . . . or John of Salisbury whose merit in opposing the ridiculous minuteness of the Schoolmen will for ever be read by intelligent minds if not with the same pleasure yet with a higher moral satisfaction than we read now the writings of Lucien as also his account of the controversies carried on by the Schoolmen not by men of no authority but men of the [f 393] highest ranks by Archbishops and Bishops as for instance whether in the Resurrection men who are fat will remain so or whether a man who has been very thin for a course of years will get more substance—or lastly whether when a man takes a pig to market who is obstinate and the man is obliged to use a rope the man drags the pig or the rope and when he speaks of the excessive clamor excited in the schools—the fury not only of the young men but of the elders . . . by . . . in his . . . we feel highly amused and when we find the eloquence with which he calls on men to exert their common sense—in which he was aided by another great man of [? his] time Eusebius who endeavours to repress this controversial spirit especially on the sacrament and on the doctrine of transubstantiation ending with this sober advice let every man take the sacrament in faith of the words and let him rely in faith for that enlightening the answer to which is promised in as far as the individuals veil is off and why then should we dispute because if the [f 394] Gospel be true that every man who asks to be enlightened in sincerity with it will learn as far as he ought why need he go to an earthly teacher or attempt to define that by words which he is assured by his Religion will be given

---

ᵒ Insertion (above line) follows erasure and presumably replaces whatever was erased

by a gradual light afforded to him but the good man failed and all those who taught the same doctrines of tolerance[p] and sober sense and let us not regret that they failed do not let us fall into the mistake of requiring that the thing should be present before the conditions of the thing were— the human mind was to be drawn out of barbarism it was to have the power of acting upon the materials before the materials were present— our powers called into actual use. Is not that the case in nature—does she not make every young animal in sport and without any purpose of utility but that of enjoyment rehearse as it were the task he is to perform in the course of after life—does not the Calf butt before the horns are there or while they are yet budding—even such is the course of providence in the education of man first of all the faculties are encountered with [f 395] as many stumblings as the babe makes in learning to walk and would that our minds were such as to contemplate them with the same love and for- bearance and so with regard to man—through[q] many errors his mind is to be cleared up he is to seek every thing in itself nature is not gone—it does not proceed in created beings with that . . . no but in created beings still one thing comes forward with mighty force ⟨and perfects itself with mighty force⟩ while other things are then in instinct but the former has gained its point—it no longer exists as interesting it has no novelty there is a dead pause like the tide at its highest—a little while it stands and trembles till an opposite direction is taken and then we must expect an- other mark of human frailty what is good will be neglected and con- founded with what is bad—the whole together is an object of reprobation till that is performed too and nature looking back takes up what has been left behind and constitutes a higher home than either so we find still the likeness between the [f 396] education of man and the likenesses of na- ture—we see too the insect—we find every thing going outwards—of every insect the internal is almost as simple as plants—the external more multifarious each insect has its shop of tools about it but with those it has insects[r] that act outwardly it constructs its nets[s]—makes its hive and be- comes the object of our profound admiration and in all that it forms but the process with which it forms its own body but we find no mark of an internal life—Nature takes a higher step and passes into the fishes and there the nervous the object by which reflection or memory is rendered probability begins—but in doing this she has lost something—all the in- sects of life—all that delight in the instinct is gone—She takes another

---

[p] First four letters of "tolerance" written over others now illegible

[q] "through" may be written over erasure

[r] "insects" altered in pencil to "instincts", perhaps by EHC

[s] "nets" altered in pencil to "nests", perhaps by EHC

step and combines both in the birds but both glorify it in a higher degree—there is the nervous system and the instinct and again[t] brings back the acts[u]—she takes another step in the animals—the four footed animals but[v] this is so great a step before she can come to her last consolation[w] that here again [f 397] we miss all not only the acts of the insects but we miss all the lovely analogies to moral feelings which are found in the birds—their mechanism their fidelity their power of imitating articulate sounds—but where she has been withdrawing from the external form the more she has been perfecting the internal organization—she has split[x] . . . the centre of action and reaction then she takes up all that she had been doing before even from the . . . up to the Elephant and by superior aid presents the materials for forming the microcosm of man who with none but the simplest forms of external power has the power of conquering the whole and all that instinct had done throughout the creation in each separate part to gain that by power of reason so as bearing in itself the best witness of higher birth no longer it but the . . . of nature but to be placed as her Lord no longer as receiving gifts but as standing forth from the naked savage up to Newton to bring whatever was within the eye within the power of the [f 398] arm and to subject to the mind that which the senses had only given him the first notices of as spies and out ministers to discover what was yet to conquer

In . . . however who was born at Iustia in Piedmont in the year 1044 and afterwards our Archbishop of Canterbury we have perhaps the proper founder of philosophy he joined with Hildebert Archbishop of Tours born in 1057—I call the proper founders of Scholastic philosophy for this reason and which will give you a further definition or rather description of Scholastic philosophy and its distinction from Greek and Roman philosophy—the Greek and Roman philosopher set out attempting by the powers of the human reason to find truth—truth he was seeking and to arrive at that was his object—the final cause of all his efforts—this could not be the case when the power of the Clergy and what was still more powerful inward conviction had declared that the truth was already found philosophy that pretended to discover truth could not have been tolerated and perhaps if we consider this—[f 399] that we were yet to be brought out of Savagery—could scarcely be rationally or humanely tolerated therefore the schoolmen stood with the truth already discovered the . . .[y] of the

---

[t] First letter of "again" written over erasure
[u] "acts" altered in pencil to "arts"   [v] "but" written over erasure
[w] "consolation" altered in pencil to "consummation", perhaps by EHC
[x] "split" written partly over erasure
[y] "amount" written in pencil in space, perhaps by EHC

sum was given to them as we give them to boys in arithmetic—the object was to prove that what faith and the Church had declared to be true
was coincident with Reason and therefore that truths already known were
rational truths—this constituted the aim and guided all the efforts of the
Schoolmen—the mode in which they put it was naturally first of all by
bringing together the opinions of wise men on such and such subjects but
yet so many and so discordant were the doctrines to be proved that nothing could be effected but by fine distinctions—the next step was therefore philosophy that employed itself in desynonimizing words—in giving them sometimes perfectly just and distinct meanings often but
apparent ones but which whether true or false laid the foundation of our
modern languages and that wonderful . . . [f 400] which in our first Writers in the popular languages we find . . . when we see an . . . which is national or which is more than national spreads over many Countries at the
same time be assured you see a manufactory of something excellent but
with all the dirt and confusion of an unripened process So was it here—
for after a time this necessarily led men from the opposition to common
sense which many of those distinctions appeared to involve and yet from
the inability to find any logical defect in the reasoning whether or not a
logical truth was necessarily an existencial one—that is whether because
a thing was logically consistent it must be necessarily existent—the
founders then I may say—the men who first presented the occasion for
this—who had been haunted with an exceeding wish to give a demonstration of the reality of the idea of the Supreme being—we ourselves still
say a proof of the existence of the Supreme being and too few attend to
the force of the words—we admit a difference between [f 401] existence[z]
and being yet that exists in our language for there is no man who would
not say it is not the essence of a circle or that a circle has all the lines from
the . . . yet few would say that a circle exists or that there is a body that
. . . perfectly equal—we ourselves therefore feel a distinction between
essence and existence this answer must puzzle one and the story which
he states of himself is a highly interesting instance of the age in which he
lived—of the connexion of superstition with metaphysical acuteness—
he long had been oppressed with this wish—he had tried to discover a
demonstration that afforded him satisfaction till he began to mistake that
this was a temptation of the enemy that it was an attack to destroy his
faith—he fasted and prayed but he still was haunted—he prayed longer
till at night in a dream a great light appeared to him and all at once he
knew not how the demonstration came forth and he awoke in full demon-

---

[z] Catchword on f 400: "ex-"; f 401 begins with "existence"

stration of it this was no other than the famous Cartesian [f 402] demonstration he found that the idea of God was the only idea of which man was capable which involved the necessity of its existence not only because man . . . and therefore implied an infinite Being as its Cause but principally from its being involved in the idea itself—for what do we mean by God but that which contains all perfectness without any negation—but existence is the perfection therefore it must ⟨contain⟩ of necessity the existence consequently the necessity . . . this was proof which we must not think much of . . . still referred to this as a something so near to human nature it could not be given up without falling into Scepticism and an utter distrust of anything in external reality coincident with our clear perception of truth

Having sent this through all the Schools and universities of Christendom there arose a monk whose name is doubtful who supported the contrary—who declared he did not see the logic that because a thing is consistent [f 403] or necessary in the idea that should imply an actual or natural existence of it and these founded the two great schools of the Schoolmen the Nominalists and the Realists—which between them we may fairly say have divided all the truths of philosophy that perhaps the human mind can ever arrive at and I here make a challenge I would almost say to point me out an opinion that has taken place since the fifteenth Century which I will not shew as clearly stated and supported in some one or other of the Nominalists or the Realists

The controversy was taken up afterwards and powerfully supported by . . . who was either a . . . or Arian in Religion but most probably the former who asserted that logic was but a higher kind of Grammar and Metaphysics a mere lexicon of general terms that all our conceptions were nothing more than mere modes of thinking perfectly empty except as far as the senses gave them substance or matter [f 404] to work on. The opposite party of course conceived this to be subversive of all religion to which Abelard who was the more celebrated scholar of . . . answered by saying this belonged to faith and that nothing was better than to give the intellect what alone the intellect could pretend—that is a religion and the senses all the rest but it was a dangerous thing to disjoin the intellect from the moral feelings or the religious—all that was to be promised would fall off at once—for what less than religion—what less than the stimulus of the hope and fear of another life could arouse men from the state in which they were—it was from ⟨Religion from⟩ the Bible from the stimulus[a] that even a childish curiosity gave that instituted . . . Botany was to

---

[a] "Bible from the stimulus" written over erasure

know what such a plant was—every Zoology was to determine what such an animal was and to discover whether[b] there was not some double sense or mystery contained in that animal—Astronomy was cultivated to understand what particular constellations existed at such a time—what the stars were that Job alluded to—in short you may trace every science of [f 405] the human mind—I mean the restoration of it in Europe to the mighty stimulus Religion gave those who would therefore make an abhorrent division between Religion and Philosophy were of course treated as heretics and though heretics they might not be in the common sense of the word yet assuredly it was for the advantage of mankind that they failed

This struggle however between those who contended that the form of the human mind or that by which man is compelled to think universally is a substance in nature—is an existential reality and those who contended as M[r] Locke did afterwards and others that they were mere impulses mere reflexes derived from the senses—continued first the realists plan[c] or those who ⟨appealing to the genus and species who⟩ appealed to the facts—that the senses could only give you the notion of a Lion but that the senses never could give you a notion of the genus of Lions—still less that the senses could give you a notion [f 406] only of the component parts of a man himself but with regard to a single individual forming[d] an individual that was derived from the mind therefore they asked in what way do we attribute thought and will to our fellow creatures by regarding nature as a . . . The other party as triumphantly shewed there was no bulwark here against every species of fanaticism against every fancy and a man might persuade himself and appeal to Thomas Aquinas who started the question how many angels could dance upon the top of a needle as an instance and there are many still more gross and the follies into which man was led by attributing to reality that which was mere play work of logic by the immense . . . names which we have been accustomed to hear with very great contempt forgetting what the Sovereigns what the Warriors were at that time over whom these men had such control—forgetting what institutions were then forming in the World or rather to say the truth talking about books [f 407] which if they have been in an old Library they probably may have seen without knowing it but of which most assuredly they never read a page but I happen to have read a considerable portion of the works of Thomas Aquinas and . . . and I should be perplexed to name any books which impressed me with a deeper sense of the

---

[b] "whether" seems written partly over erasure—of "weather"?
[c] Scribbled pencil mark below last letter of "plan"
[d] "forming" written partly over erasure

power of the human mind however they may have been misled by their partiality or by moving in one direction

Through the powers of these men aided by abler Councils . . . in the lower classes and perhaps better suited to the higher aspirations of the nobler character of man became triumphant till just about the time of the restoration of Letters Hockham our English philosopher arose—yes I say Hockham—that obscure name as it now is but which was formerly most celebrated—the object of the thunderbolts of Rome leading a life of persecution and yet still consoled by finding his opinions triumphant brought forward a system of sound philosophy—he defined [f 408] faith according to its proper nature he said that it was an anticipation of knowledge by the moral will that was indeed below science for that was what we were to enjoy as the reward of faith but far above opinion which therefore was not indeed ever attainable in its height by reason but which was constantly tricked by it and though ever flying before still in its latter steps reached it and consequently that a doctrine of faith that was against reason was absurd and a faith that was not admitted to be above reason ceased to be faith altogether inasmuch as it became one and the same with reason but what I would wish to impress is what struck me as so beautiful a definition of faith that of itself it is enough to preserve any man from fanaticism and at last secure him against . . . does not the child feeling its growth anticipate its manhood and does it not work on with a view to it— does not the child while it plays at its mothers knees yea in the touch on the mothers arm receive in love and in kindness a [f 409] pledge that that something it understands not it yet possesses the essential of sense and truth and reality combined with a reversional property something yet to come—this in reality is the pride of human reason because it is the pledge and necessary consequence of its progression

All that has been done in later times in the critical examination of the faculties by which we are to judge of both the objects of our Senses and those which are removed from us—all that speculation to rightly employ itself upon a . . . shapes by its own powers a correspondent . . . and then that larger portion of truths which are attained partly by the absurdity of supposing the Contrary and partly by the contradiction which the . . . not of our own beings—This I say was presented—no true . . . of that age indeed but yet with a clearness which has not had many modern Superiors—In our Countryman Hockham at this time the two causes were working to produce a great [f 410] [revolution]*e* in the human mind—the first was that the very satiety of a perpetual controversy concerning mere

---

e Catchword "revolution" on f 409, omitted at beginning of f 410, supplied here notions and words although it had done ample services in the formation of language ⟨and strengthening the human language⟩ and remember that this very philosophy was the Tennis Court if I may so say—it was the game of cricket that had given all the robust vigor to the greatest Statesmen and the mighty minds that existed in this Country and the whole of Europe in the reign of Richard the 3.ʳᵈ Henry the 7ᵗʰ and Henry the 8ᵗʰ and part of the time of Queen Elizabeth—it was in this school they had learnt robustness and robustness of intellect though very scanty should be the quantity of the information gained is no trifle or if it were we must admit that the under Chemist at the Royal Institution or any other person who knows five hundred facts of nature five hundred substantial pieces of knowledge of some use to mankind where Lord Bacon knew but one was a greater man than Lord Bacon and more likely to be a benefactor to his species—I mention this [f 411] because it is one of the vices of this age that we are too fond of dwelling on the vices and follies of our Ancestors—we may remember if they thought too much of giving power we have been falling into the opposite extreme of corruption till we have destroyed the tone of the stomach which it was to nourish—we have been desirous of a . . . geometry we have invented wooden Circles and tried to make the Child to feel—in short we have tried to keep up his memory as the lumber room of his Soul with guns and swords and all the implements of warfare without observing that the arm was paralyzed and the soul turned to a mere lumber room where inactive . . . remaining together brought forwards merely mists and vapours and self conceit

Extremes are produced by extremes the tyranny of Aristotle and the Aristotelian philosophy called forth the visionaries and the Mystics they abandoned all ideas and their principle was that there was an universal [f 412] life that this life was distinguished by Sympathies and Antipathies that this existed through all nature and that the proper mode of invoking nature was by attending nature by means of simple substances Out of this arose the fancy of the transmutation of metals—they believed that all the metals were the same thing in different states of growth and that by warming by bringing stimulants from . . . or contradictionᶠ from . . . they could bring forward . . . and which they believed to be no other than what they called earthly life or life in its opposite extreme—that as one extreme of life is projectile and against gravitation so as all extremes have some one middle point of indifference there was a supersensual life revealed in two ways one by phenomenal light and the other by life or gold and carrying this on they concluded as life was light so the . . . from the life would . . .

ᶠ "or contradiction" written partly over erasure

the same view therefore gave them a hope of discovering an universal remedy a power [f 413] of keeping life in the highest state conceivable of energy and on the same principle carrying on the notion of life every where and animating the universe they presented all parts of the world as having symbolical meanings—that there was no shape in nature but had its correspondent in the heavens or under the earth—that it was merely a likeness to something else and therefore capable of acting on some superior being and in this manner they introduced indeed all that was most[g] absurd in fancy or imagination but at the same time still in direct opposition to the scholastic philosophy which drew man wholly back from his senses and from the outward world into the distinctions in his own thoughts and constantly directing the human mind to found itself . . . will lead to an experimental philosophy to lead us . . . and what they called constellations—faith—watching the effects imagining[h] the possession of these things to be somewhat in the nature of ceremonies or magical invocations of them [f 414] noticing the results and ⟨so⟩ blindly leading on to other truths so important to the actual purposes of man in Society it drew Strangers minds into it infected . . . with the same notions infected with the same disposition to lying which follows an intelligence . . . a thing presented to us in Don Quixote where he begins with a grave story which he cannot bring himself to deny but goes to a magician to know whether it is true or not—so with these men they indulged themselves with these imaginations that certain indulgences became so vivid from hope that they declared they were so and afterwards many of them I believe really believed it but yet where the whole human faculties were called forth and with amazing industry something must come of it and to the Alchemists we are indebted for Chemistry as it now exists—a wonderful science I may call it for it has transmuted into reality all the dreams of polytheism and it would be difficult to find in the Arabian Nights any thing more wonderful than Chemistry has presented—so that which began [f 415] in imagination proceeding and wedding with Common sense and finally with science has ended in the gratification of it

Letters however were gradually introduced and who shall speak—who shall be worthy to describe the enthusiasm with which the Great men of Rome and Greece in the reappearance of their works were greeted in Christendom—remember how many . . . and to introduce letters and arts and sciences—compare the efforts of the Russian Court from Peter the great to the present day and[i] its existing state and then look back with hon-

---

[g] "was most" seems written over erasure
[h] First two letters of "imagining" may be written over erasure
[i] "and" seems written partly over erasure

est pride to your ancestors when the trumpet of ancient literature was blown and King and Noble and Warrior and peasant came crowding— when men gave up their pleasure exposed to every privation and with their manuscript under their arms would start from a hedge because . . . and those men were the Erasmus's the Luthers—the men who had made us all we are and whose works if well studied would make us a great deal better—This spread throughout a zeal that declared to the human mind that it was arriving at [f 416] its manhood that it was no longer to be confined to this or that study but was capable of passing off according to the will of individual genius and the social stimulus

Shortly afterwards the reformation which could not well be delayed threw open all the stores of Religion to man—there too the same mark of providence was shewn—there too was the blast of the trumpet and all those nations and all those individuals who were fitted for protestantism received it and having received it the voice seemed to have passed forth and within a few years only after Luthers death it received its outline and limits which it has not varied to this day so materially are things dependent upon the great course of events and so little is really done by individual reasons or what we are now so proud of under the name of enlightening or the spread of general information and so forth that information which is suitable to and which conforms with all its parts which in the present is wedding the past to some future that is mighty— all the rest may sometimes distinguish individuals [f 417] but it is as it were nothing in the Ocean of human concerns but assuredly the way to improve the present is not despise the past—it is a great error to idolize it but still greater to hold it in contempt Wordsworth has beautifully said the Child is the Father of the man and I would wish them to be taught to be bound each to each in natural charity

I will conclude this Lecture by a few general remarks on the ages of which we have been treating and as my next Lecture will begin with the Reformation and go on to the time of Charles the second what I mean now I will state by repeating almost a conversation that passed—"what" says an objector to me "do you hold out these middle ages as objects of admiration—what can dreaming of the past do but make men forget the duties and advantages of the present—where are your fine Chivalrous Knights—you forget their miserable vassals—there to be sure ⟨are⟩ your great displays of Priestly power but do you forget the cruel crusades and examine into the detail of life [f 418] without its comforts—with all the wretchedness that you may still find if you go into the territories between Turkey and Europe—" I answer there are always enough that is secured to us both by what is evil as well as good in nature that will be secured to us by the present and the elevation of the past is as necessary as an attention to the present the events of nature ought to be continuous many are the deformities of the middle ages but they may be well compared to the eruptions on unhealthy children they are repulsive to our feelings but where any evil exists inwardly and when the body becomes weaker and weaker it is found easy to combine the poison of the disease with the life itself and the outward counterfeits of smoothness and harmony of which the wretched inward have no partaking

That Europe is what it is could not have been in the first place but in consequence of the wisdom of Charlemagne and the other powers of Europe in imitation of him in [f 419] subordinating*ʲ* the temporal powers for a time to the spiritual powers for what interest was there but that which remained common to all the states if the Pope could not wholly prevent wars has the Protestant balance of power been more successful since it has by the necessary change of time taken from the person and turned into the balance have we gained more in that respect—but the vassals—the dreadful slavery of those ages—I am far from wishing to exculpate or palliate the evils of slavery—what makes a Slave a Slave? if I mistake not it is oppressions—it is the being in a state ⟨out⟩ of which he cannot hope to rise and he who placed where there is no motive for action but where the miserable thing he is must ever remain in the same sphere is a Slave and a pitiable one—but were the vassals of our Ancestors such— can we compare them with the miserable victims of the West Indies if so how came the Burgesses—they came from somewhere they were not original Citizens the privileges of Cities were not known till a considerable length of time had passed after [f 420] the first conquest—of whom came the great majority of the religious—the Monks and the Priests—it appears then that there were two modes by which the vassals had a hope of rising*ᵏ* either in themselves or in their Children and that they did so is evident first from the power of the Clergy and secondly from the great powers of the Burgesses Reflect only on the Hanseatic League recollect only how early the House of Commons became important—and what were those Burgesses—think of their buildings—think of the Cathedral at Strasburgh—think of the superior morality of the admirably balanced constitutions of the men of genius that were rising out of them and the refuge afforded to men of genius—see them wrongfully sometimes oppressed and sometimes wrongfully oppressing the nobility and genius but . . . and that which was to be stimulated—Consider I say too likewise not the gloomy accounts of Monkish historians only but take the picture

---

ʲ Catchword on f 418, "sub-", expanded to "subordinating" on f 419
ᵏ First letter of "rising" seems written over erasure

given by the poets of the times—surely it was not all cruelty—we find there on the contrary nothing [f 421] more frequent than such characters as that which Shakespeare has drawn in as you like it and we find . . . was predominant in the minds of men—I feel the blessings of the present time most fully but I still when I reflect on a German Town which I myself was once in and which had never been polluted by any foreign invasion and remember how strongly it struck me like something I have seen and all I have heard of good old simple times in England and compare it with the result of the manners of that same Town after it had for three years had French Troops quartered in it—how much more information there was in the Town and how much more of what was infamous in man and woman and how much shipwreck had taken place in their morality and we shall not be so apt to despise what is ancient nor admire all as good that comes under the name of modern illumination—but above all I find throughout the dark ages one striking proof of the greatness of our nature—the present man [f 422] was in all his doubtings and in all his notions subordinated to the future—Religion in thought religion in heart was with all their imperfections their guide their ultimate their supreme aid in all things we are apt to take providences as[1] history but remember that historians naturally take that which is prominent and chief but all providences are . . . We read of cruelties to the vassals—we swell with indignation at their wretched life and various instances are brought in confirmation of it and in the mean time we bless our fate and have reason to do so but greater our reason so to do if we look to ~~our~~ correspondent individuals in our own times—Great have been the advantages to this Country by commerce next to the Church it has been the great source of information—And art and Science in some measure though in a less degree but most assuredly the main support of freedom nay the very cause of freedom [f 423] as actual and as practicable throughout the Country and of that general diffusion of knowledge which if we have fewer wells now fewer reservoirs makes us have a hundred more frequent brooks which may be shallow but yet go bubbling and chattering and conveying fertility where they go to a certain extent—I feel that now you may pass from one end of England to the other and scarcely know you are twenty miles from London from the general uniformity of language habit information—I feel that by the confidence made necessary between man and man it has given a physical strength to this Country perfectly knew and unknown in any periods of the history of the world—all this I feel and feel grateful for but it has taught us to consider men our fellow Creatures

---

[1] "providences as" written partly over erasure

mere parts of the Machine—it has directed us to consider the quantity of consumable without reference to the quality of the consumer—I say it enables us to look with trifling concern at well attested facts of many thousands of little children from the age of six years old to fifteen working [f 424] from fourteen to fifteen hours out of the twenty four in a heated atmosphere of eighty five degrees or more in an air polluted by cotton flue—nay by the very effluvia from the poor little sufferers who each contribute their quota to the common contagion—I say this—and that these die off so as to leave only one in fifty and happy are those who die so escaping a miserable old age loaded with diseases as numerous as the organs of the body by which they can be attacked that arise from debility and excessive stimulants for it is not a contradiction—this is so and it is not a contradiction—they are free laborers poor little darlings and consider the Revenue—consider the money got by them but Morality! But Religion! they are all very good things—we subscribe to the Sunday Schools but you must not mention those points when it comes to a question of Commerce

LECTURE 10

Mᵣ Coleridges Lecture
Monday 1ˢᵗ March 1819

The Gothic Tribes both before and after they had received Christianity and become the founders of Christianity were strikingly distinguished from the Greeks the South Western branch of the same great family by a Federal character as opposed to a direct Republicanism or the character of a State—they in all their habits discovered a connexion without combination—they were belinked together but no part would lose its own integrity and individuality each house was to be a mans Castle—each Town owed indeed its duties and its audiences to some Noble or Prince from whom it held but still it was a whole of itself with its own rights its own Magistracies and this which marked the whole political character disclosed itself likewise in their Poetry—we find no remnants of [f 426] any poem which can be said to have a beginning a middle and an end and in which all the parts are means to some one great end with a number of successive highly interesting narrations following each other in the order of time and going to one purpose—it is in truth the same character which afterwards appeared and has given rise to the couplet verse which is precisely what I mean—if we take for instance the writings of Dryden or Ben Jonsons poems*ᵐ* you will find a series of distinct couplets all upon the same subject but each having a wholeness of itself—I have explained this because it is the character of the language marked in a smaller number of cases and the inflexes and the manifest tendency to lose this which it possessed compared with the interwoven sentences of the Romans and Greeks which doubtless permitted them a much more logical position of words according to the order of thought than a language where the grammatical must ever over rule [f 427] that position in which the mind itself brings forward the conceptions

I have made this preface for the purpose of explaining myself and being intelligible when I say that the Scholastic philosophy had two great purposes—first it introduced into all the languages of Europe as far as the lan-

---

ᵐ "Jonsons poems" written partly over erasure

788

guages were susceptible of it the power and force of Greek and Roman connexion—it forever precluded our falling—or at least it should seem to have
promised so to do—to have precluded our falling into the mere aphorism
style of the Oriental nations in which thought is heaped upon thought by
simple words of aggregation—in truth what our Schoolmen had so well labored to prepare and what the great Writers before our revolution had so
admirably elaborated and exemplified the writers since then have seemed
to take equal pains to destroy—to remove as an offence all the marks of
connexion to make [f 428] each sentence an independent one easily indeed
understood but still more easily forgotten and as these men have shewn an
utter contempt in general for whatever is ancestorial and conceived themselves to have been so abundantly wise that till some hundred years ago no
light was in the world at all it may be of some service to inform them that
this is the only mark they bear of their great Gothic Ancestors by returning
to that which it was before it had ingrafted upon it all of which it was capable—this was the first step—the second was the bringing into clear view
what in all ages clearly or obscurely conceived works in the mind the true
engines of all speculation expressed in a controversy between the Nominalists and the Realists those who conceived . . . or those terms by which
we . . . such connexions as not applicable to nature at all but mere parts of
logic and those who contended that those words appertain to certain forms
of the mind [f 429] and that those forms were truly correspondent to connexions in nature so that the mind was to be conceived of as one pole of a
line the other pole of which was in nature—the contemplative and the contemplated being as it were the positive and the negative points of the magnetic line—As soon as it had answered these purposes as soon as it had had
such an impulse given to it that it was sure to move forward by its own im-
petus and by the additional force by the celebrity the rank and influence
which it was sure to confer on the men who excelled and became eminent
in the exercise providence introduced an antidote which was to grow as the
Scholastic philosophy was losing more and more its utility and finally to
take its place when it was superannuated

    This was the other part of the Gothic mind—the inward the shaking
the Romantic character in short the genius but genius marked according
to its birthplace for it grew in rude forests amid [f 430] the inclemencies
of outward nature where man saw nothing around him but what must owe
its charms mainly to the imaginary powers with which it was surveyed—
there nothing outward marked the hands of man woods rocks and streams
huge morasses nothing wore[n] externally the face of human intellect and

---

[n] "wore" altered from another word, perhaps "more"

yet man cannot look but intellect must be either found or placed—there arose therefore among the Gothic nations a superstition or a worship of fire—imagine then that of images they had nothing like those of the Greeks they had nothing but what was to be inward and sullenly refuse to disclose itself otherwise than in terrors—so powerful was this held so strongly did the inwardness of the Gothic nature work that the first great children of genius called no doubt as by a foreign light and awaked from slumber yet with all the passionate admiration with all the gratitude that was felt for the light that had awoke them never could in the least degree approach near to the Centre—they believed [f 431] themselves imitators—they professed to follow the ancients as guides—they sometimes actually copied but nature maintained her rights and instead of the Copyists of Homer or of Virgil we have imitators indeed in Dante and Ariosto but imitators only as nature imitates herself when the same energies are excited under other circumstances and on different materials through which she is to diffuse her creative and shaping mind

Dante may be considered as a sort of Staple connecting two chains the Metaphysics and the Mysticism of the Poetic side of the Scholastic Realists whom he held in high honor and on the other side the first link of the Chain of the men of genius—It was fortunate and in all things we may trace the chain of events which it is perhaps scarcely religious to call by the name of fortunate that realism should then have been in its pride of triumph—it was so admirably adapted to give a sort of feeling and emotion and [f 432] passion to the energies in nature and at the same time connected the true form of the Scholastic Philosophy with that craving after something more substantial which soon characterized the Alchemists and the wonder workers of the same time and as admirably adapted to the occasions of mankind does this appear that nominalism under Occum should rally its forces when erudition was growing pedantry and platonism which had performed its functions was degenerating into sickly dreams—the great Patrick^o great in every respect because he was likewise eminently good and desirable even in the very height of the Scholastic Philosophy was its determined enemy—he had in truth too much of ⟨inward reality too much of⟩ tenderness too much of interest for his human brethren to find any gratification in forms of any sort in mere forms the same causes that deterred him from the law because he thought that the mere application of [f 433] universals or of general rules as drawing away the mind from that which in mind in each thing makes it itself and such as no other can be appears to have made him un-

^o "Petrarch" written in pencil above "Patrick"

just to the Schoolmen and called forward from him declamations against their spread as one of the greatest evils and a sorer barbarism under the name of philosophy than had oppressed mankind in the ages before from mere simple ignorance—in short among Patrick's prose works and especially his letters you will find all the abuse of the Schoolmen which it has been fashionable since the Reformation to heap upon them but far more pardonable was it in Patrick compared with those of later times for it is not given to man to be wholly just to his contemporaries for he is to be one in the scheme—to be warm and interested not merely to see and weigh what the beauties are or what the defects but when he feels the defect warmly to join towards its removal and when he feels an excellence to allay the flatteries with it—but who that lives in [f 434] an age which labors under the very contrary disease to that of the Scholastic age who lives in an age when thinking becomes an actual toil and when if you attempt to put three sentences together in connexion you are asked for facts though none that I have been able to ascertain knew what the meaning of the word fact is or how it is possible for a man to know how out of an immense number of circumstances that one is the fact unless he had asked himself simply first for what he was looking

A . . . the most interesting of the great men who followed Patrick was his own Scholar on the Reveniam his family name seems to have been . . . born about the year 1342 of very poor parents who yet however seized with the enthusiasm which was then beginning to spread over Christendom had sent him to the celebrated . . . who introduced him to Patrick then an old man—Patrick reared him [f 435] and treated him as a Child and perhaps there does not exist in all Biography any thing more interesting displaying more admirable traits on one part or more natural ones on the other than the letters of Patrick concerning of this John of Revenna—his first letter written to his friends in which he gives an account that a fond Father would give of a boy of twelve or thirteen he could not be much older of his tracing his distress when he was restless—while on the other the account of his vexations—the young man who had been growing restless for a time at length addressed his benefactor—I cannot stop any longer I must go away and why—first there was one excuse—he was weary of transcribing Manuscripts—but I told you when you had written so much to leave it off for a year—no he must go—but why? something or other till at last wearied by Patricks questions and kindness he declared he knew not what it was but that he was consumed with a restless wish to be moving and accordingly Patrick after having [f 436] in vain endeavored to detain him and though the young man in his passions had even behaved most ungratefully to him wounded him by words and though Patrick writes to his Father in a passion he the next day sends another letter for fear the former should have produced a bad effect in which he says—"it cannot be very wrong or I should not love him so much" and at length when he went away the affectionate recommendation that followed him all these are the happy introduction of the life and after works of a man who left no written works but who left works of an invaluable price for under him were produced almost directly or indirectly the great Scholars and Literary characters . . . in short there was scarcely a great man that had not received a part of his education from John of Revenna or had not been directly and immediately his scholars—in consequence of the zeal for knowledge which [f 437] the reputation of Patrick and the unwearied exertions of his young scholar had diffused Emmanuel . . . came from Constantinople and settled in Italy shortly afterwards followed . . . Quintilian . . . found under an old ruin a manuscript of Cicero which for a time was not legible till . . . with copies of the . . . and now in Scholastic philosophy every thing was forgotten among the young men—it was ~~they~~ an effort who could write most eloquently who could convey their thoughts most eloquently—who in short could feel most like a Roman

Still though this checked and perhaps happily checked the excess of a speculative turn it could not wholly suppress it—but philosophy assumed a form suited to the occasion and under the Patronage of the great . . . of Florence and his Sons afterwards there arose classical [f 438] philosophers passionate admirers of Plato but not of Plato . . . In treating of the Eclectic laws there was one point which I did not notice but which it is of importance that we should now attend to—Plotinus wrote against . . . Porphyry Iamblicus . . . wrote against the Christians in general but we shall entertain a very false notion if we suppose these men contended at all in the Spirit in which the Epicurean and . . . did—no in the present day these philosophers would have formed a Sect amongst us of Christians—throughout their works they speak with the highest reverence of our Lord—it never occurs to them to doubt much less to deny any of the Miracles whatever the Christians believed in point of history they believed—His Miraculous birth His Resurrection His ascension—wherein did they differ—first of all in certain points of philosophy but those were trifling however important they might appear to them—but [f 439] secondly which was of great importance they said all this is true—we reverence Christ we place him among the highest of the Gods that have descended into the human form but you do wrong in appropriating and confining this Pythagoras and Polonius were each such another—this constituted them enemies of Christianity if they were so which should teach us to look not only at what a man disbelieves but what he believes beyond or beside it for on that the nature of his belief and disbelief must depend—This was however very fascinating especially as the Eclectic philosophy was connected with the boldest purposes for the extension of the human powers for conceive what are the strongest passions of the human mind—one is the love of knowledge when it is awakened for its own sake the other is the love of power which as it is exercised as that power must be exercised in every moment for the preservation of our lives must necessarily become the [f 440] strongest and need most the discipline of the Moral law—Now the Platonic philosophy in its degenerate form after Plotinus combined both there was . . . allowed of no boundary to the human intellect—it allowed indeed most fully that many were the truths which could not be arrived at either by the senses or by the understanding or even by the reason as far as it was human but what then—there were mysteries—powers higher than those means by which they could be united positively with the Deity and live in him and in that state partake at once of his Omniscience and Omnipresence and these too were to be learned—the discipline indeed was severe the time required in the penances and the watchfulness were perfectly like those of . . . or the Brahmins but still the wished for results attached finally Plotinus we are told by Porphyry enjoyed it three times and Porphyry when sixty eight years old enjoyed it for the first time [f 441] by what faculties he came to remember this which was not only above the senses and the understanding but even above the reason or by what words or by what possible means he could have communicated this even to himself he has not been so kind as to inform us—few however must be so ambitious as to expect this last consolation but various were the seat of preferment—it was at least common for a philosopher to become connected with a Dæmon the . . . or higher air or form an intimacy with a . . . or in short with the innumerable spirits above us it was hard if he could not find a Spirit with whom he could melt like two dew drops and then becoming refreshed like a Philosopher to tell wonderful things of himself but this was still knowledge and contained within the mind and here Plotinus appears to have stopped for he certainly upon the subject of astrology reasons like a sound philosopher and speaks of magic with detestation confining himself to natural magic which appears to [f 442] be nothing more than a want of experimental philosophy

This however was of short continuance for already in the successor of Plotinus—in Porphyry who was Plotinus's immediate successor Magic is highly spoken of and the means by which it is performed and in short stories not only as gross as those which we find in our common books of magic but for the greater part they are the very same—for it is with su-

perstitious stories as it is with jokes they have a wonderful metamorphosis you may trace them in China in India in Persia—among the ancient
Greeks. You may take a story or joke and find it successively in almost
all the Countries of the civilized world—of course in each Country in its
own drapery—the same circumstances belonging to it and with the same
individual soul and I believe an edition might be given of Joe Miller or
any other Jest book that would deserve to be called the most learned book
in the World if a man were to trace each story [f 443] back to the different Writers or Heros or men of genius to whom age after age it was attributed—some have supposed it was given by some Oracle—certain
Commentators I believe are persuaded of it for the first rule I have observed in Notes on Milton and others is to take for granted that no man
had ever a thought originate in his own mind—in consequence of which
if there is any thing in a book like it before it was certainly taken from
that—and you may go on particularly by their likenesses to the time of
the Deluge and at last it amounts to this that no man had a thought but
some one found it and it has gone down as a heir loom which one man is
lucky enough to get and then another—it struck me with astonishment
when I found how devoid of power and thought our Milton is—any thing
equal to Paradise lost could not be his for there was a man who made a
poem upon it in Italy consequently this poem is the true [f 444] origin of
the Paradise Lost and so on—with regard to all the detail it is a clear point
and really with regard to certain wit and to certain stories it may be admitted without any of the ludicrous consequences that follow when applied to the production of genius

The connexion however between Philosophy and Magic did not flour-
ish so well in Italy—it met with two mighty oppositions—first of all the
passionate love for poetry whatever was chearful and whatever was elegant and next the Inquisition and the watchful eye of the Hierarchy but it
produced another effect most remarkable and which convinces us how
compleatly necessary the Reformation was not merely for the reform but
for the church from which the schism was made—there was scarcely a
man of learning in Italy at that time who was believed to be seriously a
Christian—some were open infidels that is as open as they dared to be
and in truth if we read their writings we find that before the Reformation
there being little jealousy [f 445] excited they made no great disguise of
it but the greater number were mystical Infidels of the school of Proclus
who felt the common notions of the schools and Christianity too vulgar
and in the horror they felt for superstition passed into the opposite extreme of visionary enthusiasm—it was in the North—in Germany and in
England that the Magic the Alchemistic want and desire to exercise

power by obscure means were principally noticed and this arose from that great desire for reality which marks the northern nations arising no doubt in part out of their climate but far more I am persuaded out of their institutions—nay however much it may be deemed a prejudice I would say likewise out of the original stock—the same thing which makes us domestic which makes us retire from one circle into a narrower and yet into a narrower as if the [f 446] mind within required a still stronger and a still stronger grasp to balance itself—This was shewn in the men who first led to the Reformation—it was shewn in Germany by the Bohemians who believed in the Sacrament of the cup which the Church had withheld[p] ⟨from Laymen why should it be withheld⟩ the church had encouraged a belief that it almost approached to Magic and it is curious that the fighting for a superstition that degraded the holy institution for which the controversy was should have led[q] the way to the Reformation of religion from that and from all its other true deformities

In Germany the first man and with the exception of Huss and Wickliffe and others who might be said to be the more distinct heralds of the Reformation Ritling[r] deserves to be mentioned as better known by his Latin name Caveneo now with the greatest zeal for the restoration of letters in general with a courage and an address exerted against the great enemies of all [f 447] knowledge but at the same time the main supports of the Roman hierarchy the mendicant orders—Ritling distinguished himself first by a service which will remain and which will entitle him to gratitude when all his follies and all his weaknesses will be forgotten he introduced the Hebrew Scriptures and the study of them—he did more we may say he prevented the destruction of them for upon the first dawning of Hebrew literature so great was the alarm taken by the ignorant clergy that they had begun an Inquisition among the Jews accompanied with every species of cruelty for the purpose of discovering the Hebrew manuscripts and committing them to the flames Ritling by means of the influence he had with the Emperor and by that extended correspondence which he enjoyed as an eminent Literati secured both the Jews and the Oracles of which then they had the keeping but in the commune which he had naturally with the more learned of the Jews he acquired a knowledge of the Cabala and mixed his recommendations of the [f 448] pure words of God with the most extravagant encomiums on this most sublime of philosophy

What the origin of the Cabala was I cannot pretend to tell you precisely—I know it is commonly said that it began from the 10th Century

---

[p] "withheld" written partly over erasure   [q] "have led" written partly over erasure
[r] "Reuchlin" written in pencil above "Ritling"

or even later in the middle ages—this appears to me utterly unlikely—at least I find the references to it ⟨so strong⟩ in the works of the first century—I find the same doctrines so plainly marked even in Philo Judices[s] in works which are supposed to be before the birth of our Lord that I am inclined rather to think that its origin is to be sought for about the same time that the wisdom of Solomon in our Apocrypha was written which likewise contains passages strongly cabalistical—whatever its origin was its doctrines were nearly the same as the lower Platonists a species of Pantheism was taught in a very wild form indeed but which when reduced to common sense appears to be nothing more than this that they made no essential distinction between God and his Creation [f 449] but that of the manifested and the manifestation—the Deity considered in himself and in his own essential nature they represented as three in one but the Deity as manifested—as expanding least ways they represented as the seven Spirits or the Seven Zephyrs—the last which was to be the Messiah or the Shekinah was to be the same as the second person of the Triade and to be in the Shekinah a concentration of all the Seven Spirits of the manifestation a doctrine which must have been very early indeed in the Church because we find a clear reference to it in the beginning of Apocalypse and this I confess is among my chief reasons for acceding to the Cabala a much greater degree of antiquity than is commonly done for I ~~cannot reconcile it with common sense for~~ I cannot reconcile it with common sense that the Jews who are admitted to be the inventors of this doctrine should have made a doctrine in every respect shadowing out the mysteries of Christianity [f 450] and those very mysteries which after the first conversion—which after the Apostolic times they made the stumbling ⟨block and the cause of the obstinate refusal⟩ refusal to receive our Lord it seems to me therefore that the Cabala must have a traditionary philosophy among them the likeness of which to Christianity will not be wonderful to any man who has studied the fragments of Heraclitus or believes these were derived from the mysteries that they were founded by the fanatics and that they produced it as corrupt productions from the Patriarchal religion but the Cabala likewise possessed certain combinations of sounds figures and numbers by which external nature was to be controlled and governed and this too Ritling seriously contended for and practised or at least sought for as far as he could the means of practising

Next to Ritling comes Henry Cornelius Agrippa not to be compared in interest with him but his whole life is so characteristic of the philosophy and temper of his age [f 451] as well as so interesting from his . . . he can-

---

[s] "æus" written in pencil above end of "Judices"

not be passed without some notice although almost a Century and a half had passed since the first great revival of letters yet still the number of Writers especially in the north of Europe was exceedingly small—in truth every Country had its own dark[t] age and the dark age was far lighter than that of later times even as England had its dark age when Italy was enjoying a full light—it had awakened too suddenly—had knowledge too wide for its natural effects—in short you must draw a picture full of incongruities to represent fairly the state of things in Europe about the time of the Reformation—you must take genius in all its splendor in individuals—Magnificent structures by bodies and a spirit of zeal and art throughout Society—of which we have since had but feeble or at least but morbid imitations—but we must combine with it barbarism in all the detail of social life and so gross and ignorant in the lower order ⟨as to infect the higher by rendering the lower order⟩ susceptible of so many delusions that evidence forced men [f 452] into the belief of the impossible whilst it was not considered of how little weight evidence ought to be except of him who is capable of examining and recording the circumstances under which the events had taken place—I know no other way to account for the serious solemn and minutely established details of extraordinary facts which you find not in the works of weak men or fanatics but in the writings of the greatest Scholars of the then age it seemed to be and any man who has looked into . . . law or those who have a character to maintain—it seems as if it were a peculiar species of madness as if the intense desire of power seizing hold of the mind and becoming a habit in it had given such an unnatural vividness to certain notions as to impress a belief that they had occurred as events—some of those however appear to have been what is its natural connexion mere imposture and this calls me to the character of one of the most extraordinary men that ever lived Henry Cornelius Agrippa[u]—

[f 453]   He was born at . . . at Cologne he was educated—he blended the study of the Romish Law with religion and in his first works before he was fourteen he discovered his attachment to Magic and the Occult Sciences—Soon after he removed to . . . and there he formed a Secret Society and I believe it is the first that is to be found of the many many[v] of them the laugh of young men who wished to act the Roman but some which had more serious objects as those of the Bavarian Illuminati but it is of still more interest in a moral point of view—for Agrippa believed

---

[t] "dark" seems written over erasure

[u] "Agrippa" written over erasure

[v] Last three letters of first "many" are crowded in but over-run margin; original transcription may have been "of them—many"

earnestly in the possibility of Magical arts he had persuaded himself he had produced some extraordinary effects—he sought to spread this faith with others—he erected a secret society and one of the first articles of it was that they were to pretend to do these things—to do it by conspiracy and above all things to bring great men under the belief that they would arrive at some extraordinary power but that they must [f 454] pass through all the mysteries . . . This by the letters found after his death was the plan he laid down while he was a firm believer that he should actually arrive at those powers which were to reward[w] the labors of the first greater degree—This is a lesson full of instruction indeed to shew that when the mind yearns after power by any other mode than that appointed by our Maker[x] it begins from secret deception to pass into direct and intentional imposture till the greatest and the wholesomest powers of the mind are sacrificed to the low ambition and the vile tricks of a mere Conjurer—now such was the Case with Henry Cornelius Agrippa it is not easy to conceive what that man might not have promised himself would he have preferred common sense to cunning—would he have taken the shorter way of becoming respectable instead of playing the Knave and running round that long and weary way of playing the fool—he possessed genius as a Poet—[f 455] he had uncommon acuteness as a Philosopher his remarks wherever they occur upon the powers of the human mind are wonderfully applied and are more marked even by good sense than those of his contemporaries—not only this but as a man in active life he was an excellent and commanding Statesman an admirable officer—in the different services in which he fought he distinguished himself greatly—he was created a Knight on the field and had all that could have raised him to all the honorable objects of human ambition—but what was that compared with the ambition of frightening Emperors and making them believe that you could command all the inanimate objects around them—Agrippa had fully persuaded himself that he should be able to bring over the Emperor himself and at the same time the King of France whom he calls Magnus Iovis the great Jupiter to become members of his secret Societies and submit to be placed in a lower class—in consequence of this the King wished [f 456] to have proof—one of the secret Society by the name of . . . had been entrusted with a Fortress in the Pyrenees—he behaved so cruelly to the Boors about it that they had risen and taken the fortress—it was by nature inaccessible and the King proposed to Agrippa[y] that he should win that fortress—he convinced he could not do it as it was abundantly supplied and the neighbours were friendly to the

---

[w] "reward" written partly over erasure   [x] Pencilling in right-hand margin erased
[y] "Agrippa" altered from "agrippa"

Cause—Agrippa was unwilling he was about to run away but at length ambition and that confused state of mind in which extreme anxiety a man will think and wish on a thing till at length he conjures up a belief that he can attain it—in such a state Agrippa[z] undertook the enterprize and strange to say he succeeded in what way he succeeded no man knows and it was his interest at the time to keep it concealed—he did however take possession of this fortress and in ⟨the⟩ belief of the Boors by secret arts— they described themselves as being entirely overpowered by Magic and by this diabolical Wizard by [f 457] collusion with evil spirits the poor Boors were delivered up to Massacre—Agrippa shocked and heart sick—conscience began to torment him and in the meantime news came that the party who were coming to relieve him had been seized by the Boors his Friend put to death and in short that it was impossible he could remain where he was for three days he employed a neighbouring Abbott to make peace with the Boors—they refused unless the Conjurer was given up to them still he discovered there was one passage to the Abbey but there was a lake to pass over which it was impossible to pass but by means of the Abbott sending a boat or skiff there and here we know the Magic for Agrippa informs a friend of it in a letter—he took a peasant[a] boy and by means of various herbs produced sores like the leprosy he made him a cripple and sent him back again . . . the Abbott assisted Agrippa with a boat and [f 458] he escaped but nothing would persuade him to go back to the King of France he was afraid that the King as his success was still ambiguous would set him on some other expedition and accordingly he went into Spain and Italy everywhere extending this secret Society at length he came to England where he was for a time eminently successful and as he was connecting what was good with evil studied under Colet the founder of Saint Pauls School and he declares he learned more under him of true sober theological knowledge than he knew before and yet during this time he was actively employed . . . his greater business was his founding this secret Society and connecting it with his Brothers throughout Europe it would be endless to follow this man through all his adventures his poverty his dogs and Cats that were his familiars but which he treats as the wretched means by which he was obliged to get his bread at times till at length he [f 459] wrote his recantation and he declares that he had found magic in the ordinary sense of the word to be but delusion that though he had made a great deal of money by gold making at one time he began to despair of any gold ever being

---

[z] "Agrippa" altered from "agrippa"
[a] "by" erased between "peasant" and "boy", presumably a temporary mistranscription of shorthand for "boy"

made but by cheating—by the pretence of it still he contends there is a natural magic and this natural magic—he does not merely say it would be called natural magic—if a Peasant puts his hand upon an air pump . . . no, he seems to have entertained a notion as if from the earliest times experimental Sciences were divided into two parts the one common and communicable to the whole the other essenteric, as it were or . . . to the prepared Student—the former was Mechanics . . . as what we commonly call mechanics—though he says Mechanics itself must necessarily suppose something as the ground as the universal Agent which is not mechanical but he contends besides this there is an art by [f 460] which power is communicated immediately and from the references people make to . . . and others it seems probable he would consider Electricity as one of those Magical arts and the arguments he adduced for supposing this are very strong to us now for if you remember the circumstance of Doctor Franklin calling down the lightening from Heaven and afterwards a Russian . . . attempting it and being struck dead it is remarkable that the two Priests . . . who had taught . . . that light . . . as to . . . to intreat down the lightening when it is mentioned as Pliny has said by historians of gravest name that there were particular spots with . . . and so on which at times with many religious ceremonies and rites the lightning had been brought down and this not only in Rome but in Tuscany and he assigns a reason for it that . . . their King was a Priest and that . . . was likewise Sacerdotally educated and when we find Talesis . . . imitating it we are told [f 461] of the ceremonies of . . . but mistaking them he irritated the God and though he brought down the lightening was struck dead with it the circumstance is a most particular coincidence but still more though not with regard to Electricity appear the other facts referred to and of which the Greek writers are full I allude to the Sleeps in the Temple of . . . and . . . and other Deities but more especially those of Egyptian and Phœnician origin—we find in the Greek historians of the Empire that it was habitual where persons could afford it to travel to those Temples where they prevailed on the Priests to throw them into a charmed sleep where they prescribed medicines for themselves and the God appeared to them and it was so common that I think in our present[b] records at least five of the Emperors are mentioned as having gone into the East to be thrown into these Magic sleeps and to utter Oracles in the Temple of . . . It is impossible to read [f 462] this with the minute accounts to be collected some from one and some from another whether true or not whether there is any physical agent which still remains as Galvanism did till a century ago yet

---

[b] "our present" seems written partly over erasure

undiscovered makes no difference at all in the argument but I think it is possible and most probable most highly probable . . .^{c} was known to the ~~the~~ Priests in Egypt—that it was conveyed by tradition to the latest period of the Greek Empire—we find it manifestly spoken of in . . . and in Piedmont it is mentioned . . . and it may be traced if I mistake not from the very earliest of times to the present day and this I mention as one of the characteristics of that age and as one of the modes by which philosophy through magic gradually passed into experimental Science and gave way finally itself to materialism—But a glorious period which has^d left seeds that cannot perish [f 463] took place under the first operation of these Chaotic causes—the trumpet in the revolution was blown and prepared by whatever was great and excellent and with it no doubt even the vices and the follies of mankind were forced into the same services

Perhaps the man to whom the Revolution owes the most may be said to be . . . if we speak of an immediate agent or Erasmus if we speak of one who might be called its Pioneer I have long ago given a comparison of Erasmus with a great man of the last generation If we listen I observe to a symphony of Cimarosa the present strain still seems not only to recall but almost to renew some past movement and present the same— each present movement bringing back as it were and embodying the spirit of some melody that had gone before—anticipates and seems sometimes [f 464] trying to overtake something that is to come and the musician has reached the summit of his art when having thus modified the present with the past he at the same time weds the past in the present to some prepared and corresponsive future—The auditors thoughts and feelings move under the same influence retrospection blends with anticipation and hope and memory (a female Janus) become one power with a double aspect A Similar effect the reader may produce for himself in the pages of history if he will be content called to substitute an intellectual complacency for pleasurable sensation—The events and characters of one sage^e like the strains in Music recal those of another and the variety by which each is individualized not only gives a charm and poignancy to the resemblance but likewise renders the whole more intelligible—It is not from identity of opinions or similarity of events and outward actions that a real resemblance in the radical character can be deduced on the [f 465] contrary men of great and stirring powers who are destined to mould the age in which they are born must first mould themselves upon it—Mahomet born twelve Centuries later and in the heart of Europe would not have been a false prophet—nor would a false prophet of the present generation have

^{c} "that Mesmerism" inserted into space in pencil $\quad$ ^{d} "has" written over erasure
^{e} "sage" altered in pencil to "age"

been a Mahomet in the sixth Century—I have myself therefore derived the deepest interest from a comparison of men whose characters at the first view appear widely dissimilar who yet have produced similar effects on their different ages and this by the exertion of powers which one examination will be found far more alike ~~are more~~ than the altered drapery and costume would have led us to suspect—Of the heirs of fame few are more respected by me though for very different qualities than Erasmus and Luther scarcely anyone has a larger share of my aversion than Voltaire and even of the better hearted Rosseau I was never more than a very luke warm [f 466] admirer[f]—I should perhaps too rudely affront the general opinion if I avowed my whole creed concerning the proportions of real talent between the two . . . of revealed religion now neglected as obsolete and the two modern conspirators against its authority who are still the Alpha and Omega of Continental genius yet I can never hear these two names mentioned without recalling those of our great Reformers— Those who are familiar with the works of Erasmus and we know the influence of his wit as the pioneer of the Reformation and we likewise know that by his wit aided by the vast variety of knowledge communicated in his works he had won over by anticipation so large a part of the polite and lettered world to the protestant party will be at no loss in discovering the intended Counterpart in the life and writings of the Veteran Frenchman they will see indeed that the knowledge of Erasmus was solid through [f 467] its whole extent and that of Voltaire extensive at a cheap rate by its superficiality—that the wit of the one is always bottomed on sound sense peoples and enriches the mind of the reader with an endless variety of distinct images and living interests and that his broadest laughter is very well translatable into grave and weighty truth while the wit of the Frenchman without imagery without character and without that pathos which gives the magic charm to genuine humour consists when it is most perfect in happy turns of phrase but far too often in fantastic incidents outrages of the pure imagination and the poor low trick of combining the ridiculous with the venerable where he who does not laugh abhors—Neither will they have forgotten that the object of Erasmus was to drive the thieves and mummers out of the temple while the other was [g]propelling a worse Banditti first to profane and pillage and ultimately[h] to raze it yet not [f 468] the less will they perceive that the effects remain parralel the circumstances analogous and the instruments the same in each case the effects extended over Europe were attested and augmented by the praise and patronage of Thrones and Dignities and are not to be explained but

---

[f] Catchword "ad" on f 465 followed by "admirer" on f 466
[g-h] Passage is written over erasure

by extraordinary industry and a life of literature in both instances the circumstances were supplied by an age of hopes and promises—the age of
Erasmus restless from the first vernal influences of real knowledge that
of Voltaire from the hectic of imagined superiority in the voluminous
works of both the instruments employed are chiefly those of wit and amu-
sive erudition and alike in both the errors and evils (real or imputed) in
religion and politics are the objects of the battery but here we must stop
the two men were essentially different exchanged mutually their dates of
spheres [f 469] of action yet Voltaire had he been tenfold a Voltaire could
not have made up an Erasmus and Erasmus must have emptied himself
of half his greatness and all his goodness to have become a Voltaire—
Here at least there is some likeness apparent but I might well be asked
what likeness I could find between the gigantic Luther and the sickly
dreamer of love dreams and the . . . dreams of the Misanthrope Rousseau
if I were to take them without reference to the time in which they lived I
should make such a comparison as the honest Welchman does in Henry
the fifth when he compares his Monarch to Alexander the Great but*i* there
are many points very strikingly alike Erasmus had prepared the way for
Luther by wit by polite letters by gentle raillery and Voltaire had won
over to the evil cause of infidelity all that could be won by frivolity and
superficial [f 470] knowledge but still nothing great either for good or for
evil or for evil or for good can ever be done without earnestness a Man
must employ the whole of his being to do aught effectually

Now this did Rousseau he came forward with a fulness of heart apparently he possessed naturally great sensibilities he applied these to the
sufferings of his fellow creatures he was unwilling to find the Causes
where alone they could be found in the Corruptions of our nature in the
first instance and looked for it therefore wholly in artificial institutions
and he died luckily for himself before he had seen a tenth part of the miserable effects of his doctrines—Luther with a far stronger mind but with
great sensibility and with a very hypochondraical temperament felt the
same ardour against oppression*j* as Rosseau had done indeed nothing can
be conceived more violent or more disres[f 471]pectful than Luthers first
writings just before the Peasants War had commenced—likewise he felt
no less superstition against superstitions and the difference between the
two men besides that of great genius and a heroic mind consisted in this
that Luther with all his enthusiasm and with all his natural heat of temper had still a something that balanced a something that kept him even
his full belief in the inspiration of the sacred writings—a belief in which

---

i Erasure between "but" and "there"
j Final two letters of "oppression" crowded, possibly over erasure

he sympathized with all his fellow creatures upon whom he was to act it had first an effect in humiliating the mind and secondly a great effect in rendering it kindly—but Luther was still the man of his age or he could not have removed the mountains which he had to remove he had to overthrow the Scholastic philosophy and to substitute for it the word of God—he therefore was not and could not be carrying on a process of fine reasoning [f 472] bold eloquence—that which rather knocks down an objection than stands to question it was the very means by which he was to act—in short as I have somewhere observed Luther was one of the greatest Poets that ever lived but he was so possessed by his own genius that he acted poems not wrote them—his whole life in truth was one grand poem—think you that a man could have gone through what he did—have stood alone before assembled Diets—dared Sovereigns continued with his pen scourging a Pope here and a Monarch there and treating both of them as his inferiors when at the same time he was uttering a language to the very lowest of the low which as he says himself that every man that looked at the move of his mouth said this man is speaking language to me and I know its truth—think you that a man could have done this with the cool rational language of what is now called philosophy [f 473] or philosophic . . . no—Luthers mistakes might have been superfluous but the spirit which made them inevitable was not superfluous—he believed himself most fully to be at the head of an army of the faithful whom he was to provide with weapons—with sword and shield and spear out of the Spiritual Armory of the Bible and he not only believed that the powers of the world were armed against him but that the powers of the air were leagued against him and as it was he felt as completely as if he had been in a field of battle while wielding his pen and no Warrior ever wielded a sword with greater courage than Luther wrote writings which fell like rockets and set all on fire and . . . who alone can command the elements—If in some such times as these we suppose him as I have somewhere painted him in such a mode of mind "Methinks I see him sitting the heroic student in his chamber in the Warteburgh [f 474] with his midnight lamp before him seen by the traveller in the distant plain of Bischossroda as a Star on the mountain—below it lies the Hebrew bible open on which he gazes—his brow pressing on his palm brooding over some obscure text which he desires to make plain to the simple boor and to the humble artizan and to transfer its whole force into their own natural and living tongue . . . he counts the letters he calls up the roots of each separate word and questions them as the familiar spirits of an Oracle in vain thick darkness continues to cover it . . . this must be some temptation—disappointed disheartened enraged ceasing to think yet continuing his brain . . . [f 475] in this state what if for instance he should have imagined an evil spirit what if he should actually have hurled the inkstand at his Satanic Majesty which he employed in a better way and if he had left the black stone in the wall which they shew to all travellers—it only proves that Luther lived in an age in which almost every part of philosophy had been cultivated but that which should have been its Pioneer—that by which alone it can be effectually prevented from leading first into the visionary and the enthusiastic and then into the directly superstitious and Magical till finally it ends in imposture and conjuration I mean the analysis of the mind itself as acted upon by the senses and as again reacting upon them or what is appropriately called . . . was during the whole of the middle ages wholly I might say I scarcely recollect an exception—neglected—[f 476] the consequence of this was that the greatest men and the greatest merits were no securities in that age against weaknesses that would now disgrace the ignorant themselves and it is by appealing to such weaknesses that we are taught to take away our veneration from men but for whom we should have been utterly unable even to have known that those were weaknesses but on the other hand as . . . is a necessary preparative for philosophy and as without it we have yet to arrive at the very portal and can never be secure whether we have not mistaken a post for the real^k abode that still is not philosophy nor yet is it a substitute for the same and it is in this as throughout the whole history of men he goes to two extremes before he can determine the medium . . . in the next place which begins with the time of Bacon dawned on man by Des Cartes it was carried to ⟨a⟩ great state of perfection as now it appeared to afford such [f 477] a world of information—it appeared to bring us into such a world of intimacy with our nature that men considered all was known—with a few words of connexion every thing was discovered—everything was solved—philosophy the whole wonderful world of man was to be learnt in half an hour and there was the . . . in a nutshell the consequence was a growing contempt of philosophy itself and finally for half a century . . . as Hobbes and others were avowed materialists and the other party took the predominant parts of materialism and tied them to the opposite philosophy and this passed very well he is as a sensible man I say . . . he tells you there are no truths but with the pious man—he has all the scriptures rightly but whether if one is true the other is false requires an effort of thinking which has hitherto become more and more unfashionable

Now in my next Lecture it will be my endeavor to shew the good

---

^k "real" written over now illegible letters

[f 478] and the evil of that state which was necessarily to introduce experimental philosophy which is introduced which has answered its end and[l] as I have shewn throughout these Lectures having done so begins to tell us so in an intelligible language in the evil it is now doing even by a reaction on the good effects which it produced on its former agency— This will form the subject of my next Lecture which will take in the philosophy of Lord Bacon as misunderstood and continued to the time of the Revolution taking in the counteractions by the . . . as the Counter Acts.—

---

[l] "and" written over erasure

LECTURE 11

[f 479]   Mr Coleridges Lecture[m]
                                            Monday 8th March 1819

At once the most complex and the most individual of creatures man taken
in the ideal of his humanity has been not inaptly called the Microcosm of
the world in compendium as the point to which all the lines converge from
the circumference of nature this applies to his sum of being to his powers collectively but we find him gifted as it were with a threefold mind—
the one belonging to him specifically—arising I mean necessarily out of
the peculiar mechanism of his nature and by this[n] he beholds all things
perspectively[o] from his relative position as man—the second in which
those views[p] are again modified—too often disturbed and falsified by his
particular constitution and position as this or that particular individual[q]
and the third which exists in all men prudentially[r] and in its germ though
it requires both effort from within and auspicious circum[f 480]stances
from without to evolve it into effect—By this third and highest power he
places himself on the same point as nature and contemplates all objects
himself included in their permanent and universal beings and relations
thus the Astronomer places himself in the centre of the system and looks
at all the planetary orbs as with the eye of the sun happy would it be for
us if we could at all times imitate him in his perceptions—in the intellectual or the political world—I mean to subordinate instead of
exclude—nature excludes nothing she takes up all still subjecting the
higher to the less so and ultimately subjecting all to the lower thus taken
up—but alas the contrary method exclusion instead of subordination this

----

[m] "Lect X" written above lozenge in pencil, probably in the hand of JHG

[n] "1 as man generically" written in pencil in right-hand margin, probably in the hand of
JHG

[o] First three letters of "perspectively" seem written over erasure

[p] "2 as this or that individual" written in pencil in right-hand margin, probably in the
hand of JHG

[q] "individual" written over erasure. "3. as universal" written in pencil in right-hand margin, probably in the hand of JHG

[r] "prudentially" altered in pencil to "potentially" in a different hand from previous pen-
cillings in this lect

and its result present the historian with his principal materials in whatever department his researches are directed—thus in our own past route we find a long period from the first Christian century to the sixth distinguished by a vain attempt to substitute philosophy for religion and following a more injurious endeavor to make religion supercede [f 481] philosophy[s]—As this is an error which is in truth never out of date because Religion is the interest of all men and among those who are incapable of the higher paths of intellect there are too many too proud to feel their capability I may be allowed to dwell awhile on this

What had been recorded by some individuals celebrated for purity and Christian virtues as useful discipline for himself as a part of ascetic piety was soon recommended as laws for all men and by degrees enforced as such and when it happened to meet with a congenial disposition and with warm sensibility it produced all the extravagancies which had deterred the sober from and invited the visionary to superstitions in various forms in all ages of the world I was struck in looking over some memorandum books with the character of . . . who may be fairly taken as the representative of that class of beings who would have religion without any mixture of intellect I was led to Theresa . . . by a letter of hers in [f 482] which she gives serious advice to her friend Lorenzo to keep Holy water . . . or any under whispers of temptation all which she assures him proceed from the pressure of some evil spirit felt by the soul though not evidenced by the senses—this led me to reflect on the importance of any act in strengthening and enlivening the will and I could not but think what if a mind like hers had attached any thing like a religious meaning to the Eolian harp as she did to the crucifix and the holy water what endless religious applications and accomodations all its irregular tones would produce—Her character will give the character of the whole class of those who from real piety opposed the revolution she was indeed framed by nature and favored by a very hot bed in a hot house of circumstances to become a mystic Saint of the first magnitude a mighty mother . . . first she was a woman secondly a Lady ten[f 483]derly and affectionately real—no dull no sobering or deadening reality of physical privation or pain to draw off her self consciousness of her inward goings on and . . . from her Brothers and Sisters and made a convert at eight years old of her favorite Brother next she was a Spanish Lady—reflect on the full import of that word . . . again accustomed to read the lives of Saints and Martyrs who had fought against or suffered under the Moors—At eight years old—she and her Brother were engaged to run away and go to Africa and obtain the Crown

---

[s] Catchword on f 480: "phi-"

of Martyrdom a subject which has occasioned . . . she regarded the Martyrs with more envy than admiration—they were ⟨so very⟩ unlucky*f* in getting an eternal Heaven at so easy a price—In the habit and that too without the will or knowledge of a superstitious fear of reading volumes of Romance and Chivalry to her Mother before the appearance of Don Quixotte and this all [f 484] night long to herself she had added all fancy could do by the . . . her familiar Servants—it seems she opened her fearful heart to a Spanish lover doubtless in the true . . . style and the giving audience . . . of flames and flaming conceits and anguishing despair— these seem to have been the mortal sins of which she bitterly accuses herself together with perhaps a few warm fancies and earthly loves but above all which she considers her greatest crime her aversion at fifteen years old to shut . . . to perceive how utterly unfit such a nursery . . . impassioned Theresa—what could come of it by dispelling . . . than this frame of such exquisite . . . and by the violence done to nature but her obstinate resolve to become a nun against her own wishes and against her fears arose [f 485] out of a resolve of duty finishing in a burning fever . . . from the frequent paroxysms . . . she had been reding to her over religious uncle books of the most gloomy kind of death hell and judgment which made a fearful . . . to give pleasure—she had affected to take a delight in reading them to him and thus combined an act of the will with the emotions otherwise proceeding . . . and, not so long and the . . . combine these causes only and you will see how almost impossible it was that a man so innocent and so susceptible of an imagination so lively by nature and so fever kindled by disease and its occasions . . . pleasurable approaches to bodily . . . [f 486] . . . ample explanation but what required the concurrence of many causes to produce in one by infection will spread over many till at last mankind become almost divided into knaves dupes—and visionaries and such must be the necessary effect of an attempt to disunite religion the highest object of our nature from the reason which is its highest faculty but even in this attempt which was too successful—if only instead of religion we put superstition it had in truth borrowed from a former attempt namely that of substituting philosophy for religion—it had borrowed its Theurgic right in one of their great purposes that is not to subdue nature and call forth spirits . . . but to control evil demons that were supposed to be for ever hovering round the poor Christian or like . . . were it only therefore for their endeavors to reunite reason and religion by a due subordination of the former to the latter we owe a tribute of respect to the Schoolmen from the thirteenth and fourteenth [f 487]

f "un" may have been added to "lucky" later

century—Then one general ill consequence of this was a direct application of the studies to the forms of logical thinking and because they were
treated as more than forms of thinking therefore sophistically—this is
most true and that the . . . to the great pioneers and chieftains of the Reformation yet is this to be carefully distinguished from the works themselves of the most eminent Schoolmen as Thomas Aquinas Scotus and
Occam whom those who have never read their works are ever the most
apt to accuse and speak with contempt of—I indeed am persuaded that
to the scholastic ⟨philosophy the Reformation is attributable far more than
to the revival of Classical⟩ literature except as far indeed as it produced
a general impulse and awakening over Society—nay even more to the
Scholastic philosophy than to the genial School of Platonism in Italy—

In the life of Baxter written by himself speaking of the great obligations he had to the Schoolmen he particularly instances this that ever afterwards he rendered [f 488] all indistinctness of means intolerable to him
it enforced on him—it introduced into his mind the necessity of tracing
every position as far back as either duty permitted or it was not demonstrably beyond further pursuit—but I think facts would bear me out in my
assertion that the platonism perhaps I might call it the Plotinism[u] rather
of the great Tuscan Scholars under the great . . . seems to have been un-
favorable to the Reformation strikingly so as compared with Scholastic
philosophy which was logical and analytic . . . to those of the Church it
was because there was not enough in it—they preferred paganism and
were more in danger of becoming Polytheists than Plotinists[v] and it is
well known that the greater part of them confessed to their intimates an
utter disbelief of christianity and disavowed all attachment to it except as
a substitute for the more malleable Jupiters and Junos who could [f 489]
mean anything the philosopher chose—even to this day the far greater
number of converts to the Romish Church among the educated class are
drawn into it by the attractive poetism in that church by that . . . that attracted our Cassio and the revived . . . an enthusiastic man—add too with
what favor—with what unmingled authorities the Cabalistic writings of
. . . all that was visionary and magical were received with Popes Cardinals and Bishops and that Luther and the first leaders of the Reformation
in Germany opposed the Schoolmen as the great supports of the Roman
religion—This seems to have been confined to that particular time and
did not extend into England on the Contrary our great divines found in
the writings of the Schoolmen the strongest testimonies in their favor—

---

[u] "Plotinism" written partly over erasure
[v] "Plotinists" may be written partly over erasure

There are three great instructive events in history the reflection on which perhaps more than on any other part of human history will repay us by the lessons of wisdom and caution which they imply—I mean the Reformation the Civil [f 490] War and the French Revolution—We are now come to that period of time in which we are to speak of the state in which the Reformation had left the minds of the educated class in Europe—as I have already spoken of two opposite extremes so we may divide philosophy before the time I am now speaking of and the period since then into two classes

During the whole of the middle ages and almost down to the time of the Restoration of Charles the second we discover everywhere metaphysics always acute and frequently profound but throughout estranged from not merely experimental physics generally but from its most intimate connective experimental Psychology while from the Restoration we have the opposite extreme namely experimental physics and a truly enlightened though empirical . . . Psychology estranged from and in utter contempt of all metaphysics from the former we are to deduce the explanation of a phenomena which must strike every student of the reigns of Henry 8 [f 491] Queen^w Elizabeth and Charles the first—I mean the astonishing credulity displayed by men of learning and in many respects of profound research I do not speak too strongly when I say it would be difficult to find any old woman who with a grave face would relate the stories to be found in Luther and the Divines of the English Church but especially among the Puritans combined with so much political wisdom so much Ecclesiastical research and so much genuine piety that a man must be thoughtless indeed who could find a recurrence of such facts and not seek for their explanation that explanation is undoubtedly to be found mainly in the cause I have now stated namely the absence of all psycological^x knowledge or that knowledge by which a man learns the reaction of his thoughts upon outward objects ⟨equally with the action of outward objects⟩ through his senses on his thoughts a large number of the tales which Luther tells of himself and which Baxter records both of himself and of others will be explained at once as occurring in those imperfect [f 492] states of sleep which are the true matrix—the true birth places of all the Ghosts and apparitions that history has recorded—we find for instance that in the story told of Dion and the Spirit the fury that he beheld at the end of the room or the appearance of the Spirit of Cæsar to Brutus or that which . . . has recorded of himself or which the great . . . has related all have happened under one set of circumstances—they were anx-

---

^{w} On f 490, "8" and catchword "Queen" written over erasure
^{x} "psycological" seems written partly over erasure

ious weary in cold and bodily discomfort the consequence of which is that the objects from without weakened in their influences on the senses and the sensations mean time from within being strongly excited the thoughts convert themselves into images the man believing himself to be awake precisely by the same law as our thoughts convert themselves into images the moment we fall asleep and which no less dreams no longer strike us with their wonderful nature from their frequency—from this [f 493] one circumstance—that all the well recorded stories took place under the same circumstances we could scarcely hesitate as to their solution and when a story has once had any ground of this kind and falls into a state of Society where the love of the miraculous is uppermost it will be indeed difficult in a very short time a month's time and the travel of twenty miles will convert it into a wonder which I will defy all the philosophers in the World to explain we are lucky therefore when we get hold of a well attested fact especially when we can discover it in a disguise when it has passed over many shapes and poured itself into the right one out of a multitude of mouths Fearful however was one of the results—it revived^y the notions of Witchcraft combined with all the horrors which the weaker and more powerful Religion could give to it—how it ought to humble us when we reflect that it was not in the dark ages that it was not in Countries struggling only out of barbarism but in the very morning in [f 494] the brightness of reviving letters in the age of a Kepler and a Galileo when every department of human intellect was felt and supported in its greatest splendour—it was then that the dreadful contagion of witchcraft and persecution of witches raged not in one Country but passed like a postillion through all Europe till it died in North America among the puritans of New England—no Country seems ⟨free⟩ from its ravages some of our greatest divines were the warmest advocates of these persecutions—nay boldly asserted that he who disbelieved in Witchcraft could not believe in a God—in one City alone in Germany in five years three thousand Women and Children for there were many children among them were put to death by public execution and the ⟨noble⟩ Jesuit who first raised himself against it or rather next to . . . did so on being questioned by a Prince how he came to have grey hairs answered it was the witches that had turned him grey—a smile being provoked he answered with a sigh so many hundreds [f 495] have I attended to the stake after confession with a certainty that every human being was perfectly innocent—I mention this as a proof that it is not by learning merely—no nor even by knowledge of experimental physics that the most disgraceful enthusiasm can

^{y} End of "revived" seems written over erasure

at all times be prevented—the sole prevention in reality is the recurrence to our highest philosophy—know thyself—study thy own nature but above all do no evil under the impression that you are serving God thereby

More innocent at least if equally wild was one of the two divisions of philosophy—namely the mystical which at the time I am now speaking of was so far useful that it was the antagonist to the excess of the former—It is very difficult to trace the origin of mysticism in Europe for this reason not that it is difficult to explain any visionary tendency of man a progressive animal while he is in the lower states of the progress but from an uncommon uniformity in likeness of the opinions which men wide[z] [f 496] apparently[a] even to craziness entertain from the mysteries of . . . founded shortly after Homer by the Phœnicians in all probability and which seem to have continued to the very remotest time of Platonism and to have initiated almost all the remaining pagan world—there were certainly Societies formed which under various names some known some unknown carried down these principles in a degraded form which in the time when they were doing their destined work had perhaps preserved Greece from falling into that barbarism which in all other Countries has been the effect of . . .[b] ⟨Polytheism⟩ Look to the names of the Gods worshipped at . . . and you will well understand what they are if you will conceive a system of Pantheism which describing air as a living power gave a history of its manifestations—the three lower Gods . . . with their . . . were the first three The Theologic Gods—that is those who were the [f 497] workings[c] of the Deity in manifesting itself in the formation of the World—they were otherwise called the magic Gods and it is very curious that the name may be traced in almost all the superstitions of the World wherever the Phœnicians or after them the Greeks had pierced— thus we have still the Ghebers or Fire worshippers in Persia we have the . . . or fairies of the . . . in the North of . . . and what is remarkable . . . Agricola in his account of the mines states there . . . as appearing in the same form in which the . . . are found on metals in . . . namely as . . . signifying the Deities that were bringing out disorder into order—To trace it somewhat further—another of their nature was the . . . a name still found in the vallies of Persia and from that the fairies of Europe the third name of . . . was bonæ Societæ the good members [f 498] which is still a

---

[z] Pencilled mark, probably a query concerning "wide", erased in right-hand margin
[a] Catchword on f 495: "appa"
[b] Space has words erased in it; pencilling may also have been erased in right-hand margin
[c] Catchword on f 496: "work"

name for the fairies in Scotland and in the north of England but their doctrines were still more resembling it is impossible to read Paracelsus and
compare it with what remains in Paley and elsewhere in the doctrines
taught in the mysteries without perceiving their identity A system of Pantheism it was but not irreligious—these powers had a certain dim personality attributed to them and if we could conceive them as Paley did
capable of being combined with true religious faith for Paley tells us that
the three first of their Divinities answered to the . . . or the danger represented the . . . or that which the yearning after being called forth and the
Pluto—he[d] then tells us that the next Trinity answers to the Jupiter to the
Apollo but according to others the Bacchus and to the Venus or universal love but the most mysterious consequence of which cannot be explained but by supposing some connexion the Phœnicians and the Jews—
[f 499] they introduce a wonderful character the . . . who we are told is
the first that calls out the lower Trinity which is the first says Paley becomes the lower and raises it into light—but this is the same with the second or with the higher or heavenly Trinity and as lights were still
celebrated—not as having appeared but as again appearing as the Infant
Bacchus who was to perform for man what as the Mercury he had performed for nature before he came into light and consciousness namely to
bring back the human soul again the rites of this infant Bacchus were
celebrated as the redeemer to come—so that they divided their religion
into seven Deities—we have already an eighth that was yet to appear—
the three first were the Theologic Deities representing in short the different processes of nature from an known real or merely potential[e] state—
from the Chaos in which in all Countries had originated nothing to the[f]
appearance of the Deity in his full manifestation as conscious will intellect and action and lastly as a redemptive process by which the spirit of
[f 500] man was to be called up again into its higher and heavenly state—
such were the doctrines taught by . . . but blended with a multitude of the
wildest chemical fancies which however as mysticism was not connected
with . . . was obliged to apply itself to external objects of nature but it was
applied in the same way and where a modern Chemist would talk of attractions and affinity and so forth . . . talked of . . . but it was in a belief
that every being however apparently inanimate had a life if it could be
called forth and that all along that was called but the law of likeness in
short the ground work of their philosophy was that the law of likeness

---

[d] "he" seems to have been written later over erasure; pencilled "he/" partly erased in
right-hand margin
[e] "potential" may be written over an erasure
[f] "the" written over longer erased word; short wavy line inserted after it to fill space

arising from what is called the polar principle that is that in order to manifest itself every power must appear in two opposites but these two opposites having a ground of identity were constantly striving to reunite but not being permitted to pass back to their original state which would amount to annihilation they pressed forward and [f 501] the two formed a third something and in this manner they traced in their . . . philosophy all the facts in nature and oftentimes with most wonderful and happy effects—such was the character of . . . a man who possessed a genius perhaps fully equal to that of any philosopher of more known name he was a Tutor to our famous Sir Philip Sydney and his friend Lord Bruce he came over into England and one of his exceedingly rare works which is called the . . . describes London as it then was in the time of our Elizabeth and with all the feelings which an Italian accustomed to the splendid feelings and lovely climate of Italy might be supposed to be impressed this man though a Pantheist was religious—he provoked the Priests he was seized at Rome and in the year 1601 was burnt for an atheist before his death he wrote a Latin Poem which I think in grandeur of moral has been rarely surpassed he says

"To . . . [f 502] or let them desire to be carried beyond the flaming walls of the World but we have been gifted with that genius that not blind to the light^g ⟨of the sun⟩ not deaf . . . and to the influences of the Gods we care not what the opinion of fools is concerning . . . diviners neither genius nor reason will condemn me nor the cultivated mind of true learning but ⟨the⟩ superciliousness . . . that salute the writer of a book from the threshold . . . let the sun proceed . . . moreover the species or the form of truth sought for found and manifested will bear me up and though no one understand me^h yet if with nature I am wise and under the Deity that verily is more than enough In this mode the brave man passed to his [f 503] death an Atheist and it would be well if all the Priests of Rome could have acquired his genuine piety according to his own apprehensions—his philosophy he has himself stated in these terms—there is throughout all nature an aptitude implanted that all things may be to each and to all—for everything that exists in sometime strives to be always everything that perceives any where strives to perceive everywhere and to become that universally whatever it has as an individual in short each part of nature contains in itself a germ of the omnipresence inasmuch as it still strives to be the whole and what it cannot possess at any one moment it attempts to possess by a perpetual succession of development—His notions are oftentimes highly grand—he considers himself as the Reviver of the

---

^{g} "light" seems written partly over erasure ^{h} "me" seems to have been corrected

Pythagorean system of the Universe and consequently opposed himself to Aristotle but he was the first I think of the moderns who asserted the immensity or infinity of the universe a praise that has been given falsely to Des Cartes he warmly defended and supported the Copernican system and many parts of his Chemistry [f 504] seemed wonderful in his age as anticipations of modern discoveries—he refers everything to invisible fluids or light—whatever is not light he says is a fluid but this fluid is capable of existing in fixation or as a fluid or a higher form it is capable of combining with light and then constitutes fire—he affirms the existence of an absolute vacuum which is necessary to motion but of which God is the sole plenitude and he especially explains gravity as being the necessary consequence of attraction and repulsion in a system which could exist only as far as there was a central body—The doctrine of astronomy which he teaches has been reviled even I believe of late years namely that the Sun owes its light and so forth entirely to its mass which again is reciprocally the cause and effect of its being the Central body and which is strange for situate in Italy he was not likely to observe the aurora Borealis—he states that every planet produces from itself necessarily an accumulation of inflamable matter which[i] floating in the higher regions will give at [f 505] times a light of its own and that the sun from the immense mass which it possesses beyond that of all the other planets collectively has its light by no novelty or difference of formation but solely by the production which is common to all matters of the air which he distinguishes particularly the oxygen and describes it with the greatest accuracy and the substance which he more properly[j] calls the Air—the Nitrogen—This he supposes thinning on still disposing of more and more light till at last in the higher regions it becomes light altogether and to this light in its different passages from a state of fixation upwards to its appearance as light properly he gives many of the most striking attributes of our Modern Electricity—His poetry will place him high—for there are few . . . of a very different character from Bruno was a man whose very name would excite a smile in many but I confess far from doing it in me for I have felt my own mind much[k] indebted to him and why indeed should I be ashamed of [f 506] my own Friend Jacob Behmen many indeed and gross were his delusions and such as furnished frequent occasion for the triumph of the learned over the poor ignorant Shoemaker who

---

[i] Last three letters of "inflamable" and "matter which" seem to have been inserted later, possibly partly over erasure

[j] "properly" written partly over erasure

[k] Apparent erasure in space between "mind" and "much"; pencilling (query sign or deletion sign) partly erased in right-hand margin

had dared think for himself but while we remember that those delusions were such as might be anticipated from his utter want of all intellectual discipline and from his ignorance of rational Psychology let it not be forgotten as I have noticed more than once that the latter defect he had in common with the most learned Theologians of his age—Neither with books nor with book learned men was he conversant—A meek[l] and shy quietist his intellectual powers were never stimulated into fev'rous energy by crowds of proselytes or by the ambition of Proselyting—He was an enthusiast in the strictest sense as not merely distinguished but as contradistinguished from a fanatic—Whoever is acquainted with the history of philosophy during the last two or three centuries cannot but admit that there [f 507] appears to have existed a sort of secret and tacit compact among the learned not to pass beyond a certain limit in speculative science—The privilege of free thought so highly extolled has at no time been held valid in actual practice except within this limit and not a single stride beyond it has ever been ventured without bringing obloquy on the transgressor The few men of genius among the learned class who actually did overstep this boundary as Bacon and others anxiously avoided the appearance of having ⟨so⟩ done—Therefore the true depth of science and the penetration to the inmost centre from which all the lines of knowledge diverge to their ever distant circumference was abandoned to the illiterate and the simple whom unstilled yearning and an original ebulliency of spirit had urged to the investigation of the indwelling and living ground of all things—These then because their names had never been inrolled in the guilds of[m] the learned were persecuted by the registered liverymen as interlopers on their rights and privileges—[f 508] All without distinction were branded as fanatics and phantasts—not only those whose wild and exhorbitant imaginations had actually engendered only extravagant and grotesque phantasms whose productions were for the most part poor copies and gross caricatures of genuine inspiration—but the truly inspired likewise the originals themselves and this for no other reason but because they were the unlearned men of humble and obscure occupations—When and from whom among the literati by profession have we ever heard the divine doxology repeated—I thank thee Oh Father Lord of Heaven and Earth because thou hast hid these things from the wise and prudent and hast revealed them unto babes—No the haughty Priests of learning not only banished from the schools and marts of science all who had dared draw living waters from the fountain but drove them out of the very temple which meantime the buyers and sellers and

---

[l] "meek" written partly over erasure   [m] "guilds of" seems written partly over erasure

money changers were suffered to make a den of thieves and yet it would not be [f 509] easy to discover any substantial distinction ground for this contemptuous pride in those literati who have most distinguished themselves by their scorn of Behmen De Thoyras—Geo. Fox and others unless it be that they could write orthographically make smooth periods and had the fashions of authorship literally at their fingers ends while the latter in simplicity of soul made their words immediate echo's of their feelings—Hence the frequency of those phrases among them which have been mistaken for pretences to immediate inspiration as ~~as~~ for instance— it was delivered unto me—I strove not to speak—I said I will be silent but the word was in my heart as a burning fire and so forth—Hence too[n] the unwillingness to give offence—hence the foresight and the dread of the clamours which would be raised against them so frequently avowed in the writings of these men and expressed as was natural in the words of the only book with which they were familiar Woe is me that I am become a man of strife [f 510] and a man of contention—I love peace—the Souls of men are dear unto me yet because I seek for light every one of them doth curse me—Oh it requires deeper feeling and a strong imagination than belong to most of those to whom reasoning and fluent expression have been as a trade learned in boyhood to conceive with what might with what inward strivings and commotion the perception of a new and vital truth takes possession of an uneducated man of genius—His Meditations are almost inevitably employed on the eternal or the everlasting for the World is not his friend nor the Worlds law—Need we then be surprised that under an excitement at once so strong and so unusual the mans body should sympathize with the struggles of his mind or that he should at times be so far deluded as to mistake the tumultuous sensations of his nerves and the co-existing spectres of his fancy as parts or symbols of the truths which were opening on him—But one assertion I will venture to make as suggested [f 511] by my own experience that there exist folios on the human understanding and the nature of man which would have a far juster claim to their high rank and celebrity if in the whole huge[o] volume there could be found as much fulness of heart and intellect as burst forth in many a simple page of George Fox Jacob Behmen and even of Behmen's Commentator—the warm and fervent William Law—he was indeed a stupendous human being had he received the discipline of education above all had he possessed the knowledge which would have guarded him against his own delusions—I scarcely know whether we should have had reason to attribute greater genius even to Plato himself

---

[n] "too" written over erasure   [o] "huge" written partly over erasure

when I consider that this ignorant man by the result of his own meditations presented the Newtonian system in a clearness which it certainly
had never before appeared in not even to Copernicus himself or to the
learned Bruno when I trace in him the love of action and that constant
sense of the truth that all nature [f 512] is in a perpetual evolution that
two great powers are for ever working manifesting themselves alike in
the apparently inadequate and inanimated and in intellectual nature
namely the powers by which each particular endeavours to detach itself
from nature and the counteracting powers by which nature is still bringing back each of her creatures into itself—This led him assuredly into anticipations and views of truth which will detract from many modern discoveries some part at least of their originality but above all that spirit of
love which runs through him that dread of contempt—that belief that the
potential works in us even as the actual is working on us and that not only
man but every creature contains in itself a higher being which is indeed
bedimmed under the lustre*p* of the immediate and sensual being which is
as it were its husk and outward covering but which in moments of tranquility most frequently appears in the voice of [f 513] conscience*q* but
often in high aspirations and in feelings of faith that remain afterwards as
sentiments and thoughts of consolation when I find this animating his
whole language presenting everywhere a being who had forgotten himself in the love by which he possessed all things I again and again wish
that some more enlightened friend had been present and had rescued this
man from evils I mean the error and the delusion which fortunately however his own sense of right held*r* from him for with all this though he himself prized his system mainly as explaining and inferring all the mysteries of religion—there is as there was throughout in the philosophy of that
time a tendency to Pantheism ⟨or rather it was itself a disguised Panthe-
ism⟩ in short with the exception of those who have strictly followed the
Scriptures and who will not cheat themselves by explaining this away into
a metaphor and that into an accomodation I know none who have avoided
one or the other of two evils—the one making [f 514] the World have the
same relation to God as a watch has to a Watchmaker—in truth giving
all up to secondary causes and rendering the omnipresence of the great
Being the ground of all things as well as their Creator a mere word of
honor and of pomp in the State room of the intellect or the opposite error
of carrying the omnipresence into a condition of nature with God and involving all those fearful consequences from which as I before said the

---

p "lustre" may be written partly over erasure   *q* Catchword on f 512: "con-"
           r "held" written over erasure

best refuge is not to see them—From this I cannot excuse Behmen's writings any more than I can praise or attempt or pretend to understand many of the strange fancies by which he has represented his truths—sometimes indeed one can guess at the meaning sometimes it is utter darkness and altogether he represents a great mirror[s] but placed in the shade—all the objects of nature seem to pass by but they are reflected in shadow and dimly but now and then a light passes along and the mirror in the shade[t] flashes and seems to lighten from out of its retirement

[f 515]   At this time when the downfall of the scholastic philosophy and the emancipation from the superstitions in at least the Northern parts of Europe had left the mind open and almost impelled it to real silence there arose our great Lord Bacon and at the same time nearly with him the famous Kepler—two men one of whom we all know as the beginning of truly scientific astronomy—of that science which possesses power and prophecy and which will for ever remain the greatest monument of human greatness because by laws demonstrably drawn out of his own mind he has in that mind not only light but as far as his own purposes require it controlled the mighty orbs of nature and Lord Bacon who appeared not for any one purpose but to purify the whole of the mind from all its errors by having given first that compleat analysis of the human soul without which we might have gone on for ever weighing one thing after another in scales which we had never examined and thus constantly perhaps mistaking as existing in the thing weighed [f 516] that which was really owing[u] to the scales themselves

I have in the beginning of this Lecture referred[v] in part to it when I spoke of the threefold powers with which man was gifted and of the evils which had arisen from their confusion—Lord Bacon has been commonly understood as if in his system itself he had deduced the propriety of a mode of philosophyzing of which indeed there are found in his own writings not any specimens but some recommendations which it is difficult to suppose that he himself could have been in earnest with—His own philosophy is this—he demands indeed experiment as the true ground work of all real knowledge but what does he mean by experiment he himself strongly contrasts it with the gossiping with nature as he calls it of the alchymists—the putting one thing to another in order to see if anything would come out of it—no he requires some well grounded purpose in the mind some self consistent anticipation of the result in short the prudens . . . the prudent fore[f 517]thought and enquiry which he declares to be

---

[s] "mirror" may be written over erasure   [t] "of", following "shade", largely erased
[u] "owing" seems written over erasure
[v] "referred" begun "reff", then partly erased and completed correctly

. . . the one half of one science he expressly says we do not aim at science either by the senses or by instruments so much as by experiments for the subtility of experiments is far greater than that of the sense though aided with the most exquisite^w instruments for we speak of those experiments which have been preconceived and knowingly placed and arranged to the intention and that for the purpose of that which is sought for according to art therefore says he we do not attribute much to the immediate and proper perception of the sense but we deduce the matter to this point that the sense can judge only of the experiment but it is the experiment which must inform us of the law which is the thing itself—In this instance Lord Bacons fondness for . . . has perhaps rather obscured his meaning but the sense is this that our perception can apprehend through the organs of sense only the phenomena evoked by the experiment but that same power of^x mind which out of its own laws has proposed the experiment [f 518] can judge whether in nature there is a law correspondent to the same— in order therefore to explain the different errors of men he says that there is a power which can give birth to this question he calls this the lex intellectus the lex maxime—the pure and impersonal reason freed from all the personal idols which this great Legislator of science then enumerates namely the idols of the Den of the Theatre and of the market place—he means freed from the passions the prejudices the peculiar habits of the human understanding natural or acquired but above all pure from the delusions which lead men to take the forms of mechanism . . . as a measure of nature and the Deity—in short to use the bold but happy phrase of a late ingenious French Writer he guards you against the man particular as contrasted with the general man and most truly and in strict consonance in this with Plato does the immortal Verulam . . . [f 519] render that more or less turbid or uneven not only reflects the object subjectively . . . outward senses but that there is potentially if not actually in every rational being a somewhat call it what you will the purest reason the spirit of true light and intellectual . . . expressed and everywhere supposed by Lord Bacon and that this is not only the right but the visible nature of the human mind to which it is capable of being restored is implied in the various remedies prescribed by him for its diseases . . . the true criterion between the ideas of the mind and the idols namely that the former are manifested by their adequacy to those ideas in nature which in and through them are contemplated—

[f 520]   This therefore is the true Baconic philosophy it consists^y in this in a profound meditation on those laws which the pure reason in man re-

---

^w Corrected from "exquistte" by over-writing the extra "t"
^x "power of" may be written over erasure   ^y "consists" written partly over erasure

veals to him with the confident anticipation and faith that to this will be found to correspond certain laws in nature—if there be aught that can be said to be purely in the human mind it is surely those acts of its own imagination which the Mathematician avails himself of for I need not I am sure tell you that a line upon a slate is but a picture of that act of the imagination which the mathematician alone consults—that it is the picture only is evident for never could we learn the act of the imagination or form an idea of a line in the mathematical sense from that picture[z] of it which we draw beforehand otherwise how could we draw it without depth or breadth—It becomes evidently too an act of the imagination out of these simple acts the mind still proceeding raises that wonderful[a] superstructure of Geometry and then looking abroad into nature finds that in its own nature it has been fathoming nature and that nature itself is but the [f 521] greater mirror in which he beholds his own present and his own past being in the law and learns to reverence while he feels the necessity of that one great being whose eternal reason is the ground and absolute condition of the ideas in the mind and no less the ground and the absolute Cause of all the correspondent realities in nature—the reality of nature for ever consisting in the law by which each thing is that which it is

Hence and so has Lord Bacon told us all Science approaches to its perfection in proportion as it immaterializes objects—for instance in the motion of the Heavenly bodies we in reality consider only a few obstructions of mass distance and so forth—the whole phenomena of light the materiality of which itself has been more than once doubted of as nothing but a sublime Geometry drawn by its rays while in magnetism the phenomena is altogether lost and the whole process by which we trace it is the power of intellect—we know it not as a visible but by its powers if instead of this we [f 522] are to substitute the Common notion of Lord Bacon that you are to watch every thing without having any reason for so doing and that after you have collected the facts that belong to any subject if any person could divide them and tell what could be contradicted then you may proceed to the Theory which must necessarily be false if you[b] omit any one term[c] and consequently as in all physical things the difference between them and the mathematical is that in the mathematical you can control them because they are the things of your will it follows necessarily then there can be no such thing as a physical theory nothing remains therefore but either an hypothesis which[d] if it is a thing is part

[z] "picture" miswritten, then corrected by over-writing
[a] "wonderful" miswritten, then corrected by over-writing
[b] "false if you" seems written partly over erasure
[c] "term" seems written partly over erasure
[d] "which" seems miswritten and corrected

of the problem or the discovery of some law by which our knowledge proceeds from the Centre and diverges towards by a constant approximation an ever distant circumference but feeling*e* its progress as it moves and still increasing in power as it travels onward for this a very ingenious man and a man who had a particular talent for discovery and the whole history of whose ⟨very⟩*f* active life is the best answer to his own recommendation [f 523] has proposed the following and I must again repeat that this is most frequently the opinion now of Lord Bacons philosophy—he says that before a foundation can be laid upon which anything like a sound and staple theory can be constructed you are to make yourself acquainted with a certain number of facts which I think contain three and twenty pages of which I will give you one small specimen—you are to be acquainted with the history of Potters Tobacco pipe makers . . . or furriers—Spectacle makers . . . picture drawers makers of baby heads of little bowling stones . . . I do not know whether Poets deal in this trade [f 524] Music Masters . . . Butchers Builders . . . and Cosmetics &c &c &c the truth of which" he concludes—"being all . . . in philosophy as a summary of Doctor . . . Metaphors—recipe . . . which was thought by Doctor . . . to be worthy of insertion . . . directions concerning our ideas furnish yourselves" for it is worth listening to "furnish yourselves *g*with a rich variety of ideas: acquaint yourselves with things ancient and modern things natural civil and religious*h* things of your own native land and of foreign Countries things domestic and national things past *i*present and future: and above all be well acquainted with God and yourselves learn Animal nature and the working of your own Spirits*j* . . . Such a general acquaintance with things will be of very great advantage"—certainly a most [f 525] incomparable*k* lesson—no the truth is that let any unprejudiced naturalist turn even to Lord Bacons own questions and proposals for the investigation of greater problems or to discover . . . or enquire of his own experience or historical recollection whether any important discovery was ever made in this way for though Lord Bacon never so far deviates from his own principles as not to admonish his readers that the particulars are those to be collected only—that by . . . yet so immense is their number and so various and almost endless the relations in which each is to be separately considered that the life of an antediluvian . . . or have arrived in sight in the Law which was . . . I trust I yield to none in my veneration for Lord Bacons writings proud*l* of his name we all must be as

---

e Pencilling erased in left-hand margin and after "feeling"
f "very" also written faintly in pencil in right-hand margin
g–h Written in a smaller hand as if inserted into space later
i–j Written in a smaller hand as if inserted into space later
k Catchword on f 524: "in"   *l* "proud" has been corrected

men of science—as Englishmen [f 526] we might be almost vain of him but I will not suffer nationality so far to bribe me as not to confess that there are points . . . of John Kepler as from gloom to sunshine—the beginning and the close of his life were clouded with poverty and domestic troubles while*m* . . . had left neither his head nor ~~his~~ heart for the Muses— but Kepler seemed born to prove that true genius could overcome all obstacles . . . in transitu as it were does he introduce himself to our notice . . . springs up—with what affectionate reverence does he express himself of his Master and immediate predecessor Tycho Brahe how often and how gladly . . . as Pioneers and heralds equally just to the ancients [f 527] and to his . . . we cannot avoid contrasting this generous enthusiasm . . . of Plato and Aristotle had been carried down by the stream of time like straws by their levity alone when things of weight and worth sunk to the bottom and truly so calumniously does he everywhere speak of Plato that we are obliged to believe that the manifold occupations and anxieties to which his public and professional duties engaged him and his Courtly at least his . . . must have derived his opinions of Plato and Aristotle from any source rather than from a dispassionate study of the originals themselves this however would have been a trifle but was not true of the great men themselves Plato and Aristotle were abundantly the [f 528] falsifiers*n* of their systems but it is not a trifle that those are the parts in Lord Bacons character and those the passages in his writings which have been of late more read and which are more in the mouths and minds of the common race of modern materialists than his invaluable system which differs in no other respect from that of Platos except as the objects were different except as far as that the mind was the great object in Plato and what I may call the ideal while the philosophy and the correspondence*o* of the laws of nature to the ideas of the pure reason the object of Lord Bacon— but unfortunately men had been as it were satiated with the admiration of the great men of old—the mind wanted to act upon its own stores—upon its own faculties and with this there was much of the insolence of youth— Had it remained there we should have indeed only had to travel a long road before we came back again and found we might have spared ourselves the trouble but it unfortunately extended into the moral and political character of nations—nothing was to have been known before [f 529] nothing was to be valued—all was to be created anew and from this moment the mind was led to the revival of systems which the better feelings of mankind had exploded for many many centuries and new systems that

---

m Pencilled mark partly erased in right-hand margin
n Catchword on f 527: "fal-"
o "correspondence" seems written partly over erasure

had not the least claim to originality but which have a most dreadful claim to history from the effects they have produced

These will form the subject of my next lecture—when I shall trace the state of mind in the Civil Wars under Charles the first and from thence the progress of materialism and infidelity on to the time immediately before the French Revolution and I beg to conclude with one remark namely that the influences of philosophy must not be sought for either in the lives of philosophers themselves or in the immediate effect of their writings upon the students of speculative knowledge—no we must look for it everywhere only not in their own shape for it becomes active by being diluted—it combines itself as a color as it were lying on the public [f 530] mind—as a sort of preparation for receiving thought in a particular way and excluding particular views and in this way its effect has been great ⟨indeed great in past times for good but great⟩ likewise in recent times for evil and if any one would doubt the truth of what I say let him look at the disputes in the time of Charles the first and detract from the controversies of the Calvinists and Arminians all that belongs to the Christian Gospel and leave nothing behind but the metaphysics and I suspect that spite of the Theological phrases he has left at least four fifths of the whole work untouched and that Christianity might fairly give up her claim to the bitterest controversies and resign them again to the Schools—

LECTURE 12

*p*M.̇ Coleridge's Lecture
Monday 15.th March 1819.

———————————

It is a wonderful property of the human mind that when once a momentum has been given to it in a fresh direction it pursues the new path with obstinate perseverance in all conceivable directions to its utmost extremes and by the striking consequences which arise out of those extremes it is first awakened to its error and either recalled to some former track or to some new pursuits which it immediately receives and admits to the same monopoly*q*—Thus in the thirteenth century the first science which roused the intellects of man from the torpor of barbarism which*r* as we have seen*s* in all Countries ever has been and ever must be the Case—the science of metaphysics—the non-intellica we first seek at home and what wonder the . . . should take possession of the whole mind and all truths appear trivial which could not be either [f 532] evolved out of simple principles by the same process or at least brought under the same forms of thought by perceived or imagined analogies and so in fact it was—for more than two centuries man continued to invoke the oracle of their own spirits not only concerning their own forms and mode of being but likewise concerning the laws of external nature all attempts at . . . effort of the understanding as the power of abstraction or by the imagination transferring its own experiences to every object presented from without by the former—the understanding or abstracting powers a class of phenomena was in the first place abstracted and fixed in some general term—of course this term could designate only the impressions made by the outward objects and so far therefore the effects of those objects, but having been thus generalized in a term they were then made to occupy the place of their own causes under the name of occult qualities

---

p "Lect xi" written in pencil above the lozenge, probably in the hand of JHG; it is followed by "[really Lect xii]" pencilled in by KC who initialled her insertion

q Note pencilled in right-hand margin, possibly in the hand of JHG or even of KC: But how so? The *new* path must tend in *one* direction only—towards *one* extreme—

r Altered in pencil to ", [which,]"

s Altered in pencil to "seen,"

[f 533]—thus[t] the properties peculiar to gold were abstracted from those it possessed in common with other bodies and then generalized in the term . . . and the enquirer was instructed that the essence of gold or the cause which constituted the peculiar substance called gold was the power of . . . by the latter that is by the imagination thought and will were superadded to this occult nature and every form of nature had its appropriate spirit to be controlled or conciliated by an appropriate Psychology and this was entitled the substantial[u] form thus Physic became a dull . . . and physiology . . . thus the forms of thought proceeded to act in their own emptiness with no attempt to fill or substantiate them by the information of the senses and all the branches of science formed so many sections of logic and metaphysics and so it continued till the time the Reformation sounded the second trumpet and the authority of the Schools sunk with that of the higher arcade under the intellectual [f 534] courage and activity which this great revolution had inspired—Powers once awakened cannot[v] rest in one object all the Sciences partook of the new influence and the world of the . . . by the comprehensive and enterprising genius of Bacon an Experiment is an organ of reason not less distinguished from the blind or dreaming history of the Alchymists than opposed to the barren subtleties of the schoolmen was called forth and more than this the laws explained by which experiment could be dignified into scientific experience but no sooner . . . looking at all things in the one point of view which chanced to be the predominant attraction—no sooner I observed had Lord Bacon convinced his contemporaries of the necessity of consulting their senses as well as their understandings but at the same time of consulting their reason equally with their senses than the same propensity of moving in one path and [f 535] that to the extreme was made manifest—our[w] Gilbert a man of genuine philosophical genius had no sooner magnified . . . the magnetic bodies but all things in Heaven and in earth and in the water beneath the earth were resolved into magnetic influences shortly afterwards a new light was struck by . . . Des Cartes . . . aided by the modern invention of Algebra placed the science of Mechanics on the Philosophic throne how widely this domination spread and how long continued if indeed even now it can be said to have abdicated its pretensions I need not remind you of the sublime discoveries Newton taught which

---

[t] Catchword on f 532: "—thus"; dash omitted at beginning of f 533

[u] Last three letters of "substantial" appear to be correction or later addition inserted into space

[v] Possibly "can not"

[w] "our" seems written over erasure; pencilled query mark partly erased in left-hand margin

are not less wonderful than fruitful . . . gave almost a religious sanction to the [f 536] corpuscular[x] . . . at which truth was permitted to enter the human body itself was treated of as a hydraulic machine the operations of medicine were solved and too often directed partly by gravitation and the laws of motion and partly by Chemistry which itself as far as its theory was concerned was but a branch of mechanics working by imaginary wedges angles and spheres should you chance to put your hand at any time on the principles of philosophy by De . . . you may see the phenomena of sleep explained and the results demonstrated by mathematical calculation In short from the time of Cooper whose mind was not comprehended in the vortex for he erred in the other extreme but from the time of Cooper to Newton and from that to Hartley . . . organization even of the intellect and moral being were conjured within the magic circle of mathematical formality but now a light was struck by the discovery of [f 537] electricity and in every sense of the word it may be affirmed to have the whole form of natural philosophy—close on its heels followed the momentous discovery of the causes and composition of water and the doctrine of latent heat by Black the scientific world had been prepared for a new . . . or least excited the expectation that this would be effected—a hope shot up almost instantly and as rapidly ripened into a full faith that this had been effected henceforward a new path became the common road as in the former instances to all the departments of knowledge and even to this moment ⟨it has been pursued⟩ with an eagerness and almost epidemic enthusiasm which characterises the Spirit of this age—Many and inauspicious have been the inroads of this new conqueror into the territories of our . . . terminology in homage to a life of whatever importance yet [f 538] unsettled[y] in the very ferment of imperfections discoveries either without a theory or by a theory maintained by compromise yet this very circumstance has favored it, encroachments by the gratifications which its novelty affords to our curiosity and by the genial excitement which an unsettled mind is sure to inspire and he who supposes science possesses an immunity of . . . like this knows little of human nature and how impossible it is for man to separate part of its nature wholly and entirely from the remaining parts all these causes however of every political event from their magnitude have had one tendency that of drawing men from attention to their own minds to external objects and giving them a pre-disposition to receive as the more true that which in any way makes a more vivid impression consequently a system that supplies image after image to the senses however little connected they

---

[x] Catchword on f 535: "cor"   [y] Catchword on f 537: "un-"

may be by any necessary copular will [f 539] be a formidable rival for
another which can pretend only to a logical adherence of conceptions and
which demand from men the most difficult effort in nature that of truly
and earnestly thinking

In the commencement of literature men remained for a time in that
unity with nature which gladly concedes to nature the life thought and
even purposes of man and on the other hand gives to man himself a disposition to regard himself as a part of nature soon however he must have
begun to detach himself—his dreams the very delusions of his senses
which he became acquainted with by experience must have forced him
to make a distinction between the object perceived and the percipient
Nothing however enabled him to determine to one of these a priority over
the other they were both strictly coexistent and it seems remarkable both
in ancient and in modern times the first philosophy was that of idealism
that which beginning with a courageous [f 540] scepticism[z] which I think
Des Cartes has beautifully stated when he himself gave a beautiful example of it in what he called voluntary doubt—a self-determined indetermination expressing at the same time its utter difference from the scepticism of vanity or irreligion "Nec . . . nor yet says he did I in this imitate
the sceptics who doubt only for doubting sake and seek nothing but a distinction of uncertainty for on the contrary my whole soul was engaged in
this the hope of discovering something certain In the pursuit of this therefore it was evident that success depended on an austere and faithful adherence to the principle of the mind with a careful separation and exclusion of all which appertains to the external world as far as this was
considered not as [f 541] a philosophy but as a mere introduction or discipline of the mind previous to the discovery of truth—As a natural
philosopher who directs his views wholly to external objects avoids
above all things the intermixture of mind and the properties in his knowledge as for instance all arbitrary suppositions occult qualities and the
substitution of final for efficient causes so on the other hand the philosopher who begins with the mind is equally anxious to exclude all mental
. . . he will be equally careful to . . . and by the purification of his mind of
all that does not belong to the mind itself he acquires a true sense both of
its strength and of its weakness—

We have seen in an earlier lecture that about five hundred years before
Christ Lucippus founded the Academic system or pure materialism
[f 542] in direct opposition to the Eclectic philosophy or pure idealism
and that within the next hundred years at a period rendered uncertain by

---

[z] Catchword on f 539: "scep-"

the extraordinary longevity of the individual this was enlarged by Democritus and during the interval from 312 to 270 years before Christ it was brought to that state of completion by Epicurus to which it was restored by Gassendi who was born in a village of Provence in 1592 and was after Gassendi especially applied to the explanation of humanity by Hobbs who was born at Malmesbury four years before Gassendi and who almost rivalled . . . in the length of his life the three ancient Philosophers declared the inherence of the notion and the essence at least of life and of sensation in the atoms which they assumed though they made a difference with regard to those atoms which will not be well understood unless we give the history of those atoms themselves—

[f 543]   The Eclectics had begun by demonstrating the inconsistencies that arise out of the position of motion arising from the arguments against the real external existence of space—having shewn that space involved a contradiction of a something that had the properties of nothing of course that it was a nonentity they then deduced that as motion was inconceivable without the belief of space so neither motion nor space possessed any reality the materialists who followed and who were perhaps first materialists by this outrage on their common sense were not able to combat the Eclectic Philosophers in subtlety of reasoning and they cut the knot which they could not solve and took for granted at once the existence of matter and motion without further explanation but still there were two properties of matter which demanded some solution and those were the partibility which it presented ⟨even⟩ to the senses and its resistance— Now no hypothesis suggested [f 544] itself, more probable, more plausible at least than that of atoms to answer both for while their extreme multitude and minuteness seemed every where to account to the professors[a] of matter for its divisibility ⟨on the other hand⟩[b] their hardness which they were obliged like motion to declare to be inherent and essential they gave as the true cause of the resistance of matter so that these atoms in truth were in the first place ⟨a⟩ pure fiction for no man ever pretended to have seen an ultimate particle it was merely a supposition derived from another supposition namely that of external matter but in the next place it was to account for partibility by the very circumstance of being impartible if they were asked how it was that matter was divisible they answered in consequence of the infinite multitude of ultimate particles of which it was composed if they were asked how those particles came to be ultimate and

---

[a] Last seven letters of "professors" seem written over erasure
[b] "on the other hand" has been written in pencil in right-hand margin, then partially erased

why they stopped there the answer then was if they were Atheists as in our sense of the word the old materialists were it was an [f 545] inherent eternal property—if they were theists it was a miracle—God has made them and who shall pretend as a late writer has said to quarrel with any decree of God's—certainly not, but we may quarrel with a man who chooses to affirm a miracle on his own authority this however was the ground of atoms it was nothing more than an hypothesis to expose in one thing the partibility of matter by the amazing smallness of it and the resistance or impenetrability of matter by its hardness—

But these atoms still when they had them would only account for a certain number of things either shapeless or of the same shape but among the phenomena ⟨of matter⟩ the most impressive was the manifoldness of forms—This again the system of materialism found the means of explaining by a variety of figures some of them were angular and some were round and these last forms namely the round atoms and bodies composed of them the ancient materialists [f 546] regarded[c] as motive atoms or self motive powers in short the souls and principles of all thought and motion were according to them round atoms and inasmuch as the element of fire was supposed to be composed of those round atoms likewise the soul therefore was according to them of a fiery nature in the form of warmth these round atoms appeared as life that is where a sufficient quantity was accumulated for in inanimate substances says Democritus there is still a certain quantum of warmth because there are no bodies without certain roundness but they are not vital—In this sense Democritus says there is a soul in all things—all things have a sensation in kind but the inanimate things have only a momentary sensation which being interrupted by other elementary atoms not round prevent all consciousness and all memory and even all marks of life—yet interior sensations or impressions they derived from atoms or their components that were of like [f 547] nature with the sentient and all life was but sensation which modified how has not been preserved—thus then the round atoms according to Democritus constituted souls or the power of sensation and voluntary motion but all mind is sensation which modified in the brain we are not told how becomes thinking but if modified in the region of the breast becomes feeling and in the abdomen it shewed itself only as growth or the obscure sensation of life, the mode the process of perception he explained by the effluvia, the images from every body—every body according to him sending forth images of each of its component elements and these falling on an organ of the same element as for instance water falling on the eye

---

[c] Catchword on f 545: "re-"

which he says is essentially water constitutes sight, the air falling on the ear constitutes sound and so forth but this we may safely omit it is sufficient for our purposes to know that the fundamental positions of ancient materialism were first that motion and sensation are properties of [f 548] a specific kind of atoms and that mind is but a species of sensation and all the processes of perception and of reflexion purely passive and all the acts or more accurately all the phenomena or appearances of life just as the seeming acts of a dream are wholly mechanical or produced by necessitating antecedents lastly that the distinction between these ancient materialists and the moderns from Hobbs lies mainly in this one position that the ancients accounted for the soul as the common principle of life thought and voluntary motion from a peculiar sort of atoms namely the round atoms or fire composing corpuscles while the moderns make the same things result from the organism of atoms without any assumption of a particular species or if of any yet not ab origine and consequently not immutably peculiar but the peculiarity itself produced by this self all working organization—In this assertion however I beg to be understood as speaking of the opinion common to all and the organization as being the predominant [f 549] thought though in connexion with organization the successors of Hobbs have not all confined themselves to his scheme of ⟨successive⟩ corpuscles propagating motion like billiard balls but they had had their spirits that is their irrational and inanimate solids thawed down and distilled or filtrated into living and intelligent fluids that etch and re-etch engravings on the brain for themselves to look at according to the pure materialists though they were intended by their soul to contemplate by their first inventor we have too what comes nearest to the ancient notion of hollow tubes which had been regarded formerly as tools and we have had too electric light at once the immediate object and the ultimate organ of inward vision which rises to the line like an aurora Borealis and there disporting in various shapes (as the balance of plus and minus or negative and positive is destroyed or re-established) images out both past and present but all these had been proffered as auxiliaries themselves . . . that [f 550] the modern scheme of materialism differs from that of Democritus by representing life mind and will as the result of organization not as pre-existing in the specific atom as the organization

To the best of my knowledge Des Cartes was the first Philosopher who introduced the absolute and essential heterogenei of the soul as intelligence and of body as matter—The Eclectics deduced matter and with it the mind as the mere process of thought—Democritus and his followers deduced the mind as resulting from the body while the Platonists had founded a system which at all events had the merits of being extremely poetical and which has been far more accurately as well as beautifully given by Milton than you will find it in Brooker or all the writers of philosophical history

> "Oh Adam, one Almighty is from whom
> All things proceed, and up to him return
> If not depraved from good created all
> Such to perfection, one first matter all
> [f 551] Indu'd with various forms various degrees
> Of substance, and in things that live, of life;
> But more refined, more spiritous and pure
> As nearer to him placed, or nearer tending
> Each in their several active spheres assigned
> Till body up to spirit work in bounds,
> Proportioned to each kind—So from the root
> Springs lighter the green stalk, from thence the leaves
> More æry, last the bright consummate flower
> Spirits odorous breathes: flowers & their fruit
> Man's nourishment, by gradual scale sublimed
> To vital spirits aspire,—to animal
> To intellectual, give both life and sense
> Fancy and understanding, whence the soul
> Reason receives, and reason is her being
> Discursive, or intuitive— —"

Now Des Cartes had taught an absolute and essential diversity of the soul as intelligent and of the body as matter—The assumption and the form of speaking had remained to the denial of all ⟨other⟩ properties to that of matter but that of extension on which denial the whole system of this diversity is grounded has been long exploded For since impenetrability [f 552] is intelligible only as a mode of resistance its admission places the essence of matter in an act or power which it possesses in common with spirit and body and spirit are therefore no longer absolutely heterogeneous but may without any absurdity be supposed to be different modes or degrees in perfection of a common substratum as I have just read described in the lines of Milton—"To this possibility however it was not the fashion to advert—the soul was a thinking substance and body a space filling substance yet the apparent action of each on the other pressed heavily on the philosopher on the one hand and no less heavily on the other hand pressed the evident truth that the law of causality and effect holds only between homogeneous things that is to say things having some common property and cannot extend from one world into another its opposite—A close analysis evinced it to be no less absurd than the question whether a mans affection for his wife lay north East or South west of the [f 553] love he bore towards his child for if matter be defined as a space filling substance it is evident that what cannot apply to what he predicates of space can in no degree apply to what is material Leibnitz's doctrine of a pre-established harmony which he certainly borrowed from Spinosa who had taken the hint from Des Cartes animal machine was in its common interpretation too strange to survive the inventor the next hypothesis therefore was that of recurrence to and afterwards the hypothesis of Hylozoism or that every particle of matter is essentially though not apparently alive but this was found to be the death of all essential physiology and indeed of all physical science for science requires a limitation of terms and cannot consist with the arbitrary power of multiplying attributes by occult qualities Besides the system of life in matter answers no purpose unless a difficulty can be solved by multiplying it or that we can acquire a clearer notion of our Soul by [f 554] being told that we have a million souls and that every atom of our bodies has a soul of its own but it is here as it is in many other cases man while he was persuaded that he had a soul and that he had a body and that his soul was gifted with a faculty of perceiving external objects through the medium of that body or by its organs was satisfied all was clear but when he came to ask what form has this copular is the soul diverse from the body and if so how can diverse powers act and react on each other and if it be the same in what point or degree shall we place the soul and where the body—then it is as if the sediment were at the bottom of a vessel all the water above being clear and transparent but we are not satisfied on account of the sediment, out we cannot take it and the best we can do is to shake it up not diminishing it by the least degree but for our pains rendering the whole water turbid—

Still I deny yet that it is the duty of man to despair to solve a problem till its impossibility is demonstrated [f 555] how matter can ever unite with perception—how being ever transform itself into knowing is conceivable only on one position that is if it can be shewn that the vis representativa or the Sentient is itself a species of matter, either as a property, or attribute, or a self subsistence—now that it is a property is an assumption of materialism of which permit me to say thus much in praise that it is a system which could not but be patronised if it performed what it promises but how any affection from without could metamorphose itself into perception or will the materialist has not only left incomprehensible as he found it but has made it a comprehensible absurdity—For grant that an object from without could act upon the conscious self as on

a consubstantial object yet such an affection would only engender something homogeneous with itself—motion could only propagate motion
matter has no inward—we remove one surface but to meet with
another—we can but divide a particle into particles and each particle has
the power of being again divided Let any reflecting mind make the [f 556]
experiment[d] of explaining to itself the evidence of our sensuous intuitions
from the hypothesis that in any given perception there is a something
which has been communicated to it by an impact or an impression ab
extra In the first place by the impact on the percipient or ens representans
not the object itself but only its action or effect will pass into the same
Not the iron tongue but its vibrations pass into the metal of the bell Now
in our immediate perception it is not the mere power or act of the object
but it is the object itself which is immediately present We might attempt
to explain this result by a chain of deductions and conclusions but that
first the faculties of deducing and concluding would demand an explanation and secondly there is no such intermediation by logic as cause and
effect It is the object itself not the product of a syllogism which is present
to our consciousness—or would we explain this supervention of the object by the sensation by a productive faculty set in motion by an impulse
still the transition into the percipient of the object itself from which
[f 557] the impulse proceeded assumes a power that can permeate and
wholly possess the soul

> And like a God by spiritual art,
> Be all in all and all in every part.

And how came the percipient ~~part~~ here and what is become of the wonder promising matter that was to perform all these marvels by force of
mere figure weight and motion—The most consistent proceeding of the
dogmatic materialist would be to fall back into the common rank of soul
and bodyists to affect the mysterious and declare the whole process a
revelation given and not to be understood which it would be profane to
examine too closely—But a revelation unconfirmed by miracles and a
faith not commanded by the conscience a philosopher may venture to
pass by without suspecting himself of any irreligious tendency Thus as
materialism has been generally taught it is utterly unintelligible and owes
all its proselytes to the propensity so common among men to mistake distinct images for clear conceptions and vice versa to reject as inconceivable whatever from [f 558] its own nature is unimaginable But as soon as
it becomes intelligible it ceases to be materialism—In order to explain

---

[d] Catchword on f 555: "ex-"

thinking as a material[e] phenomenon it is necessary to refine matter into a mere modification of intelligence with the two fold function of appearing and perceiving—Even so did Spinosa—even so did Priestley in his controversy with Price, he stripped matter of all its material properties substituted spiritual powers and when we expected to find a body behold we had nothing but its Ghost—the apparition of a defunct matter

Let us then re-trace our history—throughout the whole we have discovered nothing like thought the earliest materialists began with declaring all who differed from them truly out of their senses they themselves however began with hypothesis and they moved forwards as a materialist ever must do by a succession of laws as for instance from an atom fiction the first to atoms of various figures fiction the second—amongst these round atoms constituting the element of fire fiction [f 559] the third, then that the element of fire is the principle of the soul or thinking which is the fourth fiction—that sensation and thought are precisely the same which at all events is but an assertion then that this same sensation whatever it be if it be below my heart is to be one thing and if it be in the region of my heart another—but at once becomes philosophical and intellectual as soon as it passes[f] into the marrow of my skull—these may be placed each as a separate law and fiction and the whole comes at last to what—not to any thing that was meant by matter in the first sense of the word but without the slightest instruction given even in the meaning of terms without one practical consequence in science or in philosophy being deducible and with an outrage to common sense and to morality[g] it formed a complete circle of dogmatic mere unsupported assertions

The moderns were ashamed of these angular and these round atoms and they had substituted therefore [f 560] for it organization some and others life or a vital principle, we will examine both, first then what is this organization for we have been assured not in old times but even in our own that mind is a function of the brain that all our moral and intellectual being are the effects of organization which I confess has always had much the same effect upon my mind as if a man should say that building with all the included handicraft of plastering sawing planing &c were the offspring of the house and that the Mason and Carpenter were the . . . for to make A the offspring of B. where the very existence of B. as B. presupposes the Existence of A. . . . in logic—for what again I say is organization not the mere arrangement of parts as means to an end for in that sense I should call my watch organization [f 561] or a steam engine organiza-

---

[e] All but first letter of "material" seems a correction written over erasure

[f] First two letters of "passes" seem to have been corrected

[g] "morality" written over erasure

tion but we agree these are machines not organizations it appears then that if I am to attach any meaning at all to the word organization it must be distinct from mechanism in this that in all machines I suppose the power to be from without that if I take my watch there is nothing in the component parts of this watch that constitutes it peculiarly fit for a watch or produce it—there is nothing in the steam engine which of itself independent of its position would account for that position at all—organization therefore must not only be an arrangement of parts together as means to an end but it must be such an interdependence of parts each of which in its turn being means to an end as arises from within—The moment a man dies we can scarcely say he remains organized in the proper sense the powers of Chemistry are beginning to shew us that no force not even mechanical . . . to say therefore that life is the result of [f 562] organization[h] and yet at the same time to admit that organization is distinguished from mechanism only by life is assuredly what I before said to affirm a thing to be its own parent or to determine the parent to be the child of his[i] own child— in every instance we may indeed account for the difference of qualities difference of powers from organization but even there we do it only . . . not in the strict sense of the word for it is in all times incomparily more probable . . . and considered with regard to the universe produces the power itself—At all events in order to justify materialism ⟨and in materialism⟩ the assertion that life and much more that thought or will are the results of organization it would be necessary to call for a fact of organization subsisting prior to life ⟨prior⟩ to some one of the properties of life If indeed you could do that and then present a life resulting from it we will cheerfully agree with you but if you can shew an arrangement of means to an [f 563] end without life and declare it not to be mechanism and if by the superadding the idea of life that is a power from within you constitute an organization it follows self evidently that not life is the result of organization but that organization is in some way or other dependent on life as its cause—

We come then to what is life—almost all the attempts that I have seen to explain its nature presuppose the arbitrary disposition of all that surrounds us into things with life and things without life a division which is certainly quite sufficient for the common usage but far too indeterminate for a philosopher . . . of the market on the waverings of common opinion yet such has been the proceedure in the present instance by crazy logic which begins . . . has been made to define the others [f 564] by a mere reassertion of their assumed contrariety—. . . we are plainly . . . with but

[h] Catchword on f 561: "or-"   [i] "his" seems to have been inserted over erasure

one eye between them both, which each borrowed from the other as the other happened to want it but with this . . . for instance—Now that I may not be supposed to have stated . . . for my knowledge and acquaintance with the subject does not permit me to read it with—. . . I find this definition life is the sum of all the functions by which death is [f 565] resist-ed[j]—I could not after a long pause but ask myself what is the meaning this life is the sum of all the functions by which death is resisted that is that life consists in being able to live and more was I surprised when I observed the whimsical gravity with which the author has informed us that hitherto life had been sought for in abstract considerations as if four more inveterate abstractions could be brought together than the words life death function and resistance—

This is the vilest form however of modern materialism that is asserting a fact in other words and then putting the synonimes in place of the cause and the definition others have taken and observed some particular function of life as attrition or assimilation for the production of life or growth as their act of life now in the first place this would be a definition of the lowest species only of living things—it might describe a fungus but assuredly it could not describe a living man consequently [f 566] it could be no definition of life as a principle of all the other vital functions In addition to this the assimilation but in truth it merely tells us one thing that life enables animals to die not in reality what life itself is for if that be the case assimilation or attrition would convey to us some notion of life whereas we are obliged to preassume a notion of life as known[k] to understand the difference between . . . A better definition certainly as might be expected from the truly great man who produced it is the power of resisting putrescence for this is not like the former wholly unfruitful but even this definition need only be resolved into a higher formula to be found to contain little for if we say that every thing strives to preserve the state in which it is or nothing changes its state but with some resistance that will be found equally applicable to every process in Chemistry as attacked by mechanical powers and weakened [f 567] and again by those of mechanism every thing in nature and not a living body only tends to preserve its state and all we can learn is that life is a particular ⟨state⟩ that is the knowledge is assumed in the very definition which was supposed to give it but in truth it was not by the great founder supposed to give it— he knew too well what he was about he merely pointed out as a description as that most marked property which involved in itself the most fearful consequences and above all others that which will for ever

---

[j] Catchword on f 564: "re-"   [k] "known" an uncertain reading

immortalize his name an assertion justified by all facts and by all logic from within and without that to explain organization itself we must assume a principle of life independent of organization

Now where shall we seek for this principle of life we will suppose for instance that it is probable that without any reason we had made these arbitrary assertions of not merely a distinction in degree but of a distinction in kind between inanimate [f 568] and animate body we may suppose for instance with Newton that in nature there is a continual antagonism going on between an universal life and each individual composing it—we will suppose that there is a tendency throughout nature perpetually to individuate that is in each component part of nature to acquire individuality but which is as harmoniously counteracted by an attempt of nature to recall it again to the common organization—would there be aught very extraordinary in this—certainly not in the first instance because mechanism itself implies organization in the higher sense of the word namely a power from within for after the watch maker has placed the watch in its ~~due~~ due positions he looks to that power from within belonging to all the gravity which itself of course can never be the result of any mechanism for if you explained it by a subtle fluid for instance you would be asked the cause of that subtle fluid gravitating [f 569] and you must have another and another and at last you would be asked by what logic you connect power within or why a thick body should be dull and spirits of wine light and even intellectual—These were answers to no purpose mechanism leads to organization and there seems no contradiction in the supposition that mechanism in the strict sense of the word is nothing but the negative of organization for the absence of mechanism will not presuppose organization but organization ceasing mechanism commences—in short there is through all nature and we must assume it as a ground of all reasoning a perpetual tendency at once to individualize and yet to universalize or to keep—even as we find in the solar system a perpetual tendency in each planet to preserve its own individual path with a counter tendency which of itself would lead it into the common solar centre—Suppose this as I believe we must in [f 570] all reasoning to take place in the world where would be at all the extravagance of lugging in the more subtle parts of inanimate nature and in tracing their analogies and comparing them with those of life in ourselves certainly if a man were to say bona fide that that which is . . . machine accumulated is the same thing as that life which is within me he might as well have called his life by any thicker fluid or any other unappropriate thing but if in proportion as life becomes less the object of the senses in proportion as it is less capable of appearing fixed and as the body retains more and more of those properties which I notice in life and that therefore it is not impossible but that in a still higher evolution of the universal nature it may appear as life—I know no logic on earth that would point out any defect in this reasoning—It may be indeed said but where would you get this if it be said that here is an organization like the steam engine and I procure a state which in [f 571] a higher state is life and as soon as I put it in the machine plays, that would not be tenable because it would leave organization unaccounted for for organization has no other meaning than a power which instead of moving in a strait line as the mechanism does moves round upon itself in a circle and though it is an act of subsisting being the act of self reproduction is at each moment of our life the identical same act as that by which it was first established, if ever there was a first in reality—no that we should not do nor do I believe that has been asserted but it is easy when a man is anxious to express his thoughts to take one illustration and pin it down to the literal words and to draw from it all the consequences that may be drawn from every simile a sort of proceedure which excites my indignation where it does not excite my ridicule and as I said to a man I have presented a simile as a simile just as I present a candle for a light[1] [f 572] . . . or of the stench for your pains—In truth there are two errors the one places the centre in the circumference as the man who affirms life to be in the organization ⟨whereas the organization⟩ is nothing but the consequence of life nothing but the means by which and through which it displays itself—it is in truth its effects formed by the infinity of radii which proceed from that as a centre and which take collectively from the circumference The man therefore who states life to proceed from organization acts as a mathematician would who should be mad enough to assert the centre was placed in the circumference On the other hand one who would bring life from without either in the shape of a soul or any other would commit an equal fault in logic namely he would make the centre out of the circumference and besides that very unnecessarily I think confound animal life with the soul and the intellectual faculties for [f 573] I think too highly of my responsible nature to confound it with a something by which I am not distinguished from the merest animal—whatever life is in its present state it cannot be brought to account for that which is more especially constitutes us man

Now I am to state the effects of materialism in its different relations and first with respect to science there are three forms under one or the other of which all science must proceed—those are theory hypothesis or Law and it is in my intention to prove that by neither the first nor the last

---

[1] F 571 lacks catchword

of these can a materialist reason and only by the second which is hypothesis and that arbitrarily and most groundlessly—First then theory the origin of the word theorem contemplarii is to see as from an immense number of objects together in such a manner as to perceive their relations to each other—a perfect theory therefore is possible in mathematics only—the mathematician creating his terms that is determining that his [f 574] imagination*m* has had such and such acts for instance such and such lines he himself forms the terms with which he composes his proposition and consequently he knows well that there can be no more than those and no less for there being that exact number constitutes the proposition but he of course can never know by any possibility that he has exhausted all the terms if for instance in the composition and decomposition of water which is generally believed and which I think a late very eminent Physician declared to have an evidence fully equal to the mathematical science—we are told by the combustion of hydrogen and oxygen water is produced—again that if water is decomposed in a particular manner a certain proportion is oxygen and another hydrogen and that the quantities lost and gained will be perfectly equal at the sun but here it is clear in the first instance that the electrical spark is not taken in or is taken in as a mechanical agent, it may be [f 575] so but we know that the contrary theory namely that oxygen itself is only water combined with positive Electricity has been supported by very ingenious men and we have never heard of any mathematical demonstration or position whatever consequently a perfect theory is impossible in Physics but as far as we may essentially conclude for our purposes we have seen the objects which belonged to them—though it can never produce more than probability we shall discover some one which being taken for granted will serve as a support to all the rest will enable us to classify and to understand them and therefore out of every theory as far as it is a just or plausible theory there arises a just or ⟨a⟩ plausible hypothesis an hypothesis being only that fact which in a multitude of facts is observed as common to them all and which being ascertained the order and relation of all will be secured but a law will arise from an hypothesis only when having been once given it at once [f 576] supersedes*n* both hypothesis and theory—From a perfect theory arises an hypothesis that which we place under all—from a stedfast hypothesis arises a law and from a primary independent or absolute law a system

Thus Sir Isaac Newton contemplating the abstracts of material bodies as weight mass and motion and the conditions of a perfect theory as far

---

m Catchword on f 573: "im"   *n* Catchword on f 575: "super-"

as bodies are considered exclusively under the conceptions of weight mass and motion he made the bodies mathematical for he contemplated them under those conditions only which he could state abstractly and as parts of a definition From this arose his hypothesis of gravity and from this again finally the law of gravitation and thence forward neither theory nor hypothesis were further regarded nothing but the law was at all paid attention to with the law dwelt power and prophecy and by exclusive attention to the law it has been that late disciples of Sir Isaac Newton replace and others have removed all the apparent difficulties [f 577] in the theory of gravitation and turned them into the strongest confirmations of the same as they must But the progress of all great science is to labor at a law the question then is will ever Physics define . . . not as the heavenly bodies in abstract but competent to the same bodies I answer . . . and the other instruments impossible that we should ever acquire through mere observation perfect theory or in other words we can never be sure we have exhausted all the terms—that is that we have present to our knowledge all the agents and their relations but whether physics may or may not be ultimately elevated into science and prophetic power proceeding in the opposite direction that is from law to hypothesis and from hypothesis to theory the last of which will be . . . will depend of course upon the discovery [f 578] or non-discovery of such a centre and this again on the . . . and this again on whether the forms of the human conscience . . . mutatis mutandis and whether an absolute is contemplable in every dependent and finite but this is to conceal that scarcely had the present state of physics been removed from a law than the heavenly bodies appeared in the time of Kepler

Now it is clear that the materialist excludes all facts that are not immediately the objects of his senses by his very hypothesis he cannot have a theory for he determines first of all rather to place effect for cause than to concede any one thing which his reason dictates if only his senses do not at the same time give him a picture of it the law which is to come which is to fulfil how this can ever arise from mechanism which must be dependent constantly upon the accidents of the external world and therefore of all others the least fit to control it it would be useless to speak [f 579] but hypothesis or sub fictions may be had in abundance there may be atoms counteracted by atoms and these again counteracted by yet finer and so on to infinity and if only you will grant three or four moderate requests such as those Lycurgus demanded first of all atoms some one of which is a great deal larger than the others and having common powers of attraction and repulsion and these so and so modified then he will make a picture out of it having taken care that all the contents of the picture shall be put in the definitions and the assumptions before given

But if even in science it be pernicious what must its effects be in morals and in religion in religion it necessarily will lead either to atheism or to superstition—to atheism if it be driven into all its consequences for a man who affirms boldly that what the senses have not given to his mind which mind itself is but like the senses an organization of his body that he will [f 580] regard for nothing but words—that is he will look for those impressions of the senses which he is aware of and those are only the motions of articulated air—such a man cannot pretend to believe in a God—consequently *ᵒGod forbid I should say a man may not be very virtuous and pious in consequence and that the human heart will not often rescue the human headᵖ* but I say as a consequence reasonable a man cannot profess to believe in a God unless at the same time he professes to have seen him and been acquainted with him if he does that it is what we should call superstitious and if without thinking if he is a dogmatic materialist . . . by a corrupt and ignorant hierarchy he will worship statues and imagine the same power into those statues which the more philosophic materialist imagines in his composition of particles which are called organs But this would be nothing if it only left something in us to force a belief of God which cannot [f 581] be destroyed without destroying the basis of all truth that is it destroys the possibility of free agency it destroys the great distinction between the mere human and the mere animals of nature—namely the powers of originating an act—all things are brought even the powers of life are brought into a common link of causes and effect that we observe in a machine and all the powers of thought into those of life being all reasoned away into modes of sensation and the will itself nothing but a current a fancy determined by the accidental copulations of certain internal stimuli With such a being to talk of a difference between good and evil would be to blame a stone for being round or angular, the thought itself is repulsive—No the man forfeits that high principle of nature his free agency which though it reveals itself principally in his moral conduct yet is still at work in all departments of his being it is by his bold denial of this by an inward assertion I am not the creature of nature merely nor [f 582] a subject of nature but I detach myself from her—I oppose myself as man to nature and my destination is to conquer and subdue her and my destination is to be Lord of Light and Fire and the Elements and what my mind can comprehend that I will make my eye to see and what

---

ᵒ⁻ᵖ Parentheses inserted in pencil

my eye can see my mind shall instruct me to reach through the means of my hand so that every where the lower part of my nature shall be taken up into the higher and why because I am a free being I can esteem I can revere myself and as such a being I dare look forward to permanence as I have never yet called this body I but only mine even as I call my clothes so—I dare look forward to a continued consciousness to a continued progression of my powers for I am capable of the highest distinction that of being the object of the approbation of the God of the Universe which no mechanism can be—nay further I am the cause of the creation of the world for what cause to a being whose ideas are infinitely [f 583] more substantial than the things which are the results or are created from them what motive to create things that are not capable of right or wrong—what was there in them—not reality—they existed with an infinitely greater reality in the mind—the Deity knew in that which was God himself which could come from God only the will and power of becoming worthy of a return to that maker—this I say is so sacred a privilege that whatever dares to tell us that we are like the trees or like the streams, links in an inevitable chain and that the assassin is no more worthy of abhorrence than the dagger with which he murders his benefactor that man I say teaches treason against human nature and against the God of human nature shall I be told this is scepticism only—oh we have met with nothing like scepticism here we have met with truth, with nothing but the most dogmatic assertions from the time of Lucippus to Hobbs who was so far from anything like Scepticism that [f 584] he told Doctor Willis that he could demonstrate all Euclid was nonsense because he himself admitted that the eternal truth of metaphysics would be subversive of materialism and from Hobbs to . . . who having this objection made to him that if all things were dispositions of material particles or the result of them you might ask what colour such a virtue was answered with coolness yes and very properly too for as such a virtuous action is nothing but a generic term for so many particular acts which particular acts are but so many combinations of motions of a particular man which particular man must at that time have had such a coat on ~~without~~ with such and such impressions joining with that motion such was the color of his coat such was the colour of the action one would be surprised at this but looking into Condilliacs logic you will find it asserted what we have been told that a truly great man Professor Kant has justified this scepticism now that requires an answer—Kant has told us that there [f 585] are certain great truths which though they are born in the reason as ideas even as the mathematical theorems are in the pure understanding do not yet and cannot derive their reality from the reason—that in and of themselves as far as the reason was concerned merely

are certain great truths which though they
are born in the reason as ideas even as the
mathematical theorems are in the pure
understanding do not yet and cannot
derive their reality from the reason - that
in and of themselves as far as the reason
was concerned merely we should say we
cannot help from the nature of our reason
having such ideas and an existence therefore
in the reason they undoubtedly have
but whether there be any reality corres=
pondent to them whether the being of
God has likewise an existence that not our
reason can assure us - we believe it because
it is not a mere idea but a fact that
our consciousness bids us do unto others
as we would be done by and in all
things to make that a maxim of our
conduct which we can conceive without
a contradiction as being the law of
all rational being - This says he is a
fact but this being the case there is a
difference between regret and remorse
which is another fact and these would
be nonsense they would not be facts
if there were not a free will but there
                                    being
55

8. Frere manuscript, transcriber A's hand. VCL MS BT 23 f 585
Victoria University Library, Toronto; reproduced by kind permission

we should say we cannot help from the nature of our reason having such ideas and an existence therefore in the reason they undoubtedly have but whether there be any reality correspondent to them whether the being of God has likewise an existence that not our reason can assure us—we believe it because it is not a mere idea but a fact that our consciousness bids us do unto others as we would be done by and in all things to make that a maxim of our conduct which we can conceive without a contradiction as being the law of all rational being—This says he is a fact but this being the case there is a difference between regret and remorse which is another fact and these would be nonsense they would not be facts if there were not a free will but there [f 586] being a free will we should fall into an endless contradiction of nature for one part of our nature forces us to demand a value in things—that is their consequences with regard to our happiness Another part of our nature demands that there should be a worth in things, I will explain myself in a moment a man in a moment of hatred and revenge stabs me with a dagger he happens to have opened an imposthume and brings about my health that act is of value do I*q* therefore love the man or feel grateful to him, no I feel grateful to providence for using such an agent but for him nothing but detestation—why?—because one part of my nature demanded worth and could not be satisfied with the value only—again no man can pretend without insincerity to say he could . . . productive of no consequence but arising from the mind like a bubble of water bursting into nothing no, however pure they were [f 587] however*r* great the worth in the agent we should still complain of the want of value

Now our will is to a certain degree in our power and where it is not it is owing to some prior fault of ours but the consequences of that will are not in our power and hence there arises a moral interest that a being should be assumed in whom is the only will and the power that involves all consequences as one and the same which being supposed it then follows immediately that he who . . . and the consequences because his will marches under the banners of omnipotence—This is Kants scepticism it is a modest humility with regard to the powers of the intellect it was a means of curbing the pride of dogmaticism because he had seen that Des Cartes and others had their doctrines turned round and used by Spinosa and used . . . that is an unconscious something that being every where is no where that being [f 588] every thing it is nothing

But what does he say of another kind of assertion I will as literally as

---

q Punctuation (full stop or dash) inserted in pencil after "value"; "I" altered in pencil to a more unmistakably upper-case letter
r Catchword on f 586: "how-"

I can translate his words when he says the reason in things which concern super sensual objects such as the existence of God and a future state is denied the right which belongs to her to speak first then there is the door open to all fanaticism to all superstition and to atheism ⟨itself⟩ I know not says he but in some of the late writings of Jacobi and . . . I have heard of a philosophy which demonstrates the non existence of a Deity or at least asserts certain things which being granted such an idea becomes impossible I have seen them say that it is directly against reason to believe in a soul or in a free will that all consequent reasonings must necessarily lead to Spinozism that is to say to matter and thought being one and the same thing and matter having the priority so as to produce thought—by organization he goes on thus but that reason can easily give her full assent to that which [f 589] it is not in her power to produce that having herself produced the idea of a supreme being of a free will and of a future state as a consequence she can then without pretending herself to prove the reality gratefully receive such proof from revelation or from a moral and its dictates—this I can understand but when a man tells me that it is against his reason to believe such things that all argument proves the contrary and yet pretends to believe it from a principle of faith I am very glad that one thought remains to me that he may be a fanatic and not a hypocrite but one or the other must he be as none but a hypocrite or a fanatic would pretend to believe by faith not only what is above his reason but directly against it—Indeed I know no better definition of it and if you will allow me I will conclude with one little allegory if I may so express myself by which some time ago I endeavored to express my opinion between the materialist who would have nothing but what proceeded from his senses and the philosopher who thought it not beneath him to look [f 590] at the other part of his nature namely his mind and to see whether there he might not lead to some law which would render the objection from the other part of his nature intelligible I have said "Imagine the unlettered African . . . yet deep impression that his fates and fortunes are in some unknown manner connected with its contents every tent every grove . . . which however in the very height and utmost . . . the poor Indian too truly represents the state of learned . . . ignorant—arrangement guided by the light of . . . he explains to him the nature of [f 591] written words translates them for him into his native sounds and thence into the thoughts of his heart how many of these thoughts have evolved into consciousness henceforward the Book is unsealed for him the depth is opened out he communes on the spirit of the volume as a living oracle the words become transparent and he sees them as though he saw them not and then too shall we be in that state to which science in all its form is gradually leading us then will the other great Bible of God the Book of Nature become transparent to us when we regard the forms of matter as words as symbols valuable only for the meaning which they convey to us only for the life which they speak of and venerable only as being the expression an unrolled but yet a glorious fragment of the wisdom of the supreme being

LECTURE 13

^sM.^r Coleridges Lecture
Monday 22nd March 1819

I trust that the very nature of the subjects on which I am to address you will of themselves inform you that without compromising the very ends for which I stand^t here you must derive your best amusement from that degree of information which it will be in my power to impart—the subject itself cannot be ornamented or impassioned without placing you in the very state of mind subversive of the objects which I have in view There are few pursuits more instructive and not many more entertaining—I own than that of retracing the progress of a living language for a few centuries and its improvement^u as an organ and a vehicle of thought by desynomizing words—Thus as late as the restoration for instance ingenuous and [f 593] ingenious^v, ingenuity and ingenuousness were used indifferently the one for the other—propriety was the common term for propriety of behaviour for instance and for property in the sense of estate or ownership—Thus from the latin magister softened by the Italians into master we have made Mister as well as Master and thence Miss and Mistress and use them as contradistinctions^w of age and it would have been quite in the Course of the progress of language if another pronunciation which actually exists Massiter had been adopted by some great writer, Chaucer for instance, to express mastership instead of servant

This is the progress of language as society introduces new relations it introduces new distinctions and either new words are introduced or different pronunciations—Now the duty of a philosopher is to aid and com-

---

^s Above lozenge "Lect xii" written in pencil, probably in the hand of JHG, followed by "[really xiii]", pencilled in, probably by KC

^t "stand" seems written over erasure; pencilling seems erased from left-hand margin

^u Possibly "improvements"

^v Catchword on f 592: "in-"

^w Letters after "contrad" in "contradistinctions" written over erasure

plete this process as his subject demands and a distinction has perhaps almost already begun to carry an adjective to a substantive [f 594] we should say and be perfectly intelligible that Cowley was fanciful Milton imaginary Poets the Philosopher proceeds and establishes the same meaning—in fancy and imagination—for active philosophical language differs from common language in this only—or mainly at least that philosophical language does that more accurately and by an express compact which it unconsciously and as it were by a tacit compact aimed at and in part accomplished by the Common language though with less prescision and consistency—Thus in the philosophic world each contributing consistently to the finishing of that work the rudiments of which each man at large is unconsciously aiding to furnish—the mighty machinery goes on at once the . . . of the symptoms of the mind, the mind of the nation which speaks it

I have from the commencement of this Course been honored and supported by the respectful attention of my auditors[x] so much that it might well seem at once unseemly and unthankful to request it [f 595] on a particular occasion but I may request you to think with me to produce not a mere passive listening but an active concurrence for a few minutes while I define a few terms which once thoroughly understood and then borne in mind you will find little difficulty in following me or accompanying me through[y] the present lecture and here let me observe that the definitions of those terms are offered to you as verbal not as real definitions as explaining the sense in which certain terms are to be constantly employed not as positively affirming the truth and reality of the sense so expressed

I have named the pursuit of language entertaining as well as instructive and in a great number of instances it really is so but in all those subjects which require the mind to turn its attention inward upon its own operations it cannot be done without thought and thinking is an effort which habit only can render other than vain I proceed then to the definitions [f 596] first that which appears by weight or what in Chemistry is called ponderable Substance is in philosophic language body—second that which appears but not by weight or the imponderable substance is matter—thus sunshine we should not in common language call a body though we might not hesitate to call it a material phenomenon but the painter alludes to a body of sunshine because he alludes to the body laid on to produce the resemblance—thirdly that what does not appear which has no outwardness but must be either known or inferred but cannot be

---

[x] First two letters of "auditors" written over erasure; pencilled "au/" seems erased from right-hand margin

[y] First three letters of "through" written over erasure

directly perceived we call spirit or power—fourthly in speaking of the world without us as distinguished from ourselves the aggregate of phenomenon ponderable and imponderable is called nature in the passive sense—in the language of the old schools natura . . . efficient causes of the former which by Aristotle and his followers were called the actual fluid was nature in the active sense [f 597] or natura naturems fifthly on the other hand when reflecting on ourselves as intelligences and therefore individualizing Spiritual powers that which affirms its own existence and whether mediately or immediately that of our beings we call—mind—I believe if you ask yourselves you will find that is the strict sense which you have been accustomed consciously or unconsciously to attach to the word—lastly we contradistinguish the mind or the percipient power from that which it perceives the former has been very conveniently I think entitled the subject and the latter the object—hence the mind may be defined to a subject which has its own object and hence those who attribute a reality to bodies and to material phenomena independent of the mind that perceives them and yet assert equally an independent reality of the mind itself namely those who believe in both immaterial and corporeal substances or in the language of the day in soul and body both would [f 598] define the body as merely . . . an idealist would declare the material and corporeal world to be wholly subject that is to exist only as far as it is perceived in other words he the idealist—conceives a real existence to two terms only—to the natura naturams in Berkelys language to God and to the finite minds on which it acts and . . . or the bodily world being the result even as the tone between the wind and the Eolian harp I remember when I was yet young this fancy struck me wonderfully and here are some verses I wrote on the subject

> "And what if all of animated nature
> Be but Organic harps diversely framed
> That tremble into thought as o'er them sweeps
> Plastic and vast one intellectual breeze
> At once the Soul of each and God of all"

Now in and from this last view that of the idealists I mean arises the difficulty and perplexity of our metaphysical vocabulary [f 599] as long as the subject that is the percipient was opposed to the object namely the thing perceived all was clear—Again in considering the finite . . . or as the subject of becoming an immediate object to itself—but incapable of being an immediate object to itself but incapable of being an immediate object to any one other finite subject—there would be no great difficulty—a mans thoughts are known only to God and himself as reduced as a rule . . . but when not only the mind's self consciousness but all other things perceived by it are regarded as modifications of itself as disguised but actual modes of self perception—then the whole ground of the difference between subject and object appears good all is subject and the sole distinction is first between that which not only is but is [f 600] thought of by us as being such and that which indeed truly is so no less than the former but which we think of as being the contrary. By way of illustration man contemplates the image of his friend not only his recollection of the friend is in his mind but ^{z}he contemplates it as such but when his friend is present though according to the idealist that impression is as much in his mind as the former ⟨he⟩ yet considers it to be external and independent of himself secondly the distinction that^a between that which all men are by the common necessity constrained so to imagine and that which is accidental and individual as for instance all men in a sane state are compelled to see the objects which all others at least see around them as compared with the man who in a fever or delirium blends objects which no man else perceives—so that one of the elder idealists will state the subject according to his view of it that when we are awake we have a dream in common when asleep every man^b has a dream of his own ~~that is when we are awake we have a world in Common and when we are asleep~~ [f 601] ~~every man has a dream of his own~~ that is^c when we are awake we have a world in common and when we are asleep every man has a World of his own—we have only to reverse this order of thought and we shall have the opposite result that of the materialist all that is merged in the objective as the former in the subjective and these reduced as before into the general and permanent and the particular transitory— the thoughts of a tale according to the materialist differs from the tale itself not by essential invisibility or by being essentially imponderable but only because this portion of the brain is too thin and subtle to be perceptible of weight and it is truly owing to the defect of our organs that we cannot weigh our thoughts or measure our perceptions—henceforward . . . or motions thereof independent of the perception itself and the second meaning the universality of the perception as arising out of inherent laws of human nature in opposition [f 602] to the accidental state of any one individual percipient—that grass is green is an instance of the former that it appears yellow to a man in the Jaundice if such be the fact would be an instance of the latter

---

$^{z-a}$ Lineation and handwriting slightly different from surrounding text, as though passage was inserted later into space left for it

^{b} Written "everyman", but words seem likely to have been carelessly tied

^{c} Pencilled word in right-hand margin (perhaps "World") erased

Still most serious difficulties started and have been stated with incomparable clearness by Lord Bacon in his Novum organum it is thus that the human understanding itself is but an individuality in nature having its own peculiar organization and modifying all objects even its own form of self consciousness no less than the forms seen as external by its own peculiar appropriate perspective in the language of our British Plato there are not only idols of the den the theatre and the market place—the idols or delusions of our passions of our imagination and of custom and habit but idols of the res idola toribus and consequently the utmost that rational conviction can arrive to is not that this ⟨or that is⟩ true by any inherent necessity [f 603] but only that it is for man that he is compelled so to perceive and so to conceive and the deductions thus drawn can be questioned only by those who admit themselves to be deranged—that is not in the same order with their fellowmen—To what an extent this position has been carried by ancient and by modern sceptics it will be sufficient that I remind you by one observation of Mr Hume in the Essays in the form in which they first appeared namely that if spiders had been theologians they would have been under the necessity of concluding that the world had been spun and ⟨that⟩ though a philosopher . . .^d ⟨one question would⟩ would occur to every reflecting hearer pray would this spider have the power of fitting its own perception and conclusion? if so and if the spider be but a nickname for a rational being proposed for misleading the fancy by a verbal association and the spider means no more than a serious sober man arguing in defence of his Maker must there not be some other faculty above [f 604] this mechanism by which man is adapted to his present circumstances must there not be some power calling with Lord Bacon the Roman . . . the pure light with . . . call it a faith a reason must there not be some power that stands in human nature but in some participation of the external and the universal by which man is enabled to question nay to contradict^e the irresistible impressions of his own senses the necessary deductions of his own understanding to change and disqualify them as partial and . . . think you that the man who even first dared suggest to his own mind the thought that the sun did not really rise did not really move^f through the heavens but that this was the first prospect of his eye and his position only—think you that a man who diseased and beholding plainly before him such and such objects dared say that these things are not so was not at the same time conscious of something nobler than his perceptions [f 605] themselves could a machine or any part of a

---

^d Some writing seems to have been erased to create this space
^e "tr" of "contradict" seems written over erasure
^f Last two letters of "move" seem written over erasure

machine pass out of itself? if it can what becomes of the famous doctrine that our ideas have no other pretence to truth except as their generalizations or classifications and impressions passively perceived through the mechanisms of sense and sensation but I need not inform you that a numerous class of modern philosophers assert no such faculty exists the notion is a mere abortion of pride engendered in the imagination but still though I call not improperly this class numerous they yet appear numerous in consequence of their fewness of their contrariety of opinions to the feelings of mankind in general which makes me wonder so many would be found entertaining such doctrines—Still I say it must make us pause that positions asserted to differ from noise only by the sounds being articulated that positions which are affirmed to have no origin in kind but delusion[g] and which traced to their source [f 606] will be found to arise from sophisms of the mere imagination that these absurd doctrines should have been held not only by the mass of mankind in all ages but by the best and the wisest even by those whom these very philosophers are obliged to place forward in their list whenever they have occasion to enumerate the chief luminaries and benefactors of the race—that these absurd positions should be the ground work of all law so inwoven in all language that we may fairly find a materialist or an atheist to talk consistently with his own opinions any five minutes and that they should be taken for granted in every thing that distinguishes man from the brute even in the degree[h] in which he is so distinguished for these philosophers are compelled by their own principles to deny any distinction between us and the brute in kind—however be this as it may the facts remain as I have stated and if I have succeeded in rendering them intelligible and comparatively [f 607] short they will explain the subjects of this lecture which is the object with which I have stated them

I am so deeply impressed with the benefit which we all receive by the associations of love and honor with the names of great men in past times how much they make up the historical feeling of a Country and give to every individual who has cultivated his intellect a pride of heraldry far beyond that which a descendant of Julius Ceasar would enjoy if he contemplated his own family merely from himself that I shrink from violating any genuine persuasion in favor of a mans greatness and never indeed approach to it unless where I can[i] at the same moment offer him a substitute and feel at least in my own mind the belief that the pain he suffers at the moment will be more than compensated by the pleasure that fol-

---

[g] First two letters of "delusion" written over erasure
[h] First letter of "degree" seems written over erasure
[i] "can" seems written over erasure; evidence of erased pencilling in right-hand margin

lows—this I certainly feel—more especially when I speak of Mr Locke my [f 608] conscience^j bears me witness that it is not from any neglect of studying his writings or of seeking for assistance from those who have professed to do so but sincerity compels me to say that after all the study and all the assistance I could never discover any one thing to account for that prodigious impression that seems to have been made either in the novelty of the sentiments or in the system of those which are peculiar to him I verily believe myself that the case stood thus we were becoming a Commercial people we were becoming a free people in enjoyment as we had always been in right—Mr Lockes name and his services which of themselves would be sufficient to immortalize him had connected his name with that of freedom and that of the revolution from the natural attachment of old and established learned bodies to old and established political bodies which had been their protectors it was not to be wondered that those who were [f 609] supposed to teach the philosophy of past times were found mainly amongst those who supported the old forms of government it was . . . and that the same great revolution was to go on in mind that had been going on in state affairs and that as King William had completely done away with all the despotism of the Stuarts so Mr Locke had^k done away altogether with the nonsense of the schoolmen and the universalists in consequence of which people read who had never once examined the subject or thought about it and found some monstrous absurdities that they themselves had never heard of before and they found them most ably confuted to those absurdities they attributed all they had connected in their own minds with the abuses and miseries of former ages utterly neglecting the good at the time they had considered^l this as a new light stepping into the World and it is not once [f 610] or two or three times that I have heard it stated when I referred to the Writers before William the 3rd Oh you forget there was no light till Locke Milton Shakespeare and so on were forgotten—they were poets but it is clear the reign of good sense came in with Locke now one of the followers of Locke Hume who has carried the premises to the natural^m consequences has allowed^n that he did not completely understand the first book of Locke what was understood and what overthrown—but I believe it may be traced historically nearer that Des Cartes was the first man who made a direct division between man and nature the first man who made nature utterly life-

---

^{j} Catchword on f 607: "con-"
^{k} "had" seems written over erasure
^{l} First three letters of "considered" written over erasure
^{m} "natural" seems written over erasure; erased pencilling in right-hand margin
^{n} "allowed" a correction, perhaps of "followed"

less and Godless considered it as the subject of merely mechanical laws
and having emptied it of all his life and all that makes it nature in reality
he referred all the rest to what he called spirit ⟨consequently the faculty
of spirit⟩ in relation to this matter—what must be then the perception
what was it then to perceive—why it was not for mechanical laws prevented his admission of that not as the old Platonists would have said perceiving the things outward—Physiology had advanced [f 611] too far to
render that attainable he therefore conceived what he called material
ideas that is as he supposed there was in the soul causative powers which
produced images*o* for it so that there was in the brain certain modes that
preexisted*p* in itself and which determined it to receive such and such impressions rather than others and these he had called material ideas and in
consequence of their origin being in the organization itself he had named
them innate ideas in both senses—first of all the true ideas or spiritual
ones he conceived as having their birth place in the mind and those material ideas he considered innate as having their birth place in the organization but the Jesuit Grotius before Locke wrote had attacked this on the
ground that Locke proceeds on but the answer Des Cartes makes who was
a truly great man is this—I said innate not quallate I spoke of the birth
place not the time do you suppose that either I or any man in his senses
nay I will add that any man out of his senses [f 612] could imagine such
an absurdity as that men heard before they heard that they had images*q*
before they saw—these things are too absurd to be attributed to any man
in his senses much more to a philosopher but still admitting that and taking Des Cartes without his material hypothesis at all nothing can be more
simple than what he says or*r* more agreeable to common sense and what
indeed was not first said by Des Cartes it would be difficult to find anywhere among the schoolmen in which you will not find the same things
said or among the ancient metaphysicians which is simply this that there
must be a difference in the perceptions of a mouse and a man but this difference cannot be in the object perceived but in the percipient that therefore says Des Cartes we have reason to suppose that there are two sorts
of ideas or thoughts if says he two really be these are Des Cartes' own
words I am now speaking logically and as a grammarian not as a mathematician if there are two differences one is of those [f 613] thoughts or
images in which we are conscious of being passive*s* those which are im-

---

o "images" written over erasure; "image" or "images" in pencil in right-hand margin
erased
  p Written over erasure; erased pencilling in right-hand margin
  q "images" partly written over erasure; erased pencilling in right-hand margin
  r "or" seems written over erasure; erased pencilling in right-hand margin
  s First letter of "passive" written over erasure

pressed upon us whether we will or no and those as appearing to have their causes externally we call external ideas but says he there are others in which the mind is conscious of its own activity and tracing its own operations forms notions which from the place of their origin we call innate ideas—he then goes on with a definition*ᵗ* which is noticeable you may see it in his answer to Boetius by being word for word the same as Lockes definition of the reflection so that in truth the man of straw that was to be thrown down never existed but the real assertion to be opposed was not merely in substance but totidem verbis et . . . the idea in Locke's reflection

The abuse of the word idea by Des Cartes and Locke I shall not further speak of and therefore I simply say and most happy should I be to stand corrected by any man*ᵘ* who could give me better information that if you [f 614] only substitute for the phrase the ideas being derived from the senses or imprest upon the mind or in any way supposed to be brought in—for nothing can be more mechanical or pagan like than the phrases used in the Essay on the Human understanding—if for this you only substitute the word elicit namely that there are no conceptions of our mind relatively to external*ᵛ* objects but what are elicited by their circumstances and by what are supposed to be correspondent to them there would be nothing found in Locke but what is perfectly just but at the same time I must say nothing but what is perfectly what had been taught from the beginning of time to the end and with regard to the rest the grammatical part I think I took the fairest way of convincing myself that a man could I took the abridgement of his work published at Cambridge for the use of the young men at the University and having it interleaved from Des Cartes and with no other guide I wrote opposite to each paragraph the precise same [f 615] thing written before not by accident not a sort of hint that had been given but directly and connectedly the same—the question therefore amounts precisely to this—Mʳ Lockes phrases seem to say that the sun the rain the manure and so on had made the wheat had made the barley and so forth but we cannot believe that a man who was certainly a very wise man in his generation could have meant this and that he was only misled in the expressions from his not being made apprehensive of the consequences to be deduced from them if for this you substitute the assertion that a grain of wheat might remain for ever and be perfectly useless and to all purposes non apparent had it not been that the congenial sunshine and proper soil called it forth—every thing in Locke would be perfectly rational I am only standing in amazement to know what is added

---

ᵗ Last three syllables of "definition" written over erasure
ᵘ Written carelessly "anyman"   *ᵛ* "external" corrected

to it for never have I been able to learn from repeated questioning these what was done—the only answer has been did [f 616] not he overthrow innate ideas Locke is no materialist he teaches no doctrine of infidelity whatever may be deduced from them in his controversy with the Bishop of Worcester speaking of substance where the Bishop says substance can never be brought to an image . . . that which stands under every possible image precluded this—what is Lockes answer—I never denied the mind could form a just image of itself by reflection and deduction so that in truth those who have drawn the doctrines of mere materialism from Locke certainly drew what he never intended to draw and with regard to the rest I remain as before I have not yet been able to discover the ground or any ground why I should calumniate all the great men that went before him in compliment to any one idol however deserving of praise in other respects as to say that because Locke told us in defining words we ought to have distinct images or [f 617] conceptions[w] . . . which Cicero never heard of and which was a strange thing to Plato but I can very easily understand that men with far less merit than Locke and even men who wrote more entertainingly for that is a great thing—when a Book has once got a character if it should be so dull that nobody should read it afterwards it saves the reputation for centuries this we have had instances of in others many circumstances combined at the time the first was that Des Cartes had had his physical prophecies and other parts of his Mechanical system overthrown by Sir Isaac Newton but the . . . as Locks ideas of reflection therefore one great man had overthrown the physical parts and another the mathematical parts and to that circumstance we owe entirely the custom of talking of Locke and Newton to that accident entirely—the next thing [f 618] was that Voltaire and others before him both in France and in Germany had held up . . . a truly great man but as a sort of rival to our Newton and any one who has read the literary and scientific history of that time well knows that nothing in politics could excite more fury than the controversy concerning the arithmetic as to who was the inventor this again interested the natural feelings but Leibnitz supposed . . . and here again there was another connection made between Locke and Newton he was opposed ⟨to⟩ Leibnitz and the . . . which had been invented by our Newton At that time too we know well the very great heats that there were between the high Church and the low Church and at the same time the existence of a middle party who while they kept to the Church yet still favored all the tolerant opinions and in general in what was in terms the most rational [f 619] way of interpreting the religion but Locke was . . .

---

[w] Catchword on f 616: "con"

while the Clergy at large and the religious people found that in an age
when the Philosophers were beginning to be notorious as infidels there
was a man of true piety who wrote very edifying comments as they really are on the Scriptures and those won that party while the infidels such
as Voltaire and others cried him up beyond all bounds he was the true
modest man he had referred all things to the effects to mind . . . who smiling at Mr Locks deductions said they were merely amulets against Priestcraft take them in the lowest sense which Locke did not intend if you
doubt just refer to the beginning of Humes essay on cause and effect you
will find immediately the Channels made on Lockes opinions every
where it is you have no real truth but what is derived from your senses it
is in vain to talk of your ideas of reflection for what are they they must
have been originally^x in our senses or there is no ground [f 620] for
them—So many circumstances combined together as to make it a kind
of national pride in the first place and secondly the interest of almost each
of the parties to cry out Mr Locke and the effect is shewn more especially
that the most ingenious I think some of the finest works of philosophy for
that period those produced by the great Stillingfleet and others were not
merely put at once as trash out of fashion but it was said that Stillingfleet
had died of a broken heart in consequence of his defeat by Locke though
wherein the man was to become defeated till we can find how Locke differed from others is for other considerations I can therefore say this finally with regard to Locke that it was at the beginning of a time when
they felt one thing that the great advantage was to convince mankind that
the whole process of reacting upon their own thoughts or endeavoring to
deduce any truth from them was mere presumption and henceforward
men were to be entirely under the guidance of their senses this was most
favorable to a Country already busy with politics, busy [f 621] with commerce and which yet there was a pride in nature that a man would not
like^y to remain ignorant of that which had been called the Queen of Sciences which was supposed above all things to alleviate the mind which
had produced a word which a man had overthrown—had . . . that of
Philosopher what a delight to find it all nonsense that there was nothing
but what a man in three hours might know as well as the Archbishop of
Canterbury—this exactly suited the state of the nation and I believe it was
a symptom of that state of Providential Government of the world which
observed the nearer union of the Kingdoms of Europe to each other what
in a former time had been distinctions co-existing in each Country were
now to be a distinction of whole Countries formerly we were to have the

---

^{x} Last two letters of "originally" seem written over erasure
^{y} "like" written over erasure; pencilled "like/" partly erased in right-hand margin

men who employed their senses chiefly and those again who employed their brains and their spirits all in one Country the time had come when by a subdivision of labor one Country was to employ its brains another its hands [f 622] and another its senses there was a subdivision among the Countries which before had been made between the inhabitants of several Countries and this was evident in Germany Germany never had the advantages that this Country has never had that fulness of occupation by commerce never that deep interest in the affairs of the whole which constitutes the pride and is perpetually improving the faculties of Englishmen who still carry their Country home to their fire side but on the other hand it had many and great advantages of its own it was the number of its universities and the circumstance that the learned or studied men formed a sort of middle class of society correspondent to our middle Class and the very absence of nationality gave to the Germans as they became Cosmopolites as they are the only . . . the only writers truly impartial in their accounts of other nations—if they err it has been from want of information or wrong premises but never from any national [f 623] feeling whatsoever and the same cause rendering the outward world of less importance to them rendered each man of more advantage to them made them a thinking metaphysical[z] people in other words their defect for in every nation and every individual put your hand upon the defect of a nation and you will find there its excellence and upon its excellence you will find there its defect so it is the defect of Germany to be for ever reasoning and thinking and in other Countries perhaps happier to have a great aversion to thinking at all now Leibnitz first opposed Lockean Philosophy as then understood in the simplest manner in which it could be—M[r] Lockes followers had repeated there is nothing in the mind which was not before in the senses[a] Leibnitz added . . . except the mind itself and he then proceeds in his new language to demonstrate in the most beautiful manner that all those puzzling laws which appeared which Locke had in vain endeavored to draw from external [f 624] objects while in truth the very first process presupposed the knowledge of the contrary as for instance the very first process to limit a space presupposes the want of limit if I draw in my imagination a circle or a sphere I must have a preconception of the unlimited before I can examine the limits itself—he shewed[b] that all the subjects at all in controversy were the operations of the intellect

---

[z] Pencilling (delete sign referring to "a"?) partially erased in right-hand margin

[a] Short wavy line, about four letters long, separates "the" from "senses", as though space had previously been left; pencilled delete sign faintly visible in right-hand margin

[b] Last four letters of "shewed" written over erasure

itself that they were not indeed things but they were acts of mind*c* or forms
and in a manner that was as elegant as really it was forcible in demonstration he shewed that there were two points in which M*r* Lockes Philosophy was altogether disorder in that first of all which I have just now
mentioned that every one of those experiences to which he refers presupposed a certain something in the mind as the condition of that experience and he admits as Kant has afterwards done that Locke was not unaware of this that though it did not enter into his plan and though it was
afterwards [f 625] received by many of his followers yet he speaks of predisposing causes in the mind which would really amount to no more than
this the acts of the mind itself—The next point which he pressed on the
Lockeans is this all we know of matter and the external world is transient
and to everything which refers to reality we attribute a something particular the dependence upon particular time particular Space whereas there
are a whole class of truths which are distinguished by their universality
by their necessity as for instance I will take two truths but of which every
man that now hears me is as much convinced practically of one as the
other—namely the first the sun will rise to morrow and second that the
two sides of a triangle continue greater than the third side we are convinced of it but we feel the diversity of the two propositions there is no
absurdity however wild if a man were to say it is my opinion that the sun
will not rise to morrow that [f 626] in the night the system will be destroyed there is no absurdity in the thing but should a man tell you that in
a month or two the two sides of a triangle will be less than the third then
you know he is teaching a language he does not understand for madness
could not conceive or attach a meaning to the words—where is this to be
derived from—the nature of the mind itself—what is this mind reduce it
to a result of the organization of matter and it must inevitably partake of
all that is transitory in this matter of which it is a property—suppose it to
be the mind itself and not matter then we ask what in the name of wonder can be the organs of a mind what is the mechanism of the mind what
are these but vague words that can after all come to nothing more than
what we express by the word ideas*d*—what we know of our own mind
we know by its thoughts—what are the thoughts—are they for instance
particles or corpuscles we are too apt to use words derived from external
objects that I verily believe that many a man before he asked himself the
question [f 627] would imagine his mind made of thoughts as a wall is of

---

c Short wavy line, about three letters long, separates "of" from "mind"; pencilled delete
sign partially erased in right-hand margin
d "word ideas" seems written over erasure

bricks till he asks whether he ever separated a thought from a thought
whether there was a meaning in the word thought except as the mind
thinking in such a situation whether a notion of any plurality or anything
we can call construction takes place in our experience we are aware of no
such thing the mind passes on and in vain would it be to distinguish
thought from thought till we had reduced it to words and by distinction
of pen or of printer we had made them visible then our eyes recognize the
character find out divisions but the senses discover none such might be
called the Philosophy of Leibnitz in relation to Mr Locke a far higher
ground is taken as he stands on his own system

I have not felt myself allowed from the limits which my Lectures have
placed round me to enter particularly on Spinoza because the substance
of his life I could have said I have been obliged [f 628] to anticipate first
in the act of the Eliatic school the idealists of old and secondly in the act
of the new Platonists but great impressions has Spinoza made on the
minds of the learned and an impression on the Theologians and the theologic hatred of his name is one of the most incomprehensible parts of
Philosophic researches for Spinoza was originally a Jew and he held the
opinions of the most learned Jews particularly the Cabalistic philosophers
next he was of the most pure and exemplary life and it has been said of
him if he did not think as a Christian he felt and acted like one thirdly so
far from proselyting this man published not a system it was a posthumous
work published against his will but what is still more strong he was offered by a German Prince a high salary with perfect permission to preach
his doctrines without the least danger instead of accepting this he wrote
to the Prince to reprimand him for his neglect [f 629] of his duty and ask
him what right he had to abuse the confidence the Fathers of Germans
had placed in him opposite to their wish and if we come at last to the mans
own professions and service I have no doubt they were I have seen many
questions . . . to believe that not only the immediate publishers of Spinoza's writings but that Spinoza did think that his system was identical
with but that of Christianity on so subtle a point that at least it was Pantheism but in the most religious form in which it could appear for making the Deity that which is independent which is certain in and of itself
and needs no argument but which is implied in all other truth and by making all other truths dependent upon that—beyond any other system of
Pantheism it divided the Deity from the creature—On the other hand I
am far from hiding the inevitable [f 630] consequences^e of Pantheism in

^{e} Catchword on f 629: "con"

all cases whether the Pantheism of India or the solitary classes of Spinoza—he erred however where thousands had erred before him in Christian charity communicating his opinions to those only from whom he expected information and to end all the quiet family in which he lived when he was too ill to attend publicly he still kept regularly to their duty and when they come home as regularly examined them and made them repeat the sermon and comment upon it according to their impressions a character like that so unlike an infidel scarcely exists and I cannot understand the cause . . . as a dead dog—At this time Leibnitz had the courage to say that Spinozas arguments were inevitable were it not that the system of . . . could not be defended he had (that is Spinoza) affirmed there were . . . transitory as the waves of the sea having no other qualities naturally but what arise externally from their relation to each other Leibnitz thought the system [f 631] of Spinoza namely that the Deity as the great mind not merely modified into thoughts as our minds do but gave each thought a reality and that the Deity was really different from all creatures by that thing . . . his thoughts were more real than the effects of them that therefore he gave a reality to those thoughts and that whatever was possible became real not merely as thoughts nor yet by a participation of the reality but by a communication of this reality to that which was so thought by the Deity and when he was called on to explain the nature of the body and its relation to the mind he first of all joined with Spinoza in overthrowing the doctrine of Des Cartes—And here if you will permit me I will pause for a few moments on this the most interesting part of the subject as referring to the doctrine of materialism—the only argument that I believe ever really disturbs men of sincere [f 632] and sober minds is that which is derived from the seeming truth of a decay of the mind with the body we see it they say grow with the body with the organization—as the organization is affected we see it affected and when that decays this decays this is however a mere sophism of the fancy for first it asserts universally what in any sense is true only partially and certain facultys of memory may awaken into Judgment and seem to increase—again it asserts of all what holds good only of some a man from the time he has the use of his will devotes it entirely to his bodily pleasure or to his ambition or power or a desire of making money constantly and thus he occupies his mind from youth till he is feeble and do you wonder at last when the whole joke is discovered when the pleasure is no longer pleasure when the ambition has sickened and when money is representative of the world with the folly of men do you wonder that a mind so naked of all that could remain and be permanent felt at the same time a necessity of withdrawing all attention from the organs of outward [f 633] perception^f which presented no symbols of aught that any longer interested it but compare such a mind with Newton with Leibnitz who died fainting away in the act of a great discovery or trace the history of the great Greek philosophers and Poets refer to Titian and Michael Angelo and there see whether or no the picture of an old age of manhood and that which had been used to what was noble praiseworthy and permanent does not present a different picture or go into humble life take the true modest Christian who has passed a life of struggle with self will who has watched to love his neighbour as himself and who entertains a constant faith that not merely the outward body and clothings but the greater part of our intellectual vanity will be as useless in the state into which he is passing as the thoughts of a grub which has passed three years in the mud would be to the butterfly when risen out of the stream but who had past the time in what [f 634] in redering the will productive in giving the will a causative power and fitting it for a higher state—Take the . . . of which man is born observe the glory with which it is conquered and then tell us that because the memory of some insignificant circumstance is weakened or that the man can no longer talk so as to excite applauses therefore the whole mind is gone No when we are most and best ourselves all that remains and all that could decay is but the cracks on the caterpillars skin it is the loss of the caterpillar faculty which the new life of society is beginning to do without

But again it is the truth it presumes a truth of materialism which yet after the point allowed it is more than a . . . it is a begging of the question it assumes the conclusion as the very ground upon which it is to begin for suppose a fact that A and B live and decay together surely it does not follow therefore [f 635] that B is the cause of A! . . . if the mind or the power from within . . . nay all the analogy of nature is in favor . . . and in the other from without and so to it would be though A and B taken as the mind and the organization . . . the mind and body immediately by a miracle according to Des Cartes or by some Common thing between partaking of the nature both of body and soul according to one Doctor Henry Moore Now a phenomenon that admits of equal solution from four different hypotheses cannot in any common sense be thought to prove the truth of any one of them—why then does it strike—the answer is simply this because the impressions upon our senses are always more vivid and connected with sensation [f 636] than those connected with thought and this all must be struck with it who mistake vivid pictures for clear perceptions the very circumstances of this bribery in favor of the doctrine

^f Catchword on f 632: "per-"

contrasted with the fact that the doctrine is held in abhorrence by mankind in general is decisive of it for we act against a bribe in our nature this forms the last part of the Leibnitzian philosophy which rejecting . . . this was however too opposite to common sense and for Leibnitz to Kant and Voltaire . . . was all that remained the rest was falling apace into the Eclectic system . . . and from that which instead of being any Philosophy at all was a direct unmanning of the mind and rendering it incapable of any systematic thinking

In this wretched state was not only Germany when Kant arose—his merits [f 637] consisted[g] in three things namely the first was that he examined the faculties critically before he hazarded any opinions concerning the positions which such faculties had led men to establish—he entered into a real examination of the balance before he would suffer any weights to be put in the scale and thus he did as alone could be done of that time upon the ground of reflection taking the human mind only as far as it became an object of reflection—in this way he saw that there were two classes of truth received by men—the one he observed were truths of experience and were uncertain in the conviction and which increased by accumulation so that what was but faintly believed for the first month became more the second and more the third and perhaps many centuries past before it came to full perception and even here in England was susceptible of alteration and change—[f 638] other truths he perceived to be immediately insusceptible to the conviction they produced—the moment they were understood they were as certain as they would be after 100 years of attention—he perceived that the one were necessarily particular the other universal—the one necessarily contingent the others bearing in themselves the absurdity of their contrary and he affirmed therefore that here we had found a criterion of the acts of the mind or the forms which arise out of the mechanism of the mind itself and of this if I may so call it substance[h] of reality which the sensations gave to us but still he carried this to a great extent for while he admitted that there was a power in the reason of producing ideas to which there were no actual correspondents in outward nature and therefore they were only to be regarded as regulative he was then asked or rather he asked himself what would become of the ideas of God of the free will of immortality for these too were the offspring of the reason and these too it would be said were merely regulative forms to which no outward or [f 639] real correspondent[i] could be

---

[g] Catchword on f 636: "con-"
[h] Space left, about three letters wide, between "it" and "substance", possibly after erasure; partially erased pencilled delete sign faintly visible in right-hand margin
[i] First four or five letters of "correspondent" seem written over erasure

expected here then he disclosed what I may call the roof of his Christianity which rendered him truly deserving the name Philosopher and not the analysis of the mind—He says In my . . . into the whole human being—there is yet another and not only another but a far higher and nobler constituent of his being his will the practical reason and this does not announce itself by arguing but by direct command and precept—thou shalt do to others as thou wouldst be done by thou shalt act so that there shall be no contradiction in thy being and from this he deduced a direct moral necessity for the belief or the faith of reason and having first shewn that though the reason could bring nothing positively coercive in proof of religious truth which if it could it would cease to be religion and become mathematical yet they demonstrated nothing could be said with reason against them and that on the other hand there was all the analogy all [f 640] the harmony of nature all moral interests and last of all there was a positive command which if he disobeys he is at once a traitor to his nature—nay even to his common nature

Such was I think the great merits of Kant I have not mentioned a particular merit he had namely that by the first clearly shewing the nature of space and time as habits not of thinking as Leibnitz supposed by the perception he secured it . . . the Platonist of a pre-existent light on the one hand and the degrading notions of the materialists which considered it as Chemistry or an empyrical proof this was a great merit but still greater was it that he determined the nature of religious truth and its connexion with the understanding and made it felt to the full that the reason itself considered as merely intellectual was but a subordinate part[j] of our nature that there was a higher part the will and the conscience and that if the [f 641] intellect[k] of man was the cherub that flew with man it flew after the flaming seraph and but followed its track that to be good is and ever will be not a mere consequence of being wise but a necessary condition of the process—In short he determined the true meaning of Philosophy for all our knowledge may be well comprised in two terms the one philology that is to say all the pursuits in which the intellect of man is concerned in which he has a desire of arriving at that which the Logos or intellectual power can communicate—the other is Philosophy or that which comprises the Logos and including it at the same time subordinates it to the Will and thus combining the other is philosophy the love of wisdom with the wisdom of love

My time will not permit me to enter into any account of . . . as I intended but in truth I should be puzzled to give you a true account ⟨for⟩ I

---

[j] "part" seems written partly over erasure　　[k] Catchword on f 640: "in"

might at one time refer you to Kant and there I should say what . . . appears at one [f 642] time—another time to Spinosa as applied to philosophy and then again I should find him in the writings of Plotinus and still more of Proclus but most in the writings of a Jesuit who opposed the Protestants I think about the time of James the First but got silenced for it for his great object like that of . . . was to justify the worship of saints by endeavoring to convince the world that God consisted in the saints an opinion which I believe so completely won . . . heart that the last act of his life was a most extraordinary one namely that this Roman Catholic Pantheist who with a Rosary in one hand and a Bible in the other had received a call from . . . to Yenna which is a Protestant Town under Protestant government and he accepted it under these conditions that he was to have two professions that of Philosophy and that of Theology that a church should be given him to preach in the weekdays and all for the purpose of convincing the young men that their Salvation was concerned in their becoming Papists and . . . has described well the old [f 643] system he says when I was young and used to see the ceremonies of the Catholics we used to go home put on some shirts and act through the whole ceremonies with wonderful delight and I find . . . and the new converts were doing the same thing for they well knew if they held but a tenth part of what they thought it must be a bad heretic indeed that would not believe without . . . any inquisition that it was mere mockery or as one of the . . . told me . . . you think only of one sort of religion but you know in our Country we distinguish sciences into two kinds every man[1] has his bread science and at the same time his . . . science his dwelling or hobby horse—Now it is so with me says he I am teaching religion I . . . but my bread is a Roman Catholic Church and I prefer that to the other doctrines because it is more like the ancient Pagans

On Monday I deliver my last lecture and my last address to you and the public as a lecturer with a review of all the preceding course and the application of it.

---

[1] Written "everyman"

SELECTIONS FROM OWEN BARFIELD'S INTRODUCTION AND NOTES

THE HISTORY OF PHILOSOPHY

INTRODUCTION

BY OWEN BARFIELD

This excerpt from Barfield's Introduction to his ms edition is drawn from a typescript corrected by him in pen and ink. His reference notes have been normalised to conform with *Collected Coleridge* practice. It is followed by two notes from his edition.

Although it is probably inevitable that the 1818/19 course of lectures will, for the sake of brevity, be frequently referred to as Coleridge's "Philosophical Lectures", the label is a misleading one. They are definitely not lectures on philosophy but lectures on the history of philosophy, and it is well to keep this in mind when reading them. Pythagoras, we are told in Lecture 2, "began that position, the carrying on of which by Plato and the division or schism from which by Aristotle constituted the two classes of philosophers or rather of philosophy which remain to this day, and if we were to live a thousand or ten thousand years ever would remain . . .". The label Platonists and Aristotelians, of which more must be said later, derives from the history of western philosophy, but we soon realise from the lectures themselves, and still more from the marginalia in Tennemann, that its intention is much wider. Rather it signifies two different races of thinking mankind: "the *born* Conceptionists, the spiritual Children of Aristotle, and the born Ideists, or Ideatæ, the spiritual Children of Plato".[1]

If the distinction between philosophy and history of philosophy is important for a modern reader, it is not necessarily absolute at all levels. History, as so to speak a philosophy of philosophies, reveals according to the lecturer their tendency to degenerate into either narrow sectarianism or a superficial "eclecticism". Yet it is itself in a position to "collect the fragments of truth scattered through systems apparently the most incongruous". In Chapter 12 of the *Biographia Literaria*, written a year or two be-

---

[1] Note on Tennemann VIII 130: *CM* (*CC*) V.

fore 1818, Coleridge quotes Leibniz to the above effect and glosses as follows:

The deeper . . . we penetrate into the ground of things, the more truth we discover in the doctrines of the greater number of the philosophical sects. The want of *substantial* reality in the objects of the senses, according to the sceptics; the harmonies or numbers, the prototypes and ideas, to which the Pythagoreans and Platonists reduced all things; the ONE and ALL of Parmenides and Plotinus, without Spinozism; the necessary connection of things according to the Stoics, reconcileable with the spontaneity of the other schools; the vital-philosophy of the Cabalists and Hermetists, who assumed the universality of sensation; the substantial forms and entelechies of Aristotle and the schoolmen, together with the mechanical solution of all particular phenomena according to Democritus and the recent philosophers—all these we shall find united in one perspective central point, which shows regularity and a coincidence of all the parts in the very object, which from every other point of view must appear confused and distorted. The spirit of sectarianism has been hitherto our fault, and the cause of our failures. We have imprisoned our own conceptions by the lines, which we have drawn, in order to exclude the conceptions of others. J'ai trouvé que la plupart des sectes ont raison dans une bonne partie de ce qu'elles avancent, mais non pas tant en ce qu'elles nient.[2]

Platonists and Aristotelians might strike him as a convenient way of dubbing the underlying polarity, but philosophy was not, for Coleridge simply a *Disputà*. Already in the Prospectus he emphasized that the course would treat philosophy "as if it were the striving of a single mind", in Lecture 6 it is "a striving of the mind, the world of man", and in Lecture 8 he reminded his audience that he had so far considered the "different individuals, Thales and Pythagoras, or Plato and Aristotle . . . as only the same mind and in different modes or in different periods of its growth . . .".

Coleridge saw all things, including mind, in terms of process. Just as it came naturally to him to present his own opinions (in the *Biographia Literaria*) in the form of their history, so it is in these historical lectures that his view of the nature of philosophy itself, and, with that, his own philosophy, comes to expression in a way which is perhaps better suited to the subject than any other of the disparate vessels into which he was in the habit of pouring one part of it at a time. They are thus, if not an indispensable, certainly a valuable aid to the grasping of his "system".

The relation of Coleridge's maturer thought, and in particular the nature and extent of its indebtedness to that of his predecessors and contemporaries has remained a matter of dispute both before and since the discovery of the Lecture Reports by Kathleen Coburn in the 1940s and

[2] *BL (CC)* I 244, 246–7.

their publication in 1949. The voluminous reading and phenomenally re-tentive memory of the "library cormorant" perhaps made that inevitable. Was that thought a mosaic stuck together from Kant and the post-Kantian philosophers of Germany, or did it grow essentially out of Cole-ridge's understanding of pre-Enlightenment, and above all, of Greek phi-losophy? One thing that the lectures reveal very clearly is his own view of the relative importance of the ancients and the moderns. Thus, in the Prospectus the proposed "main Divisions" of the Course are seven in number; number six concludes with the "final disappearance [of philos-ophy] under Justinian", and number seven (which ultimately surfaced as Lectures 13–14) reads: "The resumption of the Aristotelian philosophy in the thirteenth century, and the successive re-appearance of the differ-ent sects from the restoration of literature to our own times". If any fur-ther evidence were needed that Coleridge regarded modern philosophy as a whole as only a re-working of disputes already settled long ago, and for the most part by the Greeks, there is the fact that the *Chronological and Historical Assistant* ends at A.D. 529. Does this mean that the life and growth of philosophy had already ceased? He does not leave us merely to *infer* the answer. In the penultimate paragraph of Lecture 8 he states explicitly that "from the rude beginning . . . to the age of Epicurus, phi-losophy had formed its circle and appeared in every possible form", and there are several other pronouncements to the same effect elsewhere in the Course. Thus, we find him explaining at the beginning of Lecture 7:

On long reflection I have determined so to divide the course as that the first half of it should present the growth of philosophy as a striving of the human mind and as presenting the utmost that as far as we know human reason itself can achieve; while in the second I endeavoured to present the effects of those discoveries made by the ancients in speculative philosophy, to demonstrate that nothing as [sensi-ble] has really been discovered in pure speculation by the moderns; at the same time, while I humbled the pride of a false originality, and took away from infi-delity its outward varnish of apparent genius and invention, still to maintain the importance of philosophy itself by exhibiting [the influence which, by pointing to] the historical facts, I can prove it to have exerted upon the structure of lan-guage, upon the language, moral feelings, and political opinions of the European nations.

During Lecture 8 Coleridge once referred to the first seven lectures as "the former course". The end of Lecture 7 and the Press Announcement of 8 both suggest that he not only actually thought of the fourteen lectures as two virtually separate courses, but that he wished his audience to do the same and, looking back on them in Lecture 14, he even referred (ac-cording to his notes) to "both my Courses". No doubt it is partly due to his imperfect health, the increasing weight of the burden the lectures laid on him and the fact that he was getting thoroughly tired of them, that the second course, or Lectures 8 to 14, is on the whole less satisfactory than the first, less vigorous, less consequential, less pulled-together, but it is also because of the difference in their subject-matter. He was still supposed to be lecturing on the history of philosophy, and philosophy no longer had a history! True philosophy had only a memory. "In the present" its only business was the very task Coleridge set himself for the last seven lectures: "to tame the vanity of the moderns by proving to you in every case I know of, that those men took up such and such opinions, but that those opinions were nothing more than what had been brought forward by such and such of the ancients as far as they were really philosophical".

In other words the business of *modern* philosophy is not the discovery of fresh truths but the refutation—not of false philosophy; that had already been done by the ancients themselves—but of the "effects" of false philosophy on the general mind. It was not necessary in Lecture 13 "to enter particularly on Spinoza" because the lecturer had been obliged to anticipate the "substance" of his life, "first in the [account] of the Eleatic school, the idealists of old, and secondly in the [account] of the new Platonists". Nor need we take as solely the effect of ill health and fatigue the sketchy treatment of German philosophy in general in the same lecture. The subject, as announced, was to have been "the GERMAN PHILOSOPHY with its bearings on the System of Locke, comprising the systems of Leibnitz, Kant and Schelling". In fact, though something is indeed said of Leibniz's critique of Locke, there is no mention of Fichte, nor of any other of the German school except Kant, who is accorded less space than had been allowed in earlier lectures to St. Theresa and Agrippa, and except Schelling, who is dismissed for lack of time and because the lecturer "should be puzzled to give you a true account". This accords very strangely both with the Announcement and with the profound respect Coleridge continued to entertain for both Schelling and Kant, but not quite so strangely with the portmanteau reference, in the passage already quoted from the *Biographia Literaria*, to "Democritus and the recent philosophers".

The *Chronological and Historical Assistant* consists of two parallel columns, one for the history of philosophy, and the other for events outside it. Definition of philosophy as a *striving* of the human mind necessarily entails a less abrupt seclusion from other human activities than is customary. The Prospectus forecasts, and the lectures realise "many and close connections of the subject with the most interesting periods of History" in both the first and the second parts of the course; especially in the second part, they often shade off into considerations of politics, ethics, religion or science. A preview of the proposed course contained in a footnote to the *Friend* describes it as (inter alia) "tracing the progress of speculative science chiefly in relation to the development of the human mind";[3] and there are many indications in the lectures as delivered—the praise of Occam, for example, the amount of space devoted to Bruno, to Böhme, to Francis Bacon, and the frequent allusions to Kepler—that it was in the direction of science (but of a science no longer based on unproven materialist assumptions) that Coleridge perceived the possibility of a future as well as a past for philosophy, one that would involve more than merely correcting for a second time the errors of the past.

According to the report in the *New Times*, Coleridge commenced his first Lecture "by disapproving of the abuse of the term philosophy applied to all investigations of the intellect—we have thus Chemical Philosophy, Astronomical Philosophy, etc". In 1812 Humphry Davy had given a public lecture entitled "The Elements of Chemical Philosophy", and Coleridge may well have had this in mind in his stricture. Although Davy had in earlier years been both his close friend and his scientific hero, and Coleridge never ceased to honour him, Davy's scientific views had been diverging from Coleridge's. In the 1809 *Friend* Davy was "the illustrious Father and Founder of philosophic Alchemy";[4] but in a marginal note on Böhme, which must be later than 1812, since it was in that year that Davy was knighted, Coleridge wrote: "Alas! Since I wrote the preceding note, H. Davy has become Sir Humphry Davy, and an *Atomist!*"[5]

There is little in the Lectures to suggest the desirability of a divorce between science and philosophy. Perhaps Coleridge would have distinguished between "chemical philosophy" and "philosophical chemistry". At all events it was part of the History of Philosophy that both mesmerism and alchemy were "modes by which philosophy, through magic, gradually passed into experimental science" and, as he himself had put it in the previous lecture, would lead to "an experimental philosophy". Here, as far at least as alchemy is concerned, Davy agreed with him, as his above-mentioned lecture makes plain, and as many subsequent writers on the history of science have done. Nevertheless it is clear that Coleridge's views on the true nature of scientific enquiry, and thus of the future of science, were different from those of Davy and his fellow scientists. If rebellion against the tyranny of Aristotle led men to the discovery that "the proper mode of invoking nature was by attaining nature by means of sim-

---

[3] *Friend (CC)* I 463.
[4] *Friend (CC)* II 252.
[5] *CM (CC)* I 572.

ple substances", it was the "visionaries and mystics" who had made that discovery, and they had done so in the confidence that "all parts of the world have symbolical meanings". In this respect Coleridge was (*pace* their aberrations) nearer to them than he was to either Lockian empiricism or atomism.

Symbolism was integral to his conception of both philosophy and science inasmuch as it was integral to his view of the nature of reality. Allusions to it are correspondingly frequent in the lectures; but since they are little more than allusions, it may be desirable to draw some of them together in a general review. Coleridge's principal published statements on symbolism had been made in the *Statesman's Manual* and *Biographia Literaria*, but his mind was busy on the subject both before and after those works appeared.[6] The opening paragraph of his Notes for the lectures, while expressing dissatisfaction with the views of G. F. Creuzer in one particular, indicates that he had been reading and absorbing the first few pages of the latter's *Symbolik und Mythologie der alten Völker*; and his most detailed exposition of the nature of a symbol, its difference from allegory, metaphor, simile, fable, myth, as well as the differences of these from each other, is to be found in *Notebooks* IV 4831 and 4832, entries that consist partly of extracts from Creuzer's book and partly of Coleridge's own gloss and comments—the latter including a long discussion of the etymology of the word *symbol* and a meticulous account of its varied significances in the works of different Greek authors.

Symbol, for Coleridge, was essentially a manifestation of the immaterial in the material, of the formless in form: Plato's ideas or Pythagoras's numbers, for example, transpiring through sensuous objects or events and thus through names and language. Thus in Lecture 4: "How the grand idea of the universe worked in him [Plato] before it found utterance! In how many obscure, and as it were oracular, sentences, in what strange symbols did it place itself!"; and in a marginal note on Tennemann on the Pythagoreans: "There exist in all things constituent and governing powers, the characters and efficiencies of which are represented to us by Numbers, as by symbolic Names, symbolic, namely, not allegorical or arbitrary, a Symbol being an essential Part of that, the whole of which it represents."[7]

The last fourteen words contain the second essential in Coleridge's concept of symbol. It is what differentiates symbol from allegory. "It is among the miseries of the present age", he had written in the *Statesman's*

---

[6] See in addition to indexes to *SM* (*CC*) and *BL* (*CC*), *CN* I 1387; II 2546, 2548; III 3325, 3954, 4058, 4253, 4503; IV 4711 and nn.

[7] Note on Tennemann I 107: *CM* (*CC*) V.

Manual, "that it recognizes no medium between *Literal* and *Metaphorical*";[8] and he saw his own concept of symbol as providing precisely that medium. An allegory, like a metaphor, is a parallel expression in one medium of something existing in another medium altogether; whereas a symbol is an actual part of the whole it represents, inasmuch as it is part of an antecedent unity from which, by the process of individuation, it has emerged. Different symbols may accordingly symbolise the same whole, and in doing so may symbolise one another. "[I]t was amongst the great Pythagorean symbols so to convey truth in part as that it might make the mind susceptible hereafter of another portion." Immaterial "wholes", from which material parts have emerged by separative projection may moreover be temporal as well as spatial. Music, for instance, "is the best symbol, perhaps, for it is as far as sight is concerned formless, and yet contains the principles of form, so that in all civilised language we borrow the proportions from it". But music is not the only, or the most important, example. "Why not at once Symbol and History?" Coleridge was later to enquire in *Aids to Reflection*.[9] So here, in Lecture 8: "Nay, even the very sacred events in which the historical part of Christianity consisted, were themselves only so many really real and historical symbols of the great truths which it was the object of Christianity to propagate". Not all objects and events however are symbols, and it is interesting that earlier in the same lecture he had hesitated between the two terms: "I cannot imagine a more expressive symbol and, as it were, allegory of this [the difference between the modern and the ancient world], than by placing before my eyes the palace of that imperial Goth [Theodoric] [frowning] opposite to the Christian temple . . . for in this I seem to have the commencement of the era as a living symbol". Perhaps he already had at the back of his mind an idea he was later to record in a notebook entry: "It will often happen, that in the extension of ~~our~~ human Knowlege what had been an *Allegory*, will become a Symbol".[10]

"Language & all *symbols*", he had noted in 1803, "give *outness* to Thoughts & this the philosophical essence & purpose of Language".[11] The relation between word as sound and word as meaning is the example most easily accessible to us of symbolism. Through realising that relation we may be led to realise the forms of nature as themselves symbols. When the unlettered savage is taught to read, "The words become transparent, and he sees through them as though he saw them not. And then too", Coleridge continues (in the concluding paragraph of Lecture 12), "shall we be in that state to which science in all its form[s] is gradu-

[8] *SM* (*CC*) 30.
[9] *AR* (*CC*) 263n.
[10] *CN* IV 4832 f 61ᵛ.
[11] *CN* I 1387.

ally leading us; then will the other great Bible of God, the book of Nature become transparent to us when we regard the forms of matter as words, as symbols valuable only . . . as being the expression, an unrolled but yet a glorious fragment, of the wisdom of the supreme Being".

Coleridge saw the evolution of both nature and knowledge in terms of individuation by progressive fragmentation, but a fragmentation that was not final or absolute. On the contrary it evinced what he described in the *Theory of Life* as "the tendency . . . at once to individuate and to connect, to detach, but so as either to retain or to reproduce attachment".[12] In the case of language the attachment of the part to the whole from which it originated is reproduced in the form of symbolical significance. Language differs from nature however in that man himself participates in the process, the fragmentation being brought about by his own partly unconscious, partly conscious mental activity. Coleridge's favourite name for that activity was "desynonymising".

It is somewhere remarked by Nietzsche that "He who finds language interesting in itself has a mind different from him who only regards it as a medium of thought." Coleridge's deep, often delighted, feeling for language, his loving contemplation both of its nature as a whole and of the seminal significance of some particular word colours all his writing, and not least these lectures, where it fuses readily with their emphatic historicism. For example, when in Lecture 14, as only summarily reported, the revived Neoplatonism of the Renaissance is described as "Platonism brooding over the birth of genius", we could be sure it is his own voice speaking even if the phrase were not confirmed by his Notes. It is one of those occasional brief flights of arrowy penetration by which that voice is unmistakeably recognisable; and we may feel through it his undoubted awareness of the slow semantic growth and metamorphosis of ancient objective Latin *Genius* into modern subjective English "genius".

The numerous observations on language that occur throughout the Lectures are however semantic rather than etymological. Coleridge's concern is with the subtle relations between living language and active thought. "Words are things. They are the great mighty instruments by which thoughts are excited and by which alone they can be [expressed] in a remembered form." [And] "There are few pursuits more instructive and not many more entertaining, I own, than that of retracing the progress of a living language for a few centuries, and its improvements as an organ and a vehicle of thought by desynonymising words."

The relation between language and thought has, on the one hand, its

12 *SW & F* (*CC*) I 517.

social aspect, since "words, the instruments of communication, are the only signs that a finite being can have of its own thoughts". Thus, in Lecture 10 Coleridge contrasts the "connection without combination" that was characteristic of both the society and the language of the Gothic tribes with the "interwoven sentences" of the Romans and Greeks. And he goes on to praise the Schoolmen for the pains they took to restore to our language "the power and force of Greek and Roman connection". (The justice of that observation may perhaps best be tested by reading a "difficult" passage in, say, Thomas Aquinas first in Latin and then in any modern English translation.) Coleridge further accuses the writers who came after the seventeenth century of taking equal pains to destroy that power and force; and his own often involved style as a writer may owe something to this judgment. It was not due simply to his personal saturation in the literature of that century and earlier; nor was it simply his excessive, sometimes preposterous, anti-Gallicism that made him write in a notebook: ". . . in the modern French Writers and their English Imitators one might suppose the necessity of the Breath to be the sole principle of punctuation, & the powers of the Breath averaged from a nation of asthmatic patients".[13]

Earlier, in Lecture 6, he had demonstrated in some detail how much the development of that lost classical power and force owed to Aristotle. The social in fact cannot be very sharply differentiated from the individual aspect. The latter energises and crystallises the former. "What is philosophy in one age is common sense in another and vice versa . . .". For the whole progress of society depends on "the whole process of the human intellect". It might even be "expressed in a dictionary" (though it is not suggested that the production of such a dictionary is a practical proposition), because "the whole progress of society, as far as it is human society, depends upon . . . the process of desynonymising".

Desynonymising (Coleridge does not himself speak of "desynonymisation"), though Herbert Spencer, as *OED* reminds us, was later to father on him that "formidable word") is first heard of in Lecture 4. By the time we have met it again in 5, 6, 9, and 13 it becomes clear that Coleridge saw in language, as he did in nature a continuous process with the tendency to progressive individuation as the law of its direction.[14] As early as 1808 he had propounded in a notebook what he there called ". . . Synonomystic, or the process of *de*-synonnomizing pseudo-synonymes, and of determining the specific mode of the Homoeoionomy of each". "To *make* real Synonymes into Homoeonymes, is the privilege of Genius,

---

[13] *CN* III 3504 f 8ᵛ–9.   [14] See *SW & F (CC)* I 516.

whether poetic or philosophic, to detect the latter in the *supposed* former the province of the genuine Philologist."[15]

He first made this insight public in the well-known passage in Chapter 4 of *Biographia Literaria* (cf Lecture 13), where he himself undertook the desynonymising of the terms *fancy* and *imagination*; and where, as we should expect, he distinguished, without dividing, the social or communal operation of the "tendency" from the individual one. For, before recommending the distinction for further use, he suggested that it was already beginning to occur as the result of "an instinct of growth, a certain collective, unconscious good sense working progressively to desynonymize" that exists in all societies.[16]

Naturally lectures on philosophy are more concerned with the desynonymising done by an individual than with unconscious good sense. When in Lecture 5 Coleridge himself desynonymises *abstraction* and *generalisation* in the presence of his audience, he may be seen as pursuing into more intricate psychological minutiae his earlier distinction between imagination and fancy. Nor is it only to psychology that desynonymising is relevant. It is needed as a remedy in the realm of ethics, Coleridge suggests, when he distinguishes *compelled* from *obliged*, or when he recalls in Lecture 4 a conversation with a hedonist friend, who had been arguing that good is another name for pleasant, and tells how he had rebuked him for making *pleasure* "a mere lazy synonym, whereas it is the business of the philosopher to desynonymise words originally equivalent, therein following and impelling the natural progress of language in civilised societies". So in Lecture 6 he selects Theodorus for mention because of "his labours in desynonymising words"; and it is because the Sceptics with their trivial conundrums were nevertheless to carry on that "business" that he refuses to dismiss them with a shrug. "The object was to guard the minds of the young pupils against the force of equivocation, of double meanings lying hid under the same word, so that an argument of a deduction drawn from one meaning shall be perfectly correct, but from the other shall be perfectly fallacious . . .".

Ideas are dim on their first appearance in the mind whether of mankind as a whole or of an individual. "In the infancy of the human mind, all our ideas are instincts; and language is happily contrived to lead us from the vague to the distinct, from the imperfect to the fully finished form . . .".[17] "[W]ithout distinction conception cannot exist . . .".[18] Desynonymising is the act of distinguishing one idea from another one, with the result that two clear ideas shall have emerged from one dim or vague one. It is a term

[15] *CN* III 3312 f 14ᵛ.
[16] *BL (CC)* I 82–4, 86n.
[17] *TM* in *SW & F (CC)* I 633.
[18] *Logic (CC)* 250.

taken from language study, but its importance is for the business of progressive thought. The "business of philosophy [is] ever to distinguish without unnaturally dividing . . .". If there are already two overlapping words (as in the case of *fancy* and *imagination*), then the unconscious has already started the business for him; if not, then it is for an individual thinker, without that help, to detect equivocation and expose it. In either case one result will be improvement of language as a means of communication and as the embodiment of mind.

It was precisely in the business of philosophy, thus conceived, that the Schoolmen, with their interminable *distinguos*, excelled. Scholasticism was a "philosophy that employed itself in desynonymising words, in giving them sometimes perfectly just and distinct meanings, often but apparent ones, but which, whether true or false, laid the foundation of our modern languages".

Thus one result of those two conspicuous qualities, his feeling for language and his evolutionary historicism, driving, so to speak, in tandem, was his being among the first to break free from that fixed and ignorant contempt of Scholasticism which had prevailed in most quarters since the Renaissance and almost everywhere since the Enlightenment. If classical philosophy had found all the answers, if express philosophy had come full circle long before the Dark and Middle Ages, the philosophic *consciousness*, the mind's attention to its own activity, was still growing. Realists and Nominalists might find little to add to the old arguments between Platonists and Aristotelians, but they were at work stating the issue more and more clearly. "I here make a challenge, I would almost say", Coleridge put it in Lecture 9, "to point me out an opinion that has taken place since the fifteenth century which I will not show as clearly stated and supported in some one or other of the Nominalists or the Realists". He saw that the Schoolmen were busy toughening the *physique* of thought—sharpening the tools of intellect by developing language towards greater and greater precision. Moreover, in doing so they were "working to produce a great revolution in the human mind" inasmuch as they were creating the very instruments by which they would later be discredited, because that had made possible a new exactness in science.

In Lecture 3 Coleridge remarked in reference to Pythagoras that sometimes "it is necessary for a man to have discovered by other means the truth of a particular position in order to learn with certainty whether a prior writer has or has not taught it"; and it has been said of Coleridge himself, that in order to grasp his views it is necessary to understand them first. If this rather suggests the old Irish advice not to enter the water before we can swim, any thoroughgoing student of Coleridge will understand what is meant. He himself, it is true, said in the Prospectus that he would prefer the majority of his audience to consist of persons whose minds were *tabula rasa*, "whose acquaintance with the History of Philosophy would commence with their attendance on the Course of Lectures here announced". In fact however anything like a proper grasp of the Course does really demand some acquaintance, if not with the history of philosophy, at least with his own leading principles, and in that respect a 20th-century reader is likely to be in a better position than most of the audience. Those leading principles fall into two classes: those that are fully expounded, usually in more than one lecture, and those which, even when they are needed as an integral part of the argument, are almost casually adduced and may well go unnoticed by anyone who has not met them more fully stated elsewhere. Examples of the latter are the difference between constitutive (or constituent) and regulative ideas; the virtual identity of mental idea with natural law; the importance of being able to distinguish without dividing; allusions to opposites, or opposite poles, or polarity such as we meet with early in Lecture 2, again in the passage on Böhme in Lecture 11 and occasionally elsewhere. As to the last, not many of his auditors were likely to have read the opening paragraphs of Chapter 13 of the *Biographia Literaria* or the note in Essay xiii of the *Friend*, whereas many modern readers, coming to the Lecture armed with some recollection of these passages and perhaps of the relevant parts of the *Theory of Life*, are in a position to accord them their full significance in the perspective which the course as a whole seeks to present.

The former class consists essentially of Coleridge's heterodox concept of mind itself and of passing observations that depend on it: his conviction, firstly, that thinking is an act, and not a passive response to stimuli, an act moreover not only of an individual intellect, still less of its physical brain, but an act of the mind of man as such. And secondly that that act is, in the last resort, one with the act which is *natura naturans*. Subject and object are one in the act of thinking, though the effect of its product (thought) is to distinguish and appear to divide them. Both in the lectures and elsewhere Coleridge repeatedly strove to implant this [concept] in the imaginations as well as in the intellects of his contemporaries. In the lectures the theme is announced as early as Lecture 2 in the section on Pythagoras, and it is heard again in most of the attacks on materialism which punctuate the course and culminate in Lecture 12. He was convinced that the removal from the common consciousness of what A. N. Whitehead was later to call "concreteness" was above all the task incumbent on the second and, so to say, un-historical period of the history of philosophy. "There is but one way", he wrote in a marginal note to

Tennemann, "to teach the doctrines of Ideas—viz. to convince the Scholar that his hitherto notions of substantial and unsubstantial are erroneous to the extreme of Error, & must be absolutely inverted to become true. . . . All short of this is but a Shifting of Error."[19]

The *philosophic consciousness*, Coleridge observed in Chapter 12 of the *Biographia Literaria*, "lies beneath or (as it were) *behind* the spontaneous consciousness natural to all reflecting beings".[20] Thus, the philosophic consciousness is not something separate from the common consciousness, rather it is the potential in the common consciousness, the "intellectual instinct" of Lecture 7, actualised. In the light of such a conviction it is not surprising that the lectures concern themselves with much in the history of mankind that lies outside the pale of philosophy as normally understood, with the progress of language by desynonymisation, with polytheism, with the Mysteries of the Cabiri, the nature of Greek democracy, the influence of monasticism, the restoration of learning, the Protestant Reformation and much else. Of the prominent position occupied by religion something more must be said later.

A 20th-century reader might with some justification object that the title of the Course should have been, not the History of Philosophy but the History of Western Philosophy. Were the lecturer anybody but Coleridge the answer would be simple enough. Oriental philosophy had only just begun to reach the West. Friedrich Schlegel's *Über die Sprache und Weisheit der Indier* (1808) was the first publication to bring it within the range of European literature, and there is no indication that Coleridge had read it, though he read and annotated a number of Schlegel's other works. In England Charles Wilkins's translation of the Bhagavad-Gita had appeared in 1775 and Sir William Jones's translation of the *Institutes of Hindu Law of the Ordinances of Menu* in 1794, but it would be no reproach to an educated man to have paid them scant attention. Coleridge of course had read them both, and it is surprising that he should have detected no affinity there with his own all-embracing idea of "the philosophic consciousness". It is true that in Chapter 5 of *Biographia Literaria* he had observed that "In Egypt, Palestine, Greece, and India the analysis of the mind had reached its noon and manhood, while experimental research was still in its dawn and infancy."[21] But it must be concluded from the severity of his strictures on the Bhagavad-Gita in Lecture 3 that, in including India among the pristine analysts of the mind, he had in view, not his own reading of Hindu texts but the presumed influ-

---

[19] Note to Tenneman, III 50–1: *CM* (*CC*) v.

[20] *BL* (*CC*) I 236.

[21] *BL* (*CC*) I 90–1.

ence of Hindu sages on Pythagoras. Is there a hint of *odium theologicum* in those uncompromisingly scornful strictures—a desire, because they might claim to be so near, to insist that they are yet so far? However it may be, he seems in this instance to have ignored the wise maxim that, if you wish to extricate a man from error, you must first do justice to his truth. Otherwise he could hardly have failed to acknowledge much in the tradition of the Gita which he himself not only approved but actively maintained: the identity in difference of subject and object, for instance, the conception of the ultimate reality as I AM and of the material world as the outward appearance of consciousness. After which he might perhaps have gone on to stigmatise the negative, or certainly undynamic, Hindu conception of outward appearance as *maya* or mere illusion. Whatever the explanation, he chose instead to interpret the vision of Arjuna, not in terms of his own objective idealism but in those of a naive realism which renders it not merely objectionable but ludicrous. And that is clearly the impression he intended, by means of an inordinately long quotation, to leave in the minds of his audience.

Coleridge's conviction that the common consciousness is connected with master-currents below the surface[22] transpires through the strongly psychological slant of his interest. Hence his readiness to expatiate on such topics as dreams, on alchemy in the past and animal magnetism in the present. Although the phrase post-dates him, it would not be unfair to describe his psychology as a "psychology of the unconscious". Research on animal magnetism was later to lie behind the work of Freud's mentor Charcot,[23] and Jung's psychology of the unconscious led him to study and to expatiate on the significance of alchemy. But the same conviction, at a point further from the unconscious and nearer to the conscious pole of that uncharted region, lies behind Coleridge's preoccupation with minutiae of the relation between thought and perception. It underlay his interest in Goethe's anti-Newtonian *Optics* and his *Farbenlehre*. It is most evident in his letters and notebooks, but it is there also in the lectures. It was, for example, in pursuit of this quarry that, as they drew to a close, he diverged for a moment in Lectures 4 and 5 into observations on the historical development of the art of painting.

Once the fundamental principles underlying Coleridge's philosophy have been grasped, the question whether a prior writer had or had not taught what he is saying at any particular moment and if so, whether he knew it, calls for some acquaintance with his actual and possible

[22] *BL* (*CC*) ch 1. *Magnetism* (1898).
[23] See A. Binet and C. Féré *Animal*

sources—what books he had annotated and what others he had read or is likely to have read. It must be remembered however that the mere fact that a prior writer consulted by him *had* taught the same lesson does not necessarily imply that Coleridge "borrowed" it from him. One may even say that the chances are he did not. As Kathleen Coburn observed in her Introduction to the 1949 edition of the Lectures, "Coleridge borrows only when his own thinking has reached almost the same point as his creditor's",[24] a truth which is well exemplified in the Lectures. It comes out in his whole *way* of expounding and explaining the particular philosopher he is dealing with at the moment. The contrast with Tennemann's aloof, Kantian detachment could hardly be greater. We detect it, for instance, as early as his handling of Pythagoras in Lecture 2. Another, and perhaps more intriguing example is his division, already referred to here, of all men into Platonists and Aristotelians.

First stated in Lecture 2 as "the introduction to all the philosophers", it recurs in the following lecture and is developed at length in Lecture 5: moreover there are eight or nine references to it in the Tennemann marginalia. It seems that he adopted the *labels* from Goethe's *Farbenlehre* published in 1808 and referred to by Coleridge in a letter to Tieck in the summer of 1817.[25] But it is equally clear that he at once applied the labels to his own previously formulated distinction between constitutive and regulative Ideas. "Whether Ideas are regulative only, according to Aristotle and Kant; or likewise CONSTITUTIVE, and one with the power and Life of Nature, according to Plato, and Plotinus . . . is the highest *problem* of Philosophy, and not part of its nomenclature", he had written in 1816 in Appendix E to the *Statesman's Manual*.[26] If it was a "problem", it was one to which he himself was so certain of the answer that when, a few years later, his attention was drawn by an enthusiastic admirer of Goethe to the latter's advocacy of research by the method of "objective thinking" (Gegenständliches Denken), so far from being impressed, Coleridge waved it aside as labouring the obvious.[27]

Goethe, in the historical survey that follows the Preface to the *Farbenlehre*, had observed that Plato and Aristotle were the first to build up anything like real systems of thought, and that their systems being preserved in their many writings, it has followed that the world "insofern sie als empfindend und denkend anzusehen ist, genöthigt war, sich Einem oder dem Andern hinzugeben, Einen oder den Andern als Meister, Lehrer, Führer anzuerkennen".[28] Coleridge on the one hand broadened

---

[24] *P Lects* 55.
[25] *CL* IV 750–1.
[26] *SM* (*CC*) 114.

[27] Note to J. C. Heinroth *Lehrbuch der Anthrolopogie CM* (*CC*) II 1025.
[28] *Zur Farbenlehre* II 141–2.

the philosophical base of the *aperçu* by identifying it with ability or inability to grasp constitutive ideas, and on the other took it beneath philosophy and into psychology by applying it not only to the philosophically inclined but also to the "common consciousness" of mankind. His "*born* Aristotelians" and "*born* Platonists" are more than pre-figurings of Jung's Extroverts and Introverts. Rather they are the two contrasted poles of mind, whose progressive synthesis is the eschatology of human evolution; pointing to an end that will only be reached when "the soul of Aristotle shall have become one with the soul of Plato . . . That is, *Graecis calendis*, or when two Fridays meet".[29]

However it may be with any particular philosophy, there is one subject which the lectures treat as, more than all others, inseparable from the history of philosophy, and that is religion. History shows, they propound, that philosophy without religion is barren, and ends in atheism; that religion without philosophy degenerates into superstition and fanaticism; that philosophy *substituted* for religion ends in polytheism. But if the two are indispensable to one another, the maintenance of a clear distinction between them is no less important than—or rather is the very condition of—their healthy union. Thus the phenomenon of the Eclectic philosophers shows "the pernicious or utterly worthless results of an attempt to confound religion with philosophy in order to mix religion itself with philosophy" (373).

On the other hand: "This I shall, I hope show: that as religion never can be philosophy, because the only true philosophy proposes religion as its end and supplement, so on the other hand there can be no true religion without philosophy, no true feelings and notions of religion among men at large without just notions of philosophy in the higher classes" (359–60).

The true relation between the two is that of a "dynamic" synthesis arising out of their origins in an antecedent unity. "In all countries", according to the *Chronological and Historical Assistant*, "the language of intellect has been posterior to, and the consequence of, settled *law* and an *established religion*". Thus, for all its essential autonomy while it lasts, the history of philosophy is conceived as an interim event in the progress of the common consciousness of humanity, away from its origin in religion and back to its end in religion.

But "religion" in this context means in effect a true, undistorted Christianity. It is evident from the lectures that Coleridge held, with St. Augustine, that the true religion, which since the incarnation and resurrec-

[29] *Logic (CC)* 206.

tion of Christ, has been named Christian, was already in existence "ab initio generis humani", from the beginning of the human race.[30] As already indicated, he saw all things, including (or rather included in) Mind, in terms of process, rather than of cause and effect, and ideally in terms of progress. In his eleventh lecture he praises Jacob Böhme for his "constant sense of the truth that all nature is in a perpetual evolution". For himself, just as, in the *Theory of Life*, he was to show himself an evolutionist, though not in the Darwinian mode, in the realm of biology, so here and elsewhere, though nowhere so near to systematically, he shows himself an evolutionist in the realm of human consciousness. Not the beginning, but the pivot of that evolution was the birth, death and resurrection of Christ.

Systematically? Coleridge often mentioned his own "system" sometimes in a passing reference but sometimes also in a context that is particularly illuminating. Conspicuous among such references is the following. It is not to be found in the lectures nor, since Gerson is not mentioned there, in the Notes to them, but it is too valuable to be left lying half-smothered in an Appendix full of adjoining but unrelated marginalia.

Gerson's & St Victoire's Contemplation is in my System = *Positive* Reason, or R. in her own Sphere as distinguished from the merely *formal* Negative Reason, R. in the lower sphere of the Understanding . . .

The simplest yet practically sufficient Order of the Mental Powers is, beginning from the

lowest	highest
Sense	Reason
Fancy	
Understanding.	Imagination
———	———
Understanding	Understanding.
Imagination	Fancy
Reason.	Sense.

Fancy and Imagination are Oscillations, *this* connecting R. and U; that connecting Sense and Understanding.[31]

Again, and more closely relevant to the lecture-course (which he must surely have had in mind while he was speaking):

My system, if I may venture to give it so fine a name, is the only attempt that I know of ever made to reduce all knowledges into harmony; it opposes no other system, but shows what was true in each, and how that which was true in the particular in each of them became error, because it was only half the truth. I have en-

---

[30] *Retractationes* I xiii 3.   (*CC*) v.
[31] Note to Tennemann VIII 960: *CM*

deavoured to unite the insulated fragments of truth and frame a perfect mirror. I show to each system that I fully understand and rightfully appreciate what that system means; but then I lift up that system to a higher point of view, from which I enable it to see its former position where it was indeed, but under another light and with different relations; so that the fragment of truth is not only acknowledged, but explained.[32]

The opening caveat here suggests that he himself sometimes had doubts whether he could claim to have a system in the customary sense at all, and critics since his death have not been slow to complain that he never succeeded in constructing one. Perhaps they are right—or perhaps we have all been mistaken in demanding one of him. Trevor Levere has maintained in his *Poetry Realized in Nature* that Coleridge was engaged throughout his life, not (like Hegel) in constructing a system, but in seeking a method.[33] If reality conceived as timeless fact can indeed be displayed by analysis, perhaps reality conceived as process must be grasped through method, in order to be known. Certainly the Essays on Method, the substance of which underlies the passage on Francis Bacon in Lecture 11, and which, as reprinted in the *Friend*, were later to make such a deep impression on Emerson, are an indispensable key to Coleridge's philosophy. Method, he there affirms, is "itself a distinct science, the immediate offspring of philosophy, and the link or *mordant* by which philosophy becomes scientific and the sciences philosophical".[34] He presents the Essays themselves "as the basis of my future philosophical and theological writings, and as the necessary introduction to the same".[35]

Thus, if some bewildered student, dismayed by the sheer quantity of Coleridge's writings now available, should inquire whether his system could be mastered, with the requisite diligence, in as little as one or two of them, one might do worse than recommend him to study the Essays on Method along with these Lectures on the History of Philosophy.

NOTES

ON THE DISTINCTION BETWEEN
ABSTRACTION AND GENERALISATION

N 25 f 49 (245 above) epitomises: "(N.b. Abst. the power simply; Gener. that power applied to classify—)". The paragraph is pregnant with C's

---

[32] *TT (CC)* I 248–9: 11 Sept 1831; the first sentence is that of the 1835 ed.
[33] Levere 221.
[34] *Friend (CC)* I 463.
[35] *Friend (CC)* I 446.

precise and repeated reflection on the border region between philosophy and psychology. The mind's *power* of abstracting and of generalising is one and the same, being in effect the power to *attend*. But whereas abstraction may result from attention to *one* impression of the senses, generalisation is always the product of attention to a number of particulars "for the purpose of forming classes". Generalisation in fact is abstraction raised to the second power, since it abstracts *relations* between particulars, which are themselves the product of abstraction, that is, between "words, names, or, if images, yet images used as words or names, that are the only and exclusive subjects of Understanding. In no instance do we understand a thing in itself; but only the name to which it is referred."[36] It was because Locke failed to realise this that he could attribute the origin of speech wholly to generalisation of sensibilia; whereas, for C, the understanding generalises "the *notices received from* the Senses in order to the construction of *Names*".[37]

A firm delineation of the two terms is rendered difficult by the fact that C does elsewhere apply the label "generalisation" to the percipient's apprehension of immediate sensibilia. In BM MS Egerton 2826 ff 24–7 he defines generalisation as "abstraction of the sense" and abstraction as "abstraction of the understanding". It would seem that the mere perception of A, as A and not B, already implies a kind of generalisation, that this gives rise to a "notice", because the understanding abstracts it from the percept itself, and that the understanding then proceeds to generalise (in the ordinary sense) these notices, as if they were actual percepts.

Thus, generalisation imparts to the particulars a factitious reality, which is at the root both of superstition and of more sophisticated but equally unwarranted attributions of causality "from the fetisch of the imbruted African to the soul-debasing errors of the fact-hunting materialist . . .".[38] "Generalization is a *Substitute for* Intuition, for the Power of *intuitive*, (that is, immediate) knowledge."[39] Abstraction without generalisation, on the other hand, is connate with imagination, and may lead to the intuiting of an Idea. Hence C's emphasis on the importance of "tracing words to their origin" as a means of emancipating the mind from "the despotism of the eye".[40] Such pure abstraction (that is, abstraction without generalisation) empowers the mind to distinguish between the "notices received from the senses" and the senses themselves—an indispensable preliminary to its apprehending "the identity of *nomen* with

---

[36] *AR (CC)* 231.
[37] *AR (CC)* 232, first set of italics added.
[38] *Friend (CC)* I 518.
[39] *AR (CC)* 275*, first set of italics added.
[40] *Logic (CC)* 242.

numen, i.e. invisible power and presence, the *nomen substantivum* of all real Objects, and the ground of their reality, independently of the Affections of Sense in the Percipient".[41] Significant as it is, C did not school himself to observe the desynonymisation in his own utterances. He frequently speaks of "abstraction or generalisation" and uses "abstraction" in contexts which would, strictly, require "generalisation". It is the same with some other technical terms, such as "powers" and "forces", or "opposite" and "contrary". There are good reasons for it. If a style of meticulous pedantry is to be avoided, words in common use must occasionally be employed without pausing then and there to point out that that use is misleading. More importantly, in a system based throughout on process and metamorphosis, verbal references cannot be fenced off from one another, terms cannot be kept as strictly univocal as in another system based on "fixities and definites" only. It remains true that grasping C's system is rendered more difficult by the fact that he never cast it into a single mould, architectonically constructed and based on consistently-adhered-to terminology.

ON HUMAN AND INTELLECTUAL INSTINCT

The seemingly casual reference here (317 above) to "a human and an intellectual instinct" masks many years of careful thinking on the subject, and there is no doubt that by the time he delivered the lectures on the history of philosophy C had come to attach clearly distinguishable meanings to *instinct*, *intellectual instinct* (or *instinctive intelligence*) and *human instinct* respectively. His *locus classicus* on the subject is the excursus "On Instinct in Connection with the Understanding" a comment on Aphorism IX "On Spiritual Religion",[42] but it constitutes only one of many animadversions on the same topic. Neither a mechanism nor a force nor a faculty, instinct functions at many levels, each of which is distinguishable, though indivisible, from the others. At all those levels it is both symptomatic of and evidence for C's whole system of interpenetrating hierarchical grades of *natura naturans*, themselves interpenetrated in different measures and manners by Reason. Cf "The Understanding acting upon and raising the animal life becomes Instinct";[43] "Now the Understanding is the Man himself, contemplated as an intelligent Creature—and the Light shineth down into his natural darkness (= blind instinct) and by its presence converts the vital instinct into Understanding . . .".[44] "The Law,

---

[41] *AR (CC)* 223, first two sets of italics added.
[42] *AR (CC)* 249–50.

[43] BM MS Egerton 2801 f 77ᵛ.
[44] *C 17th C* 692.

indeed, has not yet assumed the form of an idea in his [the chemist's] mind; it is what we have called an Instinct; it is a pursuit after unity of principle, through a diversity of forms";[45] cf the slightly different formulation in *Friend*.[46]

INDEX

All works appear under the author's name; anonymous works, newspapers, periodicals, etc are listed by title; institutions are listed under the name of the place in which they are or were located. Subentries are arranged alphabetically, sometimes in two parts, the first containing general references, and the second specific works. Hyphenated page numbers (e.g. 122–4 or 122n–4n) may refer either to an extended passage on the topic or to a series of separate references to it.

When a word is referred to rather than used (as, for example, when its meaning or etymology is discussed) it is placed within quotation marks and indexed separately. Every effort has been made to preserve Coleridge's actual words. Misleadingly irregular spellings (for example, "Clinomachus" for "Clitomachus"), circumlocutions (for example, "British Plato" for "Francis Bacon"), or alternative wordings ("intellectual son of Anac" for "Aristotle") are given in parentheses after the page number. Words whose meaning would otherwise be ambiguous may be accompanied by a parenthetical explanation: for example, "cricket (game)". In order to facilitate rational grouping, some paraphrasing has been admitted in the subentries. Greek words and phrases have been transliterated, and the term "formula(s)" has been used to denote numerical formulas, algebraic or alphabetical formulas, and diagrams.

Birth and death dates are provided when they are known, but birth dates of persons now living are not given. Names of literary characters are accompanied by the title of the work in which they appear or by the name of the author in whose work they are found: for example, "Abraham (Bible)" or "Cupid (in Apuleius)".

---

astronomy—*continued*
6; Pythagorean 66n; rejection of 666; scientific 485, 485n, 820
Asween (*Bhagavad-Gita*) 131
asylum *see* sanctuary
asymptotes 160, 160n
ataraxia 605
Atarnae 221–2, 226, 244, 704 (Atanea)
Athanasius, St, bp of Alexandria (c 296–373) 18
atheism 854, 886
and Anaximander's infinite 36; anti-philosophic 10; and Aristotle 231, 707; and atomic system 156; as consequence of materialism 534, 545, 843; Cudworth on xlvi; and the Cyrenaics 291; Democritus's avoidance of 156; earliest philosophy 24; intellectual and moral 24n; Jacobi on liii, 847; Kant on cxxxvi, 539, 539n; and materialism cxxxiii–cxxxiv; negative ciii, 266n, 292; polytheism as form of 133n; and premature definition lxxviii; of priest 602; and reliance on the senses cii–ciii; and revelation lxxxi; Schelling's 588n; and Spinoza 266n, 580n; Spinozism as 136n; of Theodore 266, 291–2, 299 (Theodosius), 724; unsuspected 126n; and Voltaire 446n; in Wisdom of Solomon lxxxix; Zeno's avoidance of 156
atheist(s)
Aristotle as 231, 707; Bruno as cxxvii, 479; Cudworth on 391n; materialists as 515, 831; negative 266, 724; Plutarch on 267n; Spinoza as 577n–8n
Athenaeum lxviin
Athenaeus of Naucratis (fl c 200) 33n
Athenians 268n
their crime against philosophy 222n; and death of Socrates 145, 225n, 667; defeated by Philip 14; their freedom of speech 496n; as grasshoppers 49, 622; naval victory over 121, 652; originally Pelasgians 51n; repentance of 225, 703; sensuality and luxury of 165; tyranny of 13; their victories 137–8
Athenodorus (1st cent A.D.) 17
Athens 223n, 295, 624n
Academy/academies 14–15, Brutus and a. xcvii, 211, 242, 695, Cicero on 211n, 242, 695, closing of 344n, distinction between two a. 211–12, 695, divisions of 210, 210n, 242, 694, first

xcvii, 201, 210, 212, 694–5, founding of 185, 684, groves of Academus 221, 221n, 701, history of the a. 242, Lyceum 15, 221–2, 221n, 244, 249, 701–2, middle 248, 248n, number of 210, 694, Peripaton 249, Plato's *see* first a.; second a. xcviii, 15, 15n, 210, 694–5, third a. 16
Areopagus 292; Aristotle at 226, 244, 704; of Christendom (Ireland) 408; constitution of 59n; corruption in 138n; decline of 735; democracy in 345n; under Demosthenes 173n; Eleatics in 153; emblem of 50n; Epicurus at 273, 729; Erigena in 379n; Gorgias in 13–14; government of 59n; justice in 185, 684; legislation at 12; its loss of genius 282; its loss of patriotism 282; and modern Jacobinism 454; people of 268n; the Peripatetic school xcix, 5, 335, 556n; philosophical advantages of 142, 157, 664 (not named); philosophy at 148n; plague at 13; Plato and A. 185–6, 684; political equilibrium in 10; the Pompeion 225n; principles in 10; Proclus to go to 298; progressiveness in 10; public spirit in 10; return of Platonists to 19; St Paul at 268, 268n, 725; schools of philosophy closed 19n, 343n; and Sparta 10; Stoa 277, 277n–8n, 297, 300, 732; tyrant of 24n; victories of 137n; Zeno and A. 277, 297, 300, 731
atom(s)
aggregate of 137n, 545; ancient theory of lxxxviii; angular 515, 524, 831, 836; Aristotle on 231; and citizens c; of Democritus 134–6, 135n, 166, 170, 198, 516, 518, 659–60, 673, 831; of difference 378, 773; different figures of cxxxii, 515, 523, 542, 831, 836, *see also* a., angular, round; Eclectics on 831; Epicurus adopts a. 272, 728; as explanation 515, 830; as fiction 135n, 515, 830, 836, *see also* a., hypothesis of; and fire 516n, 831; ground of 515, 831; history of 514, 830; hypothesis of 76, 515, 523, 547, 640, 830, *see also* a. as fiction; impenetrability of 135, 659–60; indivisible 137, 661; one larger 136, 660; largest 136, 660; Leucippus on 516n, 534, 542, 842 (Lycurgus); life in 542, 547; major 240, 713; materialist on a. 844 (organs); of matter 137, 661; and mechanical philoso-

cart-wheel 93

Casaubon, Isaac (1559–1614)
on "Hermes Trismegistus" 80n; as learned man 95n; on metre 35n; and Pythagoras 95
Of Credulity and Incredulity 471n

Cassiodorus (c 480–575) on Aristotle 405, 405n

castes
cause of 67–8, 634; effect of 67–8, 634; purpose of 68, 634

castle
bishop's 354, 765; house as 421, 421n, 788

catacomb of mummies 86

Catcott, G. (fl 1797), letter to xlvii q, xlviin

catechism 130, 233, 658, 709

categories, Aristotelian 404, 404n

caterpillar cxli, 340, 368, 582, 602, 757, 864

cathedral(s)
Milan 351, 366, 763; and sacred grove 351, 366; Strasburg 351, 366, 399, 413, 763, 785; and temples 352n, 366; York 351, 366, 763

Catherine II, the Great, empress of Russia (1729–96) 360n

Catholicism, Roman
converts to 501; corruption of 409; Crashaw converted to 468n; enduring appeal of cxxvi; errors of 501; in Europe lxxxii; on images 55, 87, 127–8 (not named), 534 (not named), 625, 656 (not named), 843 (not named); nature of 68n; non-Christian element in 468n; and paganism 153n, 591, 602, 867; and peace 413; priesthood 68, 68n, 635; Protestant attitudes to cxiii; in Protestant countries lxxxii, 68, 635; and Protestantism cxiii, 495n; Schelling as defender of 589–90, 589n, 867; and Scholasticism 468, 810; sensuality of lxxxvii; and superstition ciii, 165. *See also* Church, Roman Catholic; Church, Romish

Catholics, Roman
in Protestant countries 68, 635; rational 160; *see also* Romanists

cats 37
Agrippa's 442, 442n, 799

causality *see* cause(s)

causation, absolute principle of 215, 243, 697

cause(s)
absolute 489, 822; and effect lxxxi, 115, 259n, 520, 522, 534–5, 649, 833, 835, 843, Hume on 259, 719, and religion 260, 720; efficient 5, 27, 513, 829; of eternal will 160; final 209, 229n, 339–40, 361, 513, 693, 756–7, 829; first 171, 171n, 673; historians on 329; in history 304–5, 741; material 27, 33, 62n; objective 38; predisposing 576, 861; primary 100; second 171, 673; sufficient 556, 851 (efficient); Thales on 610; of universe 38, 268n; *see also* origin(s)

cave
of Montesino 396n; of Trophonius 74, 74n, 377, 377n, 403 (den of T.), 639, 773 (den of Polyphemus)

cavern, Epimenides in 91

Cebes (5th cent B.C.) 181n

Cellini, Benvenuto (1500–71) 245
Vita 245n

Celsus (fl c 178) 340n

Celts 23, 349, 349n, 364–5, 762

cement, higher 311, 745

centre of system 461, 807

century/centuries
eighth 403; eleventh 402; first six 462, 498, 808; sixth 403; thirteenth 5, 507, 826

ceremony/ceremonies
and alchemy 395, 783; Christian 363*; external 356, 766; and lightning 443; religious c. and revival of philosophy 356, 766; Roman Catholic 590, 867

Ceres (mythical) 473n, 624n
and yearning 475n

Cerethites 32, 32n

certainty
and positiveness cii, 260, 260n, 720; and Timon cii

Cervantes Saavedra, Miguel de (1547–1616) *Don Quixote* 396, 396n, 464, 783, 809

"chaberin" 473n

chain 365
of deductions and conclusions 522, 835; historical 455n; inevitable 535, 844; lectures as 373, 770; link(s) of 365, 424–5, 790

Chaldaea 329

chalice, Eucharistic 433n

Chambers, Ephraim (d 1740)
Cyclopaedia lin; articles: "God" 133n q, "Psychology" 501, 501n q; *see also*

in 526; Pythagoras on 79, 642–3; wooden 310, 394, 745, 782

circumference 530, 840

of knowledge 490, 823; of nature 461, 497, 807

circumstances, hot-house of 463, 808

Citium 277, 297, 731

citizen(s)

as atoms c; in commonwealth 61n; foundation of 355n; Roman 281n; and state 240–1, 714

citizenship, Spartan 10

city/cities

and Church 354, 357, 765; formation of 365; privileges of 399, 785; rise of 354–6, 765–6

Civil War, English *see* England

civilisation

acts of 311, 746; and Brahminism 718; and Christianity 718; and Church 354, 369, 765; and commerce lxxvi; corruption of Greek and Roman 282, 734; and cultivation lxxxiv, 81, 81n, 108, 348, 643, 761–2; Greek lxxx–lxxxi; Hebrew lxxx; and ideas 401n; and Mahometanism 718; in north and south 734–5; progressive state of 43; and religion 257–8, 718

claret 178, 679

Clarke, Samuel (1675–1729)

and Leibniz 581n; *see also* Newton, Isaac *Optics* tr Clarke

Clarkson, Thomas (1760–1846) 348n

letter to 462n

History of . . . the Slave Trade 348n, 360n

class(es)

in Crete 52n; duties of particular 69n; educated 468, 811; in France 52n; higher 360, 375, 378, 755, 769, 771, 773; lower 375, 392, 771, 781; middle, in England 574, 860, in Germany 574, 600, 860; and philosophy 326–7; of truth 584–5, 865; *see also* order(s)

classifications 562, 854

classifying, power of 608–9

Clavigero, Francisco Saverio (1731–87)

The History of Mexico tr C. Cullen 499n

Cleanthes (c 330–c 231 B.C.) 15

Clemens or Clement of Alexandria (c 160–215) 18, 266n

clergy

and civilisation 354, 413; constrained by doctrine 360, 769; as counter-

balance 414; disendowing 523n; ignorant 434, 795; and Jews 458; on Locke 859; nominally Christian 127, 656; power of 386, 399, 777, 785. *See also* priest(s); priesthood

clergyman, young Calvinist 381n

cleverness 530n, 573n

Clifton

lectures in xxxviiin; Pneumatic Institute 200n

Clitomachus (c 187–c 110 B.C.) 16, 253, 253n (Clinomachus), 292 (Clinomachus), 715

clouds, wings of 478n

Clown (*Twelfth Night*) lxxxi

Cluny 411

Clytus (fl 310 B.C.) 226n

coach lxxxvii

Irishman in 56n, 87; riding c. in wrong direction 56, 626

cobblers, philosophical 43

Coburn, Kathleen Hazel (1905–91) lxxii, cxliv, 872, 885

annotations by 826n, 849n; announcement lxxiiin; finds Frere ms lxvii, lxix *In Pursuit of Coleridge* lxviin; "S. T. Coleridge's Philosophical Lectures of 1818–19" lxviin; *see also* Coleridge, S. T. VI *P Lects,* IX *Inquiring Spirit,* XII *Notebooks* ed Coburn

cobweb 130, 657

codex of Cicero 429n

Codrus (11th cent B.C.?) 183, 200, 683

co-existence 247

cohesion

things resist 135, 659; thread of 241

coin(s) 351n, 474

Colchians 68n

cold 31n, 35–6, 111, 646; *see also* hot

Coleridge, Alwyne Hartley Buchanan (b 1914) lxix

Coleridge, Berkeley (1798–9) lxv

Coleridge, Derwent (1800–83) lxix

letters to 192n, 609n; as annotator of Frere ms lxxi

Coleridge, Ernest Hartley (1846–1920) 269n

annotations by lxxi, 625n–6n, 635n, 637n–8n, 644n, 646n–7n, 651n–3n, 673n, 675n, 678n, 776n–7n; death of lxix; ed C's letters lxvii, lxviin; his possession of Frere ms lxvii; transcription of mss lxxin; *see also* Coleridge, S. T. II *Poetical Works,* X *Letters* ed E. H. Coleridge

COLERIDGE, SAMUEL TAYLOR (1772–1834)

I BIOGRAPHICAL AND GENERAL: (1) Biographical (2) Definitions (3) Distinctions

II POETICAL WORKS   III PROSE WORKS

IV CONTRIBUTIONS TO NEWSPAPERS AND PERIODICALS

V ESSAYS   VI LECTURES   VII MSS   VIII PROJECTED WORKS   IX COLLECTIONS AND SELECTIONS   X LETTERS   XI MARGINALIA   XII NOTEBOOKS

I BIOGRAPHICAL AND GENERAL

(1) *Biographical*

acknowledgments, literary liv, lvii, lx; as advertiser xxxvii–xl; advice to his sons 192, 192n; alphabet, his use of letters of 150n; on animal magnetism 73n; his annuity xlvii; reading Aquinas 391, 391n–2n, 780; his associationist phase xlv; his autobiographical mode liii–liv

reading A. Baxter 469n; hears Blumenbach 73n; Böhme, acquaintance with 481n; book borrowing xlvi, xlviin, lxiv, lxivn, 456, 456n; borrowing(s) liv, lvii, lx, 884–5, attitude to 432n; in Bristol xlv; Brucker, opinion of 4n; G. Bruno, lack of access to cxxviin, importance of to C 477n, plans life of 477n, reading lin, seeks copy of 477n

moral character 44; at Christ's Hospital lxvi, 74n; claims as poet and philosopher 40; on condescending clergyman 381n; conversation lvi, with critic 678, with E. Darwin 272 (not named), 272n; Creuzer, use of lxiv–lxvi, 97n and Davy 875; Duns Scotus, knowledge of 391, 391n; in Durham 373n, 391n

his eccentricities 43; and Eichhorn 66n; his eloquence 42; and *Encyclopaedia Metropolitana* 214n; on Enfield 4n; on "enlightened" men 143n; Erigena, seeks copy of 392n; etymological speculations lixn–lxn; on evolution 887; his experience as lecturer xxxv

supports factory act 401n; his youthful fancy 557, 851; farewell address 605n; his forgetfulness 44; his French 468n, 536n; on Frere as translator 223n

reading Gassendi 513n–14n; his genius 43, 45; and Germany 343n; on Gibbon 305n; requests Goethe *Zur Farbenlehre* lxvi; at Göttingen lxiii, 73n; his use of Greek and Latin terms lix

on Hayley 432n; dispute with Hazlitt 177n; in Highgate xxxv–xxxvi; his historicism 881; on Hobbes's Homer 9n; on Homeric rhapsodes 23n; on Hume 55n, 258n–9n

idealist phase xlv; illness xxxix, 302; imagination of 40; as improviser cxix; on Indian thought 883–4; acquaintance with *Institutes of Hindu Law* 105n; on Ireland 408n; in Italy 68n; Kant, first experience of 584n

language, feeling for 878; Laplace, knowledge of 533n; lecturing xxxv–xl; his learning 43; libraries, access to xlvi–xlvii, xlviin, lx; Locke, criticism of 564n, study of 568n, 599–600; logic, class of 1822 507n

and Mackintosh xlix, attends M.'s lects xlix, xlixn, 77n, opposition to l, ln; Macpherson, views on 53n; in Malta cxxviin, 68n, 378n; and materialism 503; on mathematics 79n–80n; borrows Meiners *Lebensbeschreibungen* lxiii; his memory 873; his metaphors 41–2; on method 888; Mitford, use of lxvi–lxvii, 50n; More, knowledge of 583n

in Naples 81n; as Necessitarian 523n; on Newton 529n; his nightmares 471n; Occam, enthusiasm for 393n; reading Ocellus Lucanus 151, 151n–2n; early opinions xcvii; originality of his ideas 417

VII MSS

XII NOTEBOOKS

criterion 488, 821
of acts of mind 585, 865; Cyrenaic rejection of 289, 294; Epicurean denial of 263–4, 722; impermanence as 342, 758; lack of 211, 263–4, 294, 695, 722; Leibniz's 310n; of religion 85; scientific cxxx; true 287, 739; *see also* distinction(s)
Critias (d 403 B.C.) 200, 200n
critic(s)
and artists 61, 61n, 630; C's conversation with 177, 678; in Greece 61n; historical 49, 73, 622, 638; uninterested 587n
criticism
historic 92; system of 264, 722
Crito (5th cent B.C.) 181n
Critolaus Phaselites (2nd cent B.C.) 16
crocodiles 55, 625
Croesus (603–546 B.C.)
becomes king of Lydia 12; his collection of celebrities 26; conquered 12
Cromwell, Oliver (1599–1658), times of 355, 765
Cromwellians 355n
cross
of Christ 351, 763; elevation of 353, 764
Croton 12, 38 (Crotin), 69, 69n, 97, 107, 635 (Groto)
Crotona 105
Crotonians 70n
crown of Hiero 642n
crucible 239, 713
crucifix(es) 55n, 463, 808
Crucifixion 17
cruelty/cruelties 130, 139, 183, 258, 418, 657, 663, 682, 718
crusades cxviii, 398, 784
crystallisation lxxvii, 26, 26n
cudgel 111, 111n, 646
Cudworth, Ralph (1617–88)
The True Intellectual System of the Universe xlii, xliin, C's use of xlvi–xlvii, xlvin, ed T. Birch 79n q, 80n, 127n q, 171n, 284n q, 391n q, tr J. L. von Mosheim xlvin
Cullen, Charles (fl c 1787–9) *see* Clavigero, Francisco Saverio *The History of Mexico* tr Cullen
cultivation
progress of 345, 364, 760; *see also* civilisation
culture, European 379n
cumulative, the 606

cunning
and common sense 439, 798; and morality 61, 630
cup, Bohemian 433, 433n, 454, 795
Cupid (in Apuleius) 492n
Curetes (mythical) 32, 32n
Curley, Edwin *see* Spinoza, Baruch *Collected Works* tr Curley
curse
of Canaan 348n; of Ham 348n
Curtis, Samuel (fl 1817–18), letter to xxxviii q, xxxviiin
Curtis, Thomas (fl 1816–18), letters to 73n q, 214n, 318n q
customs 364
Celtic 349n; Gothic 346, 760; idols of 559, 853; of state 344–5, 760; *see also* habit(s)
Cuvier, Georges, baron (1769–1832) 72–3, 73n, 214, 214n, 242, 638, 697
Cybele (mythical) 341n
cycle of philosophy 11
Cynics 5, 110, 148n, 179, 204, 297, 668, 680–1
buffoonery of 330; and Christ 283, 735; and Cyrenaics xxxvii, lxxxv, xcii–xciii, 181, 199, 261–2, 295, 299, 608n, 681, 721, 731; and Lucian 330n; their way of life 148, 330n–1n
Cyprus 277, 297, 731
Cyrenaics 5, 110, 148n, 204, 265–8, 288, 292, 300, 723–4
and atheism 291; their beliefs 262n; Christ on cv; their criterion 289; and Cynics xxxvii, lxxxv, xcii–xciii, 181, 199, 261–2, 295, 299, 608n, 681, 721, 731; and Epicureans cii, civ, 274, 280, 290, 296, 729, 734; and Epicurus 276, 290; on ethics 266, 289, 724; on happiness 268, 289, 725; on immortality 269, 725; on individual as end 289; and intensity of life 290; on pain, pleasure, and indifference 288; on pleasure ciii, 274n; rejected physics and dialectics 265, 724; and science 265n; sensualism of 608, 610; and Socrates 608n; and Stoics cxliii; their way of life civ; on wisdom 278, 732
Cyrene 184, 200, 683 (Cyrenica)
"cyriologic" 82n
cyriology 82, 644
Cyrus (6th cent B.C.) 12

degeneracy, ancients on 40n
degradation 275, 730
degree 280n
Deism lxxxvii–lxxviii
  and Abelard 412n; casual lxv; and
  the Enlightenment 412n; on God 129n;
  see also theology, natural
Deist(s) xli, 128n
deity/deities
  Egyptian 444, 800; eighth 476, 814;
  Phoenician 444, 800; physiological
  476n; Samothracian 473n; seven 476,
  814; theurgic 476, 814 (Theologic);
  worship of unknown d. 424n. *See also*
  God; god(s); goddess(es)
deixis 89n
  d. theion 89, 89n
delirium 75, 229, 558, 595 (forms in
  fever), 639, 706, 852; *see also* fever(s)
dells 424n
Delos 95n
Delphi
  oracle at 65n, 94n; temple at 26
deluge, time of 432, 794
delusion(s) 599, 854
  of Böhme 481, 816–17; causes of 437,
  797; of dark ages 437, 797; mere 342,
  758; of Plotinus 322–3, 334, 752; and
  reality 562, 853; of senses 512, 533n,
  829
demagogues 38
Demeter *see* Ceres
Demetrius of Phaleron (b c 350 B.C.) 92n
democracy 138, 241, 662, 714
  and aristocracy 61n; Athenian 345n; in
  Greece 172, 674, 883; Milton and d.
  355n; Mitford on 345n; and monarchy
  38; Pythagoras opposed to 69–70, 636
Democritus (c 460–c 370 B.C.) lxxxviii–
  lxxxix, xci, cxxxii, 134–7, 134n, 170,
  198, 276, 608n, 659–61, 872, 874
  no atheist 136, 661; his atomism
  lxxxviii, 134–6, 155, 659–60, 831;
  born 12; character of lxxxviii; corporeal system of *see* D. and materialism;
  corpuscular philosophy of *see* D. and
  materialism; on effluvia 516, 831; and
  Eleatics 152; and Epicurus ciii, 272,
  276n, 295–6, 300, 309n, 609, 609n,
  727–8, 731; his followers 518, 832; on
  gravity 135n; and Leucippus 79, 513–
  17, 534n, 608n; longevity of 13, 513–
  14, 514n, 542, 830; and materialism
  136, 170, 294, 300, 513, 514n, 518,

542, 544, 661, 673, 830, 832; on mind
518, 832; on perception 516, 831; and
Pyrrho 294n; school of 155; and science 137, 661; his sect 172, 674; on
senses 294, 517, 831–2; and Sophists
156; on soul 156, 156n, 516, 542, 547–
8, 831; and Spinoza lxxxviii; Tennemann on 514n; his two problems 134,
659; and Zeno lxxxviii, 134, 165
(Xeno), 659
demon(s)
  Democritus on 137, 661; evil 466, 498,
  809; and philosopher 323, 431, 793
  (Daemon); *see also* daemon(s)
demonology 342n
"demonstration" 89n
Demosthenes (c 384–322 B.C.) 173n
  on poets 35n
den
  idols of 487, 559, 595, 821, 853; of lions
  33; of thieves 482, 818
Denis, St (d c 250) 317n
Denmark 348n
depravity, progress of 307, 743
depth(s) 27, 27n
  of science 482, 817; of our souls 507; of
  theology 282, 735; of will 58, 628
De Quincey, Thomas (1785–1859), letter to 260n
derision 61n
Descartes, René (1596–1650) cxxxi,
  232n
  and ancient metaphysicians 566, 856;
  his animal machine 520, 834; and
  Anselm cxvii, 388–9, 388n, 411,
  778–9 (not named); Article 16 520n;
  and Bruno cxxxviii, 479, 479n, 816;
  contribution of 451n; his definition
  566–7, 857; on division between man
  and nature 565, 599, 855–6; and dualism 285n, 518–19, 518n, 565n, 832–
  3; followers of 518n; on God 388n,
  778–9; and Harriott 509, 509n; on
  idea(s) ln, cxxxix, 561n, 565–8,
  565n–7n, 778–9, 856–7; on illusion
  559n; Jacobi on liii; Jesuit on 566, 856;
  Kant on 388n, 538, 846; and La Forge
  510n, 565n; and Leibniz cxl, 580n–1n;
  Leibniz and Spinoza on 580–1, 863;
  and Locke l, cxxxix, 564n, 568–70,
  570n, 599–600, 857–8; on matter
  565, 856; his mechanism 547, 827; and
  metaphysics 570, 858 (mathematical
  parts); on mind cxxxvii, 547, 582, 864;

emblem 82, 97, 644
Emerson, Ralph Waldo (1803–82) 888
Emilius *see* Paullus, Lucius Aemilius
emmetra 35, 35n
emotions
    conflict of 289; Epicureans on 262, 721
Empedocles (c 490–430 B.C.) 13, 96n
emperor(s)
    adoration of 330; and Agrippa 439, 458,
        798; loyalty to 456 (Caesar); and
        popes 353, 353n, 365, 365n, 369, 764;
        Roman 444, 800
empire
    Babylonian 92n; British 346, 761; of
        China 346, 761; Greek 444, 801; Holy
        Roman cxi; Italian 347, 761; Lower
        342n; Roman 5, 349n–50n, syn-
        cretism in 98n; western 351n
empiricism 508
    Lockean xlix, 536n, 876; and magic
        508; and quackery 547
Empusae (mythical) 526n
empyraeum, divine 477n
encyclopaedia(s) lix
    C's interest in liv; on Descartes 479n;
        definition of 214, 697; first xcviii, 214,
        697; lack of lx; and philosophy 214,
        697; of Speusippus 214, 214n, 242,
        248, 697
Encyclopaedia Metropolitana
    C's introduction to liv; C's involvement
        with lxvi, 214 (not named), 214n, 697
        (not named)
Encyclopaedists/encyclopaedists 360n
    French xlii, 332n
end 421n
endeigma 89n
enemies 61n, 91
energy
    heroic 307, 743; of love 215, 243, 697
Enfield, William (1741–97)
    abridgement of Brucker xli, xlvi–xlvii
    The History of Philosophy xlin, xlvi, 4,
        4n
Engel, Johann Jakob (1741–1802) *Der
    Philosoph für die Welt: Schriften* 238n
England
    Agrippa visits 442, 455, 799; anti-papal
        feeling in lxxxii; averse to thinking
        574, 860; character of 573n; as Chris-
        tian nation lxxxvii–lxxxviii; civil war
        in 468, 468n, 499, 501; commercial
        and political role of cxl; dark age in
        437, 458, 797; distrust of philosophy

in xliv; Erigena in 379, 382n, 408, 774;
    and Europe cxii; fairies of 474, 502,
    814; general information of 401, 786;
    and Germany 574, 860; golden age of
    intellect in 496; insularity of cxiv;
    interest in politics 343; interest in
    weather 343; magic in 433, 794; mid-
    dle class in 574; nobility in 51, 623;
    old times in 400, 786; politics and
    commerce in 564n, 574, 860; Protec-
    torate 363; religion in xliv, lxiii; Re-
    naissance in 396n; Republic of *see*
    Commonwealth; revolution in *see* rev-
    olution, English; Scholasticism in 468,
    810; truths of experience in 584–5,
    865
English
    triumph over French 570n; and Ger-
    mans 343, 759; gratified by material-
    ism 600; in November 288n; com-
    pared with Russians 81n
The English Dialect Dictionary ed
    Joseph Wright 553n–4n q
engravings on the brain 517, 543, 832
enjoyment 292
enkosmioi 341, 342n, 363, 758 (Inkos-
    meoi)
enlighteners 186n
Enlightenment/enlightenment 224–5,
    397 (enlightening), 446n, 703–4, 881
    anti-religious impulse of lxxxiii; and
    Aristotle xcvi, xcix; and astronomy
    486n; and chemistry cxviii; and Deism
    412n; errors of 239–40, 713; French
    xliv, xciii, 224n, 317n, 454n, 512n;
    and Hume lxiv; materialism of the E.
    lxxxviii; and progress cx; theorists of
    cxii; virtues of xlix–l
Ennius, Quintus (239–169 B.C.) 15
ens/entia lxxvii
    e. *representans* 522, 522n, 835; *e. vere
    realia* 393n
entelechy (entelechie)/entelechies 872
    Aristotle on xcix, 231, 231n; Barbarus
    on 231, 231n, 247, 707 (Intelika); and
    matter 231, 707–8 (Intelika); supreme
    231
entertainingness 553, 570, 849, 858
enthusiasm 456
    disgraceful 472, 812–13; and fanati-
    cism 481n; and genius 481n; with in-
    difference 481n; modern 511, 828; and
    Philo Judaeus 319n; religious 363n–
    4n; visionary 291, 433, 794

609; Kant on 585n; modern 355, 355n, 765; modern lovers of 355, 765; perfect 416; Plato's zeal for 186, 201; possibility of cxiii; rational 356n; rise of 356, 765; of speech 496n; spirit of 350n; symptom of 378n

freeman 355n

freezing 287, 738

Freja (mythical) 474n

French
character of 612–13; English triumph over 570n. *See also* France; French Revolution; language(s)

French Revolution 252, 368 (the revolution)
beginning of 224n, 360, 769; delusions of 454n; disappointment over 212n; excesses of 345n; and German morality 413–14; as great event 496n, 499, 501, 811; C's lecture on xxxviiin; and mechanical philosophy c, 240, 609, 609n, 713; period of 496; and Rousseau 448n; and Sabbath 313n; and science 499; time immediately before cxxxi, 494, 825; time of 52n, 368; Terror 448n, 612

frenzy, corybantic 319n

Frere, John Hookham (1769–1846), letters to 343n, 454n–5n, 477n
as annotator of Frere ms lxxi; C's acquaintance with lxviii; has lects reported lxviii, 223n, 302
tr Aristophanes *The Frogs* 223n

fresco in Pisa xcv

Freud, Sigmund (1856–1939) 884

friend(s)
calumny of 61, 61n, 91, 630; image of 558, 852

Friends, Society of 348n
founder of 483n

friendship, heroic 39

Frommann, Karl Friedrich Ernst (1765–1837) 590n

fruit and tree 85

Fulda *see* Abbot of Fulda

Fülleborn, Georg Gustav (1769–1803) 153, 153n

function(s)
as abstraction 526, 544, 838; sum of 526, 838

fungus 527n
life of 527, 544, 838

furies 174, 203, 676
religious and political 492

fusions 463

future and experience 125, 655

futurity and immortality 581n

Gale, Thomas (1636–1702)
ed *Opuscula mythologica et ethica* lxvi, lxvin, 116n q, 151 q, 151n–2n q, 159n, 161 q, 161n–2n q; "Testimonia" 406n q

Galen (Claudius Galenus) (c 130–c 201), birth of 17

Galileo (Galileo Galilei) (1564–1642)
age of 471, 502, 812; imprisonment of 224, 225n, 703; and Kepler 236n

Galvani, Luigi (1737–98) 510n

galvanism 444, 800

Gandharvs (*Bhagavad-Gita*) 131

garden(s)
cultivating 260n; of Eden 284n; of Epicurus 260n; olive 260, 295, 720

garment, bodily 113, 647

gases, discovery of 511, 828 (causes)

Gassendi, Pierre (1592–1655)
and Hobbes cxxxii, 542; life of 513, 513n; and materialism 513, 514n, 547 (Gasander); and *tabula rasa* 113n
De origine et varietate logicae xlii, xliin, lii; *Opera omnia* xlii, xliin, liin

Gaul
Phocaeans in 12; as Roman province 365

ge 30n

Gellius, Aulus (c 130–80) *Noctes atticae* 226n

genealogy xliii, 563n

general(s)
blinded 397n; Roman 316, 749

"generalisation" 227, 705

generalisation(s) 8, 10, 490n, 508 (general terms), 562, 826 (generalised in a term), 854
and abstraction xcix, 227, 227n, 235 (generalising power), 608–9 (power of generalising), 710 (generalising power), 880, 888–90; Aristotle's 227, 245, 247, 704; definition of 57, 227, 627, 705; and god(s) 341, 363, 757 (idea); just 176, 199, 677; and numbers lxxxiv; of observation 61, 630; progress by means of 55, 625; scheme of 236, 711; of sense impressions 596; of water 30; weaknesses of 57n

generations 30, 30n

"genesis" 25, 25n

"genial" *see* spirit, genial

genial school(s) *see* schools, genial

Gray, Thomas—*continued*
The Works ed T. J. Mathias 186n–7n,
192n q
Greece 379, 408, 416, 774
absence of conquest in 106; admiration
of 413; air of 260, 720; art of 349, 351,
762–3; artists in 61n; colonisation of
348n; connection in 453; constitu-
tion(s) of 59, 628; critics in 61n; as
cultural leader 182, 682; democracy in
172, 674; destruction of 182, 682;
Egyptians in 100; empire of 444, 801;
essence of 83, 644–5; fall of 149, 200,
670; favourable conditions of 172,
674; and France compared 59n;
freemen in 28n; genius of 96, 352, 366;
and Germany 454; great men of 396,
783; historians of 54, 236, 624, 710;
history/histories of 50–1, 172, 203,
346, 364, 499n, 623, 674, 760; before
Homer 50, 623; independence of 83,
101, 644–5; infidelity in 293–4; as intellectual Golconda 106; islands of 53,
120, 347, 624, 651, 761; language in
255, *see also* language, Greek; laws
and constitutions in lxxix, 42; legisla-
ture in 49, 100, 622; literature of 425n;
Major 59, 59n, 628; Minor 59, 59n,
628; as model 49, 622; monarchies in
59, 628; moral weakness of 172, 674;
mysteries in 472n; naming of gods in
52n; origins of 49–52, 622–3; pantheism in 126n; and Peloponnesian war
182, 199–200, 204, 682; as phenomenon in the world 182, 682; philosophers of 54, 104, 314, 581–2, 747–8,
864; philosophy in 23, 84, 607, 610,
645, 873; poetic records of lxxx; poetry in 10*, 11, 11n, 96, 457; poets in
582, 864; politics of 138, 249, 662;
polytheism in 183, 683; population of
51n; powers and thoughts of 457; pure
works of 350, 762; relaxed manners of
307, 742–3; religion in 162, 197, 692;
lack of representative government in
345, 760; republicanism in 457; re-
public(s) of 59, 100, 107, 182, 183n,
359, 628, 682, 768; and Rome 349n;
science in 146n, 349, 762; Seven Wise
Men (or Sages) of lxvi, lxxxi, 59–61,
60n–1n, 107, 629; to Solon's time 10–
11; sophistry and the overthrow of G.
610; states of 236, 710; superiority of
326, 755; temples of 352n; theology of
58, 628; tolerance in 261, 720; writ-

ings of 418. *See also* Athens; Athenians; Greek(s)
Greek(s) 57 (other race), 626 (other
race), 813
ancient stories of 431, 794; assumptions
of ancient G. 38n; and Cabiri 473; and
Christ 108 (Messiah), 291n; collective
will of 421n; earliest colony of 51,
623; and Goths 421, 457, 788; and
Hebrews lxxx, lxxxiv, cxii, cxliii, 49,
100, 106, 622; and Jew 607; origin of
100; philosophies of 310, 745; pride of
333; as race 49n; religion of 85, 85n–
6n; and Romans 349, 606, 610, 762;
their victories 137–8, 661–2. *See also*
Athens; Athenians; Greece; language,
Greek
Green, Joseph Henry (1791–1863) 168,
302, 381n, 588n–9n
annotations by lxxi, cxliin, 624n, 626n,
628n–31n, 634n–5n, 642n–3n, 645n,
651n–2n, 655n–6n, 660n–4n, 666n–
8n, 670n, 740n, 770n, 807n, 826n;
death of lxviii; on Frere ms lxviii; and
Ingleby lxviii; attends lect 22, 48; letters to lviii q, lviiin, cxlii q, cxliin,
228n–9n q, 588n–9n q; and Schelling
cxlii; his Tennemann *Geschichte*
lviii–lix, lxii
green 559, 595, 852
Gregory the Great (c 540–604)
on knowledge 374n; on learning 374
Epistolae 374n
Gregory Thaumaturgus, the Wonder-
worker (c 213–c 270)
forged works about 405, 405n
Greville, Sir Fulke, 1st baron Brooke
(1554–1628) cxlv, 815 (Bruce)
and Bruno cxxvii, 477; his writings
477n
Certaine Learned and Elegant Workes,
marginal note in 477n
Griggs, Earl Leslie (1899–1974) *see*
Coleridge, S. T. x *Collected Letters* ed
Griggs
Grimbald, St (?820–903) 379n–80n
Grotians 495n
Grotius, Hugo (Huig de Groot) (1583–
1645) 579n
ground 304, 741
grove of Hertha 351, 366
growth 527, 544, 838
grub 582, 864
Guanilo or Gaunilo (12th cent) 389n
guilt and compulsion 213, 696

heart(s)—*continued*
(hands), 657, 708; of man 308–9, 744; religion in 786; and sensation 523, 836
heat 116n
aetherial 480n; caloric or calorific 111, 111n, 115, 152, 646, 648 (calorif); latent 511, 511n, 828
heathenism 78 (heathen world), 209, 693 and Christianity 192n. *See also* paganism; pagans
heaven
and earth 333, 509; Eclectics on 324, 753; Fiddle of 432n
Heber (Bible), posterity of 349n
Hebrews 49, 57, 129–30, 130n, 434, 622, 626–7, 657, 795
their archology lxxxi; chief priests 225n; God's provision for 145, 666; and Greeks lxxx, lxxxiv, cxii, cxliii, 49, 100, 106, 622; history of 209, 693; literature of 434n (writings), 795; mss of H. destroyed 434, 795; monotheism of lxv; and moral feeling lxxx; oracles of 84, 645; origin of 100; and pagan world 40n–1n; their preparation for the Messiah 108; prophecies of 102; Pythagoras visits 95, 95n; as race 49n; records of 455n; their reliance on God lxxx; religion of 309n; and revelation 59, 140, 628, 663; role of 606n; and tradition lxxx; their writers 49, 622. *See also* Bible: Old Testament; Jews; language, Hebrew
Hecatoeus of Miletus (b 549 B.C.) 12
Hecatompolis 32, 32n
Hector (*Iliad*) 104
hedge 64, 286, 397, 418, 632, 737, 784
hedge-masters 295
hedone 147, 147n; *see also* pleasure(s)
h. en kinesei 290; *h. katastematike* 290
hedonism lxxxix
Hegel, Georg Wilhelm Friedrich (1770–1831) xlii, 888
on Schelling 588n, 590n
Briefe von und an Hegel ed J. Hoffmeister 590n q
Hegesias (c 290 B.C.) cii–ciii, cv, 262n, 266, 269n, 725 (not named)
his banishment 270, 727 (not named); on happiness 268–9, 292, 725 (not named); the *peisithanatos* 288, 288n; and Ptolemy 270, 271n, 727 (not named); silencing of 270, 271n, 288, 288n
Apocarteron (*Suicide by Starvation*) 271n

Hegesinus or Hygenus of Pergamus (fl c 185 B.C.) 15, 15n
Heidelberg 578n
height, mounting to 228, 705
Heinroth, Johann Christian August (1773–1843)
Lehrbuch der Anthropologie 216n, marginal note in 885n
heirloom and originality 432, 794
Helen of Troy (by Zeuxis) 310–11, 331, 745
Helens 238, 712
Helios (mythical) 476n
hell of heretics 405
Hellas *see* Greece
Hellespont 606
helplessness 308, 744
Helvétius, Claude Adrien (1715–71) 487n
Helvicus, Christophorus (1581–1617)
Theatrum historicum 23n
hemisphere, southern 614
Henry II, king of England (1133–89) 353n
Henry V (in Shakespeare *Henry V*) 448, 448n, 803
Henry VII, king of England (1457–1509), reign of 393, 782
Henry VIII, king of England (1491–1547) and Erasmus 447n; reign of 469, 782, 811; time of 393
hens 276, 731
Hephaestus (mythical) 473n
sons of 474n
Heracles (*The Frogs*) 223n
Heraclides (4th cent B.C.) 96n
on Pythagoras 96
Heraclitus (fl 500 B.C.) 12, 27n
deferment of discussion of 152; doctrines of 151; fragments of 436, 436n, 796; on identity of God and universe 154; as pantheist 126n; physics of 204; and Plato 183, 200, 204, 488n, 683; and Pythagoras lxxxvii, 125, 655; on sibyl 87, 88n; on sleeping and waking 558 (one of the elder idealists), 558n, 852 (one of the elder idealists); Tennemann on 126n; how to understand 152n; on world soul 126n
heraldry 350, 351n, 366, 563, 563n, 763, 854
Herbert, Edward, 1st baron Herbert of Cherbury (1583–1648)
on highest reason 561n; on innate ideas 561n; and Kant 561n; Locke on 561n;

of 54n, 106–7; imagination of 104; influence of 120, 651; as Ionian 103; language of 41; and Macpherson 53n, 104; and mysteries 54, 90, 625; and mythology 87–8; and Old Testament 41n; and Pisistratus 23–4, 24n, 53, 104, 107, 624; his poem 41; revolution after 153; and rhapsodists 23, 41; simplicity of 41; and Solon 59n; songs of 378, 403; study of 457; theogony and mythology of 53, 624; theology of 107, 651; time of 7, 10, 59n, 472, 502, 813; transmission of lxxix; unipersonality of 87; verbal changes in lxxix; works of 120n; unable to write 106n; Xenophanes on 119, 153, 651

Hymn to Apollo 51n; *Hymn to Demeter* (Ceres) 90, 90n; *Hymni et epigrammata* ed J. G. J. Hermann 51n; *Hymns* 50, 51n, 120, 651; *Iliad* 8, 25n q, 41n, 50, 53, 87, 90n, 103, 107, 107n, 623–4, date of 24n, French versions of 132, imitation of 424n, ed C. G. Heyne 53n, ed W. Trollope 53n q; *The Iliads and Odysses* tr T. Hobbes 9* q, 9n; *Odyssey* 8, 8*, 8n–9n, 90n, 96n, 103, date of 24n, French versions of 132

Homeridae 23n, 51n, 54 (not named), 120, 120n, 624 (not named), 651

homo microcosmus 331

homogeneity 77, 203 (things similar), 520–1, 641, 835

of idea and law 112, 112n, 150, 647; law of 170, 198, 671; of reason and nature 78

honey and sweetness 116, 116n, 152, 649

honeycomb 129n

honourable, the h. and the useful 174, 203, 676

Hooke, Robert (1635–1703) lv

A General Scheme, or Idea of the Present State of Natural Philosophy 490–1 q, 491n; *Posthumous Works* 490–1 q, 491n, 823 q (not named)

Hooker, Richard (1554–1600) 568n

style of 235n

hope(s) 340, 445, 757, 801

and belief 396, 783; ground of 243; loss of 308, 743; sabbath of 325, 754; St Paul on xc

Horace (Quintus Horatius Flaccus) (65–8 B.C.)

on Archytas 184, 184n, 200, 683

Odes 184n; *Satires* 328n q

horizon 36

dim 56, 100, 626

horns 384, 776

horoscopes 431n

horror vacui 198n

horse-man 34

horses 227, 705

hospitals 272, 728

hot and cold 31n, 63n

hot-house of circumstances 463, 808

hour-glass, author as 234n

house 93

as castle 421, 788

Howe, Percival Pressland (1886–1944) *see* Hazlitt, William *The Complete Works* ed Howe

Howes, Raymond Floyd (b 1903) *see* Coleridge, S. T. IX *Coleridge the Talker* ed Armour and Howes

Hufeland, Christoph Wilhelm (1762–1836) 72–3, 73n, 96, 638 (Hoffer)

Hugh of St Severino (14th cent) 428n

Hugo de Sancto Victore (Hugh of St Victor) (c 1078–1141) 412n, 482n

humanitas 216, 243 (*humanities*)

humanity, universal 345, 760

Hume, David (1711–76) 1

his debt to Aquinas 432n; attacks on 258–9, 293, 332n, 719; biography by his opponents 293; his blasphemy 560, 560n; on cause and effect 259, 572, 719, 859; and Christianity 332n; as chronicler 455n; and Creuzer lxiv–lxv; and Gibbon 332n; on God 560n; on idolatry 55n; Kant on 259n; on Locke 564–5, 572, 572n, 855, 859; on Macpherson 53n; on monotheism lxiv; his objection 259n; his opponents cii, 259n; on perception 38n; and Pyrrho 258n–9n; on religion lxiv; his saintly quality lxxxvi; and Sceptics 332; on spiders cxxxix, 560, 596, 599, 853; on theologians 560, 596, 599, 853; on tolerance 222–3, 702; on Zeno 124n

Dialogues concerning Natural Religion ed N. Kemp Smith 560n q; *Enquiries* ed L. A. Selby-Bigge 118n, 259n, 565n q; *An Enquiry concerning Human Understanding* li, 118n, 259n q, 562n, 565n q, 572n; *Essays* 560, 596, 853; *Four Dissertations* lxivn, 55n; *History of England* 223n; *The Natural History of Religion* lxiv, 55n, 222n q, 224n; "Of Knowledge and Probability" 572n; "Of the Idea of

lamp
Anaxagoras and the l. 93, 93n; midnight 377n; and oil 93, 93n
Lancaster, Joseph (1778–1838) 407n
Landolfo (16th cent) 455, 455n
Landriano, Gerard (Gerardo Landriani) bp (15th cent) 428, 429n
discovers ms of Cicero 428, 453
Landulph *see* Landolfo
Lang, Edgar Anthony (b 1896) *Ludwig Tieck's Early Concept* 589n
Langcake, Thomas (fl 1764) *see* Böhme, Jacob *The Works* ed Ward, Langcake, and Law
language(s) 111, 117, 173, 646, 650, 675
of ancient prophecies 741–2; Arabic 357n, 408, 606; Attic 116n; of Bacon 595, 853; barbarous 609; Berkeley's 557, 851; of Böhme 484, 819; C's feeling for 878; Chinese 606; and church 257–8, 718; comparison of 8n; connection in cxx, 422, 609n, 789; Dante on 387n; defect in 213, 696; its desynonymisation 553n; as disguise 614; Dorian or Doric 51n, 116n; and education 256, 717; Egyptian 82n–3n; Egyptians on world as 10n; English l. not homogeneous 255, 293, 716, spread of 346, 761, synonyms in 255, 293, 716–17; errors in 146n–7n; European 612; formation of 393, 782; foundation of modern l. 387, 778; French, C using 468n; German xlii, xlvii; Gothic 422n, 879; Greek cxliii, 8, 8n, 51n (Hellenic), 357, 408, 422, 788, absence of synonyms in 255, 293, 716, its connection 609, different from Latin 422n, is homogeneous 255, 293, 716; in Ireland 408n, knowledge of 357n, sentence-structure of 422n; Hebrew cxliii, 116n, 347, 357n, 450, 606, 610, 761, 804, dictionary 434n, grammar 434n; Hellenic *see* l., Greek; of Hesiod 8; of highest truths 606; Hindostanic 606; history of 553, 592, 849, 878; of Homer 8, 23, 41, 103; and images 88; Indian 80n; individuation in 879; inflection in cxx, 422, 422n, 788; intelligible 452, 806; Italian, Tennemann's lack of 477n; Latin cxliii, 357n, 408, 422, 788, different from Greek 422n, *see also* Romans, l. of; and law 8; logical and grammatical 422, 788; of Luther 449, 804; manda-

tory 610; mechanism of 256, 717; modern 881, sentence structure of 422n; narrative 610; and nation 610; national mind 554, 593, 850; native 387n; of Nature 270n; Nietzsche on 878; and noise 596; of numbers 80, 643; obsolete or regional 23n–4n; of old philosophy 112–13, 647; of old schools 556, 851; oppositions of 114, 648; oriental 606; philosophic(al) 304, 449, 554, 740, 804, and common l. 554, 592–3, 850; picture-l. 36n; poetic 36; poetic diction in 8; popular 387, 778; progress of 554, 849; and race 606; and religion 8, 606; since Restoration 553n; of Romans 879; of rustics 258n; Scholastic 593–4; S(h)emitic cxii, 347, 606, 761; of sensations 36n; sentence-structure 422n; Spanish 350, 366, 763; of speculation 8; structure of 304, 740; study of 555, 850; of supreme idea 88; and symbols 877; Syriac 347, 761 (Seriac); Syro-Chaldaic 116n, 606; Tartar 606; technical 256, 717; and thought 387n, 878; unconnectedness in 879; of uneducated 483, 818; word-endings 422n; word order 422, 422n; world as 55, 625. *See also* dialect(s); diction; dictionary; mood; speech
Laplace, Pierre Simon, marquis de (1749–1827) 533, 533n, 842 (replace)
Traité de mécanique céleste 533n
Larcher, Pierre Henri (1726–1812) 12, 12n
lark 287n
bird-limed 64n; and warmth 287, 287n, 739
larva 317n
"latent heat" 511n
"laugh" 438n
laugh of derision 61, 91, 630
laughter 61n, 74n
Laureati, Pietro (c 1280–c 1348) 237n
Lavoisier, Antoine Laurent (1743–97) cxxxi, 115n, 511n, 531n, 828 (not named)
on chemical phenomena 511; chemistry of 532n
Law, William (1686–1761) 484, 484n, 818
life of Böhme 484n; *Serious Call to a Devout and Holy Life* 484n; *see also* Böhme, Jacob *Works* ed Ward, Langcake, and Law

matter—*continued*
and body 508n, 555n, 832; as composition of atoms 135, 659; definition of
cxxxvi–cxxxvii, 555, 555n, 593, 850;
Descartes on 565, 856; electric 543;
and entelechy 231, 707–8 (Intileka/In-
telika); ghost of 523, 836; ground of
34; impenetrability of 547; independence of 171, 673; as indeterminate
dyad 78n; and infinity lxxvii; inflammable 480, 816; intractability of 58,
627; lacks inward 522, 835; materialists on 514–15, 830; and mind 170,
673; and number 79, 643; organisation
of 576–7, 861; partibility of 515, 547,
830; Platonist confusion over 508n;
pre-established 463n; Price on 523,
836; Priestley on 523, 836; resistance
of 515, 830; sentient as 521, 834; Spinoza on 523, 836; transience of 576,
861; wonder-promising 522, 835; *see
also* body
matter-of-factness, Socratic 260n
Matthew, St, the apostle (1st cent A.D.)
and Brothers 306, 742; and inner life
468n; on siege of Jerusalem 305–6,
741–2
Maximilian I, holy Roman emperor
(1459–1519) and Reuchlin 434, 434n,
795
maxims 234n
of Thales 28
Maximus of Tyre (Cassius Maximus
Tyrius) (2nd cent A.D.) 17
Maximus the Confessor, St (c 580–662)
405n
May, John (1775–1856), letter to xlvi q,
xlvin, 4n q
McFarland, Thomas *Coleridge and the
Pantheist Tradition* 521n, 581n
meaning of an earlier writer 117, 649
means, indistinctness of 467, 810
"measter" 554n
mechanics 443, 800
mechanism(s)
of birds 385, 777; of Descartes 547; of
man 497; of mind 596; and organisation 524n, 527 (and life), 528–9, 544,
548, 838 (and life), 839; as philosophy
523n; powers of 358, 767; science of
509, 827 (Mechanics); of sense 562,
854
medals 474
Mediator, Divine 127n
Medici, Cosimo de', the elder (1389–

1464) 429, 429n, 457, 467, 613, 613n,
792 (not named)
Medici, Giovanni de' (later pope Leo X)
(1475–1521) 237, 237n, 429 (not
named), 712, 792 (not named)
Medici, Lorenzo de', the Magnificent
(1449–92) 237, 237n, 429 (not
named), 613, 613n, 712 (Lorenzetti),
792 (not named)
Medicis, the 237n
medicine
Agrippa studied 455; Arabian 357n;
Jewish contribution to 357n; and
magic 508; operations of 510, 828;
unpleasant 177, 679
meditation
of death 82, 644; of Plato 229, 706; of
Socrates 142, 664
meditative, the m. and the contemplative
332
Mediterranean, mastery of 10, 90
medium
Christ as divine m. 283, 735; Christianity as divine m. 328; divine 328
"meeaster" 554n
"meester" 553, 553n, 592
Meetingers 221n
Megara 14, 184, 200, 683
Megarics 253, 253n, 258 (not named),
258n, 292, 299, 715
eristic thinkers 292; and Scepticism ci,
292; Timon on 253–4, 715
Meiners, Christoph (1747–1810) 7n
*Grundriss der Geschichte der Welt-
weisheit* 12, 12n; *Lebensbeschreibungen berühmter Männer* lxiii, lxiiin,
cxxi, 426n–9n q, 434n, 438n, 439n–
42n q, 454n–6n q, 496, 496n, 497 q,
497n, 499n q, C's first acquaintance
with lxiii, C's use of lxiii, cxix, omits
Huss 454n, on Politian 499n q
melancholy 74, 270, 639, 727
sublime m. of Homer 104
Melanchthon, Philip (1497–1560) 397n–
8n
melete thanatou 82, 82n, 96, 644n
Melissa 91, 91n
Melissus of Samos (5th cent B.C.) 13,
165, 652 (Melesius)
Apollodorus on 153; time of 121, 121n,
153
members, good 813
memory 394, 558 (recollection), 614n
(recalling), 782, 852 (recollection)
and age 581, 863; artificial 606n; arts of

606n; and atoms 516, 831; beginning of 385, 776; and co-presence 114n; and digestion 605; hooks and eyes of 423n; and images of place 605; in music 445, 801; and place 610

Memphis, priests at 33n

Mendelssohn, Moses (1729–86)
and Jacobi 539n; Kant on cxxxvin, 213n, 539; on philosophical controversy cxxxvi
Jerusalem oder Über religiöse Macht und Judenthum 213n; *Morgenstunden oder Vorlesungen über das Daseyn Gottes* cin, cxxxvin

mens of Anaxagoras 34n

Menu (legendary), Institutions of 105

mercantilism 25n

merchants
in Bristol xlv; Jews as 365

Mercury (mythical) 473n, 476, 476n, 814
feasts of 32, 32n; *see also* Hermes

merits, estimating 173, 675

Mesmer, Friedrich Anton (1732–1815) 72, 72n, 96, 96n, 638 (not named), 638n
Mesmerismus 72n

mesmerism 72n, 92, 318n, 444n, 875; *see also* magnetism, animal

Messiah 435–6, 796; *see also* Christ

"mēster" 554n

metal(s)
transmutation of 395, 417, 782; workers on 474n

metaphor 876–7
arithmetical 117, 650; C's 41–2; of Janus 445n; and knowledge lxxviii; literal understanding of 94; of weighbridge 525, 525n

metaphorical, the 877

metaphysicians, ancient m. and Descartes 566, 856

metaphysics 232, 547, 708
of Aristotle 234, 709; arithmetical 111–12, 646; avoidance of xcii; Cartesian 570n; and Christianity 495, 825; and common sense 163n; future 214, 697; irreconcilable theories of 412; irreligious lii; as lexicon 390, 411, 779, 827; love of 613; Mackintosh on l; and mysticism 424, 790; and poetry 374n; without psychology 451n; as science 34n, 507–8, 826–7; without science 451n, 469, 499, 501, 811; Socrates on 145n, 173, 675; supposed discoveries in li; in 13th century 507, 826

Metapontium 38

metempsychosis 66, 67n, 101, 106, 633

"method" 169n

method 4, 888
Bacon's 451, 489n; Baxter on 467n; experimental cxxxi; in fine arts 194n; idea of 169n; of natural philosopher 513n; of philosopher 513n; Plato's 186n; of scientist 513n; Socratic 173–4, 199, 201, 676

Methodism
and St Paul 291n; as stove 287n

Methodists 328
discourse of 291

metre(s) 614n
adomena and *emmetra* 35, 35n; cause of 614n; of Hobbes 9*; of Pindar 35n; regularity of 23; scansion of 35. *See also* poems; poetry

Metrodidactus *see* Aristippus, the second

Metrodorus (2nd cent B.C.) 16

Mexico, human sacrifice in 499n

Michelangelo Buonarotti (1475–1564)
Cellini's praise of 245n; and Giotto 612; and jealousy xcviii; in old age 582, 582n, 864; and Raphael 219, 219n–20n, 245n, 700; and Titian 219, 245, 245n, 700

Michelangelos 237, 712

"microcosm", man as 311, 311n, 385, 461, 461n, 497, 745, 777, 807

middle and whole 421n

middle ages 366, 469, 501, 811
admiration of 398–400, 784–6; compared with the present cxviii; contribution of 413n; deformities of 413; delusions of 450–1, 805; and jury 355n; misrepresentation of 413

migrations of descendants of Japhet 606, 610

Milan, cathedral of 351, 366, 763

Miletus 12, 25

milk 275, 730 (milky substance)

Mill, John Stuart (1806–73) 149n

millennialism cvi

millenniaries 329

millennium cvi
Christian interest in 305–6, 305n, 741–2; St Peter on 306, 742

Miller, Joe 432, 794

Miller, Walter (1864–1949) *see* Cicero *De officiis* tr Miller

mills, cotton 401n

Milnes, neighbours, letter to xxxixn

Montagu, Basil (1770–1851), letter to 186n q
Montesino, cave of (in Cervantes) 396n
mood, imperative 606
moon 66, 66n
anomalies in its motion 533n; Aristotle on transit of m. 14; Pythagoras on 633; and shadow m. 194n; size of the m. 93, 93n; and tides 346, 761
moonlight 287, 739
Pope's description of 614; reading by 397, 397n, 418; Socinianism as 287n
Moors 463, 808
moralists, outside 287, 738
morality lxxx, 235, 275n, 524, 710, 836
Celtic 349, 762; and commerce 401, 401n, 787; and cunning 61, 630; and Epicureanism 263, 300, 722; and experience 181, 681; false 614; German 350, 762; and government 360n; and intellect 356, 766; and marriage 283, 735; materialists' sacrifice of 548; as means to God-likeness 334; mediaeval 399, 785; outward 170, 673; and philosophy lxxxv; Pythagoras on lxxxv, 69–70, 610, 635–6; and reason 283, 736; and religion 85, 85n–6n, 342, 758; reliance on 56, 626; of Rome 316, 749; safe 283, 736; and sensation 274, 730; Socrates on xci–xcii, 145, 166, 190, 199, 666, 688; and taste 265, 723; theology destructive of m. 54, 625; and vice 328; comes from within 287, 738
morals 506
corruption of 212, 695; and free will 545; improvement of 69n; and materialism 534, 545, 843; natural 350, 762
morasses 424, 789
Mordecai (Bible) 304, 328, 741
More, Henry (1614–87)
on body and soul 583, 864; as Cartesian Platonist 583n; and Descartes 583n; on immortality of soul 583n; and Plotinus 583n
Philosophical Poems, marginalia on 583n; *Philosophische Werke* 583n q; *The Pre-existence of the Soul* 583n; *The Second Lash of Alazanomastix,* marginalia in 515n
Morgan, Thomas (d 1743) 128n
A Defence of Natural and Revealed Religion 128n
Morgans, time of 128, 657
Morley, Edith Julia (1875–1964) *see*

Robinson, Henry Crabb *Crabb Robinson in Germany, On Books* ed Morley
Morning Chronicle xxxvii, 22 q, 48 q, 110, 168, 208, 252, 302 q, 338 q, 372 q, 420, 460 q, 506 q, 552 q, 604 q
Morning Post 168
advertisements in xxxvi–xxxvii; editor of xlvii
mors prima 605
mors secunda 605
mosaic 873
Moses (Bible) 62n, 645n
God's answer to 606n
Mosheim, Johann Lorenz von (1694–1755) xlvin
An Ecclesiastical History tr A. Maclaine xlvi; *see also* Cudworth, Ralph *The True Intellectual System* tr Mosheim
Moslems *see* Mahometanism
Mossner, Ernest Campbell (1907–86)
The Life of David Hume lxxxvin, 259n
mother(s)
and child 392–3, 781; education by 114, 647; nature as 270, 726; of Plato 200
moths 287, 739
motion(s) 35n, 521–2, 835
as abstract 532, 841; Aristotle on 518n; and atoms 516n, 517, 542–3, 547, 832; in atoms 547; as cause of evil 58, 627; as central concept 123n; cycles of 161; denial of lxxxviii, 137, 661; Eleatics on 123, 154, 165, 514, 653–4; and gods lxxxi; Hobbes on 518n; inherence of 514, 830 (notion); laws of 510, 828; of machine 339, 361, 756; materialists on 514–15, 830; and motive power 57, 627, 841; Newton on 532; observation of lxxxi; phenomenon of 125, 654; pleasure in 290n; and reason 125, 654; and souls lxxxi; of stars 489, 510, 822; of sun 480n; unreality of 514, 830; voluntary 516–17, 543, 548, 831–2; Zeno on 123n, 257n
motives, higher and lower 334
motors, supersensual 557n
Motte, Andrew (d 1730) *see* Newton, Isaac *Mathematical Principles* tr Motte and Cajori
mountain(s)
of Norway 424n; poetic 615n
mouse and man 566, 599, 856
Mozart, Wolfgang Amadeus (1756–91)
Don Giovanni 445n

power(s)—*continued*

cxxxvii, 555, 593, 850–1; desire of 437, 797; essential 193, 690; of fixity 532n; of generalising and classifying 608–9; gravity as a p. 135n; human 341, 430, 757; of image 87n; imaginary 424, 789; individualising 594; infinite 268n; of the intellect 374, 489, 538, 587, 771, 822, 846, 866; intelligential 215, 243; interpreting p. from within 241, 714; judging men as 246; of law 533, 842; limit of 133, 144, 658, 666; love of 430, 793; magnetic 555n; mark of 358, 767; of mechanism 358, 767; motive lxxxi, 57, 532n, 627; of names 342, 758; of numbers 150, 342, 758; order of mental 887; organisation as p. 529, 840; organising 58, 628; of originating an act 534, 843; percipient 556, 594, 851; Protestant balance of 399, 413, 785; of providence 144, 666; of reason 385, 777; reconciliation of 615; representative 334; of reproduction 385n; of repulsion 240, 713; of sensation 516, 548, 831; sense of p. 135, 660; of sensibility 385n; as Spirit 598; spiritual 403, 413, 556, 851; systematic 310, 745; temporal and spiritual 398, 785; of things 393n; thinking p. 228–9, 706; of universe 240, 713; vegetative 303, 740; of will 229, 706; from within 528, 839

powerful, attacks on the p. 414

Prague 433n

Four Articles of 433n

prayer

C's 605; difficulty of 286–7, 738; every word a p. 88; inward 174, 676; object of 146n; during storm 60, 91, 629; superstitious 308, 743–4; for victory 308, 743–4

preaching 324, 753

preconception(s)

of god 267n; St Teresa's 465; of the unlimited 575, 860

predecessors, honouring 563, 854

predestination

Augustine on 410n; double 381, 381n, 410, 410n, Erigena on 381, 409n, 774, Gottschalk on 410n

prejudiced, the 225, 703

preparer for new world 200

Presbyterians li, lin

presence, real 410n

present compared to middle ages 398–400, 784–6

presentiments, incommunicable 162

preservation, tendency towards 527, 838

pre-Socratics xl

press, freedom of 355n

Price, Richard (1723–91)

C's view of 523n; and Priestley 523, 836; sophistry of 523n

and Joseph Priestley *A Free Discussion of the Doctrines of Materialism and Philosophical Necessity* 523n

pride 172

abortion of 562, 596, 854; and conscience 286, 738; empty 275, 730; family 350, 351n, 366, 763; of heraldry 563, 854; and imagination 562, 596, 854; and intellectual capacity 462, 808; modern 332; in being self-taught 272, 728; Stoic 280, 291, 313–14, 747; Zeno's 277, 732; *see also* "proud"

priest(s) 103

atheism of 602; barbarian 329; Egyptian 26, 68, 105, 323, 323n, 444, 634, 753 (not named), 801; exclusive theology of 356, 766; in Greece 162; of heathenism 224, 703; high 340, 757; Italian 350, 763; of learning 482, 817; at Memphis 33n; origin of 399, 785; power of 398, 784; Roman 162, 308, 479, 743, 815; submission to 353n. *See also* clergy; priestcraft; priesthood

priestcraft, amulets against 572, 859

priesthood 335

and Apollonius 320n; in Burma 68, 634; and conquest 107; corrupt 156; of Eclectics 325, 754; and education 94; Egyptian 42; nature of 68n; and oracles 73, 638–9; in Roman Catholic countries 68, 635; tricks of 316, 749. *See also* clergy; priest(s); priestcraft

Priestley, Joseph (1733–1804) li, lin

attack on 332n; and Hartley 562n; on Hume 259, 719; and Price 523, 836; sophistry of 523n

An Examination of Dr. Reid's Inquiry 259n; and Richard Price *A Free Discussion of the Doctrines of Materialism and Philosophical Necessity* 523n

primogeniture 9

prince(s)

German 456, 456n; happiness of 60n;

vibrations 543

vice(s) 270, 609, 726, 744

addiction to 286, 737; of our ancestors 394, 782; and Christianity 308; Condillac on 536n; degrees of cviii; equality of 280n; of Greece and Rome 307, 743; and ignorance 174, 676; and knowledge 204; modern 394, 782; philosophers on 307, 743; and religion 328; and satire 328; unchecked by comment 307, 743; and virtue(s) 101, 157, 256, 717

Victoire, St (1027–87) 887

victory/victories

Athenian 137n–8n; Greek 137–8, 661–2; prayer for 308, 744; and Sophists 138n

videri 555n

vie intérieure cxxvi, 468

Vienna 318n

St Stephen's 352n

Virgil (Publius Virgilius Maro) (70–19 B.C.)

astronomy in 163; copyists and imitators of 424, 457, 790; and Dante 424n; opposition to 375, 375n, 404, 415, 771

Georgics 163n

virgins, consecrated 352, 366, 763

viri Socratici 152

virtue(s) 178, 679

of the Antonines 233n; character of 536n; Christian 462, 808; Condillac on cxxxiv, 536, 536n, 844; definition of 279–80, 733; educing 118, 650; as end ciii–civ, 275, 291, 730; of Greece 307, 743; and happiness xc; as harmony 117n–18n; and knowledge 174–6, 201, 204, 676–7; known by virtuous conduct 152; learned by practice 118, 164, 650; as means ciii–civ, 275, 291, 730; oppressed 174, 676; and philosophy xcii; and prudence 179, 263, 289, 680, 722; and religion 176, 677; replaced by sensual gratification 335; non-Roman cxii; of Rome 307, 743; social 322, 752; Socrates and Stoics on 290–1; and suffering 342, 758; theory of 118, 650; and vice(s) *see* vice(s) and virtue(s); Zeno on 300

vis representativa 521, 834

visibility 100

visible, the 170, 671

vision(s)

beatific 334; of Ezekiel 66n; field of 228, 705; intellectual 374, 771; inward 518, 543, 832; keenest 319n; law of 493; and touch 114, 647; *see also* sight

visionary/visionaries 450, 462, 466, 468, 805, 808–10, 876

and Aristotelianism cxvii, 394, 417, 782

vocabulary

Greek and English 23, 23n; metaphysical 557, 594, 598, 851

Voetius, Gysbertus (1588–1676) and Descartes 566–7, 566n, 600 (Boetius), 856 (Grotius), 857 (Boetius)

voice, intuitive 204

volcano, intellectual 104

Volney, Constantin François, comte de (1757–1820) 86n

The Ruins 86n; *Supplément à l'Hérodote* 12n

volonté générale 487n

volonté particulière 487n

Volta, Allesandro (1745–1827) 510n

Voltaire, François Marie Arouet de (1694–1778) 360n, 583, 865

age of 447, 803; his aim 447, 802; C's aversion to 446, 802; his career 447n; and Erasmus lv, cxxii–cxxiv, 445n, 446–8, 458, 802–3; on gardening 260, 720; and infidelity 448, 571–2, 803, 859; and Leibniz 570, 858 (not named); on Locke 572n; his longevity 446n–7n; on Milton 432n; and Rousseau 446–8, 802–3; scepticism of 583n; on senses 600; superficiality of his knowledge 446–7, 802; his wit 446, 802

Candide cxxiii, 260n q; *Dictionnaire philosophique portatif* 571n; *Lettres philosophiques* 572n q

volunteer spirit 356, 356n, 66

voluptas 147, 147n; *see also* pleasure(s)

voluptuary/voluptuaries civ, 178, 276, 679, 731; *see also* Cyrenaics

Vulcan (mythical) 476n

Vulgate *see* Bible

Wade, Josiah (1761–1842), letter to 272n

wafer 376, 772

waistcoat 113, 150, 358, 647, 767

waking 558, 852

Wales, Prince of *see* George IV

wall(s)

dashing head against 274, 729; flaming 478, 815